JESUS
THE SEER

THE ORACLE

Call them forth,
Call them forth,
From the passive past.
The soothsayers and truth sayers
The yea sayers and nay sayers
The foretellers and forthtellers,
Scanning the skies,
Hoping for the horizon,
Acting out the plan
Signing forth the ban
Boon or bane
Commendation or condemnation
Blessing or curse,
Let them wrap their mantles
'Round their hoary heads
And cry: "Thus saith the Lord"
Once more
9-13-97
BW III

JESUS
THE SEER

The Progress of Prophecy

BEN WITHERINGTON III

HENDRICKSON
PUBLISHERS

Hendrickson Publishers, Inc.
P. O. Box 3473
Peabody, Massachusetts 01961–3473

© 1999 by Ben Witherington III

Printed in the United States of America

ISBN 1-56563-344-X

First printing — November 1999

Library of Congress Cataloging-in-Publication Data

Witherington, Ben, 1951–
     Jesus the seer : the progress of prophecy / Ben Witherington.
          p. cm.
     Includes bibliographical references and indexes.
     ISBN 1-56563-344-X
        1. Prophecy—Christianity—History of doctrines—Early church, ca. 30–600.
2. Prophets—Middle East—History. 3. Prophecy—History. 4. Revelation
I. Title.
BR115.P8 W57 1999
231.7′45′0901—dc21
                                                                          99-047392

Table of Contents

A Preview of Coming Attractions

THE STUDY OF PROPHECY, whether ancient Near Eastern, Hebrew, early Christian, or Greco-Roman, has taken many twists and turns in the twentieth century. Occasionally, scholarship on prophecy has been refreshed and refined by new, unexpected discoveries from such places as Mari, Deir Alla, where a tablet referring to Balaam of Beor was found, or Qumran, in the salt flats along the Dead Sea. Yet despite all this stimulus, no one to my knowledge has ever attempted a broad, cross-cultural and diachronic study of the bearing of the prophetic phenomenon on the biblical data. No one has looked at the whole to see what trends and developments took place over the course of time or what the whole might tell us about the parts.

This judgment stands in spite of the fact that a considerable amount of attention has been paid to the historical relationship of apocalyptic literature to prophetic literature. Yet even this helpful body of scholarly work has not led to an adequate analysis of the broader sweep of the social and historical phenomenon of prophecy in the eastern Mediterranean. To the contrary, the study of prophecy has become an increasingly specialized and text-oriented matter. James Ward says with reason about the study of OT prophecy, "Today the emphasis is upon the [prophetic] books themselves, and the complex literary traditions that produced them"[1] rather than on the prophets, their experience, or their original oracles. This is a 180-

---

[1] J. Ward, "The Eclipse of the Prophet in Contemporary Prophetic Studies," *USQR* 42 (1988): 97–103, here 102.

degrees reversal of the trend in the early part of this century when there was so much emphasis on prophets as unique individuals with intriguing religious experiences.[2] Increasing doubts about the historical substance and character of the biblical prophetic books is in part responsible for this shift. Psychological maximalism has been replaced by historical minimalism.

Yet, while attention to tradition history and to the redaction of prophetic books is an important task, it need not eclipse other lines of approach to the phenomenon of ancient prophecy—and for good reason. Consider the remarks of R. P. Gordon:

> While the phenomenon of the "disappearing prophet" has become a feature (indeed function) of some modern approaches to Israelite prophecy, at the same time the profile of Syro-Mesopotamian prophecy has become increasingly clear, and there are now definite cognates for the basic Hebrew word for "prophet." Against this background . . . though eighth century prophets like Amos and Hosea may not have been much interested in the title "prophet" (. . . not surprisingly when the title was used for non-Israelite prophets), they nevertheless saw themselves functioning as such. No single aspect of Israelite prophecy marks it out as distinct from its near eastern equivalents; its obvious distinctiveness derives from Israel's unique perception of God.[3]

For some time I have been working on a broad study of the social phenomenon of prophecy in the ancient Mediterranean world, realizing full well that in some respects it is an impossible task. No one can be the master of this enormous corpus of material, and so at various points I have had to simply accept that I have to stand on the shoulders of the experts in this material and rely on their critical judgments. This means that this study must be seen for what it is—a first attempt to come to grips with this vast subject, not a definitive treatment of it.

Nevertheless, having immersed myself in the scope and breadth of this material, a great deal of light has been shed for me on issues that have vexed my particular field of expertise—NT studies. For example, I have pondered why it is that such a large proportion of the Hebrew Scriptures involves prophetic books, while the NT, unless one counts the apocalyptic revelation that concludes that corpus, contains no books which could be called prophetic as a whole or even any that in the main involve collections of oracles. I believe there are also many clues about Hebrew prophecy as part of the larger ANE phenomenon, including such sites as Mari and elsewhere, which attest to a family resemblance.

While there was a range of things that prophets might do and say in the ancient world, nonetheless their activity, the form of their discourse, and the social purposes and effects of this discourse were similar in all these Mediterranean cultures, so much so that a person traveling from, say, Rome to the extremes of the eastern end of the Empire in the first century AD could speak about prophets

---

[2] See the older classic study by J. Skinner, *Prophecy and Religion: Studies in the Life of Jeremiah* (Cambridge: Cambridge University Press, 1922).

[3] R. P. Gordon, "Where Have All the Prophets Gone?" *BBR* 5 (1995): 67–86, here 67.

and prophecy and expect most audiences essentially to understand. Similarly, during the time of Jeremiah one could travel from Babylon to Jerusalem and expect the social phenomenon of prophecy to be in many, though not all, ways the same in a variety of these ANE cultures. The story of Jonah, like the story of Balaam, encourages us to look at prophecy as a cross-cultural phenomenon, with influence moving in various directions and development happening through the course of time.

I have discovered in my odyssey through the prophetic material that a great deal of loose talk has been allowed to pass for critical thinking about the nature of prophets and their utterances. For example, in my discipline, but also in OT studies, prophecy is often regarded as synonymous with preaching or with the creative handling and interpreting of earlier sacred texts. Part of this lack of clarity may be put down to confusion on the difference between prophetic utterances and the literary residue of such utterances, namely, books of prophetic material, collected and edited by scribes over the course of time. I have found it important in this study to distinguish the prophetic experience, the prophetic expression, the prophetic tradition, and prophetic corpus, all of which are part of the social phenomenon that falls under the heading of prophecy.

I have been struck repeatedly by how across a variety of cultural lines and over the course of an enormous amount of time Jews, pagans, and Christians in the eastern end of the Mediterranean crescent all seem to have had reasonably clear and similar ideas about what constituted a prophet and prophecy. To share a few of the conclusions of this study in advance, a prophet was an oracle, a mouthpiece for some divine being, and as such he or she did not speak for him- or herself but for another. A prophet might also be many other things (teacher, priest, sage), but the role of prophet could be distinguished from these other roles and functions. Prophecy, whether from Mari or Jerusalem or Delphi or Rome, was spoken in known languages, usually in poetic form, and so it was an intelligible, even if often puzzling, kind of discourse. It might involve spontaneous utterances or a reading of various omens or signs, but in either case it was not a matter of deciphering ancient texts, which was the tasks of scribes, sages, and exegetes. Furthermore, people consulted a prophet to obtain a late word from a deity about pressing or impending matters. In sociological terms the prophet must be seen as a mediatorial figure; this, therefore, makes the prophet significant but also subject to being pushed to the margins of society if the divine words involve curse rather than blessing, judgment rather than redemption. At least in the setting of Israel and early Christianity, the prophet also deliberately stands at the boundary of the community—the boundary between God and the community as well as the boundary between the community and those outside it. It is the task of the prophet to call God's people to account and to reinforce the prescribed boundaries of the community while reestablishing or reinforcing the divine-human relationship.

This takes us to another factor which has too often been underplayed in the scholarly discourse (perhaps in order to avoid the embarrassment of having to say that a particular favorite prophet was wrong). I am referring to the fact that prophecy was more often than not predictive in character, though most often its subject matter dealt with something thought to be on the near horizon, not something decades much less centuries in the future. And even when the more remote future was the subject of prophecy, the subject was raised because it was thought to have a rather direct bearing on the present. In short, ancient prophets were not armchair speculators about remote subjects. (Nostradamus, if even he were such a speculator, would not have felt comfortable in this company.)

Let me be clear from the outset that I am not just saying that a broad cross-cultural study of the social phenomenon of prophecy is illuminating. This is true and is part of the focus of this study, but one could certainly do a broad study that was simply synchronic in nature (e.g., prophecy in the eighth century BC in the ANE including Israel). I intend in this study to also pursue particular prophetic trajectories through time, which also affords a tremendously illuminating way of examining the material. The basic arrangement of this book is diachronic.

Perhaps a small sample of the value of a diachronic study of prophecy is in order at this juncture, as a partial justification for that dimension of this work. Our earliest relevant text, Isa 24:21–22, reads: "On that day the Lord will punish the host of heaven and on earth the kings of earth. They will be gathered together like prisoners in a pit they will be shut up in a prison, and after many days they will be punished." Although the identity of the host of heaven is not explicit, the contrast between them and the kings of the earth makes it likely that rebellious powers in heaven are in view (cf. Deut 32:8; Dan 10:13). There may also be something to the suggestion that these powers in heaven are seen as the ones controlling the rebellious kings and their nations.[4] What is crucial to note about this passage is the stress that these powers are put in something like an extraterrestrial prison or holding cell until the time comes for them to be punished.

The second passage from closer to the time of, if not during, the early stages of the NT era is *1 En.* 10:4–6. Here the picture of the two-stage defeat of these powers (or at least one of them) is clarified and particularized: "the Lord said to Raphael, 'Bind Azaz'el[5] hand and foot, throw him into the darkness!' And he made a hole in the desert which was in Duda'el and cast him there; he threw on top of him rugged sharp rocks. And he covered his face in order that he might not see the light; and in order that he might be sent into the great fire on the day of judgment."[6]

Our next port of call is several NT texts, the earliest being Jude. For convenience we will present these three texts in parallel columns to facilitate the comparison.

---

[4] See now the discussion of R. Bauckham, *The Fate of the Dead: Studies on Jewish and Christian Apocalypses* (Leiden: Brill, 1998), 49–80.

[5] Clearly a demonic figure; see, e.g., D. P. Wright, "Azazel," in *ABD* I, 536–37.

[6] One should compare this text to *1 En.* 10:12; 18:14–19; 21:6–10; 90:23–27; *Jub.* 5:6–10; 10:5–9.

JUDE (v. 6)	2 PETER (2:4)	1 PETER (3:19–20)
"And the angels who did not keep their own position, but left their proper dwelling, he has kept in eternal chains in deepest darkness for the judgment of the great Day."	"For if God did not spare the angels when they sinned, but cast them into hell [Tartaros] and committed them to chains of deepest darkness to be kept until the judgment."	"he [Christ] went and made a proclamation to the spirits in prison, who in former times did not obey, when God waited patiently in the days of Noah."

Obviously, the first two of these texts are more similar to one another than the third is to either one. R. Bauckham has demonstrated a likely literary link between Jude and 2 Peter, as the passages above show.[7] The first two of these texts are not obviously of christological import, though if the reference to Christ as Lord in Jude 4 prepares for v. 5, where the Lord is the one who saved the people from Egypt and then kept the angels in chains, then we have a comment on Christ's preexistence and his roles in Israel's history, drawing on Wisdom ideas not unlike what we find in 1 Cor 10:4 (cf. Wis. of Sol. 11:4) . The author of 2 Peter, however, sees God and not Christ as the one who chained the disobedient angels; this comports with the font of this tradition in Isaiah.

All these NT texts refer to Gen 6:1–4, where God was so outraged by what the angels (sons of God) did with the daughters of humanity that God brought a flood upon the earth. This Genesis context is more obvious in the 1 Pet 3 use of this material, and it is in 1 Pet 3 that we find something with christological importance. Here Christ (v. 18 makes clear this is who it is) goes and preaches to these angels in prison. Though the 1 Pet 3 text has been the basis of the creedal statement "he descended into hell" and various "second chance" theologies, it is doubtful this text has anything at all to do with such notions. Nothing is said about Christ's "descent" anywhere. We are simply told that after Christ died and was "made alive in the Spirit" he went and preached or made a proclamation to these spirits or angels. There may be a trace of this whole theological development in the hymn fragment in 1 Tim 3:16, where we hear that Christ was "vindicated in spirit." This remark is immediately followed by "seen by angels." Commentators have always thought this remark was out of place. If it referred to Christ's entry into heaven it would be better placed just before or after the last line of the hymn, which reads "taken up in glory." This reference to being seen by angels, however, may not be out of place at all if it is about Christ's visit to Tartaros. It is also not impossible that Eph 4:8 is of relevance here as well, for there it is said of Christ, quoting Ps 68:18 with alterations, "When he ascended on high, he led or made captivity itself captive."

To understand this material some knowledge of Jewish angelology and demonology is necessary. For our purposes it is necessary only to say that the powers and principalities and indeed Satan himself were believed to inhabit the realm between heaven and earth. This is one reason why the planets were sometimes assumed to be heavenly beings or angels ("the heavenly host"), and it is also why Satan is called in the NT "the ruler of the power of the air" (Eph 2:2).

---

[7] See R. J. Bauckham, *Jude and 2 Peter* (Waco: Word, 1983).

It would appear then that 1 Pet 3, far from being about a descent to humans, is about Christ's ascent to the angels on his way to heaven, at which point he proclaimed his victory over such powers and thereby made their captivity all the more permanent and their doom sure. This material then would provide us with another strand of evidence of the development of cosmic Christology or Christus Victor (over the powers), and it would show this is not simply a Pauline development. It would also provide another piece of evidence for the phenomenon whereby actions predicated of God in earlier Jewish traditions are now predicated of Christ in the NT.[8]

There is actually a remarkable coherence between these five texts with signs of development in *Enoch* in the naming of the demon in view, and in the NT in naming of the prison itself, and finally in the focus in 1 Pet 3 on the role of Christ in relationship to these beings. Yet without hearing the echoes of or allusions to the earlier prophetic texts, it is understandable how especially the text in 1 Pet 3 has been so often misread. Longitudinal studies in the trajectory of the prophetic tradition offers many such revelations.[9] What we intend to do in the main in the following study, however, is to examine larger issues concerning the nature of prophecy and the development of prophetic traditions, especially paying attention to the cross-cultural nature of the prophetic phenomenon. As we shall see, this sheds much light on the latest canonical stages of the prophetic and apocalyptic traditions and leads to some surprising conclusions.

The turn of our own era is, in various regards, an obvious time to turn once again and examine the ancient prophetic phenomenon. As I write, we have seen for several years running a wide and wild variety of end-of-the-world religious cults from North America to Switzerland and beyond, often unfortunately ending in tragedy. The fascination with prophecy, or what passes for it, remains strong even two thousand years after the time of Jesus. It is my hope that the following study may not merely further the study of ancient prophecy, but also further the discussion of whether prophecy is still a viable form of human discourse. If it accomplishes these aims I will be content.

EASTER 1999

---

[8] For a compelling study of the material in the Petrine texts which leaves little doubt that the subject is angelic beings, not human beings, who are in this dark prison and that the land of the dead or hell is not meant, see W. J. Dalton, *Christ's Proclamation to the Spirits: A Study of 1 Peter 3:18–4:6* (Rome: Pontifical Biblical Institute, 1965).

[9] Another example of this sort of approach on a larger scale but dealing with one particular tradition is found in J. T. Greene, *Balaam and His Interpreters: A Hermeneutical History of the Balaam Traditions* (Atlanta: Scholars Press, 1992).

Abbreviations

AB	Anchor Bible
ABD	*Anchor Bible Dictionary.* Ed. D. N. Freeman. 6 vols. New York, 1992
ALBO	Analecta lovaniensia biblica et orientalia
ANET	*Ancient Near Eastern Texts Relating to the Old Testament.* Ed. J. B. Pritchard. 3d ed. Princeton, 1969
ARAB	*Ancient Records of Assyria and Babylonia.* Ed. Daniel David Luckenbill. 2 vols. Chicago, 1926–1927
ARM	Archives royales de Mari
AUSS	*Andrews University Seminary Studies*
BASOR	*Bulletin of the Americans Schools of Oriental Research*
BBR	*Bulletin for Biblical Research*
BETL	Bibliotheca ephemeridum theologicarum lovaniensium
Bib	*Biblica*
BJRL	*Bulletin of the John Rylands Library*
BR	*Biblical Research*
CBQ	*Catholic Biblical Quarterly*
Colloq	*Colloquium*
DJG	*Dictionary of Jesus and the Gospels.* Ed. J. B. Green and S. McKnight. Downers Grove, 1992
DLNT	*Dictionary of the Later New Testament and Its Developments.* Ed. R. P. Martin and P. H. Davids. Downers Grove, 1997
DPL	*Dictionary of Paul and His Letters.* Ed. G. F. Hawthorne and R. P. Martin. Downers Grove, 1993
ETL	*Ephemerides theologicae lovanienses*
ExpT	*Expository Times*
FGH	*Die Fragmente der griechischen Historiker.* Ed. F. Jacoby. Leiden, 1954–1964

HR	History of Religions
HUCA	Hebrew Union College Annual
IDB	The Interpreter's Dictionary of the Bible. Ed. G. Buttrick. 4 vols. Nashville, 1962
IDBSup	Interpreter's Dictionary of the Bible: Supplementary Volume. Ed. K. Crim. Nashville, 1976
Int	Interpretation
JAOS	Journal of the American Oriental Society
JBL	Journal of Biblical Literature
JBR	Journal of Bible and Religion
JETS	Journal of the Evangelical Theological Society
JNES	Journal of Near Eastern Studies
JSOT	Journal for the Study of the Old Testament
JSS	Journal of Semitic Studies
JTC	Journal for Theology and Church
JTS	Journal of Theological Studies
NedTT	Nederlands theologisch tijdschrift
NewDocs	New Documents Illustrating Early Christianity. Ed. G. H. R. Horsley and S. Llewelyn. North Ryde, N.S.W., 1981–
NovT	Novum Testamentum
NTS	New Testament Studies
OTP	Old Testament Pseudepigrapha. Ed. J. H. Charlesworth. 2 vols. New York, 1983
PGM	Papyri graecae magicae: Die griechischen Zauberpapyri. Ed. K. Preisendanz. Berlin, 1928
ResQ	Restoration Quarterly
RevExp	Review and Expositor
RTR	Reformed Theological Review
SAA	State Archives of Assyria
SecCent	Second Century
SIG	Sylloge inscriptorium graecarum. Ed. W. Dittenberger
StTh	Studia theologica
Them	Themelios
TS	Theological Studies
TynBul	Tyndale Bulletin
TZ	Theologische Zeitschrift
USQR	Union Seminary Quarterly Review
VC	Vigiliae christianae
VT	Vetus Testamentum
WUNT	Wissenschaftliche Untersuchungen zum Neuen Testament
ZAW	Zeitschrift für die alttestamentliche Wissenschaft
ZTK	Zeitschrift für Theologie und Kirche

Dead Sea Scrolls

CD	*Damascus Document*
1QapGen	*Genesis Apocryphon*
1QH	*Hodayot (Thanksgiving Hymns)*
1QM	*War Scroll*
1QpHab	*Pesher on Habakkuk*
1QS	*Manual of Discipline (Rule of the Community)*
4QTestim	*Testimonia*
11QMelch	*Melchizedek*

Old Testament Pseudepigrapha

Ascen. Isa.	*Ascension of Isaiah*
2 Bar.	*2 Baruch*
1 En.	*1 Enoch (Ethiopian Apocalypse)*
Jub.	*Jubilees*
Odes Sol.	*Odes of Solomon*
Pss. Sol.	*Psalms of Solomon*
Sib. Or.	*Sibylline Oracles*
T. Ash.	*Testament of Asher*
T. Benj.	*Testament of Benjamin*
T. Dan.	*Testament of Daniel*
T. Jud.	*Testament of Judah*
T. Levi	*Testament of Levi*
T. Mos.	*Testament of Moses*

Mishnah, Talmud, and Related Literature

b.	tractates of the Babylonian Talmud
m.	tractates of the Mishnah
Ber.	*Berakot*
Meg.	*Megillah*
Sanh.	*Sanhedrin*
Soṭah	*Soṭah*

Other Rabbinic Works

S. ʿOlam Rab.	*Seder ʿOlam Rabbah*

Apostolic Fathers

1 Clem.	*1 Clement*
Herm. *Mand.*	Shepherd of Hermas, *Mandate*
Herm. *Sim.*	Shepherd of Hermas, *Similitude*
Herm. *Vis.*	Shepherd of Hermas, *Vision*

Ign. *Phld.*   Ignatius, *To the Philadelphians*
Ign. *Rom.*   Ignatius, *To the Romans*
Ign. *Trall.*   Ignatius, *To the Trallians*

New Testament Apocrypha and Pseudepigrapha

Gos. Thom.   *Gospel of Thomas*

Other Ancient Writings

Artemidorus Daldianus
    Onir.   *Onirocritica*
Cicero
    Div.   *De divinatione*
Constantine
    Or. sanct.   *Oratio ad sanctos*
Epiphanius
    Pan.   *Panarion (Adversus haereses)*
Eusebius
    Hist. eccl.   *Historia ecclesiastica*
    Praep. ev.   *Praeparatio evangelica*
Herodotus
    Hist.   *Historiae*
Hesiod
    Op.   *Opera et dies*
Hippolytus
    Antichr.   *De antichristo*
Iamblichus
    Myst.   *De mysteriis*
Josephus
    Ag. Ap.   *Against Apion*
    Ant.   *Jewish Antiquities*
    War   *Jewish War*
Justin
    Dial.   *Dialogue with Trypho*
Juvenal
    Sat.   *Satirae*
Pausanias
    Desc.   *Descriptions of Greece*
Philo
    Contempl.   *De vita contemplativa*
    Her.   *Quis rerum divinarum heres sit*
    Migr.   *De migratione Abrahami*
    Mos. 2   *De vita Mosis II*

Plato
   Resp.   *Respublica*
   Tim.   *Timaeus*
Plutarch
   Ant.   *Antonius*
   Caes.   *Caesar*
   Def. orac.   *De defectu oraculorum*
   Luc.   *Lucullus*
   Mor.   *Moralia*
Suetonius
   Aug.   *Divus Augustus*
   Tib.   *Tiberius*
   Vesp.   *Vespasianus*
Tacitus
   Ann.   *Annales*
   Hist.   *Historiae*
Tertullian
   An.   *De anima*
   Exh. cast.   *De exhortatione castitatis*
   Jejun.   *De jejunio adversos psychicos*
   Marc.   *Adversus Marcionem*
   Prax.   *Adversus Praxean*
   Scap.   *Ad Scapulam*
   Virg.   *De virginibus velandis*

Papyri

P.Oxy.   *The Oxyrhynchus Papyri*
P.Mich.   *Michigan Papyri*
P.Vindob.Sal.1   *Einige Wiener Papyri*, ed. R. P. Salomons

Bible Texts, Versions

LXX   Septuagint
NEB   New English Bible
NIV   New International Version
RSV   Revised Standard Version

Other Abbreviations

ad loc.   at the place discussed
ca.   about
frg.   fragment
lit.   literally
obv.   obverse (front) of a tablet
par.   parallel

Introduction

Through the Eyes of the Seer

THE STUDY OF PROPHECY HAS PROVED to be a growth industry in the last twenty-five years. This has been fueled partly by the discoveries at Mari and elsewhere, but it has also been precipitated by the growing interest in things visionary throughout Western culture in the last several decades. In a world that has a global economy and a global communications system, it is hardly surprising that there has been some impetus to take a more global or cross-cultural approach to prophecy. Now more than ever, it is possible to compare and contrast the prophetic experience, the prophetic expression, the prophetic tradition across various cultural boundaries. Yet some cross-cultural studies, because they have been too broad, or involved comparing widely divergent cultures and their prophetic components, have shed only a little light on biblical prophecy in its various forms.[1]

This book will seek to study prophecy with something of a cross-cultural approach but within limited geographical and chronological parameters. The geographical parameters are basically the eastern end of the Mediterranean crescent and the nearby Middle Eastern regions (e.g., Assyria, Babylonia, Egypt), and the chronological parameters are about 1600 BC to approximately AD 300, or a little

---

[1] Here a study such as T. Overholt's *Channels of Prophecy: The Social Dynamics of Prophetic Activity* (Minneapolis: Fortress, 1989) comes to mind; among other things, it compares the prophecy of American Indians to that of the Hebrew prophets. This is not to say that there are not some parallels, but they are insufficient to produce any significant light on biblical prophecy.

less than two thousand years. This sort of approach produces far more useful results than studies that wander further afield for parallels, precisely because all of
these Near Eastern cultures shared similar views and attitudes about a host of
subjects, including prophecy and divination. This study, then, is not limited just
to an examination of biblical prophecy, though that is where the major focus lies;
rather, it seeks to set biblical prophecy in a somewhat wider context, attempting
to see what light the larger social context may shed on the biblical phenomena.

As a prelude to the diachronic study and survey of prophecy, it will be
worthwhile to take the time to interact with an important recent study that takes
a cross-cultural and social approach to prophecy; through dialoguing with this
study, we will be able to set out and introduce to the reader some of the problems and promise of such an approach to prophecy and, hopefully, be guided
away from the pitfalls of such an approach. The study in question is L. L.
Grabbe's highly regarded work, *Priests, Prophets, Diviners, Sages.*[2]

Grabbe begins his study by surveying the most relevant biblical texts that reveal something about the nature of prophets and diviners and their arts. One tendency of Grabbe's work throughout is his suspicion of those who would try to
separate Hebrew prophets from other ancient Near East prophets as if they were
somehow distinctive, and his even greater suspicion of the use of labels of "true"
and "false" prophets within the biblical corpus itself. Thus, for instance, he takes
the story found in 1 Kgs 22:1–28 somewhat at face value. Ahab had four hundred
court prophets whom he consulted. Their leader, Zedekiah, prophesied in the
name of Yahweh, and made a prophetic sign using iron horns to make clear what
Yahweh was saying to Ahab—namely, that he would have a great victory. Grabbe's
opinion about labels is represented in the case of Micaiah, who was brought forward and predicted defeat. To account for the former prophecies, Micaiah reveals
a session of the heavenly court in which Yahweh asks how Ahab might be deceived,
and in due course a lying spirit volunteers to enter the court prophets. Grabbe
concludes, "All the prophets speak in the name of Yhwh; this includes the four
hundred court prophets. Therefore, the conflict is between two sets of prophets of
Yhwh."[3] Grabbe is obviously skeptical about the use of any sort of ideological criteria to discern the difference between a true and a false prophet.

Yet, even laying ideology aside, it can not be the case that both Micaiah
and the court prophets were doing equally good jobs of discerning the divine
will in this matter, for clearly the court prophets proved to be wrong, and
Micaiah to be right. The historical and archaeological evidence should not be ignored. It is possible to argue in the abstract that both groups of prophets could
be wrong about a particular matter (e.g., if Ahab never fought an enemy at all,
both these prophecies could be incorrect), but if indeed there was a battle, they
could not both be right. This brings up a crucial point. However difficult it may

---

[2] L. L. Grabbe, *Priests, Prophets, Diviners, Sages: A Socio-historical Study of Religious
Specialists in Ancient Israel* (Valley Forge, Penn.: Trinity, 1995).

[3] Ibid., 72.

prove to be to assess the matter, there must be some criteria by which one discerns the difference between true and false prophets, or real and non-prophets, or else one is failing to think either historically or critically about the prophetic material. All claims to be a true prophet are not equally valid. Charlatans were just as much a regular social type as true prophets in antiquity.

What this story does reveal, however, is that one can not divide true from false prophets purely on the basis of who claims to speak for Yahweh. Other criteria, including historical criteria, must be applied. The conclusion the author of the material in Kings would seem to urge is that even if one was disposed to see the court prophets as, in general, true prophets of Yahweh, in this particular matter they had been misled by a lying spirit. This brings up a further issue we will need to address—true prophets can, on occasion, speak beyond or against what God wishes them to say, and on the other hand, nonbiblical figures such as Balaam can offer true prophecy. It is not at all easy to distinguish between a true and a false prophet, and perhaps the distinguishing should actually be done at the level of prophecies rather than the prophets themselves.

More helpful is Grabbe's treatment of the Jonah stories. As Grabbe suggests, Jonah is too often ignored when the discussion turns to Hebrew prophecy, and certainly one of the major points this present book is seeking to make is that the prophecy a Hebrew prophet uttered could be *conditional* in nature. Furthermore, to a certain degree, a Hebrew prophet could resist God's call to make an unpopular prophecy. On the former score, if the audience repented in the face of the oracle, then God would perhaps withhold the judgment threatened.[4] Of course, this makes it even more difficult to discern true from false prophecy, especially when we have, in most cases, a very piecemeal knowledge of what happened after a certain prophecy was uttered. Historical evidence and literary evidence must be allowed to interact before one can make pronouncements about prophecy "failing."[5]

Grabbe offers a brief definition of a prophet. A prophet is a person who speaks in the name of a god (usually Yahweh) and claims to pass on a revelation from that god. Divine revelation is a sine qua non of prophecy.[6] On this showing, the literary creation of quasi-prophetic works involving ex eventu prophecy should probably not be seen as prophecy at all, for such efforts may well involve neither oracular prophets nor divine revelations. This point is worth pondering

---

[4] Ibid., 79–80.

[5] This is one of the major failings of R. P. Carroll's otherwise interesting study, *When Prophecy Failed: Cognitive Dissonance in the Prophetic Traditions of the Old Testament* (New York: Seabury, 1979). Carroll's particular concern is with some of the literary prophets and their predictions about the future, but he fails to deal seriously with the issue of whether some of these prophecies were intended to be conditional in nature from the outset.

[6] Grabbe, *Priests, Prophets,* 83. Compare this definition with what is said by Grabbe on p. 107: "The prophet is a mediator who claims to receive messages directly from a divinity, by various means, and communicates these messages to recipients."

further, especially when the discussion turns to apocalyptic material later in this study. On the whole, I must agree with Grabbe in his definition, and thus one must, at some point, broach the subject of non-prophetic developments based on, or prompted by, the prophetic corpus.

This leads to a brief discussion of the matter of literary prophecies, and a good point to start such a discussion is Grabbe's assessment of Akkadian literary prophecies. These prophecies generally take the form of chronicling a succession of unnamed kings and evaluating them as good or bad on the basis of what happened to the nation during their rule. There are some striking parallels with later Jewish apocalyptic, not the least in the use of ex eventu prophecy. There is, in addition, the description of present troubles that are said to be followed by some sort of idyllic future, often seen in terms of the coming of an ideal king (Marduk, Sulgi, Uruk). About these literary, ex eventu prophecies, Grabbe concludes, "There is no reason to think the literary prophecies arose from the pronouncements of a seer or ecstatic figure." Quite so, and Grabbe goes on to suggest that the distinction between literary predictive texts and real prophecy is a helpful one. I agree, and it suggests that literary predictions of the ex eventu sort should probably be seen as scribal rather than prophetic creations.[7] This, of course, raises the issue of how much of OT prophecy is in fact a literary creation, rather than a transcript of oracles. This issue will have to be faced again as this study proceeds.

Grabbe weighs in against the frequently offered characterization of prophets as social reformers and critics. This view has also led to the assumption that they are the forefathers of those who preach the social gospel. In this view, the prophets were largely forthtellers rather than foretellers. Grabbe admits that figures such as Amos do indeed offer social criticism, but in fact Amos's criticisms do not always seem terribly specific.

Prophets do, from time to time, speak in a generic way about the evils of societies—crime, immorality, idolatry, the problem of evil neighboring kingdoms or nations, and the like. But as Grabbe points out, social criticism is a staple item in Wisdom literature as well. There is nothing distinctively prophetic about such remarks, and one might also add that there is, to some degree, this kind of social criticism in non-Israelite prophecy as well. It does not set Hebrew prophecy apart from its ancient Near East prophetic surroundings, unless in the degree that self-criticism comes to the fore in Israelite prophecy.[8] Grabbe is also correct that both biblical and nonbiblical prophecies are filled with predictions about the future. One can not dismiss this as uncharacteristic of Hebrew prophets. "The designation 'social critics' applies only to some of the prophets and then only in a general way to a few of their prophecies, while 'social reformer' seems hardly appropriate to any of them"[9] unless one widens the discussion to

---

[7] Ibid., 94.
[8] Ibid., 103.
[9] Ibid., 104.

figures such as Elijah and Elisha—which will be done in this study. It will be seen that the more social-reforming sort of prophet tended to be those remembered as men of deeds, including the performance of miracles, rather than men who offered many oracles.

Although Grabbe is clearly a critical scholar, he is very leery of those who confidently think they can distinguish original oracular material from later literary expansion in the prophetic corpus. For example, he notes that the oracles against foreign nations have often been taken as secondary because it was cult prophets who offered such oracles and the Hebrew prophets we are dealing with are thought not to have been cult prophets. As Grabbe points out, this begs a whole host of questions, for clearly there were figures, such as Samuel or Jeremiah or Ezekiel, who have cultic associations or roots. When one deconstructs such criteria as are often used (e.g., certain major themes characterize a genuine oracle—woe rather than salvation oracles, for example), one is left with the rather remarkable conclusion that

> if, on the other hand, most of a book is now credited to the prophet in question—Amos, for example—such passages as messages of salvation, oracles against foreign nations, detailed forecasts about the future, predictions of a new age with millennial conditions all become part of the message of the classical prophet. The differences between the pre-classical seer, the classical prophet, the post-exilic prophet, and the apocalyptic visionary dwindle at most to matters of degree rather than kind.[10]

This is a startling conclusion, and this author is inclined to think Grabbe is right. The distinctions between the classical prophets and the later prophets, including the seers, appears to have been overdrawn, based on formal and content criteria that are dubious at best. A more holistic approach is in order when dealing with the prophetic corpus, and this study will try the experiment of being more inclusive in the analysis of the prophetic material of the various prophets and seeing what follows from such an approach.

Another subject on which Grabbe defies some common wisdom is the issue of ecstasy or trance and Israelite prophecy. Grabbe is right that, on a purely historical basis, one can not say it was only the prophets of Baal or non-Israelites prophets who experienced ecstasy or a trance state. Yet it is also true that only a distinct minority of texts in the Hebrew Scriptures suggest that biblical prophets experienced such a condition (cf. 1 Sam 10:10–11; 19:20–24; 1 Kgs 18:26–29; Ezek 1).

> Much of the time, we have no idea how the prophet received the divine message. . . . The message could have come through a trance state or it could have been a conscious composition. It could have come spontaneously or it could be the result of specific inquiry. In many cases, a variety of modes is possible, and we can only speculate on how it was received. Thus, it would be wrong to ascribe all prophetic oracles to ecstatic experiences; equally, we have no right to deny such experiences categorically to Israelite prophets.[11]

---

[10] Ibid., 106–7.
[11] Ibid., 111.

The attempt, on the one hand, to make the classical prophets fit the mold of modern rationalistic preachers will not do, but on the other hand, it is also true that the phenomenological study of trance states and ecstasy makes it evident that they can vary from heavy to light, involving more or less loss of contact with the outer world. It would appear that Israelite prophets experienced the same range of experiences found in prophets in other, nearby cultures; more important, ecstasy certainly cannot by itself help to distinguish true from false prophecy.

Grabbe rightly emphasizes that prophecy in Israel, as in the other ancient Near Eastern cultures, was not a gender-specific matter. There were certainly prophetesses in Israel, although they made up a minority of the prophetic guild. Huldah is surely one of the more notable prophetesses (2 Kgs 22:14–20). Notice that Huldah is consulted by King Josiah. Huldah responds to the inquiry by delivering an oracle of disaster, telling the king that God would judge Israel's disobedience. One may also point to the prophetess Noadiah, who opposed Nehemiah, or to Miriam (Exod 15:20), or to Deborah (Judg 4:4). From "what little is known, the only difference from the male prophets seems to be their sex. The behavior and messages of the prophetesses show no significant differences from those found among male prophets. . . . No special bias against female prophets is indicated in any of the passages where they are mentioned. This suggests that the proportion of male and female prophets in the text probably represents social reality."[12] Here it is important to note that Israel was not unusual either for the presence of prophetesses or for the roles they played in society; this shall become evident in the first chapter of this study.

The next minefield in the discussion of prophecy is the matter of divination. On first blush, one might think that divination was completely condemned in Israel (Isa 8:19; 44:25; Jer 14:14; 27:9–10; 29:8–9; Ezek 12:21–24). But what, then, is one to make of the sacred dice or lots, the consultation of Urim and Thummim for either yes or no answers (1 Sam 23:8–13; cf. Exod 28; 39)? It would appear that, as with the case of prophecy, there was bad consultation or divination for answers, and good consultation or divination. Or is it that the lots were tolerated in Israel but the prophets, as part of their critique of the cultus and the priestly apparatus, anathematized this way of controlling prophecy? Should one see in Israel an evolving critique of earlier means of getting answers from God?

It is difficult to know how to evaluate the data, but this matter needs to be revisited, not least because it even crops up in the NT in Acts 1. There would seem, however, to be this difference between genuine prophecy and divination: the latter is a human attempt to obtain an answer from God, presumably at a time when there is no spontaneous revelation from the deity about the matter. In other words, in Israel at least, it seems to serve in lieu of spontaneous

---

[12] Ibid., 115.

prophecy. It also potentially involves an element of human manipulation.[13] As such, it would seem to be subject to more human abuse and charlatanism.

It is time now to turn briefly to the issue of dreams and the receiving of revelations in dreams. On the one hand, dreams seem to be treated rather negatively in Jer 23:27–32 and 29:8; on the other hand, Daniel and Zechariah treat the matter rather differently, as does the book of Acts in the NT. It is perhaps possible to make a distinction between message dreams and symbolic dreams, the latter of which require more interpretation.[14] The evidence is such that one must say that this was a widely known means of receiving revelation throughout the entire period this book will be discussing.[15] We have clear evidence from as early as the Mari materials of revelations received in dreams (*ANET* 623). It is perhaps possible to group visions together with dreams—the former being a sort of day dream, the latter received in the night.

There is also the issue of whether a vision or dream will be made public or whether it is intended as a private revelation to the recipient. Oracles, by nature, are public in character, even if there is only an audience of one. In any event, one finds as early as 1 Sam 28:6 the suggestion that dreams and prophecy are equally means of discovering God's will, a phenomenon one also finds as late as the book of Acts, where both dreams and oracles regularly are portrayed as means of divine communication. There is clearly no blanket condemnation of dreams in the biblical or extrabiblical material relevant to this study, nor is there always a clear distinction between dreams and visions, any more than there is a clear distinction between seers and prophets in this material.

In many, if not most, respects, from a sociological point of view, it would appear that prophecy in Israel or in the Christian communities of the first century and later bore many similarities to the phenomenon found in the larger environment. One does see in the biblical tradition the shunning of certain practices, such as necromancy or witchcraft, but on the other hand, not all forms of divination would seem to have been ruled out. The question then becomes whether one places the emphasis on the similarities with the extrabiblical prophetic material or on the differences. Grabbe clearly does the former. Perhaps the current study will be able to assess the continuities and discontinuities without minimizing either. Prophecy is far too important a clue to the nature, especially the religious nature, of these ancient societies to be handled in overly simplified fashion. The reader, then, must be patient as this study allows the material to have its own say, without trying to impose a schema on the varied materials. If the reader has been exposed to new and fresh lines of thought about this venerable and variegated material, this author will be content. Clearly, this material holds an important key to understanding the biblical world. It will, then, be worth a detailed examination, to which this study now turns.

---

[13] See ibid., 136–38.

[14] See ibid., 146.

[15] On the NT period, see pp. 340–43 below.

CHAPTER 1

The Beginning of the Word

"*I*N THE BEGINNING WAS THE WORD . . ." It is a familiar and seemingly simple assertion; consequently, its profundity in a largely oral cultural environment can be overlooked. In an ancient culture the living word, the living voice, always had a certain precedence over a written word.[1] And of all the voices of antiquity, none had more power or authority than those who could speak for God or, in a pagan culture, for the gods. Indeed, those who could proffer a late word from God might well be the most important members of an ancient society.

Surprisingly, a study of prophecy in antiquity reveals that almost all ancient cultures had those who exercised roles one would call prophetic. Prophecy did not begin with the period of the Israelite monarchy, nor did it end when that monarchy was eclipsed, for even in Israel forms of prophecy carried on beyond that period of time. Nor were the prophets of Israel, any more than the NT prophets, operating in a cultural vacuum. A Balaam or a Jonah or a Paul could step over cultural boundaries and still be recognized as a sort of prophetic figure, because the social functions and roles, and to a degree even the forms and contents of the messages of prophets, were the same throughout antiquity at the eastern end of the Mediterranean.

Whether one is talking about the period of the Babylonian Empire or the Roman Empire, certain traits marked out prophetic figures such that they could be recognized throughout the region as spokesmen or spokeswomen for the divine. These individuals could

---

[1] See S. Niditch, *Oral World and Written Word: Ancient Israelite Literature* (Louisville: Westminster John Knox, 1996).

cross cultural and ethnic boundaries and still function. Indeed, prophecy was such a cross-cultural phenomenon that Babylonian kings could have Jewish prophets serving in their court, and Roman emperors might well listen to the word of an eastern and Jewish prophet before making a major decision. If one wants to understand biblical prophecy, one must be prepared to fish with a large net.

Though some cross-cultural and diachronic studies of prophecy have been undertaken in the past for at least part of the source material, it appears that no studies really take into consideration ancient Near Eastern, OT, NT, and Greco-Roman prophecy at one time. Some of the cross-cultural studies, undertaken largely by sociologists or those using sociological paradigms,[2] tend to roam too far afield and end up comparing phenomena that are too dissimilar culturally and temporally (e.g., comparing Melanesian cargo cults or Native American tribes with Israelite prophets!) to really shed much light on the ancient Mediterranean phenomenon of prophecy. Other studies analyze ancient prophecy exclusively in theological terms, with the result that cross-cultural factors and examples that could illuminate the subject are omitted.

The present study assumes that proximity in time and culture is important if we are to have enough data and cultural overlap to make sense of our subject matter. Of necessity, we must draw some temporal as well as geographical parameters for our study. The temporal parameters will be from approximately the Middle Bronze Age until the end of the third century AD, or from about the time of the Mari texts until the end of the Montanist movement. This, of course, means that this investigation will not be dealing directly with the real beginnings of prophetic phenomena in the ancient Near East, and only in a cursory way with the time when the ancestors of Israel—Abraham, Isaac, and Jacob—were thought to have lived (the Middle Bronze Period). Almost certainly, numerous prophets existed prior to the Mari prophets; furthermore, various biblical writers saw figures such as Abraham, Isaac, and Jacob in a prophetic light. The problem is that one does not possess oracles from these biblical figures, much less prophetic books, and there is only precious little other evidence that they were intermediaries for a group of people.[3] There are, of course, narratives about them, but most of these

---

[2] See, e.g., Overholt, *Channels of Prophecy;* or R. R. Wilson, *Prophecy and Society in Ancient Israel* (Philadelphia: Fortress, 1980).

[3] The story of Abraham interceding for Sodom and Gomorrah in Gen 18–19 could fall into the category of prophetic activity, as could the story of the healing of Abimelech through Abraham's prayer in Gen 20:1–18 (the only reference to Abraham as a *nabi* is in Gen 20:7), but little else in the Abrahamic material seems to suggest such activity. Or again, Jacob's dream-vision in Gen 28 might place him in the prophetic category, but this occurrence seems to be atypical of his life experiences and, in any event, is portrayed as largely a private matter that did not lead to his proclaiming things to God's people. Most any of the major figures in the Bible could be called prophets if we include any and all contact or conversation with the deity as prophetic phenomena. But such a definition is too broad. Prophets are those who manifest prophetic activity with some regularity for some period of their life. The case of Joseph is different from that of the earlier patriarchs, but

do not suggest prophetic activity on their part. Even in the case of Joseph, the having and interpreting of dreams, while a regular prophetic phenomenon, do not lead to an oracular function. Joseph could be seen as a "diviner of dreams." A similar problem exists with some of the narratives about Moses, but more will be said about him, as he does fall within the parameters of this study and manifests enough prophetic traits to make a discussion worthwhile. Yet such a study must be undertaken carefully, with a full recognition of the historical problems and of later editing, for even the most optimistic of scholarly surveys of the early history of Israelite prophets begins not with Moses but with Saul and Samuel.[4] This study must begin with the remarkable findings at Mari.[5] One of the major purposes of this chapter is to make clear both the value and the urgency of taking a cross-cultural approach to the analysis of biblical prophecy. Before doing so, however, it is important to make certain critical distinctions.

First, there is a marked difference between a mediator or an intermediary and a prophet. There are times and places at which a prophet is simply a mouthpiece for the deity and in fact does not intercede with the deity on anyone's behalf. The communication flows in one direction and is not prompted by any attempts at consultation by a human party. On the other hand, there are obviously also times when a prophet does beseech the deity or inquire of the deity on behalf of some human person or group. What needs to be emphasized about the latter is that this may be a role that a prophet plays but it is not specifically a prophetic role. Priests or kings or sages might also play such a role for a person or group of persons. Petitionary prayer or discourse is not a distinctively prophetic function. It is for this reason that I am is somewhat leery of calling a prophet an intermediary, for this term in English suggests an ambassador who exercises shuttle diplomacy between two parties. True, some central or institutional prophets did tend to function this way a good deal of the time, perhaps especially if there were no priests to approach or petition the deity. This, however, does not adequately describe the actual distinctive social function of prophets and prophetesses—namely, to speak oracles, a late word from God, to a person or group. Whether one is talking about the Mari prophets, or Israelite prophets, or the later Christian prophets, their chief and distinctive task was to speak for, or even as the instrument of, the deity.

---

most scholars think this material has been heavily edited in the light of later interests and concerns, including the interest in portraying Israel's patriarchs as prophetic figures. Joseph's dreams could indeed place him in the category of a visionary or seer, and it would appear that "seers" were not uncommon among the Jews prior to the period of classical prophecy during the monarchy.

[4] See R. Rendtorff, "Reflections on the Early History of Prophecy in Israel," in *History and Hermeneutic* (ed. R. W. Funk; New York: Harper & Row, 1967), 14–34.

[5] While there may, in the future, be sufficient evidence from the Ebla texts to warrant bringing them into the discussion, especially since they come from the third millennium BC, the claim that they provide evidence of prophecy is yet to be substantiated. See H. B. Huffmon, "Prophecy (ANE)," *IDB* 5:477–82.

Second, one must distinguish carefully between the prophetic experience, the prophetic expression, the prophetic tradition, and the prophetic corpus. Obviously, when one is talking about ancient prophets, there is no direct access to any of the first three of these items but only to the literary residue, whether in the form of the tablets at Mari, the Israelite prophetic books, the quotations of oracles in the NT, or the records of the pronouncements at Delphi. It is important to keep this point squarely in view because sometimes confusion has been created by treating these items together.

For example, only a few direct transcripts of prophetic experience have survived, although later reflections on what happened do exist. A good example of this phenomenon occurs in the book of Revelation. John of Patmos relates things he saw and heard, however, not as a transcript of an experience but, rather, as a form of exhortation and consolation to a remote group of Christian disciples. In other words, the literary residue is not a transcript but, rather, a later reflection on, and presentation of, the content of an earlier experience. What is also intriguing about this particular case is that apparently the prophetic oral expression and the period of transmission of tradition stages are skipped altogether. This material was not delivered orally by the prophet to anyone, for he was marooned—indeed, probably exiled—at the penal colony on Patmos. Rather, he put the material into an epistolary framework and sent it off as a circular letter to some churches in western Asia Minor with which he was associated. In other cases there may have been an initial proclamation followed by a long period of oral transmission of specific prophetic traditions before they became part of a prophetic corpus.

We must be sensitive to what is actually being dealt with when we approach the final form of the prophetic materials. Whether creative later editing and expansions on prophetic tradition can be called *prophecy* is debatable. For example, some of the creative exegesis of prophetic texts at Qumran does not necessarily qualify as prophecy itself but, rather, as attempts to contemporize, or apply former prophecies to a later audience. It is more a matter of hermeneutics than of new revelation from God, more a matter of creative reinterpretation or *relecture* than of inspiration. Prophets also should not be confused with their scribes or recorders, when they had them. Baruch was not Jeremiah. At its core, prophecy is a living word from the deity, and a prophet delivers that message. Figure 1-1 perhaps will illustrate some of the complexities of this matter.[6]

First, note in this schematic the difference between the solid line and the dashed lines. The revelation from God to the prophet is the fundamental and invariable component of the social situation. This may be the only component if the revelation is simply to and about the prophet himself (or herself)—for example, when God first calls the prophet or when he instructs him about something he must do. The dashed lines indicate other frequent components,

---

[6]I am here adopting and adapting a model offered by Overholt, *Channels of Prophecy,* 23.

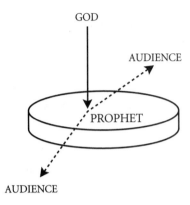

Figure 1-1

especially the delivering of a revelation by the prophet to an audience. With some regularity the prophet responds to God in regard to the revelation, or on other occasions on behalf of a third party. In the latter case, the prophet becomes an intermediary like other intermediaries. Recent sociological discussions of prophets and prophecies have added a further component to the mix, namely, the feedback from the audience to the prophet once a message is delivered. Stress is placed in the sociological discussion on how the audience authorizes or attributes authority to the prophet by accepting his word. The prophet's performance must be recognizable to a specific audience as prophetic. Yet this in fact may happen even when an audience largely or even entirely rejects a prophet's message, labeling him a false prophet. It is thus not convincing to say that a prophet must articulate thoughts, hopes, dreams, or fears that already exist in the minds of the audience. This was not always the case, especially for those, like Jeremiah, whom we might label prophets of doom because they spoke woe oracles to their own people.[7] Indeed, when we deal with peripheral prophets, or those who are not part of an institution but, rather, become external critics of an institution (e.g., Elijah and the court of Ahab and also the prophets of Baal), it was often the case that their oracles did not conform to any desires or expectations of the audience to whom they were directed. This is not to say that they were unintelligible utterances or that no one would have been positively responsive to their words. Some Israelites, and perhaps especially some prophetic understudies, may have been receptive to such negative words directed at Ahab and Jezebel. But they were not the target audience for those oracles.[8]

---

[7] But see the discussion ibid., 140ff.

[8] This brings up the interesting point that those who preserved the prophet's oracles as writings or as oral tradition seem not infrequently to have been persons who were not directly addressed by the oracles but nonetheless were affected by them and felt they were of ongoing value. At Mari we do find oracles that were originally directed to the king, preserved by the king's scribes. It is interesting that only a few of these oracles could be said to be critical of the king, and even they are only mildly critical. More often these oracles warn or inform Zimri-Lim about something that may affect him.

It will be seen that the suggestions about a prophet's role above distinguish a prophet from a diviner. Here one must agree with some of the distinctions suggested by H. Huffmon, for example, when he says a prophet is "a person who through non-technical means receives a clear and immediate message from a deity for transmission," which is to be contrasted "with learned, technical divination and the use of interpretive skills."[9] This is why, in what follows, I begin the discussion with the Mari prophets and not with the Babylonian *barum*, or diviners.

Something also must be said here in a preliminary way about prophets and prophetic signs, as well as about prophets and miracles. In regard to the latter, miracles are sometimes predicated of prophets, indeed sometimes even emphasized (cf. the Elijah and Elisha cycles). Yet it is clear enough that miracle working is not required (cf. John the Baptist); and indeed, there were healers or those with whom miracles were associated in ancient religious history who were not prophets (cf., e.g., the Jewish Hasidim at the turn of the era). This means that while a miracle may suggest the presence of a prophet, it does not necessarily do so. A Jewish sage might pray for and obtain a cure, or a messianic figure might be involved in miracle working. Finally, in regard to prophetic signs and the reading of their significance, both can occur apart from the activity of a prophet (cf., e.g., a meteorological omen and the work of a diviner), but it is fair to say that prophetic signs do often characterize the activity of prophets. They were often more than just wordsmiths.

Prophetic signs were a way to make the word visible. I agree with the recent study of Morna Hooker, who suggests that a prophetic sign is "not a visual aid intended to assist in teaching—rather, the dramatic equivalent of the spoken oracle; not an efficacious act which causes something to happen—rather, the dramatic embodiment of the divine purpose, which otherwise might well be at present hidden."[10] Such activities were engaged in by prophets with enough regularity that we are able to say that they were a normal function of prophets. What one can not say, is that the prophet *had* to perform such signs, authenticating or otherwise, in order to be a prophet. The primary and necessary task was always the spoken oracle. It will be important to keep various of these considerations in mind throughout our examination of the prophetic tradition.

I. FROM MARI TO MOSES AND BEYOND[11]

A. A Mari Old Time. It is perhaps fair to date the real beginning of cross-cultural studies of ancient Near Eastern prophecy to 1899, when the Egyptian

---

[9] H. B. Huffmon, "The Origins of Prophecy in Israel," in *Magnalia Dei: The Mighty Acts of God* (ed. F. Cross et al.; Garden City: Doubleday, 1976), 172–86, here 172.

[10] M. D. Hooker, *The Signs of a Prophet: The Prophetic Actions of Jesus* (Harrisburg, Penn.: Trinity, 1997), 38–39.

[11] I borrow here in part a title from R. P. Gordon, "From Mari to Moses: Prophecy at Mari and in Ancient Israel," in *Of Prophets' Visions and the Wisdom of Sages* (ed. H. A. McKay and D. J. A. Clines; Sheffield: JSOT Press, 1993), 63–79.

Wen Amun text was first published. This text recounts an occurrence of ecstatic prophesying in a temple at Byblos in the eleventh century BC, complete with a stick figure drawing of the prophet, depicted as if he had just picked up a live electrical wire! This text, dating close to the time of Saul, set in motion a whole series of queries and inquiries about the possible correlations between Egyptian and Israelite prophecy. Little did scholars know at that point that there would come to light in the twentieth century a far more significant finding that, had the Qumran material not been discovered, would have to be seen as the most significant archaeological finding of relevance to the Bible in modern times. I am referring to the finding of the royal archives at Mari.

Mari is the ancient name of Tell Hariri, a site located in northwest Mesopotamia on the middle Euphrates River, about thirty-one miles north of the current border between Syria and Iraq. The site was first excavated by A. Parrot, and since 1979 by J. Magueron; the results are nothing less than staggering. Not only have the city and its palace been uncovered, but also an archive including some twenty thousand cuneiform tablets (largely administrative texts, letters, and treaty documents from the Lim dynasty, which ruled during the last half of the life span of Mari's existence).[12] Our concern is with the texts that mention various sorts of prophetic figures and activity and especially with the material that has been appearing in a series of volumes since 1988 under the title *Archives épistolaires de Mari I/1* (=ARMT 26/1).

Perhaps it will be well to deal with one of the most startling discoveries to date, namely, the presence of an Akkadian cognate of the Hebrew word for "prophet" *(nabi)* in text 216 (A.2209). A court functionary says that he assembled these prophetic figures *(lu nabi-i mes sa ha-na-mes)* the day after he arrived at Asmad in order to discover whether it would be safe for the king to engage in a ritual lustration outside the city walls. This finding of the cognate of *nabi* was especially interesting in light of the fact that at the Syrian city of Emar there are occurrences of the form *munabbiatu* in thirteenth-century BC texts, referring to what appear to be prophetesses associated with the goddess Ishara (texts 373:97, 379:12, 383:10, 406:5).[13] The importance of this cross-cultural phenomenon should not be underestimated. Not only do we find terminology for prophets similar to what we find in the OT from a period well before the era of classical prophecy; we also find the practice of consulting such figures about the future.

---

[12] For a general description of the site and the findings, see J. Magueron, "Mari (Archaeology)," *ABD* 4:525–29.

[13] See the discussion by Gordon, "From Mari to Moses," 65; and the more detailed discussion by D. E. Fleming, "The Etymological Origins of the Hebrew *nabi:* The One Who Invokes God," *CBQ* 55 (1993): 217–24; and his "Nabu and Munabbiatu: Two New Syrian Religious Personnel," *JAOS* 113 (1993): 175–83. It is interesting that Fleming suggests that in these contexts the cognate terminology seems to speak, in the main, of one who calls upon the deity, not one who is called by that deity. Perhaps this is one of the reasons that Moses is called a *nabi* in the Deuteronomistic traditions but not elsewhere in the Pentateuch.

There is general agreement that this terminology, like the Hebrew *nabi*, etymologically ultimately comes from the verb "to call," though there is debate as to whether it suggests that the prophet is a person called by a god, or one who calls upon the deity (as an intercessor).[14]

The two most common terms used for prophets at Mari are *apilum* and *muhhum* (or *mahhum*). These and other such terms refer to professional prophetic figures. The term *apilum* (and female equivalent *apiltum*) means something like "cultic functionary" or "answerer" whereas the *mahhum/muhhum* or his female counterpart the *muhhutum* is the ecstatic. The term *kumrum* means "priest" and *qabbatum* "prophetess."[15] It is clear that some of these terms go back much further than 1800 BC, for we find in an old Akkadian text the term *mahhum* for a court prophet who is given a dole of grain by a ruler.[16] It is interesting that at Mari and elsewhere the *mahhum* seems to be connected to both temple and palace. Again we find evidence of the ecstatics not merely at Mari but also at Susa, Larsa, and Tell ed-Der under the term *mahhum* or its cognate, and the evidence for both women and men ecstatics is clear. Being a prophet, whether in the ancient Near East or in the Greco-Roman world, was never apparently a gender-specific role.

The evidence from Mari further attests that the ecstatics there did not serve just one deity but could be involved with several, such as Nergal or Itur-Mer or Dagan (see ARM 3 40, 21, 333). That all the ecstatics have Akkadian names (e.g., Irra-gamil, Ea-masi) suggests that the origins of such prophets and prophetesses was from farther east than Mari. It is also possible to give a job description of what the ecstatics did at Mari: (1) they delivered oracles; (2) they participated in cultic rituals; (3) they received rations. The first of these is the most well-attested function. The messages they gave to Zimri-Lim, the king, included advice concerning the maintenance of sacrifices (see ARM 3 40) or warnings about potential danger if the king should leave Mari on a new expedition (ARM 10 50).[17]

On some occasions the *muhhum* becomes simply the mouthpiece for the deity, with the deity (Annunitum or Dagan) speaking in the first person (cf. ARM 10 7, 8, 50 and A. 455). There is evidence of visions and dreams being experienced by the Mari prophets; in one case a prophet reports having heard a discussion among the gods of the circle of Ea (text 208 or A.2233; cf. the dream experience of the prophet in the temple of Dagan in text 233 or A.15). It is interesting that the *muhhum* was also like OT prophets in another regard—he or she would perform symbolic actions to illustrate or dramatize a word from the

---

[14] See the discussion by R. P. Gordon, "Where Have All the Prophets Gone?" *BBR* 5 (1995): 67–86, here 73ff.

[15] I am indebted here to the discussion by B. E. Beyer, "Aspects of Religious Life at Mari" (Ph.D. diss., Hebrew Union College, 1985), 203ff.

[16] Ibid., 204.

[17] See ibid., 206–7.

deity. Thus text 206 (A.963) refers to a *muhhum* who devours a raw lamb and announces a devouring that threatens the country.

The prophets at Mari would regularly offer authentications of their prophecies by sending along with their prophecies either a lock of hair or material from the fringe of a garment (see A.455, ARM 6 45, and ARM 10, 7, 8 and 50).[18] This suggests that the *muhhum* had distinctive apparel that could be recognized by the king or there is a possibility that the hair or fringe was involved in some ritual upon the receipt of the message.[19] But this practice of sending hair or fringes was also used by an *apiltum* as well. While one might think that this ritual would indicate that the prophet was at some distance from the king, this may well not be the case, in view of the fact that various *muhhum* are listed on the ration lists receiving a dole, which suggests that they are in or near the palace. On the other hand, text 206 is quite clear that the prophet gave his oracle in the city gate to the elders of the city, rather than to the king directly or through a royal messenger.[20] The conclusions of Beyer about the *muhhum* are fully warranted: "The ecstatic of Old Babylonian Mari—whether *muhhum* or *muhhutum*—played a prominent role in society. The ecstatic's oracles, containing warnings, blessings, and instructions for proper worship, often influenced the lives of the Mari kingdom's ruling family. As did so many other religious personnel, the ecstatic received rations from the palace."[21]

The ration lists are also helpful in that they indicate that the ecstatic prophet was regularly connected with one particular deity, for the formula we find in the list reads, "*X* item(s) (for) [personal name] ecstatic of [deity name]" (see ARM 21 333:34, 43). There is also evidence from ARM 25:142 of a reward being offered to a prophet, presumably for a favorable or true prophecy, in this case a silver ring.

It is appropriate to say a bit more about the content and form of the oracles. It should not be thought that prophecy at Mari was simply identified with divination or that, on the other hand, it excluded it. To the contrary, prophecy often came in the form of a warning that divination was in order. For example, in text 204 (lines 22–26) Inib-shina, a prophetess, says, "Let my star [i.e., the king] have an omen taken, and let my star act according to his omens. Let my star take care of himself." This is very similar to a warning by this same prophetess in text 197 that urges not going into a city without taking an omen. In short,

---

[18] It has been suggested that the term *qammatum* indicated the hairy condition of the prophetess. From a much later period we can see that, in a Greco-Roman setting, hair becomes an issue when a woman prophesies in Corinth (1 Cor 11:2–16, on which see B. Witherington, *Conflict and Community in Corinth* [Grand Rapids: Eerdmans, 1995], ad loc.).

[19] See E. Noort, *Untersuchungen zum Gottesbeschied Mari: Die Mari prophetie in der alttestamentlichen Forschung* (Neukirchen-Vluyn: Neukirchener, 1977), 83–86.

[20] See the discussion by S. B. Parker, "Prophecy at Mari and in Israel," *VT* 43 (1, 1993): 50–68, here 60–61.

[21] Beyer, "Aspects," 209–10.

prophecy could prompt divination and reinforce it, which may suggest that divination was the more usual form of prophecy at Mari, or at least was thought to be the more reliable and so had the last word. It is interesting that in text 207 there is reflected a clear suspicion of prophecies that have been given in response to a solicitation (and perhaps an inducement of a gift or some food or wine). Here Queen Shibtu, who has solicited oracles about her husband's fate, reassures him, "Perhaps my lord will say: 'She used guile to make them speak.' One does not *make* them speak! Some speak, some resist" (lines 35–39).[22] Spontaneous oracles apparently were less suspect than solicited ones, and as Parker says, there was apparently a need "institutionalized in extispicy to check and control for possible misreadings of the divine message by the prophet, as by the diviner."[23]

In regard to the form of the oracles, text 207 strongly suggests that at least some of the oracles originally had a poetic character:

> My lord raised the staff.
> Against Ishme-Dagan he raised the staff,
> saying,
> With the staff I shall overcome you.
> Struggle as much as you want.
> In the struggle I shall overcome you. (2.13–17)[24]

When one compares this text with various oracles from other ancient Near Eastern cultures, it appears that it was a normal characteristic of prophecy that it take a poetic form. D. N. Freedman puts it this way: "From time immemorial the language of heaven and of heroes has been poetic in form. . . . The basic and persistent medium of classic religion and revelation is poetry."[25] This is an important reminder not least because some of the most archaic portions of the Pentateuch are poems, and while not all poems are prophecies, nevertheless, when we are dealing with the Song of the Sea in Exod 15 or the Song of Deborah in Judg 5 or the oracles of Balaam in Num 23–24—all of which have been dated to the twelfth or eleventh centuries BC[26] and all of which are attributed to figures who are called prophets or prophetesses in the larger context of these poems—we seem to be dealing with prophecy.

There is, in fact, another dimension to this phenomenon that bears mentioning now. It is not an accident that the material in Exod 15 and Judg 5 are called songs, for they are said in Exod 15:1 and Judg 5:1 to be sung to God's people. We must reckon with the possibility that some prophetic oracles were

---

[22] See Parker, "Prophecy at Mari," 64.

[23] Ibid., 67.

[24] See the discussions by Gordon, "Where Have All the Prophets Gone?" 76; and Parker, "Prophecy at Mari," 57–60.

[25] D. N. Freedman, "Pottery, Poetry, and Prophecy: An Essay on Biblical Poetry," *JBL* 96 (1, 1977): 5–26, here 15.

[26] See ibid., 18.

sung from a very early period in the history of Israel.[27] This is of no little importance for our discussions not only because, at a later point in Israel's history, we
hear of singers who are considered prophets (in Chronicles) but also because
when we get to the material that came from the earliest Jewish Christians,
namely, some of the christological hymns, it would appear that we have a much
later manifestation of prophetic oracles in poetic form meant to be sung.

B. Malamat's Musings.   A. Malamat has been especially helpful in indicating
both the most revealing elements from the Mari texts and the light that the Mari
material sheds on Israelite prophecy.[28] Some of the most helpful observations that
arise from a close examination of his study need to be repeated at this juncture.
First, the evidence about prophecy at Mari suggests that many prophets spoke to
or about the king, but since this material comes from a royal archive, we can not
say that Mari prophets did not also address others and other sorts of social situations. Second, as Malamat stresses, over half the prophecies at Mari were revealed
in dreams. This sort of prophecy especially required authentication; hence, in the
dream-revelation texts the following pattern is regularly discernible: (1) mention
of the male or female dreamer; (2) the opening formula of the dream, "(I saw) in
my dream" (cf. Gen 40:9, 16; 41:17); (3) the content of the dream, based on a visual or, more often, an auditory experience; (4) the communicator's comments,
often including a lock of hair or the hem of a garment. As Malamat says, the latter
were personal elements that may have served as an identity confirmation card.[29]
Prophecy, then, could come either in the form of a dream or vision, or as a revelation given while one was awake and conscious. It would appear dream revelations
were considered somewhat more suspect.

Third, clearly enough from the content of the Mari prophecies, prophets
functioned especially at a time of crisis (in this case the coming danger was from
Babylon itself and Hammurabi).[30] The oracles are typically oracles of assurance
from the deity to the king and often involve the phrase "fear not." Their func-

---

[27] See the conclusion of R. E. Clements, *Old Testament Prophecy: From Oracle to
Canon* (Louisville: Westminster John Knox, 1996), 2: "Against Gunkel's earlier conclusion, that the psalmists were simply imitating the prophetic style, the weight of evidence
points to the conclusion that the relationship between prophecy and psalmody had at one
time been very close. Accordingly, where liturgical forms and modes of address appear in
prophecy, this points back to a situation in which central cultic origin and association of
the prophets themselves has shaped the traditions."

[28] See especially A. Malamat, *Mari and the Israelite Experience* (Oxford: Oxford University Press, 1989).

[29] Ibid., 93.

[30] See Huffmon, "Prophecy," 479: "A number of the oracles are public, even in the
presence of the assembly of the elders. The connection of the oracles with times of political
and personal (royal) crisis is even clearer with the publication of the additional texts [i.e.,
those published since 1988]. Also, the initiatives that the prophets can take—especially the
'official' speakers—are striking."

tion is, in part, to suggest the loyalty and reliability and power of the deity.[31] The crisis context is an especially important insight to remember when we are dealing with Israelite prophecy. Fourth, both women and men were designated as and functioned as prophets. Their prophecies were primarily political or social in character. Fifth, prophecy and divination were not seen as competing forms of knowing about the future but mutually reinforcing forms, with divination apparently given something of an edge in reliability. Sixth, prophets were often remunerated for their services, whether with food or with valuable gifts, and apparently they came to expect this.[32] Seventh, there appears to have been an ecstatic component to the prophetic experience at Mari, and as in the Hebrew Scriptures, spontaneous, unsolicited prophecy was not uncommon.[33] Last, the terminology used to describe prophets at Mari, when compared to the terminology for such figures in other Semitic cultures of a later period, suggests a phenomenon that was culturewide, not subculture specific. Israelite prophecy must not be evaluated in isolation from the prophetic phenomena found among its neighbors. This last conclusion becomes even more evident when we consider the material from Deir 'Alla about Balaam.

II. BALAAM THE SEER AND THE SIGNIFICANCE OF DEIR 'ALLA

A. Balaam's Angst. There was a time in the study of Hebrew prophecy that various scholars doubted the historical existence of the interesting figure named Balaam that shows up in Num 22–24. But when in 1967 an inscription, written by a non-Israelite on plaster, from about 700 BC was found not in Israel but at Tell Deir 'Alla in the East Jordan Valley near Ammon, such conclusions had to be revised. The most important part of this find comes in what is called "Combination I," which may be translated as follows:[34]

> The account of [Balaam son of Beo]r who was a seer of the gods [*hazeh 'ilahin*]. The gods came to him in the night, and he saw a vision like an oracle of El. Then they said to [Balaa]m son of Beor: "Thus he will do/make [   ] hereafter (?), which [   ]." And Balaam arose the next day [   ] from [   ] But he was not ab[le to   ] and he wept grievously. And his people came up to him [and said to] him: "Balaam, son of Beor, why are you fasting and crying?" And he said to them: "Sit down! I will tell you what the Sadda[yyin have done.] Now come see the works of the gods! The g[o]ds gathered together; and Saddayyin took their places in the assembly." And they said to S[   ]: "Sew up, bolt up the heavens in your cloud, ordaining darkness instead of eternal light! And put the dark [se]al on your bolt, and do not remove

---

[31] See ibid., 481.

[32] See the discussion in Malamat, *Mari and the Israelite Experience*, 83ff.

[33] That it is a phenomenon only at Mari and in Israel, as Malamat, ibid., 79, suggests, is not at all clear.

[34] Here I am following the careful translation work of J. A. Hackett, *The Balaam Text from Deir 'Alla* (Chico, Calif.: Scholars Press, 1980), 29.

it forever! For the swift reproaches the griffin-vulture and the voice of vultures sings out. The sto[rk] the young of the NHS-bird (?) and claws up young herons. The swallow tears at the dove and the sparrow [ ] the rod, and instead of the ewes it is the staff that is led. Hares eat [a wo]lf (?) [ ] drink wine and hyenas give heed to chastisement. The whelps of the f [ox] laughs at the wise. And the poor woman prepares myrrh while the priestess [ ] for the prince, a tattered loincloth. The respected one (now) respects (others) and the one who gave respect is (now) re[spected] and the deaf hear from afar. [and the ? of (?)] a fool see visions. The constraint of the offspring [ ] the leopard. The piglet chases the you[ng of] (?) . . ."

The text, of course, has many imponderables and uncertainties, but certain things are evident about it.[35] First, it is clearly about Balaam, the same Balaam referred to in Numbers. Second, he is clearly seen as a famous prophet or seer. He requires no introduction in this text. "This fact implies that his name is well known to the people to whom the inscription was addressed, so we may infer that his was a tradition of long standing."[36] He has received, in this case, a revelation, a word about a meeting of the divine council in which the gods are upset about the state of earthly affairs. Balaam's reaction makes clear that the implications of the heavenly council's decision are tragic for his clients. The heavens have been shut up, and this means that chaos and darkness and all sorts of reversals of normal order will prevail upon the earth.[37]

B. Balaam As Seer.   Several aspects of this text are crucial for the discussion of the Balaam traditions, as well as other prophetic traditions in the OT. First, Balaam is called by a term that is related to the Hebrew word *hozeh,* or "seer." This seems to have been the preferred term for such a figure in the earlier stages of Israelite prophecy (cf., e.g., Samuel). Second, both the notion of the heavenly council and the prophetic access to it characterize not only various extrabiblical traditions, such as this one, but also various biblical ones as well (see, e.g., 1 Kgs 22:19–23; Isa 6:1–2; Pss 29; 82:1–8; 89:6–9; Job 1:6; 2:1). We also find this notion in the NT at various points (cf. 2 Cor 12:1–10 and various texts in the book of Revelation). Third, the prophet is portrayed here as one who has received bad news and finds it incumbent on himself to deliver it, which causes him no end of grief. This comports well with the portrait of Balaam in Numbers, in which he makes evident that he must proclaim the words, whether blessing or curse, that God has given him to proclaim. The Balaam of the Deir 'Alla tradition and of the OT is one who is a reluctant prophet when it comes to being the bearer of bad news for his clients.

---

[35] One of the major debates about this text is its language. Is it a dialect closer to Aramaic, or is it some South Canaanite dialect like that which existed in the first half of the first millennium BC?

[36] Hackett, *The Balaam Text,* 125.

[37] See the discussion of M. S. Moore, *The Balaam Traditions: Their Character and Development* (Atlanta: Scholars Press, 1990), 78ff.

Finally, the apparent home region of Balaam in the biblical traditions comports with the locale of the Deir 'Alla text.

Our scrutiny of the Mari texts and the Deir 'Alla text reveals both the benefits and the necessity, at this juncture, of reading the biblical data in the light of such material. It also prepares us for a closer examination of some of the earliest Israelite prophetic traditions—the Moses traditions, the Deborah traditions, and the Balaam traditions, to which we now turn.

III. MOSES THE REMARKABLE INTERMEDIARY

A. Was Moses a Prophet?   Surprisingly, a close inspection of the Pentateuch reveals next to no discussion about prophets and prophecy, especially if one leaves Deut 13 and 18 temporarily out of our purview. By this I do not merely mean that the terminology for prophets or prophetesses doesn't come up much, though that is true ("prophet" or "prophets" is mentioned once in Gen 20:7, once in Exod 7:1, and once in Num 11:29 and 12:6, and a prophetess is mentioned once in Exod 15:20; only Deuteronomy has significant use of the terminology, and then only in three places—Deut 13:1, 3, 5; 18:15, 18, 20, 22; and 34:10). I also mean that the subject does not come up for discussion except in Deuteronomy, and even there it is a rather briefly mentioned topic. This is very surprising if in fact the Pentateuch was put together during or after the monarchial period, as most scholars think. Even more surprising, if the Pentateuch does come out of or after the age of the classical prophets, is the fact that very little effort is made to portray Moses as a prophet in the Pentateuch. We must examine this curious fact in some detail.

The first question concerning Moses is, Does he really deserve to be called a prophet in the first place? This question must be raised on two grounds especially. First, in the call material in Exod 4–6 we must come to grips with the fact that it is said that Moses is uncircumcised of lips, which means, at the least, that he is a poor speaker or possibly also slow of speech, perhaps having a speech impediment (tongue-tied) (see 4:10–11). In other words, he is not well equipped to be a wordsmith or an oracle. Second, we have the remarkable fact that while nothing is said of Moses being a prophet, Aaron is described as the mouth of Moses (4:16): "He shall indeed speak for you to the people; he shall serve as a mouth for you and you shall serve as God for him." Later only Aaron is actually called a *nabi* (7:1). In short, Moses will serve as the intermediary between God and Aaron, conveying God's words to Aaron, but Aaron will serve as the prophet to God's people and others. That Moses was commissioned to be a leader and bring the Israelites out of Egypt is clear. Equally clear is that Moses and Aaron are empowered to do great signs before Israel and Pharaoh—authenticating or validating miracles. This was the very sort of thing Jesus refused to do for those who challenged his words and actions. What is not clear is whether Moses was commissioned to be a prophet.

If we consider for a moment the usual way of evaluating the material in Exodus, something peculiar comes to light. Customarily it is argued that, because

of later priestly interests, Aaron has been added to various passages in this earliest material from the Moses saga, presumably in order to establish the precedence of the Aaronic priesthood.[38] But the evidence itself suggests there are two
good reasons for doubting this conclusion, at least insofar as the recounting of
the Exodus-Sinai events is concerned: (1) knowing what we know about the stature of Moses in the eyes of later Judean writers both during and after the
monarchial period, it is difficult to think that a later redactor would construct
things in such a way as to steal Moses' thunder, time and again, simply in order
to support a particular tradition about the priesthood; (2) there is no real effort
to present Aaron as a priestly figure before the golden-calf episode in Exodus. To
the contrary, he is clearly presented as a prophetic figure up to that point, and a
priestly figure afterwards. The latter observation needs to be demonstrated.[39]

A customary feature of some call narratives in the Hebrew Scriptures is
that the one called expresses his inadequacy for, or reluctance to take up, the
commissioned task (Judg 6:14–15; 1 Sam 10:20–24; 1 Kgs 3:5–9; Isa 6:5–8; Jer
1:4–10).[40] In this regard, Moses is no different. Especially plain is Exod 4:10,
where Moses is presented as saying, "Forgive me Lord, I am no man of words—I
never have been nor have I become so, in spite of all you have said to your servant—for I am heavy of lip and thick of tongue." J. H. Tigray has analyzed closely
the key phrase, comparing it to various parallels, especially Akkadian ones, and
has shown that Moses is claiming a medical exception to this call. It is not just
that he is not an eloquent speaker; he has a speech impediment of some sort.[41]
Even when Yahweh states that Yahweh is the one who made the mouth and will
be with Moses, Moses responds and, in effect, asks God to send someone else.
Notice what follows this exchange at Exod 4:14–16. Yahweh speaks again and
says, "Is there not Aaron your brother, the Levite? I know that he is an eloquent
speaker. . . . You will speak to him, and put words into his mouth. And I am with
your mouth and with his mouth, and I will instruct you both as to what you are
to do. He will speak on your behalf to the people, and so he will be as a mouth
for you and you will be as a god to him."

---

[38] See the discussion in J. I. Durham, *Exodus* (Waco: Word, 1987), 47ff.; his explanation is rather typical.

[39] The distinction between the presentation of Aaron in the narrative portions of the
Pentateuch and that in the cultic material, especially in Leviticus and Numbers but also in
Exodus, has often been noted (see A. Cody, *A History of the Old Testament Priesthood*
[Rome: Pontifical Biblical Institute, 1969], 146–74), but I am referring to the distinction
made in the early and later narrative material in Exodus.

[40] See the discussion by N. Habel, "The Form and Significance of the Call Narratives," *ZAW* 77 (1965): 297–323.

[41] J. H. Tigray, "'Heavy of Mouth' and 'Heavy of Tongue': On Moses' Speech Difficulty," *BASOR* 231 (1978): 57–65. Tigray notes that Maimonides saw the problem here
clearly: a prophet is someone who has to be able to speak clearly and distinctly. Indeed,
Maimonides spoke of bodily as well as spiritual perfection as the prerequisite for being a
prophet (see p. 62).

This extremely interesting exchange suggests several things. Although it is mentioned in passing that Aaron is a Levite, there is absolutely no discussion of his activities in that role here. Rather, here he is presented as Moses' mouthpiece or spokesman. Notice that the implication of this passage is that Moses will not be the spokesman, or at least not the primary spokesman, to God's people and others—rather, Aaron will fulfill this role. Moses will speak to Aaron in such an authoritative manner that it will be as if God had spoken directly to Aaron and Aaron were a prophet of Yahweh. Moses is the intermediary and Aaron the prophet. I would urge that it is no accident that later in Exodus, at 7:1–2, it is Aaron and not Moses who is called the prophet, for one is not a prophet in any full sense unless one speaks God's word to God's people. One could, in effect, see Moses and Aaron as a sort of dynamic duo, with each completing half the task of being God's spokesman. Neither, by himself, is adequate to the task, but together they are. This conclusion is supported by a close analysis of the material that follows the call material in Exod 4.

First, notice that at Exod 4:30 the text is quite clear that when the elders of Israel were gathered, "Aaron spoke all the words that Yahweh had spoken to Moses, and did the signs before the eyes of God's people."[42] Here Aaron is not merely presented as the spokesman but as the one who performs the legitimizing prophetic signs. It is important to bear this early material in Exod 4 in mind throughout one's reading of the account of the exodus and Sinai events, as they set the precedent for the reader and set up certain expectations of a pattern that will only be alluded to in passing in the later material. The reader is supposed to recall this material throughout and assume that things are still operating in this manner in regard to Aaron's or Moses, roles unless the text makes a point of saying something else.

Nor is it only in the call narrative that Moses protests that he is not a public speaker, which means we can not merely treat it as a typical feature of that genre of material which the author has no special interest in emphasizing. To the contrary, Exod 6:12 portrays Moses as once again protesting to Yahweh that the sons of Israel have failed to pay any attention to him: "Now behold—the sons of Israel paid no attention to me [see 6:9]. How is Pharaoh going to pay attention to me, especially with my uncircumcision of lips." In short, even when Moses tried to speak on his own, he was a failure and was ignored. The response to such a protest in Exod 4:13 was that Yahweh sent both Moses and Aaron and ordered them together to speak to Pharaoh and bring forth the sons of Israel from Egypt.[43]

---

[42] Typically, Durham, *Exodus*, 59, wants to treat Exod 4:30 as a later pro-Aaronic insertion. But another reading of the text makes better sense of the narrative flow and the point of view of the writer.

[43] This text is of course sometimes seen as an independent Priestly account of Moses, commission. If this is correct it makes clear that two different sources presented Moses as inadequate by himself to be an oracle of Yahweh. I personally, however, do not find this analysis fully compelling. Clearly, the final editor of this book did not view it that way, for he is building up a picture of Moses through some use of repetition to stress the main characteristics of this servant of Yahweh.

Exodus 6:28–7:2 offers the clearest and fullest presentation of the pattern we have already noted. Once again Moses says right to Yahweh's face, "Now behold—I am a clumsy speaker; just how is Pharaoh going to pay attention to me?" Yahweh replies, "See here, I give you, a god, to Pharaoh, and Aaron will be your prophet. You are to speak all I order you to speak and Aaron your brother is to speak to Pharaoh." This is the only use of the term "prophet" in the entire book, and strong stress here is placed on the fact that Aaron is the prophet and that this is so because he will be the one to speak to Pharaoh just as he was the one to speak to Israel and its leaders. Moses, however, is, in extraordinary fashion, affirmed once more to be like God in relationship to Aaron and even indirectly in relationship to Pharaoh. In view of the Egyptian belief about Pharaoh being a god upon the earth, one wonders if we should not see this as a counterpolemic, but in any case Moses is presented as God's agent—one authorized with the message and the power of God, which he in turn will pass on to his brother the prophet.

As Durham points out, this material comes directly after the genealogical passage, which has as its function justifying Aaron as an equal partner with Moses.[44] Just so, and it is not convincing to argue that the stature of Moses would be diminished in this fashion in the same age that produced material such as we find in Deut 34:10 (or later for that matter). I submit that such a portrayal of Aaron must be primitive and in contact with the original thrust of the material before the exaltation of the role of Moses, including his prophetic role (cf. Deut 18; 34), had become common practice. I agree with Durham that "we have allowed centuries of the glorification of Moses," begun even in the biblical period, to color over much of our interpretation of the Exodus narratives. We need to note with more precision the amount of attention really given to Moses, how flawed a hero he actually is, "and how at every crucial point, the presence of Moses is either forgotten or at least obscured by the Presence of Yahweh."[45]

Our next passage of consequence is Exod 7:10, where we are told that when Moses and Aaron came before Pharaoh, they did exactly as Yahweh had ordered; then it is said, "Aaron threw his staff right in front of Pharaoh and right in front of his court, and immediately it turned into a monstrous snake." Nothing is said of Moses casting the staff down. This same pattern is reiterated at v. 19, where God commands Moses, "Tell Aaron, take your staff and thrust out your hands against the waters of Egypt." We are then told at v. 20, "Thus Moses and Aaron did exactly as Yahweh had ordered and he raised high the staff and struck the water of the Nile." The stress is, of course, on the fact that God is acting through these intermediaries, but as for the human agent who is actually speaking to or acting before Pharaoh, it appears, to this point in the narrative, to

---

[44] Durham, *Exodus*, 84.

[45] Ibid., 86. A variety of efforts has been undertaken to survey the role of Moses. Cf. D. Daiches, *Moses: The Man and His Vision* (New York: Praeger, 1975); H. Cazelles and A. Gelin, *Moïse, L'homme de l'alliance* (Paris: Desclée, 1955).

have been Aaron rather than Moses. This is also exactly what we find at the point of recounting the frog plague at 8:1–2 (vv. 5–6 in the Hebrew) and also in the story of the plague of gnats (8:12–15). It is Aaron who stretches out the staff and the gnats appear. At the same time, we begin to see a stress on Moses being the one who intercedes with God through prayer to call off a plague (8:9–10), a pattern that will recur and receive more stress as the narrative goes on.

B. Moses Speaks Up.   A partial change occurs in the narrative at Exod 8:16–28. Here for the first time, we have a repeated use of the phrases "Moses said" or "Moses replied" in regard to the conversation with Pharaoh. But how is this to be evaluated? Verse 21 reports that Moses and Aaron were summoned and spoken to, and it would be natural to assume that the narrator expects his audience to see the same procedure as before still in practice—Moses speaks to Aaron (presumably in Hebrew) and Aaron speaks to Pharaoh. Once again the theme of Moses interceding and stopping a plague is presented at vv. 26–27.

The presentation of the sixth plague at 9:8–12 brings a further change. God commands both Moses and Aaron to scoop up ash, but then it is said, "Moses is to fling it toward heaven in the sight of Pharaoh." Verse 10 says that "they" both scooped it up but then Moses flung the ash heavenward. It is possible that we are meant to think that Moses here performs the prophetic sign without the aid of Aaron. Perhaps this is so because it did not require speaking but, rather, only acting. We may ask but can not answer what Aaron did with his handful of ash. When we get to the seventh plague at v. 23, we hear about Moses thrusting forth his staff, apparently without the aid of Aaron, and hail falls.

But lest we think that the narrator is easing Aaron gradually into the background or out of the story, when it comes time to speak again to Pharaoh, we find at 10:3 the words "So Moses came, and Aaron, to Pharaoh. They said to him, 'Thus says Yahweh, the God of the Hebrews, "Just how long . . ."'" Here we have a clear use of the oracular formula "thus says Yahweh," and it seems reasonable to conclude, in view of the earlier pattern in Exodus, that we are meant to see Aaron as speaking to Pharaoh, while Moses speaks to Aaron. This joint effort is highlighted by the fact that when we get to the ninth prophetic sign or plague, once again the text mentions only Moses thrusting out his hand to bring about the darkness (v. 22). When the tenth and final plague is spoken of, we finally have reference only to Moses speaking to Pharaoh at 11:4. Yet we can not be sure even here. The text goes on to say that it was Moses and Aaron who did all these wondrous signs in Pharaoh's presence (11:10). There is no attempt by the final editor to exclude Aaron even at this point in the narrative.

The narrative of the Passover in 12:1–28 is framed by a reference to Yahweh speaking to and commanding both Moses and Aaron (vv. 1, 28; cf. v. 43), and in the midst of this narrative we hear of Moses speaking God's commands to Israel (v. 21). Is this simply a shorthand way of saying what has been said before—that God spoke to Moses, and Aaron completed the conversation with God's people—or are we to see Moses as actually speaking to God's people? One could argue that it is the latter, for now the stigma of Moses' slow speech or

tongued-tied condition has been overcome because Moses has proved himself
through the course of the plagues to be a leader. Yet once again, when we have
the final encounter between Pharaoh and the Israelite leadership, v. 31 says the
Egyptian ruler spoke to both Moses and Aaron.

Beginning with 13:1, Aaron is scarcely mentioned in the narrative, but
then we are no longer talking about the exodus events any longer. The entire sequence from Exod 3 to 12 is about the process that led to the liberation of Israel
from bondage in Egypt. Aaron plays a crucial role in all these events. Thereafter,
the focus is clearly on Moses. It is, however, interesting that when Moses leads
the male Israelites in the victory ode recorded at 15:1–18, nothing is said about
Moses being a prophet or acting in a prophetic manner, but when in turn we
hear about the leading of the women in a similar ode at 15:20–21, Miriam, the
sister of Aaron, is explicitly called a prophetess *(nebiah)*. It is also intriguing that
we are told that Moses sang with the sons of Israel (15:1), while Miriam sang to
the Israelite women.

There has been considerable debate as to whether originally Miriam sang
such an ode and that it was also predicated later of Moses, in view of the fact that
the odes appear to have been identical. But as Durham says, "either version could
be contemporary with the event; neither version has to be."[46] This is the only
place in Exodus where Miriam is mentioned, and it is generally agreed that this
magnificent song is very ancient. For our purposes it is important to stress three
things: (1) it is unlikely that a later editor of the tradition would have added Miriam to the story, and doubly unlikely he would have done so just to have her reiterate an ode already sung by Moses; (2) here, as also in Judg 4–5, there is a
connection between prophecy or being a prophetic figure and a song sung to
God; (3) if one must choose, it is far more likely that this is originally an oracle
of Miriam rather than of Moses, in view of the later glorification of Moses, but if
in fact we are meant to think that both sang such an ode, then Miriam is presented as a leader figure for at least the women, like unto Moses. Indeed, she
speaks authoritatively to the women while Moses simply sings with them. It is
unlikely that this fact, which gives Miriam a certain precedence over Moses, is
the product of later editing.

After the victory ode we have the accounts of the wilderness wandering
period, and here Moses is to the fore, but Aaron does appear occasionally
when something must be *spoken* to the Israelites. For example, at 16:2 the
people grumble against Moses and Aaron, and then Moses and Aaron speak to
the Israelites (v. 6). Indeed, we find once more the old pattern at v. 9, where
we hear, "Then Moses said to Aaron, 'Say to the whole company of the sons of
Israel. . . .'" And v. 10 makes clear it is only Aaron who is speaking to them on
this occasion.

It is interesting that even when there begins to be an account of Aaron's
priestly roles, the relationship of Moses and Aaron continues to be the same as it

---

[46] Durham, *Exodus,* 209.

was earlier. Thus at 16:32–36 Moses instructs Aaron and Aaron places an omer of manna in God's presence, and it is noted at v. 34 that "just as Yahweh instructed Moses, Aaron set the jar." It is Moses alone who hears from Yahweh, and it is Aaron alone who acts upon Moses' instructions. Between the two of them, the whole of what God wants is accomplished. This sort of teamwork is even enhanced at one point during the battle with the Amalekites when Moses' hands become weary and Aaron and the previously unmentioned Hur hold up Moses' arms so that Joshua may prevail (17:12).

We have already had occasion to mention Moses' role as an intermediary, interceding with God to stop the various plagues. Moses is presented in a similar sort of advocacy role in 18:13–27, where Israelites come to Moses asking for decisions in judicial matters: "the people come to me to make inquiry of God" (v. 15). Jethro even calls Moses an advocate before God (v. 19). Notice that this role is not said to be a specifically prophetic role. Notice, too, that Moses heeds the advice of Jethro and delegates authority to various others to take on the judicial functions while Moses remains the advocate before God. In the case of difficult decisions, the matter was to be brought directly to Moses, presumably because it required prayer and consultation with Yahweh (v. 26). This advocacy or intermediary role is seen particularly clearly at Sinai, where Moses "declared the words of the people to Yahweh" (19:9). It is interesting that at 19:24 both Moses and Aaron are allowed to go up Sinai to hear from God; this gives the impression that they were both present when the ten words of Yahweh were given (ch. 20).

As things turn out, the Israelites can not bear to hear from God directly, so they insist to Moses that he speak to the people but that Yahweh speak to Moses (20:19). It may be that Moses is also presented as the messenger who will lead Israel toward the promised land and with whom God's presence dwells (23:20–22), but most commentators take this as a reference to the messenger or angel of Yahweh. Notice that even as late as 24:1 it is still Moses and Aaron, as well as others, who are to make the covenant with Yahweh, but with only Moses himself drawing close to God to do so.

C. Aaron the Priest.   It is really not until Exod 27:20ff. that we begin to see Aaron not merely as the alter ego or partner of Moses or the completer of the Mosaic ministry but as a priest who has his own distinct tasks. These tasks are to be inherited by Aaron's descendants as well. They include the wearing of the breastplate with the sacred dice in it (Urim and Thummim—28:30). We do not know how exactly these dice or stones or gems were used, but they seem to have been for some sort of divining of God's will (Num 27:21; Deut 33:8; 1 Sam 28:6; Ezek 2:63; Neh 7:65). The practice of seeking answers or oracles by the rolling of stones with positive and negative values on them is widely attested in the ancient Near East.[47] It is, then, appropriate that they are first given to Aaron the prophetic figure, for in

---

[47] See E. Reiner, "Fortune-telling in Mesopotamia," *JNES* 19 (1960): 22–35.

the ancient Near East we have already seen how the two distinguishable functions of prophesying and divining the future could be seen as supplements of one another.[48] The later description of the consecration of Aaron and his kin makes clear not only the superior position of Moses but also the important priestly role Aaron and his family are to fulfill (Exod 40:12–13). Paradoxically, perhaps the ultimate testimony to just how important a leader Aaron was comes when Moses is on Sinai too long and the people turn to Aaron to make "gods who can lead us" (Exod 32:1).

Our discussion of Moses and Aaron in the exodus traditions has led to some surprising revelations, the main one of which is that Aaron and Miriam are presented as the prophetic figures, while Moses, in the main, is presented as God's agent or intermediary, who communicates with Aaron, and as the people's intermediary, praying to God to end or begin one or another divine act. This entire portrayal looks primitive, for it in no way tries to conform Moses to later notions about what a prophet should be, or be doing. Only a minority of the material mentions Moses' speaking or prophetic-sign activity. Aaron, on the other hand, appears as one who, in both word and deed, is seen as a prophet right up until the point when he is anointed and made a priest by Moses. Especially interesting is the fact that Miriam also is presented as a prophetic figure, and this is connected with her singing a victory ode, something Moses also does, only he does it with the Israelites and in his case it is not connected to the prophetic office. In view of all this, a scrutiny of the material in Numbers and Deuteronomy on prophets and on Moses as a prophet is required. One of the questions we must keep steadily in view is, If a later editor in fact dealt with Exodus and Numbers at all, why is there so little trace of the Moses-as-prophet notion in this earlier material?

Two texts in Numbers deserve some attention before we focus on the material in Deut 13 and 18. In Num 11, Moses is instructed by Yahweh to call together the seventy leaders of the people, and God will take some of the Spirit that is upon Moses and place it upon these leaders so that they can help Moses bear the leadership load. As in Exodus, we are told at Num 11:25 that God came down in a cloud and spoke with Moses, then transferred some of the Spirit on Moses to these other leaders, with the result that they prophesied. The same happened to the two leaders who remained in camp, Eldad and Medad, even though they did not gather with Moses and the other leaders around the tabernacle.

Notice, however, that v. 25 says literally, "and when the Spirit rested upon them they prophesied. But they did so no more." This was a onetime phenomenon, and it would appear that the function of it was to demonstrate to Israel that in fact these men had been endowed by Yahweh to share the burden of leadership. This is why commentators have often made the suggestion that we are dealing with an authenticating sort of prophetic ecstasy here (cf. 1 Sam 10:10–13;

---

[48] See pp. 13–19 above.

19:20–24),[49] and the focus is on the genuineness of the experience, not on the oracular outcome. Notice that nothing is said about what these leaders prophesied, if indeed they uttered intelligible oracles. "The author seems anxious to stress that this is a once-for-all experience associated with their installation in office."[50] As Ashley reminds us, this is the only place in the Pentateuch where we have the verb "to prophesy," and it is more natural—since the verb does indeed mean to act the prophet and there is no mention of what these leaders said—to assume that the focus is on ecstatic behavior: "The elders behaved in some way that accredited them as prophets."[51]

To the suggestion that Moses should make Eldad and Medad stop prophesying, presumably out of a concern that they might divert or dilute the authority of Moses over the people, Moses rejoins in a somewhat wistful manner, "O that Yahweh would make all Yahweh's people prophets and that Yahweh would put his Spirit upon them" (v. 30). This sounds like the reply of one tired of shouldering all the burden.

It is difficult to know precisely what to make of this story. It would appear that the prophetic experience was of limited duration and only served the function of demonstrating to God's people that these truly were leaders who could help Moses fulfill his responsibilities. The connection between God's Spirit, which rested on Moses, and prophecy is interesting. The question is whether we are meant to see the following connection—the Spirit that enabled Moses to be a prophet was now partially transferred to these other leaders and so they prophesied. Or is it, rather, that the Spirit, which enables not only prophecy but all true leadership, is simply shown to be on these leaders through their undeniable prophetic experience? In the latter case, we are not talking about the transfer or widening of the prophetic office but, rather, the transfer of the Spirit, which manifests divine activity in this way among many others, for the Spirit in the Hebrew Scriptures is so often the Spirit of prophecy. In any event, Moses' wish is not granted, and v. 30 reminds us that authentic prophets are those whom Yahweh has raised up, placing upon them his Spirit.

This leads us to the important passage in 12:1–9. Here again the issue of prophecy arises, but a rather clear distinction is made between Moses, to whom Yahweh speaks "mouth to mouth," and prophets, to whom God manifests himself in visions and dreams. What prompts this pronouncement by God is that Aaron and Miriam, the two main prophetic figures, have criticized God's servant Moses because he married a Cushite woman. They go on to say, "Is it true that God has spoken simply and solely to Moses? Has he not also spoken through us?" (v. 2). Yahweh does not deny that he has spoken through an Aaron or a Miriam, but he distinguishes the sort of prophetic revelation they have received from the kind of communication Moses has had from and with God. The effect

---

[49] See, e.g., P. J. Budd, *Numbers* (Waco: Word, 1984), 128.
[50] Ibid.
[51] T. R. Ashley, *The Book of Numbers* (Grand Rapids: Eerdmans, 1993), 214.

of this is to distinguish Moses from the prophets, not identify him with them. It is important to note that while in Exodus the clear pattern is of God speaking to Moses, who in turn speaks to Aaron, nonetheless there are a few pentateuchal texts that suggest God occasionally spoke directly with Aaron (see Exod 4:27; Lev 10:8; Num 8:20, 18:1).

For our purposes, it is crucial to note the obvious distinction between Moses' "mouth-to-mouth" communication with God and the visionary nature of what a normal prophet receives. The summary description of the prophets' revelations as visions and dreams comports with the idea that the term *hozeh*, "seer," reflects the earlier stages of the prophetic phenomenon, at least in Israel. The labeling of this phenomenon as prophecy with the suggestion of its indirectness and figurativeness, as compared with Moses' direct oral communication, also points to an early stage in the prophetic experience of Israel.[52] We are now prepared to consider closely the material in Deuteronomy.

D. Unprofitable Prophets.   Deuteronomy 13:1–5 is, of course, not a text about Moses or Aaron but, rather, contains instructions about how Israel is to deal with misleading or mischievous prophets or diviners that might lead God's people astray. The first point is to determine whether the author of this material has in mind foreign prophets, such as a Balaam, or Israelite ones, and while we can not be certain, it would appear that the former is in view. This is so because here prophets are grouped together with those who "divine by dreams," and these prophets or diviners are promising signs and wonders or, more to the point, omens that will foreshadow and foretell the future.[53] Deuteronomy 13:1 is important, for it bears witness to the distinction we have already noticed in the Mari material, namely, that while prophets and diviners both deal in words about the future, their modi operandi can be distinguished. They have related tasks, but they can in fact be distinguished: prophets receive oracles or visions from God, diviners look for or seek out signs in the heavens or on earth about what a god's will might be. Here the focus is on those who divine by dreams. It is not clear whether we are to think of the diviner as having the dream and then interpreting it, or—more likely—being a diviner or interpreter of other person's dreams (cf., e.g., the roles of Joseph and Daniel in the Hebrew Scriptures). Notice that nothing is said about these prophets being unable to actually perform the tasks they undertake. Indeed, it is suggested that they might well be able to accurately predict a coming sign or portent or omen. Nevertheless, the true Israelite is not to pay attention to them if the intent of all this is to lead God's people to go and worship false gods.

There was, in fact, a wide variety in the types of diviner in antiquity, ranging from ornithomantics to oneiromantics to necromantics.[54] The first of

---

[52] See ibid., 224ff.

[53] My colleague Dr. Bill Arnold has suggested that Israelite false prophets might well have functioned as diviners—see 1 Kgs 22.

[54] See the helpful discussion by Moore, *The Balaam Traditions*, 47ff.

these divined the future by examining or releasing birds and studying their flight; the second divined by interpreting dreams; the last consulted the spirits of the dead. The first of these also read the entrails of animals, such as lambs. This ancient practice predated the rise of Roman culture. It is important to bear this in mind when we come to discuss Greek and Roman prophecy and divination.[55] The second sort of diviner seems to be in view in Deut 13. This text does not suggest that such diviners or prophets were simply charlatans in the sense that they were faking having revelations or foreseeing things that were to come. The issue here is whether their use and interpretation of such phenomena led to the worship of the true God or of false gods. This, of course, makes clear that the test applied in Deut 18, to which we now turn, could not stand as the only litmus test of who was or wasn't a true prophet.

We have already seen from various Exodus texts and also Num 12:6–8 that there was a basis in the tradition not only for a distinction between diviners and prophets but also for a distinction between ordinary prophets and an intermediary such as Moses. This has led various scholars, including H.-J. Kraus, to make a rather clear distinction between Moses, who, as a covenant mediator, is clearly superior, and ordinary prophets.[56]

Deuteronomy 18:15–22 comes at the end of a somewhat lengthy discussion of religious functionaries. The last of these to be mentioned are prophets. We must first deal with the textual issue of whether 18:15 is to be seen as a reference to a prophet or to prophets, perhaps a succession of them. The reason there is some question about this is that while the Hebrew noun here is in the singular, it seems to be in a collective form, in which case it would refer to a class of persons or a succession of prophets.[57] This is the first time in all of the Pentateuch that Moses is called a prophet; there will be one more occurrence at Deut 34:10.

The concern of this text seems, clearly enough, to be with the succession after Moses and particularly how the people of God will receive a true word from Yahweh. A promise is given that such prophets (or such a prophet) will be raised up by God from the midst of God's people and God will put his words in those prophets' mouths. These prophets will be like Moses in this respect, but the comparative terminology also suggests they will be unlike him as well. The authority of such a prophet who speaks God's word and in God's name is such that if one disobeys such words, one has disobeyed God and will be held accountable by God.

There was, however, a problem. How was one to actually know that a particular prophet was speaking Yahweh's words? Two criteria are mentioned

---

[55] On this see pp. 296–301 below.

[56] See the classic discussion in H.-J. Kraus, *Die prophetische Verkündigung des Rechts in Israel* (Zollikon, Switzerland: EVZ, 1957). A revised form of his thesis is found in his *Worship in Israel* (Richmond: John Knox, 1966).

[57] See, e.g., P. C. Craigie, *The Book of Deuteronomy* (Grand Rapids: Eerdmans, 1976), 262ff.; or P. D. Miller, *Deuteronomy* (Louisville: John Knox, 1990), 151ff.

for discerning true from false prophets: (1) if they prophesy in the name of other gods, they are false prophets; (2) if they speak in the name of the true God but say what God has not commanded, they are false prophets. Still, the question is, How could one tell in the latter case? The only secondary criterion listed is that if a prophecy does not come true (lit., "if the word is not," i.e., has no substance), the spokesman has not spoken under Yahweh's inspiration or guidance. What is added at the end of the passage is intriguing: such a prophet has spoken presumptuously. This suggests that a prophet might undertake to speak under his own initiative for Yahweh and this created the need for criteria to determine what had and had not come from Yahweh. The prophet must be commanded to speak before he should speak, but in fact sometimes he acted on his own. The penalty for false prophecy, whether in the name of another god or in Yahweh's name, was severe—death. This also suggests that a significant problem existed in determining true from false oracles, which in turn suggests an environment in which there were a considerable number of prophets among or around God's people. The severity of the penalty reflects the belief that the prohibition against idolatry had been breached when such prophecy was uttered. This passage must be set clearly over against the prohibitions in Deut 18:9–14. Here we find exhortations against various forms of divination known in the surrounding nations—children made to pass through fire, augury, soothsaying of some sort, sorcery, the casting of spells, the consultation of spirits of the dead, or the seeking of oracles from such dead persons. Israel is strictly prohibited from paying attention to diviners of any of these sorts.

This raises major questions about what we are to make of Urim and Thummim. Was this not also a means of divining God's will? Was this acceptable divination as opposed to unacceptable non-Israelite forms of the same thing? We can not really tell, since we are nowhere told specifically what was done with Urim and Thummim.

In any event, Miller is right to stress that what this passage says about prophecy comports with the general view in the Pentateuch that God's word comes true precisely because God is a God of history, and indeed the only God who is in charge of history. Only Yahweh's words about the future really have substance, for he is in control of that future.[58] If we ask how Deuteronomy 13 and 18 may be reconciled when the former text suggests that a false or foreign prophet could foresee something that actually would come to pass, perhaps the best answer is that the "authentic divine word on the lips of the prophet is one that is confirmed by history and consistent with all the Lord's other words as set forth in the Mosaic instruction and focused in the demand for exclusive worship of the Lord."[59]

---

[58] Miller, *Deuteronomy*, 153–54.
[59] Ibid., 154.

Whether one thinks that this passage in Deut 18 was originally about a series of prophets or, as with later messianic interpretation, referred to one, or especially to one latter-day Moses figure (see Acts 3:22–23), it strongly suggests that the prophetic office was one that was periodically filled in Israel. It was not a continuous institution; rather, God from time to time had to raise up a prophet in the land when a late or urgent word was needed, especially in times of crisis. It was precisely this lack of an institutionalized, and so controllable, nature of many, if not most, prophets and prophecy that made it necessary to have instructions such as we find in Deut 13 and 18. Prophets (or at least peripheral rather than central, institutionalized ones) were always the wild cards in the deck of regular religious functionaries. In terms of social necessity, if one was going to rule out all, or almost all, forms of divination, one needed to have the assurance that there was still a way to receive guidance from God on an ongoing basis. That means would be prophecy.[60]

It is intriguing that the last word in the Pentateuch on the promise mentioned in Deut 18, a word that is clearly retrospective and probably encompasses a considerable passage of time, is that "never since has there arisen a prophet in Israel like Moses, whom the Lord knew face to face" (Deut 34:10). It adds that he was unequaled in the performance of terrifying signs and wonders both in Egypt against Pharaoh and before and on behalf of Israel. Absolutely nothing is said here about Moses being an oracle or wordsmith. The stress is on Moses' intimate relationship with God and his mighty deeds. This is, I submit, what the Deuteronomist means, in the main, in calling Moses a prophet, something no other book in the Pentateuch does. Yet this writer is quite capable of seeing that Moses was an intermediary and mediator of a higher sort than those ordinarily called prophets in the writer's own time.

This lack of precision of terminology is only what one would expect when the subject is the earliest stages of Israel's history. The writers were looking for adequate and analogous terms to indicate the great significance of Moses. Early figures such as Moses and Aaron, in fact, played a variety of roles that were not always typical of prophets in the classical period. They were thus difficult to categorize, and this was more the case with Moses than with Aaron, whom the tradition is more comfortable in labeling a prophet because he was indeed an oracle—one who spoke God's word regularly to the people and to others. As for Moses, perhaps in the end he was called a *nabi* in the Deuteronomistic material in part because the term has a sense close to what we find in the cognate language at Emar—one who calls upon God and intercedes for the people.[61] As we shall soon see, other early figures, such as Deborah, also fulfilled a variety of roles that made them likewise difficult to pigeonhole in terms of their social titles and roles.

---

[60] See the helpful discussion in Wilson, *Prophecy and Society,* 160ff.

[61] See pp. 14–15 above.

IV. BALAAM THE RELUCTANT SEER

A. Balaam Redux.   On any showing, the material we find in Num 22–24 is remarkable.[62] Rather like the material in Daniel, only in reverse, we find an apparently non-Israelite prophet prophesying to God's people. This story bears witness to the cross-cultural nature of the prophetic phenomenon in the ancient Near East.[63] A word from God could come from unlikely sources. It is interesting that the locale of this block of material, in the plains of Moab (which is also the locale for all of Deuteronomy), in fact suits what we know of Balaam's place of origin, or at least of operation. But what are we to make of Balaam? Is he indeed a true prophet of Yahweh? Is he a pagan prophet but one God chose to use, as God later used Cyrus? Did he begin as a prophet of Yahweh and finish as something else? Consider for a moment the conclusions of W. F. Albright:

> We may, accordingly, conclude that Balaam was really a North-Syrian diviner from the Euphrates Valley, that he spent some time at the Moabite court, that he became a convert to Yahwism, and that he later abandoned Israel and joined the Midianites in fighting against the Yahwists (Num. 31:8, 16). We may also infer that the Oracles preserved in Num 23–24 were attributed to him from a date as early as the twelfth century, and that there is no reason why they may not be authentic, or may not at least reflect the atmosphere of his age.[64]

This seems to make sense of all the data, yet one is left wondering whether Balaam was just a professional prophetic opportunist who changed sides depending on which way the wind blew. Notice that when later biblical texts refer to the material in Num 22–24, the judgment passed in these texts seems as neutral as that of these chapters (cf. Deut 23:4–5; Josh 24:9–10; Mic 6:4–5; Neh 13:2). But when there is reference to Balaam's subsequent activities, the judgment becomes clearly negative (Josh 13:22; 2 Pet 2:15–16; Jude 11; Rev 2:14). It would appear that, by and large, the material in Num 22–24 does not intend to

---

[62] The attempt to divide this material into at least two sources, J and E, on the basis of the use of the divine names has proved to be largely unprofitable, as W. F. Albright showed some time ago, but there may well be something to the common view that the narrative traditions were formed independently of the oracles. See the discussion in Budd, *Numbers,* 258ff. For our purposes, what is significant is that both the narrative and the oracles portray Balaam in the same way, as a seer and as a sometime diviner as well. J. Sturdy, *Numbers* (Cambridge: Cambridge University Press, 1972), 157–58, argues well that the later oracles are in fact dependent on the earlier ones, such that to divide the first two from the second two misses the increasing firmness and confidence of Balaam's oracles. This makes it implausible to reverse the order of the prophecies, placing those in Num 24 before those in Num 23. Apart from the donkey story, the narrative appears to be a coherent and continuous whole. So also Budd, *Numbers,* 259.

[63] This is in no way surprising in light of the names of the Mari prophets and the probability of their ultimate family origins outside that great city.

[64] W. F. Albright, "The Oracles of Balaam," *JBL* 63 (1944): 207–33, here 233.

paint Balaam as a false prophet, but at least the story of the donkey portrays him as obtuse, or less visionary than even the beast he is riding upon.

Yet it has been urged that the story is an independent tradition inserted into this cycle of material. For example, T. R. Ashley argues that the "text of chs. 22–24 is not concerned to pronounce on the matter. Balaam's character is incidental to the story."[65] Yet the story also clearly depicts Balaam as participating in pagan rites (22:40–23:3; 23:14–15, 29–30) and looking for omens (24:1), a practice forbidden to Israelite prophets, at least at a later date (Deut 18:9–14). If we are to evaluate Balaam's roles, he is not just depicted as prophet but also as a diviner and possibly even as an exorcist.[66] Some scholars have found the comparison of Balaam with the Babylonian *barum,* or diviners, profitable, especially since he both has night visions and does indeed seek out omens and try to read signs of the times. The Hebrew Bible, in fact, never calls Balaam a prophet, and the report of visions places him more in the category of a seer, in any case. The description of Balaam's characteristic behavior is telling:

> Oracle *(ne'um)* of Balaam, Beor's son,
> Oracle of the man whose eye is true;
> Oracle of one who hears El's words
> And knows the knowledge of Elyon;
> Who sees *(yehezeh)* the vision *(mahazeh)* of Shaddai,
> Who falls down but has eyes uncovered. (Num 24:3–4, 15–16)

This description needs to be analyzed carefully. While there is mention of Balaam hearing El's words, the stress is clearly on the fact that he sees, that he has visions, and that, as a result, he speaks oracles as the mouthpiece of the deity. Notice that we are told he sees truly and then presumably speaks truly. The last line is especially interesting, suggesting an ecstatic experience that leads to this gaining of second sight or visionary insight, or, better said, the ecstatic state places Balaam in the position for the god to give him a revelation, to uncover his eyes and let him see something. It is noteworthy that at Num 24:1–2 Balaam does not go to practice divination, for example by casting lots; rather, we are told that God's Spirit came upon him. The word for "oracle" here, *ne'um,* is almost always used in the Hebrew Bible of Yahweh's words and is found regularly with prophetic oracles (see Isa 14:22; Ezek 13:6–7; Hos 2:13, 16, 21; Jonah 2:12; Mic 4:6). This may be intended to suggest a transition in Balaam's career from pagan diviner to prophet of Yahweh, but we can not be sure.

As R. Wilson has pointed out, this description has links with both Israelite prophecy and with the descriptions found at Deir 'Alla. Both sources apply the root *h.z.h.* to Balaam. The nonbiblical text calls him a visionary of the gods to whom the gods spoke at night. What is surely implied by both the biblical and nonbiblical material is that Balaam was a professional intermediary, an

---

[65] Ashley, *Numbers,* 434–35; following others, he argues for the independence of the Balaam's donkey story.

[66] See Moore, *The Balaam Traditions,* 47ff.

internationally known conveyor of oracular blessings and curses, prophecies and visions. Notice especially the reference to fees for divination *(q'samim)* sent by Balak (Num 22:7), which makes the clear categorization of Balaam as a diviner at Josh 13:22 understandable.[67] Yet the roles of prophet and diviner, while related in regard to their function, should be distinguished, as is clearly done at Mari. If you are uncertain of the validity of a prophecy or do not like the oracle, or if simply there is no prophet around, you go to the diviner to get a second and, hopefully, a different opinion derived by different means (cf., e.g., the practice at Mari and the example of Saul and the medium at Endor).

B. The Origins of the Oracles.   There is really no need to analyze in detail Balaam's oracles, but several pertinent remarks are in order. First, they are clearly typical of ancient Near Eastern oracles pronounced against an enemy before battle,[68] and as such, they are the prologue to which the victory ode that we find in Judg 5 is the epilogue. Second, the archaic character of the Hebrew in these oracles is beyond question.[69] They are surely not compositions from the monarchial period. Third, they are in poetic form, which is, in the vast majority of cases, typical of such ancient Near Eastern prophecy, whether Israelite or otherwise.[70] Fourth, as is typical of such prophecy, it focuses on historical matters of weight that are, by and large, either present or on the near horizon. The prophecy, however, is full of images and metaphorical enough to make it useful in other and later times and settings as well, including for messianic reflection and application. This was especially the case with Num 24:17, which was applied much later to Bar Kokhba during the Jewish revolt in the second century AD. Fifth, the allusion back to the exodus-Sinai events at Num 24:8 should not be ignored. This is not likely a later insertion. The prophet knows he is dealing with a specific people whom a specific God has rescued and helped in the past and whom God has made "uncursable," so to speak. The allusion to the history of Israel is also often common in later Israelite prophecy as well and reflects a certain historical consciousness. Lastly, the judgment of Craigie deserves to be repeated: "Whatever our conclusions concerning Balaam's nature and office, he had a certain integrity in his art. The point of significance is the compatibility of Balaam's position with the great Deuteronomic principle that whoever blessed Israel would be blessed, and whoever cursed Israel would be cursed. Balaam's view of Israel is quite in harmony with the normative biblical tradition concerning Israel's religion at this period."[71] This may, in

---

[67] See the discussion by Wilson, *Prophecy and Society,* 147–50.

[68] See A. Haldar, *Associations of Cult Prophets amongst the Ancient Semites* (Uppsala: Almqvist & Wiksell, 1945).

[69] Besides Albright, "The Oracles of Balaam," 207ff., see P. Craigie, "The Conquest and Early Hebrew Poetry," *TynBul* 20 (1969): 76–94.

[70] Albright's rendering of them into English in "The Oracles of Balaam," 224–25, makes this especially clear for those unfamiliar with Hebrew.

[71] Craigie, "The Conquest and Early Hebrew Poetry," 92.

part, be due to judicious editing by a later Israelite redactor, but on the whole, these oracles seem relatively free from such tampering.

What I would want to stress about this early prophetic material is that the case of Balaam is, in various regards, like the case of Moses, whom we have already referred to, and the case of Deborah, whom we will consider in a moment. These important figures all play more than one social role, with the prophetic role only being a part of the picture. Balaam was also a diviner, a natural companion to his other role of prophet or seer. Moses was not merely an intermediary but also a charismatic leader, and Deborah was also a judge as well as a prophetess. A variety of roles and functions were assumed by these persons.

It would appear that, in this early period at least in Israel, it was not possible to simply make a living as a prophet or prophetess. There was no court or king to which one could attach oneself, as was the case at Mari or at Babylon. While it would be wrong to say that the era of prophecy did not begin in Israel until the rise of the monarchy, it is true that there were no central and full-time prophets before that time, unless one counts Balaam, but of course he would have been attached to non-Israelite courts. Deborah comes as close as possible to being a central prophet, in that she is involved in the leadership structure of Israel as it existed in the time of the judges. We must turn to her remarkable story at this juncture.

V. DEBORAH—POWERFUL PROPHETESS

A. Seeking the Historical Deborah.   In the NT era, one of the most commented on and elaborated upon stories of the OT seems to have been the story of Deborah (see Josephus, *Ant.* 5.198–209; *Pseudo-Philo* 30–31), not least because of the role a woman plays in the story. Indeed, it has been argued that the feminist theme is the key to the very structure of Judg 4.[72] It will pay us, then, to give the story some scrutiny at this point, since the woman in question is portrayed as playing a prophetic role.

The consensus of OT scholars appears to be that there is no reason to doubt, and several reasons to affirm, that there was a historical figure named Deborah who was a prophetess (called specifically a *nebiah*) and judge during the earliest stages of Israel's life in the promised land. For one thing, we now have historical evidence from close to this period of time, from Mari, that demonstrates that prophetesses could be involved in the political process of ancient Near Eastern nations.[73] For another, it is not likely that in a patriarchal environment there would be any good reason to invent the idea of a female prophet, much less one that proves to be the catalyst leading to her people's triumph over a significant foe. Notice that at Judg 4:4 we have what Boling calls exclamatory

---

[72] B. Lindars, "Deborah's Song: Women in the Old Testament," *BJRL* 65 (1982–1983): 158–75, here 160.

[73] See R. G. Boling, " Deborah," *ABD* 2:113.

syntax, indicating both surprise and a positive value judgment that it was true she was a prophetess.[74] In the third place, it is generally agreed that the ode in Judg 5 is extremely ancient, being full of archaic language, and in this ode Deborah speaks in the first person. Most commentators still think it may well go back in some form to Deborah herself.[75] In the fourth place, as B. Lindars points out, we should likely see Judg 4 and 5 as independent sources about the same events; this provides further confirmation of the historical substance of the roles attributed to Deborah.[76]

The actions of Deborah in "judging" may refer to her offering oracular responses to inquiries under her palm tree, in addition to whatever judicial decisions she may have rendered. Block suggests, "Deborah's prophetic status and not her judicial office led the 'sons of Israel' to come to her at the palm between Ramah and Bethel."[77] In doing this, she would be much like other seers who were available for consultation during a crisis. Whether this is so or not, we do have two oracles attributed to Deborah and delivered to Barak son of Abinoam at Judg 4:6–7 and 4:14. What is notable about these oracles is that they involve a direct command from Yahweh in which God speaks in the first person and the future is revealed: Sisera will fall into the hand of Barak. (The command and promise are simply reiterated in a slightly different form at v. 14.) It is noteworthy that it is here in ch. 4, and not in ch. 5, that Deborah is both portrayed as and called a prophetic figure. It may be of some importance that prophets and diviners were regularly consulted *before* someone went into battle during this period, and Deborah is likely to have fulfilled such a role in this case.[78] Her accompanying of Barak into battle would presumably have been as the mouthpiece and representative of Yahweh, the real commander in chief.[79] The question, then, becomes whether the famous Ode of Deborah should also be seen as an example of her prophetic activity. There are some reasons for hesitation about this conclusion.

---

[74] R. G. Boling, *Judges* (Garden City: Doubleday, 1975), 94.

[75] See, e.g., ibid., 94ff.; G. F. Moore, *Judges* (Edinburgh: T&T Clark, 1966), 130ff.; A. Cundall, *Judges* (Downers Grove, Ill.: InterVarsity, 1968), 82ff. Freedman, "Pottery, Poetry," 18–19, dates the present form of the ode to the second half of the twelfth century BC.

[76] See Lindars, "Deborah's Song," 159.

[77] D. L. Block, "Deborah among the Judges: The Perspective of a Hebrew Historian," in *Faith, Tradition, and History* (ed. A. R. Millard et al.; Winona Lake, Ind.: Eisenbrauns, 1994), 240. Her locale was a strategic spot that made her available for consultation with Israelites from all over the land. Indeed Block, p. 241, suggests that being stationed near Bethel made her an alternative to the consultation with God through the priest's use of Urim and Thummim. He adds, "The fact that the Israelites came to her instead of the priest reflects the failure of the established institution to maintain contact with God."

[78] See ibid., 244. Besides the obvious examples from Mari, consider also a near contemporary of Deborah—Shalmaneser I of Assyria (1274–1245 BC), who resorts to divination before going into battle. See ibid., 244.

[79] See ibid., 252.

B. Deborah's Ode to Joy.   Notice in the first place that the ode is, in fact, attributed at Judg 5:1 to both Deborah and Barak, who is not said anywhere to be a prophet. In the second place, Deborah is spoken of in the third person at v. 7, but at v. 12 Deborah is exhorted to sing a song. In any event, it is clear that this poem is not an oracle, for at v. 3 we are told that this is an ode sung to Yahweh and the first-person reference there is to the singer. It is intriguing that Deborah is identified in this poem as a "mother in Israel" (v. 7), which probably is not just another way of calling her a prophetess (see 2 Sam 20:19).[80] This indicates some kind of leadership role, and about this verse Boling says, "Deborah is lauded for providing the prophetic answer to the concern of inquiring leaders of Israel. This verse anticipates the concluding scene where 'Sisera's mother' propounds the question and the 'wise' women provide the incorrect answer (vv. 28–30)."[81]

Block is right to stress that Deborah must have been a remarkable woman, especially in view of the difficulty of the times in which she lived and the general lack of leadership among her people.[82] This is made even further evident from the fact that she alone among the judges is portrayed in an unequivocally positive light and was the only one in the service of Yahweh before her engagement in an act of delivering Israel.[83] Notice, too, that a shaming device seems to frame the story, which highlights the role of women. In the first place, Barak must be goaded into action by a woman, and precisely because of this we are told that Sisera will in the end fall into the hands of a woman. It is a woman who initiates the action and a woman who finishes off the foe, an utterly humiliating result for Sisera and a somewhat humbling situation for Barak. Lindars puts it this way: "The real point is the connection between Deborah's taunt to Barak and the fulfillment of her prophecy in Jael's deed. . . . The prowess of a woman is prophesied by contrast with the cowardly reluctance of Barak."[84]

What can we conclude from this material about Deborah? There was a historical memory that a prophetess offered oracles by that name in early Israel. Yet she also played a political role, offering leadership and support for Barak during this crucial period. Furthermore, it was remembered that she offered a victory ode after the fact. This association of the prophetess not only with oracles but also with odes may provide us with a certain precedent in Israel for the phenomenon we find elsewhere, of prophets singing or singers prophesying.[85] Her political activities remind us that prophets often functioned in relationship to the political and religious structures in Israel even when they were not, as Deborah may well have been, central prophets, a part of the existing leadership structure.

---

[80] Lindars, "Deborah's Song," 168, notes the contrast between the mother of Israel, who protects and delivers her people, and the mother of Sisera, who can do nothing but wait and hope in vain.

[81] Boling, *Judges*, 109.

[82] Block, "Deborah," 231.

[83] See ibid., 236.

[84] Lindars, "Deborah's Song," 162, 164.

[85] See pp. 52–56 below.

The later activities of Nathan in the south or Elijah and Elisha in the north should not seem surprising in light of this material. Finally, the unreservedly positive portrayal of Deborah here, alone among all the "judges," reminds us that the prophetic office, based as it was on revelation and inspiration rather than gender, provided opportunities for women to function as leaders among God's people, even in the most patriarchal periods of Israel's history.

As we draw this discussion to a close, it will be useful to consider how Josephus views Deborah. He is quite clear in calling her a προφῆτις, and he says at *Ant.* 5.201 that the Israelites came to her so that she would intercede with God and they would then not be destroyed by the Canaanites. In other words, her role is viewed as a prophet or intermediary rather than as a judge. Notice how he adds to the story his own androcentric viewpoint by having Deborah upbraid Barak: "You resign to a woman a rank that God has bestowed on you; nevertheless I do not decline it" (*Ant.* 5.203). Again, later he contrasts the cowardly Barak and Israelites with Deborah, who restrained them from retiring from the task and indeed ordered them to deliver battle on that very day without delay (*Ant.* 5.204). He brings the story of Jael and Sisera to a conclusion by saying, "thus did this victory redound, as Deborah foretold, to a woman's glory" (*Ant.* 5.209). Josephus believed that prophecy was important; indeed, he saw himself as occasionally filling that role.[86] What is important for our purposes is that he viewed what Deborah was doing in the same vein as he viewed what he and other first-century AD prophets were doing. There was in his mind a continuity in the prophetic office, tasks, and expressions through the ages.

VI. CONCLUSIONS

In this all too cursory survey of early prophetic phenomena in the ancient Near East both within and outside Israel, we have learned much. We have learned that prophecy certainly did not begin during the monarchial period either within or outside Israel. This is not an insignificant finding, as it means we must reckon with the role prophecy played throughout the history of Israel, even if there are historical difficulties with the most ancient source material.

We have further learned that there is plenty of justification for treating prophecy as a cross-cultural phenomenon. Not only the similarity in terminology about prophets in these various cultures but also the concrete examples of figures such as Balaam encourage us to do so. True prophecy, by which is meant prophecy that comes true or is fulfilled, could come from a non-Israelite prophet, and on the other hand, a recognized prophet of Yahweh could, in fact, utter false prophecies. In any event, there was great respect for, and belief in, prophecy throughout the ancient Near East in this early period. Indeed, the

---

[86] See pp. 294–96 below.

evidence suggests that prophecy was a vital phenomenon even well before the Middle Bronze Age.

A third important observation is that because prophecy existed in Israel before the monarchy (and, as we shall see later, after the monarchy), it is not simply a function of some court official, for we have noted evidence that, at Mari as well, some of the prophets and prophetesses seem to have been outsiders to the court. The sociological distinction between central and peripheral prophets becomes an important one for Israel with the rise of the monarchy, but it is not applied very easily to the premonarchial situation. For example, do we wish to call Deborah a central prophet simply because she was both a judge and one who spoke for Yahweh, or is this, as seems more likely, an example of her assuming multiple roles in Israelite society? It would appear from the study of early figures such as Deborah or Aaron or Moses that such leaders did indeed fulfill a variety of roles for their people.

The examination of the material pertaining to Moses led to the somewhat surprising conclusion that, on the whole, Moses is portrayed as an intermediary or mediator but not usually as a prophet. Not all of those who intercede with God for a people are prophets. Indeed, some of the traditions we noted made a distinction between Moses, who related to God face-to-face, and prophets, who were one step removed from such a relation and simply heard or saw a word from Yahweh from time to time. Moses and Aaron together are, however, portrayed as fulfilling the prophetic office, with Aaron offering the oracles to the audience. We must, it appears, allow for some fluidity and flexibility in the use of terms such as *nabi*, especially in this early period. We must also recognize that both women and men could and did fulfill the prophetic roles as far back as we can go with our source material, and as we shall see, this continued to be the case throughout the history of Israel and then early Christianity.

In regard to the relationship of prophecy and divination, we saw reason in the materials from Mari for making a distinction between the two phenomena, although clearly they are related to one another. There is also no reason to deny that at least some forms of divination seem to have been employed by Israelites at various stages of their history.[87] Divination comes in response to consultation, and at Mari it appears to have been used as a means of confirming a prophetic oracle. This may suggest that divination was seen as a more secure means of getting answers from the deity, at least in that culture. To judge from the biblical material, Israelites seem to have thought prophecy was more reliable than divination.

Already in this early period we have seen clear evidence that prophecy could and did regularly come in poetic form, and there are some hints that those who prophesied also offered songs (e.g., Deborah) and that possibly music was regularly associated with the prophetic phenomenon. Whatever form oracles came in, it appears that they were not always taken on face value but various

---

[87] See pp. 43–44 below.

means or criteria were used to weigh or test the validity of the utterance, including the use of divination to accomplish this confirmation. It is notable that, in these oral cultures, prophecies nevertheless seem to have often been written down and kept even in this early period, presumably because they were seen to have some lasting value.

There are, at the end of the day, of course, some significant differences in the prophetic phenomenon in the early Israelite period from that which we find at Mari and elsewhere in the ancient Near East, precisely because in these extrabiblical examples prophecy is focused on the court or the king whereas Israelite prophecy seems to have been initially focused on the people. There are also theological differences affecting the utterances of a Deborah, on the one hand, or a Mari prophet, on the other. Monotheistic tendencies do affect how one views the potential source and, to some degree, the content of prophecy. But at the same time, there are many similarities in the oracles of weal and woe that are offered by prophets in all of these cultures of the ancient Near East, as will become even more evident in our next chapter.

CHAPTER 2

Keepers of the Flame:
The Early Israelite Prophetic Experience

*I*N THE FIRST CHAPTER, THE ROLES prophets and prophetesses played in the earliest period of Israel's history were discussed. In various ways, this experience was anomalous, for there was no king or court to which prophets could or would be attached in Israel at this time, unlike the case at Mari or Babylon and elsewhere in the ancient Near East. It is to be expected that when the monarchy appeared in Israel, the roles of prophets would take on features more in common with those of prophets in surrounding cultures, where they were regularly attached to courts.

But what we do not find is prophetic figures serving as diviners as well as court prophets in Israel. Rather, priests seem to have fulfilled the role of providing answers to specific inquiries through the use of Urim and Thummim (see Deut 33:8; Num 27:21). One of the sorts of inquiry that seems to have been made is about the selection of goats for the sacrifices on the Day of Atonement (see Lev 16:7–10). A king, such as David, could also consult the priest for answers to specific questions in the absence of a prophetic figure (1 Sam 23:9–12). It is interesting that there is no evidence that Urim and Thummim were used for divination after the reign of David (cf. Neh 7:65).

This evidence is mentioned now because there is so little of it. There was something about the rise to prominence of the prophetic office in Israel that seems to have made divination a minor practice there, apparently almost entirely eclipsing it. Nor does it appear to have been ever identified as a function of prophets; rather, it was always associated with the priest, which is not surprising in view of the

Aaronic traditions we examined in the last chapter. On the whole, the following comment by D. Aune is fully warranted and deserves to be heeded: "Inspired prophecy . . . consists of comprehensible verbal messages from the supernatural world conveyed through an inspired medium who may be designated a prophet. Divination, on the other hand, consists of the interpretation of coded messages from the supernatural world conveyed through various kinds of symbols. Both inspired prophecy and divination may be solicited or unsolicited."[1] Furthermore, the experiences of prophets and those of priestly diviners can not really be compared. Prophets are the receivers of compelling and demanding communications within themselves; diviners are the exegetes of external phenomena. Prophets offer oracles grounded sometimes in auditory, sometimes in visual, experiences; diviners give interpretations of things seen in the material world.

But it would be getting ahead of the discussion to suggest that there was a clear-cut distinction between priests and/or leader figures and those who fulfilled the prophetic roles in Israel. Samuel has been seen as the prototypical prophet who set the mold for those who followed him. But Samuel, like those before him, is connected, in the traditions about him, not only with the priesthood and the cultic center but also with the activity of judging. Before the real rise of the monarchy, we still see leader figures, including prophets fulfilling an interesting array of roles.

Furthermore, Samuel is portrayed, in the main, as a seer (hozeh/ro'eh) and indirectly called such (1 Sam 9:9), although he is also called by the term that later became standard for such figures (nabi, 3:20). Probably, the use of the latter term reflects a stage in Israel's history when it is self-consciously attempting to portray itself as on a par with other international powers, and so even the more pancultural terminology for prophet comes to the fore. Aune puts it this way: "During the monarchial period (1000–586 BC) the term nabi' tended to displace the older terms hozeh and ro'eh . . . though all three terms continued to be used interchangably (2 Sam. 24:11; 2 Kgs 17:13 . . . ; Is. 29:10; Amos 7:12)."[2] Finally, we must also not overlook the fact that for the first time, in the case of Samuel, we also find the title "man of God" applied to a prophetic figure.[3]

I. THE SAGA OF SAMUEL

There are many difficulties in dealing with the narrative material about Samuel and Saul, not the least of which are the textual problems, but for the

---

[1] D. Aune, *Prophecy in Early Christianity and the Ancient Mediterranean World* (Grand Rapids: Eerdmans, 1983), 82.

[2] Ibid., 83.

[3] D. L. Petersen, *The Roles of Israel's Prophets* (Sheffield: JSOT Press, 1981), 63, has tried to argue that *nabi* refers to northern, while *hozeh* refers to southern prophets. He argues *nabi* is used positively only in the book of one northern prophet—Hosea. This judgment requires one to ignore: (1) the evidence in the former prophets; (2) the historical appendix to Isaiah (Isa 36–39). Cf. Isa 3:12; 9:14; 28:7.

purposes of this study, what is crucial is to examine the material that has to do with prophecy and prophets. The basic lineaments of this material are not in dispute. What is in dispute is whether, in their original form, the Samuel traditions portrayed Samuel as a prophet at all. As G. W. Ramsey has remarked, it has been suggested that "the mantle of prophecy was cast upon Samuel by later handlers of the tradition. Prior to the composition of the final (Deuteronomistic) version of 1 Samuel, it is hypothesized, there was an edition prepared by prophetic circles, which developed the character of Samuel into a figure who speaks and behaves like prophets of a later era."[4] Some of the principal exponents of this theory are G. Fohrer, B. Birch, and P. K. McCarter.[5]

These assessments all share one major thing in common: they were made before the real impact of the Mari discoveries and were based on a general skepticism about the existence of oracular prophecy before the monarchial period not only in Israel but elsewhere. There are, however, other problems with this thesis as well: (1) We have no solid evidence for prophetic circles creating or modifying stories about earlier non-prophetic figures; (2) nor do we have clear evidence for a prophet's disciples creating such prophetic traditions. (3) As R. E. Clements has pointed out, when no two scholars can agree what were supposedly the original words and deeds of a figure such as Samuel and what are later accretions, we are not encouraged to think that such readings of the tradition history are very accurate or helpful. But more important, as Clements also stresses, if Samuel *was* a prophetic figure, such a free handling of what he said and did by disciples or later prophets is unlikely. Both of these groups, above all, would have known that such a practice

> obliterates the sense of uniqueness and unrepeatable divine inspiration that the great prophet possessed. If his words could simply be repeated, adapted, and imitated by later disciples [or prophets], then the unique inspiration which was claimed for him was of no great importance. . . . The singling out of particular prophets as the unique and distinctive revealers of God's will toward the people of Israel was fundamental to the retention of their sayings.

In short, if "anyone could speak or write prophecy, then the very uniqueness of the prophet was undermined."[6] (4) One would think that later Israelite prophets, who themselves had received such unique inspiration and revelation from God, would be least likely to retroject such sayings and material into the mouth of an earlier prophet such as Samuel. They were far more likely to have stories written

---

[4] G. W. Ramsey, "Samuel," *ABD* 5:954–57, here 955.

[5] G. Fohrer makes this suggestion in his *Introduction to the Old Testament* (trans. D. E. Green; Nashville: Abingdon, 1968), and he is followed by B. Birch, *The Rise of the Israelite Monarchy: The Growth and Development of 1 Samuel 7–15* (Missoula: Scholars Press, 1976); and P. K. McCarter, *1 Samuel* (AB 8; Garden City: Doubleday, 1980).

[6] Clements, *Old Testament Prophecy*, 11–15; the quotes are from p. 14.

about themselves and their own words.[7] (5) In fact, Samuel does not by and large behave like prophetic figures of later eras. He also acts as priest and judge, and probably such multiple roles suggest a premonarchial figure. Furthermore, Samuel is certainly not portrayed as one of the "writing" prophets but, rather, as a seer. (6) The parenthetical remarks of the final editor of this material do not suggest that there was any tendency in the later handling of the material to try to create prophetic traditions about earlier figures. To the contrary, such remarks suggest an emphasis on little prophetic activity in the earlier period (see 1 Sam 3:1; cf. 9:9, journeying to see the seer). Indeed, Samuel is singled out as the one named prophetic figure for the whole land (1 Sam 3:20). It is thus unlikely that the prophetic traditions about Samuel have no grounding in his actual life and work.

Consider now several aspects of the portrayal of Samuel. When we first meet Samuel—both in 1 Sam 1, when we hear of his offering as a Nazirite, and in 2:11, 18—there is a strong emphasis on his being a priest or a priest in training. He is living at the cultic site, he is wearing a linen ephod, and he is said to be ministering to Yahweh in the presence of Eli the priest. Nothing prior to this point in the narrative or in this initial reference suggests that Samuel is or will be a prophetic figure. Furthermore, when he receives his "call" from God, he not only mistakes who is calling him but also what it is about. The story suggests that the prophetic role comes unexpectedly and without preparation. This is hardly the sort of portrait one would expect if a later writer from the period of classical prophecy, seeing Samuel as a prototype, was attempting to present Samuel as being prepared all along for a familiar prophetic role by God. What is stressed is that Samuel was both growing up physically and growing in God's favor during this period (cf. 2:21b–26).[8]

The "call" narrative of 3:1–4:1a requires closer scrutiny. It must be kept steadily in view that the narrative characterizes Samuel by contrasting him with Eli and his sons. The final editor of this material stresses from the outset that prophetic experience, the reception of words or visions from God, was rare during this period of Israelite history (3:1). Then, too, the priesthood was too wicked to reform. Thus the prophetic word was given in a new way to a Nazirite boy, who delivered it to Eli and thereby brought the priestly service of Eli and his kin to an end.

It is possible to see 3:1 as an explanation for why Samuel was bewildered and did not know what was happening to him. There is, however, some debate

---

[7] Very similar sorts of objections can be made to the theories of E. Boring that later Christian prophets retrojected utterances they had received from the exalted Lord into the mouth of the Jesus portrayed in the Gospel narratives. If they were indeed words of the exalted Christ, they did not need such a means of accreditation, nor would have the oracles of later Israelite prophets need to be predicated of figures such as Samuel. See pp. 321–27 below on Boring.

[8] The latter text is the basis of Luke 2:52 and, as such, may be further evidence of Luke's attempt to portray Jesus as a prophetic figure, but one could also argue that it portrays him as some sort of sage or teacher from God, since he is presented as arguing with the Jewish teachers in the temple complex. See pp. 330–35 below.

as to what we should make of the Hebrew word *nifrats*. The word could mean either "frequent" or possibly "widespread." If it is the former, it is talking about how often prophecy happened; if it is the latter, it is talking about the scope of prophetic activity in Israel during this period.[9] Either way, we are speaking about prophetic activity being unusual, whether because it only rarely happened or because there were few prophets and they apparently did little itinerating. A way beyond this dilemma is possible if "word of the Lord" and "vision" are not seen as simple synonyms. The former refers to something a prophet hears, the latter to something a prophet sees. About the former, auditory experience, it is said to be rare or infrequent and thus precious (cf. Isa 13:12). About the latter, visionary experience, it is said to be not widespread. Both suggest a paucity of recent communication from God to Israel. Samuel's experience is, then, meant to be seen as unexpected and anomalous. "Thus we are not to suppose that Samuel (or even Eli) is unusually obtuse in his initial failure to realize what was transpiring."[10] Yet the author wants to make clear that Samuel had indeed received the same sort of communication as other genuine prophets. It was the "Word of Yahweh" that Samuel would receive, a technical phrase for revelations given to a prophet.[11]

One of the more influential theories about the story of Samuel's call suggests that he experienced an "auditory message dream theophany."[12] There are problems with at least several major features of this assessment. First, although Samuel is in the holy place, we find nothing in this story remotely like the experience recorded in Isa 6, where Isaiah indeed had a vision of God. There do not appear to be any visual components to this communication, which is surely an essential feature of a "God-appearing."[13] Yet equally clearly we are meant to see this as the experience of a seer—1 Sam 3:15 says Samuel was afraid to relate the word or message that he had seen, and v. 10 speaks of Yahweh coming and standing at the holy place, although apparently Samuel does not see God.[14] Second, it is not at all clear we are meant to see this communication as being conveyed in a dream. If Samuel is asleep, then this communication comes to him from outside himself and wakes him up! So much is this the case that he repeatedly runs to Eli to see if he has called him. True, the formal features of a call

---

[9] See the discussion in R. W. Klein, *1 Samuel* (Waco: Word, 1983), 31–32.

[10] McCarter, *1 Samuel*, 97.

[11] See Klein, *1 Samuel*, 32

[12] See R. Gnuse, "A Reconsideration of the Form-Critical Structure in 1 Samuel 3: An Ancient Near Eastern Dream Theophany," in *1978 SBL Annual Meeting Abstracts* (Missoula: Scholars Press, 1978).

[13] 1 Sam 3:21, a concluding editorial comment, should not be allowed to determine how we assess this narrative. Notice, in any case, that this verse does not say that Yahweh appeared to Samuel but that he appeared in Shiloh and that he revealed himself to Samuel.

[14] This feature is not uncommon with seers and refers to the seeing of the communication, like writing on the wall. The seeing of Yahweh is not necessarily involved, and it is the latter that makes a theophany.

narrative are present: (1) God calls someone by name; (2) there is a formulaic response—"speak Lord, your servant listens"; and (3) there is further communication, usually entailing some sort of commission.

It has been debated as to whether vv. 11–14 can be seen as a commissioning scene. At the least, it can be called Samuel's first prophetic experience,[15] and
in fact these verses do indirectly involve a commission to Samuel. He must speak
God's word, even though it involves the unpleasant task of bearing bad tidings to
Eli about his family. The unique feature that affects the formal elements is that
Samuel is a boy and therefore reluctant to communicate such news to his respected elder and priestly overseer, Eli.

The third important feature of this story is that Samuel is instructed to
refer to himself as God's servant (vv. 9–10). This was to become a typical term
for a prophet, and indeed so typical that a whole portion of the Isaianic corpus
uses it to speak of its prophetic figure. While the terminology is also used in
the Moses narrative material and therefore can have a wider sense than just
"prophet," nonetheless the term is important because it says something about the
relationship of the prophet to God.

The prophet is not an initiator of this particular relationship with God,
nor of the particular tasks that he will undertake, nor of the words he will speak.
He is a person under authority who can only speak and act at the behest of his
Master, just as in the normal slave-master relationship. The initiative, like the
source of the communication, lies outside the prophet. Being a prophet is not so
much a vocation pursued as something that happens to a person quite apart
from his or her plans or will. In the case of Samuel, there is no preparation for
this prophetic role. To the contrary, he is being prepared to be a priest. Yet the
experience is compelling enough that the prophet feels he must speak or act as
instructed.

This brings to light another interesting feature of this story. Although
Samuel had heard God's word, still he had some choice about whether he would
speak it. God had not simply turned Samuel into a megaphone; there was some
human will involved in responding properly. Fear, in Samuel's case, inhibits his
relaying the message to Eli right away (vv. 15–17). Notice, too, the stress that he
did not leave out a single word of what Yahweh had said. This is the proper thing
for an oracle to do, but again it seems to be implied that he could have done otherwise.[16]

The way of describing the prophet's situation in v. 19 becomes quite typical. God is with Samuel, and therefore his fame continues to grow through time.
God will not allow one of Samuel's word to "fall to the ground" or become

---

[15] See the discussion of W. Richter, *Die sogenannten vorprophetische Berufsberichte*
(Göttingen: Vandenhoeck & Ruprecht, 1970).

[16] See M. J. Buss, "The Social Psychology of Prophecy," in *Prophecy: Essays Presented
to Georg Fohrer on His Sixty-fifth Birthday, 6 September 1980* (ed. J. A. Emerton; Berlin: de
Gruyter, 1980), 1–11.

groundless.[17] Indeed, the text says that the whole of the land, from the northern cultic center in Dan to the southern border at Beersheba came to know that at Shiloh God had established a significant prophetic figure in Samuel. The frequency of God's coming to Shiloh is linked to the presence of the true prophet in that sanctuary.

This story raises again, in a significant way, the question of the etymological overtones of the word *nabi*. Does it refer to one who calls upon God or the reverse—one called by God? The stress here on being audibly called by God leads one to suspect that when we arrive at v. 20, we are meant to think that Samuel is the "called one" of Yahweh, endowed with a special relationship and special communication from God. McCarter is likely on the right path when he says that *nabi* is "a noun of an archaic passive formation denoting 'one summoned (for a special assignment or office).' Cf. the Akkadian verb *nabu*, 'call by name, call to duty,' used especially of the calling of men by gods. Hebrew *nabi* may thus connote 'one called to duty by a god.'"[18] The very fact that Samuel's duties are not restricted to that of an oracle giver but, rather, also include being a priest, warrior, governor, and judge (see 7:2–17) suggests an earlier stage in the history of Israel, a premonarchial stage when judges were still needed and kings were not yet to be found.[19] "Joshua was Moses' successor, the 'servant of God'. But he is never called prophet, nor is he a priest. Here is more than a Joshua. Here, too, we have something more than the prophets of later times, who stood in the midst of the people as the spokesmen of God, but in other respects were still on their periphery."[20] Samuel, then, is a prototype of what Wilson has called a central prophet.[21]

Whether one agrees with my assessment above or sees this presentation of Samuel as a retrospective glance from a much later period, it is difficult not to see here a strong emphasis on Samuel's experience being prototypical and, in some ways, paradigmatic of Israel's prophets. This in itself raises questions about how we are to assess Saul, especially since nothing suggests that Samuel's call experience is ecstatic in character. To Saul we now turn.

II. SAUL SEARCHING

The material in 1 Sam 8ff. is undoubtedly some of the most important, historically speaking, in this entire book, for it chronicles the transition from the

---

[17] See H. W. Hertzberg, *1 and 2 Samuel: A Commentary* (trans. John Bowden; Philadelphia: Westminster, 1960), 42. McCarter, *1 Samuel*, 99, says that it means letting nothing he said prove false, thus showing that Samuel meets the later Deuteronomistic standards, on which see pp. 30–32 above.

[18] McCarter, *1 Samuel*, 99.

[19] See McCarter, ibid., who recognizes the diversity of roles but does not draw the proper conclusions about what sort of social situation this material suggests.

[20] Hertzberg, *1 and 2 Samuel*, 43.

[21] See Wilson, *Prophecy and Society*, 85ff.

period of the judges to the monarchy, a transition in which Samuel plays no little part. What is important for our purposes is to recognize that the insistence on a king by Israel is presented in this material as a rejection of the kingship of Yahweh, a rejection of theocracy and, in one sense, also a rejection of the adequacy of God plus judge/prophet as a plan for ruling God's people. God will accede to having a *nagid* over his people, a prince but not a king. The problem is that the people will see him as a king and call him such and, in due course if not immediately, this is how the potentate will see himself. In this context Samuel will play the role of anointer of the human ruler, a role to be taken up later by Elijah and Elisha in the northern part of the land.

The editing of this material becomes especially clear at 9:9–11, where the editorial comment found at v. 9 indicates that prophetic figures *used* to be called seers but apparently in the editor's time a prophet was called a man of God. Yet in the story at vv. 11–21, Samuel is addressed as a *ro'eh,* a seer, and calls himself the same. For our purposes, vv. 15ff. are also important, for they indicate to us that a prophet may receive a personal revelation, in this case about Saul, that he is not called upon to proclaim or relate to someone else but that, rather, is to be the basis of his own future actions. The prophetic experience of revelation and the prophetic expression of oracles must be distinguished.

Notice that a seer is someone whom one can go to and consult with and ask questions of (v. 9). This practice unites both ancient Near Eastern prophets, such as Samuel, and Greek prophetic figures, such as the oracle at Delphi. They were the persons to whom one would go to receive an answer from God, and as such they could serve as intermediaries, although, at least in the case of seers, in the biblical tradition this was not their primary function. Notice, too, how the communication of God to Samuel is described at v. 15. It reads literally, "Yahweh had uncovered Samuel's ear." The emphasis, then, is on the auditory nature of the revelation, even though Samuel is called a seer in this passage. McCarter also suggests that this idiomatic expression "implies disclosure of something previously unknown to or even kept secret from the hearer (as in 20:2, 12 [MT], 13; 22:8 [bis], 17)."[22]

About the notion of a man of God, McCarter helpfully summarizes that he was

> a professional holy man. He was thought of as possessing special skills and powers enabling him to invoke the aid of supernatural forces. His role in society is best illustrated by reference to the stories about Elijah and Elisha, who might be categorized as paradigmatic men of God. The miracles ascribed to them include healings of the sick or even dead . . . provision of much food from little . . . and so on. To be sure Elijah and Elisha also prophesy. . . . But the designation "man of God" . . . itself carries none of the special force of "prophet" (*nabi'*).[23]

At 1 Sam 10 there is the interesting tale of Saul's anointing and the confirmation of his anointing in the encounter with a band of ecstatic prophets. The

---

[22] McCarter, *1 Samuel,* 178.
[23] Ibid., 175.

anointing of Saul is presented as a prophetic sign act, symbolizing the fact that God would anoint Saul.[24] That it is a sign and not an act of magic, nor a sacrament, nor the actual empowering anointing becomes clear when one notes that not only is the anointing accompanied by a prophecy of a future anointing; in addition, it is only through a later encounter with the band of prophets that Saul becomes a changed man and prophesies.

This conclusion goes against the suggestion of various scholars that prophetic symbolic acts necessarily participated in the reality that they symbolized. It is true there might be a close connection, in some cases, between prophetic sign and the thing symbolized. For example, this seems surely to be the case with the anointing of David at 1 Sam 16:13, which reads, "so Samuel took the horn of oil and anointed him in the midst of his brothers, and the spirit of Yahweh rushed upon him from that day forward." Yet even here it is not made clear that the anointing was the means by which the spirit of God came, and this seems clearly not to be the case with Saul. Thus, at most on some occasions, there seems to have been a close correlation or connection between a prophetic sign and the reality it symbolized. Hooker puts things aptly:

> Perhaps it would be better to speak, on the one hand, of prophetic actions which mediate manifestations of divine power in events that bring with them either salvation or judgment, and on the other, of prophetic actions which point to a divine activity which cannot otherwise be observed at present. . . . The prophetic actions in the first group are understood as leading to epiphanies: God is at work through the prophet, and what takes place is a manifestation of God's power. The actions in the second group are also manifestations—not direct manifestations of divine *power*, but manifestations of the divine *will*. Like prophetic oracles, these prophetic actions unveil God's purposes.[25]

Something more needs to be said about anointing at this juncture. Anointing in Israel, while sometimes associated with priestly figures (Exod 40:12–15), was in the main a royal ritual. First Samuel reports the anointing of Saul and David, then in 1 Kgs 1:39 we hear of the anointing of Solomon, and so on. As we have already noted, prophetic figures might often be involved in an act of pouring or smearing some kind of oil (1 Sam 10:1 would seem to suggest vegetable oil) on the one who would be king,[26] but they themselves were not symbolically anointed figures. The relationship between anointing and the reception of the spirit of prophecy needs careful discussion because, while prophets certainly manifested the inspiration of God's spirit, they were not anointed figures and, while anointed figures were regularly kings in Israel, they were seldom prophets, manifesting the inspiration of the spirit in their lives. It is the king who came to be known as God's anointed one, or *meshiah*, not some prophetic figure.[27]

---

[24] On prophetic sign acts, see pp. 238–44 above.

[25] Hooker, *Signs of a Prophet*, 3.

[26] See Exod 30:22–25, which seems to offer a sort of recipe for anointing oil, including olive oil with spices in it, such as myrrh, cinnamon, sweet cane, and cassia.

[27] See the discussion in McCarter, *1 Samuel*, 178.

First Samuel 10:5–6 is extremely important for this study. On the basis of these verses and some parallels from prophetic material outside the Hebrew Scriptures, elaborate theories have been conjured up about prophets and ecstasy. Perhaps the most influential of such theories within biblical circles is that of J. Lindblom in his classic work *Prophecy in Ancient Israel*.[28] It will be well if we consider some of his remarks at this juncture. At the outset of his study, he stresses that "the prophet is compelled by the spirit. . . . He has lost the freedom of the ordinary man and is forced to follow the orders of the deity. He must say what has been given him to say and go where he is commanded to go. Few things are so characteristic of prophets, wherever we meet them in the world of religion, as the feeling of being under a superhuman and supernatural constraint."[29] He goes on to emphasize that, in the case of prophets, inspiration tends to pass over into ecstasy:

> In religious ecstasy, consciousness is entirely filled with the presence of God, with ideas and feelings belonging to the divine sphere. The soul is lifted up into the exalted region of divine revelation, and the lower world with its sensations momentarily disappears. There are various means to induce such a mental rapture: intoxication of different kinds, fasts, flagellation, dancing, music and so on. . . . It must be kept in mind that ecstasy has many degrees. There is an ecstasy which involves a total extinction of the normal consciousness, a complete insensibility and anesthesia. There is also an ecstasy which approximates to a normal fit of absence of mind or intense excitement. . . . This inspired exaltation has in the prophets a tendency to pass over into a real ecstasy of a more or less intense nature, lethargic or orgiastic.[30]

Prophetic figures, both ancient and modern, have been known to have intense ecstatic experiences, whether one is thinking of ancient figures, such as the band of prophets described in 1 Sam 10, or much more modern figures, such as the Islamic whirling dervishes or some of those who have experienced the "Toronto Blessing." One can say it is a regular feature of the prophetic experience. What one can not say is that it is a universal experience of all prophets at all times, especially if by ecstasy one means the extreme end of the spectrum, where consciousness is lost or—better said—it is taken over by some sort of spiritual presence.

Sociological analyses of this phenomenon have tended to stress that this sort of behavior has the function of credentialing, or authenticating that a particular person is a true prophet. Wilson, for example, says, "The behavior conforms to the society's expectations about how possessed individuals act. Similar 'uncontrolled' symptoms are exhibited initially by *all* possessed individuals in the society, and in this way the society is able to recognize that possession rather than illness [or madness] is involved."[31]

---

[28] J. Lindblom, *Prophecy in Ancient Israel* (Philadelphia: Fortress, 1962).

[29] Ibid., 2.

[30] Ibid., 5.

[31] Wilson, *Prophecy and Society*, 64.

There are, however, problems in simply subsuming the prophetic experience under the category of ecstasy, or suggesting that manifesting ecstatic behavior in public was necessarily intended by the prophetic figure—a deliberately chosen demonstration or proof of one's authentic prophetic character. It is one thing to talk about the effect of manifesting such behavior in public, and another to speak of intent. There is also a problem in simply amalgamating all prophetic experience from whatever age or culture under one heading. These dangers are recognized quite well by McCarter:

> The hand that shaped the stories of Samuel and Saul viewed the prophet as a sober mediator between God and man, whose leadership responsibilities were unlimited except by the divine will itself and whose complete integration into the social structure could therefore be taken for granted. But here [i.e., in 1 Sam 10] we encounter another aspect of the phenomenon of prophecy. These prophets, like Samuel, are recipients of divine inspiration, but in them it expresses itself in the form of ecstatic practices of an orgiastic type, *which set them apart from other individuals. . . .* By all accounts such behavior is highly contagious, as Saul himself discovers.[32]

Caution, then, is required so as not to lump together all prophets, or all prophetic experiences, or all forms of prophetic expression but still to be open to all insights that can be gained from a cross-cultural approach to analyzing prophecy.

First Samuel 10:5–6 refers to a band of prophets. Nothing here is said about these prophets having a particular leader figure, as if this were a prophet with his disciples or other prophets in training, although we can not rule out such an idea (see pp. 94–99 below). In any case, the emphasis is on the collective nature of the group and the fact that all could be called prophets and all manifested the same sort of phenomena. In an age where gender, geography, and generation were seen as the fundamental building blocks of society, prophets always posed a threat to the status quo. The function of the concluding remark at 1 Sam 10:12—"But who is their father?"—could be meant to emphasize the skepticism of such a culture about those who claimed authority and power outside the regular channels of gender, geography, and generation. Hertzberg says that this is a contemptuous and dismissive remark that means in essence, "But where have they come from?" The implication is, Why should we recognize them or the legitimacy of their experiences?[33]

There is, however, another way of viewing v. 12. The question about the prophets might mean, "But who is their leader?" since elsewhere we do hear about groups called sons of prophets (2 Kgs 2:12; 6:21; 13:14) and since at 1 Sam 19:20 we see Samuel depicted as the leader of some sort of prophetic guild.[34] It is interesting, then, that Saul is simply said to be among or one of the

---

[32] McCarter, *1 Samuel,* 182; emphasis mine.

[33] Hertzberg, *1 and 2 Samuel,* 86: "The proverb means, 'How does a reasonable man, well placed in civic life, come to be in this eccentric company?' "

[34] See the discussion by P. R. Ackroyd, *The First Book of Samuel* (Cambridge: Cambridge University Press, 1971).

prophets, not the leader of them, even though he has just been anointed to be a prince over Israel. J. G. Williams has plausibly argued that the phrase "But who is their father/leader?" suggests that if one knows the leader of the group, then one knows why Saul is with these prophets, and the leader of this group is Samuel. In short, Samuel orchestrated this whole affair to authenticate Saul as a leader.[35]

Another important feature of this narrative is the connection of this band of prophets with music and musical instruments. Notice that v. 5 says Saul will encounter a group of prophets coming down from the high place prophesying and in front of them will be a variety of musical instruments. This suggests they are accompanied by musicians. There seems to be some connection between music and the prophets being able to or induced to prophesy, since the spirit of prophecy comes on Elisha when music is played (2 Kgs 3:15–16), and notice that an evil spirit rushes on Saul when David plays the lyre for him (1 Sam 18:10). The instruments in question are harps, tambourines, woodwinds, and lyre, or in short, percussion, stringed, and woodwind instruments—a regular marching band. McCarter stresses that the woodwind instrument in particular was regularly associated with extremely emotional occasions.[36] If there was indeed a long-standing connection between music and prophecy, it would not be surprising that some prophecies were delivered in the form of songs, something not only this text but the general poetic character of prophecy, and the later references to singers prophesying seem to suggest.[37]

Here a word is in order about the spirit of Yahweh. What seems to be meant by this phrase is Yahweh's presence, which brings with it Yahweh's power, authority, words, and knowledge. The phrase *ruah Yahweh* could, of course, be equally well rendered the "breath" or "wind of Yahweh." Thus McCarter stresses that it "refers in such situations to the vital force of the deity, that is, to the invigorating power of God as experienced by a human being."[38] This empowerment can lead to deeds of great power (Judg 14:6, 19; 15:14; 1 Sam 11:6) or words of great power (compare 1 Sam 10:10 with 16:13–14).

What, in the end, will be the effect on Saul of the spirit of Yahweh rushing upon him? The result is mentioned twice (vv. 6, 9). It is first said that he will be turned into another man; in short, it will be a life-transforming experience. Nothing here is said about Saul losing his sense of self but, rather, of his gaining a new sense of self or, indeed, gaining a new self. The issue here is not about loss of consciousness or self-consciousness through ecstasy but, rather, about the

---

[35] J. G. Williams, "The Prophetic 'Father': A Brief Explanation of the Term 'Sons of the Prophets,' " *JBL* 85 (1966): 344–48, here 347.

[36] McCarter, *1 Samuel*, 182.

[37] On which see below pp. 62–65.

[38] McCarter, *1 Samuel*, 182.

personality transformation that the prophetic experience wrought.[39] Verse 9 puts the matter a bit differently; it says, literally, "God turned another heart to him," which presumably means that God gave him another heart. Hertzberg raises the issue whether this refers to a conversion of some sort, and he dismisses the notion by concluding that this merely meant that Saul had been made ready by this experience to accept God's interventions in the future.[40] There may be something to the latter suggestion, but the stress surely lies on Saul being a changed man because of the impact and influence of God's presence and power in his life. At the least, this is the conversion of Saul to a new vocation, authenticated by the prophetic experience.

By 1 Sam 12 we are already hearing about Samuel's farewell, and we have had very little indication of the sort of oracles this seer may have proclaimed. The same can be said of Saul. What was important in the case of the latter was that he manifested prophetic phenomena, authenticating that God was with him.

Yet one more item of importance comes to light from a close scrutiny of ch. 10. It was when Saul came to the hill of God, where a leader of the Philistines was, and approached the city that Saul met a band of prophets. Saul was a Benjaminite, living in territory that bordered on regions belonging to the Philistines. Like Samson after him, he was likely used to fraternizing and associating with those of another religious culture. It is possible that we are meant to think of this band of prophets not as Israelite prophets but as Philistine prophets. This might explain not only their unexpected number (in light of what was earlier said about Samuel) but also the possible skepticism expressed about them in the question about the father, and possibly even the apparent skepticism about Saul being a prophet or associating with this group of persons.[41] If this conjecture is right, it may provide for us one additional piece of information supporting the notion that the prophetic situation in this region was fluid, with prophets operating in cross-cultural situations.[42] There may also be some latent irony as well. Saul begins his public career associating with a foreign prophetic band, near the end of his tenure he consults a medium at Endor, and in between he bans such people from the land! Saul is seen as an inconsistent, spiritually suspect, and deeply flawed leader—the very sort a flawed people with polytheistic leanings would prefer. On the other hand, in light of a text such as 19:20, the prophetic

---

[39] In short, I am doubtful about anachronistically applying modern notions about spirit possession or possession trance to the ancient prophets; such an application hinges, in part, on taking the term *hitnabbe* to mean "rave" rather than "prophesy." But see S. B. Parker, "Possession Trance and Prophecy in Pre-exilic Israel," *VT* 28 (1978): 271–85.

[40] Hertzberg, *1 and 2 Samuel*, 86.

[41] Saul's later association with the medium of Endor may also be an indicator that he associated from time to time with prophets and diviners of neighboring cultures.

[42] This conjecture makes better sense of the text than does the suggestion of McCarter, *1 Samuel*, 182, following others, that the mention of the Philistine prefect is immaterial at this point. To the contrary, it signals that we should recognize we are dealing with a cross-cultural situation.

band Saul encounters may be Israelite prophets.[43] We can not be sure. We must consider a few more texts to see if this conjecture has merit.

We must first consider a few points on 1 Sam 15. First, it is not entirely true that there are no oracles attributed to Samuel. In fact, at vv. 2–3 there are both the messenger formula ("Thus says Yahweh") and the record of a specific oracle commanding the smiting of the Amalekites by Saul and his troops. This may be contrasted with the revelation that comes to Samuel himself at 15:10, not for proclamation but for information that motivates him to act. Secondly, the oracle about the Amalekites calls for the execution of the *herem*, the holy war against this tribe. If one is prompted to ask why, it is because they were the chief opponents of the Israelites during their wilderness wandering period and it was this tribe primarily that sought to deny Israel entrance into the promised land (see Exod 17:8–17).[44] The oracle is a political one, involving military actions, but it is also a theological one, for what is involved is a holy war, where there is utter destruction and sacrifice of the opponent to the Lord and no booty or spoils are allowed for Israel to keep. This practice is known elsewhere in the ancient Near East. For example, there is the story of Mesha, the king of Moab, who took men, women, servants, and children from Israel and devoted them to destruction as an offering to the god Ashtar-Chemosh.[45] Thirdly, there is, then, nothing in this oracle that distinguishes it in content from the practices of other ancient peoples, except that the biblical God is involved. It is important to remember that the theology of the ban, or total destruction order *(herem)*, turns up again later in the context of prophetic actions and oracles at 1 Kgs 20:42, and in fact it is implicit in the earlier Elijah narrative material in 1 Kgs 19. This may be taken as early evidence that Israelite prophets saw themselves as the prosecutors of the covenant lawsuit, urging Israel to keep its stipulations and requirements, stipulations we find enshrined in a later form in Deut 20.

First Samuel 15:10 reminds us once more of the difference between prophetic experience and prophetic expression, with this text dealing only with the former. Klein makes the interesting observation that we should compare Yahweh's regret over making Saul a ruler here with the regret of God over making humankind at Gen 6:6–7. The problem is that Saul does not fully carry out the ban, and so does not fully carry out or establish God's word. "This represents a backsliding, or a turning away from Yahweh (. . . cf. Num. 14.43; 32.15;

---

[43] One wonders if, since prophets were basically just messengers, there were bands of prophets who were prepared to be the mouthpieces for whatever deity enlisted their services. The case of Balaam, discussed in the previous chapter, raises precisely this sort of question. Prophets might serve a particular deity, but in a polytheistic environment, if they were not Israelite prophets, they might be prepared to serve Yahweh as well as other gods, like mediums at the beck and call of whatever spirit chooses them. One wonders if the band of prophets Saul encountered was of this sort.

[44] See Hertzberg, *1 and 2 Samuel*, 124.

[45] See the Moabite Stone inscription in *ANET*, 320.

Josh. 22.16, 18; Jer. 3.19).".[46] What this story tells us is that the election of God is not irrevocable; God can always decide to choose a more suitable instrument or implementer of the divine will. What is remarkable is that Samuel disagrees with God's rejection of Saul and spends all night crying to the Lord, presumably pleading for God to reconsider.[47] The prophet is not just a mouthpiece of God but also, from time to time, an intercessor; but in this case it is all of no avail, and this does not necessarily reflect negatively on the true prophetic character of Samuel. It simply shows he had a personal relationship with Yahweh and felt free to discuss and argue things with God.

First Samuel 19:18–24 confronts us once more with the issues of prophecy, ecstasy, and the roles of Samuel and of Saul. This story, however, comes from much later in the story, at a time when Saul is already out of favor with Yahweh and David's star is on the rise, even though he is on the run. One of the interesting aspects of this passage that distinguishes it from the similar one in ch. 10 is that here it is implied that prophets lived in camps. A *nahweh* was originally a shepherd's camp that would be pitched outside a city (see Jer 33:12), but here the term is used of the band of prophets that Samuel is presiding over when Saul's emissaries come to take David captive.[48]

The prophets are depicted here as having some sort of assembly or conclave over which Samuel is "standing holding a position," which means standing in a position of authority—presiding.[49] The prophets are prophesying, and the spirit of God is so palpably present that when Saul's emissaries come near, they catch the "fever," for the activity is contagious. They are overcome by Yahweh's spirit and totally fail to accomplish what Saul sent them for. The focus here is not just on the experience of ecstasy but on the activity of prophesying, and McCarter simply confuses the matter by suggesting that prophecy in this case *is* group ecstasy. It would be more accurate to say that group ecstasy prompts prophecy.[50] As Wilson points out, the niphal of the verb "prophesy" means the delivery of a prophetic oracle, not merely the experience of ecstasy.[51]

Saul, in frustration, himself goes to the camp of the prophets. The closer he gets, the more the spirit of Yahweh influences him, and he finds himself prophesying as he heads toward the camp near Samuel's hometown of Ramah. The experience of the spirit is so overpowering that when he reaches the camp, he strips off his clothes and prophesies in front of the prophets and lies naked before them for an entire day and night. The story is meant to show who is in charge of the situation and how impotent Saul is to resist God's will for David.

---

[46] Klein, *1 Samuel*, 151.

[47] See the discussion by Hertzberg, *1 and 2 Samuel*, 126.

[48] See the discussion by A. Malamat, "The Origins of Statecraft in the Israelite Monarchy," in *The Biblical Archaeologist Reader 3* (ed. E. F. Campbell et al.; Garden City: Doubleday, 1970), 195–99.

[49] See McCarter, *1 Samuel*, 329.

[50] Ibid.

[51] Wilson, *Prophecy and Society*, 138; cf. Klein, *1 Samuel*, 198.

Indeed, since nakedness was seen as shameful in this ancient Near Eastern culture, one must see this as a story about the shaming of a once great man.

First Samuel 19:24 says that it was this episode that actually prompted
some to ask if Saul was a prophet. This may suggest that the earlier story in ch.
10, insofar as it records the same phenomenon, is in fact a doublet or variant of
this story. Yet the stories are different enough to allow the possibility that they
record two episodes. "The spirit of Yahweh now haunts him rather than helps
him. And in contrast to the encounter described in 10:10–12, here he meets the
prophetic troop as an unwelcome intruder, indeed as an enemy. He is now more
a victim of prophetic inspiration than a beneficiary of it."[52] Wilson, in fact,
thinks the answer to the question "Is Saul among the prophets?" is meant to be
"no" here, yet clearly the narrator presents Saul doing the same thing as the other
prophets.[53] In any event, this prophetic interlude allows David time to escape
from Saul once more. It is very interesting that nothing whatsoever is said or implied here about David being a prophet or being caught up in the prophetic
experience.

The last passage of relevance for this discussion is 28:3–25. Our concern in
this story is not the demise of Saul, though the story is clearly meant to depict
the nadir of Saul's spiritual pilgrimage, but the consultation with the medium at
Endor and the way this is clearly contrasted with what is seen as acceptable
means of gaining insight from God about a situation—through dreams, through
Urim and Thummim, or through prophets (v. 6). Yet the story makes clear that
Saul consulted these legitimized means first but could get no response from God
and so turned to the very means that he had expelled from the land—mediums.
The story, then, is laden with irony and is meant to depict a portrait of a desper-
ate man. This tale is not about a time when there are no prophets in the land, as
is sometimes said. It is, rather, about a figure to whom God no longer gives
guidance.

The story begins at v. 3 by saying that Saul had banished all "ghostwives"
from the land. The term refers to a female necromancer. It is interesting that the
Hebrew terms *obot* and *yidde'onim* are most often referred to in tandem (Lev
19:31; 20:6, 27; 2 Kgs 21:6; 23:24). Originally the terms referred to the departed
spirits who spoke to some humans, but by extension the terms came to be used
of those through whom such spirits spoke, namely, necromancers. Notice that
the implied polemic here is not against any and all forms of divination, since it is
suggested that consulting Urim and Thummim is acceptable. The issue here is
that Saul has gone to a medium who relies on a forbidden sort of divination. He
commands the woman, "divine for me by a ghost."[54]

Notice also that the story does not suggest that this medium is unable to
speak with the dead. She is not portrayed as a charlatan. To the contrary, she has

---

[52] McCarter, *1 Samuel*, 329. It is possible, as McCarter suggests, that this story is
from a different source than the one found in 1 Sam 10, and one hostile to Saul.

[53] Wilson, *Prophecy and Society*, 183.

[54] See McCarter, *1 Samuel*, 421.

a real encounter with the departed spirit of Samuel, who is not at all pleased to be disturbed. The story does not suggest that the woman was incapable of doing what Saul requested. Rather, it suggests that Saul simply had no business pursuing this information in this manner. Yet ironically, Saul obtained answers by this means when all other means of consultation had proved fruitless. Saul consulted a true prophet through a prohibited but nonetheless effective means. What is assumed throughout is that a departed person, especially a departed true prophet, will have clear insight and access to what God is about to do.

When the spirit of the departed Samuel is summoned, he comes up from below, from Sheol, the land of departed spirits. He is recognizable by his robe or mantle, which is wrapped around his form (cf. 2:19; 15:27). The medium recoils because what she sees is a godlike figure (28:13). The use of the term *elohim* of a human being is found only here in the OT. Although he has been disturbed, nonetheless Samuel is still a true prophet even beyond the grave, for he tells the truth about what is happening and what is about to happen with Saul.[55]

Notice the cross-cultural dimensions to this story. Saul must slip behind enemy lines to consult this woman. Necromancy was the sort of activity for which the Philistine diviners were noted (6:2; contrast 15:23). Thus, the lawmaker becomes the lawbreaker in regard to mediums; notice the extra irony in Saul swearing by Yahweh (28:10) as he promises no harm will come to this woman for this activity.[56] This story makes evident that there was a whole spectrum of means by which the ancients sought to learn about the future. Divination was, in the Israelite culture, distinguishable from prophecy, and certain forms of divination were proscribed. Nonetheless, even the proscribed form of divination is not seen as an ineffective means of gaining information on what is true or will come true. In this regard the Israelite perspective does not differ from that at Mari or elsewhere in the ancient Near East. What distinguishes the Israelite perspective is the proscribing of certain forms of divination.

III. CONCLUSIONS

M. J. Buss, in a study of the social psychology of prophecy, makes the following observation:

> As a group increases in size, at first a single part-time or full-time religious specialist emerges . . . then religious duties are divided between priests and diviners, and finally several classes of priests and diviners or prophets are formed. This pattern of development also appears in Israelite society. Although early Israel existed within the orbit of elaborately organized states, its constituent groups were small enough so that there was little occasion for assigning priestly, prophetic, and judicial functions

---

[55] On the cult of the dead, see T. J. Lewis, *Cults of the Dead in Ancient Israel and Ugarit* (Atlanta: Scholars Press, 1989).

[56] See the discussion by Klein, *1 Samuel,* 267.

to different persons. Thus early figures—including the patriarchs, Moses, and Samuel—are appropriately pictured as executing a variety of tasks.[57]

This comment is apt, as the study in this chapter of Samuel and Saul has demonstrated. Before the establishment of the monarchy, a variety of leader figures assumed a variety of roles. Delineation of roles in Israel seems to come to the fore only in the time of David. This does not mean, however, that there were no prophetic figures among the Israelites before David. It simply means that there were no professional prophets or court prophets who could be simply characterized by this sort of descriptor and not another one.

This chapter has also brought out important points about the issues of ecstasy and about bands of prophets. It may not be the case that ecstasy was unknown among Israelite prophets, but the story of Saul could be interpreted to mean that he had associated himself with a band of Philistine prophets. On the other hand, Samuel also seems to have been involved with a band of prophets, and it could be the same as the one Saul was associated with. What can not be said is that there is clear evidence in this material either that all true prophets had ecstatic experiences or that they did not. It would appear that some did and some did not.

The role of music in providing an ethos for ecstasy comes to the fore in the Saul stories. Already in the last chapter, evidence was present that prophets could also be singers (e.g., Deborah), and in the Samuel and Saul pericopes, music seems to be something that can induce a trancelike state. This has to do with prophetic experience, but could it also have to do with prophetic expression, such that prophets in this state felt led to express their oracles in the same sort of poetic form that songs took in that era? It is not possible to give a definitive answer to such a question, and perhaps it is safer at this juncture simply to recognize the connection between music and prophetic ecstasy.

The story of the call Samuel received would seem to be presented as something of a paradigm, for later generations, of how a prophet came to be a prophet in the first place. Yet there are anomalies in this story as well. On the one hand, there would be later figures, such as Ezekiel, who have associations with the priesthood but are called away from this role in order to fulfill another. What the priest and the prophet share in common is that they are mediators between the people and God, those authorized to go into the presence of God and empowered to come back to the people with aid or answers. The transition from one role to the other is not such a sharp one as one might think. On the other hand, in Samuel we have the case of a Nazirite boy who becomes a prophet and by his first oracle brings a priestly line down. One must weigh both the continuity and discontinuity between this story and other call narratives.

In regard to the issue of divination and prophecy, the Israelite traditions examined in this chapter continue to support a distinction between the two phenomena, and the Saul story in particular suggests that divination was seen as a last

---

[57] Buss, "Social Psychology," 4.

resort if there were no real prophets to consult. But what this material does *not* suggest is that divination was an ineffective means of consulting the spirits of the dead. To the contrary, the story intimates that Saul had an encounter with the not-too-pleased-to-be-disturbed shade of Samuel. When we deal with prophecy and divination, we are dealing with spiritual phenomena that appear in many of the ancient Near Eastern cultures in a variety of forms. If we must conjecture, Israelites were forbidden to consult necromancers perhaps not merely because of the potential for erroneous information or charlatanism but because Israel was called to a higher and more intimate relationship with God through prophets and intermediaries (e.g., Moses). Seeking after mediums was taken as a clear sign of a spiritual breakdown in that intimate relationship. In the next chapter, we will see prophets attempting to repair such breaches in the divine-human relationship by confrontational prophetic speech acts.

CHAPTER 3

Courting the Prophets:

Prophets and the Early Monarchy

THE DESIRE OF ISRAEL TO BE LIKE other nations in having a monarchy inevitably led to an emulation of other ancient Near Eastern monarchies. One of the ways this manifested itself in due course was that Israel, like the Babylonians or those who dwelled at Mari, saw a need for court prophets, apparently in addition to regular advisers, such as Abner. It is almost never the court prophets in Israel, however, who challenge the king about his behavior or actions. Beginning with the Elijah and Elisha cycle and continuing on into the period of the writing prophets, there were a series of peripheral prophets who were often critical of the behavior of the monarch and provided an independent audit of the spiritual state of affairs in the palace and in the nation in general. A possible exception to this rule about court and peripheral prophets is the very first prominent prophetic figure to arise once the Davidic monarchy was established—Nathan. These early prophets of the monarchial period must be examined closely, for they provide a precedent for somewhat later figures such as Amos or Micah or Hosea.

I. NATHAN—A PROPHET AFTER GOD'S OWN HEART

A. Good Housekeeping.   Hardly any text in the corpus of Samuel material was to prove of more importance, in the long run, than 2 Sam 7. This is shown clearly enough by the various places in which material from this text appears. For example, there is the later but parallel version found in 1 Chron 17:1–15, a poetic recension in Ps 89:19–27 (which has led some to wonder whether this isn't the earlier form of this oracle), and Ps 132 (perhaps a yet further recension).[1] There are also the echoes of, and allusions to, this text in the NT.[2] It will accordingly require some close attention.

The role of Nathan must first be evaluated. He appears for the first time in 2 Sam 7, at the crucial juncture when King David is contemplating building Yahweh some kind of temple; he reappears during the Bathsheba crisis (2 Sam 12) and then appears one final time during the succession crisis in 1 Kgs 1:11–27. In all these cases the prophet appears as a sort of crisis intervention specialist, coming to warn of, or head off, disaster.[3] At the outset, Nathan is simply with the king (2 Sam 7:2); that the text does not say that Nathan, while undertaking some other task, was called to go and speak to the king suggests his affiliation with, or at least his access to, the court in some capacity. Equally, the account in 1 Kgs 1 likewise suggests that Nathan is a prophet with clear access to the royal family and that his words were valued. He was a prophet who prophesied with some regularity to or for the king, since he is concerned about the legitimate succession of the royal line and is apparently known well enough to Bathsheba to not only have ready access to her but give counsel that will be immediately received.

The references to Nathan being sent to David at 1 Sam 12:1 and Nathan going to his own home at 12:5 do not necessarily contradict the impression that Nathan was a prophet involved with the court, for at this early stage in the monarchy, it may be doubted that there was anything like official residences adjoining the king's palace for the king's officials. Nothing, however, suggests that Nathan was one of a group or band or guild of prophets associated with the monarch, nor is there anything to suggest Nathan presided over such a group. Furthermore, there is nothing in this narrative material to suggest that David was seen as a prophet who had an association with Nathan because of a shared experience or prophetic function, unlike the case with Saul and the aforementioned band of prophets.

Yet however new it may have been for an Israelite ruler to have a prophetic consultant, this was certainly nothing new in the ancient Near East. Importantly, there is clear evidence that prophets involved in court life might well share oracles about the worrisome issue of succession. One must distinguish, however, between a court prophet as a regular day-to-day functionary of a king and a prophet who had the ear of the king and was from time to time consulted by, or brought a message to, the king. All the evidence about Nathan suggests he was the latter sort of figure, not unlike some of the prophets brought in and paid for an oracle at Mari.

In this regard one may, to some extent, contrast Nathan with the seer Gad, who is referred to in 2 Sam 24. Gad is introduced to us at the outset in v. 11 as

---

[1] See the discussion of A. Malamat, "Mari Prophecy and Nathan's Dynastic Oracle," in *Prophecy* (ed. Emerton), 68–82.

[2] See pp. 332–43 below.

[3] Even in the case of 2 Sam 7, it appears that the function of the dynastic oracle is, in part, to prevent David from making the major mistake of trying to build God a house.

"David's seer." This suggests an ongoing consulting relationship with the court. By contrast, Nathan is never called David's seer. Yet Gad, like Nathan, is also no mere yes-man; indeed, he is the bearer of the bad tidings that God's judgment is about to fall upon the land, and David must choose which form it will take (vv. 12–17). Thereafter, it is also Gad who directs David to make the proper atoning sacrifice that will avert further plague from destroying Israel. David is allowed to build an altar on a threshing floor and make sacrifice, even though previously he had not been allowed to build a temple. Gad, like Nathan, is not merely a prophet of doom but also a crisis intervention specialist helping the ruler to cope with and overcome the judgment that is to fall on sin. Yet, again, the fact that he is called David's seer must suggest that he had a more permanent in-house relationship with David than did Nathan. At this juncture, a brief return to the illuminating material from Mari is in order.

The document in question has been labeled A.1121, and the following is a quote from the critical portion of it. The prophet says:

> My lord, in the presence of [. . .]-men,
> Told me to deliver the *zukrum* (pastureland) as follows:
> "Never shall he break (his agreement) with me.
> I have brought witnesses for him. Let my lord know this."
>
> Through oracles, Adad, Lord of Kallassu,
> [spoke] to me as follows: "Am I not
> [Ad]ad, Lord of Kallassu, who
> reared him (the king) between my testicles and restored him to the throne
> of his father's house? After I restored him to the throne
> of his father's house, I have again given him a residence.
> Now since I restored him to the throne of his father's house,
> I will take from him an estate.
> Should he not give (the estate),
> am I not master of throne, territory, and city?
> What I have given, I shall take away. If (he does) otherwise, and
> Satisfies my desire, I shall give him throne upon throne,
> house upon house, territory upon territory,
> city upon city.
> And I shall give him the land
> From the rising (of the sun) to its setting."
> This is what the *apilu*-diviners said, and in the oracles
> It stands up constantly. Now moreover,
> The *apilum*-diviner of Adad, Lord of Kallassu,
> is standing guard over the tent-shrine of Alahtum to (be) an estate.
> Let my lord know this.[4]

There is, in addition, another oracle also to King Zimri-Lim, numbered A. 2731, which provides confirmation that the deity Adad was, in fact, demanding

---

[4] I am here following Malamat's translation in "Mari Prophecy," 69, with minor variation.

tribute or sacrifice in the form of livestock and a *nihlatum,* which apparently means an estate, because the god had restored Zimri-Lim to his throne and en-sured his succession.[5] The historical situation was that Zimri-Lim had spent nearly two decades in exile while his land was being ruled by an Assyrian gover-nor but that he succeeded in regaining his throne after this long hiatus.

For the purposes of this study, the crux of the matter has to do with the patronage and reciprocity cycle being established by these oracles. The god in question makes a demand and then a conditional promise to Zimri-Lim in re-gard to land or property. Adad expects some land and animals dedicated for sa-cred purposes, and indeed there may even be reference to a tent shrine that is to be replaced by a more permanent sort of dwelling place for the deity—the *nihlatum.*[6] Adad says he has restored to Zimri-Lim his royal residence and in turn will take from him an estate. Notice, however, the conditional nature of things. Adad adds that *if* he does not give the estate, then "What I have given, I shall take away. [On the other hand,] *if* (he does) otherwise, and satisfies my de-sire I shall give him throne upon throne, house upon house, territory upon terri-tory, city upon city. And I shall give him the land from the rising (of the sun) to its setting."

The one who conveys this oracle is apparently the *apilu*-diviner. Yet notice the lines that say, "This is what the *apilum*-diviners said, and in the oracles / It stands up constantly." This suggests the same sort of two-step process seen in the earlier discussion of Mari and prophecy,[7] only there oracles were confirmed by diviner's inquiries whereas here diviner's words seem to be confirmed by oracles. In any case, the diviner is what we would call an official or court figure, for he is the one who stands guard over the tent-shrine. The word *apilum* itself suggests an "answerer," that is, one who responds to inquiries, and therefore a diviner rather than a prophet per se.

This raises another interesting point. In view of the evidence from Mari about prophets being paid for their oracles, one wonders if, while diviners were court figures, prophets were often not in this society. The prophet seems to have a more tenuous and less ongoing relationship with Zimri-Lim than the diviner. This is very close to what we find in the case of Nathan, who, while he apparently from time to time came and spoke to David or Bathsheba, particularly at times of crisis, was not necessarily a regular participant in the day-to-day operation of the court as an adviser, such as an Abner or Ahithophel would be.

The difference between what one finds at Mari and what this study is about to explore in 2 Sam 7 is, at the most fundamental level, the fact that Yahweh does not want David to build him a house, but, rather, has graciously provided a "house" in both senses for David, whereas Adad does indeed want

---

[5] It is possible that the Adad of Kallassu is not the same as the Adad lord of Halab mentioned in the second oracle, in which case two deities were making such claims upon Zimri-Lim.

[6] See Malamat, "Mari Prophecy," 75.

[7] See pp. 14–19 above.

reciprocity in a material way. One must, however, raise here the issue of whether the dynastic oracle in ch. 7 is conditional or unconditional. Is it part of a covenantal arrangement and therefore promissory in nature, depending on the keeping of the stipulations, or is it an unconditional grant? In the Ps 132 recension of the oracle we find the words "if your sons keep my covenant and my decrees that I shall teach them, their sons also, forevermore, shall sit on your throne." This remark immediately follows the "sure" oath of God to David that God will not take back the promise to set one of his sons on the throne. If, in fact, the oracle in 2 Sam 7 is seen as part of a covenantal or treaty arrangement that ultimately involved stipulations, then it, too, was conditional.[8]

Notice that we have the familial imagery used about the relationship between King Zimri-Lim and the deity. The deity is the father of the king, who came forth from his loins. As Malamat says, this is indeed a conventional metaphor used throughout the ancient Near East for the relationship between deities and rulers (also between lords and servants, or overlords and client kings). This imagery is used in 2 Sam 7; Ps 2:7; Ps 89:26–27; and 1 Chron 20:10, 28:6 of either David or Solomon.[9] The mention of an expansive domain given to the king at Mari finds a near parallel in 2 Sam 7 with the promise of progeny on the throne and a domain to rule. Yet there is a difference, too, for the emphasis in 2 Sam 7 is on a protected rather than an expansive realm. In some ways, the most important parallel between the Mari oracle and 2 Sam 7 is the fact that they both reflect an ideological change from a tent to a house mentality in terms of sacred space set apart for the deity, which in turn reflects the social change from a more nomadic to a more sedentary culture. With this background in mind, 2 Sam 7 must be more closely examined.

Part of the difficulty in analyzing vv. 1–17 is that most scholars think that, at the very least, there are several layers of tradition here, including at least two oracular traditions from different times in Israel's history. The most plausible of these theories is that of F. M. Cross, who contended that there are basically three sources here: (1) the original anti-temple oracle of Nathan in vv. 1–7, (2) the eternal decree of Davidic kingship from a later period in vv. 11b–16, and (3) a Deuteronomistic editorial link in vv. 8–11a.[10] The discussion has been ably summed up by McCarter, but it shows that there is nothing approaching a con-

---

[8] This study will take a position that many OT scholars, though perhaps not the majority, would not—namely, that there was indeed a united monarchy and that one is dealing with traditions of some historical substance in these chronicles. I am well aware of the work of W. Dever, B. Halpern, and others but am unpersuaded by extremely minimalist approaches to these matters. Here, however, is not the place for a detailed response to their positions. It can only be pointed out here that there are equally competent and critical OT scholars who take an approach quite similar to that found in this study.

[9] See Malamat, "Mari Prophecy," 80.

[10] F. M. Cross, *Canaanite Myth and Hebrew Ethic* (Cambridge: Harvard University Press, 1973), 249–60.

sensus on these matters. Indeed, one critical scholar, S. Mowinckel, even argued that the oracle, as a whole, is a literary unity.[11]

It is important to see if sense can be made out of the text as it stands, allowing for some later editorial work. This approach is especially important in a diachronic study such as ours because later use of these traditions in the biblical era was innocent of modern literary criticism and would have taken these texts as literary wholes. The point is that if they were able to make sense of these texts as wholes, then perhaps we can as well. Equally important, the trend in scholarship in the last several decades is to take much more seriously the suggestion that at least some of this material comes from a situation in the lives of Nathan and David. Especially favoring this last conclusion is the fact that the historical review of these texts, while it looks back on the period of the judges, in fact looks forward to the Davidic dynasty. Had this historical review been written up much later—for example, well after there were any Davidic ancestors on the throne— one would have expected the oracle of Nathan to have been edited differently or not to have emphasized a "forever" component. McCarter has shown that there are too many differences between our account and the Egyptian *Königsnovelle* stories—about kings devising a plan to build or restore a temple—for our narrative to be modeled on such stories. Even formal similarities with such stories cease with v. 3, and of course ours is not a story about David successfully building a temple.[12]

The narrative opens at v. 1 with David having a break from all his many military activities and political intrigues and finally resting on his laurels a bit. But he is concerned because he is living in a splendid mansion made of cedar and the holy ark still remains in a tent shrine. Nathan, who is present with the king and hears or overhears his remarks, gives him his own advice—"Do whatever you have in mind, for Yahweh is with you." This is not an oracle but simply advice, and it is advice given on the basis of the previous track record of God blessing David's endeavors. Notice that neither David nor Nathan says anything explicit about building a temple. It is one of the repeated refrains of the story of David, especially in its early parts, that God is with him. This phrase is found at 1 Sam 16:18; 17:37; 18:14, 28 and 2 Sam 5:10. It is found also in Judg 2:18 and elsewhere in texts thought to reflect Deuteronomistic editing. But, as McCarter, says there is no reason to see this phrase as an exclusively Deuteronomistic expression.[13] The sense of Nathan's remark, then, is that whatever good deed the king is going to put his hand to is likely to prosper because Yahweh has been blessing his activities.

Yet in fact, Nathan's remark, based on the track record of David, stands in need of correction. One can not always judge what is appropriate to do on the

---

[11] See P. K. McCarter, *2 Samuel* (Garden City: Doubleday, 1984), 211–31; and S. Mowinckel, *He That Cometh* (New York: Abingdon, 1956).

[12] See McCarter, *2 Samuel*, 212–15.

[13] Ibid., 201. See its use elsewhere to indicate divine favor—e.g., Gen 26:3, and of Samuel in 1 Sam 3:19.

basis of analysis of the past, and the author of this material wants to make a distinction between human reasoning and the word of God. David's reasoning made sense to Nathan, for David wished to honor God better and was ashamed that he was in a more honorable abode than the ark was. Yet there was a problem because David now viewed himself as in the position of being the benefactor and God being the beneficiary of his royal largesse. The major contrast in what follows is not between temple and tent, or even David and Solomon, but rather between "you" and "me," with the latter being Yahweh. It is Yahweh who is the benefactor, not David, and he will determine the future, the fate of David's house, not the other way around.

Perhaps too much has been made of the contrast between Nathan's advice and the oracle he receives shortly thereafter. Prophets were human beings, and they, too, could be corrected by God. "That David should propose such a grandiose gesture of patronage toward Yahweh—who is, as he has always been (cf. vv. 8–9a), David's patron—is taken as an affront. Yahweh has always moved about freely in a tent, never taking up residence in a temple. David's concern about the lack of a temple (v. 2) is groundless, as should be obvious from the fact that Yahweh has never chastised any of Israel's previous leaders for failing to provide one."[14] Nathan's advice is understandable because of the blessing of David's previous activities by God, but he was not speaking for God before the reception of the oracle. His response should not be seen as a mere polite formality, in view of its echoing of a major theme in these narratives,[15] and in any case, Nathan will demonstrate in ch. 12 that he is no mere sycophant.

It can not be stressed enough that in the ancient Near East it was precisely by the constructing of cities and temples that a king became the organizer, protector, and controller of a country, its people, and its political and religious life. The "Good Shepherd," as such ancient kings were called, was at once chief executive, high priest, supreme commander of the army, and supreme-court judge all rolled into one. The city of a great king had a cosmological aspect—it became the abode of the god. "Because the temple as the visible expression of his domain was, at the same time, the king's property, the capital was the ruling center of both the god and his vice regent . . . the king. There [it was natural that] temple and palace should be seen as two aspects of the same phenomenon; together they constituted the essence of the state."[16] The suggestion of David, then, must be seen as something of a power move, trying to consolidate all power into his control. But Yahweh would not be domesticated. There may also be a further factor. H. K. Uhlshofer has suggested that Nathan opposed David's plan to build a temple because of the political instability in Israel at the time. In short, another

---

[14] Ibid., 197.

[15] Against M. Noth, "David and Israel in II Samuel VII," in *The Laws in the Pentateuch and Other Studies* (trans. D. R. Ap-Thomas; Edinburgh: Oliver & Boyd, 1966), 250–59.

[16] G. W. Ahlstrom, *Royal Administration and National Religion in Ancient Palestine* (Leiden: E. J. Brill, 1982), 3–20.

major issue was the timing of the suggestion, not just the underlying motives of the suggestion. In this view, Nathan's oracle shows the way forward to stability through a dynasty, which in turn will allow a temple to be built. This reading is not wholly convincing in light of the complaint of Yahweh to David, focusing on "you" and "me."[17]

Verse 4 indicates the reception of the oracle by Nathan at night, which apparently was frequently the time when such messages were given.[18] It is possible that Nathan received this word in a dream, but we are not told so. Notice several features about what precedes the oracle: (1) The messenger formula *ko amar yahweh*. This formula was one originally used by servants in the ancient Near East carrying messages from their lords to a third party. The messenger needed to repeat verbatim what he had been told to say, and so the message was delivered in the first person, prefaced by a formula such as "This is what [name of person] has said" (see Gen 45:9). (2) David, like Moses before him, is called God's servant. It is difficult to know whether the appellation here is simply a reflection of the older biblical tradition or is instead following the ancient Near Eastern tradition of calling a king some deity's servant.[19] In either case, it indicates that David is in the service of Yahweh and under Yahweh's directions. Yahweh is not in the service of David, as one for whom David might do favors.

The beginning of the oracle sets the tone for what follows. The very first Hebrew sentence is notable for its use of emphatic pronouns—"you" and "me." The first of these is "you," and so attention is focused squarely on David's behavior. The pronoun "you" here possibly indicates that the negation concerns primarily the person (i.e., David) rather than the action itself (i.e., the building of the temple). The sentence is, in effect, a rhetorical question that implies by its construction a negative answer. Verses 6–7 indicate that heretofore Yahweh has not had, nor has he needed, a temple to dwell in. There seems clearly to be a contrast between "dwelling" and "going" or "wandering," focusing on the mobility of God and thus the lack of need for a permanent dwelling place. There can be little doubt that a fixed cultic building was often associated with the localization of a god's presence in the ancient Near East (see 1 Kgs 8:12–13). But a localized presence also meant a presence readily at the beck and call of those who dwelt nearby, including especially the royal family. Yahweh, however, was not to be domesticated or "*house*broken." Yahweh, to the contrary, was sovereign and free in regard to locality. As Anderson points out, any attempt to manipulate Yahweh through the manipulation of the ark always ended in disaster (cf. 1 Sam 4–6; 2 Sam 6), and presumably the same would be the case if one attempted to

---

[17] H. K. Uhlshofer, "Nathan's Opposition to David's Intention to Build a Temple in the Light of Selected Ancient Near Eastern Texts" (Ph.D. diss., Boston University, 1977), iiiff.

[18] See pp. 46–47 above and the discussion of 1 Sam 3.

[19] On the ancient Near Eastern context of the use of the term for kings, see R. deVaux, *The Bible and the Ancient Near East* (Garden City: Doubleday, 1971), 155–56.

manipulate Yahweh by trying to confine God to a particular locale.[20] The issue, then, once more seems to be the person who wants to build this temple and, by implication, his motivation for doing so. Was David already thinking like an ancient Near Eastern monarch? It is thus possible to argue that v. 13a was an original part of the oracle, for Solomon is a different person and might have different motives for building a house for Yahweh. Nonetheless, most scholars think it is a later addition, not least because it disturbs the poetic structure of vv. 12–13b, and the case against its originality is rather strong.

Verses 8–11 stand in contrast with vv. 4–7. Instead of David building God a house, the reverse will be the case. There is an issue of what to make of the verb tenses in this portion of the oracle. Verses 8–9a seem clearly to be referring to past activities (from the perspective of the time of the giving of this oracle), but vv. 9b–11 have often perplexed interpreters. What is to be made of the series of perfect verbs often attached to conjunctions? The normal way to render these would be as perfective futures (future from the perspective of the prophet but treated as a completed action because God is guaranteeing in advance these things will come to pass). While commentators such as Hertzberg have argued that the actions are things that had already happened even at the time Nathan was speaking,[21] as McCarter says, much hinges on the interpretation of the word *maqom*, which literally means a place. Those who interpret this part of the prophecy as referring to past activities take the word to refer to the promised land itself. Yet it is quite possible to take the word in the specialized sense of cult place (see Deut 12:5). In support of this interpretation is the exegesis of this oracle at Qumran in 4QFlor, where it is said, "This . . . is the house that [. . .] in time to come," referring to the final eschatological temple.[22] If this is correct, then even if v. 13a is a later parenthetical insertion, it would simply be a further explication of what is implicit in v. 10. Also possibly in favor of this interpretation is the fact that when the speaker refers to the land in v. 9b, he uses *eretz* and then uses *maqom* immediately thereafter to refer to something else, namely, the Temple Mount.

Verses 8–9, then, chronicle the rags-to-riches story of how a sovereign God plucked David out of a sheep pasture and made him a chosen leader over Israel. This entailed God remaining with David wherever he went (just as God was with Moses) and scattering his enemies. This portion of the oracle ends with the emphatic assertion that Yahweh will make David's name and fame great in the land. The emphasis is on David owing Yahweh everything both in the past and in the future. The force of v. 9, by implication, is that David need not try to establish his own fame in the land—for instance, by building a great temple. God will accomplish the elevation of David's status.

We must offer a somewhat literal translation of v. 10 at this point—"I shall fix a place for Israel my people and plant them, so they will remain where they

---

[20] A. A. Anderson, *2 Samuel* (Waco: Word, 1989), 120.

[21] See Hertzberg, *1 and 2 Samuel*, 283ff.

[22] See A. Gelston, "A Note on 2 Samuel 7.10," *ZAW* 84 (1973): 92–94.

(now) are and never again be disturbed, and nefarious men will no longer abuse it [i.e., the holy place] as in the past, in the days when I appointed judges over my people Israel." The first point of note is that the people, including David, belong to Yahweh, not the other way around, and Yahweh has established for them a holy place where they can worship God in spirit and in truth, in peace and quiet. What establishes Israel is its God and its right relationship with its God. But it is not just Israel that has been disturbed in the past but also the relationship of Israel with God through the poor service of its priests. The reference to nefarious men is vague, and only the context can adequately provide clues to its meaning. It could be a general reference to Israel's enemies who have oppressed it. In view of the discussion of the holy place, an allusion to the time at the end of the period of the judges (see v. 11a) and to the corrupt sons of Eli (Hophni and Phinehas), as McCarter has suggested, makes very good sense at this juncture.[23] After all, the only holy place or Israelite cult shrine mentioned in the earlier part of the Samuel literature is the one at Shiloh, and the analogies between some of the roles of Samuel and of Nathan are considerable.

The point is that Israel had not been able on its own to establish a holy house and thus David should not expect that, by taking the initiative, he could do so. Rather, Yahweh must be the one who takes the initiative. It is by Yahweh establishing a holy place in the midst of a holy land and by Yahweh planting his people on such a holy hill that they will finally find and have well-being, peace, *shalom*, and not just peace in the abstract but even peace from all their enemies. It is by Israel dwelling within the very presence of God that it will be kept safe. Here in v. 11b we have a rather clear statement that when Israel is living according to the will of God and on the basis of the divine guidance and initiative, all manner of things will be well.[24]

At v. 11c the final portion of the oracle begins. Instead of David informing God about what is about to happen in regard to God's house, God will inform David about the future of his house, namely, that Yahweh will build a house for David.[25] The position of the word *bayit* is emphatic and, in view of its preceding the verb, necessarily retrospective. The echo of the first part of the oracle in vv. 5–7 is deliberate. What this may suggest is that David's real motive for building a temple was, in fact, to enhance and establish his own house, his own family line. Here *bayit* refers not to a building but to David's family line. David already had a palace, as vv. 1–2 made clear. There is something of an ironic twist here because, of course, David already has both a wife and children, indeed a large

---

[23] See McCarter, *2 Samuel,* 204.

[24] The attempt to see this part of the oracle as simply about a promise of land must be deemed implausible. It is true that the metaphorical language about planting and the like is the sort of language one hears elsewhere in relationship to Yahweh giving his people a land, but the context here is about David's building God a house, a point too often underplayed.

[25] Notice again the "you" and "he" contrast as at the beginning of the oracle— "Yahweh discloses to *you* that as for a house, *he* will build it."

family (3:2–5; 5:13–16). Yet the heir through whom the Davidic line will continue has not yet been born.

Throughout vv. 12–16 we have third person singular pronouns,[26] as was the case in the middle portion of the oracle, where the translation "him" as "them" was offered, since the singular was used in a collective sense. The question arises here again whether the singular noun *zera*, "offspring," has a collective sense implying ongoing progeny of several generations, or whether only the very next generation, and perhaps a particular one among that generation, is in mind. Verse 13a answers this question by making this prophecy refer clearly to Solomon, but this verse may be a later particularizing of what was a more general tradition, by the insertion of a parenthetical explanatory remark.

But if one goes the other route and assumes that this prophecy was, in fact, about a particular heir not yet born, this raises interesting questions about the reference to the words "and I shall keep his throne forever stable." If the reference is to Solomon, this would presumably imply stability throughout Solomon's reign, not a promise of an eternal dynasty. The phrase *ad olam* or the variant *le olam* occurs some seven times in ch. 7, which shows clearly the concern for stability, and perhaps even for permanency. This is hardly surprising in the Davidic era, since Israel had just experienced the instability of first having a ruler such as Saul and then watching the demise and death of both Saul and his family. But what really does this Hebrew phrase, which we translate "forever," mean? In 2:30 it is used in reference to a divine promise of priesthood to Eli's house, which is then revoked because of the wickedness of his sons. Are these immutable promises or only permanent promises contingent upon certain stipulations and kinds of responses? Is this the rhetoric of dynasty or a sure commitment from Yahweh?[27] If "forever" really means an irrevocable guarantee of Davidic dynasty, then why is there need for vv. 14b–15a?

It is telling that in one of the earliest interpretations of this oracle we find a proviso not spelled out in ch. 7. Psalm 132:11–12 clearly interprets the promise of royal offspring given to David as immutable, but the promise to further generations of his descendants is contingent—"The Lord swore to David a sure oath from which he will not turn back: 'One of the sons of your body I will set on your throne. If your sons keep my covenant and decrees that I shall teach them, their sons also, forevermore shall sit on your throne.'" Part of the difficulty of dealing with this entire issue is the question whether covenant theology underlies any and all of Yahweh's promises. If this is indeed the case, then Yahweh's immutable promises are always to be taken as contingent upon the fulfillment of

---

[26] Except where *naqar* seems to require the translation "it," referring to the cult place.

[27] See the discussion in K. Seybold, *Das davidische Königtum im Zeugnis der Propheten* (Göttingen: Vandenhoeck & Ruprecht, 1972), 33f. and n. 52; and especially M. Tsevat, "Studies in the Book of Samuel. III. The Steadfast House: What Was David Promised in II Samuel 7.13b–16?" *HUCA* 34 (1963): 71–82; and idem, "The House of David in Nathan's Prophecy," *Bib* 46 (1965): 353–56.

the stipulations of the covenant and upon the avoidance of suffering its sanctions. God is not obligated if the human partner violates the terms of the treaty. Notice again that the psalm assumes that a particular progeny was meant by the promise in 2 Sam 7, while a rather different impression is gained from a close reading of Ps 89:27–37. It is not easy to resolve this matter, but it seems, on the whole, that 2 Sam 7:11b–16, even if one takes v. 13a as a later editorial clarification, is about, and focuses on, a particular individual descendant of David, although there are things at least implied about that future king's descendants as well.

Verse 12 assures David of what will happen when he dies. He does not need to worry about establishing a permanent name for himself by building Yahweh a grand house of cedar. Yahweh will raise up the appropriate seed of David after him and establish his kingship. David does not need to be either king maker or name maker to assure his enduring legacy. Yahweh will establish the throne of this successor so that it is absolutely stable, at least throughout the reign of the successor, but more may be implied as well. This promise of unbroken rule by the successor is based on a promise of unbroken relationship. If v. 13a was an original part of this oracle, then it was meant as a sign to David of God's earnestness about keeping the divine promise concerning the successor and the enduring name of the Davidic line. "Though you will not build me a house, nonetheless *he* will."

In v. 14 the language of kinship ties is applied to the relationship between David's successor and Yahweh. The language used here is not about physical descent from a deity; it is the language of adoption.[28] This is seen most clearly at Ps 2:7, where during the coronation ceremony the divine voice says to the king, "You are my son; today I beget [i.e., adopt] you." As McCarter suggests, one of the primary purposes of such a pronouncement is that the king could qualify for the royal inheritance or patrimony God wishes to bestow.[29] This is why Ps 2 continues, "Ask me and I shall grant the nations as your estate." We have extrabiblical evidence that kings of Damascus in the ninth century BC took the name "Son of Hadad" (cf. 1 Kgs 15:18 = 2 Chron 16:2).[30]

M. Weinfeld makes clear that the model for this sort of discussion was the ancient Near Eastern relationship between a lord or king and a loyal vassal or client king. Grants of lands or a "house" were made legal and permanent by fictive kinship because through such adoption they then became patrimonial in character.[31] The point here would be that the promise Yahweh makes to David of permanency is made sure through the adoption of his heir as God's son.

---

[28] See W. Schlisske, *Gottessöhne und Gottesohn im Alten Testament* (Stuttgart: Kohlhammer, 1973): 109–10.

[29] McCarter, *2 Samuel*, 207.

[30] See ibid.; and F. M. Cross, "The Stele Dedicated to Melcarth by Ben-Hadad of Damascus," *BASOR* 205 (1972): 36–42.

[31] See M. Weinfeld, "The Covenant of Grant in the OT and in the ANE," *JAOS* 90 (1970): 184–203; and "Covenant, Davidic," *IDBSup* 188–92.

"There will always be a fief . . . in Jerusalem for David" (see 1 Kgs 11:36; 15:4; 2 Kgs 8:19).[32]

But if the heir of David is going to be treated as Yahweh's son, this will also mean that this heir must undergo Yahweh's discipline when necessary. The imagery here comes from the normal ancient form of disciplining of wayward children (see Prov 3:11–12, which compares the discipline of the Lord to the discipline of a father). Yet such disciplinary action will not mean that God's promises will no longer apply. Even ancient lord-vassal property agreements could occasionally be inalienable. Weinfeld cites the following example from a thirteenth-century Hittite king to one Ulmi-Tesup: "After you, your son and grandson will possess it, nobody will take it away from them. If one of your descendants sins . . . the king will prosecute him at his court. . . . But nobody will take away from Ulmi-Tesup either his house or his land."[33] In short, David's heir will have both the duties and the privileges of a son and will be treated as such—never forsaken but, if necessary, disciplined.[34]

Notice in v. 15 the use of the term *hesed,* which refers to the sort of love and loyalty that exist within a covenantal relationship. It is a keeping of faith to a person to whom one has already commited oneself. The term, then, does not necessarily connote undeserved or unmerited benefit, although that also may be true, but, rather, a sort of loyalty that one has promised to give, whether the party in question deserves it or not.[35]

The oracle concludes with a contrast between what was the case with Saul, who is not mentioned by name (and thus is shamed), and what will be the case with David's heir. Yet there is something ominous about the reference to God's withdrawing of his covenant favor or loyalty to Saul, and perhaps it is meant as a sort of sanction to insure good behavior by the heir. [36] Verse 16 reiterates the promise of the security of David's line and assures that this will be so because Yahweh will care for David's royal house. God will build it, maintain it, and guarantee it perpetuation. It is hardly likely, knowing what we do about the subsequent history of the Davidic monarchy, that these sorts of claims first arose at a time after the demise of the Davidic line in Israel, especially since one could debate whether "seed" refers just to Solomon or to Solomon and his descendants. It is indeed possible, if the promise is about Solomon in particular, to conclude, as does Tsevat, that while "dynasticism is introduced into Israel, . . . the innovation is only a qualitative one; quantity, i.e., the duration of the dynasty, is not involved." This would explain why David in his prayerful response

---

[32] McCarter, *2 Samuel,* 207.

[33] Weinfeld, "Covenant of Grant," 189.

[34] So ibid., 192–93; and Weinfeld, "Covenant, Davidic," 191.

[35] See the discussion in K. D. Sakenfeld, *The Meaning of Hesed in the Hebrew Bible: An Inquiry* (Missoula: Scholars Press, 1978), 139–45.

[36] See Anderson, *2 Samuel,* 122: "Although the word covenant does not occur in Nathan's oracle, it is presupposed if not alluded to, in v. 15 since *hesed* 'good-will' 'covenant loyalty' . . . may well denote the essence of a covenant."

asks that his dynasty be a lasting one. "The response presupposes the dynastic principle and extends it in prayer by introducing the element of duration. Unconditionality, i.e., placing the dynasty beyond good and evil, is outside of its pale."[37]

Verse 17 indicates that Nathan fulfilled his responsibility of giving David a true account of all these words and of this vision. This way of putting it, coupled with the earlier reference to night, may suggest that Nathan received this oracle while dreaming. Notice the distinction between the genuine prophetic experience and the prophetic expression. There is a time lag between the two, and Nathan would hardly be implicitly commended, as he is here, if it were not possible for the prophetic expression to David to have been at variance with the prophetic vision. A true prophet is one who reports faithfully just what he has heard and seen. There is no historical evidence that David was disobedient to the heavenly vision. If one asks why Israel later thought it was inappropriate for David to build a temple when a temple would in due course be built, the answer given in 1 Kgs 5:3–5 is that David was a man of warfare but that the king named after the Hebrew word for "peace" ruled during an era when such military activities had ceased and so a house for Yahweh could be built. But before then there would be difficult times for David, and Nathan would have to be the bearer of bad tidings yet again.

B. "You're the Man!" It has sometimes been urged that "in the beginning was the woe oracle," or that the woe oracle and the salvation oracle could never be mixed, or that sapiential and prophetic materials could not be intermingled. But history seldom happens according to discrete form-critical categories, and we have already seen an oracle in 2 Sam 7 that includes both denials and affirmations, both prohibitions and promises. What we find in 2 Sam 12 is a combination—a *mashal* followed by a prophetic oracle.

Meshalim were figurative or metaphorical speech forms that were sapiential in character. They ranged, in actual form, from riddles to aphorisms to short analogies to parables and even to allegories.[38] It is interesting that the parabolic or allegorical form of sapiential speech seems to have been found especially useful by Jewish prophets (compare 2 Sam 12 with Isa 5:1–7 and Ezek 17:1–10). In 2 Sam 12 we are dealing with a particular kind of parable that has been dubbed a juridical parable.[39] There are other possible examples of this sort of parable in the OT in 2 Sam 14:1–20, in 1 Kgs 20:35–43, and again in Isa 5:1–7.

---

[37] Tsevat, "The House of David in Nathan's Prophecy," 356. Tsevat rightly stresses that the text of Nathan's prophecy continually uses the singular where biblical style would lead us to expect the plural if generations (plural) of posterity were in view.

[38] See B. Witherington, *Jesus the Sage and the Pilgrimage of Wisdom* (Minneapolis: Fortress, 1994).

[39] See U. Simon, "The Poor Man's Ewe-Lamb: An Example of a Juridical Parable," *Bib* 48 (1967): 207–42.

The basic way a juridical parable works is not different from how various other parables work. Not every part of the parable is analogous to the situation it is being used to address, but there is a close enough correspondence between some elements in the situation and some in the parable to make the latter an effective, if indirect, way of addressing the difficulties of the former. There is a common structure shared by most juridical parables: (1) an introduction, (2) a reference to a fictive legal case or situation calling for judicial action, (3) a judgment elicited, and (4) the judgment then applied to the guilty party.[40] The parable serves in our case to disguise a real-life judicial matter with the intent of getting the guilty party to pass judgment on himself.[41]

The background to the delivery of this parable is the famous David and Bathsheba affair, which displeased Yahweh and prompted Yahweh to send Nathan to confront the king. There are various features of the parable that would likely have appealed to David. In the first place, it is about an owner of a lamb, and David had previously been a shepherd, well aware how important a shepherd's sheep were for his survival, especially if he was a poor person with a limited flock. David would have likely identified with that poor sheep owner. In the second place, the parable seems, on the surface, to affirm the king's rightful position of power by asking him to pass judgment in a legal matter. It also appeals to his own sense of justice or fairness; this sense is not absent from some of the stories about his own trials and tribulations during the reign of Saul. David is portrayed in this earlier material as a man of some conscience.

As McCarter points out, the parable stresses that David's crime involves, among other things, the sin of abuse of power, of taking what rightfully belonged to another simply because one has the power to do so.[42] As such, it falls under the category of the most heinous form of such theft—the disenfranchising of the poor by the rich. Israel's tradition was that the king was supposed to be the advocate for the poor and helpless and prevent their abuse and disenfranchisement (see Ps 72:2–14). But Samuel had warned Israel that kings tended to be the epitome of self-serving people—they simply took and took and took (see 1 Sam 8:11–18).[43]

There is debate about what should be made of the phrase "a son of death" in 2 Sam 12:5. McCarter argues that one should translate it something like "a fiend of hell" and see the phrase as characterizing the man's behavior rather than condemning the man to death.[44] The phrase, however, is usually rendered "deserves to die" (RSV, NEB, NIV) with a meaning similar to the modern cry of outrage "He ought to be shot." McCarter's rendering, however, does not wrestle seriously enough with the other occurrences of the phrase—for

---

[40] See Anderson, *2 Samuel*, 160.

[41] See Simon, "The Poor Man's Ewe-Lamb," 208.

[42] McCarter, *2 Samuel*, 299.

[43] Ibid.

[44] Ibid.

example, in 1 Sam 20:31–32, where Saul calls David "a son of death" and Jonathan asks why he should be put to death. There is a similar usage in 1 Sam 26:16.[45] What is important to note is that this exclamation by David does not amount to a legal pronouncement but, rather, to a personal evaluation or judgment.[46] Therefore, v. 6 does not contradict a legal judgment passed in v. 5, because an executed person could no longer make restitution for a crime. David insists on a sevenfold restitution on the grounds not only of the crime but also of the lack of compassion that lies behind the crime. Sevenfold is likely not to be taken literally but means something like a complete or perfect restitution.[47] It is interesting that in the Mosaic law (Exod 21:37) fourfold restitution was required for the theft of a sheep, so we may take David's exclamation as an example of his sense that an extreme injustice has been done. It is equally intriguing that in the Talmud (b. *Yoma* 22b) David's case is related quite specifically to the law in Exod 21:37; it states that David made fourfold restitution through the death of four children—Bathsheba's first child, Tamar, Amnon, and Abishalom. But, of course, David's crime was far greater than sheep stealing. It involved adultery and then plotting to have someone murdered. Hertzberg stresses that "Nathan's 'You are the man,' one of the 'most apt' sayings in the Bible, takes up the verdict spoken by David without having to state it explicitly: it is a death sentence . . . [that] is only annulled on David's acknowledgement of his guilt and not before. Until that point it stands, as otherwise it would not be necessary for it to be taken back."[48] Once David has, in effect, passed judgment on himself, it is at this juncture only that Nathan reveals that David himself is the culprit. Instead of David formally passing sentence on someone, Yahweh passes sentence on David in the form of a judgment oracle pronounced by Nathan.

The judgment oracle is preceded by the prophetic messenger formula at v. 7a, making clear that what follows is not merely the opinion of Nathan but the judgment of God. The consequences of David's sins of adultery and murder are enormous. In the first place, David's selfish and sinful actions amount to enormous ingratitude. God had given David so much—he had plucked him out of the sheep pasture and anointed him king, he had repeatedly rescued him from Saul, he had given him Saul's house and household, including Saul's wives and concubines, he had given him both the house of Israel and of Judah, and he would have given him more if this had been insufficient. There is no evidence in the OT that David ever married any of Saul's wives, but there was indeed a practice in the ancient Near East of taking and sexually using the women of one's enemies in order to demonstrate one's absolute power over a conquered enemy (cf.

---

[45] See A. Phillips, "The Interpretation of 2 Sam. xii.5–6," *VT* 16 (1966): 242–44.

[46] See Anderson, *2 Samuel*, 162.

[47] See McCarter, *2 Samuel*, 299. See also R. A. Carlson, *David the Chosen King: A Traditio-historical Approach to the Second Book of Samuel* (Stockholm: Almqvist & Wiksell, 1964), 152–57.

[48] Hertzberg, *1 and 2 Samuel*, 313.

2 Sam 16:20ff.).[49] This, too, was a major shaming technique in an honor-and-shame culture.

David's crimes amounted to a rejection or despising of God's word, which spoke clearly in the prohibition of murder and adultery in the Ten Commandments. The punishment for David's crimes will include the sword never departing from his house thereafter, trouble within his own house, and public humiliation and shaming, so that what David did in private will be done to him in public by his "neighbor" (indeed by his own son!). David's response to Nathan is brief and to the point—"I have sinned against the Lord." He might rightfully have expected to be executed for such crimes under the *lex talionis* of a life for a life. But Nathan makes clear that God's justice is tempered by mercy—David will not die, Yahweh will transfer his sin. Nevertheless, even with forgiveness and remission of personal punishment, David will by no means escape the moral consequences of his sin. Most immediately he will lose the child created in lust with Bathsheba. Yahweh can not allow one who represents him, his own anointed, to get away with such sins. "If a man like David, the anointed one, 'with whom the Lord is,' allows himself to be guilty of such offenses, then the Lord's cause is seriously damaged."[50]

Several details of this judgment oracle and the response to it by David deserve closer attention. Notice that there are two portions of this oracle—vv. 7–10 and vv. 11–12—both prefaced by the messenger formula. It is possible that these were two different judgment oracles originally pronounced on different occasions. The first of these rehearses the benefits given by God to David and accuses David of despising God's word and of striking down Uriah and taking his wife, and since David chose to live by the sword, the sword will not depart from his own house. The second oracle, or portion of the oracle, makes more specific the sort of trouble David should expect and stresses how he will be publicly shamed for his actions. The pericope then concludes with a direct pronouncement by Nathan of the most specific and horrendous of all punishments—the immediate loss of the child he and Bathsheba were about to have, and so the potential cutting off of his dynasty.

The sword David has wielded will be turned against him: Amnon will die by the sword (14:23–29), Absalom will take up the sword against David and die by it (18:15), and Adonijah will die by the sword (1 Kgs 2:25). As McCarter says, David's own words come back to haunt him—"sometimes the sword devours one way, sometimes another" (11:25).[51] One can not avoid the echoes of the earlier oracle in ch. 7 here. In both oracles the house of David comes to the fore; only now, instead of being built by Yahweh, it will undergo some demolition. In both oracles there is the issue of David's name; only in ch. 12 the issue is the

---

[49] See M. Tsevat, "Marriage and Monarchial Legitimacy in Ugarit and Israel," *JSS* 3 (1958): 237–43.

[50] Hertzberg, *1 and 2 Samuel*, 315.

[51] McCarter, *2 Samuel*, 300.

shaming of that name. Yet Yahweh has "transferred" David's sin to another,[52] so that he will not die at this juncture. Notice that sin can not simply be forgiven; it must indeed be atoned for because Yahweh is a righteous God, a God of justice. It has been suggested that Ps 51 is an early commentary on this story. If this is correct, then David's sorrow for his sin was much more profound than the conclusion of our narrative seems to suggest. Once again, as in the previous passage, David submits to the verdict pronounced by Nathan.

C. Nothing Succeeds Like Succession.   A final passage involving Nathan finds David near the point of death. At issue in 1 Kgs 1 is the succession to the throne, since David's health is failing. Adonijah desires to be king and goes and offers sacrifice near the En-rogel spring, inviting those who would be sympathetic to his wishes to attend the sacrifice and subsequent feast. But the text is clear that Nathan the prophet was not invited (v. 10). In this case, Nathan does not confront David directly. Rather, he works through Bathsheba and supports her words and pleas. "How adroitly Nathan plays upon the instincts of Bathsheba as a mother and rival wife in his reference to Adonijah as 'the son of Haggith'!"[53] Obviously, Nathan has a personal stake in these matters on two scores: (1) he had previously been a sort of godparent to Solomon and was responsible for passing on to him the religiously significant name Jedidiah ("Beloved of the Lord"), which ultimately was what Yahweh had told the prophet to call him (2 Sam 12:25); (2) since Nathan had been excluded from the royal party of Adonijah, his own future—and perhaps even his own life—was on the line should Adonijah become king.

Notice, too, that he does obeisance before David (v. 23) and calls himself David's servant; in due course David calls upon him and Zadok the priest to anoint Solomon king over Israel. But the subsequent narrative mentions only Zadok doing the anointing (v. 39).[54] Perhaps we are meant to think of the beginning of the separation of the priestly and prophetic roles. In any case, here more than in either of the two previous texts, Nathan appears to be a regular functionary of the court, concerned about those in power maintaining it and securing a particular sort of dynastic succession. Here he is not critic of the king but crisis intervention specialist with the wisdom to know how to handle and defuse the problem. Thus S. J. De Vries is right to say of Nathan in this text, "His role seems more political-institutional than charismatic-prophetic, yet he does act to superintend politics in the name of a transcendental purpose."[55]

---

[52] On *he'ebir* as "transferred" rather than just "has put away," compare this text with 3:10 and 24:10; and see G. Gerlmann, "Schuld und Sühne: Erwägungen zu 2 Sam. 12," in *Beiträge zur alttestamentlichen Theologie: Festschrift für Walther Zimmerli* (ed. H. Donner et al.; Göttingen: Vandenhoeck & Ruprecht, 1977), 132–39, here 133–34.

[53] J. Gray, *1 and 2 Kings* (Philadelphia: Westminster, 1970), 87.

[54] Which, as J. A. Montgomery and H. S. Gehman, *The Book of Kings* (Edinburgh: T&T Clark, 1951), 77, point out, is good reason to think that the reference to Nathan is original at v. 34.

[55] S. J. De Vries, *1 Kings* (Waco: Word, 1985), 14.

It is not clear whether we are meant to see Nathan as a subtle manipulator of the king, but clearly Nathan's speech, which is not an oracle, contains dramatic hyperbole and irony in order to spur David to action. The text had not previously told us that Adonijah's compatriots were hailing him king. Probably we should not take the opening of v. 24 to be a question but, rather, as an ironic assertion offered in respectful form, as if Nathan can not believe what he has heard about the happening at En-rogel spring. The action of Nathan, however, in another sense is truly ironic, for its effect is to take the succession to the throne out of the realm of the charismatic picking of a new king from generation to generation by Yahweh and to place it into a more institutional dynastic mode, or as Tsevat says, it entails "the stabilization of kingship by making it independent of the charisma."[56]

This completes our study of Nathan's role as prophet in the early monarchy. One can not say of Nathan that he was simply David's yes-man, yet one can perhaps conclude that whether he started out as such or not, in the end Nathan was surely a central and court prophet, not least because he helped to establish the dynastic principle. There is no evidence that Nathan received his revelations from God through some sort of ecstatic experience; instead there is a hint in 2 Sam 7 that he may have received them through dreams. There is also no evidence that Nathan was part of a guild or school of prophets. Nathan was not limited to the relaying of oracles: he also was capable of crafting a parable or offering a dramatic speech. It should be clear from an examination of all of the reported speech of Nathan that he was indeed involved in the political process and his oracles focused on that process. His focus was not on the distant future but on the immediate future of David and his kin. Nathan is not like Samuel in that he does not serve as a priest as well as a prophet. It is perhaps in Nathan that we began to sense a division of labor whereas, before the monarchy and in its incipient stages, prophets were also a variety of other things as well—judges, priests, leaders. What we find in the Nathan material does, however, prepare us in some respects for the next stop in our journey—examining the Elijah and Elisha cycles.

II. THE ELIJAH PRINCIPLE

A. Prophetic Cycles or Prophetic Circles?   Certainly some of the most fascinating material in the Hebrew Scriptures involving prophets is the cycles of material—interspersed in the narratives that make up 1 Kgs 17–2 Kgs 13—about two prophets from the north and the Transjordan region. Within this corpus there are about six episodes that involve Elijah and eighteen that involve Elisha. These prophets began to operate almost a hundred years after the time of Nathan and were thus living during the troubled times of the divided monarchy, times that were especially difficult in the portion of the Holy Land that came to be called Israel. The material of concern to us reflects the severe tensions in society under

---

[56] Tsevat, "The House of David in Nathan's Prophecy," 356.

the dynasty founded by Omri, which lasted for a generation (forty years—ca. 882–842 BC). Omri had chosen, like Solomon, to pursue international alliances to strengthen his regime; this entailed, among other things, intermarriage with the royal family in Phoenicia to the north. Thus was Ahab, the son of Omri, married to Jezebel, the daughter of King Ethbaal of Tyre. Both parties profited economically and militarily from the alliance, for they both lived in volatile times, with the creeping shadow of Assyria looming larger and larger.

The net effect, however, of this cross-cultural approach to rule was syncretism, or at least polytheism, as an approach to religion. Jezebel came as a strong supporter of Baal, the fertility deity that was supposed to make both the earth and human beings fecund. This god of the crops and crop cycle was easy for an agrarian people to relate to, while Yahweh, who was a God of historical events and happenings, seemed to have less to do with day-to-day life. Into the midst of this tug of war for land, food, and the hearts of Israelites came Elijah and Elisha as ardent and uncompromising supporters of Yahweh and Yahwism.[57] Needless to say, their relationship with the Omris was an adversarial one, and there is no case to be made for seeing them as central or court prophets. Their locale, their demeanor, their activities all bespeak peripheral prophets operating in a crisis mode, which suggests that they saw the leadership of their land as not merely dysfunctional but in the process of commiting apostasy. These traditions must be evaluated bearing these points in mind.

The form-critical analysis of the Elijah and Elisha material has gone through various phases with no clear consensus emerging.[58] Should one see this material as saga or legend? Either judgment implies that the material went through a very long period of traditionalizing and editing before it reached the form in which we now find it. Some have suggested that this material is biographical in character, at least in the case of Elisha, whom we know a bit more about than Elijah. The problem with all of these suggestions is that these narratives do not in fact seem much different in character from the other historical narratives found in the Historical Books and, furthermore, they present a rather full-orbed portrait of these two, including tales that are unflattering. This material is not the stuff of mere hagiography or hero-worship and should not be compared to the medieval lives of the saints.

The fact that there are miracle narratives within the Elijah and Elisha cycle says something about the content of some of these stories but precious little about their form-critical categorization, unless one is prepared to categorize them on the basis of content. This is in fact the suggestion of A. Rofe.[59] Yet even

---

[57] See the helpful discussion by T. H. Renteria, "The Elijah/Elisha Stories: A Sociocultural Analysis of Prophets and People in Ninth-Century B.C.E. Israel," in *Elijah and Elisha in Socioliterary Perspective* (ed. R. B. Coote; Atlanta: Scholars Press, 1992), 75–126.

[58] See B. O. Long, *1 Kings with an Introduction to Historical Literature* (Grand Rapids: Eerdmans, 1984), 174ff.

[59] See A. Rofe, "The Classification of the Prophetical Stories," *JBL* 89 (1970): 427–40.

this approach falls short because it does not take into consideration the polemical edge of various of these stories, which are seen by L. Broneer as apologetic tales deliberately shaped to show that what people sought from Baal could only be had from Yahweh.[60] The historical focus of these stories is important, as they show how prophets functioned within a particular social and religious and historical matrix, and the interest of the author is not primarily on the prophets' lives. Details are only included when they are germane to the story itself, which has a historical thrust or point, not a biographical point. For example, Elisha's family and background do not come into the picture at all except in the service of showing how he was called to be a prophet of Yahweh and thereby called away from his family. That is to say, the issue here is the instruments Yahweh will use to deal with Baalism, not the vita of Elisha or Elijah.

There is, however, a rather significant tendency to portray Elijah especially as a prophet in the mold of Moses, perhaps even the prophet predicted to come in the Mosaic corpus.[61] Like Moses, Elijah makes a pilgrimage to Mount Horeb, like Moses he battles a people largely unfaithful to Yahweh, like Moses he makes fundamental challenges to the powers that be, like Moses he is a man of powerful prayer and intervention, and like Moses his end involves the miraculous.[62]

One of the most prevalent conjectures about this material is that it was preserved initially, at least as oral tradition, by the prophetic guild that seems to have been associated with Elijah in particular, however much it may have been later edited to suit Deuteronomistic needs and agendas. This is a reasonable working hypothesis, but then the question becomes why some of the same themes, grammatical style, concepts, and vocabulary seem to be imbedded in both the prophetic portions of 1 Kgs 17–2 Kgs 13 and the portions that do not mention Elijah and Elisha. Whatever the origins and stages this material went through, it now provides an important glimpse of Hebrew prophets operating in a volatile situation when the monarchy and the land are in danger. It may also provide some clues about a possible developing difference between Ephraimite, or northern, Yahwistic prophets and Judahite, or southern, ones. Specifically, it may suggest a prophetic tradition that links itself directly with Moses without any reference or allegiance to the southern and Davidic traditions. This may prove important when we examine that latter-day prophetic figure—Jesus of Nazareth.

B. Elijah—a Prophet out of Bounds.   Our first block of texts for scrutiny is the material in 1 Kgs 17–19, which makes up the bulk of the Elijah traditions. The first question of importance is raised by the very first verse of this material—17:1,

---

[60] L. Broneer, *The Stories of Elijah and Elisha* (Leiden: E. J. Brill, 1968).

[61] On this Deuteronomistic material see pp. 30–33 above.

[62] See, for instance, H. Gese, "Bemerkungen zur Sinai-Tradition," *ZAW* 79 (1967): 137–54; and R. P. Carroll, "Assyrian Prophecies: Some Remarks on Prophetic Succession in Ancient Israel," *VT* 19 (1969): 400–415.

which speaks of Elijah's origins. We are told he is from Gilead, the territory east of the Jordan River and south of the River Yarmuk, which territory seems to have been wild and largely unsettled during this period. Is it possible to be more specific? Most commentators have taken the term found in this verse to refer to an as yet undiscovered place, Tishbe, but this depends on the vocalization of the Hebrew. If one vocalizes with *o* instead of *i*, then we have a term meaning "settler," presumably a comment on Elijah's not being from the region in which we find him prophesying.[63] For what it is worth, both the LXX and Josephus, who follows it, make the disputed word a proper name and therefore a place name ("Elijah the Tishbite from Tishbeh in Galilee"; cf. *Ant.* 8.319). It is possible, then, that we have somewhat of a cross-cultural situation here, with Elijah being a real outsider to Israel. Be that as it may, there is no doubt about his Yahwistic faith, and indeed his name—which means "Yahweh is my God"—if it was given him at birth, suggests the faith of his parents as well.[64] It must be remembered that, probably for hundreds of years, there had been loyal Jews who had not chosen to move into the promised land but, rather, resided on the far side of the Jordan.

The story begins with a situation of drought and so of approaching famine. The prophet is ordered by Yahweh to go find Wadi Cherith, east of the Jordan, and hide himself there, where he would receive bread and flesh and could drink from what was left of the brook. Besides being economically precarious, seasons of drought were also religiously precarious times, especially for fertility deities who were supposed to provide both crops and the means of supporting them, namely, rain. Indeed, the times are so precarious that only those, like Elijah, who are at the water source and are being fed miraculously, in this case by ravens,[65] will be fit and well provided for. The story shows God's provision and care for his prophet, in preparation for what God will command him to do.

The word of God comes again to Elijah once the wadi goes dry, not so that he may proclaim it but so that he may obey it. He is ordered to yet another locale outside the promised land—Zarephath, on the Mediterranean coast seven miles south of Sidon. There he will be provided for by a widow, which in itself is also something of a miracle, for in a time of drought, she would surely be one of the first to feel the pinch. If this is a test of Elijah's faithfulness to follow God's word, it is an interesting one. As it happens, this widow thinks she is going out to prepare a last meal for herself and her son, so she too is being tested in this situation. Elijah simply orders the woman to bring him water and then a little bread. But when the widow complains to the prophet about her extreme situation, he urges her not to fear but to do as he asked, and he then reinforces this with his first oracle—"Thus says Yahweh, God of Israel: 'The jar of meal shall not fail, nor the flask of oil give out until the day that Yahweh gives rain upon the

---

[63] See De Vries, *1 Kings,* 216.

[64] See Broneer, *Stories,* 19ff.

[65] There is nothing to commend the pointing of the key term to read "Arabs" rather than "ravens" by Gray, *1 and 2 Kings,* 378–79, and none of the versions or more recent commentaries follow him. See, e.g., De Vries, *1 Kings,* 216.

face of the ground.' " The story concludes by confirming the prophet's word and by saying that the widow, and presumably her son and the prophet, ate for days (*yamim*), presumably meaning a considerable period of time.

What is this story really about? Some commentators have suggested that these stories are quite amoral in character, without a message beyond the glorification of the prophet. There is reason to doubt this conclusion. The prophet is in perilous times but is being provided for by Yahweh through remarkable and indeed unlikely means. Furthermore, we are told that Elijah is hiding, but from what or from whom? It is precisely in these sorts of times that a ruler would in desperation call upon a prophet to beseech his god for rain. But Elijah has been ordered to make himself unavailable and, while being obedient, is himself being taken care of. This suggests a situation where Yahweh is alienated from the rulers of Yahweh's people and is indeed very angry with those rulers.

The proof that this interpretation is correct comes from the very first verse of this passage, in which, before making himself scarce, Elijah, the outlander, goes before Ahab (in Samaria?) and tells him, "By the life of Yahweh, God of Israel, before whom I stand, there shall be neither dew nor rain throughout these years except at my express word!" As De Vries says, this is Yahweh's challenge to Baal by way of Ahab.[66] While Ahab might see this as the clash of the Titans, it proves to be no contest at all. Incidentally from this story we also learn of God's provision for the marginalized, such as the widow and her son, during difficult and dangerous times. This becomes even more evident in the next episode of the saga, even though the story can also be called a prophetic-legitimation tale.

The issue in this story, as in the previous one, is both the identity and the nature of the true God and then, by extension, the identity of Elijah as a true man of God. It is not a "quite extraneous prophetic legitimation narrative" added here by some clumsy redactor.[67] The story follows quite naturally from the previous one, as it tells a further incident from a time when Elijah was sojourning in Zarephath and having regular contact with a certain widow, apparently as a boarder in her house. The story indicates that the power of Yahweh is great, even extending to bringing the dead back to life, and, equally important, it extends beyond a particular locale, indeed beyond the boundaries of the Holy Land. This is made clear by the fact that it is Yahweh, to whom Elijah prays—and not Elijah himself—who brings the life back into the young man.

The story is especially poignant because a widow's only ongoing means of support in her old age would be her son. Ancient Near Eastern law was such that it would be difficult, if not impossible, for the widow to inherit property or maintain the property she and her son shared. The effects of the famine could be reversed, even when they resulted in the sickness and death of a person, because Yahweh had power over life and death. Another telling portion of this story is the refutation of the theology of cause and effect, which suggests that sickness and death are necessarily a punishment from God for some sin that has been

---

[66] De Vries, *1 Kings*, 216.
[67] Contra De Vries, ibid., 221.

committed. The widow assumes that the holy man has come as a sort of grim reaper or angel of death from his God to punish her for her sin.

The action of Elijah is not an example of sympathetic magic but, rather, a prophetic sign act,[68] asking Yahweh to act by transferring life back into the son's lifeless body. "It is an 'acted out' way of saying, 'Let his lifeless body be as my lively body.' "[69] The widow, then, becomes witness of the results of a mighty miracle of God that at once both refutes her theology of the nexus between sin and sickness and confirms that Elijah is indeed a man or prophet of a mighty God, one who speaks the truth about Yahweh.

As Broneer stresses, the prophets of Yahweh were apparently regularly involved with, or consulted about, matters of healing (cf. 1 Kgs 14:1–13; 2 Kgs 8:9; Isa 38:1–21).[70] The connection between virtue and health was widely assumed in the ancient Near East, and it was assumed that no one knew more about it or was a better practicioner of virtue than a holy man, who therefore presumably would understand matters of health as well. The converse was also assumed. If someone performed a miracle, he or she must be some sort of holy man, though not necessarily a prophet. Here, however, there is a tight connection between the word of Yahweh and the activity or deeds of his prophet. What the miracle showed was not only the character of Elijah but also that the word of Yahweh was in his mouth.[71]

C. Showdown on Mount Carmel.

In what was apparently the third year of the famine (1 Kgs 18:1), Elijah is once more summoned to speak to Ahab. The word that Elijah receives at this juncture is instructions for himself involving a promise, and not an oracle to be proclaimed. He is to appear before Ahab, and there is a promise of rain. It is said at 18:2 that, by this juncture, the famine caused by the drought is severe in Samaria. The point of this remark is to indicate that even Ahab is feeling the pinch at his capital at this point. A new figure appears, Obadiah, who is said to be exceedingly reverential toward Yahweh. Obadiah is "over the house" (v. 3; see also 4:6), which would seem to mean that he is the caretaker of the royal house and properties, including the land that is now parched.[72] Verse 4 is one of the most revealing comments in the entire chapter. It is explained that there were originally a large number of court prophets in Ahab's court who were Yahwists and that, despite the purge of these prophets undertaken by Jezebel, there were still Yahwists in the court. Obadiah is said to have hidden one hundred of these prophets in caves, feeding them with bread and water. This indicates that his natural sympathies would be with someone like Elijah.

---

[68] See p. 13 above.

[69] De Vries, *1 Kings*, 222.

[70] Broneer, *Stories*, 100.

[71] See Montgomery and Gehman, *Kings*, 296.

[72] The phrase has sometimes been thought to refer to the chamberlain, in charge of just the house itself (see Gray, *1 and 2 Kings*, 133), but it probably has a wider reference; see De Vries, *1 Kings*, 70.

Ahab and Obadiah are reduced to scouring the land, looking for pasture for the animals, and in the course of this activity, Obadiah looks up and sees Elijah coming to meet him. He does obeisance to Elijah and calls him "lord Elijah," indicating the extreme respect he has for the prophet. In various respects Obadiah is the natural middleman for Elijah to approach in order to reach Ahab. Notice the parallel in form but the strong contrast in content between the way Obadiah addresses Elijah here and the later address by Ahab himself to Elijah, "Is that you O, Israel's hex" (v. 17). Initially Obadiah protests that he can not deliver the message that he has run into Elijah, for it will mean his own death, especially since Ahab has been frantically searching the land for Elijah. If Obadiah comes to the site of this meeting, "Yahweh's spirit will take you off I know not where" (v. 12), and this will result in Ahab venting his frustrations on Obadiah. Obadiah reminds Elijah that he is a loyal Yahwist and has revered Elijah himself since youth. The implicit plea in all this is, "Please do your own dirty work; bear your own tidings to the king." Nonetheless, Elijah tells Obadiah to announce his presence to the king, and he will meet with him.

Elijah swears an oath at v. 15, using the name *Yahweh Sabaot*—Yahweh Lord of hosts, or possibly Lord of the armies, as 1 Sam 17:45 suggests. It is interesting that this divine name elsewhere appears regularly in oracles and may indeed have been the regular divine name used at Shiloh by Samuel and Eli (1 Sam 1:31; 4:4). Notice here in v. 15, as before, the reference to Elijah standing before Yahweh. The image is of the prophet being part of the heavenly council and standing before God on his throne. The implication is that Yahweh is watching and will hold Elijah accountable to keep his word.

The meeting begins with invective by Ahab, calling Elijah one who has put a spell on Israel, and thus in essence calling him a magician. But Elijah turns the tables and makes clear that it is Ahab's own disloyalty to God that has provoked this temporal punishment. His abandonment of the very first commandment and his pursuit of other gods have caused a curse to fall on the land. What Elijah intends to do is not merely announce the return of rain but produce a showdown between himself and the multitudinous prophets of Baal (450) and of Asherah (400). It is interesting that it is the latter who are said to dine at Jezebel's table. But it is not just a showdown between Elijah and these other prophets; it is one between Yahweh and these foreign deities. The story is not so much about legitimation of a prophet as about vindication and confirmation of a deity.

The reference to Baals (plural) refers to the various local manifestations of the god, and we find at vv. 18–19 also a reference to Baal and Asherah, a pairing known from Ugaritic texts. Notice that, according to 1 Kgs 16:31, Jezebel's father was the priest of the goddess Ashtart, who corresponded to Asherah.[73] What most concerns us, however, is the reference to numerous pagan prophets who are devotees of Baal and Asherah. The term *nabi*, probably a more generic term for "prophet,"[74] is used here of these prophets. As Gray says, "The use of the

---

[73] See the discussion in Montgomery and Gehman, *Kings,* 300.

[74] See pp. 14–15, 44–45 above.

same word *nebi'im* to denote the prophets of Yahweh and the devotees of Baal indicates that the two groups had certain features in common."[75] But what features? It surely can not be the rituals of imitative magic that we find the prophets of Baal practicing in order to force their deity to act.

It is interesting that Elijah is set on proving his deity's reality and superiority by making it more difficult to accomplish the task of setting the sacrifice on fire, whereas his opponents are busy trying to do whatever they can to encourage or make easier their god's task. They sought "on behalf of the community to promote a new effusion of life after rain by the release of the life-essence, their own blood."[76] Could it be, then, that the term *nabi* is used of Elijah and of these prophets because they shared ecstatic religious experiences? This is possible, but nothing in our text strongly suggests that this characterized Elijah's prophetic experience. In view of the cross-cultural evidence, one should be leery of too quickly assuming that "prophet" equals "ecstatic." For example, the Mesopotamian evidence shows a clear distinction between the *mahhu*, or ecstatic, and the *baru*, or seer. The *mahhu* could communicate the will of God in addition to the *baru*, and this, not ecstatic experiences, is what they shared in common. It is likely that what Elijah shared in common with these other prophets was the receiving and communication of oracles or, in the case of diviners, answers to questions. This is why the term *nabi* was used. It indicated a specific prophetic function, not a specific type of prophetic experience. We must also not be too hasty in identifying ecstasy with rituals of sympathetic magic, although it appears both were involved in this case.

If one asks why Elijah chose Mount Carmel for the showdown, it is perhaps because this is where Obadiah had hidden the Yahwistic prophets. Elijah was not as outnumbered as it may have seemed on the surface of things. Notice that v. 20 says that Ahab summoned all the baalistic prophets from all over Israel, which suggests the proliferation of shrines to this god throughout the land. Elijah indeed apparently sees himself as alone among the active Yahwistic prophets (v. 22). On paper it should have been no contest—one Yahwistic prophet beseeching his God, compared to the many prophets of Baal trying to reach theirs. The story is further evidence of how prophetic activity was shared across all cultural and religious boundaries in the ancient Near East, such that prophets from one culture could be recognized as prophets in another because of shared functions and activities and, of course, also because all of these cultures influenced each other.

There was an especial urgency for the prophets to demonstrate the potency of their god, for nothing could be worse than urging allegiance to a fertility god that couldn't give rain! The ultimate humiliation in an honor-and-shame culture was that one's gods were incapable of helping the people. The urgency would be even greater at Carmel, for the particular Baal worshiped in this vicinity was likely Hadad, the god who in Canaanite mythology was said to have

---

[75] Gray, *1 and 2 Kings,* 393.
[76] Ibid.

subdued the chaos waters, thus preserving life, vegetation, and order in nature. Mount Carmel was the spot that would first get whatever rain might come off the ocean, and it was noted, as a result, for its verdancy (see Amos 1:2).[77]

The challenge that Elijah issues is directed to his own people, not in the first place to the king or to these other prophets. He asks them how long they would hobble about on two religious crutches (i.e., Baal and Yahweh). The image is a poignant one and suggests that the reliance on a plurality of deities prevents one from walking straight on one's own. It disables, rather than enables, normal walking. Since the same verb, *pasah*, is used in both v. 21 and v. 26 and since, in the latter text, it seems to mean a sort of ritual dance that involves hopping, the image becomes even more interesting. Elijah is ridiculing the "lame" rituals of Baal that Israel has been seduced into practicing.

Elijah gives the prophets of Baal the first opportunity to vindicate their deity. They offer the ox in sacrifice and cry out until noon to Baal for an answer. At this juncture Elijah ridicules their god, suggesting that perhaps he has gone to the restroom or is off on a journey or is asleep. Yet despite even louder cries and rituals of imitative magic where these prophets gashed themselves, absolutely nothing transpired. Once the impotence or possibly even nonexistence of this god has been suggested by this outcome, Elijah then draws to himself the Israelites. In a prophetic sign act, he repairs the broken-down altar of Yahweh, using twelve stones symbolizing, as v. 31 indicates, the twelve tribes. The image suggests that Israel could only be united if it offered itself wholeheartedly to Yahweh.

The remainder of the story is too familiar to need repeating in detail, but a few points are in order. Notice that Elijah invokes Yahweh as the God of Abraham, Isaac, *and Israel,* the other name for Jacob. Verse 36 must be compared to v. 31, where we are reminded that Jacob was given the name Israel and that therefore the tribes descending from Jacob and named after the special name God gave him should be serving the same God Jacob served. Elijah beseeches Yahweh to demonstrate he is both the God of Israel and God in Israel. And when fire falls from heaven on the sacrifice and the people respond with their statement of faith—"Yahweh is God, Yahweh is God"—Elijah seizes the moment and has all the prophets of Baal taken to the Kishon spring down the mountainside and executed by the people. Presumably, this was not done on the top of Mount Carmel so as not to defile the newly reconsecrated holy place.

The reader is meant to think that the king was watching this entire spectacle and thus Elijah could address him on the spot at the end of all this. Once the land has been cleansed of baalistic prophets, the rain returns to nourish the earth. The problem in Israel was not primarily a meteorological but a spiritual one. Ahab is warned to eat quickly and hitch up his chariot lest he be left stuck in the mud on the way to Jezreel. Various commentators have spoken about the posture Elijah assumes, with his head between his knees, and in all probability it reflects a posture of profound and determined prayer.[78] Like Moses, Elijah is a

---

[77] See ibid., 395–96.

[78] See De Vries, *1 Kings,* 217–19.

man of God, one who stands in the very presence of God and therefore can intercede for the people effectively, but even Elijah could not prevail in prayer on the matter of rain until the spiritual problem troubling Israel, the problem of syncretism and polytheism, had begun to be dealt with.

Is there yet another miracle in v. 46, or just an extraordinary God-aided human feat? Gray says, "Elijah's outrunning Ahab's chariot to Jezreel is taken as an example of abnormal physical effort characteristic of the ecstatic experience of the prophet, and this is supported by the statement that 'the hand of Yahweh was upon him,' which regularly describes prophetic ecstasy in Ezekiel."[79] Yet one must recognize that we may be meant to think, as Gray adds, that while Elijah could run cross-country the seventeen miles to the city that housed the summer palace of the Omride kings, Ahab had to stick to the roads, now subject to flash flooding. Whichever may have been the case, clearly God was with Elijah, and the reader is meant to see him arriving ahead of the king at the royal city in triumph.

D. The Flight of the Tishbite.   What a contrast is found in 1 Kgs 18 compared with the very next episode of the saga in ch. 19. The latter story reveals an all too human Elijah, who runs from the threats of Queen Jezebel and gives way to despair only shortly after his greatest victory over the prophets of Baal. Notice the naming ritual that Jezebel engages in at v. 2—"if you are Elijah [whose name means 'Yahweh is my God'], I am Jezebel [whose name means 'Where is Prince Baal,' referring to the resurrection of the deity]." There is, however, clearly a parody here in the Hebrew, for *'i-zebel* literally seems to mean "Where is the dung?" or, if pointed, *'i-zebul*, it means "no nobility."[80] In any case, Jezebel offers an imprecation and an oath that clearly frighten the prophet enough to make him run. One wonders if we are meant to think back to the cycle's beginning, which suggested Elijah was hiding. Was he by nature a timid and fearful man?

One possible answer to this question is given by R. B. Allen, who points out that most Hebrew manuscripts have the verbal form *wayyar* ("and he saw") as opposed to *wayyira* ("and he was afraid"). Allen argues that Elijah was not afraid but, rather, his spirit was broken because he saw that, despite his great victory over the prophets of Baal, the monarchy was not going to change and this depressed him so much he fled from the scene, feeling that he had accomplished nothing. This may well be the correct reading of the situation, in which case Elijah was a broken but not a fearful man at this juncture.[81]

Elijah's gloom is not lifted even by the miraculous provision of food in the desert. Elijah treks all the way from the northern part of the Holy Land to Beersheba, the southernmost town in Judah,[82] and from there to Mount Horeb,

---

[79] Gray, *1 and 2 Kings*, 404.

[80] Ibid., 368, 407.

[81] R. B. Allen, "Elijah the Broken Prophet," *JETS* 22 (3, 1979): 193–202.

[82] As Gray, *1 and 2 Kings,* 407 says, the mention of Beersheba as belonging to Judah suggests that our source here is surely from before 722 BC, when the Assyrians overran the northern part of the Holy Land.

a good forty or more days' and nights' journey.[83] Note that it was not his plan to go all the way to the mountain of God. He simply wanted go off into the desert and be allowed to die. This is clear especially from his dismissal of his servant as well as from his prayer. It was through the prodding of the *malak Yahweh*, the messenger of Yahweh, that he ate and drank and made the further journey to Horeb, where he had a close encounter of the first kind with Yahweh.

This encounter is interesting in several respects. First of all, had Elijah merely wanted to communicate with God, such a trek would not have been necessary, since he had received oracles in Israel. Elijah's initial thought had been escape from the territory of Queen Jezebel, and then of escape from life itself. Notice, however, that he does not try to take his own life but, rather, asks Yahweh to take it from him.

When Elijah finally arrives at Horeb, he enters a cave, much as the Yahwistic prophets apparently did on Mount Carmel, and Yahweh then speaks to him, asking him what his business is at the holy mountain. As it turns out, Elijah appears to be there to complain to God. He protests his extreme zeal for Yahweh's cause, but it has granted him, in his view, little headway with the wayward Israelites, who continue to forsake the covenant, overturn Yahwistic altars like the one on Carmel, and slay Yahwistic prophets. In short, there appears to be no profit in being a true prophet. In a bit of angst-filled hyperbole, Elijah complains that he is the only faithful one left and now someone is seeking to kill him as well. We see here that one man's zeal is not enough to change a people or the course of a nation. They must be willing to be changed.

Verse 11 is interesting because here Elijah is ordered to go out and stand on the mountain before the Lord. We have noticed that previously Elijah characterized himself as one who stood before Yahweh. As with the case of Moses, God passes by in front of Elijah, leaving in his wake wind, earthquake, fire, and finally a gentle breeze. It is said emphatically that Yahweh and Yahweh's will could not be discerned or found in any of these natural phenomena, however remarkable. Yahweh and Yahweh's will are known through his word and actions in history. Yahweh once more repeats his initial question to Elijah, and Elijah repeats the same reply, as if nothing had passed in between the two dialogues. It is then that Yahweh gives Elijah a specific commission to return to the north of the land and anoint Hazael king over Syria (see 2 Kgs 8:7–15), Jehu king over Israel (2 Kgs 9:1–13), and Elisha as a prophet to take Elijah's place (see 1 Kgs 19:19–21). There is no other record of the anointing of a prophet successor in the Hebrew Scriptures, and the subsequent accounts do not say anything about either Hazael or Elisha being literally anointed by Elijah. This leads to the suggestion that we should not overpress the term *masah*, which could simply mean "set apart" or "appoint." The word from Yahweh ends with the reassurance that there are several thousand Israelites who have still remained faithful to God. Is this a "You will be replaced; go back to work for a while and appoint the neces-

---

[83] Technically, the text suggests that it was forty-one days' and nights' journey, since he was a day into the desert when he got the call to go on.

sary leadership to take over when you are gone" speech? It would seem so, especially in light of what immediately follows this story in vv. 19–21 and the conclusion of the Elijah cycle in 2 Kgs 1–2. Whatever else one says about 1 Kgs 19, this story is not the kind one would expect if the Elijah cycle was an exercise in hagiography, and we are not encouraged in such a direction by the story in the Elisha cycle about the children and the bears (2 Kgs 2:23–25) either.

The events that are recounted in 1 Kgs 19–2 Kgs 2 would seem to be out of order, or else Elijah performed the tasks assigned to him in an order different from that in which they were mentioned in the commission. In any case, we note immediately that Elijah comes upon Elisha while he is plowing and simply throws his mantle over him, a prophetic symbolic act suggesting a transfer of office. That this should probably not be seen as an example of a belief in contact magic, or the transfer of power by touching a holy person's clothes, becomes clear in the story about Elijah's ascension, where only then does Elisha ask for a double portion of Elijah's spirit or vital force. Elijah's gesture would be all the more clear if prophets wore some sort of recognizable robe or mantle.[84] It is interesting, however, that Elisha is not called a prophet until 2 Kgs 9:1. At 1 Kgs 19:16, Elisha is said to be from Abel-Meholah (cf. Judg 7:22; 1 Kgs 7:22), a city said by Eusebius to be located ten miles south of Beth-Shean in the Jordan Valley. If this is correct, once more this is a prophet from the region that was neither Israel per se nor Judah per se, but a border region.

It is not clear how we should read Elijah's response to the request by Elisha to go and kiss his mother and father goodbye. There are, however one takes it, the clear overtones that the demands of the prophetic call are unconditional. Gray plausibly suggests the translation "Go back, but (remember) what I have done to you," taking *ki* as an adversative particle. The first action of Elisha as a prophet is itself a prophetic sign act. The taking of the yoke as firewood and the oxen as food symbolizes a very clear break with his old life. It is a farewell banquet with his fellow workers (and his family?) that serves as a rite of passage. Then arising, he follows Elijah and serves him. The successor must first be a servant of the master prophet. This way of putting the matter clearly echoes the Mosaic tradition, where Joshua is said to be the minister or personal servant of Moses (Exod 24:13). What needs to be seen when we read this entire saga is that Elijah is clearly portrayed as the primary prophetic figure and Elisha is seen as a lesser figure, though still a prophet. It is Elijah who is like Moses, while Elisha is simply like Elijah. This clearly was how Jews later read this story, including the author of Malachi.

The narrative in 1 Kgs 20:43–21:29 appears to be an independent tradition and one out of order. Elijah is introduced again, as if for the first time, and Ahab is identified as the king of Israel, as if the hearers did not know this. The story, however, is interesting for our purposes in two regards: (1) It reveals something of the prophetic process by which Elijah receives an oracle and then goes forth and proclaims it. But not only does he receive an oracle that he is to repeat

---

[84] See pp. 58–59 above.

verbatim; he also receives instructions about what and how and to whom he is to deliver the oracle. This distinction is important, for personal instructions are just as much revelation as oracles are, but they are not repeated or proclaimed. Yahweh reveals to Elijah the evil that Ahab is doing and sends him into action. (2) It also shows that although Yahweh's words of judgment are stern and the oracle seems to be an unconditional announcement of certain and imminent doom, nonetheless vv. 27–29 make clear that how Ahab responds to this oracle will at least determine when the judgment would come and also, in part, on whom it would fall. Repentance, if it does not make Yahweh change his mind, nonetheless may defer or deflect the blow.

Notice again that the concluding word of Yahweh to Elijah in v. 29 is not for proclamation but so that the prophet will know what God is doing and why. Yet such a way of acting without public explanation would leave Elijah wide open to the charge of being a false prophet. Indeed, all God's prophets could be accused of such if, every time a threat of judgment has as its response repentance, the oracle of doom is not enacted, or at least deferred. This is one of the factors that makes it exceedingly difficult to decide what amounts to a false prophecy or an unfulfilled prophecy. The matter would be simpler if all prophecies were clear and unconditional in character, but this very narrative strongly suggests this is not how Israelites viewed the matter.

E. *"And Now, a Message from Your Alternate Prophet of Doom."*   The narrative about Micaiah, the prophet of doom in 1 Kgs 22:1–40, is of concern for this study only at a few points. "The appearance of an otherwise unknown Micaiah vouches for the originality of the story, and is evidence of a wider range of literary composition among the sons of the prophets than might have been expected."[85] Notice that the in-house or court prophets in this case are indeed portrayed as yesmen, who only prophesy sweetness and light in the future for Ahab (v. 6). The reference here to four hundred prophets once again suggests that there was great concern to know about the future in advance and that prophets or diviners were the ones to be consulted on such matters. In uncertain times, there would be great demand for prophets. Notice that it is not Ahab but Jehoshaphat who is suspicious of their promise of victory at Ramoth-Gilead, and he asks for a second opinion. Intriguingly, Ahab refers not to Elijah or to Obadiah but to one Micaiah son of Imlah, whom he detests "because he does not prophesy good concerning me" (v. 7). Yet he is summoned and initially seems to confirm the favorable judgment of the court prophets (v. 15). He has been encouraged by the messenger who came and got him to fall in line with what the earlier prophets had said, but he protested that he must say what God gave him to say. But to judge from v. 23, Yahweh, in fact, had inspired the other prophets by means of a "lying spirit" to tell Ahab what he wanted to here. The same might be said of Micaiah's initial words in v. 15. Yet when Micaiah is abjured upon an oath by Ahab to speak the truth, he tells a tale of all Israel scattered upon the mountains by their foes and leaderless, like sheep

[85] Montgomery and Gehman, *Kings*, 336.

without a shepherd, and their having nothing to do but wander home. Since the term "shepherd" was a not uncommon euphemism for the king in the ancient Near East (see, e.g., Zech 13:7), the implications of the oracle are clearly bad for the king. This poetic oracle will show up again in the Gospel material. This may suggest that his first words to the king were intended to be ironic and were heard that way by the king,[86] or as De Vries suggests, Micaiah was expressing his patriotic hopes in the form of the usual ideology.[87] If so, the rebuke of the king brought him back to his senses. His job was to be an oracle proclaimer, not a people pleaser.

The description of the heavenly council by Micaiah found in vv. 18–27 is intriguing. Montgomery and Gehman rightly stress that we see here the precedents for the sort of visionary accounts we find in Amos 1–2 or Isa 6 and thus that we should definitely not make too great a distinction between the somewhat later writing prophets and these prophets in their prophetic experience and expression.[88] Yahweh is on his throne, surrounded by supernatural beings or spirits. Yahweh asks for a volunteer who will deceive Ahab so that he will fall in battle. One volunteers to be a lying spirit inspiring Ahab's court prophets. The image is of a God who is in control of all that transpires. Nothing is left to chance or luck. Whether a lying spirit or the spirit of truth in the mouth of Micaiah, it all ultimately goes back to Yahweh and Yahweh's plan for the demise of Ahab.

But if a prophet is given an oracle of deceit, does this make him a false prophet or simply a faithful messenger relating what he has been given to say? These stories are complex and can not easily be reduced to simple formulaic analysis. For his pains, Micaiah is first publicly disgraced by being slapped and then incarcerated.

His parting remark is that if Ahab returns safe and sound, then Yahweh has not spoken by Micaiah. The ultimate test of a true prophet is usually that if his words come true, he or she is authentic. This is not always an accurate test in view of conditional oracles and unpredictable responses to them. The poetic oracle that Micaiah offered was, of course, ambiguous—it could be about another king, and in fact in 2 Kgs 9 we learn that those who lost their lives at Ramoth-Gilead were the son of Ahab (Joram) and the son of Jehoshaphat (Ahaziah).

This raises another possibility that needs contemplation: a true prophet could offer a true oracle, but the oracle itself, because of its poetic or metaphorical form, could be capable of several applications or interpretations. The hearers might listen and misapply it, and then, when it did not happen to those to whom they thought it applied, they might assume that the prophecy was false. They would be wrong, and the words would later come back to haunt them. This story may provide an example of such a case. In any event, we see here a foreshadowing of the later antipathy between some court prophets and those

---

[86] See ibid., 338.

[87] De Vries, *1 Kings*, 268.

[88] Montgomery and Gehman, *Kings*, 336.

who became the canonical prophets—for instance, between Jeremiah and Hana-niah.[89] It must have been confusing, deciding who to believe when there was a variety of prophetic opinions.

F. Fire from Heaven.   There is an episode about Elijah and his adversarial rela-tionship with the apostate house of Omri, this time with Ahaziah, involving a death oracle or curse in 1 Kgs 1:2–18. The depiction of Elijah in this story is the same as we have seen before: he is an uncompromising Yahwist who calls into question every attempt by the monarch to consult other deities, in this case Baal-zebub of Ekron. The description of Elijah here is a bit more revealing; he is de-scribed as a hairy man, girt with a leather belt around his waist. M. Cogan and H. Tadmor stress that *ba'al 'se'ar* only can mean a hairy man, rather than a hairy or shaggy garment. It is true that Elijah is said to have worn a mantle (1 Kgs 19:13, 19; 2 Kgs 2:8, 13, 14), and it may have even been a hairy one (see Zech 13:4), but as these scholars emphasize, if all prophets wore hairy mantles, this would not have distinguished Elijah, and he would not have been recognizable from this descrip-tion.[90] There is the further point, made by T. R. Hobbs, that Elijah would indeed have been distinguishable from his fellow prophet Elisha by being called the hairy one, for Elisha was bald.[91]

G. Elijah's Ascension and Succession.   One of the most dramatic and moving narratives in the entire historical portion of the Hebrew Scriptures is the story of Elijah's ascension in 2 Kgs 2:1–25, a story that has echoes in Luke 24 and Acts 1. It serves both as a conclusion to the Elijah cycle and as the effective beginning of the Elisha cycle. We have here the only clear suggestion in the OT of something like a regular form of prophetic succession. Certainly this is the only saga about one prophet tapping another as his successor.[92] Notice that although Elisha is intro-duced before the story, nonetheless he does not succeed Elijah until after Elijah is taken up *and* Elisha receives a double portion of Elijah's spirit.[93] As Carroll stresses, it is important not to think in too linear a fashion about the prophets. On the one hand, there were the official court prophets, and on the other hand, there were peripheral prophets consulted from time to time by a king and visiting and commenting to the king without invitation on other occasions. There was no sin-gular line of the prophets, not least because there was no singular sort of prophet.[94] There was a variety of prophetic figures: some operated in groups, some as individuals; some were seers, some were not; some were court prophets, some were not; some were miracle workers, some were not; some were men, some

---

[89] See Gray, *1 and 2 Kings,* 449.

[90] M. Cogan and H. Tadmor, *II Kings* (New York: Doubleday, 1988), 26.

[91] T. R. Hobbs, *2 Kings* (Waco: Word, 1985), 10.

[92] See Carroll, "The Elijah-Elisha Sagas," 403.

[93] A later echo of this is found in Acts 1, where Jesus is taken up and the disciples all receive the plenitude of the Spirit once Jesus is gone.

[94] Carroll, "The Elijah-Elisha Sagas," 414–15.

were women; some seem to have had ecstatic experiences, some seem not to have had such experiences. All shared one thing—they were called upon to speak about the future and were from time to time inspired to offer oracles.

The narrative begins with Elijah and Elisha on the move from Gilgal, and Elijah seems to be attempting to leave Elisha behind, but Elisha will have none of it. The successor swears an oath, "As Yahweh lives and as your soul lives I will certainly not forsake you." Thus, despite Elijah's request to be left alone, they travel on to Bethel, where they meet a group called the sons of the prophets. Care must be taken in analyzing this group. The earlier band of prophets that Saul and Samuel were involved with are not called sons of the prophets, and the two groups are not necessarily to be identified with each other. This, in turn, means that one can not assume what Lindblom and others have assumed—that all or most of the prophets in the early monarchy were organized in guilds or bands that had leaders who trained their disciples in ecstatic exercises and practices. The basis for this conclusion entails not only the amalgamation of 2 Kgs 2 with the earlier material in Samuel but also a rather serious anachronism—assuming Hebrew prophetic guilds were like the much later Islamic guilds of whirling dervishes.[95]

On the other hand, we also can not assume that the phrase "sons of the prophets" simply means lay supporters of the prophets.[96] To the contrary, vv. 3–4 suggest that they also have the prescience that prophets were noted for. The phrase "sons of the prophets" is, with one exception, always used in the Elisha material, and we certainly cannot generalize about all prophets from this experience. For example, Lindblom suggests, on the basis of the baldness of Elisha, that it was normal for prophets to be tonsured and, from material in 1 Kgs 20:35 and 2 Kgs 1:8, 2:22–24, that they all had distinguishing tatoos and clothing.[97] But as Cogan and Tadmor point out, we would rather have expected them to be like Elijah, hairy, for this was an accepted feature of Jewish asceticism as the laws of the Nazirite suggests (cf. Num 6:5 and Judg 13:5). Notice, too, that the ritual cutting or shaping of hair is also prohibited in Mosaic law (Lev 19:24; 21:5).[98] As Josephus concluded, the sons of prophets are likely prophets in training, or disciples of the great prophets just as Elisha was of Elijah (see *Ant.* 9.28, 106). It is not surprising in this context that Elijah should have been called Elisha's spiritual father. We should probably also distinguish the plural phrase "sons of the prophets" from the phrase "son of a prophet" in Amos 7:14, for when a single prophet's disciple is mentioned, he is called "one of the sons of the prophets" (1 Kgs 20:35), not "a son of a prophet." The phrase in Amos would

---

[95] See Lindblom, *Prophecy in Ancient Israel,* 69–71; Gray, *1 and 2 Kings,* 474; G. von Rad, *Old Testament Theology* (2 vols.; New York: Harper & Row, 1965), 2:25–32. Wilson, *Prophecy and Society,* 141, is correct that there is no evidence the sons of prophets were ecstatics.

[96] Against Hobbs, *2 Kings,* 25–27.

[97] Lindblom, *Prophecy in Ancient Israel,* 69–71; cf. Gray, *1 and 2 Kings,* 480.

[98] See Cogan and Tadmor, *2 Kings,* 38.

seem to be simply another way of speaking of a prophet, though it can not be ruled out entirely that "son of a prophet" means a prophet in training. As J. G. Williams has stressed, the phrase "sons of the prophets" does not appear in our sources before the reign of Ahab or after the time Elisha unless Amos 7:14 is an example of it (cf. 1 Kgs 20:35; 2 Kgs 2:3, 5, 7, 15; 4:1, 38; 5:22; 6:1; 9:1), and it is only used to describe northern prophets.[99] What little can be said about the relationship between Elisha and the sons of the prophets has been aptly summed up by D. L. Petersen: " . . . only the Elisha narratives are of help in charting the contours of the group–holy man dynamic. . . . The leader was held responsible for food (2 Kings 4:38–41, 42–44), for housing (2 Kings 6:1–7), for health (2 Kings 4:38–41), and for relatives of deceased group members (2 Kings 4:1–7)."[100]

Verse 5 indicates that both Elisha and the sons of the prophets are aware that this is the day Elijah will be taken from them, which explains why Elisha is sticking to Elijah like glue. The verse suggests that Elisha is annoyed that the sons of the prophets bring the matter up, as if speaking about it only makes the matter worse. At Jericho, once again Elijah trys to shed Elisha, but the disciple is having none of it. It appears that the some fifty representatives of the sons of the prophets attempted to provide a human barricade to Elijah's progress; at this point, Elijah and Elisha turned and faced the Jordan, Elijah struck the Jordan with his mantle, the waters parted, and they crossed over on dry ground (v. 8). Here is another parallel with the Mosaic traditions.

At vv. 9–10 Elijah gives Elisha an opportunity to ask for some sort of prophetic inheritance. Elisha requests a double portion of Elijah's spirit. The language here does not mean that he wants twice as much "spirit" as Elijah had; rather, it is the language of inheritance, for the phrase "double portion" or "double share" is found at Deut 21:17. The upshot is that Elisha is requesting to receive the portion of the eldest son and asking for the status of being the legitimate heir of Elijah and of his prophetic role. But as Williams suggests, the text is dealing not just with a transfer of prophetic office but with a transfer of leadership over an organized group of prophets, who have as their mission the restoration of Yahwism in Israel and thus are concerned with gaining a king who will maintain an exclusive loyalty to Yahweh.[101] It is not for Elijah to dispense, but he informs Elisha that if he sees Elijah taken up, he will in fact receive what he asks for (which is said to be a difficult request).

As the two prophets continued on their journey and continued discussing matters, we are told that a fiery chariot and fiery horses came between them and Elijah went up in the storm into heaven. As Cogan and Tadmor point out, the Hebrew does not necessarily suggest a whirlwind, for *se'ara* means literally a storm.[102] This phenomenon is sometimes associated with a theophany (Job 38:1; 40:6), but it is also associated with divine punishment (Jer 23:19; Zech 9:14; Ps

---

[99] Williams, "The Prophetic 'Father,' " 345.

[100] Petersen, *Roles of Israel's Prophets,* 48.

[101] Ibid., 345.

[102] Cogan and Tadmor, *2 Kings,* 31.

83:16). Nothing specific is said in our text about God appearing, but in view of the traditions about God being a warrior who would ride in his chariot on the clouds (cf. Ps 104:3–4; Exod 15:1–3; Judg 5:4–5),[103] it is probably implied here.

Elisha's response to this theophany is to cry out repeatedly, "My father, my father! The chariots of Israel and its horsemen!" There has been much debate about this phrase, but it must be seen in the context of the holy-war traditions. Elijah was an agent of God's holy war against false gods and apostasy. Yahweh sent fire from heaven on Mount Carmel, and again it fell from heaven when the agents of the apostate king came after Elijah (2 Kgs 1:9ff.). Fire as well as rain are the weapons of the divine warrior, and chariots of fire are the natural vehicles for his agents and his own person. The cry comes up again at 2 Kgs 13:14 at the end of the Elisha cycle, where it is a cry of despair as Elisha is about to die. Perhaps the phrase had become famous as associated with dramatic transitions involving God's prophets. Elisha calls Elijah his father twice. The paternal terminology was sometimes applied to a group's leader (2 Kgs 2:12; 13:14; cf. 1 Sam 10:12), but here it connotes a special relationship between Elisha and Elijah. He had left everything and followed Elijah. Elijah had become his parent and indeed his family.[104]

The further response of Elisha, rending his clothes in grief, may suggest that his outcry was also part of an expression of grief, as it is at 13:14. But Elisha was not to be consumed with grief. He picks up the mantle of Elijah, which had fallen when Elijah was taken up. Immediately Elisha repeats the prophetic act of Elijah and strikes the water with Elijah's mantle. He cries out, "Where is the Lord, the God of Elijah?" This exclamation, if it is a true question, is a question that is immediately answered by the parting of the waters, and at the same time the action confirms that the God of Elijah is with Elisha and that thus he is an authentic Yahwistic prophet.

It would appear that Elisha donned Elijah's robe, and this may explain the reaction of the sons of the prophets, who say, "the spirit of Elijah rests on Elisha." Thus Elisha's status is confirmed both to himself and to his compatriots. He will assume not only the relationship Elijah had with God but also the relationship Elijah had with these prophetic disciples. They do obeisance before Elisha, showing their respect for him and willingness to subordinate themselves to him. But what then comes out of their mouths shows them to be neophytes. Their proposal is to send fifty strong men to see if the windstorm has dropped Elijah somewhere on one of the nearby mountains or in some valley! This shows not only their great love for Elijah but perhaps a bit of the Middle Eastern concern that Elijah receive a proper burial, for it was the duty of every "son" to make sure his father or mother received a proper burial. At first Elisha rejects the proposal, perhaps because he knows it will be a pointless search, but then he is shamed into relenting and allowing them to search for Elijah. The three-day

---

[103] T. Longman and D. Reid, *God Is a Warrior* (Downers Grove, Ill.: InterVarsity, 1995): 67ff.

[104] See the discussion by Williams, "The Prophetic 'Father.'"

search produced no results, except an "I told you so" from Elisha when the search party returns.

Yet it must be borne in mind that there was no precedent, even in the Mosaic stories, for an ascension. Even the Enoch tradition does not directly suggest a bodily ascension. There was, then, no precedent for this event. It is interesting that a later Jewish tradition found in Sir 48:9 claimed that Elijah did not ascend to heaven but waited in some interim state or condition to return as forerunner of the Messiah. In view of 2 Chron 21:12–15 (which reports a letter sent to King Joram by Elijah, while our story indicates he disappeared during the reign of Jehoshaphat), it is understandable why Josephus (*Ant.* 9.99) would urge that Elijah simply disappeared at this juncture instead of ascending into heaven. Did the Chronicler already know of such a tradition of Elijah's temporary disappearance? Notice, too, how 1 Macc 2:58 speaks of Elijah ascending "as if into heaven."

Perhaps this scene has been best summed up by Cogan and Tadmor:

> As during his life, Elijah is portrayed as an elusive wanderer, appearing and disappearing at a moment's notice . . . so in his death it was told that he vanished from among men for all time. Enoch "was taken by God" (Gen. 5:24), but Elijah is the only biblical personality of whom it is said that he "ascended to heaven in a storm" (vv. 1, 11). By utilizing this image, the prophet's followers invested him with the quality of eternal life, surpassing even Moses, the father of all prophets, who died and was buried (albeit by God himself: Deut. 34:5–6). It was this quality which became the dominant motif in the later Elijah legends.[105]

The remainder of 2 Kgs 2 provides the reader with two miracle tales that further validate that Elisha is a man on whom the spirit of God rests. One may be said to be a positive, the other a punitive, miracle. The first involves the bad water that in turn makes the land unfruitful. Elisha remedies this problem, oddly enough, with salt, which is not used elsewhere in the OT as a healing agent. Indeed, salt is sown in the land in Judg 9:45 to produce just the opposite effect—making the land unfruitful. But undoubtedly, we should read this story in light of the story of Moses sweetening the waters at Marah (Exod 15:23–25). Thus Elisha, too, is a prophet like Moses.[106]

The second story, at 2:23–25, involves, however, a punitive miracle that has no parallel in the Mosaic corpus. Notice that this destruction of the boys is accomplished by issuing a curse in Yahweh's name. While it is true that this story reveals that this is a true prophet who can effectively use the divine name, it is also true that this tale, like the one at 1:2–18, likely involves an abuse of power. God has bestowed his power or spirit upon the prophet, but the gift can be misused, as indeed it was by Elijah on occasion. This is not the sort of story of which hagiography is made.

R. G. Messner has made a valiant attempt to offer another reading of this text, pointing out that the terminology need not suggest children were involved

---

[105] Cogan and Tadmor, *2 Kings*, 33–34.
[106] See Gray, *1 and 2 Kings*, 477ff.

but, rather, young men and that they represented the syncretistic views of Bethel and spoke abusively to the prophet (the accusation of baldness was considered a significant shaming device in a culture where hair was a sign of power and virility in men, and of fertility in women), suggesting he should ascend like Elijah and leave them alone. He then adds that God is responsible for what happens to the young men, that Elisha simply invokes God's action.[107] While Messner may be right in pointing out certain mitigating details, so that Elisha's actions should be seen in the proper context of an honor-and-shame setting, nonetheless he ignores the point that God's spirit was upon Elisha, empowering him to act as he would, or not to act at all. Therefore, the responsibility for the action must lie at Elisha's door.

While it would be possible to analyze the further stories of Elisha's miracles, they add nothing to what we have learned already in our analysis of the Elijah cycle and the beginning of the Elisha cycle. Indeed, some of the miracle tales, as has often been noted, are virtual doublets of stories we found in the Elijah cycle (stories about a widow's oil, about bringing a child back to life), and the others focus on the miraculous element in itself, telling tales about floating ax heads and the curative power of Elisha's bones (cf. 2 Kgs 4–6; 13). In fact, none of these stories portray Elisha as an oracle to any significant degree. Instead the emphasis is almost entirely on his being a holy man of God (4:9). Nor is there as great an emphasis on Elisha's battle with apostasy in the land or with false prophets compared with Elijah's similar battle, although there is a telling moment, in the story of the attempted capture of Elisha by the king of Aram, when Elisha's servant is allowed to see the chariots of fire and horses surrounding and protecting the prophet (6:17)—a further indication of the divine-warrior tradition and that Elisha, too, is seen as the agent of God's holy war, which is being waged not only against enemies without but also against traitors and apostates within Israel. Although there is no record of Elisha offering any extended oracles, it is interesting that his life ends with his instructing King Joash to perform what amounts to a prophetic sign act of future destruction of, or victory over, Aram (13:14–19). It seems clear that one is meant to see Elijah and Elisha as a different breed of prophet where prophetic sign acts and miracles come to the fore and oracles recede into the background. It will be well to bear this in mind when we move finally to a discussion of the writing prophets, who, for the most part, are not like Elijah and Elisha in regard to the matter of miracles and indeed are not, for the most part, northern prophets either. The northern tradition seems to have produced Moses-like figures who were more holy men than oracular prophets, more sign prophets than bestowers of symbolic utterances.

III. CONCLUSIONS

This chapter has analyzed the material that may give insight into the role of prophets during the first three hundred or so years of the monarchy, including

---

[107] R. G. Messner, "Elisha and the Bears," *Grace Journal* 3 (1962): 12–24.

during some of the divided monarchy. Examples of both central prophets, with close connections to the court (Nathan), and peripheral prophets (Elijah and Elisha) have been scrutinized. The Elijah-Elisha cycle of traditions also bears witness to court prophets in the northern kingdom. These traditions provide evidence of prophets fulfilling a variety of roles in Israelite history: (1) crisis intervention specialists, (2) offerers of oracles, (3) tellers of symbolic tales or performers of prophetic signs, (4) workers of miracles. There is very little here, in terms of social functions, that can not be paralleled with data from other ancient Near Eastern cultures, though of course in the service of other deities. The crucial prophetic material in 2 Sam 7 about dynastic succession is quite similar in content and form to the traditions cited from Mari. Once there was an Israelite monarchy, it would appear likely that Israelite prophecy became more, rather than less, like other ancient Near Eastern prophecy. The problem in Israel, however, was that, for a variety of reasons, there were not long, stable reigns of kings for generation after generation and so prophets in Israel repeatedly found themselves playing the role of prosecutors of the covenant lawsuit or the role of crisis intervention specialists. They do not, then, appear as simply court yes-men, and often they were more severely critical of the monarch than any other known prophetic group in the ancient Near East.

Several notable conclusions can be drawn from the Nathan traditions: (1) Nothing suggests he was part of a band or guild of prophets. Prophets in Israel could act as individuals or as part of a group. (2) Nothing suggests that Nathan's relationship to David was like that of Samuel to Saul. Nathan was not a king-maker, nor does the evidence suggest that David became a part of some prophetic band. (3) Nathan was a prophet with clear access to the royal family, and his words were valued. He was a prophet who prophesied with some regularity to or for the king, for he was concerned about the legitimate succession of the royal line and was apparently known well enough to Bathsheba not only to have ready access to her but to give counsel that would be immediately received. Yet one can distinguish between Gad, who is David's official seer, and Nathan.

One of the more revealing insights comes right at the beginning of the Nathan material at 2 Sam 7:1. David proposes to undertake building Yahweh a building, and Nathan, speaking on the basis of his own judgment, concurs. This contrasts with the oracle Nathan gives thereafter. There was a difference between personal advice and the reception of an oracle, and an Israelite prophet could offer either or both. Not everything a prophet said was prophetic or inspired. There is, furthermore, this difference between what one finds in 2 Sam 7 and what one finds in the Mari oracle: for whatever reason, David is not to build his God a house; rather, his God will establish David's house and lineage. The issues of lineage, land, temple, and people are not to be adjudicated by David as if he were just another ancient Near Eastern monarch.

The issue of covenantal relationships begins to enter the discussion of prophecy in the Nathan material. If indeed Nathan is the prosecutor of the covenantal lawsuit and, in fact, the proclaimer of a new covenantal arrangement between David and Yahweh, this raises the important issue of the conditional nature of his prophecy of succession. Does God make David an unconditional promise of perpetuity for the royal line, or is it only an unconditional promise that David's son will inherit the throne, or are these promises conditional? The evidence could be read in several different ways, but what seems clear is that the more prophecy is linked to covenantal arrangements, the more likely it is that the prophecies involve some conditions that must be fulfilled by the recipients. Curse or blessing sanctions, in the form of woe or weal oracles, come into play depending on how the vassal responds to God's demands. Psalm 132, clearly enough, did not see all the promises of progeny to David as unconditional.

There was the suggestion in the Nathan material that there was a difference between prophetic experience and prophetic expression. It was intimated that Nathan may have received his oracle in a dream, but there was a lag between that reception and his proclamation to David. A decision also had to be taken about whether and in what form to make the proclamation. There is no suggestion that Nathan's dream was in parabolic form, although it may have been. On the other hand, the parable may be the prophet's compositional response to the dream. There is no hint of ecstatic experience in the case of Nathan. He is deeply involved in Israel's political process, dealing with issues of land, temple, marriage, and succession. He is not a sage spinning generic parabolic maxims. Yet his range of expression to convey the prophetic word includes *meshalim*. He is a crucial figure at the beginning of Israelite monarchial history.

The stories about Elijah and Elisha come from a rather later period but also show how prophets were involved in the political process, only in this case during the divided monarchy and in the north. It seems clear that their stories have been written up with an awareness of the Mosaic tradition, such that Elijah especially is portrayed as the latter-day Mosaic prophet. Like Moses, Elijah makes a pilgrimage to Mount Horeb, like Moses he battles a people largely unfaithful to Yahweh, like Moses he makes fundamental challenges to the powers that be, like Moses he is a man of powerful prayer and intervention, and like Moses his end involves the miraculous. This, in part, explains the enormous interest in Elijah much later in early Jewish literature, in the NT, and in the literature that arose in Judaism and Christianity after the NT era.[108]

In the Elijah cycle especially, the prophet is portrayed as sought after to solve crises such as drought or death. The focus is on the prophet as a man of deeds rather than the prophet as oracle, although there is some material dealing with oracles. It is not clear from the material itself whether the reader is meant to see in Elijah and Elisha the establishment of a different sort of prophetic tradition, in particular, a northern tradition, but certainly their efforts would later be seen as precedent-setting.

Especially the Elijah traditions portray the prophetic situation as complex. There were various Yahwistic prophets, some court prophets, some like Elijah, and there was conflict over what God's will and word were for the king. Was a

---

[108] See, e.g., M. E. Stone and J. Strugnell, *The Books of Elijah, Parts 1–2* (Missoula: Scholars Press, 1979).

prophet who deliberately delivered a "lying oracle" a false prophet or simply doing his job? Were there means besides historical verification after the fact to distinguish the false from the true prognosticators? The presence of numerous prophets of Baal in the north adds further complexity to the situation, even if there seems to have been some temporary resolution of the matter after the confrontation on Mount Carmel.

Despite a scholarly tradition suggesting that the Elijah and Elisha stories are amoral in character and biographical in interest, it seems more likely that we should see these stories in a different light. The focus is on the activity of God through the prophets and Yahweh's tenuous relationship with his people. The stories also make evident that the empowerment of God's spirit does not lead to automatic activity. Rather, the prophet has choice over how he will use or even abuse the power given to him. Elijah and Elisha were so known as men of power that these stories mainly portray them as being sought for their aid rather than for their knowledge.

From this material, some important points are learned about the prophetic guild or "sons of the prophets," a tradition that should not be too readily identified with the bands of prophets mentioned in the Samuel traditions. The earlier band of prophets that Saul and Samuel were involved with is not called sons of the prophets, and the two groups are not necessarily to be identified. This, in turn, means that one can not assume that all or most of the prophets in the early monarchy were organized in guilds or bands that had leaders who trained their disciples in ecstatic exercises and practices. The basis for such a conclusion entails the doubtful amalgamation of 2 Kgs 2 with the earlier material in Samuel.

We cannot assume that the phrase "sons of the prophets" means lay supporters of the prophets. Second Kings 2:3–4 suggests they also have the prescience prophets were noted for. The phrase "sons of the prophets" is, with one exception, always used in the Elisha material, and we certainly cannot generalize about all prophets from this experience. As Josephus concluded, the sons of prophets are likely prophets in training, or disciples of the great prophets just as Elisha was in relationship to Elijah (see *Ant.* 9.28, 106). It is not surprising in this context that Elijah should have been called Elisha's spiritual father. We should probably distinguish the plural phrase "sons of the prophets" from the phrase "son of a prophet" in Amos 7:14, for when a single prophet's disciple is mentioned he is called "one of the sons of the prophets" (1 Kgs 20:35), not "a son of a prophet." The phrase "sons of the prophets" does not appear in our sources before the reign of Ahab or after the time Elisha unless Amos. 7:14 is an example of it (cf. 1 Kgs 20:35; 2 Kgs 2:3, 5, 7, 15; 4:1, 38; 5:22, 6:1; 9:1), and it is only used to describe northern prophets. One must be careful how one uses such material to speak about an ongoing guild or tradition of the prophets.

It is perhaps worth stressing that Elijah and Elisha appear to be a different breed of prophet where prophetic sign acts and miracles come to the fore and oracles recede into the background. It will be well to bear this in mind when this study moves on to a discussion of the writing prophets, who for the most part are not like Elijah and Elisha in regard to the matter of miracles, and indeed are not for the most part northern prophets either. The northern tradition seems to have produced Mosaic like figures who were more general holy men than just oracular prophets, more sign prophets than bestowers of symbolic utterances, more mediators and intercessors than oracles. But unlike Moses, Elijah and Elisha are peripheral prophets, not court prophets or leaders of the people of Israel writ large. They have a following, but it is a limited and specialized one, and most of the narratives suggest they operate alone. This last fact seems also to characterize the writing prophets, to whom this study turns in the next chapter.

CHAPTER 4

Prophets of Holy Writ:

From Amos to the Exile

T IS ONE OF THE SINGULAR PROBLEMS of most studies of Hebrew prophets and prophecy that the discussion normally begins and frequently ends with the prophets of the eighth century BC and beyond, with no account of the earlier period or, for that matter, no account of the larger cross-cultural prophetic culture that had been extant for centuries.[1] In a cursory fashion in the first three chapters in this study, there has been an effort to demonstrate how to remedy that problem. This is not to say that there was no attention being paid by scholars to the indebtedness of the writing prophets to the earlier prophetic and even legal traditions. G. von Rad, for example, popularized the view that the prophets depended heavily on earlier traditions of various sorts, including legal traditions.[2] This, however, was more a matter of source criticism than a reckoning with social realia. It needs to be stressed that Amos, Hosea, Micah, Isaiah, and others were aware that they stood in a line of prophets that, though we can not speak of anything like prophetic succession over a long period of time, nonetheless served a significant ongoing social function in Israel and in Judah.[3]

---

[1] See, e.g., G. M. Tucker, "Prophecy and Prophetic Literature," in *The Hebrew Bible and Its Modern Interpreters* (ed. G. M. Tucker and D. A. Knight; Philadelphia: Fortress, 1985), 325–68.

[2] See G. von Rad, *The Message of the Prophets* (San Francisco: HarperCollins, 1962), 15ff.

[3] On the relationship of this material to Deuteronomistic interests, see K. Zobel, *Prophetie und Deuteronomium* (Berlin: de Gruyter, 1992).

The Hebrew prophets were not like itinerant revival preachers who, once in a long while, came to town for a few days and then were never heard from again. Nor, for the most part, was their target audience the general populace. They were, rather, the figures who called Israel's leadership to accountability, as we already have seen in the cases of Samuel, Nathan, and Elijah, and this continued to be so right through the time of Jeremiah. It is a thesis of this work that one of the major reasons for the sea change in prophecy and its character, beginning with the exile and then continuing into the postexilic situation, is that the Hebrew prophets themselves had to assume different social roles. *There were no kings or controlling ruler figures to address when correction of God's people was sought.* Social realia dramatically affected both the form and the content of prophetic expression. It appears also to have affected prophetic experience with the increase of visionary and apocalyptic elements in prophecy. But it is premature to bring this up here.

When one arrives at the writing prophets, this is in some ways a gain, but also in some ways a loss. It is a gain because here one is often listening to, despite some editing, the authentic voices of Hebrew prophets expressed in oracles. But the gain is also a loss because without much, and in some cases without any, narrative material to accompany the oracles, these prophets have tended to be treated as talking heads, heralds without a heritage, messengers without a movement, wordsmiths who were all talk and no action, or finally as part of a stream of prophetic tradition. In what follows, something will be said not only about the words of Amos, Micah, Hosea, Isaiah or Jeremiah, and others but also about the social world they spoke out of and addressed. While biography is seldom possible, in these cases social matrix and level and function can nonetheless be recovered.

In his landmark study on the writing prophets, K. Koch asserts from the very outset, "A prophet addresses himself to the future."[4] Whether one calls it prescience or foreknowledge or revelation, the prophets, in a culture and time that focused so heavily on the past and on precedent, attempted to warn about or celebrate what was to come. Once we have conceded this point and then further conceded that at least some prophets on some occasions spoke accurately about what would happen in the future, we are then faced with the issue of ex eventu prophecy. Is ex eventu prophecy a failure of faith, does it reflect the loss of inspiration, is it merely a reflection of the transition from classical prophecy to apocalyptic? How can one tell when one has come across an example of ex eventu prophecy?

These sorts of questions must be faced on various occasions in this study, and Koch may provide a helpful clue. It has usually and correctly been thought that if we are able to isolate oracular forms, then it may be possible to discern later redaction or making prophecies more specific in light of the events themselves. But this still would not constitute an ex eventu prophecy per se. Koch, however, suggests that the prophets must be seen as independent thinkers who

---

[4] K. Koch, *The Prophets* (2 vols.; Philadelphia: Fortress, 1983), 1:1.

"in a process of what I should like to term 'subsequent insight,' give a rational form to what they have already become certain of intuitively."[5] In other words, the gap between prophetic experience and prophetic expression must be taken seriously especially with the writing prophets.

The placing of the oracles of these prophets into writing reflects a belief that there is some enduring value to what has been already spoken and reflected upon, and the very writing down of these prophecies may indeed have encouraged further reflection, refinement, and clarification. In this case, the prophetic corpus becomes a stimulus to further prophetic reflection.

I would suggest that if it fits in anywhere, ex eventu prophecy does so in this category of further prophetic or apocalyptic reflection on earlier oracular material, because it was believed that some of those ancient oracles had finally found a correlate in the recent past experiences of God's people. But there may well be good reason not to see ex eventu prophecy as prophecy at all, properly speaking, but, rather, as written commentary in prophetic clothing or as non-prophetic scribal expansions on the basis of earlier prophetic material. One must bear these things in mind as we explore the world of the so-called writing prophets.[6]

I. FROM FIGS TO BURNT OFFERINGS: FROM AMOS TO MICAH

A. A is for Amos.   Whatever else one might wish to say, the period from the middle of the eighth century until about 685 BC was a remarkably fertile time for the Hebrew prophetic movement. This is a good-news, bad-news situation because, in general, the more prophetic activity, the greater the likelihood that God's people were in the midst of or facing various social crises. The Hebrew writing prophets were not, for the most part, conveyors of sweetness and light or reassurers that all manner of things were and would be well. In what follows, some core samplings will be taken from the writing prophets, asking questions about the character, content, and form of their messages and what these convey about prophetic experience, expression, tradition, and now finally the prophetic corpus.

---

[5] Ibid., 1:vii.

[6] Clearly enough, ex eventu prophecy is a literary, not an oracular, phenomenon, for it is linked to and dependent upon the literary phenomenon of attributing a work to an ancient legendary figure. It shows the strong social belief of a society that the opinions of the ancients mattered much in deciphering contemporary experience. It may be asked whether ex eventu prophecy should even be considered prophecy, as opposed to commentary on some social situation using a prophetic form as a literary device. In short, it could be seen as commentary that uses the form of oracles to make its point but does not derive from prophetic experience or prophetic oracular expression. One suspects that the reason ex eventu prophecy has even been considered as prophecy at all is the dominance of literary critical examinations of ancient Hebrew prophecy that focus too one-sidedly on form as the determinant of the genre and function and character of a particular expression.

It is generally agreed by scholars that Amos was the first Hebrew prophet to have his oracles gathered together in a book. Amos prophesied in the period leading up to the demise of the northern kingdom, Israel, and he warned of that coming demise. The only portion of Amos that is in the third person and speaks about his mission says this: "Amos conspires against you at the center of the house of Israel. The land can not comprehend all his words. For thus has said Amos: 'Through the sword shall Jeroboam die and Israel shall surely be deported from its land'" (7:10–11). These are, in fact, words of warning from Amaziah the priest to Jeroboam about the essence of Amos's message. The inclusion of this material in this book shows that, in all likelihood, Amos was not the collector and editor of his own material. Indeed, it is likely it was collected and edited in the south after the fall of Israel—which leads to the next important point about Amos.

If ever a prophet fit the description of a peripheral rather than a central or court prophet, Amos would be the person. Amos 1:1 indicates that he comes from the small village of Tekoa about six miles south of Bethlehem, and 7:15 suggests he was called from there, from being a supervisor of a group of shepherds (1:1; 7:14–15), to being a prophet. Yet he does not prophesy in the south but, rather, in the north! This is not all that surprising, however, when we remember our earlier discussions of the cross-cultural range of prophetic figures.[7] Judging from 7:14–15, his call can probably be dated rather precisely between 765 and 760 BC.[8] His ministry seems to have been of short duration, perhaps only a year, and its locus was the shrine at Bethel (7:10–17) and the capital city of Samaria (3:9; 4:1; 6:1). Even a cursory study of Amos's oracles reveals a man with an understanding of the political and religious problems of the day in Israel, a grasp of ancient history and international relationships. His overarching concern and complaint is about a lack of justice and faithfulness in Israel, which will lead to its doom. Correctly, G. V. Smith argues that it would be wrong simply to paint Amos as yet another Judean nationalist who cast aspersions on his northern cousins, suggesting they were beyond the pale. Nor was Amos a cult prophet in the south who simply ranted and raved about the competition at Bethel. The very fact of Amos's ministry suggests a grave concern on his part to warn Israel and try to help set it back on the right course. These warnings, however, seem to have gone largely unheeded, with disastrous results.[9] Let us examine, then, some of Amos's oracular material.

The first two chapters of Amos belong together and involve a litany of judgment pronounced by Yahweh (noting the "thus says Yahweh" formula at 1:3, 6, 9, 11, 13; 2:1, 4, 6) on Damascus, Gaza, Ashdod, Ashkelon, Ekron, Tyre, and Edom, on the Ammonites, the Moabites, and then surprisingly on Judah and then on Israel. The arrangement is one of judgment on cities, then on peoples, with God's people mentioned last but included within the purview of

---

[7] See pp. 8–20 above.
[8] See the discussion by G. V. Smith, *Amos* (Grand Rapids: Zondervan, 1989), 3ff.
[9] See ibid., 3–4.

God's judgment. The image here is of God looking around from Jerusalem in all directions (see 1:2) and not liking what he sees either near or far. Yahweh is an equal-opportunity judger of cities and nations, his own not exempted. Each city or people seems to get its own oracle of judgment, and the initial form of each oracle is the same—"For three transgressions of . . . and for four"—followed by a list of destructive acts Yahweh will perform, and concluded with the phrase "says the Lord."[10] If one asks about the social effect of these oracles, one must bear in mind their order—with judgment on Israel mentioned last. If indeed this oracle or series of oracles was delivered in the north, one can imagine they were well received up until the surprise ending. Amos indicates that the Hebrew prophets believed that God held not only individuals, such as leaders, but also cities and nations accountable for their actions.

Though by no means the only signal, the poetic form of Amos's oracles suggests its prophetic character, something not easily appreciated in English translation. This feature of many prophetic oracles makes it unsurprising that one also finds the use of colorful metaphors, images (even bizarre ones), and other nonliteral devices in Amos and elsewhere. It also suggests that plebian attempts to read prophecy in an overly literal manner are often the products of category mistakes. One can not fault a prophet for not being literal if the intent and nature of his discourse was metaphorical. On the other hand, metaphorical images, such as a basket of summer fruit, are often meant to refer to actual historical conditions or circumstances, whether already existing or impending ones. Rhetorical questions using metaphorical expressions often point to lurking historical dangers of an analogous kind. The situation, then, is complex, and the poetic form of oracles adds to the complexity of the situation.[11]

There are some important clues in Amos to the way prophecy came about. For example, in 3:1 Amos refers to what God has already spoken against Israel. The pronouncement of doom has already been made by Yahweh in the heavenly council, and the prophet has overheard it. It is the job of the prophet to announce to Israel what God has already decided and said. It is, in various ways, already a fait accompli. The prophet, then, is not simply the voice of God speaking to Israel on the spot but, rather, the conveyor or announcer of what God has already said and determined elsewhere. In this regard, the later, written form of these oracles does not differ from such an announcement in that it is an expression after the original utterance of the oracle.

In 3:3–8 there is a series of rhetorical questions, all of which suggest a situation of peril for some vulnerable creature. This augurs disaster for Israel, with Yahweh as the bringer of destruction. It is interesting that in v. 7 we are told

---

[10] The exceptions to this rule are Tyre, Edom, and Judah, and there does not seem to be any particular reason why.

[11] Sometimes the reader may be forgiven for finding Hebrew prophecy difficult to decipher, not so much because it is coded language but because of the deliberately general or even vague character of various utterances, which were capable of being interpreted or applied in different ways. But Hebrew prophecy was not alone in having these traits.

God does nothing without revealing what he has in mind to his servants the prophets. But why would God do that, unless the intent was to explain or make evident the theological character and importance of the coming events? Judgment must be seen to be judgment, not merely an unfortunate happenstance. Notice also that Amos refers to "God's secret," which must be revealed to be known. This suggests that the character of the history of God's people is not evident without prophetic interpretation of what is, or is to come. Even the prophet can not see judgment coming unless it is revealed to him. Here may be the precursor of the notion of apocalyptic secrets that the visionary must see and then be aided to interpret.

Amos 7 provides another intriguing glimpse into the prophetic experience. Here Yahweh shows Amos various possible scenarios—a locust plague, or a fire destroying the land of Israel—but here Amos intercedes and Yahweh relents. We are reminded of the earlier experiences of other of God's servants, such as Abraham or Moses. But on the third occasion Amos is showed a wall and a plumb line, with Yahweh measuring Israel for destruction, and there is no promise to relent. In each of these cases the prophet has seen something metaphorical in character (he is not just a hearer of God's word; he is a visionary), but only in one case does it augur something that actually transpires on the historical plane. The vision in vv. 7–9 is reinforced by a subsequent one about a basket of summer fruit at 8:1–3, which relies not on analogy but on a phonological form of wordplay (*qayts* can be understood to refer to summer fruit, but with the pronunciation *qets* it could be understood to be a reference to *et qets,* "the end"). Amos had both seen and heard something that suggested impending doom.

Not surprisingly, such pronouncements as these by Amos did not make him a popular person with the powers that be in Israel. In 7:10–15 this results in a famous confrontation between Amos and Amaziah, the priest of the shrine at Bethel, which is seen as the center of the house of Israel. Amaziah has understood Amos's utterances to entail both the violent death of King Jeroboam and Israel's going forth into exile. Notice that Amaziah recognizes Amos as a seer and calls him such *(hozeh).* Amos's much controverted reply at v. 14 finds him repudiating that he is or was either a *nabi* (prophet) or a *nabi's* son by trade and claiming to be, rather, a dresser of sycamore fig trees and a herdsman. But this utterance must be seen within its context.

Here the detailed analysis of H. W. Wolff is helpful. As Wolff points out, Amos has already said at 3:8 that when Yahweh speaks to someone, that person must prophesy, regardless of previous activity or profession. Thus, although the Hebrew does not indicate a particular tense for the nominal clauses and so, for example, the Greek OT (LXX; only Chrysostom and afterwards render it "I am") at this point translates, "I was neither a prophet nor . . . ," Amos's statement must be seen as an adequate response to the statement of Amaziah about Amos's present activities in Israel. Hence, the present-tense translation is likely correct. Wolff is surely right that there are no polemics here in regard to the terminology used for prophets. When Amos is called a seer or visionary, he, denying that he is a prophet, responds using the more generic term *nabi,* but he does not deny performing the activity of a *nabi—hinabeh*. The point, as Wolff correctly argues, is that Amos is distinguishing between the profession of prophet and the fact that anyone can be endowed and impelled by Yahweh to prophesy on a given occasion or for a specific, limited period of time. Amos was one such person: he had another profession, had never been a disciple of a prophet or a professional prophet, and yet had felt compelled to speak out.[12]

Amaziah has assumed that Amos is a professional prophet and has urged him to go practice his art and "earn his bread" back where he came from—in Judah (7:12). Amos's response is that he is not a professional prophet at all, simply a person God called on this occasion to convey God's word. The issue here, then, probably isn't about a contrast between the term *hozeh* and the term *nabi*, as if there were a critique of the latter term here. Amaziah is doing the critiquing here, and yet he probably does not use the term *hozeh* in a derogatory sense. "The problem is not in the designation or title [either by Amaziah or Amos], but in the characterization of the position. In effect, Amaziah accuses Amos of being a professional prophet, one who earns his living by his utterances."[13] The net effect of Amos's reply is that he distances himself from both professional prophets and perhaps also prophetic guilds, if the phrase "son of a prophet" refers to such a guild. "Amos reveals himself as a lone figure, one who is unclassifiable, but with a unitary focus and guided by a personal vision. His mandate came from God himself, who took him from following the flock—a cliché out of Israel's past but one that was packed with tradition and power. Israel's history was largely shaped by ex-shepherds"—particularly Moses and David.[14]

It follows from the above discussion that, in regard to prophets, there was always the potential of a wild card, a person who was neither a court prophet nor even a regular recognized prophetic figure of any other sort but who nonetheless, for some limited duration of time, was impelled to prophesy. The "charismatic" nature of this activity made it impossible for institutional figures such as priests or kings to control entirely the prophetic office.

There was thus a source of power and authority in the ancient Near East that was not entirely within the control of existing ruling figures, and understandably this often made them nervous or angry or even violent. Part-time prophetic figures such as Amos were often on the periphery of society and its institutions but were summoned to the center to make one or more proclamations. This did not make them popular figures, and doubtless the conjecture is correct that the utterances of Amos were preserved only in the south, not at the venue where they were actually uttered, for obvious reasons. If it is true that Amos's utterances were the first to be collected into a prophetic book (as opposed to prophetic utterances that made up a minority of some other kind of

---

[12] See H. W. Wolff, *Joel and Amos* (Philadelphia: Fortress, 1977), 312–14.

[13] F. I. Andersen and D. N. Freedman, *Amos* (New York: Doubleday, 1989), 788.

[14] Ibid., 790.

literature, such as historical narrative), then already at the beginning of the collection and codification of such material the secondary nature of such a process is evident. There would necessarily have been a time lapse between when Amos uttered these prophecies and when they were written down and collected in the south.

Furthermore, the written collection would have a social function distinctly different from that of the original oral proclamations. The latter were intended to warn Israel about coming disaster in the form of the "Day of the Lord," a temporal incursion of divine judgment. That day was apparently anticipated as something positive, such as a day of rescue from enemies, and Amos had to disabuse his audience of this notion. But when the prophecies were written down, at whatever remove from the time of the original utterances,[15] and placed into a book to be read by Judahites, they lost their power of immediacy or direct address but could still serve as a salutary warning to go and do otherwise lest a similar fate befall the south. They could also serve several other purposes, some of them political, for these oracles might well bolster a case by southern rulers against their northern neighbors in regard to their infidelity to Yahweh. These points must be borne in mind as the period of the writing prophets is investigated.

B. The Rock from Which Micah Was Hewn.   Here, as elsewhere in this study, the major concern is not so much with the content of this or that oracle as with the nature of the prophetic phenomenon—the experience, the expression, the tradition, and the corpus. There is also concern with the social function of prophets and their oracles, and we are especially helped along the way by self-reflective comments that indicate something about the process of inspiration or expression, or the reception and preservation of oracles.

Micah, on any showing, is a near contemporary of Amos. Presumably, if Mic 1:10–16 is any guide, he prophesied just a little later and longer than Amos, presumably until at least 701 BC, when Sennacherib marched on Jerusalem. There is confirmation from Jer 26:18 that Micah did indeed prophesy the fall of Jerusalem, during the reign of Hezekiah (715–687 BC). The strong similarity betweeen Amos 8:5–6 and Mic 6:10–11 may suggest familiarity by Micah with the oracles of that slightly earlier seer. It is also possible that Micah knows something of the oracles of Isaiah, or vice versa (compare Isa 2:2–4 with Mic 4:1–5). It would appear that in Micah can be seen the real beginnings of a viable prophetic tradition in which later prophets use motifs, ideas, and even the words of earlier prophets to good effect as authoritative sources. This notion should be

---

[15] Amos 1:1 indicates that Amos made these pronouncements "two years before the earthquake," possibly that of ca. 760 BC. This remark is also significant because it indicates a lapse of a number of some years between the time Amos 1:1 was written and the time Amos had prophesied. We can not tell how much editing went on in the interim, but we can say that at least the arrangement of the material suggests something other than a bare transcript in chronological order of what Amos originally said.

evaluated by a comparison with one of the great prophetic messages found in the writing prophets:

Amos 5:21–24	Mic 6:6–8	Hos 6:5–6
I hate, I despise your festivals, and I take no delight in your solemn assemblies. Even though you offer me your burnt offerings and grain offerings, I will not accept them; and the offerings of well-being of your fatted animals I will not look upon. Take away from me the noise of your songs; I will not listen to the melody of your harps. But let justice roll down like waters, and righteousness like an ever-flowing stream.	With what shall I come before the LORD, and bow myself before God on high? Shall I come before him with burnt offerings, with calves a year old? Will the LORD be pleased with thousands of rams, with ten thousands of rivers of oil? . . . He has told you, O mortal, what is good; and what does the LORD require of you but to do justice, and to love kindness, and to walk humbly with your God?	Therefore I have hewn them by the prophets, I have killed them by the words of my mouth, and my judgment goes forth as the light. For I desire steadfast love and not sacrifice, the knowledge of God rather than burnt offerings.

Here is the basic expression of what was to be called the ethical monotheism of the writing prophets. Although it may seem obvious to those in the Judeo-Christian tradition that there should be a connection between one's ethical behavior and one's worship practices, this was not always—perhaps not often—understood in antiquity. In Greco-Roman religion, for example, appeasing the gods was seen primarily as a matter of rituals perfectly performed, not a matter of revision of one's character or one's behavior outside worship. The Jewish and Christian prophetic traditions often stand out in this regard. The point that needs to be stressed here is that Yahweh expects his own character to be reflected in the lives of his people, and the divine character involves justice, righteousness, covenant loyalty, kindness, mercy.

Obviously the texts cited above are not identical, but the criticism especially of burnt offerings in all three is clear, as is the offering of the alternative that God truly desires, whether it is characterized as justice or kindness or covenant love and loyalty. The incongruity between how God's people worship and how they live is so great that the hypocrisy of even costly worship through sacrifices of burnt offerings is apparent. Sometimes this tradition has been seen as antisacramental per se, but this is to overlook the comparative character of the tradition. Only in the Hosea version of the tradition may there be something of an antisacramental overtone. The issue here is not formal versus informal worship but, rather, the positive doing of good by humans, which truly reflects God's own character, as opposed to the use of worship as some sort of protection against judgment by an unrepentant and unrighteous people. God's demands for righteous character can not be bought off by expensive sacrifices meant to atone for past sins.

It seems clear that the closer one gets to the exile, the wider the gap between life and lips, between worship and service, and thus the function of the prophet becomes increasingly to utter oracles of impending doom, to act as a miner cutting stony hearts down to size. But was it possible for preexilic prophets who were authentic and not false prophets to utter oracles of future salvation as well? Was there not a longing for a better day even during the preexilic period?

This question has often been answered in the negative, in part because it has been assumed that prophets did not speak—or almost never—of the more remote future but only of what was impending. It is also sometimes assumed that before the exile only false prophets offered oracles of salvation. For example, the detailed and helpful formal analysis by C. Westermann basically assumes such a division, so that prophets of salvation were a later exilic and postexilic phenomenon if they were true prophets.[16] The problem with this assessment is severalfold: (1) There were no original pure types of oracles, from a formal point of view, such that judgment and mercy or justice and salvation could never be spoken of in the same oracle or by the same prophet. True enough, some oracles could be almost entirely judgment oracles or almost entirely salvation oracles, but there could also be oracles of a mixed type. Earlier in this study, this mixed phenomenon has been seen to be the case as early as the oracles from Mari, where mostly positive oracles could also include words of warning about possible disaster, and there is no reason to assume this would not also occasionally be the case in preexilic Israel as well.[17] (2) If indeed it is correct to suggest, on the basis of the covenant lawsuit *(rib)* pattern, that prophets were, to some extent, prosecutors of the covenant law, then it is in order to point out that there were both oath curses and blessings attached to the end of such ancient Near Eastern covenants. There is no reason why one or more oracles could not expound on one or both of these aspects of the covenant in the same proclamation. (3) There was already in the late monarchial preexilic period such a sense of the gap between the ideal and reality in terms of rulers that sociologically one should not be surprised to find the beginnings of a hope for a more trustworthy and Torah-true ruler on the lips of some of the preexilic prophets who spoke during these dark and ominous days.

This seems to be found in the oracles in Mic 3:5–5:6, where a definite contrast is set up between the impending doom that is on the near horizon and the hope for a more ideal ruler who can only come after judgment. God's people have gone too far wrong to avoid all judgment; on the other hand, Yahweh still wishes to preserve at least a remnant and later revive his people. The light can only come at the end of a long dark tunnel, but the prophet sees both coming.

Koch astutely observes, "A good many of the prophecies of salvation [in Micah] sound so fresh and individual that it is hard to put them down to the

---

[16] See, e.g., C. Westermann, *Prophetic Oracles of Salvation in the Old Testament* (Louisville: Westminster, 1991), 7ff.

[17] See pp. 13–20 above.

generalizing trend of later centuries. It is also surprising that in a passage like 7.14–17 Yahweh is associated solely with North Israelite landscapes like Carmel, Bashan, and Gilead."[18] Furthermore, as Koch adds, the ability to perceive impending doom on the part of Micah through Yahweh's withdrawal of presence and protection carries with it the ability to perceive presence and ongoing concern, and thus one must ask "how, then, the partial divine withdrawal could be perceived *with any certainty* unless the spokesman of doom, Micah, had also become the spokesman of God's magnanimity. But this in its turn means attributing some prospects of salvation to Micah."[19] Thus he includes Mic 5:1–6 among the authentic oracles of this prophet. At the very least, among the salvation sayings in this book, this is the one that most clearly has oracular form.[20] A brief examination of it is in order.

Precisely in the context of making clear that judgment will soon fall on God's people comes a dramatic salvation oracle about a leader who comes from a particular clan of Judah—Bethlehem Ephrathah—after judgment has fallen. It is not said at what remove from the time of judgment this saving figure will appear, but one is told that God will give his people up to the invaders until the time when this savior figure is born (v. 2). Salvation arises only beyond judgment, a not uncommon theme in the prophets. The leader figure is presented as a shepherd figure who will rule on the basis of Yahweh's power and in the majesty of Yahweh's name. In other words, the leader is radically dependent on his God, and it is to Yahweh that the credit and glory accrue. Dwelling safely in the land is what is promised because this ruler will be great to the ends of the earth.

Some of the details of 5:1–5 bear a closer look. The clan of Bethlehem is called not merely small but insignificant (cf. Ps 68:27).[21] Elsewhere Ephrathah and Bethlehem seem to be closely associated if not identified (Ruth 1:2; 4:11; cf. Gen 35:18; 48:7 [Ephrath]). What is crucial about this designation is that this is the place of David's birth, and so this coming ruler is cast as a Davidic figure, like David a shepherd of his people. But J. L. Mays is likely right when he stresses that this text provides something of a qualification of the earlier oracle of Nathan (2 Sam 7),[22] for here the idea of a succession is ignored and the concept of a new beginning is enunciated, but paradoxically this beginning is one that goes back to the very starting point, so that this ruler's origins are from of old, or from ancient days.[23] This is possibly a reference to the first Adam in the garden of Eden,[24] but in view of the time of David being called "ancient days" in Amos

---

[18] Koch, *The Prophets*, 1:102–3.

[19] Ibid., 1:103, italics mine.

[20] See ibid., 1:102.

[21] Note the difference from what we find in Matt. 2:6—"not the least among the clans."

[22] On this see pp. 69–75 above.

[23] J. L. Mays, *Micah* (Philadelphia: Westminster, 1976), 115.

[24] See R. L. Smith, *Micah-Malachi* (Waco: Word, 1984), 44.

9:11 and in view of the other possible dependencies of Micah on Amos, this is probably what is meant here. At least a part of Mic 5:3 has been seen as a later accretion referring to return from exile, and this may be so,[25] but if Micah was capable of foreseeing not only judgment but salvation beyond judgment, in view of the regular policies of deportation of leaders by the Assyrians and later the Babylonians, it is not impossible Micah foresaw some coming back from exile at the time when the ruler figure was to be born.

Verse 4 is redolent with the language of the Psalms about the ideal king "standing against all the changes and challenges of history (Ps 72.5)."[26] Since this shepherd ruler will be ruling by God's power and not by his own, "his reign will be an expression, not a replacement of YHWH's kingship."[27] Peace and security will be provided by this ruler, his greatness being such that none dare challenge him. Notice that this ruler is never called king, for the prophet upholds the theocratic ideal that God is the one who is truly ruling.

If we ask why the prophet is so general in this pronouncement, with only the reference to Bethlehem providing some specificity (and even then this is likely a generic reference to the Davidic line), Koch suggests,

> It is not the function of a prophet to point the details of this new turn of events, for he is talking to listeners who will no longer be affected by it, since by then they themselves will have perished. But there is certainly a point in establishing assertively ("but you," adversative), parallel to the statements about the downfall, that things will not come to an end either for God or for his chosen people. The prophet himself may draw the assurance from this that with the *dabar* (word) he is proclaiming he is not merely evoking a chaos that will swallow everything up, even if he cannot cherish any further hope for his own individual salvation.[28]

The lack of specificity in what was to be later called messianic oracles also had another effect. It opened the door for many to claim to fulfill such promises or prophecies.

One final passage from Micah bears some scrutiny because of what it reveals about the conception of prophets at this time—Mic 3:5–8. There is a clear contrast between the professional prophets or central prophets, who continue to proclaim peace and claim sustenance from those to whom they dispense oracles, and Micah himself. Notice that it is not said that they never had visions from God but that there would be no more visions given to them because of their false pronouncements. They will be disgraced or shamed because they have no late word from God for his people. Also, it is suggested in v. 6 that visions tend to come at night. There is also a paralleling, but yet a distinguishing, in v. 7 between seers on the one hand and diviners on the other.[29]

---

[25] See Mays, *Micah,* 113.

[26] Ibid., 117.

[27] Ibid.

[28] Koch, *The Prophets,* 1:105.

[29] On this distinction, see pp. 3–5 above.

In contrast to all these prophets of peace stands Micah, for whom there is no lack of inspiration and power. He is filled with God's spirit, power, and righteousness to proclaim to Jacob his sins. Inspiration and power come to those who faithfully proclaim the words given them. It is important to recognize that during this period, as is true both before and after, it was common for prophets to have visions and to be called either seers or *nebi'im*. There can be no hard and fast distinction between preexilic and exilic or postexilic prophets on this score. Possibly it is the *nature* of the visions, which change during and after the exile and lead to the rise of apocalyptic, but we get ahead of ourselves. We must turn at this point to consider the two towering prophetic figures who take us up to the exilic period—Isaiah and Jeremiah.

II. ISAIAH—THE MAN OF PURIFIED LIPS

Despite the vicissitudes of the discussion about the parsing of the book of Isaiah, there is little dispute among scholars that there was a historical prophet named Isaiah whose oral proclamations were the catalyst for the composition of this book. Nor is there any significant debate that this Isaiah's message mainly was addressed to Judahites and was relevant for Jerusalem and Judah (Isa 1:1; 2:1). Two of the major narrative sections of the book depict Isaiah as having considerable authority in the royal house and in political affairs (6:1–8:23; 36:1–39:8). Isaiah, then, may be seen as, in various respects, like Nathan, but the opposite of Amos. He is a central prophet from the south prophesying to his own people and rulers. The indications are that, also unlike Amos, Isaiah had a remarkably long career as a prophet, offering oracles during the reigns of Kings Uzziah (when Amos and Hosea also prophesied), Jotham, Ahaz, and Hezekiah, or from about 740 BC to just after the turn of the next century (700 BC), and perhaps even longer.

Much depends on how one views the so-called call narrative in Isa 6. On the one hand, if this is indeed a call narrative, why is it placed in the sixth chapter of Isaiah? The view is now fairly common among scholars that "Chap. 6 is not an inaugural call, but a commission for a specific task from the heavenly council, given in the year King Uzziah died."[30] If this is correct, then Isaiah may well have prophesied during the reign of Uzziah, but it was that transitional time in the year of Uzziah's death, when worries about the future of a nation would be at a peak, that Isaiah received this particular revelation.

The revelation he received on this occasion suggests a variety of things. First, it suggests that the prophet sees a continuity between the visible and invisible realms, such that the temple on earth was at least the forecourt of the heavenly dwelling place. Second, Isaiah has a vision not only of God's great holiness but of his own uncleanness and sinfulness, embedded as he is in a people of un-

---

[30] See C. R. Seitz, "Isaiah, Book of (First Isaiah)," *ABD* 3:472–88, here 479; cf. Koch, *The Prophets,* 1:108–11.

clean lips and lives. But there was also a cathartic component to this experience—Isaiah was cleansed of his sin, and so made a suitable vessel to undertake a new commission of proclaiming an oracle of judgment on a wayward people. Indeed, one could even say that Isaiah becomes a vehicle through which Israel's heart is hardened, or at least was fortified in its existing hardness. As Koch points out, this is not an event that takes place before time began; it has nothing to do with the later doctrine of double predestination.[31] The judgment is aimed at the whole people of God and is an act initiated and fulfilled in history. The existence of further and subsequent oracles that are not all doom and gloom (e.g., in chs. 7–11) suggests that this temporal judgment is not to be seen as God's last word to or about even this generation of Israelites.

It must be kept steadily in view that the oracles we find in chs. 1–39, or at least the majority of them, presuppose the ongoing historical difficulties caused by the aggressive policies of Assyrian rulers in the region. Seitz offers the following timetable:

(1) Tiglath-pileser—744 –727 BC
(2) Syro-Ephraimite debacle—734–732 BC
(3) Shalmaneser V—726–722 BC
(4) Sargon II—721–705 BC
(5) Fall of Israel (northern kingdom)—721 BC
(6) Sennacherib—704–681 BC
(7) Assyrian assault on Judah—701

Isaiah prophesied in perilous times, and his prophecies had everything to do with the particular predicaments his people now found themselves in, in both their political and their religious aspects. Notice that, from the outset, the entire book is categorized as a book of vision, containing things that Isaiah had seen *(hozeh)*. Roughly speaking, this book of visions is assembled in chronological order in chs. 1–39, such that chs. 1–5 seem to deal with Uzziah's reign, chs. 6–8 with Ahaz's reign, and chs. 9–14 with Ahaz's reign, while chs. 20–22 deal with Hezekiah's reign, and chs. 36–39 with the end of this period or its sequel.[32] One should be aware, then, that there seem to have been considerable periods of silence in Isaiah's life, along with periods of pronouncements. Isaiah embodies most of the major elements we have come to associate with such prophetic figures—a receiver of revelations and visions, a proclaimer of oracles, an enacter of signs and symbolic messages, and, like Nathan, another central prophet, even an offerer of occasional parables. It is time to examine more carefully a sampling of the material in this book.

Isaiah 5:1–7 is the famous song or parable of the vineyard. This text falls in a section of the book (chs. 1–5) that seems introductory and general in character,

---

[31] Koch, *The Prophets,* 1:11–12.
[32] See the discussion by J. D. W. Watts, *Isaiah 1–33* (Waco: Word, 1985), 5–8.

as opposed to the more specific oracles found in chs. 7–12.[33] They deal with broad or underlying issues and causes, behaviors and consequences, that explain, in part, the character of the message Isaiah must proclaim. Chapter 5, in particular, is a poignant portrait of Israel's moral condition as the Assyrian threat begins to loom on the horizon. Here, as in the parable of the ewe lamb by Nathan (2 Sam 12),[34] the hearers are set up to pronounce judgment on themselves.

Meshalim were metaphorical forms of speech that could make one or several points in an indirect manner. It needs to be recognized that the making of a hard and fast distinction between parable and allegory is a modern obsession, and in fact there was a sliding scale from stories having one major point to those having several points, involving several symbolic elements.[35] The parable in Isa 5 seems to have one major point—that Israel, as God's vineyard that God has planted, nurtured, and protected, has not produced the sort of fruit God expected of his people. But just as God has protected Israel, building a watchtower in the vineyard, now God would tear down the protective hedge around the vineyard, leaving it vulnerable to attack by outsiders. Verse 7 not only makes the parable's essential referent clear (vineyard = house of Israel); it also makes evident what fruit God had expected—righteousness and justice.

Although it is hardly evident in English translation, this "song" is in poetic form, with assonance, alliteration, and even some rhyme, for all three verbs in v. 3 end in -*ehu* and they are vocalized the same. This song is clearly not an oracle, at least in vv. 1–2, for they are not in the first person. Yet Yahweh speaks for himself in vv. 3–6, and then once again the prophet speaks in v. 7 in his own voice. What this masterful piece of verse shows is another way in which a prophet could use poetry to express God's word. Whether poetic oracle or poetic parable, it was still a way of conveying God's word. But equally important, we find here a clear association of poetry, song, and God speaking in direct speech (vv. 3–6). The prophets were not just poets or wordsmiths; they were also on occasion songsmiths or even parabolists. This warns us against too peremptorily ruling out forms of expression as non-prophetic simply because they have non-oracular elements or form. Chapter 5 also provides something of a warrant to examine other songs in the Judeo-Christian tradition to see if they might not also be prophecies after a fashion.[36]

If one looks a bit more closely at 5:1–7, it becomes clear just how prophetic this material is, not merely because it accurately foreshadows the coming downfall of Jerusalem and Judah but because it takes the form of a complaint of accusation in a court of justice handling family matters. The prophet is the prosecutor of the covenant lawsuit, or better said, both the prophet and Yahweh are. But there is yet more, for here the prophet appears to take on the role of the

---

[33] See J. Oswalt, *Isaiah 1–39* (Grand Rapids: Eerdmans, 1986), 151ff.

[34] See pp. 75–79 above.

[35] See my discussion of ancient parables in Witherington, *Jesus the Sage*, 147ff.

[36] See pp. 37–42 above and pp. 293–300 below.

bridegroom's friend and advocate who takes up the groom's cause. Some scholars have thought that Israel in the narrower sense is meant here, and so what is foreshadowed is the fall of Samaria in 721. This is possible, but unlikely in view not only of the prescript in 1:1 but also of the texts leading up to ch. 5 in which Jerusalem and Judah are criticized and called the house of Israel (cf. 1:2–9, where Israel and the daughter of Zion are equated, or 1:21–26, where Jerusalem as a city of unrighteousness is critiqued but its God is called the Mighty One of Israel). Isaiah directed his oracles to Judah and was concerned with her fate.

It is entirely possible to call Isaiah a sign prophet, not only because he undertook such signs as going about naked for three years (ch. 20) but also because he named his own children in symbolic fashion, foreshadowing the future of God's people. Sign acts are revelations of God's will or plan or purposes. As such, these signs should not be seen as either magic or merely acted parables but, rather, dramatic presentations of the truth—of the way things are or are about to be. As Hooker puts it:

> Drama, oracle, event and record are all . . . different modes of one reality. . . . Each of them is a manifestation of the underlying divine intention. Only if God's will changes—perhaps because men and women repent—can the future be different. But that does not mean that the prophetic actions were mistaken. The oracle spoken in the name of the Lord, the prophetic drama and the vision, were all of them authentic because they represented a reality that had its being in God.[37]

To the extent that any such oracles or signs were intended as warnings given in the midst of a living relationship between God and Israel, if the relationship changed, if the warnings were heeded, then indeed God might not carry out his plan as he had previously designed to do. There is a difference between a false prophecy and one that does not come to pass because a warning was heeded or a relationship changed. All of this needs to be kept in mind when one examines the famous and much debated passage found in 7:10–17.

The context of this material is a dialogue between King Ahaz and Yahweh through the mediation of the prophet Isaiah. Ahaz is encouraged to ask for a sign, but he refuses to do so on the pretense of not wanting to put God to the test. Nonetheless, God determines to give him one anyway. It is, in fact, Ahaz who is being put to the test here, and he is found wanting in sufficient faith and trust in his God. The birth of a child to be called "God-with-us" is announced, and it is stated that before the child comes of an age where he is morally discerning, the two lands or powers (in this case likely Samaria and Damascus; cf. 8:4) that Ahaz has been fretting about will already be desolate. J. Oswalt has suggested that perhaps this passage is the more poetic form of an oracle that has its prosaic counterpart in 8:1–4. If this is correct, then Maher-shalal-hash-baz is indeed Immanuel and both refer to Isaiah's own child, who was apparently born not long after these utterances and lived to see the demise of the aforementioned

---

[37] Hooker, *Signs of a Prophet*, 4.

cities at the hands of Assyria.[38] But it is also possible—and this was a more frequent interpretation in antiquity as well as today—that the reference in ch. 7 is
to Hezekiah, and in various ways this makes better sense of 7:14.[39] In any case,
the context of these oracles makes evident that Isaiah does not have in mind
some events in the distant future but, rather, those which would affect and could
be a sign for King Ahaz.

Several other key features of the Immanuel oracle deserve comment. Verse
14 indicates that an *almah* will conceive. This term does not have the specificity
of the Hebrew term *betulah,* nor the generality of the term *ishsa,* which simply
means "woman." The term *betulah* clearly focuses on the virginity of the
woman, while *almah* likely includes this concept whenever the term is used in a
positive context.[40] Clearly it refers to a nubile woman who would be assumed to
be a virgin unless otherwise specified, for the term is not used of married women
in the OT. This leads to the question, Was Isaiah not married when this oracle
was given, but was married when the one in 8:1–4 was given? This seems unlikely
in view of 7:3. Isaiah 8:1–4 refers to Isaiah going to a prophetess and her conceiv-
ing a child. In view of 7:3, it seems unlikely that the reference in 7:14 is to Isaiah
seeking out an unmarried woman, marrying her, and impregnating her. This
means that we likely should distinguish between the oracle in ch. 7 and the one
in ch. 8. In any case, the children of both Isaiah and Ahaz (?) are made to bear
symbolic names—"God with us" in the latter case, and "a remnant shall return"
and also "the spoil speeds, the prey hastes" in the case of Isaiah's offspring.[41]

Notice in 8:16 the command from Isaiah to his own disciples to seal up the
oracular testimony and teaching and thereby not pass it on. The reference to Isaiah's disciples is revealing and indicates a context in which his oracles may have
been written down, collected, preserved and eventually passed on to future generations. This text provides prima facia evidence for a pedagogical context in
which prophetic traditions would be passed on and prophetic books might be
created, for it is the disciples in whom the testimony is to be sealed.

Equally interesting is the contrast with what is mentioned at 8:19. If
prophecy is not available, or even if it is, an unfaithful people will not wait on
Yahweh to speak (as does Isaiah, v. 17) but will turn to alternate sources of information about the future—necromancy, the consulting of the spirits of the departed human beings who dwell in Sheol. Notice the way the communication of
such spirits is characterized—chirping or muttering, as opposed to the plain and
clear speech of Yahweh. It apparently was a rather widespread belief that the

---

[38] See Oswalt, *Isaiah 1–39,* 213–14.

[39] See the helpful discussion by D. Schibler, "Messianism and Messianic Prophecy
in Isaiah 1–12 and 28–33," in *The Lord's Anointed* (ed. P. E. Satterthwaite et al.; Carlisle:
Paternoster, 1995), 87–104.

[40] See B. Witherington, "Birth of Jesus," *DJG,* 63–64.

[41] The reference to children in 8:18 favors the suggestion that two different children
are in view in chs. 7 and 8.

dead spoke in birdlike and whispered voices.[42] Here the prophet has in mind a clear distinction between such consultations and listening to oracles conveyed through a prophet. Once again divining and prophecy are seen as distinct and distinguishable although they purport to convey similar sorts of information, and one means is seen as more effective and clearer than the other. First Samuel 28:7–20 reveals that such beliefs about the dead, as well as about prophecy and divination, persisted throughout this era, whether we are speaking of 1100 BC or 700 BC.[43]

Whatever may be said about the oracles in Isa 7 and 8, when one reaches those in chs. 9 and 11, it is clear that we are not simply dealing with a description either of an extant historical person of Isaiah's day or one likely to have appeared in that period. The former oracle speaks of a time of endless peace for God's people and a king with power and influence far exceeding even those of David or Solomon. Even allowing for the hyperbole involved in poetic license and even if one suggests that the titles in 9:6 are to be seen as throne names rather than actual character descriptions, there is clearly a good deal of idealization here. The same came be said for the oracle in ch. 11, where in vv. 6–9 we hear not only of a return of an Edenic state to the world but a spread of the knowledge of God throughout the earth. The earlier oracles had a certain specificity to them and could be correlated with some historical circumstances of Isaiah's period, but these oracles are more general and reflect an idealization not characteristic of the other oracles. They raise the question whether prophets, perhaps when they despaired of current human monarchs, did not occasionally look forward into a more remote future in order to be able to hold out at least some future hope for a people still in distress and about to be faced with disaster. It appears to me that they did do so on occasion, though only rarely. It will be well to keep in mind a general rule of thumb about such oracles: the more proximate the subject matter, the more specific and sober the prediction; the more remote the subject, the more general and idealized the portrait.

When we examine ch. 9 in the Hebrew, we notice immediately the perfect tenses, which give the passage a timeless appearance.[44] They may be called prophetic perfects, indicating a certainty about things that have not yet transpired. This stands in stark contrast to what we find in 6:11–21, 7:8, or 8:7, where there is a clear time frame or time-bound character to the material. Chapter 9 has, however, this much specificity: the good news would bring honor to a region in

---

[42] Cf. "The Descent of Ishtar to the Netherworld," obv. 10 (*ANET,* 107); "The Gilgamesh Epic" 7.4.38–39 (*ANET,* 87); Virgil, *Aeneid* 6.492.3; Homer, *Iliad* 23.101; Horace, *Satires* 1.1.8.40. These texts remind us of several important points: (1) beliefs about foretelling the future and beliefs about the dead crossed many cultural lines and were passed through many generations; (2) the Greek and Roman cultures were the inheritors of many such ancient Near Eastern traditions. I owe all of these references to Oswalt, *Isaiah 1–39,* 237 and n. 31.

[43] See Watts, *Isaiah 1–33,* 126–27.

[44] See ibid., 135.

the north, Galilee of the nations, which had previously endured contempt (8:23). Whether the great light will break forth there first or whether this new ideal monarch will once more unite the region (which fell first to Assyria) with the south in a reestablishment of the true Davidic kingdom, this expression of hope is comprehensive in that it is for the whole land.

The picture here seems to be of a boy king who nonetheless will bring an end to all wars, a picture perhaps indebted to the Davidic saga about the exploits of the shepherd boy in his encounter with Goliath. That this ruler is a child seems important to Isaiah, for it comes up again in 11:6, 8. If one allows that the prophet is talking about the ideal ruler, using ideal terms, then it is not absolutely necessary to conclude that the lofty titles in 9:6 are simply throne names. For one thing, there is no historical evidence that such lofty names, implying divinity, were ever applied to Israelite kings in the monarchial period, whatever may have been the practice in Egypt or Assyria. Hebrews did not believe their king was more than a mortal, and the Davidic tradition in particular, both in the narrative material in Samuel and in the Psalms, stresses the kings' all too fallible human nature.

In the second place, this material does not seem to be a coronation ode, but rather a birth announcement. The figure in question deserves these titles from birth, not from the point of ascent to the throne (contrast Ps 2:7).[45] It is perhaps a measure of Isaiah's despair over all too mortal and fallible human kings such as Ahaz that he paints the ideal king in divine terms. This ruler is to be a wonder of a counselor (which is what the Hebrew says literally), impressing all with the depth of his wisdom. Although the phrase *el gibbor* has been the subject of no little debate as to its meaning, clearly elsewhere in the Bible the phrase means "mighty God," referring to the deity, not to a merely great hero (Isa 10:21; Deut 10:17; Jer 32:18), and it may well do so in 9:6 also. This shows the extent of the idealization here.

While many ancient kings claimed to be father of their people, Isaiah goes one step beyond this by speaking of an everlasting Father. One might write this off as royal boasting typical of the ancient Near East, except that we do not typically find these sorts of claims made in Israel.[46] This king will be a Prince of Peace, not only in the way he rules but because he will bring an end to wars. He will be a king to end all kings, for of his reign there will be no end. The warriors' garments will be fit only for burning when this ruler appears. This ruler will sit on the throne of David.

Watts has correctly pointed out that the material we find in chs. 9 and 11 is not in typical oracular form. There is no "thus says Yahweh" formula, and in fact the deity is usually spoken of in the third person. This material, then, might more accurately be called prophetic poetry about the future. Chapter 11, like ch. 9, focuses again on the Davidic character of the coming one. Characterized as a shoot from the stump of Jesse or a branch that comes forth from Jesse's root, this sug-

---

[45] See Oswalt, *Isaiah 1–39*, 246–48.
[46] Ibid.

gests not a vision of succession but of regeneration after a period when the Davidic tree has been cut down and left for dead. This is the vision of one who has experienced the truncated nature of the monarchy in his own day. The reviving agency is not heredity but, rather, the spirit of the Lord, which rests on this monarch and brings him wisdom and understanding. He will be the ultimate just ruler, so much so that nations will come seeking his counsel (11:10). Even nature will be pacified during his reign. Just as there were echoes of the Davidic saga in ch. 9, here one hears resonances from the story of Solomon, only amplified. The words of O. Kaiser give perspective on this passage: "Isaiah has clearly recognized that the ruling house of David in no sense fitted this picture. Consequently, God would once again make a complete new beginning."[47] A similar conclusion is reached by Schibler, following von Rad.[48] Yet the beginning is not without continuity with the past, since it is still a shoot of *Jesse* that is to come.

Our final exploration within First Isaiah will be of chs. 24–27, the so-called Little Apocalypse. This material is often thought to offer insights into the origins of apocalyptic literature, but this probably entails an overreading of the evidence.[49] There are no visions here of heaven, nor any mention of an angelic mediator, nor any clearly apocalyptic images or metaphors. It seems, rather, to be an example of prophecy that focuses on matters we would call eschatological, such as resurrection.

Whether one sees this as going back to Isaiah himself or as the product of one of his disciples,[50] it still clearly predates the apocalyptic material in Daniel and Zechariah and perhaps even predates the material in chs. 40–66. There is considerable debate about the unity of this material, but a goodly number of critical scholars are convinced that this passage should be treated as a whole.[51] Although the form of this material is poetic, it is not specifically oracular, with the exception of a few verses (e.g., 27:2–5). Nor does one find the formula "thus says Yahweh," which usually introduces oracles, or any indication that this is visionary material. As for its focus, it is entirely earthly (although it entails the sea beasts as well, 27:1), dealing with a catastrophic judgment and with some restoration of God's people thereafter. The expansive scope of both judgment and redemption warrants it being called eschatological in character, but not apocalyptic by any normal definition of the term, whether one thinks of the form or features or even the content of this segment of the Isaianic corpus.

The picture of complete devastation when God comes to judge is clear enough in ch. 24. There will be nowhere to run and nowhere to hide from the

---

[47] O. Kaiser, *Isaiah 1–12* (Philadelphia: Westminster, 1972), 160.

[48] See Schibler, "Messianism and Messianic Prophecy," 102; cf. von Rad, *Old Testament Theology,* 2:170.

[49] See W. R. Millar, "Isaiah 24–27 (Little Apocalypse)," *ABD* 3:488–90; and cf. P. D. Hanson, *The Dawn of Apocalyptic* (Philadelphia: Fortress, 1979).

[50] Especially ch. 27 has been seen as exilic or even postexilic in character, promising, as it does, restoration from Assyrian exile.

[51] See, e.g., Lindblom, Anderson, Ringgren, Redditt, and Watts.

fury. There may be a hint at vv. 21–23 that not just the kings of the earth but also the wicked heavenly hosts will be judged, so complete and cosmic is the scope of this judgment. But they are not judged immediately. They are placed in a dungeon of sorts and await sentencing. These hosts must submit in due course to the Lord of Hosts, who will reign in glory from Mount Zion. More will be said about these enigmatic but influential few verses later in this study.[52]

Here it is important to point out that it is possible to read the phrase "the host in the heights," as Watts does, as "the army in the highlands," in which case the reference is to a mundane force, not a cosmic one that is being judged.[53] It must be said, however, that this is not how later Judeo-Christian interpreters within the biblical era understood the text (cf., e.g., Jude 6 or 2 Pet 2:4). But elsewhere even in the OT, this phrase is used for either stars (Jer 33:22; Neh 9:6) or for pagan gods (2 Chron 33:5) and so not for earthly forces.[54] This train of thought is further reinforced if with Oswalt we see the reference in Isa 24:23 to the Silver One and the Hot One as alluding to the moon and the sun, both of which were seen as deities in various areas of the ancient Near East (cf., e.g., the god Sin).[55] The important point to make about this text, even if we interpret these verses to be about the judging of angelic beings, is that this in itself does not make these chapters apocalyptic in character. Discussions of angels and their role in the drama of redemptive judgment can be found both within and outside apocalyptic literature. The same can be said about the theme of catastrophic judgment followed by restoration or redemption.

Isaiah 25 speaks, among other things, about a feast set up by God on Zion for all peoples. This feast is possible because of Yahweh's universal rule from Zion as a result of his having judged the earth and eliminated the opposition or resistance. But who or what is the real enemy here? It is said in v. 7 that God will swallow up the shroud that engulfs all people, the shadow that overshadows all, which seems to be further defined in v. 8a as death itself. Perhaps one may see the reference to "the face of the shroud" as a reference to a burial shroud or a mourning garment.[56] God will remove the disgrace of a people and wipe tears from every face. The feast, then, would seem to be a celebration of God's victory over death and disgrace—the forces that produce tragedy and tears in human lives—which is of a piece with a rendering of 26:19 as, "Your dead will live! My corpses will rise!"[57] The means of victory over death is resurrection of the dead. But again this victory celebration on Zion is for all peoples, not just for Israel. God will find a way to stop the cycle of violence and death by overcoming it with a permanent dispensation of life. This victory is necessary if God is also to abolish disgrace and grief, since "as long as people die, there can be no end to

---

[52] See pp. x–xii above and pp. 226–29 below.

[53] See Watts, *Isaiah 1–33*, 325.

[54] See O. Kaiser, *Isaiah 13–39* (Philadelphia: Westminster, 1972), 192–93.

[55] Oswalt, *Isaiah 1–39*, 455.

[56] See ibid., 457.

[57] See Watts, *Isaiah 1–33*, 337–39.

mourning and suffering upon this earth."[58] It is probably also correct to conclude that the author has in mind the shame of God's people from having been
subject to being conquered and deported. Once God has his victory over the
alien powers that have subjugated God's people and God rules from Zion in full
power, it will most certainly be time to celebrate.

Kaiser is likely correct that 25:6–8 owes something to the tradition of the
pilgrimage of the nations to Zion for a festival, bringing with them gifts and services (Ps 96:7f.; Isa 45:14, 23; 60:3ff.; 61:5–6; 66:12). This central idea in the passage will indeed appear in a later apocalyptic context in Zech 14:16ff. The text
teaches that God cares enough to provide the very best sort of feast with the best
food and wine. Oswalt is probably right to suggest that the author is drawing on
the ancient Near Eastern imagery of the inaugural banquet where the newly
crowned and ruling king sets the tone for his dominion by holding a feast for all
and bestowing benefits (cf. 1 Sam 11:15; 1 Kgs 1:9–25).[59] It is not surprising that
later Christian reflection on this passage saw in it a reference to the conquering
of death by means of the resurrection of Jesus on Zion and the victory celebration that was appropriate thereafter. But the author has in mind the time when
God's will shall be fully done on earth as it is in heaven, not just in the life of one
individual, such as Jesus, but in the world as a whole.

But it is reiterated in Isa 26 that this great victory feast and indeed resurrection only come after death, destruction, and judgment. Verse 21 is quite explicit in its warning for God's people to duck for cover when God comes forth
from his place to punish the earth's inhabitants for their wickedness. Even on
God's people is placed a severe chastening (v. 16), causing them to cry out in
prayer, and God responds to the cry with the promise "Your dead shall live, their
corpses [or, my corpse] shall rise. O dwellers in the dust, awake and sing for joy!
For your dew is a radiant dew, and the earth will give birth to those long dead"
(v. 19). This verse is, in some regards, a reiteration of what was announced at the
banquet in 25:7–8. "It is significant that the dead are recognized as belonging to
Israel *and* to Yahweh."[60] Dew is the key to life in Israel; in particular, during the
long dry seasons it keeps vegetation alive. It is important to see in 26:19 a response of God to the praying community of faith (vv. 16ff.). The common understanding of the underworld in the ancient Near East was not merely that the
shades of the dead dwelt in the ground but that the underworld was a dusty and
shadowy place where the conditions of the grave or tomb prevailed (cf. Job
21:26; Ps 22:16). This is clearly illustrated in the poem called "The Descent of
Ishtar to the Netherworld," which speaks of going down to the dark house
"wherein the entrants are bereft of li[ght]. Where dust is their fare and clay their
food . . . (and where) over door and bolt is spread dust."[61]

---

[58] Kaiser, *Isaiah 13–39*, 201.

[59] Oswalt, *Isaiah 1–39*, 463.

[60] Watts, *Isaiah 1–33*, 342.

[61] Excerpts from "The Descent of Ishtar to the Netherworld," lines 4–11 (*ANET*,
107). See the discussion by Oswalt, *Isaiah 1–39*, 487.

Kaiser, like many other scholars, concludes that since there is a clear reference to resurrection in 25:8 and 26:19, these verses must necessarily be later interpolations into the Isaianic corpus. They, along with Dan 12 and perhaps Eccl 3:19ff., provide the only clear references to resurrection of individual persons in the OT.[62] But there is no textual or literary reason to see these verses as later insertions. The belief in resurrection began at some point in the history of God's people, and there is no reason that it could not have been something they turned to in the wake of the devastation the Assyrians brought on various peoples and various parts of the Holy Land. They were certainly some of the most ruthless warriors of antiquity, leaving long trails of the dead in their wake as they marched to the sea from Mesopotamia.

Isaiah 27 concludes this cycle of material, and it is an appropriate place for us to draw to a close this discussion of the Isaianic corpus, returning as it does to the theme of God's vineyard, which was discussed earlier in our treatment of ch. 5. If indeed this material goes back to either Isaiah or his disciples, this chapter suggests that the material is likely written from exile or with knowledge of exile, for v. 13 speaks of a great trumpet being blown on that day and "those lost in the land of Assyria and those who were driven out to the land of Egypt will come and worship the Lord on the holy mountain at Jerusalem."[63]

This chapter begins with a reference to a widespread ancient Near Eastern myth—the story of a high god and his struggle with a sea/chaos monster. The idea is found not only in the Babylonian creation story about Tiamat but also in the Ugaritic epic about the defeat of Lotan, as well as in Hittite literature.[64] For our purposes, it is important to indicate that Leviathan is a symbol of evil and chaos that must be subdued, but the tendency in Hebrew literature is to demythologize such images by linking them to historical events, in this case the future final day of reckoning on earth. What needs to be said about this image is that it predates any apocalyptic literature, Israelite or otherwise. It is true that it is reused in apocalyptic contexts (*T. Ash.* 7:3; *Pss. Sol.* 2:25; Rev 20:2), but it also appears in nonapocalyptic contexts (Ps 106:26; Job 40:25). As Kaiser suggests, there is no attempt here to suggest that the sea monster represents a particular evil empire or empires; rather, this verse would seem to be about the conquering of evil and chaos, which lie behind and induce human misery and suffering.[65]

The important point to note about 27:2–6 is the either-or character of the remarks. If God's vineyard produces thorns, he will burn it up, but there is an alternative—"or else let it cling to me for protection, let it make peace with me." The relationally dependent character of such utterances is clear. There is nothing inevitable or foreordained about God's judgment of his people. It is an action taken on the basis of how Israel relates to its God. Exile is seen as a

---

[62] See Kaiser, *Isaiah 13–39*, 218ff.

[63] It is possible to translate here "the dead of the land of Assyria," but the next clause makes unlikely that this is a reference to non-Israelites.

[64] See e.g., *ANET*, 66–68; 125–26.

[65] See Kaiser, *Isaiah 1–33*, 222

means of punishing infidelity to Yahweh, but God's judgment of his people is not to be simply equated with God's judgment of others with whom God has no covenant.

If this interpretation is correct, then one need not see this passage as a complete antithesis to ch. 5, where judgment on an unfruitful vineyard is proclaimed. Kaiser is probably right to see the thorns or briars as within the vineyard and not an outside intrusion.[66] On the other hand, it is possible, though less likely, to see here the promise that God will protect his vineyard against the encroachment of thorns and thistles, just the opposite of ch. 5, where God tears the protective hedge down.[67]

In either case the relationally dependent nature of the pronouncement seems clear. Verse 9 especially reminds us that God indeed has judged and will judge his people but also that perhaps through exile there will be expiation for Jacob, and so in the end God will not treat them like any other nation. Before turning to another Hebrew prophet who knew something about judgment on Israel and the threat of exile, Jeremiah, it is apropos to take a glimpse at what was going on in prophetic literature of this period elsewhere in the ancient Near East—in particular, Assyria, which has been regularly mentioned in this discussion.

III. ASSYRIAN SEERS AND DIVINERS—COURTING THE KING'S FAVOR

There is now a large body of material from the time of the reigns of Esarhaddon (681–669 BC) and Assurbanipal (668–627 BC) that sheds light on prophecy and divination in this kingdom.[68] The material suggests a large group of diviners in the Assyrian court. Not surprisingly, much of the material that is extant about them suggests they focused on matters of national security and military policy. The god would be asked questions such as "Will M[ugal]lu, the Melidian, st[rive and plan]? Will he mobilize a powerful army against Mannuki . . . and the magnates and army of Assyria?"[69] The diviner may well consult the astrologist and provide the king with an answer such as "If Jupiter stands [behind the moon] there [will be] hostility in the land."[70] There were other experts, medical experts, who would be called upon to speak about what the omens said about matters of health, human fertility, and the like. One of the major social functions of such persons was to keep the king on the straight and narrow and

---

[66] Ibid., 224–25.

[67] See the discussion by Watts, *Isaiah 1–33*, 350; Oswalt, *Isaiah 1–39*, 494.

[68] This section is indebted to the work of L. Grabbe and of C. Vondergeest for guidance about which texts are of relevance to this discussion.

[69] I. Starr, *Queries to the Sungod: Divination and Politics in Sargonid Assyria* (SAA 4; Helsinki: Helsinki University Press, 1990), no. 5.

[70] Starr, *Archives X*, no. 84.

in the good graces of various gods. Omens warned that the king was going astray or was about to.[71]

Assyrian prophets can be distinguished from these other diviners in that the former have some sort of experience, such as a vision or audition or dream, that leads to a communication from a god that must be conveyed, typically, to the king. There are now tablets available containing prophecies, and other tablets containing what Esarhaddon or Assurbanipal had to say about prophets.[72] Most of the former sort of material is simply composed of quotations of oracles, leaving us with little data about the prophetic experience. The latter material is a little more illuminating in that we find that Esarhaddon relied on both omens and prophecies (clearly distinguished) to justify his coming and taking the throne vacated in 681 BC by the assassination of Sennacherib: "Favorable omens in the sky and on the earth came to me. Oracles of prophets, messages of the gods and goddess, were constantly sent to me and encouraged my heart."[73] We are reminded of the succession oracle given to David when we read the oracle given to Esarhaddon at his coronation ceremony: "But when you drink from this water, you will remember me and keep this covenant which I have made on behalf of Esarhaddon."[74] The similarities to 2 Sam 7 are even stronger when the goddess Ishtar reassures Esarhaddon, "I will give long days and everlasting years to Esarhaddon my king. . . . I am your great midwife; I am your excellent wet nurse. For long days and everlasting years I have established your throne under the great heavens. . . . I am mindful of you, I have loved you greatly."[75] Most of the oracles, however, are of the military sort, such as when the god says, "I will finish the land of Gomer like (I finished) Elam . . . I will break the thorn, I will pluck the bramble into a tuft of wool, I will turn the wasps into squash . . . I will carry you on my hip like a nurse, I will put you between my breasts (like) a pomegranate . . . As for you, have no fear, my calf, whom I (have) rear(ed)."[76] This is not unlike some of the oracles examined above from First Isaiah. There are no preserved oracles that are critical of the king, but there is indirect evidence that there must have been some. Hear what is said: "If you hear any evil, improper, ugly word which is not seemly nor good to Assurbanipal . . . from the mouth of the prophet, an ecstatic, an inquirer of oracles, or from the mouth of any human being at all, you

---

[71] See C. Vondergeest, "A Question of Loyalty: Prophets and Kings in Israel and Mesopotamia" (paper presented at Duke University, December 12, 1998). This material and much other of relevance for this discussion will appear in Vondergeest's forthcoming doctoral dissertation.

[72] See S. Parpola, *Assyrian Prophecies* (SAA 9; Helsinki: Helsinki University Press, 1997).

[73] M. Nissinen, *References to Prophecy in Neo-Assyrian Sources* (SAA 7; Helsinki: Helsinki University Press, 1998), 14.

[74] Parpola, *Assyrian Prophecies*, 3.4.

[75] Ibid., 1.6; cf. Isa 45:5, "I am Yahweh . . ."

[76] Parpola, *Assyrian Prophecies*, 7.

shall not conceal it but come and report it to Assurbanipal, the great crown prince designate, son of Esarhaddon, king of Assyria."[77]

It has been pointed out by Grabbe that, of the dozen or so prophetic figures named in the Assyrian tablets, over half are women; this may, however, be because the evidence available concerns the goddess Ishtar.[78] Also, all the oracles are directed to the king. Yet the similarities to the material already studied in this chapter are noteworthy in form, in some of the content, and in the distinction between diviners and prophets.

IV. JEREMIAH—GOING TO THE WELL ONE TOO MANY TIMES

The prophet most often associated with laments and prophecies of doom and gloom is Jeremiah. His dates correspond approximately with the last half-century of Judah's nationhood (640–587 BC), but he outlived the downfall of Jerusalem in 587 BC and apparently lived to old age in exile with other Jews in Egypt. Jeremiah knew about not only the devastation wrought by the Assyrians; he also saw the rise to power of Babylon and the havoc that empire wreaked on his land.

Jeremiah was born the son of Hilkiah, a priest at Anathoth, a village only a few miles north of Jerusalem. It is not clear from Jer 1:2, 4 whether Jeremiah was called in boyhood to be a prophet in 627 BC (the thirteenth year of Josiah and the year that the Assyrian ruler Assurbanipal died) or whether this was the year that Jeremiah was born. Jeremiah 1:5 seems to suggest that the reference in v. 2 is to the date of Jeremiah's birth, for he was called from the womb. In any case, the call is not fulfilled until later (v. 12).

It was after the discovery of the law book during the reign of Josiah in 622 BC that Jeremiah was authorized to begin his prophetic career. Somewhere along the way he had moved from Anathoth to Jerusalem and possibly had been trained and had become literate at a scribal school there.[79] W. Holladay may be right that the prophet was born when the reforms of Josiah were well along and that the move of Hilkiah and his family to Jerusalem came as a result of those reforms, which included the centralization of the cult.[80]

Wherever he may have learned his craft, Jeremiah is clearly one of the most skilled communicators and capable poets among all of Israel's prophets. Jeremiah trots out the whole arsenal of rhetorical devices and poetic effects, uses signs, and even embodies in his own life his message about impending suffering and judgment. It is clear from his own accounts and pronouncements that he is especially indebted to the traditions about Moses and Samuel in the way he conceives his prophetic call, roles, and activities. Being from a priestly family and

---

[77] Ibid., 33.

[78] Grabbe, *Priests, Prophets,* 91–92.

[79] On all this, see J. R. Lundbom, "Jeremiah," *ABD* 3:684–98.

[80] W. Holladay, *Jeremiah 1* (Philadelphia: Fortress, 1986), 1ff.

growing up not far from the priestly center where Samuel was called may, in part, explain some of this influence.

But another influence in the book of Jeremiah has led to all sorts of speculations about later Deuteronomistic editors, and indeed even composers, of a good deal of what we find in Jeremiah.[81] Holladay is probably right that these conjectures far outstrip the evidence and that there is another very plausible reason Deuteronomistic echoes are found in this book. Jeremiah grew up during the reign of Josiah, when Deuteronomistic reforms were being implemented. Holladay suggests that one of those reforms was the reciting of Deuteronomy at the Feast of Tabernacles, which transpired every seven years (thus in the fall of 622, 615, 608, 601, 594, and 587). Jeremiah's oracles may, in part, correspond to these, and in any case, as a supporter of what Josiah was doing, it is no surprise that his own oracles might take on a Deuteronomistic flavor.[82] It is even possible that Jeremiah saw himself as that latter-day prophet of which Moses spoke in Deut 18:15. But Jeremiah is only one central prophet among others, and it appears he was in a distinct minority when it came to proclaiming the downfall of Jerusalem at the hands of the Babylonians. When his chief opponent, the court prophet Hananiah, dropped dead (Jer 28:17), which could have been seen as a stunning vindication of Jeremiah's prophecies, there seems to have continued to be opposition to his ministry, even from his own family. Jeremiah's life after the time of Josiah was, by and large, one long jeremiad. There seems to have been no prophet for whom biography and prophecy were so intermingled, which explains why there is so much biographical material in the book of Jeremiah. For example, the collection of confessions from 11:18 through chapter 20 should be seen not as a reflection of an interest by later editors in the psychology of being a Hebrew prophet but, rather, as Jeremiah's way of vindicating that he was a true prophet.[83]

After all the years of doom-and-gloom prophecy, it appears to have been near the end of Jeremiah's time in Jerusalem, after the fall of the city and the burning of the temple, that Jeremiah was finally able to utter an oracle of promise, since Jerusalem had now endured the judgment: the famous new-covenant prophecy in 31:31–37, uttered on the last occasion when Deuteronomy was recited, in the autumn of 587.[84] Although this is an oracle of hope, it also indicates the death of the old hope shared by Jeremiah that a reform based on Deuteronomy would redeem and renew God's people.

The book called Jeremiah is not a book per se but an anthology of anthologies, in some ways like the book of Psalms. It involves a variety of smaller collections of a range of materials—oracles, liturgies, biographical passages, confessions, and other things as well. The social function of the book must be dis-

---

[81] See especially the discussions of R. P. Carroll in his commentary *Jeremiah* (Philadelphia: Fortress, 1986).

[82] See Holladay, *Jeremiah 1*, 3ff.

[83] So rightly ibid., 8–9.

[84] Ibid.

tinguished from the social functions of these varied materials in the life and time of Jeremiah. One must ask why such a disparate collection of materials, so full of bad news for Israel, would have been kept. The answer must, in part, be to warn God's people against making the same mistake again, the mistake of assuming they were immune to God's judgments. But this material was also kept to remind them that the message of true prophets is not just "Here comes the judge" but also that restoration and redemption or even a new covenantal arrangement are possible after judgment. It would appear that the initiative to begin collecting and preserving the oracles of Jeremiah was first taken by Baruch, Jeremiah's scribe, during the prophet's lifetime (ch. 36), perhaps about 605 BC, but the process continued for some time after the prophet's death.[85] The task of this examination of Jeremiah is to investigate some of the rich variety of material found in this book and see what it reveals to us about prophecy and the roles of prophets at this time.

In the discussion of Isa 6 it was concluded that this Isaianic text probably is not a call narrative but a further commissioning in the midst of a prophetic career. The same can not be said about the material in Jer 1, and it is perhaps no accident that when Paul chooses to speak of his own call/conversion in Gal 1, there are echoes of Jer 1. The first thing to be noticed about the material in Jeremiah is that the contents of the book are described as "the words of Jeremiah . . . to whom the word of the Lord came," which may be contrasted with, for instance the beginning of the book of Hosea, which speaks of the word of the Lord that came to Hosea (compare Hos 1:1 with Joel 1:1). This is perhaps because, as with the case of Amos (see Amos 1:1), the content of the book involves a good deal of prophetic reflection and other material that in general would not be called oracles. Indeed, the majority of the book is not simply oracles. Like Amos, Jeremiah is both seer and auditor of the divine communication.

The basic call narrative can be found in Jer 1:4–10, and it is followed by the recounting of two visions Jeremiah had, very much like those of Amos, only now they concern what is looming on the horizon for Judah. Each will be examined in turn. In the first passage we find a first-person account of a dialogue between Jeremiah and God. While this passage has some similarities with Ezek 1–3, the primary similarities are with the stories of the calling of Moses and of Samuel. The form-critical attempt to delineate a clear *Gattung* of call narratives on the basis of Isa 6, Jer 1, and Ezek 1 has shown that there is no singular pattern, for otherwise one would have expected much greater similarity between these accounts.[86] Note, for instance, in the case of the Jeremiah narrative that there is no indication of the social location of this call, unlike the case with Isa 6 (in the temple) or Ezek 1 (by the river Chebar). This suggests that the primary reason Jeremiah begins as it does is not an interest in biography but, rather, the intent to validate Jeremiah as a prophet in advance of presenting his prophetic material.

---

[85] See P. Craigie, *Jeremiah 1–25* (Waco: Word, 1991), xl–xli.
[86] See ibid., 8.

The case for arguing that Jeremiah's call is being presented in a Mosaic vein here has several components. First, God's promise to put words in Jeremiah's mouth not only echoes the similar promise made to Moses[87] but is most similar to the words concerning the coming prophet in Deut 18:18. Second, there is Jeremiah's reluctance and expression of inadequacy, which is very reminiscent of the Mosaic call narrative, although the latter's reluctance was for different reasons. The youthfulness of Jeremiah (who describes himself as a boy here, not a man) may be compared to what we found in the story of Samuel in 1 Sam 2:18. In Jeremiah's case, as in the case with Moses (but not Samuel), what is being recounted is a private experience—a direct encounter with God, without mediating or interpreting figures. In "this narrative, Jeremiah is not the messenger but the one to whom the message is addressed. And the narrative is essentially in prose form, rather than the poetic form common to oracles."[88]

Is Jeremiah here presented with a fait accompli, since he is told that he was set aside from before his conception for the task of being a prophet to God's people? The answer is, "Not quite," because Jeremiah must respond positively on his own to this announcement. Although "in freedom Jeremiah could have resisted the call, it is equally clear that he could only discover the meaning of his birth and mortal existence in responding to the call."[89] The issue here, in any case, is the life vocation of Jeremiah, not his personal salvation.

But what was this vocation? What did it mean that he was called to be a prophet to the nations (cf. Jer 1:5, 10)? If we look at the rest of the book of Jeremiah, we see that he was a prophet to Judah. On the whole, the suggestion that he was meant to be a prophet who spoke about Judah within the setting of international relations commends itself. In other words, he would take a cross-cultural perspective of what God intended for these ancient Near Eastern countries, including not only Judah and Israel but also Assyria, Babylon, Egypt, and other nations. Thus, finding the foreign-nation oracles in chs. 46–51 is not a surprise, nor is the fact that most oracles are directed to Judah, though with one eye on the broader national horizon.

Jeremiah's objections, on the basis of both age and his lack of ability in view of the nature of the task, are overruled in much the same fashion as with Moses in Exod 3:11–4:12. We are told that God touched Jeremiah's mouth, as in the case of the prophet Isaiah; with Jeremiah, however, the effect is not cleansing but, rather, putting words in his mouth (Jer 1:9). There is also another call narrative echoed in this Jeremiah text—the call of Gideon, found in Judg 6. Gideon was not called to be a prophet but, rather, a leader of God's people, which is primarily the case with Moses as well.[90] This necessarily raises the question whether Jer 1 is a specifically prophetic call narrative or a more general call to leadership,

---

[87] See pp. 22–25 above.

[88] Craigie, *Jeremiah 1–25*, 10.

[89] Ibid.

[90] See pp. 26–28 above.

which in this case manifests itself by Jeremiah taking on the role of prophet.[91] I think the latter is the case, and so it is questionable whether we are meant to find a paradigmatic prophetic-call narrative here or in the story of Moses. The crucial assurance "I will be with you" here most nearly echoes Judg 6:16, and less proximately Exod 3:12.

The reassurance was necessary not merely because of Jeremiah's age and inexperience but also because of the nature of what he must proclaim. The six verbs found in Jer 1:10 (pluck up, break down, destroy, overthrow, build, and plant) indicate God's sovereign dealings with nations, and it is noteworthy that only the last two are positive verbs. This roughly corresponds to the pattern— judgment followed by restoration or redemption—that this study has already noted in prophetic literature. It has been suggested that these six verbs provide the essential outline or shape of this book in terms of the arrangement of the material (cf. 18:7–10; 24:6; 31:27–28; 42:10; 45:4).[92] Thus the book will mainly be about the coming downfall of Jerusalem and Judah but also in due course, at the end, about its restoration. There is a decidedly ominous tone to v. 8, which suggests that Jeremiah will have to be rescued after he delivers such a message. This was to prove all too true.

The second major section of this opening salvo is found in vv. 11–19, which concern two visions, or perhaps two items seen in one vision. The format of this part of the narrative is very similar to what we have already seen in Amos 7, not only in the format of the narrative itself but in the way the images are presented. For example, there is wordplay in v. 11 between the Hebrew words *shaqed* and *shoqed*, the former referring to an almond-tree branch, the latter to watching. The connection is purely a verbal one, depending on assonance. What Jeremiah saw was the almond-tree branch, but the message was about God watching and waiting to perform his word. There may be some connection here between Jeremiah's hometown and this vision, for the town then, as now, was noted for its almond trees, and it may be germane that they are the first to blossom in the spring.[93]

The second vision, however, has a more direct connection with the message being conveyed. Jeremiah sees a boiling pot tilted from the north in the direction of the south. This betokens the looming threat from an enemy, coming from the north, who is about to endanger all the residents in the promised land. There is also a sinister element in this part of the narrative as well, for at v. 17 one hears, "gird up your loins; stand up and tell everything that I command you; do not break down before them or I will break you before them." On the other hand, in the next verse God promises to fortify Jeremiah against all those who may assail him for his message—including princes, priests, and the people. Verse

---

[91] See the perceptive discussion by Holladay, *Jeremiah 1*, 27–31.

[92] W. Brueggemann, *Jeremiah 1–25: To Pluck Up and to Tear Down* (Grand Rapids: Eerdmans, 1988), 24.

[93] See the discussion by J. A. Thompson, *The Book of Jeremiah* (Grand Rapids: Eerdmans, 1980), 153.

19 even says that although they will "fight" against Jeremiah, God will deliver him. The message might be that God is looking for the first opportunity to implement God's plan of judgment. The second vision, however, goes a step further, suggesting that the boiling pot has already begun to be tipped over and Judah and Jerusalem were about to be in hot water! But Jeremiah himself would also be in hot water, for his audience would tend to blame or even abuse the messenger. This is, in part, understandable even on the basis of our text, for, as v. 10 suggests, Jeremiah is not merely the announcer of the truth but one whom God has placed over nations and kingdoms, such that when he speaks God's word, things will come to pass. All the more reason why Jeremiah would need industrial-strength fortification.

The next text for consideration is the famous temple sermon of ch. 7, although it would be better called a temple oracle. It is a prose oracle or oracles. This oracle comes with the command to stand in the temple gate and deliver it. At issue here is the notion of the invulnerability of Jerusalem because the temple—and thus the true God's presence—dwells there. There is some question how v. 3 should be translated. Is it to be rendered "Amend your ways and works and I will dwell in this place" or "Amend your ways and works and I will make you to dwell in this place"? The issue here is one of revocalization, and on balance it appears that the former translation is correct,[94] but at v. 7 the proper reading may be either "then I will dwell with you" or more likely "then I will make you dwell." The issue in the former verse is God's presence in the temple; the issue at the end of the segment is the people's continued dwelling in the land.

What is not evident in v. 3 is made evident in v. 7—that God is offering a conditional promise. If Israel will amend its ways and forsake idolatry and immorality and injustice, then it will be true both that God will dwell with them and that they will continue to dwell in the land. Here once again we are confronted with the conditional nature of a good deal of oracular material, and it is well to remember that this means that if the condition in the protasis of the statement was not met, then the promise in the apodosis of the statement would not necessarily be fulfilled, and certainly would not *have* to be fulfilled for God's word to be true. In other words, conditional prophecies do not raise the same sort of issues of potential falsity as unconditional ones would.

In part, what is also at issue, especially in vv. 8–11, is the concept of sanctuary—the notion that no matter what one may have done outside the temple, if one ran into the temple and perhaps grasped the horns of the altar and claimed sanctuary, one would be safe. This ancient practice (cf. 1 Kgs 1:50–51; 2:28) was apparently applied on a national scale to mean that, by extension, even if the Hebrews violated all the Ten Commandments outside the temple but continued to support the temple ritual, make pilgrimages, and offer sacrifices in Jerusalem, the land would be safe because the temple and God's presence there would still protect the land. This protection was assumed to be unconditional, not depend-

---

[94] See Holladay, *Jeremiah 1,* 236ff.

ent on Israel's behavior. In effect, the temple had become a refuge for immoral people, a robbers' cave where those who had acted unethically could go and hide and not suffer judgment for their actions.[95] "The torah violators attempt to hide in the sanctity of the ritual. The temple becomes a means of cover-up for the destructive way life is lived in the real world."[96] In a devastating analogy, Jeremiah says that the doctrine of unconditional invincibility was all wrong and that what happened to the legitimate sanctuary at Shiloh would indeed happen to the temple in Jerusalem. The verdict of God in v. 14 is clear. In view of the persistent failure of God's people to respond to God's righteous demands, even a house called by Yahweh's name will have done to it what befell the sanctuary at Shiloh. God's people, a holy city, even God's house are not immune to judgment if wickedness has replaced holiness. But not just the temple will fall: "I will cast you out of my sight, just as I cast all of your kinsfolk, all the offspring of Ephraim" (v. 15). What had happened to the northern tribes would happen to Judah as well.

One of the more powerful passages in the entire book of Jeremiah is found in 18:1–11, the famous story of the potter and the clay, where a scene from real life is taken as an object lesson for how God can and will relate to God's people. The story begins with a command given to Jeremiah himself. He is to make a trip down to the potter's house, with a promise that he will hear God's words in that place. The emphasis in the observation found in v. 4 seems to be on the malleability of the clay pot in the hands of the potter. Even a flawed pot can be reworked, as seems good to the potter, into another vessel. By "flawed" what appears to be meant is that the clay itself was not suitable for the potter's purposes.[97]

The lesson drawn from what Jeremiah observed is that God can do with Israel or, for that matter, any nation what the potter did with the clay. God can make or break a nation; it is like putty in God's hands. But as it happens, what God does with a nation is at least in part dependent on how that nation relates to God's call and message to it. "Yahweh the potter was dealing with a clay that was resistant to his purpose."[98] So the clay turns out not to be mere putty in the potter's hand.

If God declares judgment for a nation but the nation repents of its evil, then God will not implement the judgment. The reverse is also true. The

---

[95] As Holladay, ibid., 246, says, the word *parits* refers not just to a robber but to a brigand, one who commits acts of violence in order to steal (cf. Ezek 7:22; 18:10; Ps 17:4; Dan 11:14). The image, then, is not merely of those who want to steal a blessing from God that is not rightfully theirs in view of their conduct but of those who wrap themselves in the cloak of true religion not only to avoid suffering the just consequences of their actions but to continue to practice such idolatrous and immoral activities in the world and not have to mend their ways. God, in this case, becomes something of a security blanket for the wicked.

[96] Brueggemann, *Jeremiah 1–25*, 76.

[97] See Thompson, *Jeremiah*, 432.

[98] Ibid., 433.

"moral" to the story and lesson is given in v. 11: God is shaping and devising a plan against Israel, but at the same time God is issuing a final summons to repent. If the latter is heeded, the former will not be implemented. God's contingency plans should not be taken as matters written in stone, because again they are part of an ongoing relationship that has various ups and downs and conditional promises and plans. The issue here is not so much God changing his mind as God changing his promised treatment in the wake of a change in behavior by a group of people. "Yahweh's responsive sovereignty and Judah's determinative obedience are both constitutive of Judah's life."[99]

But repentance was not to be in the case of Judah. "In such circumstances . . . only the refining influences of judgment could avail to make them amenable again to the potter's touch."[100] Holladay's summary about this passage is exceedingly apt, and it tells us a good deal about how Jeremiah views the relationship of God to the chosen people and indeed to humans in general.

> First, the clay is not altogether passive. . . . The process of shaping pottery is therefore an extraordinarily apt analogy for the work of Yahweh with his people: though he is sovereign, the people have a will of their own which they exert against him. Second, Yahweh can change his mind if the decision of his people warrants it. . . . Yahweh has a "plan" . . . which he intends . . . but whether he puts it into operation or not depends upon whether or not the people turn from their evil way: if they will, he will not. . . . This is the lesson of the potter. Some pots turn out fine the first time. Some do not, so the potter changes his tactics. It is a striking presentation of divine sovereignty and human freedom."[101]

Though the material thus far considered is not lacking in pathos, it pales in comparison to what is found in 20:7–18—the great lament and curse of Jeremiah in regard to his own existence—which brings to a climax the so-called confessions. This material is not an oracle, but it is nonetheless some of the most revealing material in the entire book. We find Jeremiah hemmed in between his people and his God. If he proclaims God's word of judgment, he becomes a laughingstock and subject to abuse by those who should most be thankful for his words of warning. If he fails to proclaim God's word, he is eaten up from the inside out, for God's word burns within him. It is possible, from a literary point of view, to divide this material into two sections—a song of lament in vv. 7–13 followed by a curse in vv. 14–18. But this fails to explain why the two sections have been so strikingly juxtaposed here; thus, while these two sections will be analyzed separately, we must address the issue of juxtaposition thereafter.

Jeremiah 20:7–13 takes on the classical form of a lament, and it is in a *qinah* rhythm for the most part. It moves from complaint to words of assurance and finally to praise (v. 13). There is considerable debate about the very first major verb of the lament—*patah*. There is no doubt that the verb could mean

---

99 Brueggemann, *Jeremiah 1–25*, 161.

100 Thompson, *Jeremiah*, 435.

101 Holladay, *Jeremiah 1*, 515.

"deceive" (2 Sam 3:25), and it is used elsewhere of God deceiving a prophet (1 Kgs 22:20–22; cf. Ezek 14:9), but a case has been made for the translation "persuade" or "try to persuade."[102] On the whole, the case fails to convince, for this is a lament and Jeremiah is feeling misused or misled by Yahweh. He has proclaimed the fall of Jerusalem and it has not transpired, and now he is a laughingstock; he has been shamed and humiliated in the presence of his own people and family. It has even been suggested that the verb has the sense of "seduced," which, when coupled with the second verb, "overpowered," indicates Jeremiah's sense of being compelled to proclaim doom and gloom for Jerusalem and Judah.

There is no doubt that the verb "overpowered" is crucial in this lament. We find this verb in vv. 7, 9, 10, and 11. Yahweh has overcome Jeremiah. Jeremiah can not overcome Yahweh. Jeremiah's detractors have not overcome him. This lament could easily be entitled "We Shall Overcome Some Day." Another strong word that occurs more than once is "vengeance," first directed by Jeremiah's enemies against him in v. 10 and then directed by Jeremiah to Yahweh against these enemies in v. 12. Despite all the strong language in this lament, which is not uncharacteristic of such Hebrew laments, as a quick glance at the Psalms will show (cf., e.g., Pss 13 and 22), it must be stressed that Jeremiah is speaking to God. He is not taking his life or his troubles in his own hands, but he is placing them in God's hands. He is complaining to the highest court and looking outside himself for help and deliverance.

Jeremiah is caught in an intolerable bind. Whenever he proclaims "violence and destruction," it leads to his being continually reproached and an object of derision, but this also means it has become a horror to Jeremiah himself to proclaim it, precisely because of his great love for his people and for Jerusalem. Yet just when Jeremiah decides not to proclaim doom and gloom any longer, God's word burns within him and will not leave him alone. It is like fire in his bones, and Jeremiah becomes weary trying to hold it in, trying to refrain from pronouncing judgment. It is significant that the prophet sees God's word as an inner fire, something already within him, rather than an outer power or force seeking to enter his mind and heart. It is not that Jeremiah does not know what God's word is in this situation or that God has ceased to speak to him. He knows all too well but does not wish to proclaim it.

Things have become so bad that, according to v. 10, even Jeremiah's close friends (and family?) are watching for Jeremiah to stumble, trying to trip him up and entice him to cease the judgment oracles. But according to v. 11, Jeremiah has confidence that God the divine warrior will assist him and that it is his detractors, not he, who will ultimately stumble and be shamed. "Their eternal dishonor will never be forgotten."

It is interesting that the particular terminology used here, "dread warrior," is not found elsewhere used of God. In fact, the adjective is always used elsewhere of enemies (cf. 15:21). It may be that this reflects Jeremiah's mixed feelings

---

[102] See D. J. A. Clines and D. M. Gunn, "Form: Occasion and Redaction in Jeremiah 20," *ZAW* 88 (1976): 390–409; and Craigie, *Jeremiah 1–25*, 270ff.

about Yahweh at this juncture. It is even possibly that Jeremiah has the line of a popular psalm in mind (see Ps 78:65–66).[103] In v. 12 Jeremiah pleads with God to take vengeance on his foes and so vindicate the prophet, "for to you I have commited my cause." In other words, God's honor, and not just that of the prophet, is at stake. I submit that this is the lament of a central or court prophet who under normal circumstances would expect to be honored and supported by rulers, friends, and family in Jerusalem and the vicinity. But these are not normal circumstances. Verse 13 is a rather traditional positive closure to such a lament (cf. the positive ending of Ps 22), where Jeremiah asserts that God is the one who delivers righteous but needy people such as himself from the hands of evildoers. It is possible that we should see this as ironic in view of what follows in vv. 14–18, or it can be an assertion of naked faith, against the prevailing wind of his situation. "Jeremiah cannot find satisfaction in the public arena, nor in social relations. He is finally driven to face the theological reality of his life and vocation. He is driven to God as his 'only source of comfort and strength.'"[104]

After v. 13 however, vv. 14–18 come as something of a shock. The juxtaposition of this passage with the previous one is abrupt and shows that Jeremiah's reaction to his situation is complex. He relies on the conventional forms in which to lament and praise God, but they are not enough to express his anguish and anger. The juxtaposition of these passages reveals faith under an enormous amount of duress. Jeremiah wants to praise God and rely on God, but life is so difficult and raw that he curses the very day he was born. He wishes sometimes he had never been created. Notice, as Bruggemann rightly points out, that this curse is not addressed to God or even his parents.[105] Jeremiah is not asking for God to curse him or for anyone else to do so, nor does he curse God or his parents.

As in Job 3, there is here a wish to have never existed. Jeremiah honestly states it would have been better not to be born than to have come to this horrible state of affairs. There may be some reflection here on the fact that he was called by God from the womb. He cannot rue the day he was called to be a prophet as some occurrence subsequent to birth; he can only rue the day he was born. "As Jeremiah himself is rejected as a messenger, so Jeremiah would reject the messenger who caused him to be present and known in the world. Jeremiah knows all about messengers being rejected, and he wishes his birth message had never been delivered."[106] Jeremiah narrowly avoids the law's prohibition of cursing parents (Deut 27:16) by cursing the messenger that brought the news from the midwife to his father about his birth. In the end, Holladay is likely right that both v. 14 and v. 15 have a declarative, rather than imperative, function.[107] By this is meant that Jeremiah is not here uttering a curse or a wish but, rather, stat-

---

[103] See Holladay, *Jeremiah 1*, 557.
[104] Brueggemann, *Jeremiah 1–25*, 176.
[105] Ibid., 177.
[106] Ibid., 178.
[107] Holladay, *Jeremiah 1*, 561.

ing facts—the day of his birth was cursed, and the messenger who gave the birth announcement as well. In an interesting way, this material rounds off the confessions of Jeremiah and should be compared with the opening confession in 15:10–21. It is clear from such material that being a prophet was not only a difficult vocation; in an honor-and-shame culture it became an almost unbearable one for those who honestly proclaimed judgment on their own people. Since honor was a higher value than life itself in such a culture, it is understandable why a shamed and abused Jeremiah would indeed have wished to have never lived rather than come to this impasse.[108] That Jeremiah eventually got beyond this impasse is indicated by the continuation of the material in this book, in particular the positive content we find in 31:31–34.

With 31:31–34 we are once more dealing with an oracle. But it is entirely an oracle of promise and hope, not one of judgment. The first and most important thing to say about this oracle is that it is the only place in the entire Hebrew Scriptures that there is mention of a *new* covenant. The emphasis is placed on discontinuity with the past through the use of the phrase "not like," referring to the Mosaic covenant (v. 32), and the phrase "not anymore" (v. 34 twice).

Some understanding of covenant theology is required to make sense of this passage. First of all, this is not a parity covenant or an agreement between equals but, rather, a lord-vassal covenant. Just as God had been their Lord in Egypt (v. 32), God would continue to be so, and thus it is entirely in the Lord's hands to initiate this new arrangement. But Yahweh had chosen to treat his people not just as slaves or vassals who would be considered property but as his people; indeed, if we read the key verb in v. 32 *(bealti)* to mean "I had mastered them as a husband,"[109] then God is talking about initiating a marriage covenant. In a patriarchal world such covenants were one-sided affairs in which the bride had no real say about the proceedings.

Several key points need to be made about this new arrangement: (1) Like the old arrangement, this covenant is with Israel, not with some new spouse, some new group of people. (2) Nevertheless, the arrangement will be quite different from the old one. There will be full, not partial, knowledge of the Lord, and this intimate knowledge will be available directly to all, presumably without the requirement of human mediators. (3) Perhaps most crucial, this new arrangement is only possible because *(ki)* God has forgiven his people's sins. The curse sanctions of the old covenant have come into play and judgment has been exacted (Deut 28), but it is probable that, as Brueggemann suggests, the affront of both Israel and Judah could never have been completely expiated or atoned for by some temporal and temporary judgment, however severely it may have affected some individuals.[110] God has, then, on the basis of his own graciousness,

---

[108] See W. McKane, *Jeremiah I* (Edinburgh: T&T Clark, 1986), 486.

[109] See G. L. Keown, P. J. Scalise, and T. G. Smothers, *Jeremiah 26–52* (Waco: Word, 1995), 132.

[110] Brueggemann, *Jeremiah 26–52: To Build and to Plant* (Grand Rapids: Eerdmans, 1991), 72.

decided to "cut a new covenant," as the language of 31:31 actually says, referring to the practice of cutting the agreement into stone or some other medium of lasting character.[111] God has no obligation to recovenant with this people once the old covenant sanctions were brought into play. Yet God chooses to restart this relationship on the basis of God's unmerited forgiveness of past sins and so to institute a new arrangement that would not require a continued payment for past sins. (4) This covenant is not inaugurated at the time Jeremiah is speaking; rather, it will be instituted at some undisclosed time in the future, "after those days" (v. 33). (5) It will involve the placing of God's law in, or the inscribing of God's law on, human hearts. (6) The result of this process of changing the manner in which, and the degree to which, God's people will know God is that all of God's people, without regard to social status or standing or educational background, will know God intimately and he will truly be their God. This, in effect, would put priests, prophets, diviners, teachers, and other mediators out of business.[112] (7) God promises, as his part of the relationship, not only to forgive God's people but also "to remember their sin no more." (8) The covenant is with both Israel and Judah, not just the southern tribes, and so it bids fair to reunite the whole Hebrew people.

It needs also to be kept in view that by "heart" the author means the control center of the human personality—the seat of thought, will, and emotions. He is, then, not talking just about an inward experience of God, although that is part of the matter, but also about an actual inward knowledge of God and God's will, motivating the human will to respond accordingly. Finally, it is worth pointing out that if Holladay is right about Jeremiah's support for Deuteronomistic reforms early in his life, here he has reached a stage of recognition that such a reform would not, in fact, accomplish what God requires. An entirely new covenant and a new way of knowing and relating to God were necessary, and the necessary prerequisite to all of this was God's forgiving Israel's past sins. Needless to say, there is nothing in the rest of Jeremiah, nor, for that matter, in the later prophetic corpus, to suggest such a covenant was instituted in that era.

Jeremiah, then, should not be seen simply as a prophet of doom and gloom, although most of his oracles were of that character. Like other Hebrew prophets, he also believed in redemption beyond judgment, and this belief is manifested in the new-covenant oracle. It is also a measure of Jeremiah's love for his people that he was so reluctant to prophesy judgment on them. Jeremiah's modus operandi was varied, involving both prose and poetry, both signs and oracles, both symbols and personal embodiment of the message. A great debt is owed to Baruch and perhaps others for preserving the pronouncements of Jeremiah. They reveal that the tasks of a true prophet, dedicated to sharing the word of God about the future whether bad or good, were never easy and often left the practitioner a shamed or persecuted person. Under such circumstances, it is all the more remarkable that much of the book of Jeremiah has been preserved.

---

[111] See Keown, Scalise, and Smothers, *Jeremiah 26–52*, 131.
[112] See Thompson, *Jeremiah*, 581

V. CONCLUSIONS

A lot of ground has been covered in this chapter, and some fresh light has been shed on the prophetic phenomenon. As with other nations, Israel's prophets spoke, in the main, to the leadership of the nation. Their concerns were similar to, sometimes even nearly identical with, the military and political concerns of prophets elsewhere in the ancient Near East. So long as there was a monarchy, the social roles of prophets in Israel were much like the roles assumed by prophets elsewhere.

Koch was surely right that the subject matter for most prophecy was the future, albeit, more often than not, the near future. Whether one calls it prescience or foreknowledge or revelation, the prophets, in a culture and time that focused so heavily on the past and on precedent, attempted to warn about or celebrate what was to come. Sometimes these prophets even spoke in an idealized way about the more remote future. Although there was an oral prophetic tradition that prophets such as Jeremiah drew on to help conceptualize their own roles, once one reaches the stage of putting the oracles down in writing, it then became possible for non-prophetic expansion of prophetic material to happen. If it fits in anywhere, ex eventu prophecy fits in this category of further prophetic or apocalyptic reflection on earlier inscripted oracular material, because it was believed that some of those ancient oracles had finally found a correlate in the recent past experiences of God's people. But there may well be good reason not to see ex eventu prophecy as prophecy at all, properly speaking, but, rather, as written commentary in prophetic clothing or as non-prophetic scribal expansions on the basis of earlier prophetic material.

The prophets were crisis intervention specialists. This, in turn, meant that the more Israel faced crisis, the more need there was for reflection on Israel's future, and thus the need for prophecy. The plethora of prophetic works from the eighth century BC on indicates the ongoing social dysfunction of life in Israel and especially of political and economic life. The northern part of the promised land was the first to face serious crisis after the monarchy divided, and thus it is not surprising that the first of the prophets to have an extended collection of his oracles put down in writing was a prophet who addressed that situation even though he was from the south.

The ministry of Amos seems to have been short, but clearly someone thought it crucial enough to enshrine his oracles in a book. Perhaps it was hoped that Judah would learn the lessons that Israel had refused to learn through the proclamation of Amos. Even a cursory study of Amos's oracles reveals a man with an understanding of the political and religious problems of the day in Israel and with a grasp of ancient history and international relationships. His overarching concern and complaint were about a lack of justice and faithfulness in Israel, which would lead to its doom. Amos is especially interesting because he is, to some extent, a cross-cultural prophet (if one can speak of Israel and Judah having distinguishable cultures) and he prophesied with one eye on the wider ancient Near Eastern horizon. He would speak about Israel in the context of oracles delivered about the surrounding nations.

The poetic form of Amos's oracles suggests its prophetic character. This feature of many prophetic oracles makes it unsurprising that one also finds the use of colorful metaphors, images (even bizarre ones), and other nonliteral devices in Amos and elsewhere. It also suggests that plebian attempts to read prophecy in an overly literal manner are often the products of category mistakes. One can not fault a prophet for not being literal if the intent and nature of his discourse was metaphorical. On the other hand, metaphorical images, such as a basket of summer fruit, are often meant to refer to actual historical conditions or circumstances, whether existing or impending. Rhetorical questions using metaphorical expressions often point to lurking historical dangers of an analogous kind. The situation, then, is complex, and the poetic form of oracles adds to the complexity of the situation.

Amos 3 suggests that Amos, like others, had prophetic experiences that allowed him to overhear the deliberations of the heavenly council. The prophet was to announce to Israel what God has already decided and said. The prophet thus is not simply the voice of God speaking to Israel on the spot but, rather, the announcer of what God has already said and determined. The later, written form of these oracles is like such an announcement in that it is an expression after the original utterance of the oracle. But the prophet knows only what is revealed to him. Yet there is also a dynamic interaction between the prophet and his God, so that texts such as Amos 7 indicate that the prophet's intervention could possibly head off imminent judgment. Yahweh shows Amos various possible scenarios—a locust plague, or a fire destroying the land of Israel—but here Amos intercedes and Yahweh relents. Amos is showed a wall and a plumb line, with Yahweh measuring Israel for destruction, and there is no promise to relent. Insufficient attention to the relational context of prophecy and also to its often conditional nature can lead to all sorts of false conclusions about false prophecy. Amos was no court or central prophet, not a professional at all, but, rather, a peripheral prophet, yet his oracles had the same weight and force and form as of those who were more recognized and prophesied over a longer period of time.

In Mic 6:6–8 there comes the glimmering of a prophetic tradition that included a critique of the religious and political apparatus of God's people in terms of the demands of Yahweh for justice and mercy. This tradition of ethical monotheism is important, but it should not be used to suggest that the Hebrew prophets were basically antisacramental in emphasis. Their concern was with the substitution of formal religion for personal religion or, better said, with public religious acts in lieu of the embodiment of the qualities God expected to be enshrined in the nation's leaders and people. The issue here is the doing of good by humans, which truly reflects God's own character, as opposed to the use of worship as some sort of protection against judgment. God's demands for righteous character could not be bought off by expensive sacrifices.

In Mic 5:1–6 we find an example of a prophecy about a more remote solution to Israel's problems. Like many such prophecies, it comes in highly idealized form, and its focus is on a monarch who will finally fulfill the roles Yahweh intended for Israel's ruler. This tradition was to find increasing expression in the exilic and postexilic situations as present leaders so clearly failed to meet hopes and expectations. There is reason to challenge the form-critical dictums about preexilic prophets not offering oracles of salvation or about there not being oracles that might be mixed in character, involving both judgment and salvation. Koch was likely right that there were oracles that spoke of redemption beyond or after judgment even in the preexilic period.

In Mic 3:5–8 there is a contrast between the professional prophets or central prophets, who continue to proclaim peace and claim sustenance from those to whom they dispense oracles, and Micah himself. There would be no more visions given to them because of their false pronouncements. They will be shamed because they have no late word from God for his people. It would be interesting to know *how* the oracles from prophets such as Micah or Amos were preserved when they were not court prophets nor represented the courtly tradition. One can only assume there was a strong tradition of passing down prophetic oracles even if they were uncongenial to the current monarch's policies or behavior. It is easier to understand how, during exilic or postexilic times, the social conditions were such that preserving such oracles would be seen as advisable to remind Israelites why they were in their current predicament.

Prophecy was, more often than not, in poetic form, and thus it is not surprising that it was often highly metaphorical and full of images. Prophets could offer up not only oracles but songs, not only songs but various forms of *meshalim* or metaphorical speech ranging from riddles, to taunts, to aphorisms, to proverbs, and even to the occasional parable. In some of this they were drawing on the sapiential traditions to enhance their literary vocabulary and possibilities. Already in Amos there was evidence of the use of pregnant metaphors, but in First Isaiah one finds all that plus much more—even material sometimes thought to be bordering on apocalyptic but that would be better called eschatological material.

A comparison and contrast between Isa 6 and Jer 1 suggest that the former is not an initial-call narrative but, rather, a commissioning to a new task, whereas Jer 1 is more properly designated a call narrative (as would be Ezek 1–2). These sorts of narratives let us know that the prophetic expression is indeed grounded in prophetic experience. Real prophecy is not a mere literary exercise.

Isaiah is an interesting case, not least because he was a court prophet who prophesied over a wide expanse of time and through various royal reigns. His oracles were about both judgment and redemption, and even, on rare occasion, apparently about redemption beyond both judgment and death. Isaiah 27:2–6 manifests the conditional, the either-or character of many prophetic oracles. If God's vineyard produces thorns, he will destroy it, but there is an alternative—"or else let it cling to me for protection, let it make peace with me." The relationally conditioned character of such utterances is clear. There is nothing inevitable or foreordained about God's judgment, for it is an action taken on the basis of how Israel relates to its God.

The Neo-Assyrian oracles and texts about prophecy and divination provide a glimpse at the wider context in which Hebrew prophecy was given. The apparently much greater reliance on divination in Assyria (involving many court diviners of various sorts) in contrast to Israel is noteworthy. The dual tradition of prophecy in Israel (both critical and affirmative of the court and monarch) also stands in contrast to what one finds in the Assyrian materials.

The book of Jeremiah provides one of the most comprehensive glimpses into the nature of Hebrew prophecy. Once again the prophet is at odds with the powers that be and sees his task of proclaiming doom and gloom an onerous one. But he has been called even from the womb, and there is no escaping his duty, or at least none without experiencing fire in his bones. The prophet takes no delight in informing his family, friends, and fellow Judahites that Jerusalem and Judah are about to go down for the count, and yet God requires that he warn them.

Both the experience of Jeremiah and that of other major writing prophets, such as Isaiah, suggest a strong visual element in the communications they received from God. The prophet is expected to reflect on the meaning of images, such as a cauldron in the north tipped in a southerly direction, or a potter forming a clay pot, or, in the case of Isaiah, a vineyard with its hedge broken down, or, in the case of Amos, a basket of summer fruit. Sometimes the significance of such visions lies in word association, sometimes in the pictographic symbol itself (boiling cauldron being tipped over = Judah is about to be in hot water).

It is Jeremiah who, alone among the prophets, offers an oracle about a new covenant. But the dark underside of this oracle is the assumption of a fundamental rupture in the relationship between God and God's people that required a starting over again. The Hebrew prophets, no matter how gloomy the majority of their oracles, still seem to have believed in a light at the end of the tunnel, whether one is thinking of Isaiah's thoughts on resurrection, or Micah's ideal shepherd monarch, or Jeremiah's new covenant. How stark this stands in contrast to the Assyrian oracles, which basically refused to reckon with the possibility of defeat or inappropriate behavior by the monarch and therefore felt no need to speak of redemption beyond judgment, light beyond the darkness. In the next chapter we must turn to even more profound musings about light beyond darkness, the darkness of the exile and the postexilic state.

CHAPTER 5

Exilic Dreams of Grandeur

"BY THE RIVERS OF BABYLON—there we sat down and there we wept when we remembered Zion. On the willows there we hung up our harps. For there our captors asked of us songs and our tormentors asked for mirth saying: 'Sing us one of the songs of Zion!' How could we sing the Lord's song in a foreign land?" (Ps 137:1–4). It was a very real question, and one might well have also asked, "How can we prophesy in a foreign land?" Yet surprisingly, as the psalm above shows and as the material below will demonstrate, the inspiration to compose poetic songs and oracles and visions had not dried up. God's people had not lost their voice or even entirely their religious bearings while in exile.

But a new sort of prophecy or at least a new development of prophecy would indeed arise during the Babylonian exile, and it came to be called apocalyptic. In some ways, the turn to more visionary and otherworldly prophetic forms is not surprising. An Israelite prophet in Babylon had no monarch or court or temple or holy city to focus on or prophesy to, no religious pilgrimages to go on while there, and no people in charge of their own destiny to speak to. Only journeys of the soul or in the mind's eye would be possible if royal persons, holy temple, holy place, holy land, and a free people with viable religious choices were to be "seen" and spoken of.

True, such an exilic prophet could come to deal with a court, but it would be the court of a foreign king. It would not be the same. A Jewish prophet in exile could see the future of the holy land only in dreams or visions and the like, not by going down to a potter's house within that land and musing on the land's future. This social situation provides a partial explanation for the rise of Jewish apocalyptic prophecy. What happens to a hope deferred? It becomes the stuff of dreams and visions and prophetic songs of longing. It is the intent of this chapter to examine the two greatest bodies of exilic prophecy—the material found in Isa 40–55 and the material found in the book of Ezekiel.

I. ISAIAH, PART TWO—THE SEQUEL

Certainly one of the most difficult and indeed intractable problems in all of OT studies is the matter of what to do with Isa 40–55. The notion of the greatest body of poetic prophecy or prophetic poetry in the OT coming from an anonymous source is difficult to grasp or comprehend. In the history of Israelite prophecy up to this juncture, all the prophecy studied was tagged to particular prophetic figures, all of whom had personal names. Pseudonymity at least presents us with an attribution, but the so-called Second Isaiah material does not do so. And it is clear that the assemblers of the Hebrew Scripture themselves were not comfortable with leaving this great body of literature free-floating, without prophetic attribution and location. This is why there is still something to be said for the bold attempt, made most recently by Oswalt, to argue that this material does, in some manner, go back to the historical Isaiah.[1] This conclusion is supported by the observation that there is a theological connection and continuity between Isa 1–39 and 40–55, such that "II Isaiah theologically is seen to be organically derived from I Isaiah."[2] Furthermore, as for Third Isaiah (Isa 56–66), no less a scholar than R. Rendtorff has stressed that this material is so dependent on First and Second Isaiah that it can hardly have had an independent existence.[3] The central themes introduced in the first thirty-nine chapters are developed in Isa 40–66.

But if the historical Isaiah in fact spoke all of this material, this means that he not merely spoke about the future but addressed people in the future about their current situation. This would be unprecedented, entailing a conception of prophecy that does not pertain elsewhere in the prophetic material that has already been examined. It would be prophecy without a social location, prophecy without anything like an immediate audience, a prophecy set loose from its immediate historical moorings. Does the issue, then, finally come down to whether one conceives it possible that the divine would actually reveal the future in advance to a prophetic figure? I think not; for many, if not most, scholars recognize that Amos and Jeremiah did correctly foresee and speak about the fall of Israel and Judah respectively. The issue is the more difficult one of social and historical location for the material.

---

[1] See J. Oswalt, *The Book of Isaiah 40–66* (Grand Rapids: Eerdmans, 1998), 6ff.

[2] W. Brueggemann, "Unity and Dynamic in the Isaiah Tradition," *JSOT* 29 (1984): 89–107, here 96.

[3] R. Rendtorff, "Zur Komposition des Buches Jesaja," *VT* 34 (1984): 295–320, here 320.

The speaker in chs. 40ff. addresses the exiles about their future. Everywhere else the bond between prophet and his own audience is not severed in the earlier Hebrew prophecy, even if and when the prophet spoke about the future. Even messages about the more remote future in the earlier portion of Isaiah were juxtaposed with those about the more proximate future or present to show the connections between them (cf., e.g., chs. 7–11). There is nothing like this in chs. 40ff. They address the exilic situation and its sequel with the return to the land. If Isaiah himself wrote this, he did not live long enough to have contact with either of these settings.

One must ask, then, why the divine would choose to operate in this peculiar fashion in this particular case, especially when there is the clear example of Ezekiel, which shows it was not necessary to rely on the names of ancient prophetic luminaries during the Babylonian exile in order to come up with prophetic discourse. To the surprise of Ezekiel and others, God was still speaking as a living voice to God's people even though they were in exile. There was no need for a voice from the past to be conjured up in order to address their particular situation. And I can not help but wonder if the difficulties faced here are not, in part, attributable to a too ready assimilation or amalgamation of the prophetic experience, the prophetic expression, the prophetic tradition, and the prophetic corpus.

In the case of the material in chs. 40–55, one is dealing with a body of literature that is indeed dependent on chs. 1–39. If a towering figure such as Isaiah had disciples, and it is apparent he did,[4] then there is no reason that there could not have been a passing on of the Isaiah tradition for a considerable period of time, and a development of the Isaianic themes and ideas and diction during this time period.

What this would mean is that in chs. 40ff. we are not entirely dealing with the same sort of prophetic phenomenon as we are in chs. 1–39. Disciples of prophets are not necessarily prophets—they may simply be students and in time educators, even scholars—but at least one of them, perhaps a student of one of these original disciples and tradents of the Isaiah material, may have become a "son of a prophet," and a "like father (or grandfather), like son" prophetic phenomenon could have transpired along the lines of what was the case with Elijah and Elisha. Inspired both by his learning and transmitting of the Isaianic material and by God as God spoke to him directly, this latter-day Isaianic prophet spoke within a prophetic tradition, reflecting his heavy indebtedness to the human font of this stream of material. We may perhaps find some confirmation for this view from 50:4, where God is said to have dispensed the tongue of the learned to "me." Isaiah 8:16 and 54:13 show that the learned are always disciples in the Isaianic tradition. But the disciple has been given a tongue to be a teacher as well. Like a later teacher, the Teacher of Righteousness, this teacher preferred to remain anonymous and so keep the focus on the content of what God had said through him.

---

[4] See pp. 120–21 above.

A close analysis of chs. 40–55 will show that only a portion of this material is oracular, in the sense of God speaking in the first person. Very often it is the prophet speaking of God in the third person and to the people. This mixture of oracular and prophetic reflection and poetry has surfaced before, but here it is especially in evidence. Perhaps precisely because of the heavy indebtedness to Isaiah, and since the real issue was whether this was a word from God or not (not whether it was by this particular prophet or not), this prophet does not reveal himself and his individual situation. This is not, however, merely a matter of adaptation and imitation of Isaiah by a latter-day disciple.[5] There are also direct inspiration and expression. It is the combination of these factors that goes into making up the Isa 40–55 discourse, and this is, in some ways, analogous to the influence of the Deuteronomic material on Jeremiah's own oracles and discourse.[6]

This process may, in part, be especially understandable as an exilic phenomenon. Here is a figure, called today Second Isaiah, for whom hope lay in continuity with the past and clear vision about the future, but not in a close analysis or revelation of the present. The sordid character of the exile did not need to be belabored for those who experienced it. Rather, buried in a precious Isaiah scroll or in learned Isaiah traditions that had been brought into exile by someone, God had spoken afresh to this person and urged him to continue to sing forth in an Isaianic mode. He succeeded brilliantly, and his words not only were remembered but were recorded and brought back to Jerusalem when the Hebrews finally returned from exile. But the compilation of the Isaianic corpus as we know it was a later process. As Clements says, "Prophets were primarily preachers and speakers and . . . the process of collecting and shaping their words into book form was a secondary process."[7] The primary concern of what follows is with the prophetic expression rather than with the tradition history or the process of final redaction. It would appear that this material originated sometime after the rise of the Persian conqueror Cyrus (Isa 45:1) but before the final demise of the Babylonian Empire (46:1–47:15), and so perhaps in the middle of the sixth century BC.

The opening salvo in chs. 40–55 indicated that God would use unconventional means to lead God's exiled people back to Jerusalem. The construction order is given for a superhighway right through the desert, straight as a crow flies, through the Syrian-Arabian Desert to Jerusalem. There would be no return by the usual caravan routes that Abraham and others followed up to Damascus and then down into the promised land. The good news was that Israel's days of forced labor were over and it would soon be time for God to lead them home.

---

[5] Hence the complaint of Clements, *Old Testament Prophecy,* 11ff., is in part answered about the issue of inspiration and prophetic uniqueness.

[6] See the discussion in Y. Gitay, *Prophecy and Persuasion: A Study of Isaiah 40–48* (Bonn: Linguistica Biblica, 1981), 52–55.

[7] Clements, *Old Testament Prophecy,* 12.

Indeed, if the mid-sixth-century date for Second Isaiah is correct, once Cyrus had conquered the Babylonians, many of the Israelites would be on their way home within less than a biblical generation. This Isaianic figure had been absolutely correct about Cyrus overcoming the Babylonians and about the sea change that would happen in the status of God's people thereafter. Figures such as Nehemiah would rise to the position of King Cyrus's cupbearer and then would help lead the new exodus back to Jerusalem and Judah.

Probably, one should see ch. 40 as an introduction to the entirety of chs. 40–55, although several major themes (e.g., witness, the Servant, and salvation of the nations) are not found in this chapter. The themes of comfort and of the highway have occurred before in Isaiah (cf. ch. 12 on the former; 11:19, 33 on the latter). One must also see in this chapter a commissioning. The order goes out for someone to act as a herald, and the response by the author is, "What shall I cry?" (v. 6),[8] which in effect means, "What shall I proclaim?"[9] There are indeed some notable[10] parallels with the commissioning scene in ch. 6: the calling voice (compare 40:3 with 6:3); all flesh will see God's glory (compare 40:5 with 6:3); the response of the prophet (compare 40:6 with 6:11); and the message seeming to be the exact reverse of the message in ch. 6 (compare 40:9 with 6:11).[11] Finally, if 49:5–6 is about the prophet himself, in the study of ch. 6 we saw reasons to suggest there a distinction between the time of the initial call and this special commissioning.[12] There is no reason this could not be the case here as well. Clearly, this chapter establishes that the theme of this section will be redemption and restoration for Israel, chiefly by means of judgment on Babylon by Cyrus. God's redemptive judgment occurs in such fashion here that Israel no longer must face judgment but their tormentors must. God's judgment and redemption make two things clear: while human beings are like grass that readily perishes, God's word endures forever and prevails.

The reason for Israel feeling comfort is that God will break into human history and lead them back to the promised land. We may see a reprise of this initial theme at 52:7–10. The prophet means rescue and restoration of a people when he speaks of salvation. He is not referring to the conversion of individuals to the true faith. Just as the actual rescue is an unexpected event of grace, so also the path of deliverance—a highway made straight through the desert is likewise a surprise. "Vv. 3–5 depicted the irresistible, triumphal march of the universe's King. Nothing in the world can deter him, not deserts, mountains or valleys. He

---

[8] See Habel, "Form and Significance," 314–16.

[9] C. Westermann, *Isaiah 40–66* (Philadelphia: Westminster, 1975), 40–41.

[10] Oswalt, *Isaiah 40–66*, 48.

[11] Here the argument of D. L. Petersen, *Late Israelite Prophecy: Studies in Deutero-Prophetic Literature and in Chronicles* (Missoula: Scholars Press, 1977), 20–22, fails to convince when he tries to argue there is no call or commissioning material here vis à vis the author of this material.

[12] See pp. 116–20 above.

is [an] unstoppable reality."[13] In a vivid image in vv. 9–10, Jerusalem itself becomes the herald to Judah, standing on top of Mount Zion and announcing, "Here is your God." This in turn is followed by the image of God as the shepherd who will feed, carry, and gently lead his flock. There is, then, a twofold announcement of the good news—first to those in exile, and then to the remnant that was still in Judah and beyond it to the nations.[14]

It is interesting that nothing in the Hebrew text speaks of a voice crying in the wilderness, though both the later LXX and the OT chose to read the text this way. Rather, the imperative is used: "In the wilderness pave the way." Before Israel can leave exile, the way must be prepared.[15] It has been suggested that here is the Israelite counterpart to the Babylonian great processional highway. Indeed, the city of Babylon had at its heart the place where the highway of the gods and the highway of kings met. Consider the following excerpt from a Babylonian hymn:

> From hostile Elam he entered upon a road of jubilation,
> a path of rejoicing . . . of success to Su-an-na.
> The people of the land saw his towering figure,
> the ruler in (his) splendor.
> Hasten to go out, (Nabu), son of Bel,
> you who know the ways and the customs.
> Make his way good, renew his road,
> make his path straight, hew him out a trail.[16]

The theme of the Servant is not found in the opening material in ch. 40, but it soon appears, and with it the controversy as to whom or what the *ebed* terminology refers.[17] There is little debate that some of the twenty uses of the term "servant" in chs. 40–55 refer to Israel; indeed, there is general agreement that thirteen of these references do so. The real question is about the remaining seven, which occur within the Servant Songs, found in 42:1–4, 49:1–6, 50:4–9, and 52:13–53:12. It is notable that the plural term "servants" occurs nowhere before ch. 53 and, starting with 54:17, occurs eleven straight times without the singular, referring in each case to the people of God. In addition, it can be pointed out that the phrase "my servant" occurs twelve times in chs. 40–55, "his servant" occurs three times (44:26; 48:20; 50:10), and simply the term "servant" occurs five times (42:19; 44:21; 49:5, 6, 7).[18]

---

[13] Oswalt, *Isaiah 40–66*, 52.

[14] See G. A. F. Knight, *Isaiah 40–55: Servant Theology* (Grand Rapids: Eerdmans, 1984), 15–17.

[15] Westermann, *Isaiah 40–66*, 36–37.

[16] This is quoted, ibid., 38, from an unspecified source.

[17] Two of the more helpful surveys of the debate are C. G. Kruse, "The Servant Songs: Interpretive Trends since C. R. North," *SBT* 8 (1978): 1–27; and for a fuller treatment, H. Haag, *Der Gottesknecht bei Deuterojesaja* (Darmstadt: Wissenschaftliche, 1985).

[18] On all this, see the helpful analysis by G. P. Hugenberger, "The Servant of the Lord in the 'Servant Songs' of Isaiah: A Second Moses Figure," in *The Lord's Anointed* (ed. Satterthwaite et al.), 105–40.

Part of the debate hinges on whether one thinks these songs were originally separate entities that have been integrated into chs. 40–55, or are integral
parts of Second Isaiah, authored by the same person who composed the rest of
this material. It was the views of B. Duhm at the end of the last century that first
brought to prominence the theory that the Servant Songs are compositions separate from, and later than, the rest of chs. 40–55.[19] This view has of late been seriously challenged on the basis of the continuity of style, vocabulary, and content
that all of chs. 40–55 shares. It was also Duhm who urged that the Servant in
these songs was clearly an individual, not the nation of Israel. Among those
scholars who think the Servant Songs refer to an individual, there is no consensus as to which individual is meant—the prophet himself, Cyrus, Moses, a latter-
day Moses-like figure, one of the other famous prophets (Jeremiah?), or a future
messianic figure. There is evidence that this issue was debated even in the biblical
era. The Ethiopian eunuch was not the only person asking, "Does the prophet
refer to himself or someone else?" (Acts 8:34).

Some internal clues within the songs themselves help sift out some of the
options. In the first place, ch. 53 makes clear that the Servant is a human being
or group of humans, subject to suffering and death. In the crucial passage 49:1–7
one finds both an individual called Israel and "my servant" (v. 3), and a group to
whom this Servant ministers, which is also called Israel in this same text (v. 5).
The person in question is clearly a Hebrew and so part of Israel, and yet he can
be called Israel as well. In 42:3 the Servant is differentiated from the bruised reed
and dimly burning wick, both of which seem to refer to Israelites with tender
consciences. There is a similar distinction in both 42:6 and 49:8, where the Servant will be made a "covenant for the people," and this may be compared to a
similar remark in 53:8. "Accordingly, an identification of the Servant with Israel
is excluded because the 'he' who was 'cut off' [in ch. 53] cannot have the same
referent as 'my people.'"[20] Notice, too, finally that whenever the pronouns "we"
or "our" or "us" appear without explicit identification, it is always the individual
speaking on behalf of the people of Israel, with whom he identifies (cf. 42:24;
53:1ff.).

The question then becomes, Who is this individual? One might think immediately that since Isaiah himself is identified as "my servant" in 20:3, this provides us with an answer. Isaiah 44:26 would seem to refer to Isaiah, to Second
Isaiah, or to prophets such as them. But at the same time, in a text such as ch.
53, if we allow that the "we" or "us" is the prophet speaking on behalf of Israel
(see, e.g., 53:6), then this person is distinguished from the "he" or "him" who
suffers. One might also find it stretching things considerably to suggest that the
prophet was the one called upon to establish justice upon the earth, as the Servant is called to do in ch. 42. The exaltation of the Servant in 52:13 and 53:12
also fits poorly with an identification with a simple prophet. J. L. McKenzie also

---

[19] B. Duhm, *Das Buch Jesaja* (Göttingen: Vandenhoeck & Ruprecht, 1892).

[20] Hugenberger, "The Servant of the Lord," 110, to which this discussion is particularly indebted.

makes a good point when he asks why the prophet, who has so thoroughly hidden himself behind his message in the rest of chs. 40–55, should suddenly be so personal about himself in the Servant Songs.[21] It seems clear that the Servant is neither just the prophetic speaker of this material, who today is called Second Isaiah, nor simply just a prophetic figure in general. This Servant is also some kind of leader or ruler figure.

The traditional messianic interpretation of the Servant Songs has suggested that the figure here is the promised offspring of David referred to in chs. 7, 9, and 11. But frankly, apart from a hint of it in ch. 53, there is an absolute absence of royal imagery applied to the Servant in chs. 40–55, in contrast to the frequent use of the same in chs. 1–39.[22] It would be passing strange to call a king the slave of rulers, as is done of the Servant in 49:7. Instead of royal imagery, we regularly have prophetic imagery applied to this Servant, and he is said to be a teacher (42:4), a role that is not attributed to kings in the Hebrew Scriptures.

Perhaps one clue to the identity of this Servant is that in the earliest postcanonical interpretation of the Servant Song material, Rabbi Simlai quoted ch. 53 and applied it to Moses (b. *Soṭah* 14a). But the author of the Servant Songs is not simply engaged in retrospection here; he is looking forward, and this raises the question whether the Servant might indeed be the prophet like Moses, an interpretation that seems to be suggested in 11QMelch 18–25. The material in Isa 49 is reminiscent of what was said about Moses when he was called "servant," bearing in mind that Moses was especially called God's servant about forty times, eighteen of the twenty-three times in the form "Servant of Yahweh" (the other five to David), and all four of the times the phrase "Servant of God" occurs. Isa 49 is also reminiscent of what was said in Jer 1 about that prophet.

Notice also that the task of being a light to the nations is assigned to this Servant, which is close to what is said about Jeremiah (a prophet of the nations),[23] but this task is clearly one that Israel as a nation elsewhere had been given. This combination of Mosaic traits and prophetic traits well suits the idea that the Servant is the latter-day Mosaic figure, and it must be remembered that there is some evidence that Jeremiah may have seen himself in this light.[24] The prevalent second-exodus imagery throughout chs. 40–55 also supports this connection.[25] The later material in 63:11–19 also supports this view, for when the people look for a deliverer, they look for a latter-day Moses figure and Moses is called "his servant" in that passage. Finally, it will be remembered that in Moses various roles coalesced. He was a mediator; he functioned sometimes as a priest; he spoke God's word; though not a king, he exercised rule and authority over

---

[21] J. L. McKenzie, *Second Isaiah* (Garden City: Doubleday, 1968), xlvii.

[22] Hugenberger, "The Servant of the Lord," 117.

[23] See pp. 130–35 above.

[24] See pp. 130–40 above.

[25] See Hugenberger, "The Servant of the Lord," 124–28.

God's people; he was a judge; he was the people's representative. The portrait of the Servant likewise suggests such a figure in whom such roles coalesce.

It follows from all of this that the Servant is apparently some sort of leader figure, like a Moses or like a Jeremiah, who has some particular representative role in relationship to Israel. He appears in the same chapters as does the theme of the new exodus from exile. R. J. Clifford puts it this way: "Servants, such as Moses, Joshua, the king of the Deuteronomic ideal (Deut. 17:14–20), and the preexilic prophets, are models of obedience for Israel. In this sense, the servant can be at the same time an obedient friend of Yahweh and the nation. The obedient servant is what Israel is called to be."[26] At the same time, Israel has not been all that God wanted it to be, and so there is a sense in which its representative must fulfill its role and also absorb punishment in its stead. Isaiah 52:13–53:12 is surely about some sort of vicarious act by the Servant. At the same time, there is no evidence that either Isaiah or Second Isaiah or Jeremiah or Moses fulfilled the role described in this most controversial of all Servant Songs. While Moses certainly experienced rejection by God's people, he never died for their sins. The Servant of these songs, then, is in all likelihood an individual, the promised prophet like unto Moses, who, like Moses, would come and represent God to the nation and the nation to God, fulfilling roles that had been originally expected of the nation. It is Cyrus, not the Servant, who is called "my anointed," or messiah. The Mosaic and prophetic—rather than the royal—traditions are, in the main, those applied to this future figure in these songs. This study must now turn to some of the details of the songs.

Isaiah 42 announces the theme of the Servant and his relationship with God. Here a particular individual is designated as God's Servant, and God promises to uphold him. The manner in which this transpires is that God puts his spirit upon his Servant, and imbues him with the the authority and power that the spirit brings; the Servant will bring forth justice to the nations. As Oswalt says, this role of doing *mishpat* distinguishes this Servant from the role predicated of Israel the nation as God's Servant.[27] Notably, this Servant will not come like the prophets of doom, lifting up their voices in the streets and thundering condemnation. To the contrary, he will deal gently with those who are damaged and those whose light is flickering or burning low. Nonetheless, he will bring forth justice, never wearying until he accomplishes this task.

But how will he accomplish this task if he does not come as a warrior king or as a prophet whose very words enact and inaugurate judgment? Verse 4b says that the coastlands wait for his teaching. The role of the Servant is further explicated in vv. 5–9, which could be seen as the second stanza of this first song. Verse 5 serves as a preamble to the oracular material of vv. 6–9. The preamble affirms the sovereignty of God as the creator of all things and persons (cf. 40:12–26). Verse 6, however, turns specifically to God's call and enabling of the Servant. Precisely because God is the Lord of all, God has called the Servant in

---

[26] R. J. Clifford, "Isaiah, Book of (Second Isaiah)," *ABD* 3:500.

[27] Oswalt, *Isaiah 40–66*, 109.

righteousness, has taken him by the hand, and has given him as a covenant to the people and a light to the nations (v. 6b). The first thing to note about this interesting verse is that the verbs "call" and "take by the hand" are the very same as those applied to Israel as a people in 41:9. But what does it mean that the Servant has been given as a covenant of the people? Sense can be made out of this if one compares the next clause, where the Servant is a light to the nations. It suggests that the Servant has a more intimate and binding relationship to Israel than to the nations. Like Moses, the Servant establishes a new relationship, a covenantal relationship with God's people. Isaiah 49:5–8 will make even clearer that the Servant has a mission to Israel. But the obligation of God's people to enlighten and thus save the nations now also falls on the Servant.[28]

Verse 7 indicates that the particular focus of the ministry of the Servant in Israel will be directed to the least, last, and lost—to open eyes that are blind, bring prisoners out of dark prisons. God affirms this agenda again in v. 8 being the Lord, with the implication that God is perfectly capable of doing these new things. Verse 9 indicates also that God will reveal new things to the Servant. God will tell the Servant in advance about these new things. This indirectly suggests the Servant's prophetic role—he is to teach and to prophesy about the coming new things. It is not revealed here what these new things are, but soon enough we hear about the surprising role of Cyrus as an anointed liberator of God's people; in addition, however, one also hears of a suffering Servant. Both come as complete surprises.[29]

The second Servant Song is found in 49:1–6. By this point in chs. 40–55, Cyrus has already been revealed as God's anointed one and his role has been delineated (ch. 45). In ch. 49 the Servant speaks for himself to faraway people about his calling. As Oswalt points out, this reiteration of some of the content already given in the first song is natural if the intervening material in 42:10–ch. 48 was in fact about something else.[30]

The call of the Servant did not come in the midst of life but, indeed, before he was born. He was called and named by God while he was still in his mother's womb. The reference to the womb surely supports the contention that this Servant is not the nation but an individual.[31] This indicates that God has claimed and shaped the very nature of this Servant. Notice that it is particularly the mouth of the Servant that has been enabled by God—it will be like a sharp sword. The Servant himself will be like a highly polished arrow, so penetrating and powerful will be his words and his very presence. The image of the arrow may also suggest the wide range and scope of the Servant's ministry.[32] The image of the Servant being hidden away in the quiver may indicate that he will suddenly appear as from nowhere when God sends him forth. Before then, he will

---

[28] See Knight, *Isaiah 40–55*, 48.

[29] See Westermann, *Isaiah 40–66*, 99–101.

[30] Oswalt, *Isaiah 40–66*, 288.

[31] Ibid., 289.

[32] Westermann, *Isaiah 40–66*, 209.

be nowhere to be seen. What God said to the Servant was that he was indeed *his* Servant, his Israel (i.e., chosen one), in whom God will truly and finally be glorified. The Servant will function as Israel should have functioned. While it was Cyrus's job to help God's people return to the land, it was the Servant's job to help them return to the Lord and—even beyond that—to save the world! In fact, strictly speaking, the grammar of the Hebrew here suggests the translation, "I have appointed you . . . to be my salvation to the ends of the earth."[33]

Surprisingly the Servant replies to God in v. 4 that his own efforts are fruitless and he has wasted his time and strength, even though his cause and reward are with God. Verse 5 specifies quite clearly that the Servant is not the nation of Israel, for it is his task to bring Jacob back to God, to regather Israel to God, to raise up the tribes of the chosen people, to restore the survivors of Israel (vv. 5b, 6a). But God has decided it is too light a thing for the Servant to simply be engaged in that task. He will also be given as a light to the nations so that God's salvation may reach the ends of the earth. One may perhaps see three stages in the career of the Servant—he is called and equipped (vv. 1–3), he despairs of his first task (v. 4), he is given a further task in relation to the nations (vv. 5–6).[34] This brings us back to the beginning of this song, in which the faraway peoples were addressed. Thus, the Servant is depicted as already undertaking this further task at the beginning of the song.[35]

The third Servant Song is found at 50:4–9. If it has not dawned on the reader before, it certainly becomes clear here that the effect of the Servant Songs is intended to be cumulative and they must be read in their current sequence. In ch. 49 one hears something of the frustrations and depression of the Servant. There are open opposition and abuse by some of those who have heard the Servant. Furthermore, in this song some additional information can be learned about the Servant as both learner (being a good listener when God speaks) and as teacher. In v. 4 it is said of the Servant that he is given the tongue of a disciple, which is to say, the tongue of one who recites verbatim what he has heard and learned. Here is a figure who accomplishes his mission by speech.[36] It is interesting that it is only in the book of Isaiah that the substantive *limmudim* occurs, meaning "learners" or "disciples" (cf. 8:16–17).[37] He is able to sustain the weary by his words; in other words, he is a sort of pastor (cf. 40:28–29 on the term "weary").[38] The key, however, to his even having words to say is that morning by morning God opens his ears and instructs him. His ear has been trained to listen like a disciple.[39]

---

[33] See Oswalt, *Isaiah 40–66*, 294.

[34] Knight, *Isaiah 40–55*, 130–31, fails to grasp the subtle interplay between the individual servant as representative of Israel and Israel the nation.

[35] See Westermann, *Isaiah 40–66*, 207.

[36] See McKenzie, *Second Isaiah*, 116–17.

[37] Knight, *Isaiah 40–55*, 144.

[38] John D. W. Watts, *Isaiah 34–66* (WBC 35; Waco: Word, 1987), 201.

[39] Westermann, *Isaiah 40–66*, 228–29.

Westermann rightly stresses that here we have a very accurate description of the way prophecy worked in Israel. It is a matter of, first, being trained by God to listen, then listening intently to God, and, finally, like the disciple of a great teacher in antiquity, simply reciting verbatim what one has heard. "The special characteristic of the prophetic office is the very fact that the prophet wakens his ear 'morning by morning,' and must continually allow it to be opened by God, in order to have 'an answer to give to the weary.' The entire inability to exercise any control over the reception and transmission of a word that has no establishment in which it is at home, is here the expression of the chief characteristic of the prophetic office of the word."[40]

But in fact, when he has spoken, there have been vulgar, insulting, shaming responses. What is described in v. 6 is the sort of negative response one would expect to an uncomfortable teaching or prophetic oracle in the ancient Near East, where negative responses often took the form not only of verbal rejection (insults) but of gestures (spitting) and even of physical violence of a minor sort, intended more to shame than to harm (pulling the beard, striking with a hand or a garment). "The most telling insult that the East could perpetrate on a man in order to insult him and so render him inferior, or even just to put him in his place, was to pluck the hairs from his *beard* (cf. Neh. 13:25)."[41]

But attempts at shaming and success at shaming are two different things. The Servant says in v. 7 that because God has helped him, he has not been disgraced regardless of his audience's conduct. Because God is with him, he has simply become more determined in the face of opposition. He sets his face like flint, knowing that in the highest court he will be vindicated. The Servant calls out those who would contend with or confront him or accuse him of being guilty of something—those who are adversaries—and he does so without fear because his vindicator is near to hand. God is his advocate in court. The Lord is his help, and eventually the opposition will wear itself out like an old coat.

Nevertheless, the Servant has had something of a Jeremiah-like experience with his audience (cf. Jer 11:20; 15:15, 16; 17:14; 20:11, 12; 18:23), and there is an element of the lament in this third Servant Song.[42] But the complaint here pales in comparison with what is coming in the final Servant Song. In concluding the discussion of the third song, it is worth pointing out that in this song alone do we find the phrase "Sovereign Lord," and here we have it four times. It seems to be present to stress that God is in control of what is happening to the Servant and thus that God's sovereignty is the basis of the Servant's courage to go ahead with his mission and his confidence that he will be vindicated.[43]

Certainly, one of the most discussed passages in all the Hebrew Scriptures is the fourth Servant Song, found at 52:13–53:12. Almost everything about the song is debated, including the form of the original text itself. Some important

---

[40] Ibid., 229.
[41] Knight, *Isaiah 40–55*, 145.
[42] Westermann, *Isaiah 40–66*, 226–27.
[43] Oswalt, *Isaiah 40–66*, 323.

things have been learned about the Servant prior to this song, but we are not entirely prepared for what we find in this concluding song. Yes, the reader has been informed about the Servant's suffering in the third Servant Song, but not to the degree that is presented here. Indeed, the various repeated themes that are found here are all amplified to a new level, and this includes the notions of "the worldwide consequences of his work after apparent failure, the lack of understanding, the willingness to undergo undeserved suffering, the certain success."[44]

Equally clearly, the literary art is taken to a new level, for this climactic song is not just the longest of the songs but a carefully crafted five stanzas of three verses each (52:13–15; 53:1–3; 53:4–6; 53:7–9; 53:10–12). The first and last stanzas are oracular in character as God speaks words of commendation about the Servant; the second and third stanzas are spoken by those who caused the Servant's suffering; and the fourth stanza is in the third person as the author gives a commentary evaluating the Servant's unjust fate. The heart of this song is the contrast between God's evaluation of the Servant and that of those human beings other than the author, who were in part responsible for the Servant's suffering. There is also a strong contrast between the Servant's exaltation by God and his humiliation and suffering at the hands of human beings. These two contrasts are connected. If the humans had had God's perspective on the Servant, the Servant might not have had to undergo the humiliation and suffering he did at their hands.[45]

In the previous chapter, dealing with the earlier Isaianic material about the ideal ruler, there were a certain generality and opacity to the material, which have led to some of the current debate and have equally led to suggestions of multivalency.[46] The same may be the case with this material in the fourth Servant Song. This is not surprising when a prophet feels led to speak about the more distant future, which does not have clear moorings in his present or near future. Because of the use of this material in the OT and the interpretation of ch. 53 by both modern Christians and Jews, there has been a tendency among scholars to try to say more than they should about what the text can *not* mean, in order to peremptorily rule out of court interpretations of the text they personally find offensive or find inconsistent with their own assumptions about what is true or false about Hebrew prophecy, about the nature of God, or about the possibility of vicarious or substitutionary suffering, to mention but a few contentious subjects. The focus here will instead be on what the text *does* say, leaving the implications and applications for debates in other contexts.

The fourth Servant Song begins as the first one did, with the words "Behold my Servant." The focus is, from the outset, to be on this individual, and from the outset the focus is on the contrast between now and the future. The Servant will be exalted and lifted up, but that is only after his suffering. And his

---

[44] Ibid., 376.

[45] On these contrasts see P. Raabe, "The Effect of Repetition in the Suffering Servant Song," *JBL* 103 (1984): 77–81.

[46] See pp. 118–25 above.

suffering involves considerable disfigurement, such that some who see it are astonished. This would seem to go beyond what scourging and beard pulling could accomplish (ch. 49). We are told his appearance was marred beyond recognition. He hardly appeared human. As Westermann says, this means the Servant has suffered severely, so that he has been seriously disfigured by it, causing people to shudder in horror.[47]

In an honor-and-shame culture, such an appearance not only would cause revulsion but would prompt many to assume that this person was cursed by God, probably a notable sinner and at the very least ritually unclean, and so to be shunned or even ostracized from society. The reaction in the ancient Near East would be just the opposite of that to someone who was tall and handsome (cf., e.g., the story of Saul). That such a disfigured person should be exalted by God is unheard of, new and shocking in such a setting. As Knight says, in a strongly hierarchial culture, the opinion of the king quickly becomes the opinion of the country: if the king is astonished or impressed or appalled, the nation will immediately also have to take notice. Our author "is obviously aware that the best strategy one can employ in the propagation of an idea is to begin with the man at the top."[48]

The Servant, then, will startle not only ordinary Jewish mortals but also many nations, including kings. It is not just the appearance of the Servant that astonishes; it is that God has chosen this unlikely person to accomplish God's saving purposes. As McKenzie says, the theme that unites all these Servant Songs is the saving acts of Yahweh, and these acts involve both Israel and the nations.[49] Unlike Israel, the nations have not had advance notice about this saving work through the Servant. They had not been told about it and so they had not heard of it, but nonetheless they will be forced to contemplate it. It must be stressed, though, that what certain people say about the Servant is largely irrelevant. What matters is what God (and the author) says about the Servant.

As Westermann says, the account of what some say about the Servant (53:1–11a) is set within the framework of what God says about him (52:13ff.; 53:11b–12). Both sections speak of the Servant's humiliation and exaltation but from very different points of view.[50] In God's view, the Servant is and will be successful in his mission and, as a result, will be *high* and *lifted up*. These two terms in combination are used elsewhere in the OT, but in this book and in each case they are used to describe God (cf. 6:1; 33:10; 57:15). The same can be said about the use of the language of exaltation here. Isaiah 2:6–22 speaks strongly against the exaltation of any mere mortal. Thus it appears from the outset of this song that we are being told that the Servant will be given a divine position and condition that is not suitable for any mere mortal, although at the same time we

---

[47] Westermann, *Isaiah 40–66*, 259.
[48] Knight, *Isaiah 40–55*, 167.
[49] McKenzie, *Second Isaiah*, 133.
[50] Westermann, *Isaiah 40–66*, 255.

are being told how very mortal and frail this Servant is.[51] This Mosaic prophetic figure is no ordinary prophet or even a normal human leader. And he will pursue an unheard-of means to win over the world—he will choose to lose all things, give his life, choose to die in an apparently shameful way in order to gain all.

The second stanza of this Servant Song begins at 53:1, but it continues the theme found at the end of the first stanza. At the beginning and end of this stanza there is the "we" who are astonished at what they have heard about the Servant and who have held him of no account. But is this "we" Israel, or is it the Gentile nations? A case can be made for either; on the whole, however, the theme of the one with a marred appearance that a particular group finds repulsive appears in both stanzas, and in the first it was the many Israelites who commented on his marred appearance. Thus, the prophet is speaking for Israel in 53:1—he is one of those who is shocked to hear about this remarkable phenomenon.[52] The phrase "the arm of the Lord," like the phrase "the hand of the Lord," is a common one and refers to God's saving power. The image is of a warrior who has thrown off his cloak and bared his mighty arm and hand (compare 40:10; 48:14; 51:5; 52:10 with 5:25; 9:11, 16, 20; 10:4; 50:2; 51:9). The interesting juxtaposition here is that God's power is being revealed through weakness, through the weak Servant.

Two analogies are used in 53:2 to describe the Servant: he grew up like a young plant, suggesting tenderness and vulnerability, but he was like a root out of dry ground, again suggesting vulnerability but also the element of surprise. The root came up where it was not expected. Westermann suggests that both analogies imply that the Servant grew up parched and without strength or sap.[53] "Instead of bursting on the scene like a mighty oak or a fruit tree in full bloom, he appears as a *sprout* or 'sucker,' the normally unwanted shoot that springs up from an exposed root of a tree."[54] This image may perhaps be correlated with the shoot from the stump of Jesse, found earlier in 11:1.[55] The second half of the verse indicates that the Servant had no form or beauty that would cause one to take notice of him in a positive way or find him desirable. Beauty was seen as the sign of blessing from God (cf. Gen 39:6b; 1 Sam 16:18), and so a marred form would signal the opposite. But this sapling grew up under the watchful eye of God, who would ensure that he became and did what he was designed to become and do.

Not surprisingly, with the form and visage the Servant had, he was despised and rejected by others; suffering and infirmity were his regular companions. Notice that the emphasis falls on the word "despised," which occurs at the beginning and the end of this verse. Yet as Oswalt says, the Hebrew term here

---

[51] See Oswalt, *Isaiah 40–66*, 378–79.

[52] Ibid., 381.

[53] Westermann, *Isaiah 40–66*, 261.

[54] Oswalt, *Isaiah 40–66*, 382.

[55] See Knight, *Isaiah 40–55*, 169.

basically means someone worthless and so unworthy of notice. His lot in life was, to a real extent, determined by how people reacted to him. There is some dispute whether the text reads "as one who hides his face from us" or "as one from whom others hide their faces." It could be either.

In an honor-and-shame culture, it was normal for the disfigured or diseased to hide their form so that they would not be immediately shunned or rejected by others, but the text could also mean that the Servant's features were so repulsive that people instinctively turned their face in another direction so as to not have to see the ugliness. The evil-eye conventions of antiquity might also come into play here, for it was widely believed that if you looked at or allowed the gaze of a sick or repulsive or cursed person, you too might be blighted.[56] There is a very close affinity here with the language of the Psalms, especially Ps 22:24.[57] Interestingly, in the psalm one hears the opposite—that God did not despise the suffering psalmist nor hide his face from him. This leads to a third possibility—that people would not support the Servant or give him help in his distress. The effect of the Servant's form and his being despised is that he was alienated from his own people and community. He tred a lonely path, isolated from those who should have appreciated and esteemed him.

The third stanza, in 53:4–6, pushes matters a step further. Here it is indicated that the sufferings of the Servant were not his own just due, much less his own fault, but that he suffered for the iniquities of the community. As McKenzie says, it is not clear whether suffering caused by illness or suffering caused by physical violence is in view (or perhaps both), but what is clear is that it was unmerited, undeserved by the Servant.[58] The belief in the integral connection between an individual's lot of sin and suffering (if one suffers, it is because one has sinned) is being rejected here. Yet there is clearly a connection of a different sort—the Servant suffers because he has been pierced by "our transgressions," he has been crushed for or by "our iniquities."

Clearly, it is here and in vv. 10–12 that the issue of the Servant's substitutionary suffering becomes a live issue. The text seems to strongly suggest that the Servant suffers not just *as a result* of the sins of the people but also *in the place of* the people.[59] It will not do to simply say that the Servant suffers with God's people, because the text speaks of him unjustly suffering for "our" transgressions, as if he were like the scapegoat in the Levitical ritual. Second, the Servant has been clearly identified in these songs with God's saving purposes, with the arm of the Lord. "But if the Servant is merely the prophet who suffers because of his people, that identification is impossible."[60]

---

[56] See B. Witherington, *Grace in Galatia* (Edinburgh: T&T Clark, 1997), on Gal 4:13–14.

[57] See Westermann, *Isaiah 40–66*, 262.

[58] McKenzie, *Second Isaiah*, 133.

[59] See rightly Oswalt, *Isaiah 40–66*, 385.

[60] Ibid.

The "we" assumed that the Servant was afflicted by God for his own sins, but in fact he was afflicted for "our sins." "We" saw him as weak and sick, but in fact it was "our" weakness and sickness he was bearing and enduring. The verbs here about carrying and bearing come from the Levitical cultic material. The animal carries *(nasa)* the sins of the one who offers that animal in sacrifice, and thereby deflects the punishment from falling on the offerer (Lev 5:1, 17; 10:17; 16:22; 17:16; 20:19; Num 9:13; 14:34). Furthermore, the verb *sabal* refers to a suffering of something on behalf of, and in place of, someone else (Isa 46:4, 7; Lam 5:7). The element of vicariousness can not be eliminated from this text. "The Servant is not suffering *with* his people (however unjustly), but *for* them."[61]

This person was pierced through as a result of his people's rebellion, and as the text says literally, "in his welts, it is healed to us." His suffering produces their healing, his suffering makes it unnecessary for them to be punished for their sins. "Upon him was the punishment that made us whole." The end of this stanza reminds the audience that their behavior has been as careless as that of sheep, which quite easily lose their way by being so self-absorbed that they simply go their own way. But these sheep will not have to pay for their errors and foibles, because the Lord has laid on the Servant the punishment for their iniquity. "The prophet clearly sees an innocent Israelite who rescues his fellow Israelites from suffering by bearing their suffering himself."[62] This suffering, then, is not in vain, for it wards off penal suffering for the sheep. The "thing that was new and revolutionary for the present speakers was the fact that in this case suffering which gave power to be a substitute and to atone was found residing in a quite ordinary, feeble and inconsiderable person whose suffering, disfiguring as it was, had brought him into contempt and abhorrence."[63]

The fourth stanza (vv. 7–9) will tell us something of how the Servant responded to all this suffering and finally to an unjust death. This section makes quite clear that we are not just talking about a suffering Servant but, rather, also a dying and dead Servant, and in fact one who died violently and was shamed even in his burial. At the beginning of this stanza the sheep metaphor is continued—the Servant is like a sheep led to the slaughter. Like an animal that is in a very frightening position, whether being sheared or being killed, he was completely silent, never opening his mouth. He did not plead, he did not protest, he did not break down. Sheep are nondefensive and often submissive by nature. The Servant was as innocent as a lamb, but he was in the midst of a bunch of merciless and mercenary people. One other thing about sheep may suggest why this metaphor is extended in this song—they were the chief sacrificial animal (cf. Jer 11:19).

---

[61] Ibid., 386. Here and throughout this section, I am following Oswalt, who has seen most clearly the implications of this material.

[62] McKenzie, *Second Isaiah*, 134.

[63] Westermann, *Isaiah 40–66*, 263.

Verse 7 sets the tone by stressing that the Servant was oppressed, a note re-iterated at the beginning of v. 8. There was nothing just about the way he was treated. Oswalt is probably right that the second verb in v. 8 means "he was humbling himself," which comports with the sheep metaphor but also suggests some intentionality on the part of the Servant.[64] This behavior of the Servant was in spite of the fact that he was taken away from a place where he might have been protected or justice might have been rendered. Verse 8 is full of textual and grammatical difficulties, but on balance the second half of the verse seems to mean, "and his descendants, who has considered them?" No "one has consid-ered that the Servant was left without children in a culture where to die childless was to have lived an utterly futile existence."[65] This comports well with the re-verse of this proposition, which one finds in v. 10c and which speaks of his off-spring. The clause in v. 8 that speaks of his being cut off from the land of the living makes clear that his life was cut short—it was by no means a natural death. But it begins to emerge in this verse that there was someone else behind the Servant's death other than just wicked human beings, for clearly enough *they* were not offering the Servant up as an atonement for Israel's sins. Thus, when it says, "he was stricken for the transgressions of my people," the author seems al-ready to be implying that there was indeed a specific purpose to his death—God's purpose.

But it was not enough for the wicked that they killed the Servant. They then added insult to injury by making his grave with the wicked. "Shame was part and parcel of the Servant's suffering. Shame also attaches to his death. He was buried with malefactors and miscreants. This is the verse that makes two things clear. First, the report has an individual, one single [person] in view. And at the same time it shows perfectly plainly that the one about whom the report is made had actually died and been buried."[66] The further explication is that he was buried with a rich person, or possibly the text reads that his death was like that of a rich person. In favor of the latter is that there is in the biblical tradition some association of wealth and wickedness (cf. the parable of the Rich Man and Lazarus). This death and shameful burial happened even though the Servant had done no violence and there was no deceit in his mouth. The end of this stanza returns us to the beginning, about what comes out of the Servant's mouth. It will be remembered that in the third Servant Song the stress was on his having the tongue of a disciple. Nothing malicious, nothing deceptive came out of his mouth, and indeed in his last hours absolutely nothing came out of his mouth despite the horrible way he was treated.

The final stanza of the final Servant Song brings the entire song cycle to a dramatic conclusion and climax. Verse 10 begins with a *waw* adversative, which in a lament would normally signal a turning point in the song.[67] Indeed, there is

---

[64] Oswalt, *Isaiah 40–66*, 391.

[65] Ibid., 395.

[66] Westermann, *Isaiah 40–66*, 266.

[67] See ibid.

a change at this juncture, from a tone of mourning to one of exaltation. We need to be clear, as Westermann rightly stresses, that the subject of what follows in vv. 10–12 is not merely deliverance *from* death, a frequent theme in the Psalms (Ps 18:4–5; 69:1–2, 14–15; 88:3–6), but deliverance *after* or *beyond* death. McKenzie is also right to stress that the "scope both of the Servant's atoning suffering and of his vindication go beyond any historical persons or events of ancient Israel known to us."[68] No human being in ancient Israel played the role of the scapegoat (Lev 16:21–22), but the Servant is said to have done so here.[69]

The final stanza begins, however, on a somber note—"yet it was the will of God to crush him with pain (or disease)."[70] Whatever else one chooses to say about it, this phrase means that the Servant was not just a victim of the accidents of history or the maliciousness of wicked human beings. He wasn't just in the wrong place at the wrong time. God's will was involved in this horrible death. But even so, as the next clause makes clear, it would be for naught if human beings did not react properly to this event. The second clause reads "if you make his life a guilt offering." The conditional particle here needs to be left in the text, in all probability.[71] The "you" is surely those who might benefit from this death if they relate to it properly.

The point is that God wants human beings to have an atonement for their sins to offer up, and this Servant is the means of it. God's purpose will be fully realized only if people relate to the death of the Servant in such a manner.[72] There is, however, another way to read the main Hebrew verb here, which results in the translation, "when he makes himself an offering for sin" (NRSV). This makes sense and it may well be right, but it requires we take the conditional particle to mean "when" rather than "if." The key here, however, would seem to be that we have a reference to the guilt offering, an offering for deliberate sin, knowingly incurred, and thus an offering that had to be offered by the person responsible for the sin (Lev 5:1–19).[73] This favors the "if you . . ." translation, in which case the author here is engaging the audience directly and telling them how they must relate to this sacrifice for it to accomplish the purpose that God intended.

It is interesting that the next clause focuses on the benefits of this death for the Servant himself—"he shall see his offspring and prolong his days; through

---

[68] McKenzie, *Second Isaiah,* 136.

[69] See, e.g., even Koch, *The Prophets,* 2:141: "Does the Servant himself become the scapegoat in his own person? Is it to him that Israel's tremendous sphere of sin is transferred, so that he may go to his death carrying it (*nasa,* v. 4)? The song which is sung by people professing faith in Yahweh, suggests something of the kind."

[70] It is interesting that the *Isaiah Scroll* (4QIsaª) has "that he might pierce him."

[71] See M. Dahood, "Isaiah 53.8–12 and Masoretic Misconstructions," *Bib* 63 (1982): 566–70; and J. Battenfield, "Isaiah 63.10: Taking the 'if' out of the Sacrifice of the Servant," *VT* 32 (1982): 485.

[72] See rightly Oswalt, *Isaiah 40–66,* 401.

[73] Ibid., 402.

him the will of the Lord shall prosper." Here are the first signs of the great reversal. The Servant died without children and was buried without honor. The key terms applied to him here are the usual barometers in Israelite society of a person blessed by God—long life and progeny (Ps 21:4; 34:12; 127:3–5; 128:6; Prov 17:6). This successful conclusion only happens because the Servant became a sacrificial offering for some people, and they in turn became his offspring, his extended family. Thus, the reference to "seed" must be taken in a metaphorical sense here, and it is possible that the reference to length of days should be as well. On the whole, however, there does seem to be a reference to resurrection here, for it is only beyond death that the Servant gets these benefits and it would be difficult to see how these metaphors are appropriate if the author only had in mind heavenly compensation for the Servant after his exaltation. As Koch says, "This sounds like resurrection, which would make Isa. 53 the earliest passage in the Old Testament in which such a hope is expressed (apart from Ezek. 34:23? . . .)."[74] The Servant, then, is said to live again, beyond death, see his descendants, and acquire a not inconsiderable inheritance. But it is not the Servant's will but the will of the Lord that will be coming to fruition and prospering when all this transpires.

Nonetheless, the Servant will have a sense of accomplishment when he sees the results and benefits of his death, knowing it has not all been for naught. There is light at the end of his anguish. The second half of v. 11 restates what has already been suggested, but in different terms. The Servant will make people righteous, in the sense of achieving for them right standing with God through his atoning sacrifice, through bearing the people's iniquities or sins, and he is able to do this precisely because he is the Righteous One. The sacrifice must be perfect and unblemished to accomplish such a result, and the Servant was an innocent and blameless man. In a fitting comparison, Oswalt notes what the Servant accomplishes in comparison with God's anointed one Cyrus—the latter restored Israel to its land a physical return, the former made it possible for Israel to come home to its God, a homecoming of the heart.[75]

The last verse of the Servant Songs, v. 12 tells of the consequences of all this for the Servant himself—"Therefore I will allot him a portion with the great and he shall divide the spoil with the strong." The image here is of a victory parade, and to the victors go the spoils. This figure, then, is more than an ordinary prophet. He is here seen as a conquering hero, but the war he fought was not waged with the normal weapons of an Israelite soldier. The Servant is more like Moses than David in what he has accomplished and, to some extent, in the means he used to do so—bearing with a difficult people and interceding for them. Verse 12b reiterates one more time the reason God has so favored the Servant: he poured out his life *(nefesh)* to the point of death and endured being numbered with the transgressors, and yet he was not one of them but was merely intervening for them. "This does not mean, as some . . . imagine, that he

---

[74] Koch, *The Prophets*, 2:142.
[75] Oswalt, *Isaiah 40–66*, 405.

made prayers of intercession for them, but that with his life, his suffering and his death, he took their place and underwent their punishment in their stead."[76] God has exalted him because he fulfilled the purposes for which God intended his life. It is clear that this conclusion to the greatest of the Servant Songs provides some of the basis for the conclusion of the greatest of the Christ hymns, found in Phil 2.

The lofty themes and forms of expression we find in these Servant Songs would be difficult to surpass. Many scholars rightly see this material as the apex of traditional Hebrew prophetic expression. But in a way, these songs were surpassed, at least in the scope of their subject matter, in protoapocalyptic literature, which opened windows to the heavenly realities rather than just provide penetrating insights into earthly ones. This study must turn now to the beginnings of apocalyptic in the visions of a priest and prophet known as Ezekiel.

II. EZEKIEL AND THE CHARIOT OF GOD

Though perhaps from a generation before Second Isaiah, Ezekiel's prophecy portends the direction that Hebrew prophecy was increasingly going to take in the postexilic age—namely, an apocalyptic direction—and so we must deal with this text before moving on to the postexilic period. In his landmark study on apocalyptic, P. D. Hanson argued at some length that apocalyptic, and in particular apocalyptic eschatology, developed out of the prophetic tradition in the late sixth and early fifth centuries BC.[77] He sought to pinpoint the prophetic tradition of Second and Third Isaiah and Zech 9–14 as the tradition out of which apocalyptic emerged, while he saw Ezekiel and Zech 1–8 as something separate and only occasionally using apocalyptic motifs to legitimate a particular political agenda. The latter conclusion will not stand close scrutiny, for, as R. J. Bauckham has rightly pointed out, Zech 9–14 seems to be rather heavily dependent on the traditions we find in Ezekiel.[78] Nevertheless, Hanson's major conclusion—that apocalyptic developed primarily out of the prophetic tradition—is widely accepted today as correct. I would, however, demur at the conclusion that apocalyptic did not arise until the postexilic period. It seems that its social origins must be pushed back further.

At the heart of apocalyptic thought is the notion that God, and God alone, can rectify a world, a situation gone so very wrong. In other words, it is a theocratic vision of how positive change can and will come for God's people and the human race. It affirms repeatedly the solution of direct divine intervention and therefore not surprisingly focuses, to a great extent, on things transcendent and on the interface between the heavenly and the earthly. While the auditory dimension of prophecy is not by any means left behind, nevertheless the visual or

---

[76] Westermann, *Isaiah 40–66*, 269.

[77] Hanson, *Dawn of Apocalyptic*.

[78] R. J. Bauckham, "The Rise of Apocalyptic," *Them* 4 (2, 1979): 10–23.

visionary prophetic experience comes much more to the fore, and in all cases what is seen, whether heavenly or earthly realities, is described in metaphorical and often hyperbolic terms. Whether one thinks of tours of the otherworld or images of cosmic transformation of this world, there is a constant presentation of visual stimuli. What had prompted this focus more on the visionary prophetic experience than on simply the auditory? Why this considerably greater emphasis on otherworldly realities? Here social analysis of the prophetic experience can be of help.

Once we get to the exile, the previously crucial distinction between central and peripheral prophets does not much help, except when we are dealing with a figure such as Daniel, who plays a role in a foreign ruler's court. Peripheral prophets were always on the margins and often marginalized by society even further, but what happens when all of Israel lives on the margins of an alien society? What happens when temple and territory can no longer be a concrete and visible focus at the heart of one's religion? What happens when a prophet can very seldom say, "Thus saith Yahweh," in any positive way about some reality in the present? Perhaps the focus of the prophet turns both upward and outward—to distant places and more remote times. In the situation of the marginalization of a whole subculture in exile, keeping hope alive entailed focusing on the vertical and the horizontal perspectives. This does not necessarily include eschatology because sometimes the horizontal perspective is totally eclipsed in favor of a focus on the otherworldly. Thus, we can not say that eschatology stands at the heart of all apocalyptic literature.

It is no accident that the beginnings of a full-blown belief in a positive afterlife, whether above or beyond in the resurrection, first comes to light only in the exilic material. This has already been seen in the material we examined in Second Isaiah. My contention is that apocalyptic literature arose as a prophetic means of expressing such beliefs about the afterlife and the otherworld. It may also have arisen in response to the lack of a sense of God's presence and activity in the present situation in exile. The necessary presence of otherworldly mediators in this literature, such as angels, even between a prophet and his God in various cases, suggests the sense of distance from the divine. Apocalyptic literature is always minority literature, and it assumes a condition of cultural deprivation and often of crisis, such that without some form of divine intervention, things can not possibly get better. It assumes the opposite of *Realpolitik*.

In Second Isaiah there are songs, and insofar as they envisioned a solution, they were not closely tied to any particular historical experience in the prophet's own life or that of his audience. These songs do not constitute a program to be realized by the prophet or his audience. They constitute a hope for the future, even though that hope is born out of great suffering and arrives and arises only beyond that suffering. The solution is not escape to heaven but help from heaven "in that day." In other words, it has not lost its historical moorings, but it has no faith in history itself or its human processes. Nevertheless, the otherworldly reality and its images do not come to the fore—the fate of the Servant on earth is its focus. This is eschatology without the form of apocalyptic but with idealization. In Ezekiel, by contrast, we have apocalyptic both in its otherworldly and in its afterworldly dimensions (cf. Ezek 40–48).

It appears that apocalyptic, if one can speak of it already existing in Ezekiel, was born out of a shocking intervention of God in the prophet's own life. The visionary call—at an unexpected time in an unlikely place—that we find in Ezek 1–2 suggests that before he could express apocalyptic, he had first to experience apocalyptic.[79] My contention is that apocalyptic is not in the first place a literary exercise entailing the recycling or interpreting of Israelite prophetic motifs, ancient Near Eastern images and ideas, and a jumble of other things, although this is part of what is going on when the time comes for expression of experience. Apocalyptic is in the first place a visionary experience that then has social and literary forms of expression. And the spiritual experience of a Hebrew in exile, probably far more than the Babylonian setting (though this may provide a partial font of images and ideas), explains what we find especially in Ezek 1–2.

The book of Ezekiel begins with a very specific reckoning of time. Like a prisoner counting the days in jail by marking the wall, Ezekiel knew exactly when he had this unexpected vision from above. It was in 593 BC, or probably four to five years into his experience of exile. But the date is possibly significant also because Ezekiel had reached the age when he, as a member of a family in a priestly line, should have been a priest serving full time in the temple in Jerusalem.[80] He could not now go to the temple and enter the holy of holies, but the One whose presence was believed to reside there now came and visited Ezekiel where he was.[81]

Ezekiel in 1:1 describes the experience in visual terms—"the heavens were opened and I saw visions of God." It is interesting that the expression "the heavens were opened" is found only here in the OT, and B. Vawter and L. J. Hoppe are likely right that it refers to the necessary preconditions for such a vision instead of being a literal description of what the prophet saw.[82] Notice as well that the prophet refers to visions in the plural. The call experience was to be the beginning of a series of experiences of God for Ezekiel. It is also interesting that the expression "the hand of the Lord" shows up in v. 3, although here it seems to mean not God's redemptive work but his presence in Ezekiel's life, his endorsement for Ezekiel's life.[83]

The first issue of importance in chs. 1–3 is what kind of call and/or commissioning narrative we may be dealing with. W. Zimmerli has shown that there

---

[79] Notice the rather similar situation of John of Patmos, cut off from the locus of his previous religious activities and community.

[80] See the discussion by W. Eichrodt, *Ezekiel* (Philadelphia: Westminster, 1970), 52ff.

[81] See the discussion in W. H. Brownlee, *Ezekiel 1–19* (Waco: Word, 1986), 3–4.

[82] B. Vawter and L. J. Hoppe, *Ezekiel: A New Heart* (Grand Rapids: Eerdmans, 1991), 25.

[83] Cf. the similar phrase in Second Isaiah, pp. 150–55 above.

seem to have been two sorts of prophetic call or commissioning narratives, and he seeks to locate the one in Ezekiel in the stream of tradition found in 1 Kgs 22:19–21 and Isa 6, as opposed, for instance, to a more word- than vision-centered account, such as we find in Jeremiah.[84] What he is able to show is that some combination of vision plus commissioning seems to have been an original feature of such accounts. The difficulty with his analysis is that although the visionary elements are similar in 1 Kgs 22 and Isa 6, the former text is not an account of a call or commissioning of a prophet but a commissioning of a heavenly spirit to enter a prophet and speak in a specific fashion, whereas in Isa 6, as has already been discussed,[85] what we find is a "recommissioning" for a new task of someone who had already been a prophet. This is, in all probability, not the case with Ezekiel. Here there is a visionary call plus a commissioning. There is another difference as well. While in Isa 6, as in 1 Kgs 22, we have a disclosure of what is going on in the heavenly council, here God is on the move and appearing in Babylon to Ezekiel. The one who has moved in the Ezekiel account is God; the prophet is not taken up in a vision into the heavenly court. It is, however, interesting that a vision was what led to the recommissioning of a prophet to a new work (Isaiah) and of a priest to become a prophet (Ezekiel).

There is a further difference. The imagery and ideas of the heavenly council were long-standing, and there is nothing particularly apocalyptic about them. But the vision of a chariot being borne up by living creatures of various odd sorts—not angels as in Isa 6—within a set of wheels is clearly symbolic and metaphorical rather than descriptive in nature. We are now dealing with disclosure rather than descriptive models of reality, and disclosure transpires through incredible images, analogies, and the like. In short, we have arrived here at the doorstep of apocalyptic visions.

It needs to be kept in mind that visions, as opposed to dreams, are normally communications that come to a prophet in the day, when he is awake and alert. Some might call them quite literally daydreams, but in each case they seem to intrude on the consciousness from somewhere else instead of representing something the prophet was already mulling over or thinking about. This is surely the implication of the phrase "the heavens were opened." One of the features of this vision—and indeed of most apocalyptic visions—that must be stressed is that we keep hearing the language of analogy ("like," "something like," "looked like"—vv. 4, 5, 7, 13, 16, 22, 24, 26, 27) as the prophet is groping for adequate words to describe what he sees. This is the nature of such nonliteral disclosure language.

In terms of the overall contours of the vision Ezekiel had, one may make a contrast between the glorious vision he has of God and the painful words he has to swallow and to convey to Israel. The vision is of a mobile and sovereign God who can appear to Ezekiel wherever he is and can give him a vision of God's sovereignty over all the creatures of the earth, including the human ones. The im-

---

[84] W. Zimmerli, *Ezekiel 1* (Philadelphia: Fortress, 1979), 97–100.
[85] See pp. 116–18 above.

ages are glorious and overwhelming to Ezekiel, and they make clear to him that God is still on God's throne. Despite how things appear at the mundane level, Yahweh is still the God of his people and aims to rule them even in exile. But there is much more to this vision than the summary thus offered.

For one thing, this vision, like the vision in Isa 6, is of a present reality; it does not, at least initially in its visual component, include the conveying of information about the future. For another, it is possible to suggest that the four living creatures are actually a good deal more than representatives of the created order. They have some resemblance to several of the demigods or gods of Babylonia. One suggestion is that they represent the *karibu,* the half-human, half-beast angelic monsters who in Mesopotamia were guardians of sacred places and signs of the divine presence.[86] A more specific suggestion is that this is a depiction of the main Babylonian gods—Marduk was a bull with the face of an ox, Nergal had a lion face and was the god of the underworld, Ninib had the face of an eagle and was the god of war, and finally the revealer god, Nabu, had the face of a human.[87] Eichrodt even suggests that we are talking about stone images of creatures that are seen as throne bearers in the ancient Near East.[88]

Ezekiel's vision has animals that each have all four faces, but it is quite possible that he had seen such sculptures during his time in Babylon. If so, his vision comes to him in a permutated form, involving images he had already seen or contemplated elsewhere. This material in the vision is characterized by pictographic language. If in fact the vision was meant to conjure up foreign gods or demigods, then the point would be that Yahweh is lord over them, even in Babylon—a message of reassurance. Clearly, the image is not of quadrupeds but of creatures that stand upright, and so of creatures of a higher order, like the lion-human or ox-human images seen in Babylon and Assyria.[89] Their function here seems to be similar to that of the cherubim that bore up the ark according to the Israelite tradition (see 1 Sam 4:4; 2 Sam 6:2; 2 Kgs 19:14–15).

Although there is a strong emphasis on glory in the vision account in Isa 6, it pales in comparison with what is depicted here in Ezekiel, for, as Brownlee says, this appears to be the only example of a technicolor vision in the Hebrew Scriptures, with a strong stress not only on the image of a rainbow but on a rainbow of colors reflected in the various items in the vision—the wheels gleam with topaz (v. 16), the throne is like a sapphire stone (v. 26), and there is also reference to burnished bronze feet or legs (v. 7).[90] It may be that the rainbow image (v. 28) and the rainbow of colors in the vision were meant to convey the same message as the bow in the clouds was meant to convey to Noah: God will no more judge humans, in this case the chosen people, in such a severe fashion (Gen 9:11–13). One wonders, too, if the mention of the animal images in the

---

[86] See Vawter and Hoppe, *Ezekiel,* 26–27.
[87] See Brownlee, *Ezekiel 1–19,* 11.
[88] Eichrodt, *Ezekiel,* 55.
[89] Ibid.
[90] Brownlee, *Ezekiel 1–19,* 11.

vision also conjured up the Noah tradition, for God's covenant with Noah was made also with every living creature. Notice, too, the connection between these stories in regard to the storm clouds, which begin Ezekiel's vision and recede at the end of the Noahic story.[91] If the dome over the heads of the creatures is an image of the dome of the sky, this is further evidence along these lines.[92] Perhaps these reassuring connotations were necessary at the beginning of this revelation precisely because God would go on to speak to Ezekiel about some further judgment on God's people (see below).

Something more needs to be said about the living creatures and the movement of the throne chariot. As in the vision of Isa 6, the creatures of Ezek 1:11 seem to have multiple pairs of wings—two that cover their bodies and particularly the genitals, two that are spread out above their heads (cf. Isa 6:2, where there are three pairs of wings, and Rev 4). Unlike in Isaiah, here these creatures do not cover their eyes, not needing to shield themselves from God's glory because they are shielded already by the dome over their heads and are, in any case, looking straight ahead. They do not see the ineffable, nor do they wish to be entirely seen. A glimpse of glory is sufficient for the prophet, yet even this is overwhelming.[93]

In spite of the wings and the reference to wheels, the main means by which the entire mammoth construction appears to be moving is by the spirit of God. The Hebrew term *ruah,* like the Greek *pneuma,* can mean breath, wind, or spirit, but the point, in any case, is that the creatures are not the propellers nor are they self-propelled. It is God's spirit that is moving and guiding this vehicle. But v. 21 says that this spirit or animating principle was in the creatures and then, by transfer, in the wheels next to them. The idea seems to be that of God's presence permeating the entire thing, both the animate and the inanimate parts. Still, according to v. 24, the creatures do use their wings, and it creates the sound of the moving of enormous waters, or a sound like the thunder of God or the tumult of a battle. Yet as grand as this is, it pales in comparison with the Almighty, who is described in ever more allusive language beginning with v. 25.

One first hears about the voice of the Almighty (v. 25), which comes from above the heads of the creatures. It is literally over their heads. God is known first by the divine speaking. Notice the reticence to describe an image of God—it is something like the image of a human person seated up there. In addition to the qualifier "something like," the term "image" is used to indicate another step removed from the reality itself. The word for "image" used here is neither *pesel,* which suggests a carved image, nor *selem,* which would also suggest something cut out, but *damot.* The former two would be avoided because of associations with idolatry, with graven images of pagan deities. The feet and lower torso of the figure seem to be sheathed in fire, and the upper torso is sheathed in

---

[91] Eichrodt, *Ezekiel,* 58.

[92] See Brownlee, *Ezekiel 1–19,* 13.

[93] See ibid., 12.

gleaming amber.[94] What surrounds all of this is splendor, but notice the three degrees of qualification in v. 28 of what was seen—this was the appearance of the likeness of the glory of Yahweh (the appearance of the likeness of God's glorious presence). Ezekiel is far more reticent than Isaiah to claim he has "seen the Lord high and lifted up."

> To what he has seen he applies the widely used term *kabod,* i.e., the glorious form assumed by the divine presence. This, according to the priestly view, dwelt only in the tabernacle, or in the holy of holies of the temple at Zion (Ex. 40.34; Lev. 9.6, 23; Num. 14.10; 16.19; I Kgs. 8.11; II Chron. 7.1). But now he sees that it is not indissolubly tied to those places, but is manifesting itself, by preference, to a lost and banished one like himself. Yet this reflected image of the heavenly glory of Yahweh . . . imparts a revelation of him, shows, not the national God of Zion to whom Israel lays an exclusive claim, but the Lord, free from all earthly limitations, and able to command the whole universe.[95]

The vision is so overwhelming that Ezekiel falls on his face but then hears a voice clearly speaking to him. It appears that what Ezekiel is claiming is that he encountered God in a vision of a replica of God's throne chariot (cf. Ps 68:4, 33; 104:3), because, for example, the firmament or dome is not the real sky but only an image of it.[96] The vision is followed by an audition. Scholars are divided about whether the audition was originally connected with the vision, but it seems likely it was, in view of the stress on the voice toward the end of the vision. Yet it is still quite possible that the scroll vision is a later confirmatory event.[97]

It is important to recognize the similarity of elements in the calls of Jeremiah and of Ezekiel. Both have visions, although Jeremiah's occur after, rather than before, the audition. Both receive a commission proper (Jer 1:4–5; Ezek 2:1–5). Both receive an exhortation to encourage them to undertake their assigned tasks (Jer 1:7–8, 17b; Ezek 2:6–7). Both are said to be equipped for the task (Jer 1:9, 18–19; Ezek 2:8–3:9). In both it is said that Yahweh stretches out his hand to the prophet (Jer 1:9; Ezek 2:9; cf. 8:3). Clearly, these are call narratives, as opposed to a recommissioning account, as in Isa 6. Yet there is a sense in which Ezekiel, who was in a priestly line, is being retooled for a new task.

In Ezek 2:1–7, for the first time God addresses Ezekiel as *ben adam.* The phrase will occur about ninety times in this book if one counts the strengthened form of the address,[98] and it occurs once in Dan 8:17, not to be confused with the reference in Aramaic to the *bar enasha* in the apocalyptic vision of Dan 7:13. Here and elsewhere the phrase, as in Ps 8:4, seems clearly to suggest the contrast between God and the prophet, with emphasis on the latter's mortality and

---

[94] Ibid., 14.
[95] Eichrodt, *Ezekiel,* 58–59.
[96] See Brownlee, *Ezekiel 1–19,* 18.
[97] Ibid., 22.
[98] See Zimmerli, *Ezekiel 1,* 131.

fraility. Vawter puts it this way: "Particularly in divine communication, its purpose is to call attention to all that otherwise separates the revealer from the one who receives revelation."[99]

This address comes at the point when Ezekiel has prostrated himself before God, indicating that he understands his weakness and subordinate standing before the Almighty. Notice, too, that it takes the power of God's spirit to lift him up and set him on his feet, so overwhelmed was Ezekiel. Furthermore, *ben adam* is not something Ezekiel calls himself; it is how the deity addresses the prophet, and it contrasts strikingly with the fact that God had addressed Jeremiah and Amos by their proper names. The prophet is not being addressed in his individuality but as a representative of a class of beings—humankind. "The Spirit, the breath of divine life, will penetrate his feeble body, in the same way as it gives new life to all created things, or returns to bestow new life upon that which its departure has menaced with death (Ps. 104.29f; Job 34.14; Judg. 15.19; 1 Sam. 30.12). God must therefore at every step continue to aid and support by his gifts the man upon whom he has imposed such a task."[100]

The commission that Ezekiel receives has several peculiar features. In the first place, he has come into exile with residents of Jerusalem and Judea, yet he is told immediately that he is sent to the people of Israel. This suggests that God intends to start over with the people of God as a whole. There would be no more of these divisions of Israel and Judah. As Zimmerli reminds us, the verb *shalah* occurs at the crucial juncture of call narratives because the very essence of being a prophet is that one becomes a dispatched agent of the Almighty, an agent who must go forth and proclaim some message (cf. Jer 1:7; Isa 6:8). To say to such a person that Yahweh has not sent him is the severest critique one could offer (compare Ezek 13:6 with Jer 28:15; 43:2). When a prophet wants to claim authorization, he says, "Yahweh has sent me" (Zech 2:12–15).[101] This raises important questions about the title "sent one" for such people, because in the OT era this is precisely what *apostolos* means. Did the early apostles see themselves as the successors to, or the continuation of, the prophetic office? This issue will be addressed in due course, but for now we must agree with Zimmerli's conclusion that "the title 'sent one' best fits the prophet's consciousness of his office."[102]

The message that comes to Ezekiel is in no way sugarcoated. Israel is described as a bunch of rebels who remain rebels right up to the very day Ezekiel received this commission. In other words, Ezekiel was being prepared to deal with recalcitrants, and although his audience was already in exile, his task would not entail his simply offering them oracles of hope and salvation.

Ezekiel 2:4 makes abundantly clear that Ezekiel is being commissioned to be a prophet. He will use the messenger formula in advance of his proclamations to signal his role and intent—"Thus says the Lord God. . . ." The effect of the

---

[99] Vawter and Hoppe, *Ezekiel*, 30.
[100] Eichrodt, *Ezekiel*, 61.
[101] Zimmerli, *Ezekiel 1*, 132.
[102] Ibid.

proclamation may not be successful, but whether Israel hears or refuses to hear, they will know that a prophet has been in their midst. Ezekiel is counseled not to be afraid of this stubborn people or of their negative responses. Unlike the rebellious people, Ezekiel is to be obedient, and open his mouth and receive what God will feed him with—a handwritten papyrus (and thus edible) scroll full of words of lamentation and woe on the front and on the back. It has been suggested by Zimmerli and Vawter that Ezekiel may have been present as an eighteen-year-old priest when the king burned Jeremiah's scroll of woe in 604 BC (see Jer 36).[103] Notice that the text says literally, "eat what you find here," rather than, "eat the scroll"; the former might signify to take the contents of the scroll into one's inner being. In this case, we find both literal and nonliteral elements in this vision. At any rate, the total consumption of what is given to him indicates Ezekiel's complete submission to God's command.[104] One need not think of Ezekiel literally eating a scroll, as this is still an account of a visionary encounter.

Whether or not this vision is, in part, based on reminiscences, Ezekiel does receive what is offered, and he indicates that paradoxically the taste of it was sweet in his mouth.[105] On the surface, his commission might seem easy— he doesn't have to deal with foreigners or foreign languages. Unfortunately, however, he must deal with something far more difficult than a linguistic and cultural barrier. He must deal with spiritual barriers to the reception of his message. He will have to convey these words of woe to a hardheaded and hard-hearted people, and in preparation for doing so, God is going to make him hardheaded as well—"See, I have made your face hard against their faces and your forehead hard against their foreheads" (3:8). Ezekiel is being prepared for a head-butting contest.

We are then told that the spirit that moved the throne chariot also lifted up Ezekiel and carted him off to an undisclosed location. The vision left him, and in due course he found himself sitting with his fellow exiles, saying nothing for seven days, he was so stunned by this experience. Nevertheless, we are told that internally he was extremely upset—"I went in bitterness in the heat of my spirit, the hand of the Lord being strong upon me"(cf. Jer 15:17). This seems very similar to what was said about Jeremiah,[106] and in both cases the call upon the life of the prophet is not experienced as a pleasant thing, nor, for that matter, is his ministry seen as an optional undertaking. Instead of producing euphoria and pride, it produces bitterness and shame. It is an onerous task. Just how onerous is conveyed more fully in 3:16–21 when Ezekiel is told that he must be the bearer of bad news to wicked people, that he must be like a sentinel standing

---

[103] Ibid., 137; Vawter and Hoppe, *Ezekiel*, 32.

[104] See Brownlee, *Ezekiel 1–19*, 32.

[105] See the additional remark in Rev 10:8–11, where John finds the words sweet in the mouth but a real cause for stomachache once they go down.

[106] See pp. 136–38 above.

on a watchtower, who has done his duty only when he has properly warned those he guards of what is coming.

The watchman theme is an important one in this book (cf. 18:24–25; 33:7–18), as it suggests the mediatorial role of the prophet, guarding an endangered and vulnerable people, but of course the guard in question is himself very vulnerable, he is "son of man." As Eichrodt says, none of this suggests that this revelation was a product of Ezekiel's own imagination and desires. Indeed, "he, more intensively than any other prophet, finds his experience as a prophet claiming and controlling his body."[107]

We could analyze here various of the judgment oracles that follow the call and commissioning of Ezekiel, but we would discover that they differ very little from other such oracles by Israel's prophets both in form and in content. For example, we could analyze the poetic structure, wordplay, and content of "The End" judgment oracle in 7:1–4 and discover that the themes in this oracle, like those in the other oracles in this chapter, are by now familiar ones. They deal with God putting an end to Israel's unfaithfulness by bringing judgment, and there are various echoes of earlier material in Amos, Jeremiah, and elsewhere. There is, however, this difference in procedure: unlike in the case of Amos, where judgment is pronounced first on other nations and then on God's people, Ezekiel begins by pronouncing judgment on God's own.

It must suffice to say about such traditional oracular material that a good deal of what one finds in Ezekiel is much like the material in the earlier writing prophets, which is to say that such a large portion of this book is not apocalyptic in character, that one can not really call it an apocalyptic book. Nevertheless, one should not underplay the visionary character of a good deal of the material as well, whether one thinks of Ezekiel's throne chariot vision, or his insights into what is happening in Jerusalem while he is away, or his vision of the new temple.

The focus here will be on some of the prophetic sign acts and parabolic or allegorical material in Ezekiel, for they betoken the increasingly metaphorical, symbolic, and visionary character that Hebrew prophecy was to take from the seventh century BC on. Ezekiel 4–5 provides us with two formidable examples of prophetic sign acts—the portrayal of the siege of Jerusalem and depiction of the sword against Jerusalem. It is not necessary to conclude that these prophetic sign acts must have occurred at a time before the exile simply because they would not be depicting the future if they were done in exile. As Hooker says, some prophetic sign acts depict divine activity that is not presently observable and, in some cases, may well have happened or begun in the past. The point of such depictions for the exiles would, in part, be that God's people still had not learned the lessons they should have about God's judgment on their unfaithfulness when Babylon besieged Jerusalem and that therefore they still faced the prospect of God's judgments. But these oracles would also be about judgment for those left behind in Jerusalem who continued to be unfaithful. These sign acts are not pri-

---

[107] Eichrodt, *Ezekiel*, 64.

marily revelations of God's present power at work where the prophet is but, rather, of God's divine purpose and will.[108]

Chapter 4 begins with the command for Ezekiel to take a piece of clay—which could be used equally for bricks or for tablets in Babylon (*lebenah;* cf. Gen 11:3)—on which he is to depict a city under siege, presumably in this case Jerusalem.[109] Verses 1–2 are clearly in poetic form, involving nearly perfect examples of assonance, rhythm, and some alliteration even though they are instructions. Brownlee has plausibly suggested, in light of the copper cauldron allegory in ch. 24,[110] that they constitute a work song sung during construction of the model of the city.[111] If this is correct, then there are two further examples of prophets offering oracles in poetic fashion, as songs.

Ezekiel goes so far as to depict the siege not only by lying on his side for a prolonged period of time (a symbol in which the agent of Yahweh "lays siege," depicting God doing the same) but also by fashioning siege engines, siege ramps, armed camps, and the like and placing them around the representation of the city. "Turning his face steadfastly towards the city is evidently a gesture representing the attitude taken up by his divine Lord."[112] The image of the siege is intensified with the addition of the iron griddle (which is literally what the text says in v. 3). Israel is about to be fried.

Equally menacing are the symbolic acts depicted in ch. 5. The cutting of hair, in itself, does not seem to be a sinister act, but it is very often a symbol of mourning. But one does not normally cut hair with a sword. Furthermore, this symbol is about God shaving a group of people, and so it must be seen as a shaming gesture. The dual reference to sword and barber's razor suggests that the former is the symbol of the cutting implement to be used against God's people and the latter is the implement Ezekiel is to use to perform this sign. One may be meant to think of Isa 7:20, in which Assyria is depicted as a razor that will completely shave Jerusalem and Judah. But here the issue is only the head hair, including the beard.

The bizarre part of this symbol comes in the instructions on what Ezekiel is to do with this hair. First he is to weigh the hair and divide it into three even piles. One must bear in mind that weighing and numbering are regular symbols of judgment (Dan 5:27; Prov 21:2). Then Ezkiel is to burn a third of the hair in the midst of his model of besieged Jerusalem, take his knife and cut up hair all around the model, and then finally scatter one-third to the wind. Apparently

---

[108] See Hooker, *Signs of a Prophet*, 3: "Sometimes these dramatic actions refer, not to future events, but to something that has already taken place or that is now taking place: when Ezekiel lay on his side, the time of punishment for Israel had already begun."

[109] Various scholars take the specific reference to Jerusalem as a later gloss, but the textual evidence does not support this conclusion. But see Zimmerli, *Ezekiel 1*, 148.

[110] Chapter 24 is in the form of a work song that Ezekiel sings while performing the symbol. See below.

[111] Brownlee, *Ezekiel 1–19*, 61.

[112] Eichrodt, *Ezekiel*, 83.

some is to be held in reserve from these three piles so that it may be sown into the skirt or hem of Ezekiel's robe. This last suggests the exiles who are to survive and are now surviving in Babylon.

The point of this sign act is once again to connect the exiles with what has happened and will happen in Jerusalem—some are destroyed, some are scattered, some are protected as if hidden in the hem of a garment.[113] The latter will avoid the sword, or at least any further contact with it. There may be some reference here to the fact that the hem of the garment was where the fringe, or *tallith*, was placed, indicating faithfulness to God's word (Num 15:37–40). Those preserved would be the ones who were faithful. Those scattered may represent the new exiles who are to join Ezekiel and company, who are already in Babylon.[114] This portion of the passage may be called "Israel has a close shave and is nearly destroyed." Such symbolic acts are not, in principle, different in function from the telling of a parable or allegory, for they serve to reveal some truth about Israel's relationship with God and God's will for it. It is appropriate for the discussion to turn now to the allegory of the cauldron in 24:1–14.

This passage is quite rightly classified as an allegory, and it shows beyond reasonable doubt that such a form was most certainly a part of the prophetic repertoire. It is doubtful that a radical distinction should be made between this form of metaphorical expression and what we find in parables. The main difference is that there are more correspondences between certain details in an allegory and a particular message or situation than is the case with a parable, and in order to make these points, an allegory becomes more a matter of artifice and less true to life as a story than many parables. This allegory completes what Ezekiel already said in a negative vein in ch. 22 about the coming judgment on Jerusalem and its people.

The prophecy of Ezekiel in 24:1–14 reflects on what will happen to those in Jerusalem when Nebuchadnezzar comes calling and besieges the city.[115] It seems clear from this text that Ezekiel was part of the first vanguard who were deported to Babylon around 597 BC and that the fall of the city itself transpired a considerable period of time after he had left the city. This oracle can in fact be dated to January 15, 588 BC (cf. 2 Kgs 25:1). "The Babylonian invaders stood as the final link in a moral chain of cause and effect."[116] Scholars have been divided over how to read this text—that is, whether it can be seen to be a true oracle or whether the remarkable correspondence between the oracle and what happened to Jerusalem is the result of later redactional work on an originally more generic oracle.[117]

---

[113] This symbolic act would not seem to have anything to do with the gesture, known elsewhere in the ancient Near East, in which a prophets cuts off a lock of his hair and sends it with his oracle to the king, presumably as a sign of authentication. See pp. 13–19 above.

[114] See Vawter and Hoppe, *Ezekiel*, 46.

[115] The messenger formula at v. 15 indicates that v. 14 is the end of this unit.

[116] L. Allen, *Ezekiel 20–48* (Waco: Word, 1990), 60.

[117] See Vawter and Hoppe, *Ezekiel*, 114.

In this "allegory"[118] the following correspondences become clear: Israel, or more particularly Jerusalem (cf. 22:2–5), is clearly the pot that God has been lighting the fire under. Fire, on the one hand, can be purgative and thus purifying, but on the other hand, it can simply consume. God had hoped that the fire would burn off the rust in the pot, but in vain. The rust represents Israel's sin and impurities. The pieces of meat put into the pot represent God's people, and the choicest pieces would be the pick of the flock that was still left behind in Jerusalem. It appears that one is meant to think of Ezek 11:7, where the meat in the cauldron represents those slain there. "There may indeed be some irony here in the stress on the 'choicest'—the most distinguished were by no means exempt from [God's] culinary exercise."[119] But this meat had much blood in it, which may, in part, be a reference to bloody deeds of those remaining in Jerusalem ("for the blood she shed is inside it," v. 7).

God has set in broad daylight these wicked bloody deeds ("I have placed the blood she shed on a bare rock, so that it may not be covered"). God had attempted to purge Israel before, but to no avail, and thus now the fire must be used for judgment without mercy ("I will not refrain, I will not spare, I will not relent," v. 14). There will be not merely suffering or deportation but also a conflagration in the city. Not only the rust but the cauldron itself will be eliminated in the coming fire.[120] Ezekiel means to make clear to his fellow exiles that they can not set their hopes on those left behind or on the so-called Holy City. Their trust must be in God alone. As Zimmerli puts it, "In that this prophecy, however, was proclaimed among the exiles, it destroyed all the comforting hopes which believed that they would soon go back to a Jerusalem which had been spared the judgement."[121]

Although it is by no means the first of the salvation oracles or visions in Ezekiel (cf., e.g., 34:11–16 about God as the shepherd who seeks and brings back the lost), the vision about the valley of dry bones, found in 37:1–14, is clearly the most memorable. The imagery in this apocalyptic vision is far less exotic than what was found in ch. 1, and it is less difficult to decipher. It is not about the resurrection of individuals but about the resurrection of a people, and thus the imagery must be seen as metaphorical. It is a message of hope to despairing exiles that restoration of the people and to the land will happen by a miracle of God's power and grace.[122] The sharing of this vision with his fellow exiles is part of Ezekiel's attempt "to convince his fellow exiles that God's power was about to restore Judah to its land, the source of its life."[123] The metaphorical character of

---

[118] The term *mashal* can refer to a variety of forms of metaphorical speech, including what is today called parable, allegory, riddle, and even aphorism. For its use in Ezekiel, see 17:2; 21:5; 24:3.

[119] Allen, *Ezekiel 20–48*, 59.

[120] See Eichrodt, *Ezekiel*, 339.

[121] Zimmerli, *Ezekiel 1*, 500.

[122] Eichrodt, *Ezekiel*, 509.

[123] Vawter and Hoppe, *Ezekiel*, 165.

the vision is made especially clear in vv. 11–14. The latter passage, too, is an allegory or parable, with an analogy being drawn between the land of exile and a grave, and the spiritual condition of Israel and death. But Israel will not live unless God's breath or spirit rests within them. Nevertheless, even though the vision is not about a literal resurrection, it seems to presuppose a knowledge of the concept of resurrection of the dead, which would not be surprising in light of the earlier discussions in this study about the growth of understanding about the afterlife in the exilic period.[124]

The scene, as the prophet sees it, is of the aftermath of the carnage of war. He is transported to a valley full of very dry bones, indicating persons long since dead. It is interesting that this is the only nondated vision in this book, but it does seem to have come at a point after the fall of Jerusalem, when all natural hopes of the exiles had been dashed, but before the return to the land. The structure of this passage is quite straightforward, with the account of the vision proper given in vv. 1–10 and an interpretation of the vision in the form of an oracle given in vv. 11–14. Thus we have here the interesting combination of vision and oracle in sequence, a combination not always found even in apocalyptic material.

When Ezekiel wants to indicate the onset of a visionary or oracular experience, he uses the phrase "the hand of the Lord was upon me" (cf. 1:3). He speaks of psychic transport to another place, or to use the words of Eichrodt, the "experience of the vision begins with Ezekiel being seized . . . by an ecstatic trance in which the prophet's mind is made to serve a reality other than itself." [125] The language suggests total absorption in the experience.[126] Notice God's command to Ezekiel to speak to the bones and make known their reconstitution in v. 4. Here as elsewhere the vision includes a commission to speak. The process found here is that the prophet first speaks to the bones, which come back together as skeletons, then sinews and flesh are added, then the prophet speaks to the four winds to blow on or into the human forms and bring them to life. The human form without an élan vital does not constitute a living person or a people.[127] Reconstitution without revivification avails not at all. In a sense, this passage is a showcase example of the various ways one can use the Hebrew term *ruah*. As Vawter says, in v. 1 it refers to God's spirit, in v. 5 to breath or the animating principle within human beings, and finally in v. 9 to an external force, the winds.[128] To some extent, the image here is quite similar to the story of the original creation of Adam, who was first formed and then into whom life was breathed (cf. Gen 2:7).

It has often been debated how one should take the response of Ezekiel to the initial question of God—"Can these bones live?" Is Ezekiel expressing simple

---

[124] See above pp. 150–55 on Isa 55.

[125] Eichrodt, *Ezekiel*, 507.

[126] That this ecstatic sort of experience was not the exclusive provenance of the apocalyptic prophets is shown by 1 Kgs 18:12, 46; 2 Kgs 2:16. See Allen, *Ezekiel 20–48*, 184.

[127] See Eichrodt, *Ezekiel*, 508.

[128] Vawter and Hoppe, *Ezekiel*, 166.

ignorance (like our "God only knows"), or doubt, or is he offering a response of faith when he says, "You alone know, Lord" (v. 3)? Purely on the basis of common sense and normal reasoning, it would have been understandable for him, when confronted with the scene of exceedingly dry bones indicating those long since dead, not to have expressed any confidence in the likelihood of revivification. Perhaps this is why Allen suggests that Ezekiel's actual meaning is, "You know as well as I do" (the situation appears hopeless).[129] But if this is Ezekiel's meaning, then God is about to make clear that he knows more than the prophet.

This vision indicates that Israel plays no part in its own revival. It is solely an act of God's grace and power, like a literal resurrection. With the turning of the discussion to graves in v. 12b, it is understandable how some have seen here a reference to literal resurrection. But v. 14 brings us back more clearly into the realm of the metaphorical, where it is a matter of being restored to the land. Notice that once this restoration transpires, it is only then that God's people will realize again that Israel's God is Lord of all (v. 14). "As ever in the book of Ezekiel, salvation is to be a means to a divine end. The redeeming act of God would bring with it the revelation of his true self."[130] It appears there is an echo of 36:27–28 here in v. 14.

In any event, here Ezekiel is seen not merely as a proclaimer but as one who might have an active role in the restoration of Israel, for it is the prophet who is called upon to prophesy to both the bones and breath so that new life can happen to Israel. The vision reminds one and all that God can kill but God can also bring back to life (Deut 32:39; 1 Sam 2:6). It is striking that a much later Jewish prophet saw in this text a promise of the eschatological revival of Israel as Israel is reincorporated into a community of Jew and Gentile united in Christ (Rom 11:15). Here in Ezekiel, as in Second Isaiah, when prophets prophesy about a future remote from their own situation and time, the prophecy becomes more general in substance, more metaphorical or parabolic in form, more apocalyptic in character, and thus more otherworldly and afterworldly in its assumption about how and when salvation can truly and fully come.

III. CONCLUSIONS

Without question, two of the greatest of the writing prophets were the authors of the material in Second Isaiah and Ezekiel. Their prophetic material has in common a growing belief in the otherworld and the afterworld, which affects the character of their pronouncements. But these prophets have expressed their understanding of the transcendent differently from each other. Second Isaiah offers highly lyrical material often focusing on an idealized leader figure such as Moses. Ezekiel uses striking and often bizarre images to speak about the transcendent and the future. In the latter prophet's work one can glimpse the

---

[129] Allen, *Ezekiel 20–48*, 185.
[130] Ibid., 187

birth of apocalyptic, but one would never accuse Second Isaiah of being an apocalypticist. The poetic form of oracles is found in both prophets' work, but this is far less often the case with the material examined from Ezekiel than with the material examined from Second Isaiah.

Second Isaiah stands in a tradition of prophetic material and consciously draws upon it, but is far from just a tradent or slavish imitator. Rather, the man was an inspired prophet in his own right. At Isa 50:4 God is said to have dispensed the tongue of the learned to this prophet. Isaiah 8:16 and 54:13 show that the learned are always disciples in the Isaianic tradition. But the disciple has been given a tongue to be a teacher as well. Like a later teacher, namely, the Teacher of Righteousness, this teacher preferred to remain anonymous and so have the focus be kept on the content of what God had said through him.

A close analysis of Isa 40–55 will show that only a portion of this material is oracular in the sense of God speaking in the first person. Very often it is the prophet speaking of God in the third person and to the people. This mixture of the oracular and prophetic reflection and poetry is especially in evidence in Second Isaiah. Perhaps precisely because of the heavy indebtedness to Isaiah, and since the real issue was whether this was a word from God, this prophet does not reveal himself and his individual situation. Nor, for that matter, does he reveal the identity of the main character of his songs and oracles—the Servant.

What we can say about the Servant is that he appears to be an individual, and the combination of Mosaic traits and prophetic traits well suits the idea that the Servant is a latter-day Mosaic figure, not a Davidic figure. The prevalent second-exodus imagery throughout Isa 40–55 also supports this connection. The most intriguing part about the depiction of the Servant is that he is a truly human and suffering figure and yet he performs roles and receives plaudits more appropriate for a transcendent figure. There is also the distinctive emphasis on his making atonement for other persons' sins. God has chosen an unlikely person to achieve the divine salvific purposes. Like Moses, the Servant establishes a new relationship, a covenantal relationship with God's people. Isaiah 49:5–8 makes clear that the Servant has a mission to Israel, but the obligation of God's people to enlighten and thus save the nations now falls also on the Servant. The final Servant Song offers some of the most exalted and intricate poetry in all the Hebrew canon, and it suggests that inspiration must include not only prophetic experience but also prophetic expression after reflection.

Of Ezekiel one may say that, in some ways, the turn to more visionary and otherworldly prophetic forms is not surprising. In Babylon Ezekiel had no monarch or court or temple or holy city to focus on or to prophesy to, no religious pilgrimages to go on while there, and no people in charge of their own destiny to speak to. Only journeys in the mind's eye would be possible if royal persons, holy temple, holy place, holy land, and a free people with viable religious choices were to be spoken of.

While the book of Ezekiel is not an apocalypse, we find the beginnings of apocalyptic visionary material in this work, spawned by the prophet's experience, but also the expression reflects his marginalized social situation and the hope for a remedy. Although his poetry may not be as exalted as that of Second Isaiah, Ezekiel is a prophet who uses a much wider array of literary devices to reach his audience, including oracles, songs, parables, allegories, and riddles. In addition, he performs prophetic signs and gestures, dramatizing or even embodying the message he conveys. Such symbolic acts are not, in principle, different in function than the telling of a parable or allegory, for they serve to reveal some truth about Israel's relationship with God and God's will for it. Ezekiel's visions, whether of the dry bones or of the temple, are in various ways just as idealized as those of Second Isaiah, but they differ in that, in the main, they do not focus on a particular individual as a solution to Israel's problems. The hope that Ezekiel offers is hope beyond even more judgment, even on recalcitrant Jerusalem, and in this regard Ezekiel shares much in common with Jeremiah; both have a rather priestly fixation with the fate of Jerusalem, including the temple. In the next chapter, the progress of prophecy will be pursued a step further into the postexilic age, which is the age of the rise of full-blown apocalyptic as a form of prophetic utterance.

CHAPTER 6

Vital Visions or the Dying of the Light?

The best part of a lifetime separated the deportations of 597 and the first return in 538 BC. The common feeling among the exiles was that they might as well be dead. Their bones were dried up and their hope gone (Ezek 37:11). From a human standpoint they were right. It would have been hard to find any reasonable ground for hope, but to Ezekiel came a vision of resurrection. God would recreate His people, reunite the two kingdoms under a Davidic head and set His sanctuary among them once and for all (Ezek. 37). . . . Cyrus was designated as the anointed of the Lord to fulfil His purpose. Suddenly there was a glorious future ahead because they had an incomparable God who saw fit to forgive the past and plan redemption.[1]

I. NIGHT VISIONS ABOUT EXILIC DAYS, ESCHATOLOGICAL SONGS FIT FOR A KING— ZECHARIAH

The rather glowing report above of the postexilic situation and hope fails to deal with the fact that restoration had come to Israel only after painful and costly judgment. It was not merely a matter of forgive and forget. It was, rather, restoration after judgment. The prophets of the postexilic situation were not likely to forget this fact, and indeed their utterances are full of words of both woe and weal. The visionary and metaphorical vein of apocalyptic will be mined even further in the postexilic age, but not to the exclusion of more traditional

---

[1] J. Baldwin, *Haggai, Zechariah, Malachi* (Downers Grove, Ill.: Inter-Varsity, 1972), 13–14.

oracular prophecy. For evidence of this conclusion, one need look no further than the book of Zechariah, which, like Ezekiel, reflects both something new and something old in the prophetic genre. The main concern of this study is with the new, with the direction prophecy was taking in the postexilic situation, and so this chapter will concentrate on some of the visionary material in Zech 1–8 as well as some of the more obscure oracular material in Zech 9–14, which may in fact come from a different and possibly later hand than that of Zechariah himself.[2]

Perhaps the most crucial thing to be said about the postexilic situation is that things had not, by the time this material was written, turned out like the glorious vision one sees at the end of Ezekiel, despite the best efforts of Ezra, Nehemiah, and others. Indeed, the marginalized situation continued despite the return to the promised land. The social climate from 525 BC or so until the time of the Maccabees was such that it could quite readily produce apocalyptic visions and literature.

G. W. E. Nickelsburg, paraphrasing and to some extent following P. D. Hanson, comments,

> Ancient apocalyptic movements have a common *social setting* in which a group experiences alienation due to the disintegration of the life-sustaining socio-religious structures and their supporting myths. Institutional structures may be physically destroyed or a community may find itself excluded from the dominant society and its symbolic universe. The results are chaos, a cultural vacuum, and intolerable strain on the community of the disenfranchised. In their *response* to this setting of alienation, members of apocalyptic movements create a new symbolic universe that replaces the one dominant in the social system responsible for the alienation. The response of apocalyptic eschatology allows the community to maintain a sense of identity and a vision of their ultimate vindication in the face of social structures and historical events that deny that identity and the plausibility of that vision. True identity is derived not from the structures and institutions of the society but from God's redemptive acts, which are effected on the cosmic level. Apocalyptic movements may express their opposition in a variety of forms. They may withdraw and form a new society based on a symbolic utopian universe. They may yield to opposition and go underground and express their identity in a symbolic sub-universe. They may respond with violence, become a revolutionary community, and construct a symbolic counter-universe.[3]

---

[2] R. L. Smith, *Micah-Malachi* (Waco: Word, 1984), 169ff., is right to point out how very different the material is in Zech 1–8 as opposed to Zech 9–14. The first part of the book is well dated, and visions are tagged to specific historical situations or dates seven times. In chs. 9–14 there are no dates, and the prophet's name is also left behind. There are also no more references to Darius the king, or any king for that matter. A time of peace seems to be present in the earlier chapters, but in chs. 9–14 we seem to be dealing with a time of war. Some have even seen in chs. 9–14 a reference to Alexander the Great's invasion of Palestine in 333 BC. Were this material to go back to Zechariah himself, it could have a date no earlier than the last part of the sixth century.

[3] G. W. E. Nickelsburg, "Social Aspects of Palestinian Jewish Apocalypticism," in *Apocalypticism in the Mediterranean World and the Near East* (ed. D. Hellholm; Tübingen: Mohr, 1989), 641–54, here 645.

There is a considerable amount of insight in this quotation, and one of the things it makes evident is that the fact of apocalyptic visions continuing to appear in the postexilic situation shows that a return to the land was not the solution to all the problems. Speaking of Haggai and Zech 1–8, C. and E. Meyers suggest that more "than any other factor, the absence of any realistic opportunity to restore the monarchy influenced the content of their utterances. The hegemony of Persia in all local affairs is presupposed by both prophets."[4] This also, in part, explains why prophecy in the postexilic age has a different character from that during the time of the monarchy. The prophet is not able to address a particular Jewish ruler as responsible for the direction of the nation. Since the fate of the nation is not entirely in Jewish hands and the prophet does not share a universe of discourse with those who rule, the focus must be on God, the people, and their interrelationship. Another factor coloring the prophecy is the prophet's own background and situation. In the case of Zechariah, he was a priestly descendent who is now called to be a prophet (cf. Ezekiel) but who still has great concern for the priesthood and the temple and hopes both can be fully reestablished. These concerns are clearly reflected in the visions that one finds in the first half of this book, and unlike some of Ezekiel's visions or Second Isaiah's song, the ones found here have a concreteness in regard to names, which suggests they are about the near horizon.

The first point of note is that these are visions that come to Zechariah in the night (1:7). It is not, however, said that these are dreams, for the prophet is awake and alert (contrast Daniel as a dream interpreter). Notice also that these eight night visions come to someone who is already a prophet; hence there is no evidence here of a real call narrative. In addition, the prophet is in something of a quandary to figure out what the vision might mean, and so here, for the first time in this sort of material, we have an interpreting angel or messenger of God provided to illuminate the matter.

Some scholars have taken the presence of the interpreting angel as a clear sign that here, for the first time, one is really dealing with apocalyptic. But there is already such a figure in Ezek 40–48, and in any case, one must distinguish between the term "apocalyptic," used to described a literary form that is found here, and the phrase "an apocalyptic book," for clearly enough there is some nonapocalyptic material in this book. Even Zech 1–8 could not simply be called an apocalypse. Perhaps it is sufficient to call these eight visions apocalyptic visions rather than merely protoapocalyptic ones. This means that, at the very least, one can not say that apocalyptic first arises in Judaism in the Maccabean period but, as has already been suggested in this study, in the exilic and early postexilic period if not before (see the Isaiah apocalypse).

In the first vision, Zechariah sees a man on a red horse in a grove of myrtle trees and behind him horses in three different colors. Notice that the interpretation of the vision does not come from the angel per se but from the man in the

---

[4] C. Meyers and E. Meyers, *Haggai, Zechariah 1–8* (AB 25B; New York: Doubleday, 1987), xl.

vision whom Zechariah sees and who informs the prophet that what he is seeing is those whom God has sent to patrol the earth. Then the patrols in the vision report to the angel rather than to the prophet that they have searched and found the whole world at peace. It is then the angel who beseeches God about how long God will continue to be angry with Jerusalem and Judah, who have experienced his wrath for seventy years (588–518 BC?).[5]

Nevertheless God is now angry with the nations who are at rest and is prepared to turn and comfort Jerusalem and Judah and rebuild the temple and the Holy City (v. 16). In addition, in v. 17 there is a promise of prosperity for the cities of Judah as God again chooses to favor Jerusalem and Zion. There is some confusion in this vision, but it appears that the interpreting angel (who appears throughout these visions—1:18; 2:3; 4:1; 5:5; 6:4) is one figure and the man on the red horse is another. It is possible that the angel of the Lord (v. 14) should be identified with the man on the red horse.[6]

What can be made of this vision? Its purpose seems to be to reassure and comfort those who have returned from exile that the temple and city will be rebuilt soon.[7] It is possible, as Baldwin suggests, that since the horsemen represent God's emissary, one is to envision them encamped in a myrtle grove in the Kidron Valley outside Jerusalem, indicating that God's presence is near the city but not yet in it, for the temple is as yet not rebuilt.[8] A mere return without rebuilding did not constitute a fulfillment of such prophecies as Jer 29:10. In fact, the rebuilding was to take at least another eighty years (cf. Neh 7:4; 11:1).

Nonetheless the pledge, conveyed by Ezekiel (43:5), of the return of God's spirit to the Holy City must have been a promise the exiles had clung to. Notice that the election of Jerusalem hinges on the presence of the temple and God within it. The imagery of messenger horsemen may have been taken from the Persian ruler's practice of using such mounted messengers to keep him informed about matters of state in his far-flung empire. Horses were used almost exclusively for military purposes in the ancient Near East, except in the case of royalty. Donkeys were the normal means of human transportation in the region.[9] Thus, one must view this as a reconnaissance mission for the Almighty, who rules all the earth. Notice that this vision has many similarities to the last of the eight visions, in which there are found emissaries going out on horseback.

---

[5] This seems to have been a traditional number for a period in which a deity is angry with a city or people. From this same period comes an Esarhaddon inscription on black stone from about 681–669 BC indicating that Marduk would be angry with his land until seventy years had been accomplished. See E. Lipinski, "Recherches sur le livre de Zecharie," *VT* 29 (1970): 38.

[6] See Meyers and Meyers, *Haggai, Zechariah 1–8*, 115.

[7] Smith, *Micah-Malachi*, 191, suggests an allusion to the message of comfort in Second Isaiah at Isa 40.

[8] Baldwin, *Haggai, Zechariah, Malachi*, 95.

[9] See Meyers and Meyers, *Haggai, Zechariah 1–8*, 113.

The impression left by this vision is that Zechariah is one step removed from direct communication with God and hence in need of an intermediary to help interpret and, indeed, to hear things. This sense of distance from the Holy Other tends to characterize a good deal of apocalyptic literature. Meyers and Meyers are quite right to stress the novelty of the formula we find in Zech 1:13–14. God conveys words of comfort to the angel who is talking with Zechariah. It is this angel, not God, who in turn says to Zechariah, "Proclaim this message: 'Thus says the Lord of hosts: "I am very jealous." ' "[10] It may, in part, be because of this sense of distance that some in early Judaism saw the telltale signs of the dying of the light of revelation during the postexilic period.

If the first vision was meant to signal and encourage the restoration of the city and temple, the vision in 3:1–10 has to do with the restoration of the high priest's office and, even more importantly, Judah's spiritual standing before God, who must deal with their guilt. It is interesting that in this vision there is neither the presence nor apparently the need for the interpreting angel. Instead we have the angel of the Lord facing off against "the Adversary," the accusing angel. The word "Satan" is a transliteration of the Hebrew term for adversary, and the definite article here and elsewhere makes clear it is not a proper name but a descriptive noun (cf. Job 1:6–12; 2:1–7; Rev 12:10). Nevertheless the presence of a sort of angelic figure very different from the angel of the Lord, who speaks for the Lord, is interesting and suggests that belief in both good and dubious angelic figures was widespread at this stage in the development of prophecy. Notice how the accuser is rebuked by the Lord here.

It is interesting that the priest is presented as a singed and dirty figure and is called "a brand plucked from the burning," a phrase already used in Amos 4:11 of a remnant of Israel. The phrase connotes a dramatic rescue, perhaps even a last-minute rescue from a conflagration, in this case from God's judgment. Here we have a priest rescued from the burning refuse heap, and so a priesthood rescued from absolute destruction and termination. Baldwin aptly comments that this priest represents "all that remains from the furnace of the exile."[11] "The saying has particular relevance to Joshua because his grandfather, Seraiah, was among those who were slaughtered by Nebuchadnezzar (2 Kngs. 25.18–21 . . .). The fact that Joshua survived in exile to return to Jerusalem in the capacity of high priest is hardly accidental, according to the prophet."[12]

The priest's robes were tainted not just by exile but also by the iniquity of God's people, including presumably his own.[13] This priest is named Joshua, which surely identifies him with the original priestly returnee from exile (Neh 12:4; Hag 1:1; Ezra 3:2, 8; 5:2).[14] In other words, this is not an idealized or com-

---

[10] Ibid., 119.

[11] Baldwin, *Haggai, Zechariah, Malachi,* 114.

[12] Meyers and Meyers, *Haggai, Zechariah 1–8,* 187.

[13] Meyers and Meyers, ibid., 188, may be right that the priest is seen as tainted by his time of exile in an unclean land.

[14] See ibid., 16.

ing figure but an already well-known one who is to take on an important role in the restoration of the temple precincts and the temple operation. This point makes very evident that the vision is not about the distant future. Joshua is called here literally the "great" priest, which surely means the high priest.

It seems probable that the verb "standing before" indicates that this vision gives a glimpse of what is transpiring in the heavenly council or court, and thus should be compared to the scene in Job 1, where we also find the presence of the Adversary, although here we also have the Advocate (i.e., the angel of the Lord). One must envision a trial scene, perhaps with the high priest on trial as a representative of the people and the Adversary accusing him of not properly keeping the people's relationship with God "clean." The angel of the Lord has the priest's filthy clothes removed, presumably by other angelic attendants, and this act is clearly interpreted as follows: "See, I have taken your guilt away from you and I will clothe you with festal apparel" (v. 4). Notice that it is God who cleanses him; the priest does nothing but receive these actions. Thus the high priest is not merely acquitted; he is given a new role in restored Israel.[15] Interestingly, at this point in the vision, Zechariah becomes an active participant urging that a clean turban be put on his head as well, presumably making clear his high office and official status (cf. the use of the term in other figurative contexts, such as Job 29:14; Isa 62:3). What is happening to Joshua is his cleansing, reinstatement, and recommissioning.[16] A conditional promise is given to this high priest, Joshua, once he has been freshly clad. If he walks in God's ways and keep his requirements, he shall rule in the earthly temple and have access to the heavenly courts as well on behalf of God's people.

At v. 8 a new figure is introduced into the vision—"my servant the Branch." He undoubtedly is a promised future ruler figure, presumably Davidic (cf. "the shoot of Jesse," Isa 11:1). It appears Zechariah and/or his audience knows about what Jeremiah said about the Branch (Jer 23:5; 33:15). There will, in addition, be a remarkable stone with seven facets,[17] which will be inscribed and set before Joshua. The inscribed nature of the stone suggests a cornerstone, presumably of the new temple.[18] Presumably its appearance will be that which indicates that God has removed the guilt from the land in a single day. When that transpires, it will be a day of rejoicing and gladness, a day for the Branch, the priest, and indeed one and all to invite each other to come under the arbor and the fig tree and celebrate. "The proverbial picture of everyone inviting *his neighbour under his vine* . . . (1Ki. 4.25; 2 Ki. 18.31; Mi. 4.4) represents the acme

---

[15] H. Mitchell et al., *Haggai, Zechariah, Malachi, Jonah* (Edinburgh: T&T Clark, 1912), 147.

[16] Smith, *Micah-Malachi*, 200.

[17] Another possible translation is "springs," in which case an allusion to the rock from which water came forth for Moses could be in mind, but this is uncertain. See ibid., 200–202.

[18] See Mitchell et al., *Haggai, Zechariah, Malachi, Jonah*, 156.

of contentment for which the Israelite longed. While every[one] would have a place to call his own, his joy would be to share it with others."[19]

Turning now to chs. 9–14, immediately we see how very different this material is from that found in chs. 1–8. Here there are songs and oracles rather than night visions, and some of them, at least, lack the historical particularity of some of the visions. The first text to examine is 9:9–10. These verses are familiar to those who know the Gospels, as they are cited in several places (cf. Matt 21:5; John 12:15; Luke 19:38). Here we find some sort of sung entrance liturgy, and it bears the closest resemblance to what is found in the Psalms or in Second Isaiah. In fact, it appears at one point to be citing Ps 72:8, if the influence does not go in the other direction. There is no question about the poetic character of this material; it could stand alone in its own right, "but it follows not only the triumphant theme but also the poetic structure of the preceding section, reverting to the 2+2 rhythm with which the chapter opened."[20] For this reason among others, some scholars have sought to take 9:1–10 together as a single unit. Even if this is the case, v. 9 begins a subunit within the passage, and we will focus on it. It may be, as D. L. Petersen suggests, that the imperatives in this unit presuppose and are based on the indicatives in the earlier part of this chapter.[21]

The passage begins with an exhortation to daughter Zion/Jerusalem. The city—and especially its holy hill—is personified as like maidens who should exult when they see their king returning to town. The verb "rejoice" in its form is found only in the poetic books of the Hebrew Scriptures and signals the poetic nature of what follows.[22] Coupled with the verb "exult" (see 2:10), it suggests an atmosphere of great excitement and expectation. There may here be an echo of Mic 4:10, where we also find two imperatives and the reference to daughter Zion. The imagery, in any case, suggests dependency. "Just as unmarried daughters cannot act independently of their parents, so Yahweh's people must rely on God and on the king who is coming for their future to be arranged."[23] Notice that this chapter suggests that before the king can come and rule in the city, God's presence must be reestablished in the temple (see vv. 1–8).[24]

The voice of the herald is heard before the city gates crying out, "Behold, your king is coming" (see the entrance liturgy in Ps 24:7–10). There is a widespread belief among scholars that this passage must be seen as an eschatological

---

[19] Baldwin, *Haggai, Zechariah, Malachi*, 118.

[20] Ibid., 163.

[21] D. L. Petersen, *Zechariah 9–14 and Malachi: A Commentary* (Louisville: Westminster, 1995), 56.

[22] See Meyers and Meyers, *Zechariah 9–14* (AB 25C; New York: Doubleday, 1993), 121.

[23] Ibid.

[24] Petersen, *Zechariah 9–14 and Malachi*, 58, rightly says that the "logic of the poems in Zechariah 9 suggests that the presence of the king depends on the prior presence of the deity in Jerusalem (Zech. 9:8)."

one, looking toward the future ultimate king.[25] This explains the more general character of the poem. Notice the nonmilitary tone of this entrance and this king, a tone that also pervades chs. 1–8, especially the familiar theme "not by might, and not by power; but with my spirit, said Yahweh of Hosts" (4:6). It appears the fact that Zerubbabel could only be a client ruler or governor simply whetted the appetite for reflecting on a true king who would come. In any case, in the ancient Near East, accession of a new ruler was often viewed as a time when a new era of shalom began. Consider, for example, what is said of the Assyrian king Assurbanipal:

> At the proclamation of my honored name, the four regions (of the world) were glad and rejoiced. . . . The hurled (*lit.*, on-coming) weapons of the enemy sank to the ground. The well-organized (enemy) broke their battle line. Their sharp lances came to a stop (*lit.*, rested), they brought their drawn (*lit.*, filled) bows to rest. . . . No deed of violence was committed. The lands were quiet (*lit.*, inhabited an abode of rest). The four regions (of the world) were in perfect order. . . . [26]

The poem offers three terms to describe the coming king. He will be righteous or triumphant, rescued or vindicated, humble or poor. The meaning of the key terms here depends on how one reads the context. What is not in debate is that this royal figure comes to town on a donkey rather than a warhorse, and this may help us grasp the meaning of the three descriptive terms here. It seems probable that the term *saddiq* here means not only that this ruler is the rightful or legitimate king but also that he is the ideal king (see Isa 11:4), the right man for the job. In view of the subsequent reference to the cessation of hostilities, it would make sense that *(w)enosha* here has the sense of "triumphant" or "victorious." It appears to mean that God has triumphed and therefore the king has been rescued or vindicated.[27] The king's victory is dependent on divine activity on his behalf.

The third descriptive term occurs in 7:10, where it refers to someone of low economic status and so of humble station (not a comment on his self-understanding). On the other hand, texts such as Num 12:3 suggest that the term has to do with one's piety, more particularly with having the right and submissive attitude and relationship with one's God (again, not an attitude about self or toward one's subjects). "Although kings hardly exhibited humility toward their subjects or enemies, they were expected to be pious and humble to their god, upon whom they depended for victory in battle."[28] Petersen suggests that Second Isaiah has influenced this aspect of the portrait (see Isa 49:13; 51:21; 54:11).[29]

---

[25] See, e.g., Meyers and Meyers, *Haggai and Zechariah 1–8*, 123; Smith, *Micah-Malachi*, 255–56.

[26] Cited in *ARAB*, 2 §987.

[27] See Meyers and Meyers, *Haggai and Zechariah 1–8*, 126–27.

[28] Meyers and Meyers, *Zechariah 9–14*, 128.

[29] Petersen, *Zechariah 9–14 and Malachi*, 58

It was a well-known practice for ancient Near Eastern royalty to ride in a royal procession on a mule, and there may be an echo here of Gen 49:10ff. or the story of David returning to Jerusalem after quelling Absalom's rebellion (see 2 Sam 15:19).[30] Whatever else this gesture is meant to convey, it surely gives the impression that this king comes in peace, in contrast to the horses and chariots in the earlier visions, which suggest a military situation. "By substituting non-military animals for horses, the prophet is reversing the power imagery associated with a king's rule. In the eschatological future, the restoration of the Davidic monarchy will radically alter the notion of kingship—the future king will not exert exploitative domination or foster socioeconomic elitism."[31] There may, then, also be the sense that riding on a donkey, which was the normal beast for travel of all persons in the ancient Near East, signals an identifying with the common person—an anti-elitist gesture. The king is riding on a particular kind of ass, a young one, which further accentuates the anti-elitist significance of the gesture, but nonetheless a purebred one and so suitable for a righteous king.[32] All warfare will be "cut off," such that neither the northern part of the land nor the southern part will need or use the weapons and equipment of war. At the same time, this king will not merely pacify his own land and reunite it into one; he will also promise peace to the non-Jewish nations. But more is also involved, for this king will, in fact, rule these nations, from sea to shining sea (cf. 14:8), from the Euphrates[33] to the Mediterranean, and even to the ends of the earth.[34] A worldwide rule of the known world is envisioned.

The second passage to be examined is also poetic in form and is found in Zech 13:7–9. Here is a resumption of the shepherd theme found in 9:16, 10:2–3, and especially 11:3–17. But it must be doubted that the subject of this poem is the same as in ch. 11, where the subject is a worthless shepherd, not, as here, a person who is seen as a positive associate of God.[35] Strikingly, God calls for the sword to strike God's own shepherd. This shepherd is also called "the man who stands next to me," in essence God's right-hand man.

In light of 1 Kgs 22:17, it is virtually certain that the author is talking about a ruler. In addition, this is never the sort of language used of God's prophets. They do not have that degree of intimacy with God, and when they die, their death does not have the effect on God's people that the death of this

---

[30] See Smith, *Micah-Malachi*, 257; Lipinski, "Recherches sur le livre de Zecharie," 51–52.

[31] Meyers and Meyers, *Zechariah 9–14*, 129–30.

[32] Baldwin, *Haggai, Zechariah, Malachi*, 166.

[33] See Mitchell et al., *Haggai, Zechariah, Malachi, Jonah*, 275.

[34] It is not impossible that the reference to the river is a reference to the cosmic sea that nourishes the Holy City (cf. Ps 46:4; Ezek 47:1; Zech 14:8; Rev 22). See Smith, *Micah-Malachi*, 257.

[35] But see the older discussion by Mitchell et al., *Haggai, Zechariah, Malachi, Jonah*, 253–54, 317–19; Meyers and Meyers, *Haggai and Zechariah 1–8*, 384–85; Petersen, *Zechariah 9–14 and Malachi*, 129–30.

figure will.[36] The closest parallel in the prophetic corpus to the thought of Zech 13:7 is Isa 53:10—"it was the will of the Lord to bruise him."[37] When it is seen that the prophets considered it possible for God to strike down God's own favored ruler, the rationale for moving this passage elsewhere or connecting it to Zech 11 is eliminated.[38] For the sheep, the results of the demise of the shepherd are disastrous. They are leaderless, and indeed it appears the purpose of striking the shepherd is that they might be scattered. In an act that appears merciless on the surface, even the little sheep will feel the wrath of God, such that in the entire land two-thirds will perish.

The one-third that remain will, in addition, be put through a refiner's fire. The imagery here of smelting is a common one in the prophets for spiritual purification (cf. Jer 6:27–30; 9:6; Isa 48:10; Ezek 22:17–22; and especially Mal 3:2–3). It should be noted that only precious metals are subjected to such a refinement, and so the image is of something exceedingly valuable to the smelter. Thus, this suffering is meant to have a constructive purpose: they will return to a positive relationship that God filled with positive acts of naming. The end result of this process is that the sheep will call on their master, God, and God will answer and call them "my people," to which they respond, "The Lord is our God." There are two sides to any relationship; both must be loving and willing participants.[39] The language here is that of a covenant renewal by the two parties concerned (cf. Exod 6:7; Jer 31:33; Zech 8:8; Hos 2:23).[40] The hope expressed here is that after the striking of the shepherd, the judgment on two-thirds, and the refining of the one-third, there can be an enduring covenantal relationship between God and God's people.

Notice the general character of this song. The prophet is not specific about the identity of this shepherd who will be struck down. This, of course, made the prophecy far more serviceable in future generations, and indeed the prophecy seems to have an eschatological character from its inception. It must be stressed that here, as elsewhere in the prophetic corpus, redemption of the remnant comes after and beyond suffering and tribulation. Even the remnant is not spared this tribulation. Nonetheless the emphasis must be placed on the fact that this is an eschatological word of hope about salvation beyond judgment or a period of tribulation.[41]

---

[36] See rightly Meyers and Meyers, *Haggai and Zechariah 1–8*, 386–87.

[37] What is missed by Meyers and Meyers, ibid., 387, is that they assume that this shepherd ruler must have been personally guilty for God to strike him down. But if Isa 53:10 is a parallel, this need not be the case.

[38] It seems clear in the older discussion by Mitchell et al., *Haggai, Zechariah, Malachi, Jonah*, 318, that this is what motivates the scissors-and-paste approach here—a view of God that is found objectionable. But exilic and postexilic texts such as Ezek 21:9–12 do indeed speak of God striking Israel and its leaders down with the sword.

[39] See Baldwin, *Haggai, Zechariah, Malachi*, 198.

[40] Mitchell et al., *Haggai, Zechariah, Malachi, Jonah*, 318.

[41] See Smith, *Micah-Malachi*, 283.

There is a history of what can broadly be called messianic interpretation of this passage in Judaism, beginning at least as early as the *Damascus Document* (CD 19:5–9), where it may be that the Teacher of Righteousness is seen as the shepherd whom the poor ones of the flock watch as he is struck down. Ibn Ezra, on the other hand, saw Zech 13:7 as a reference to the messiah ben Joseph, the precursor messiah.[42] This sort of interpretation by Jewish exegetes continued into the Middle Ages.

II. DANIEL AND THE CONVERGENCE OF WISDOM, PROPHECY, AND APOCALYPTIC

Easily the most controverted of all the books that could be called prophetic in character is Daniel. Indeed, the book of Daniel has spent more time in the critic's den than its main character is said to have spent in the lion's den. It is not my intent to enter the fray about the authorship or date of Daniel except to say that clearly this book could not have arisen before the exile and that even if various of its traditions indeed go back to the exile, it appears, in its present form, to be a postexilic work written after apocalyptic was a viable and vital form of Hebrew expression.[43]

A majority of scholars rank it as the latest of all the material we have thus far discussed in this book. It is noteworthy that when the canon of the Hebrew Scriptures was assembled, this book was placed among the Writings, or the third division of Tanak, and not among the prophetic books. This may also suggest the lateness of the book, for the Writings seem to have been the last section of that canon to take a definite shape. Notice that the Jewish evaluation of the work in b. *Meg.* 3a says that Zechariah, Haggai, and Malachi are prophets but Daniel is not. This reflects the later Jewish polemic against visionaries and diviners. Nevertheless, clearly the Daniel corpus was enormously popular and influential well into the first century AD and beyond, both with Jews and later with Christians. The versions include various materials not included in the Hebrew Bible (but found in the Roman Catholic canon)—two long

---

[42] Ibid., 284.

[43] We should not dismiss the traditions, found in Ezek 14:14 and 28:3, about a figure named Daniel, which suggest there was in Hebrew circles such a figure, famous for his righteousness and wisdom. Nothing in Ezekiel necessarily suggests that Ezekiel means an ancient luminary when he mentions Daniel. He could be a famous contemporary. He appears to be associated with Noah and Job because all three were known for their upright character and the knowledge they gained from God. Nothing is said about them being of the same era in antiquity. Thus, I have doubts about the identification of the Jew Daniel with the Ugaritic Dnil. Would Hebrews such as Ezekiel really suggest that a pagan was famous for his righteousness? I think this is less probable than the alternative suggested above. Nonetheless it is not impossible that Ezekiel is referring to a legendary non-Jewish figure. See Zimmerli, *Ezekiel 1,* 314–15, for the discussion; and J. J. Collins, *Daniel* (Minneapolis: Fortress, 1993), 1ff.

prayers in Dan 3, the story of Susanna, and the story of Bel and the Serpent. It is possible that the reference to Daniel in *1 En.* 6:7 or *Sib. Or.* 3 provides us with a terminus ad quem for the book of Daniel, but even this is uncertain. The primary concern of this discussion, however, is with the character of the material we must examine, and we will also consider some of the ways that Daniel is portrayed—that is, as some combination of sage and seer, just as the book itself is an interesting amalgam of sapiential, prophetic, and apocalyptic material.

It is important at the outset to acknowledge that some scholars think that apocalyptic literature is not really prophecy at all but rather the redaction and reuse of prophecy—or at least forms and ideas that appear prophetic—for other purposes. Others see apocalyptic as the child of prophecy, attempting to prolong the usefulness of historical prophecy in an age when there was little or none of the latter. For instance, A. LeCocque suggests that apocalyptic "is the prolongation of prophecy and, in a sense, its replacement by a suprahistorical speculation on the basis of contemporary events."[44] The problem with this characterization is that prophecy had always had something to say about the spiritual (or as some prefer to call it, the supernatural) realm because it always had something to say about God and divine activity. Furthermore, at least as early as Isa 6 and probably much earlier, prophecy had already had a visionary component and possessed an air of revealing the secret or unknown, and by the time of the Isaiah apocalypse and Ezekiel, it was already using bizarre apocalyptic images. The book of Daniel is not the font of apocalyptic material, and only the second half of the book (chs. 7–12) could be called an apocalypse.

Nor is it clear historically that chs. 7–12 arose in an age when prophecy had ended and been superseded by apocalyptic. It is methodologically unsound to take later estimates, in some cases much later estimates, at face value as the truth about an earlier age and its prophecy. It is true that in Sir 49:10 the Twelve Prophets constitute a closed category, but against this Ben Sira presents himself and others like him as prophetic sages (Sir 39:1–5)![45] The much later material—for example, in *b. Meg.* 14a and *S. ʿOlam Rab.* 20–21 (cf. also *m. ʾAbot* 1.1; Pr Azar 3:28)—which suggests there were only forty-eight prophets and seven prophetesses in Israelite history, or that in *j. Soṭah* 13.2, which speaks of the Spirit leaving Israel when the last prophet died, and in *b. Sanh.* 11a can not be taken as historical fact. The judgment of D. Aune must be heeded:

> The rabbinic sages regarded themselves as the only legitimate interpreters and expounders of the Mosaic Torah, a role they had inherited from the canonical prophets who in turn were the successors of Moses. Since the sages did not consider themselves inspired spokesmen for divine revelations but rather traditionists, the view that prophecy had ceased was a means of legitimating their role as successors

---

[44] A. LeCocque, *Daniel in His Time* (Columbia: University of South Carolina Press, 1988), 4.

[45] That Ben Sira does not use Daniel proves nothing. Absence of evidence is not the same as evidence of absence.

of Moses and the prophets. Although these and other rabbinic texts make it clear that some rabbis did hold that prophecy had ceased during the Second Temple period, the view had a theoretical character and was only one view among many. According to other rabbinic traditions, famous rabbis claimed the gift of prophecy.[46]

Aune rightly adds, "It has become increasingly recognized that prophecy did not disappear in Judaism during the Hellenistic and Roman periods, but that it was alive and well, though in a form considerably different from that of classical OT prophecy."[47]

Although Josephus, *Ag. Ap.* 1.8, could be taken to suggest that prophecy is over and done with, this is the same Josephus who presents himself as a prophet and correctly predicts the rise of Vespasian to the Roman throne. Finally, the material in 1 Macc 4:46 and 9:27 should be compared with 1 Macc 14:41. Clearly, in 1 Macc 9:27 and 1 Macc 4:46, it was believed that a certain kind of prophet, in particular the court prophet who confronted the king, had disappeared from the landscape. But 1 Macc 14:41 makes quite clear that they were looking for another sort of prophet to arise and that Simon would be the leader pro tempore until he did. Eschatological prophets were of a different ilk than court prophets, as were peripheral prophets. Seers were of a different ilk than traditional oracular prophets. Movements such as the one at Qumran and the Jesus movement reflect a living and lively belief in the continued existence of prophecy, even if it took forms unlike some of those found in classical prophecy.

But the book of Daniel, like Ezekiel and Zechariah, suggests that traditional prophecy continued to exist alongside this new emphasis or development, which scholars today call apocalyptic, within the prophetic traditions. It is not surprising that, with a setting in Mesopotamia, the particular form of prophecy that is to the fore is visions rather than oracles. The question is whether apocalyptic visions can be characterized in general as "suprahistorical speculation based on current events." As a book such as Revelation shows, apocalyptic is sometimes about events seen as future, as were some of the more generalized and idealized forms of prophecy also.

Nothing said thus far is meant to deny that some apocalyptic works did sometimes employ pseudonymity as a vehicle for ex eventu prophecy (veiled descriptions of a current reality). One can hardly think otherwise in the case of some of the Enochic material or *4 Ezra*. The question is whether this is the case with Daniel.[48] Here it must be stressed that apocalyptic should not be categorized as the replacement for prophecy, as if prophecy had ceased. It makes far better sense to see it as one interesting and distinctive development within the ongoing Jewish prophetic tradition, since this study has already dealt with

---

[46] Aune, *Prophecy in Early Christianity*, 104.

[47] Ibid.

[48] It is, of course, possible that a book might be pseudonymous or anonymous but not include ex eventu prophecy at all.

apocalyptic visions within otherwise prophetic books such as Ezekiel and Zechariah.[49]

What, then, does one make of the case that Dan 7–12 can simply be described as ex eventu prophecy? This case hinges, to a great degree, upon a certain interpretation of ch. 11 (and also ch. 8), in particular vv. 34–45, which are seen to allude to events down to and including the committing of the abomination of desolation by Antiochus Epiphanes in the temple of Jerusalem in December 167 BC. But the narrative of the death of this ruler in vv. 40–45 does not comport with the evidence we have elsewhere about the demise of Antiochus Epiphanes. This means, at the least, that this event was in the future when the author wrote this material, yet he felt free to speak about it in the same fashion as he spoke about the other material. In other words, he was willing to risk some predictions such that even this section of Daniel could not simply be categorized as ex eventu prophecy. This raises the question whether the immediately preceding material *must* be seen as ex eventu prophecy.

The answer to this is no. Indeed, ch. 11 could be said to represent a very normal description of ancient Near Eastern or even Greek or Roman war tactics for shaming a foreign nation and proving its gods impotent—profaning the gods' temple and abolishing their sacrifices to accomplish the latter; pillaging, plundering, burning, maiming, killing, and deportation to accomplish the former. A conqueror uses the typical ancient Near Eastern or Greek or Roman propaganda to proclaim himself a god, as is shown by his victories, and insists, in the final act of humiliation, that the conquered must worship the god or gods the conqueror specifies. While this description could certainly apply to Antiochus Epiphanes, it could also apply to Nebuchadnezzar or later Roman conquerors, especially with the rise of the emperor cult. Antiochus Epiphanes was not the only ruler who ever defiled and then destroyed a temple. The material in ch. 11 is general enough in character to suit several such tyrants, but this is often the nature of apocalyptic, which is a study in deliberate generality or multivalency. It is no surprise under these circumstances that a Josephus or a Qumranite could peruse Daniel and see the last beastly empire as referring to Rome rather than the successors of Alexander. Such is always possible with general and ambiguous material. It is patient of several possible interpretations and applications.

On the other side of the coin, however, is the more specific material in ch. 8. There is the tale of a he-goat that comes from the west, becomes a great power

---

[49] The issue of apocalypse as a genre will be dealt with in pp. 217–19 below. I am also leery of the characterization of all of the literature of revelation in the Hellenistic world as pseudepigraphic in character. Some of the material in the sibylline oracles, as in the Orphic and Hermetic oracles, definitely is ex eventu prophecy. Some of it is probably not, and more certainly, some of the material from the oracle at Delphi that was also written down was not ex eventu prophecy at all but prophecy addressing a current or impending situation, as was true of the prophecy offered at other shrines in the Greco-Roman world. Cf. pp. 296–300 below.

over against a ram, then is cut down, and instead of him there are four conspicuous horns dividing up the worldwide empire. One of these horns, the one from the south, exalts himself, stops the sacrifice, and overthrows the sanctuary in the promised land. A specific time limit is then stated before the proper sacrifice and temple proceedings will be restored. Daniel requires angelic help in understanding this vision, and he is told at v. 20 that this is about the kings of Media and Persia and that the he-goat is the king of Greece. The four horns represent four kingdoms that will result from the dividing of the vast realm of the king of Greece, but they will not have his power. After this, v. 23 speaks of a king of bold countenance, understanding riddles, very powerful and successful in his acts of destruction even against the people of the saints, who will magnify himself and finally only be broken by God. At the end of this vision and even after the explanation, Daniel states that he is appalled by the vision and fails to understand it (v. 27).

It is difficult not to hear this more specific account in ch. 8 as a reference to Alexander the Great, to his successors, particularly Antiochus Epiphanes, and then to an unspecified great king who follows him. It is understandable why early interpreters saw in this a reference to the Hellenistic and then the Roman periods of history, which affected early Jews.

This leaves several questions. Does the greater specificity of this vision indicate that the author already has specific knowledge of at least Alexander and Antiochus, if not also of events beyond that period? If so, the case for ex eventu prophecy has considerable strength, especially in light of what we know about other similar apocalyptic literature that uses this literary device. Furthermore, since the prophecy here refers, for some reason, to Median as well as Persian kings (rather than Babylonian and Persian ones), does the author really know the Babylonian and Persian period? If this is actual predictive prophecy like earlier Hebrew predictive prophecy, a student of this material would expect one of two things—when the prophecy is specific, the prophet is speaking of his own time or that which is imminent in his time, but when the prophecy is more generalized or idealized in character, the further horizon, perhaps even the eschatological horizon, is in view.

The problem with ch. 8 is that it appears to be specific while *also* apparently speaking about end-time events. It is thus an enigma and unlike what this study has found before this in Hebrew prophecy, even in Zechariah or Ezekiel, in this regard. It seems in this case best to argue that we may be confronted with a hybrid form of material in Daniel, one that had a considerable tradition history.

If the traditions in 9:24–27 in the Old Greek translation of Daniel (ca. 150 BC) were made more specific in order to make very clear a reference to Antiochus Epiphanes, it could suggest that ch. 8 itself was augmented from its original Hebrew (or Aramaic?) form at an early date to point directly to the Greek empire and Alexander's successors. Nonetheless, the case for ex eventu prophecy in chs. 8 and 11 can not be lightly dismissed. One must balance the possibility of ex eventu prophecy here with the fact that even in chs. 8–12 there is some visionary material that is more generalized in character and seems to focus on the more distant and eschatological horizon. Thus, one can not rule out the possibility either that there is ex eventu prophecy in these texts or that the more specific references to Greek and Hellenistic rulers in ch. 8 in particular are later ex eventu editorial work.

Suppose, then, for a moment that it is the case, as the majority of scholars think, that at least some of the material in chs. 8 and 11 is an example of ex eventu prophecy. It does not follow from this that all of the rest of chs. 7–12 is of the same ilk, especially if it is true that Daniel is a composite work incorporating a variety of traditions of various ages.[50] At the very least, the composite and hybrid character of Daniel requires that we evaluate the famous son of man prophecy in ch. 7 with an open mind and not simply assume it is an example of ex eventu prophecy, as can be argued more strongly for other parts of chs. 7–12. It is in order at this point to ask if there are any telltale signs that ch. 7 perhaps deserves a different sort of treatment than the material that follows it in chs. 8–12. Indeed, one must ask if ch. 7 was originally the climax of the material in the earlier part of Daniel and should not be grouped with chs. 8–12.

In my view, the answer to these questions is yes on several grounds. In the first place, there are linguistic grounds for placing ch. 7 with what precedes it rather than with what follows. It is in Aramaic, as is the material since 2:4b. If language is any guide to sources, then certainly ch. 7 belongs with the earlier material.[51] Second, it seems clear that ch. 7 is dependent on ch. 2. This is why J. Collins argues that ch. 7 is in Aramaic, although he thinks ch. 7 was composed later to imitate the style of the Aramaic in chs. 2–6. His argument, however, is unconvincing. There are no telltale signs of a later Aramaic in ch. 7 than what we find in chs. 2–6, and furthermore, Collins allows that chs. 8–12 may come from a somewhat later time than ch. 7.[52] In fact, the Aramaic throughout chs. 2–7 is clearly Imperial Aramaic, the lingua franca of the ancient Near East between the sixth and second centuries BC.[53] If one follows J. Fitzmyer's dating system, the Aramaic of Daniel can not date later than 200 BC or earlier than 600 BC. This at least means Dan 2–7 was written *prior* to the Antiochus Epiphanes debacle, and perhaps well prior to it.[54]

---

[50] On the nature of Daniel as composite from a variety of historical dates, see Collins, *Daniel,* 24.

[51] Recently my colleague B. T. Arnold has suggested that the change in language is a literary device in a bilingual environment and that it has to do not with source material but the issue of "point of view" (à la B. Uspensky). See B. T. Arnold, "The Use of Aramaic in the Hebrew Bible: Another Look at Bilingualism in Ezra and Daniel," *JNST* 22 (2, 1996): 1–16. As he recognizes, ch. 7 is a real problem for this theory, not least because of the character and content of that section. If the issue were really a matter of point of view, Daniel should be speaking in Hebrew in ch. 7. One suspects at the end of the day that the author of this material was innocent of such sophisticated literary approaches as espoused by Uspensky.

[52] See Collins, *Daniel,* 24–25.

[53] See J. Goldingay, *Daniel* (Waco: Word, 1989), xxv.

[54] On the dating system, see J. A. Fitzmyer and D. J. Harrington, eds., *A Manual of Palestinian Aramaic Texts* (Rome: Pontifical Biblical Press, 1987), and Fitzmyer and S. A. Kaufman, *An Aramaic Bibliography* (Baltimore: Johns Hopkins University Press, 1992).

Third, only chs. 8–12 are presented directly in the first person. Chapter 7 is introduced with the same third-person style as the earlier chapters before it turns to direct speech. In other words, the beginning of ch. 7 makes clear that it goes with what has come before. Fourth, Josephus, who was in a position to evaluate early Jewish prophecy, makes a clear distinction between chs. 8–12 and what has come before. He says, in commenting on the beginning of ch. 8, that Daniel "left behind writings in which he made plain to us the accuracy and faithfulness to truth of his prophecies" (*Ant.* 10.267, Whiston). That he does not include ch. 7 in with chs. 8–12 suggests that he considers it either transitional or belonging with what has come before.[55] This is for good reason. Chapter 7 continues the story about King Belshazzar and relates a dream vision that Daniel had in the first year of his rule. It was a vision about four beastly empires followed by a humane one ruled by one like a son of man. None of the four kingdoms in the vision are clearly identified with Medes, Babylonians, Persians, Greeks, or anyone else.[56] Indeed, to make sense, the vision depends on what has been said earlier in ch. 2 about the king's vision.

Fifth, at the end of only ch. 7 do we have these words: "Here is the end of the matter." This is clearly a signal that a particular section of a work, if not the whole work, is concluded. Comparing Jer 51:64, we find a similar formula at the end of the oracles of Jeremiah. Ecclesiastes 12:13, an especially clear parallel, signals the end of the entire book: "The end of the matter; all has been heard." The formula, then, was used to signal the end of the orally delivered words (whether aphorisms, oracles, or visions) of some person, in this case Daniel. Sixth, it will not do to make a radical literary division between tales in chs. 1–6 and visions in 7–12. In chs. 2ff. Nebuchadnezzar has the same sort of dream visions as one finds in the case of Daniel in ch. 7.

Furthermore, the description before and the reaction afterward is closely similar in the case of the king and Daniel. For example, 2:1 tells us that Nebuchadnezzar "dreamed such dreams that his spirit was troubled and his sleep left him." After the interpretation of his vision by Daniel, we hear at 2:46 that the king "fell on his face, worshiped Daniel." Daniel 7:1 says of Daniel that he "had a dream and visions of his head as he lay in bed," and at the end of the vision he says, "As for me, Daniel, my spirit was troubled within me, and the visions in my head terrified me" (cf. also 7:28 and also the reaction Daniel had in 4:19 to Nebuchadnezzar's second dream vision). Daniel also must consult a diviner to understand the vision, just as Nebuchadnezzar had consulted Daniel, but Daniel's consultant is a heavenly attendant, presumably in the heavenly court. His reaction to such visions is basically the same as King

---

[55] It is understandable, too, that Josephus is silent about ch. 7 in general, just as he is silent about the stone that crushes the iron empire, because he was the guest of the Romans in Rome and, like other early Jews, he likely interpreted the stone and son of man materials messianically and considered the iron empire to refer to Rome.

[56] The only real clue from the earlier material comes in 2:36–45, where the first kingdom is identified with the Babylonians and their king, Nebuchadnezzar.

Nebuchadnezzar's, and he needs just as much help interpreting his vision. But Nebuchadnezzar's vision is one of destruction, while Daniel's is of a promised future kingdom for God's people and their representative after the earlier destruction.

Finally, there is the close similarity between the words of Darius in 6:26–27 and what Daniel says in 7:14. The former text says that God's kingdom will never be destroyed and God's dominion has no end; this is a very close match to "His dominion is an everlasting dominion that shall not pass away, and his kingship is one that will never be destroyed." Daniel 6:26–27 provides an important fore-shadowing and clue to the meaning of the vision in ch. 7, for this description ap-plies only to the kingdom of the living God in 6:26–27. In other words, the author is talking about the same kingdom in both cases, and one must assume a close identification between the one like a son of man and the living God if the former is to rule God's everlasting dominion.

In short, the visions do not begin in ch. 7; rather, Daniel's vision is seen as a continuation of the revelations of God in visions that had previously been given to the pagan rulers. Therefore, ch. 7 can not be separated from chs. 1–6 on the grounds that the visions are beginning at ch. 7. Even Collins at one point is forced to admit that the "concentric arrangement of chaps. 2–7 is highly com-patible with the hypothesis that an Aramaic book, consisting of chaps. 1–7 or 2–7, circulated independently."[57] Indeed, in his earlier work on the form of Dan-iel, Collins was prepared to say that the "most plausible explanation is that an original collection of Aramaic stories was expanded by the addition of the He-brew revelations in chs. 8–12. This much has been generally accepted, despite H. H. Rowley's famous defense of the unity of the whole book."[58] Just so, and I conclude that Daniel is indeed a composite book and that it can not be demon-strated that there is any ex eventu prophecy in 2:4a–ch. 7.[59] The material in chs. 8–12, from whatever hand, is added later and may represent ex eventu prophecy, but even this is uncertain, and in any case it is not relevant, since this study must focus on ch. 7.

As for the genre of Daniel, it hardly seems possible to call the entire book an apocalypse any more than we could with Zechariah. This description would do no justice to the sapiential character of most of chs. 1–6. What we must say is

---

[57] Collins, *Daniel*, 35.

[58] J. J. Collins, *Daniel, with an Introduction to Apocalyptic Literature* (Grand Rapids: Eerdmans, 1984), 29. I accept the point of Collins that a purely synchronic study of Daniel dies the death of a thousand qualifications in terms of the adding of later glosses. The diachronic approach makes much better sense of both the canonical and the noncanonical parts of this corpus.

[59] Notice the admission by Collins, *Daniel*, 47, that in chs. 1–6 "we lack the specific allusions that would enable us to ground the tales, either individually or taken together, in a specific time and place," by which he means a time and place other than the Babylonian and Persian period, which the stories are said to be ostensibly about. The same can be said of ch. 7.

that the book is hybrid in form, not fitting neatly into one specific literary genre, and that it includes some apocalyptic visions, especially in its second half.[60] The suggestion that the Hebrew portions of the book were added later makes good sense, for there are clear connections between them. Goldingay notes that ch. 1 is closely linked to the ending of the book in chs. 10–12 by the term "discerning," the visionary's self-designation, and a number of linguistic parallels with Gen 41 in both places.[61] Against the attempt to separate the beginning Hebrew section from that at the end of the book by claiming that 1:1–2:4a was originally composed in Aramaic is the observation that this hardly accounts for the fact that there is wordplay at various points, particularly at 1:8, that requires the Hebrew and would not work otherwise.

Something must be said about the portrayal of Daniel in chs. 1–7 before we consider the text of ch. 7. Daniel is clearly portrayed in this work as a sage, a diviner, a visionary, and also a sometime administrator of the realm. He is called a wise man or sage, but what is meant is that he can discern the meaning of dreams, visions, signs of the times (5:14). He is an expert in mantic, not proverbial or aphoristic, wisdom. Such figures were well known and often part of a king's court in the ancient Near East, as has already been seen in the discussions of Mari and other courts.[62] In other words, Daniel represents not merely an apocalyptic seer but a *baru*, one of the oldest known sorts of sapiential and prophetic figures from this region.[63] He differs from other such figures in the apocalyptic character of some of his visions. The story here, then, has echoes of the wider context and, in particular, the cross-cultural roles that prophets or diviners could play in such societies.

Within that wider context, however, it has often been noted that there are various parallels between the portrayal of Daniel here and that of Joseph in the Pentateuch. Both Daniel and Joseph were carted off into exile and became court diviners and administrators of the realm. The key to this in both cases is the ability to interpret dreams, but it must be remembered that both Joseph and Daniel are also portrayed as having dreams. Both Daniel and Joseph are said to have God's spirit in them (Dan 5:11, 14; Gen 41:38), and indicate that the ability to interpret dreams comes from God. Both wear a chain of office around their necks (Dan 5:29; Gen 41:42). There are comments made in both cases about their being handsome (Dan 1:4; Gen 39:6). Both are said to be distressed by a dream, through use of the same verb (Dan 2:1; Gen 41:8). It seems likely that the author of this Daniel material knew and was influenced by the portrayal of Joseph.[64] If this is so, then the portrayal in chs. 1–7 would not

---

[60] Thus, it can not be neatly slotted into the category of either a prophetic or an apocalyptic or a sapiential book. It seems to have the least in common with the first of these, if by prophetic one means classic nonvisionary oracular material.

[61] Goldingay, *Daniel*, 327.

[62] See pp. 13–20 above.

[63] See pp. 86–87 above.

[64] See Collins, *Daniel*, 39.

likely have been complete without the recounting of a dream vision that Daniel himself had received.

The portrait of Daniel in the book of the same name suggests that, far from being an ancient luminary like a Noah, he was someone born in Israel immediately prior to the southern exile and deported as a young man by Nebuchadnezzar and that he had a remarkably long tenure as a courtier from the reign of Nebuchadnezzar to the reign of Cyrus, in other words, from one end of the exile to the other—about seventy years.[65] There is no suggestion he lived long enough to return to Jerusalem in the late sixth century BC or that he lived long before the exile. LeCocque is right that the stories that we find in chs. 1–6 bear some rather clear resemblances to the Elijah and Elisha sagas.[66] But there is this difference: those northern prophets perform miracles, while Daniel simply has miracles happen to him. There is, however, this further similarity: at Dan 5:17 and in the story of Elisha and Naaman in 2 Kgs 5, Daniel and Elisha each indicate the authenticity of their gift by refusing funds and so make clear they are not prophets working for personal gain.[67]

On Daniel as a *hasid*, or wise man, one hears not only about his excellent wisdom but that the spirit of God is within him, that he fears God, that he is a righteous man, that he is something of an ascetic, and so on (cf. Dan 1; 4:9; 5:14). Insofar as one may talk about Daniel as a prophet, he must be seen in the mold of Zechariah. These are prophets who reflect the beginnings of the apocalyptic tradition in their visions but do not produce an apocalypse per se. Daniel is, like Ezekiel, an ecstatic whose visions not merely transport and transform and transfix him but indeed frighten him (compare Ezek 1–3 with Dan 7:15, 28; cf. Dan 8:18, 27; 10:9–10, 16–17). It is important, however, not to distinguish too sharply Daniel's being a sage and from his being a seer. As Koch reminds us, Daniel's wisdom does not lie merely in solving riddles, such as the writing on the wall of the palace, but in revealing mysteries about the historical process and its ultimate end and aim (2:22).[68]

The hybrid character of things, involving the convergence of the wisdom and prophetic traditions and roles, best explains both the book of Daniel and its legacy in a later era, affecting figures as diverse as Jesus ben Sira and Jesus of Nazareth. The stories in chs. 1–6 are, in the first instance, stories about an

---

[65] I find remarkable the comment of LeCocque, *Daniel in His Time*, 183, about the portrayal of Daniel: "The author's silence on his hero's origins is purposeful. It leaves them in the dark and thus confirms the legendary character stressed already by Ezekiel 14:14; 28:3 where Daniel is an ancient holy man associated with the patriarchs Noah, Job." In the first place, the implicit suggestion of ch. 1 is surely that Daniel was born and brought up in Judah shortly before the exile. In the second place, nothing in those Ezekiel texts suggests Daniel was an ancient luminary. He is said to be like these other figures in his righteousness and wisdom; nothing is said or suggested about his antiquity.

[66] See pp. 80–99 above.

[67] The same might also be the motivation of a much later prophetic figure—Paul.

[68] K. Koch, "Is Daniel among the Prophets?" *Int* 39 (1985): 117–30.

astounding prophetic sage who has the ability to discern the meaning of things ranging from riddles to dreams. They are not mere court tales.

The international character of the wisdom tradition, rather than the cross-cultural aspect of the prophetic tradition, best explains what we find in chs. 1–7. Daniel appears much like the font of wisdom in the Jewish tradition as he is portrayed in 1 Kgs 3–10—namely, like Solomon. The sapiential tales in Kings showing the king's wisdom are not unlike those here in Daniel. This is why the placing of this work among the Writings is, in various ways, an understandable and apt move. It is perhaps also why one does not have recorded here a call narrative for Daniel, for sages were not so much called as they were persons who acquired wisdom—in Daniel's case, through assiduous attention to God in prayer and other acts of devotion.

It is right, as Le Cocque points out, that in a sense Daniel is a throwback to earlier models of a prophet, for he is a diviner and one involved with mantic, not proverbial, wisdom. Yet the content that he interprets and then also his own visions are no throwback—they are apocalyptic in form and, to some degree, in content as well. With this in mind, the discussion turns now to ch. 7.

Daniel 7 provides the climax of a chiastically arranged series of material that encompasses all the Aramaic portion of Daniel. The structure is as follows:

> ch. 2: A vision of four kingdoms and their end (Nebuchadnezzar)
>> ch. 3: Faithfulness and a miraculous rescue (the three friends)
>>> ch. 4: Judgment previewed and experienced (Nebuchadnezzar)
>>> ch. 5: Judgment previewed and experienced (Belshazzar)
>> ch. 6: Faithfulness and a miraculous rescue (Daniel)
> ch. 7: A vision of four kingdoms and their end (Daniel).[69]

This structure not only encourages us to read ch. 7 in light of ch. 2, both chapters being about symbolic dreams referring to four realms, but it will be observed that the story line moves from less to more focus on Daniel's own experiences. It moves from the experiences of the pagan rulers to those of the Hebrew prophetic sage, just as it moves from beastly kingdoms and kings who end up acting like beasts to one ruled by a son of man, or human figure. The progression through these chapters is also a logical one. First the pagan ruler is told that he has his position from the true God. But chs. 3–6 portrays such rulers as trying to make themselves into gods and so becoming beastly. Daniel 7 presupposes all this and shows the outcome: a divine kingdom must supplant all of this with a ruler of God's own choosing who will not exalt himself but yet be exalted. Notice, too, the sequence from dream statue in ch. 2 to real one in ch. 3 and from real animals in ch. 6 to dream ones in ch. 7. Peoples of every race were first impelled to bow before the human statue (3:4; 5:19), but in due course they will have to bow before the real human figure (7:14).[70]

---

[69] Here I follow Goldingay, *Daniel*, 158.

[70] Ibid., 158–59.

The material in ch. 7 contains repeated use of stock formulas, chiefly with the repetition of the term "watched" (vv. 2, 4, 5, 6, 7, 8, 11, 13), emphasizing that this is something that Daniel saw "in my vision during the night." Images keep appearing before his mind's eye—he is a passive recipient of them. The whole of the chapter is an interesting mix of prose and poetry, but it is important to note that the climax of the vision is marked by the use of poetic parallelisms, assonance, rhythm, and repetition, with vv. 9–10 possibly identifiable as straight poetry, and v. 14 as well. This suggests that at least the climax of this vision did come to some prophetic figure as a revelation; as has been seen so many times before in this study, genuine prophecy, especially in the Hebrew tradition, took poetic form.[71] There is one contrast that will bear further reflection, but it needs to be mentioned now. The natural balance in vv. 1–4 should be that creatures come up from the sea and the human figure comes down from and with the clouds. The issue is where the final-judgment scene is envisioned as taking place, and I will suggest that, as elsewhere in the prophetic corpus, the *Yom Yahweh*, which involves judgment for some and redemption for others, is seen as transpiring on earth, not in heaven. At the end of human history, court is held where the offenders and the vindicated are.

It is crucial to note the motifs that are repeated in this chapter and those that are interpreted, for both of these factors signal importance in the author's mind. For example, there is no interpretation here of the first three animals, but in part this is because ch. 7 depends on ch. 2, where at least it is made plain that the first beast is Babylon. Notice also that in ch. 7 there is no depiction of the horn's punishment. The only matter mentioned four times in the chapter is the new dominion for God's saints (vv. 14, 18, 22b, 27), but the final beast, the ten horns, the small horn, and the divine judgment come up three times each (e.g., on judgment, cf. vv. 9, 10, 22a, 26a).[72] Bearing these things in mind, it is time to work through the chapter and see how it develops.

Daniel 7 ostensibly appears to record a dream that Daniel had during the time of the coregency of Belshazzar and the absentee king Nabonidus and so somewhere around 550 BC or shortly thereafter.[73] What so clearly distinguishes this dream vision from what we find in chs. 8–12 is that here there is no specific reference to the introduction of abominations either into the temple worship or alternatively to temple worship, unlike what we find in 8:13, 9:27, and 11:31. This vision also clearly suggests that divine deliverance for Israel is still in the future. In short, although the vision may begin with Daniel's present, it clearly finishes in the future, indeed in the eschatological future, not necessarily the near future, and as such must be seen, in regard to content, as like other idealized or generalized prophecies of the remoter future already examined in Second Isaiah, Ezekiel, and Zechariah. Apocalyptic images and forms are used here as in some

---

[71] See pp. 66–69 above.

[72] Goldingay, *Daniel*, 155.

[73] See the discussion in S. B. Reid, *Enoch and Daniel: A Form Critical and Sociological Study of Historical Apocalypses* (Berkeley: Bibal, 1989), 83–92.

of those places, but here for the first time, one sees them full-blown. Daniel 7 begins to cross the line, providing the formal pattern for apocalyptic, and it is no accident that chs. 8–12 were later added directly to this material. Like later apocalyptic literature, the emphasis will be placed here in Daniel on the fact that things will be rectified for the saints on earth only when there is direct divine intervention in some form.

This vision comes at a perilous time for Babylon because while Nabonidus was away at Tema, Belshazzar and the empire were vulnerable, and one knows that it was at this very time in 550–549 BC that Cyrus had a tremendous victory over the Median king Astyages.[74] It was indeed an appropriate time for such a vision, as trouble was lurking for Belshazzar on the near horizon.

It is interesting how the Aramaic reads here: "Daniel saw a dream, even visions of his head on his bed." The emphasis here suggests no pneumatic transport but a phenomenon much like that found in Zechariah. The mention of writing the dream down indicates that its message was not just for Daniel alone (cf. 8:26; 12:4, 9; Isa 8:1, 16; 30:18; Jer 30:2; 36:2; 51:60; Ezek 43:11). Prophetic experience flows quickly into prophetic expression, but in this case not in an oral form. The account of the dream vision has a very clear framing device. The end of v. 1 can be translated, "the head [or start] of the matter [or account]," and v. 28, "the end of the matter [or account]." The latter also serves the purpose of signaling the ending of the Aramaic source.

The vision begins with Daniel watching four winds of heaven stirring up the great sea, the Mediterranean (cf. 1QapGen 21:16). And the result of this is that four great and distinctive beasts are dredged up out of the chaos waters. Two things are being affirmed here. First, God is in control of this whole historical process—these are divine winds that stir this up. Second, this is the beginning of the theme of order out of chaos. As in ch. 2, it is affirmed that God has set up governments; the question is whether they will follow God's blueprint or go their own way. That *beasts* show up out of the chaos waters is not promising for good things to happen, at least from the perspective of God's people. Baldwin rightly notes the close similarities here of "I saw in my night vision" to Zech 1:8, and the reference to the four winds of heaven is like what we find in Zech 2:6 and 6:5 (cf. Dan 8:8; 11:4).[75] Of course, the four winds come from all four major directions of the compass. There seems also to be some familiarity here with Isaiah's notion that the nations are like a troubled, restless sea (Isa 17:12–13).[76]

But Daniel's vision is not about human history as a whole but about history as beginning in his own time and continuing on into the future. It is very

---

[74] See G. Hasel, "The First and Third Years of Belshazzar (Dan. 7.1; 8.1)," *AUSS* 15 (1977): 173–92.

[75] J. Baldwin, *Daniel* (Downers Grove, Ill.: InterVarsity, 1987), 138.

[76] The "universal" scope of the vision is, of course, from the ancient Near Eastern perspective; the great sea is thus the Mediterranean, and the vision is of the then known world, not the world known today.

possible that this vision is partly shaped by the author's knowledge of the *Enuma Elish*, the Babylonian mythological poem of creation, in which Marduk uses four winds to stir up and corner Tiamat, the monster of the great sea. As Collins avers, one must think mythologically here because, from any point of view, including Israel's, neither the Babylonian empire nor its immediate successor could be said to rise out of the sea in the west. Rather, the sea here represents not a geographical location but a mythical description of a world in chaos, needing order.[77] The empires are viewed as like the chaos monsters that were thought to dwell in such a vast sea (cf. Isa 27:1; 51:9–11).

The emphasis in v. 3 is on the hugeness of the animals, hence the vastness of the empires, in comparison particularly with Israel. The closest parallel to the animals mentioned beginning in v. 4 is found not in extrabiblical literature but in Hos 13:7–8, where lion, leopard, bear, and then an unidentified wild beast are mentioned as a comparison to Yahweh and as part of a divine threat. The emphasis is on the ferociousness and power of these beasts in both our text and Hos 13, and there may also be some reminiscence of the notion of Israel's enemies being like brutal beasts—another prophetic idea (Ezek 34). One finds this even more fully played out in the so-called animal apocalypse in *1 En.* 85–90.[78]

It may also be germane that in Babylon there were represented winged lions and similar beasts on public buildings.[79] Thus, it is not likely a coincidence that the first beast Daniel sees is like a lion with wings of an eagle, and this beast, according to the earlier cues in ch. 2, is to be identified with Babylon just as the golden head of the four-part statue was to be so identified. The lion, of course, was king of beasts, and this may suggest that the first beastly empire is less animalistic and that then there is a progressive degeneration in the next three. This may also comport with the partially favorable portrait of the Babylonian court in the early chapters of the book and certainly makes sense of the next comment in v. 4—namely, that the lion was given the heart of a human being and had its wings plucked. As a likely reference to the restoration of Nebuchadnezzar in ch. 4, it makes him a more human ruler.[80] This makes good sense of what is also said at the end of the verse about this creature being made to stand on two feet and so walk as a human. We may also compare Jer 49:19, 22, where lion and eagle characterize Nebuchadnezzar.

Verse 5 describes the second beast. It is made very clear that this is "a different animal," not just another symbolic representation of the same one. This one is a bear, standing up with bones already in its mouth, and it is commanded to get up and eat a lot of meat. The image is of an animal about to pounce on more prey.[81] Nothing here associates this beast with a specific kingdom, and it is

---

[77] Collins, *Daniel*, 294–95.

[78] The animal apocalypse can be taken to be influenced by Daniel rather than the converse. See the next chapter.

[79] See pp. 198–202 above.

[80] See Collins, *Daniel*, 297.

[81] Baldwin, *Daniel*, 139

unwarranted to read into it the later material in Daniel.[82] The image of bears in the OT is of highly dangerous and carnivorous creatures (see 2 Kgs 2:24). Collins and those who do not try to overallegorize the text at this point (referring the three ribs to three kings or kingdoms) should be followed, for the author is striving for a vivid picture of an animal devouring its prey, as in Amos 3:12.[83] In other words, what is helpful is to interpret the text in light of earlier prophetic material, not later apocalyptic material that involves ex eventu prophecy.

The third animal in the vision is a leopard, also a carnivore but, unlike the bear, known for its speed (cf. Hab 1:8—the Babylonian army is seen as faster than a leopard). But this leopard also had the power of flight, with four bird wings on its back, making it doubly quick on land or by air. This animal had four heads and "authority was given to it." Perhaps one may see the winged leopard as analogous to the winged lion of Mesopotamian art.[84] In any case, the old guesses that this represented Alexander and Greece because of the speed of his conquest could also be predicated of Cyrus for the same reason. The author does not specify or speculate. The symbol is general and plastic. The four heads, if they remind of anything, suggest a knowledge of Ezekiel's vision where there were four-headed creatures. Inasmuch as one has seen the number four earlier in the vision suggest universality and in Dan 2:29 the third kingdom is said to have universal rule, this is likely the point here as well. This universal scope is also why the authority of this kingdom is stressed. Again it is God who so authorizes such kings and kingdoms.

The fourth animal, mentioned in vv. 7–8, is the most fearsome of all, and we are told it acted differently than the other beastly kingdoms, but we are not told in what way it differed. One feature of this last beast rings a bell—its iron teeth, which seem to allude to the layer of iron in the statue in ch. 2. This beast is described as terrible, dreadful, and exceedingly strong. As in Zech 1:18–21 (2:1–4), we should see the reference to horns as a reference to strength. The more horns, the more strength. This beast had five times the natural animal's number of horns, and so perhaps five times its strength.[85] The reference to horns, then, does not require us to think that our author knew anything about Seleucid coins with rulers who had horned helmets on their heads.[86] Whatever else one may want to say about these four beasts, one can only agree that the "writer was not encouraged to see in history evolutionary progress."[87] Notice, too, that this last monster is not identified with any known creature, much as in the case of Hos 13:5–6, where the fourth animal is also unspecified.

---

[82] E.g., O. Ploger, *Das Buch Daniel* (Gütersloh: Mohn, 1965), ad loc., links the bear's clumsiness with the Medes' lack of historical achievement. But of this our text implies nothing. It does not even suggest a lumbering bear. Rather, it depicts a killing machine.

[83] Collins, *Daniel*, 298.

[84] Ibid.

[85] See Baldwin, *Daniel*, 140.

[86] Against the suggestion of Collins, *Daniel*, 299.

[87] Ibid.

From the midst of the ten horns comes forth yet another horn, a little one that is seen to grow right before the eyes of the visionary. The little horn uproots three of the horns and has eyes and a mouth making grand pronouncements. Isaiah 37:23 characterizes the behavior of Sennacherib in this very fashion, and in Isa 10:12–13 the king of Assyria is said to be arrogant of look and word. In other words, there are prophetic precedents that explain this use of imagery; we need not look to later Hellenistic events. Nothing said about the little horn here is suggestive of Antiochus Epiphanes in particular. What we can say with more certainty is that the eyes suggest intelligence and powers of observation,[88] something a Hebrew would not likely predicate of that most insensitive of anti-Semites, Antiochus Epiphanes. The author is not writing about a particular, already known person. The description is typical rather than personal, and it suggests an intelligent and powerful usurper of some who are already in power. It more nearly fits a Herod the Great than an Antiochus Epiphanes, but neither is specifically alluded to here. In any event, the fourth animal has, like the first animal, elements in his appearance that suggest he is more than an animal.[89]

The poetry proper begins with vv. 9–10, and it has often been suggested that this material is taken from an older hymn or poem. Whereas in the description of the beasts there were chains of synonyms, here there are short phrases in poetic parallelism (clothing white as snow, hair like pure wool). There is, however, no need for the suggestion that older material is cited here.[90] It can just as well be that the author has chosen simply to present the prophetic vision received in an unadorned or transcript fashion here but the earlier material in the chapter has been carefully edited to make it largely prosaic. The form also suggests that the author sees this climax of the vision in vv. 9–10 and 13–14 as the heart of the matter, deserving to be presented verbatim or nearly so in prophetic form, to make evident its divine source.

The next stage in Daniel's vision contains a court scene. The Almighty could not brook such injustice being perpetrated upon the earth, and especially upon God's people for so long. Thus the day of reckoning has come. But the question immediately raised is where this courtroom drama unfolds. It could be a scene in heaven, and this is indeed how the account in *1 En.* 14 seems to have exegeted Dan 7.[91]

---

[88] See Baldwin, *Daniel*, 140.

[89] Goldingay, *Daniel*, 164. For those keen on specifying the four empires, it needs to be stressed that not only in ch. 8, in the later part of the book, but also in ch. 6, where we find references to the one law of the Medo-Persian empire, and finally in 5:28, where we hear of the Babylonian kingdom being given to both Medes and Persians, the author or final editor of this work seems to insist on treating Media and Persia as two parts of one empire.

[90] See Collins, *Daniel*, 299–300.

[91] The account in *1 En.* 14 is far more elaborate than what is found here, which suggests its dependence on Daniel and not the other way around. The one thing that is notably absent in the later account in *First Enoch* is the courtroom setting, which is not

But several factors must count against this. The courtroom scene, coupled with the motif of the final judgment of nations, favors an earthly setting. There are various prophetic texts indicating that God comes forth from heaven to judge the earth (Zech 14:5; Joel 3:12; Jer 49:38; cf. Ps 96:13). Furthermore, what is depicted in a portion of ch. 7 is a royal-investiture ceremony for a human figure who would supersede the beastly rulers. The obvious venue for such a scene would be earth, not heaven. The judgment scene that is also referred to in vv. 11–12 and 23–27 likewise most naturally would transpire where those who are being judged reside—on (or under the) earth. Goldingay rightly says that there is no reason to think that the scene, which is on earth as described in vv. 2–8, has suddenly shifted to heaven, especially since v. 9 implies a continuing of perspective.[92] The case has been made forcefully by M. Casey, who has argued that the setting for this judgment scene is not merely earth but Israel. This is where the fourth beast that comes forth from the sea onto the promised land will be confronted. The phrase "seeing the Son of Man coming upon [or in] the clouds of heaven," then, suggests a theophanic scene with a descent from heaven.[93] Finally, v. 22 says that the Ancient of Days came, which suggests that the scene must be on earth.[94]

Although thrones are mentioned immediately, only one is said to take his seat at first, and he is called "the Ancient of Days," or as Goldingay puts it, "one advanced in years." The phrase clearly refers to one of great antiquity (cf. Ps 9:7; 29:10; 90:2l; Sir 25:4).[95] The later clarification in *1 En.* 47.3 refers to the "Head" or "Source of Days." But here the focus is on someone venerable and wise. In a culture where great age was revered rather than youth, it is not surprising to find God described in this fashion. The seating of the rest of God's court takes place afterwards (v. 10), and only then the books are opened, the records of deeds consulted, and the leaders of the evil empires either executed (the little horn) or put on notice that their days are numbered (the animals).[96]

The Almighty is described as having clothing like white snow and hair like lamb's wool. The description is meant to indicate extreme purity (see Ps 51:7). Neither God nor the divine judgment could be accused of being tainted.

---

surprising since Enoch has ascended to heaven, while God's final judgment in earlier Israelite tradition is to happen on earth.

[92] Goldingay, *Daniel*, 164.

[93] M. Casey, *Son of Man: The Interpretation and Influence of Daniel 7* (London: SPCK, 1979), 28ff. This view is given further substantiation by K. Müller, "Der Menschensohn im Danielzyklus," in *Jesus und der Menschensohn* (ed. R. Pesch et al.; Freiburg: Herder, 1975), 37–80. He places especial stress on the way the participial construction favors reading this as a descent from heaven.

[94] See G. R. Beasley-Murray, "The Interpretation of Daniel 7," *CBQ* 45 (1983): 44–58.

[95] Goldingay, *Daniel*, 142.

[96] If, as seems likely, this includes the ruler of the first empire, the lion figure, it suggests that this prophecy may have been given at a time before his death, and certainly before the death of the other animalistic rulers of kingdoms.

The evidence elsewhere speaks of God's books prepared for the judgment day (Exod 32:32; Ps 56:8; Mal 3:16). The throne is also described, and there seems to be some indebtedness to Ezek 1 here especially if one translates, "his throne was fiery flames, and its wheels were burning fire." As if this were not threatening enough, we are told that a stream of fire issued from the divine presence. Fire is a natural symbol of judgment and is frequently used as such in the OT (Deut 4:4; Ps 18:9–14; 50:3; 97:3). Lightning is an appropriate symbol of the sudden destructive power of judgment issuing from a holy and powerful source.[97]

The judgment that is to be rendered against the beastly rulers and realms is to be final. As Collins suggests, it is reasonable to conclude that the execution here is by order of the court.[98] The little horn is first executed and then cremated, and the other beastly rulers are stripped of their dominions. This is the necessary prelude to what is found in vv. 13–14, for the human figure will be able to exercise world rule only if the other rulers are either dead or stripped of power. Verses 11–12 are once again in prose, as if the beastly kingdoms did not merit elevated oracular speech but the dominion of God does. The restrained and more primitive nature of the judgment scene here becomes clear when we compare *1 En.* 90:20–27, where wicked stars, shepherds, and even sheep are thrown into a fiery pit (cf. 1QS 2:8; 4:13; CD 2:5). Here in Dan 7, because "the beast symbolizes a kingdom, the emphasis is on destruction rather than on the eternal punishment of individuals in hell."[99]

Verses 13–14 are clearly some of the most controverted verses in the entire Scriptures, and here I can mention only the major interpretive moves and the reasons for the present study's conclusions. The lengthy formula that introduces the scene indicates a major new subject is to be treated.[100] There is precious little debate that the phrase "one like a son of man" means "one like a human being." But the very comparative nature of the phrase might suggest a description of a being that only appears to be human, whether an angelic or a divine figure, and in fact is more than human. This possibility is raised because in Ezek 1 such an analogy is drawn in describing the Almighty.[101] The possibility is perhaps given further support by the fact that we seem to have a theophany described here (cf. Isa 19:1; Ps 18:9–12). The problem, of course, with the conclusion that God is being described here is that this figure comes to a court where God as the Ancient of Days is already seated.

Not surprisingly, some have thus concluded that an angelic figure is meant, not only because of where the Son of man comes from but also because of texts such as 8:15, where Gabriel is described as having the likeness of a man, and one could also compare similar data in 10:5 and 12:5–7. One could also

---

[97] Goldingay, *Daniel*, 166.
[98] Collins, *Daniel*, 303.
[99] Ibid., 304.
[100] Goldingay, *Daniel*, 167.
[101] See pp. 169–70 above.

compare the description of the fourth figure in the furnace at 3:25, who is called a "man" (i.e., a person), having the appearance of a son of the gods. In the later apocalyptic literature, there are such analogies applied to angels in *1 En.* 87:2; 90:14, 17, 22. Thus, Collins and others have a case when they urge that the text is referring to an angelic figure.[102]

Against the use of the evidence from at least the parables of Enoch is the point that in that very text the son of man is revealed to be a human being—Enoch himself. Against the use of material in Dan 8–12 is the likelihood that these chapters were added later to the Danielic Aramaic corpus. As for 3:25, the Aramaic says that this figure has an appearance of a son of the gods, not of a son of man. Furthermore, 7:27 says that the final dominion is given to human beings—the people of the saints of the most high—not to an angel. It is possible that the reference to *qedoshim* is itself a reference to angels, but then one must envision a dominion given on earth to a head angel (the son of man figure) and his angelic host. But how would this be a message of comfort and triumph for God's people continuing to live in the mundane sphere?[103] It seems far more likely that beastly human rulers would be replaced at a tribunal on earth by a humane human ruler.[104] Furthermore, in 7:25, when the little horn is said to wear out the holy ones of the most high, are we really to envision a human ruler waging war against angels? How would such angelic beings be devastated by a change in feast days and the law? If, on the other hand, these holy ones are human beings, why should one think otherwise about the son of man figure? What Israel hoped for is what they had possessed during the monarchy—a king who would rule on their behalf.

Against the suggestion that corporate Israel is meant by "the son of man" is the observation that previously the beastly empires all had heads and they were not simply synonymous with those heads. One would expect the pattern to play out the same way in 7:13–14. Furthermore, the son of man is to rule a dominion of God's people as well as all other peoples and nations once he has come on the clouds from heaven. He is not synonymous with his dominion of the ruled. Finally, corporate Israel coming on clouds from heaven is hardly a likely image to be employed here. We are thus left with the notion of a representative figure who is like a human being yet comes from heaven and furthermore can be bequeathed an everlasting dominion, something that could not in truth be said of the beastly rulers. The interpretation and application of this text to an individual is found already in the parables of Enoch and, of course, also in the NT.

---

[102] See Collins, *Daniel,* 305–6.

[103] See B. Witherington, *The Christology of Jesus* (Minneapolis: Fortress, 1990), 238ff.

[104] The logic of the narrative moves away from the sort of heavenly speculations and focus that we find in later apocalyptic literature and places this text closer to the earlier prophetic material, which expects a resolution of matters on earth, one involving a human ruler, however much endowed with divine power and authority.

Here this figure is treated as royalty by God in the investiture scene, and he partakes of both human and more-than-human traits and actions.[105] Notice, too, that no part of the description here suggests animal features. This figure entirely resembles a human being.[106] He is given authority that in 2:44–45 is said to be from God and indeed was God's own. Thus, he is given the power the pagan rulers of world empire once exercised (2:37; 5:19; 6:25) and is given an even more lasting and vast domain. It is worth stressing that, elsewhere in the biblical tradition, angels are never given such dominions on earth to rule nor are the people of the earth expected to serve angels, as is said here of the Son of man figure. One wonders if there is an echo here of the mandate given to the first human being in Genesis to fill the earth and subdue it and to rule over all its creatures. Yet Goldingay is right to stress that "if the humanlike figure is the anointed, the anointed as Daniel pictures him now has a very transcendent dimension. If the idea of the anointed moves between a God pole and a human pole, this humanlike figure is at the former."[107]

A few loose ends from vv. 13–14 need to be tied up at this juncture. The Son of man figure is said to be presented to the Almighty. Presumably, it is those myriads mentioned as serving and attending the Almighty in v. 10 who are at this scene doing the presenting. Notice, too, that the Son of man figure not merely is given kingship and a dominion to rule but is also said to be given glory—the divine presence. All three of these necessary equippings are what make it mandatory that peoples and nations serve him.

He is the deity's agent or representative and so should be served as the deity is served. Like the deity's, his dominion is everlasting and indestructible, and his power is divine. Of only a divine or quasi-divine figure could a Hebrew say this, unless we are meant to take this as simply rhetorical hyperbole. But however hyperbolic the description here, the Jews in exile had really experienced the pagan empires as beastly and were looking for an equally real remedy on the historical plane so that justice would finally be done on earth as in heaven. It is doubtful, then, that this should be seen as a supramundane description of what is or will be true in heaven rather than on earth, or merely hyperbolic words of encouragement "full of sound and fury, [but] signifying nothing."

First offered in vv. 15–18, the interpretation of the vision is given once Daniel has asked one of the (angelic?) attendants to explain. The vision is said to have deeply troubled Daniel and frightened him, just as their dream visions frightened pagan rulers.[108] He is also clueless about the meaning without interpretive help. Notice that the same verb, "alarmed" or "terrified," is used of Daniel here as of the previous recipients of night visions in 2:1; 4:1 (cf. also 8:27). The author is not suggesting that Daniel's experience is any different from the

---

[105] For a fuller discussion of the linguistic evidence about *bar enasha* and *ben adam,* cf. Witherington, *Christology of Jesus,* 238–47.

[106] Goldingay, *Daniel,* 168.

[107] Ibid., 170.

[108] See pp. 199–200 above.

kings' either in the form of message received or in reaction to it. This, in turn, raises the important question whether a vision recipient is ipso facto a prophet or whether it is also necessary that the individual be a vision interpreter before being called such. If the former is the case, then even the pagan rulers in Daniel could be called prophets, or even Pharaoh in Gen 41:8. This conclusion is doubtful, and so one must conclude that the mere having of visions does not make one a prophet unless we simply define prophet as seer.

Daniel is said to approach God's entourage to get an interpretation of what he has seen, and we may compare other texts that talk about the attendants or angels or spirits of the heavenly court who serve various functions (1 Kgs 22:21; Isa 6:6), but the closest parallel is probably the interpreting angel found in Zech 1:9–19. This feature was to become a stock item in apocalyptic material, and it suggests that the meaning of apocalyptic material was never deemed to be self-evident to any human recipient however spiritually perceptive, even if one was a prophetic sage like Daniel.[109] We may compare the function of the interpreting angels in the earlier material in Ezek 40–48 as well as Zech 1–6. There is a significant difference, however, between what is seen here and what we find in chs. 8–12. In the latter texts the interpretation is given on divine initiative, whereas here and in the earlier apocalyptic material it is the recipient who requests interpretive help. This places ch. 7 with the earlier material rather than with chs. 8–12.[110]

The initial interpretation offered in vv. 17–18 is tantalizingly brief. Four beasts represent four kings arising out of the earth (notice, not out of the sea). This makes clear that the author was using "sea" in a mythical sense earlier, and one is not necessarily to think of empires coming from across the Mediterranean. Verse 18 makes a contrast with v. 17—but the holy ones of the Most High will receive "the Kingdom" and possess it forever. Notice that, even in the interpretation here, absolutely nothing is said to indicate specifically which pagan kingdoms are in mind. The point is that, after them all, it is *the kingdom* that comes from God and is given to God's people forever.

If we examine closely what ch. 7 and ch. 8 say about the little horn, it will be seen that the message is notably different and that only in the latter chapter is an allusion to Antiochus Epiphanes clear or likely. In ch. 8 the small horn emerges after the appearance of four previous horns, whereas in the vision in ch.

---

[109] Nevertheless, Collins, *Daniel*, 311–12, probably makes too much of the distinction between Daniel as interpreter for the kings and the angel as interpreter. He says that this signals a change in genre. But Daniel receives his insight from God. He is a prophetic sage, not an ordinary person. His interpretations are not merely his own. Collins is, however, right that an angelic interpreter is a standard feature of Jewish apocalypses. It is worth suggesting that the difference here has to do with who the recipient of the vision is: Daniel is in intimate fellowship with the God who reveals these truths; the pagan king is not, and can not call on angel interpreters for assistance. There is no suggestion, however, that the kings had B-grade or distorted visions rather than true ones.

[110] See Goldingay, *Daniel*, 173.

7 ten horns are followed by a little horn, which seems to supplant three of them. In ch. 8 the little horn clearly grows from one of the four previous ones, like the offshoot from an earlier tree, and so not unlike the relationship between Antiochus and Alexander. The later interpretation of ch. 7 in *Sib. Or.* 3:388–400 also makes the mistake of amalgamating chs. 7 and 8 and reading the earlier chapter in light of the later one.[111]

The phrase "holy ones of the Most High" occurs only in 7:18, 22, 25, and 28. There is a near equivalent from the later Qumran material (CD 20:8), but it is likely to be indebted to our material. Most often in the OT "holy ones," as a term by itself, denotes heavenly beings (Ps 89:5–7; Job 5:1; 15:15; Hos 12:1; Zech 14:5), and we find the same usage outside the canon (Sir 42:17; Wis 10:10; *Jub.* 17:11; 1 QapGen 2:1). Yet usage of the phrase as meaning God's people is familiar both early and late (cf., e.g., Ps 34 and 1QM 12:8–9), and Dan 7:27 seems to require a reference to humans both here and at the end of the chapter. Logic suggests this as well, for would the author really be arguing for the bequeathal of a kingdom to angels, and even if so, how would this comfort the audience of Daniel?

No one, in any case, would be arguing about this matter if the author of ch. 7 had been more specific about the identity of the holy ones, but as is the case with the Son of man, so with the holy ones. The vision and its interpretation in ch. 7 are general in character, not specific, leaving a fertile field for guessing commentators who refuse to take seriously the intended lack of specificity here or its intended multivalency. After struggling to wring specificity out of this vision, one then reads conclusions like that of Goldingay: "But the vision leaves unclear whether the holy ones who are destined to rule are Israel's celestial protagonists, or their protagonists mingling among Israel, or Israelites who are dead but glorified, or living Israelites viewed as having supernatural significance now. Perhaps the visionary did not know"![112] The most we can really say is that God's kingdom will triumph and this will affect God's people in a positive way, and it appears the agent of that triumph is their God's representative—the one like a Son of man.

In vv. 19–22 there is a reiteration, with some addition of detail, about what has already been said about the beasts, the ten horns, and the little horn. At v. 21 we learn that the little horn waged war on the holy ones and was prevailing until the Ancient of Days came and gave judgment for the holy ones, who then gained the kingdom. Verses 23–27 returns to poetry with alliteration, and the piling up of synonyms for emphasis.[113] The little horn is also said to speak words against the Most High in v. 25 and attempt to change the sacred seasons and law, and God's people will be delivered into his hands for a specified amount of time,

---

[111] It is interesting that in 2 Esd 12:10–12 God explains to Ezra that Rome is the fourth kingdom but that Daniel was not given this interpretation in his own day. Certainly, no such specificity of any kind is forthcoming to Daniel in ch. 7.

[112] Goldingay, *Daniel*, 178.

[113] See Baldwin, *Daniel*, 147.

after which the court shall sit in judgment and he will be stripped of his dominion, and dominion of a different order will be given to God's people. It is interesting that v. 27 adds that there will still be other kingdoms in the world but that
they shall serve and obey the everlasting dominion. It is the same old tale of woe
followed by weal, trial followed by triumph, judgment on God's people at the
hands of foreign rulers who worship other gods and try to change God's captive
people and their religious allegiances, followed by redemption and restoration finally into an everlasting godly dominion. This same basic story line, of course, is
found in earlier prophetic material in Amos, Jeremiah, Micah, Second Isaiah,
Ezekiel, and Zechariah. What is different here is that the triumph of the people
(v. 27) is seen to happen through the intervention of God in the person of an in-
vested agent—who is here alone called "one like a son of man," the one like a
human being (v. 14). The story ends with Daniel ghostly pale, very much afraid,
but like the good prophetic sage, he was keeping and pondering the meaning of
all this in his mind. There are signs that an ongoing pondering of this material
and an attempt to apply it began as early as the Hebrew material found in chs.
8–12, and then perhaps shortly after that in *1 Enoch* and the *Sibylline Oracles*, at
Qumran, in the NT, by early Jewish commentators, and by others as well. The vision in ch. 7 captured the imagination of many, for they saw in it hope for the
future of God's people in a world of beastly empires that oppressed them. Such a
general and universal hope struck a chord in many generations, beginning
at least as early as the Maccabees. Thus, our study must turn to the intertestamental age, in which we find full-blown apocalyptic books. But first a few
conclusions to this chapter must be offered.

III. CONCLUSIONS

The visionary and metaphorical vein of apocalyptic was mined even further in the postexilic age but not to the exclusion of more traditional oracular
prophecy. When a dream is deferred, one looks to the further horizon for help.
The social climate from 525 BC or so until the time of the Maccabees was such
that it could quite readily produce apocalyptic visions and literature. The signal
fact that in the postexilic situation most of the literature speaks of the past or of
the less immediate future is a telltale sign that the present is not what the
prophet would have hoped. In the case of Zechariah, there were some prophetic
utterances that spoke to his own situation and talked of hope for that situation,
but it is not an accident that most of his visions speak of a more distant, different solution to the dilemmas of God's people.

It is interesting to compare and contrast the sort of visionary material we
find in the first half of Zechariah and in Daniel. The former has night visions,
while the latter has dreams or, better said, visionary material received within a
dream. The former focuses on the people of God and their religious issues, the
latter on beastly world empires and the final solution of a kingdom ruled by a
humane human one. The former focuses on what is happening in the promised

land, the latter on what is happening in exile at least until the final solution will come. Yet both see a singular human figure endowed by God as the focus of that final solution. Zechariah suggests he will be unlike previous rulers in that he will come in and bring peace, and Daniel suggests he will be different because he will not partake of the beastly character of other empires and emperors. Yet both Zechariah and Daniel require interpretive help, whether it be from an interpreting angel or from another higher source, to understand such offbeat and highly metaphorical visions or dreams. When the times are out of joint, even the visionaries need help to see.

In terms of the social roles of the two prophets Zechariah and Daniel, they are depicted differently. Zechariah is a prophet with priestly connections, while Daniel appears more as a court sage and diviner of dreams. Yet both could be designated central prophets of a sort. The differences between them may, in part, be explained by the different foci of their ministries—the hierarchy of postexilic Israel or a foreign court.

The theme of God's sovereignty unites the prophecies of these two figures. Both wish to stress, as does much of apocalyptic literature, that God is still in control even though things appear bleak. In the case of neither Zechariah nor Daniel is there an abandonment of history. For Daniel the kingdom will indeed finally come on earth through the agency of the Son of Man, while for Zechariah the vision is even more focused on the Holy City, the holy temple, and therefore on God's holy, Davidic anointed one. Yet like the Son of Man figure, Zechariah's king is a humble or poor man, clearly a vulnerable figure.

This chapter has suggested a different way of reading Dan 1–7 that does not neglect its apocalyptic dimensions but recognizes and stresses that it is a hybrid form of material—one part prophecy, one part sapiential tales, one part apocalyptic. If ch. 7 is allowed to be seen as the end of the original and earliest portion of the Danielic corpus, then one must reckon with the material not involving ex eventu prophecy, even in ch. 7. It is the final form of the book of Daniel, with the added material in Hebrew, that becomes the precedent and paradigm for apocalyptic literature, not the Aramaic material by itself, which is found in the first half of the book. Yet this study must now turn to the apocalyptic works that did take the canonical form of Daniel as something of a precedent and impetus for, among other things, the creation of ex eventu prophecy, the first of which we find already in chs. 8–12.

CHAPTER 7

Apocalypse—Then

LTHOUGH IT CAN NOT BE SAID THAT PROPHECY died during the time between the Testaments, it certainly took some new forms, and the most interesting of these is the apocalypse. Traditional oracular prophecy using a messenger formula seems to have been almost unrepresented during this period;[1] we can only speak of the proliferation of visions and dreams, and in particular apocalyptic ones. As D. Petersen suggests, this is in part to be explained by the close connection between the monarchy and prophecy in Israel, as in other ancient Near Eastern situations.[2] When the social situation changed drastically, forms of discourse changed as well.[3] The prophet in exile could no longer function as counselor to the king, and there seems also to have been a strong backlash against traditional prophets who had spoken false words of hope. The sentiment in this age was, it is better to have no prophet rather than a false one (cf. Zech 13:2–6; Jer 23:34–40).[4]

---

[1] As Richard Bauckham has pointed out to me in conversation, there are no prophets, writing in their own name in the Second Temple period, who produce documents like the classical writing prophets, and indeed no written sources of this kind assembled by such prophets' disciples. Clearly something significant is different about this era in regard to things prophetic.

[2] Petersen, *Late Israelite Prophecy*, 1–3. Following F. M. Cross he stresses that the rise of apocalyptic should be connected with the fall of the southern monarchy.

[3] See E. Hammershaimb, *Some Aspects of Old Testament Prophecy from Isaiah to Malachi* (Copenhagen: Rosenkilde og Bagger, 1966), 109—change in society causes change in prophetic form.

[4] See Petersen, *Late Israelite Prophecy*, 34–37. Note in Zechariah the *mode* of prophecy is only visions.

We must also speak of the literary exercise of creating apocalyptic literature using the devices of pseudonymity and ex eventu prophecy, although not all of it included these traits. But even apocalyptic literature sometimes contained both ex eventu prophecy and predictions about what lay in the future from the time of the author. Thus, although the question has been broached in previous chapters, this study must finally ask and answer more fully this question: what is an apocalypse, and what counts as apocalyptic literature?

I. APOCALYPSE, APOCALYPTIC VISIONS, APOCALYPTIC MIND-SET

Apocalyptic visions existed within prophetic texts before the Hellenistic era, as has already been seen in Ezekiel, Zechariah, and Dan 1–7. We may wish to call this protoapocalyptic material, but it clearly does not manifest enough of the usual traits of an apocalypse to allow us to label these books in this way. It seems clear that such visionary material first appears on the Hebrew scene during the Babylonian exile, and already at the outset it manifests some influences from that environment.[5] In particular, there seems to be a use of creation and combat myths, periodization of history, and mythical monsters from the Babylonian and Persian sources. Hebrew apocalyptic material was to prove to be highly synthetic in character, acting like a vortex, sucking in materials from all directions (including Greco-Roman sources from the Hellenistic age onward) and transforming them into images and stories and ideas that were compatible with the Jewish faith.

Clearly, there were social factors involved in these developments within the prophetic tradition. The exile and the calamities that followed it up into the second century AD are the factors that most contributed to the formation of both counterorder Wisdom literature and apocalyptic literature, and these two streams of tradition continually cross-fertilized, for both sorts of literature deal with theodicy and justice issues. As a result of this concern, apocalyptic literature also focuses on the final resolution of such issues either in the otherworld or at the *eschaton* or both.

Apocalyptic literature, then, was not just a matter of experiencing a foreign stimulus and drawing on outside sources and ideas, because if we must speak of the main or primary sources of Hebrew apocalyptic material, it is found in Hebrew prophetic and sapiential material. By the time we arrive at a full-blown apocalypse and can begin to ask genre questions, there has already been a considerable confluence of materials and concepts drawn from these various sources. A perfect example of this is the earliest apocalypse—the final form of the book of Daniel.

---

[5] See R. J. Clifford, "The Roots of Apocalypticism in Near Eastern Myth," and A. Hultgard, "Persian Apocalypticism," in *The Encyclopedia of Apocalypticism* (ed. J. J. Collins; 3 vols.; New York: Continuum, 1998), 1:3–38 and 39–83, respectively.

Without much doubt, the material in Dan 1–6, or even 1–7, would never have been labeled an apocalypse by itself. It would have been seen as a series of sapiential court tales about a prophetic sage named Daniel, who both interpreted visions and had the occasional apocalyptic vision. To judge from the tradition history (e.g., the addition of the Bel and the Serpent story), this book was a work in progress for a long time. When the apocalyptic material in chs. 8–12 was added to the earlier material, without interspersing it with more sapiential tales, a new hybrid genre was being born that would contain at its heart apocalyptic visions (whether of the genuine or ex eventu variety or both). One can not stress too strongly that it is not possible to say either that Hebrew wisdom or prophecy or external influences alone were the parent of this literature. The narrative section generally owes more to the wisdom material, and the apocalyptic visions generally owe more to prophetic and mythological sources.[6] We must be content with calling an apocalypse a beast with the head of a lion, the body of an eagle, and the feet of a human—a mixed breed.

But we can say in addition that apocalyptic literature arose at a time when the sort of wisdom material that was being written and was most popular was counterorder wisdom of the Job and Ecclesiastes variety, not the older and more traditional proverbial and aphoristic material. Apocalyptic material, such as we find in Job, was often to include narrative dialogues between a sage/righteous man and the divine about issues of theodicy, theocracy, and theology. This was true not merely at the beginning of the period when apocalypses were written but well into the Roman era.

Even in a work as late as *4 Ezra*, usually dated after AD 70, there are dialogues between a Jewish seer and God about the justification for all the calamities that had happened to God's people. Furthermore, Christian works, or works redacted by Christians, as well as Jewish ones manifest this pattern as well. The *Apocalypse of Abraham* and the *Ascension of Isaiah* have this pattern. Note also that *1 En.* 1–36 (Book of Watchers) combines stories about the Watchers with Enoch's revelations—a mixture of narrative and apocalyptic passages. One is thus left with the odd fact that the final form of Daniel, itself of mixed genre, became the genre model for a type of apocalypse consisting of (1) stories about the seer and (2) revelations given to the seer.

How, then, is one to define "apocalypse"? This study simply follows the Society of Biblical Literature Seminar's definition, hammered out by many scholars over a long period of reflection on the whole corpus of material. An apocalypse as a literary form is "a genre of revelatory literature with a narrative framework, in which a revelation is mediated by an otherworldly being to a human recipient, disclosing a transcendent reality which is both temporal, insofar as it envisages eschatological salvation, and spatial insofar as it involves another, supernatural world"[7] This sort of literature, more often than not, intends

---

[6] On this literature and its enormous influence on the early Christian movement, see Witherington, *Jesus the Sage.*

[7] J. J. Collins, ed., *Apocalypse: The Morphology of a Genre, Semeia* 14 (1979): 9.

to interpret present mundane reality in light of both the supernatural world and the future.[8] Thus, even a book such as Revelation begins clearly with the situation of the churches of John's own day and tries to help them exegete and endure their own experiences without losing faith or heart, by broadening their perspective both upward and forward. It is also the case that this is minority literature written for persons enduring at least some intellectual, if not also social and physical, crisis at the time.

It is a mistake, however, to think that certain eschatological ideas are, in themselves, necessarily the heart of what apocalyptic is all about. The eschatological ideas we find in apocalypses are also found all through early Jewish and Christian literature, much of which is not in the form of an apocalypse. Apocalyptic is primarily a matter of the use of a distinctive form—visions with bizarre and hyperbolic metaphors and images. Some apocalypses focus almost exclusively on otherworldly journeys without saying anything about the end of human history. Historical apocalypses are not the pattern for, or representative of, the whole genre. What is at the heart of apocalyptic is the unveiling or revealing of secrets and truths about God's perspective on a variety of matters, particularly justice and theodicy matters raised by God's people. We must keep steadily in view the fact that apocalyptic forms of prophecy, rather than traditional forms, are what dominate the era from the second century BC to the second century AD, and this is the era when we see the rise not only of the Pharisaic movement and the Jesus movement but also of other sectarian offshoots of Judaism, such as the Qumran movement and the John the Baptist movement.

What all these movements shared is a strong belief that they lived in the age of the fulfillment of earlier prophecies, and thus in an age when it was appropriate to look for some final answers not only about the future but about the afterlife or otherworld. It is my view that perhaps the major cause of the shift from traditional prophecy to apocalyptic is this conviction about living in the age of fulfillment. Apocalyptic is far more about fulfillment than it is about prediction, and even when it deals with predictions of the end, it dares to do so because it is convinced that the final things have *already* been set in motion.

Apocalyptic is written with an eschatological and/or otherworldly mind-set, but it brings that mind-set to bear on a host of issues and topics, only some of which are eschatological. In fact, when one gets beyond AD 70, the historical apocalypses start to disappear from Jewish literature, and in the second century AD the same can be said for Christian literature. In the latter case, the focus turns to more strictly otherworldly matters and journeys, culminating in the final great work of early Christian apocalyptic—Dante's *Divine Comedy*. In light of the above, it is appropriate to examine some samples of early apocalyptic material that will take us up to the NT era—specifically Dan 8–12 and the final form of that book, some of the material found in *1 Enoch,* and some of the third book of *Sibylline Oracles*. Some of the relevant material from Qumran, and then material about John the Baptist, must also be scrutinized.

---

[8] Collins, *Encyclopedia*, xiii.

II. THE WORLD ACCORDING TO DANIEL

In the previous chapter, some preliminary remarks were made about Dan 8 and 11,[9] but here the focus must be on some of the features in this material that were to help set the pattern for later apocalyptic works. What we find in this material is not just the general periodization of history into epochs associated with particular empires and rulers but the much more specific practice of setting time limits or dates, and this is coupled with a greater specificity about the individuals or things the apocalyptic images refer to. In addition, even the interpreting angel and other angels suddenly are given names. We can only wonder if, in an age of anxiety about the future for Abraham's descendants, this specificity reflects the earnest desire for greater certainty about such matters. These sorts of practices were not characteristic of earlier Hebrew prophecy when it spoke about the more distant future. The material we find, for example, in Second Isaiah is clearly idealized and general and avoids the very sort of specificity mentioned above.

Consider, for example, the dialogue in Dan 10 between Daniel and the angel Gabriel. Here it is explained that Daniel is in conflict with the "prince of Persia" but that soon "the prince of Greece" will come, yet Daniel should not despair, for he will be aided by the angelic patron saint of the nation Israel—"Michael your prince." As J. J. Collins points out here, we see that conflicts "on earth are understood as reflections of struggles between their patron angels"[10] or, perhaps better said, are seen as the cosmic dimension of the same struggle Daniel and his people are having. In addition, our author is bold enough to clearly extend the struggle he is now observing not only into the next age but into the final future. Although the named empires may be succeeded by one more unnamed empire, nevertheless the end will happen after that. Michael will finally prevail (12:1), and resurrection and judgment will follow. Notice also the far greater specificity about the shape of the end and the afterlife than was found even in Dan 7. Chapters 8–12 are an extension, an amplification, a clarification of what is found in ch. 7, and this is the characteristic of pseudonymous apocalyptic works: the recycling of earlier prophetic material (oracles and visions and images and ideas) not primarily in order to validate further predictions the author wants to make but primarily to say, "This is that; we are in the age of fulfillment."

In ch. 9 we find a reuse of Jeremiah's prophecy that Jerusalem will be laid waste for seventy years (Jer 25:11–12). Of course, the prophecy of Jeremiah was for his own age and people, who were staring down the barrel of the gun, as it were, of exile. How, then, would the author reuse this material? The angel Gabriel appears to explain that, in fact, the seventy years were really seventy weeks of years (490 years). As Collins rightly stresses, ch. 9 "shows the importance of Biblical prophecy in apocalyptic thought."[11]

---

[9] See pp. 196–200 above.

[10] Collins, *Encyclopedia,* 143–44.

[11] Ibid., 144.

If we step back to ch. 8 for a moment, several more insights come to light. First, the vision according to 8:1 is subsequent to the one Daniel received in ch. 7. Second, it gives us a clear social setting in Susa, where Daniel sees a ram with two horns, presumably the kingdoms of Media and Persia. But then from the west the he-goat comes across the entire earth with great rapidity. The ram could not withstand the charge of the he-goat, but thereafter, at the height of the power of the he-goat, his horn was broken, and in its place came up four horns toward the four winds. From out of them came a little horn that grew great toward the south, the east, and the promised land. It is very difficult not to hear this as a description of the events involving Alexander the Great and then Antiochus Epiphanes. Antiochus is depicted as a sacrilegious person who acts arrogantly even toward God and the patron angel of Israel, taking away the burnt offering and overthrowing the sanctuary place. The fault, however, chiefly lay with Israel itself—these things happened because of its wickedness. These actions are called the abomination that makes desolate (v. 13). Then in v. 14 there is an apparently clear time reference as to how long this abomination will last—2,300 days and nights—and then the temple will be restored. Daniel is informed in no uncertain terms that this vision is about the time of the end (v. 17). Undoubtedly, this is how Hebrews living through the nightmare of Antiochus Epiphanes felt.

In the interpretation offered by the angel, various specifics are made clear. The ram with two horns was indeed the Median and Persian empire (v. 20). The he-goat was the king of Greece (v. 21). The four little horns represent four kingdoms that resulted from the breakup of Alexander's empire, but what was of especial concern to Israel was the Seleucids and the Ptolemies. It is said about these four kingdoms that they will not have the power of the king of Greece, and indeed this was what happened. A fuller poetic description of the misdeeds and treachery of Antiochus is given in vv. 23–25 with the reassurance that eventually he will be broken, but not by human hands. At the end of this interpretation of the vision, two things are added that were not said at the end of Dan 7—a command to seal up the vision, for it refers to "many days from now" (v. 26), and then the admission by Daniel that, even after the interpretation of the angel, he did not understand it (v. 27).

Here for the very first time we have material that has the specificity that only prophecy about the near horizon had in earlier Jewish prophecy, yet it presents itself as about a more remote time. To punctuate this literary device, there is the command to seal it up, as if to admit that prophecy this specific could not be meaningfully given to a general public that far in advance nor could the seer himself understand it! Here surely is a different situation from that which produced the vision in ch, 7. Here the author indeed uses a literary device in order to make comments about the Hellenistic age in which he lives. His point is not to claim to offer prophecy about a distant horizon but to reveal fulfillment of what God long had in mind for God's people in the author's age. His audience is being reassured that God is still in control even though the times seem out of joint.

In short, ch. 8 is a redaction of ch. 7 with the benefit of a large amount of hindsight, and perhaps a bit of foresight as well. It appears that the author of this material somewhat tips his hand in ch. 9, for he says that shame "as at this day, falls on *us*, the people of Judah, the inhabitants of Jerusalem, and all Israel, those who are near and those who are far away in all the lands to which you have driven *them*" (v. 7; my italics). He is not in Daniel's situation but, rather, writes from a Jerusalem-centric perspective, thinking about those out in the exile as faraway and as "them." He has seen the calamities wrought by Antiochus up close and is doing theodicy. He is explaining why such bad things have happened to God's people—namely, because of their sins and unfaithfulness. In short, this is theology dressed in the garb of visions and their interpretation. What is most urgent is to reread and apply prophecies such as those of Jeremiah and those earlier attributed to Daniel and to make some sense out of Israel's current situation. The prayer in ch. 9 is an earnest and timely one for such Jews in the Hellenistic age—"let your face shine upon your desolated sanctuary. Open your eyes and look at our desolation and the city that bears your name. We do not present our supplication on the basis of our righteousness but on the ground of your great mercies." It is "our desolation" in Jerusalem that the author is feeling.

The scenario is repeated with some variations and additions in ch. 11, where once more we hear about the Hellenistic age and the struggles between Seleucids and Ptolemies and where once again the desecration of the Jerusalem temple is recounted in the same terms (v. 31). And now we hear even more clearly that this king shall exalt himself and consider himself greater than any god (v. 36). But he will only prosper until the specific "time of wrath" against Israel is over (v. 36). God is still in control.

It is noteworthy that nothing is said in chs. 8–11 about the Son of man figure. The author is too fixated on his own day and its disasters to look much beyond it. He is able to conceive of deliverance only by direct divine intervention, in this case by the angel Michael (12:1). When that happens, the resurrection of many who sleep in the dust will happen—a resurrection of the righteous and the wicked (12:2) The most urgent concern, however, seems to be how long it will be after the abomination of desolation that the proper sacrifices will be restored so that Hebrews may once more properly honor God.

Three numerical statements are made—it will be a time, two times, and a half time before the power is restored to Israel to control its cultus (v. 7); it will be 1,290 days (v. 11), but the blessing will not really happen for God's people unless they endure for 1,335 days. The fact that these numbers differ suggests strongly that their function is not to pinpoint an exact time but to indicate that Israel's God, being sovereign, has it under control and that oppression will indeed come to an end "in due time," with the enemies of God's people getting their just due. The fixation in all this material on when and why does not characterize chs. 1–7, but then one is dealing with a literary phenomenon that has a different function than traditional prophecy, whether in oracular or visionary form.

The material in both the Aramaic and the Hebrew portions of Daniel was destined to have an enormous impact both on more traditional apocalyptic prophecy, such as one finds in Revelation, and on apocalyptic of the pseudonymous–ex eventu variety. The important point to stress, as this discussion is brought to a close, is that apocalyptic was a diverse hybrid phenomenon that could incorporate both real and literary prophecy or one or the other.

III. TAKEN UP WITH ENOCH

Clearly enough, when one is dealing with the age in which Daniel took its final form and at least some of the Enochic material arose, apocalyptic was still in very much of an experimental stage. The paint was still wet. For example, only in the Book of the Watchers in *1 Enoch* is there an otherworldly journey of a very distinctive ilk.[12] Furthermore, the portrayal of Enoch is just as much a hybrid as the book itself—he is seer, sage, scribe, mediator, and then world judge. The historical apocalypses were to take their cues primarily from Daniel, while the apocalypses that focus on otherworldly journeys and tours seem to owe more to some of the Enochic material. Yet all of this literature shares in common the function of seeking to inform, encourage, and exhort God's people in troubled times, using apocalyptic images, metaphors, and forms of discourse.[13]

Scholars are in agreement that the book known as *1 Enoch,* a book about the length of Isaiah, is in fact a composite of several works and that it has an extended tradition history, with the earliest portions of the work likely written as early as the third century BC and the latest portions of it (possibly the Similitudes) dating to the first century AD. It would be incorrect, then, to simply call *1 Enoch* an apocalypse. Rather, it contains apocalyptic material and visions, and there are portions that approximate a whole apocalypse, at least in short form. The literary conceit that binds the entire work together is that Enoch, having been taken up into heaven by God, is taking a tour of the otherworld, and indeed of the universe, and being informed about various things, including earthly things, from the divine perspective.

What is generally considered to be the earliest portion of this work is the so-called Astronomical Book of Enoch (chs. 72–82), which informs Enoch about various astronomical and geographical matters. Enoch is being conducted on this heavenly tour by an angel named Uriel. "Fundamental to the treatise is a solar calendar of 364 days, i.e., four seasons of ninety days each, plus one day

---

[12] See ibid., 146.

[13] It would be a mistake to assume that apocalyptic literature was all that arose as a result of the influence of Daniel in this era. There is in the Greek version of Daniel a ch. 14, which returns to the sort of sapiential court tales demonstrating Daniel's divine wisdom and favor that are found in the Aramaic portion of Daniel. Both sapiential and apocalyptic traditions were inspired and influenced by Daniel.

added to each season."[14] Enoch is also being informed about the various ranks, authorities, and positions of the heavenly bodies. Uriel is also said to be the one who informed Enoch about the "years of the world unto eternity, until the new creation which abides forever is created" (72:1). Enoch is informed about the rising and setting of the sun and moon, how they move, the twelve winds and their gates, the four compass points, the seven high mountains and great rivers, and in general the astronomical laws.

The purpose of all this is not that Enoch may have arcane knowledge but that he may understand the effect of the heavenly bodies on earthly matters, including human matters. The author is, on the one hand, concerned to preserve monotheism and so deny the stars are gods but, on the other hand, admits the influence of the stars on earth and its inhabitants. For example, 80:6 says,

> Many of the chiefs of the stars shall make errors in respect to the orders given to them; they shall change their courses and functions and not appear during the seasons which have been prescribed to them. All the order of the stars shall harden (in disposition) against the sinners and the conscience of those that dwell upon the earth. They (the stars) shall err against them (the sinners) and modify their courses. Then the sinners will err and take them (the stars) to be gods.

Enoch is sent back to earth to convey this knowledge to his son Methuselah so that his descendants will be wise and live righteous lives in accord not with the influence of the stars but with the law of God. This apocalypse is clearly of the otherworldly-journey sort, and it shares with apocalyptic literature in general the interpreting angel, the revelation of arcane secrets, and the hortatory purpose of exhorting God's people to live righteous lives because there is indeed a God of judgment and justice and there are indeed potential evil influences, even of a cosmic sort, out there.

It is possible that the so-called Book of the Watchers (chs. 1–36) comes from the same early date as the Astronomical Book, namely, the third century BC, but some scholars would date this somewhat later. In any event, this book contains apocalyptic material and traits (cf. chs. 1, 10–11, 14–15, 17–36) but is not, as a whole, in the form of apocalyptic visions, for it also involves sapiential material—for example, in 1:9–5:4, where nature's obedience and human disobedience to God's order are contrasted. Notice, too, how, at the very beginning of the book, the theophanic description reflects deep indebtedness to earlier scriptural material (e.g., Deut 33 in 1:3–4; the oracle formula from Balaam's oracles in 1:2–3b; cf. Num 24:15–17).[15] Thus, right from the beginning of this work, its hybrid nature is clear. What Enoch is said to be dealing with are *meshalim* (parables, proverbs, aphorisms, riddles—in general, parabolic and metaphorical speech), which are the provenance of sages, and visions, which are the provenance of seers. Enoch will be cast as a prophetic sage or a sapiential seer just as

---

[14] G. W. E. Nickelsburg, "Enoch, First Book of," *ABD* 2:509.
[15] Ibid.

Daniel was, but Enoch will have far more than just night visions. He will get the grand tour of the other world.

Enoch was an antedeluvian figure (Gen 5), and it is interesting to see how the judgment on the earth in the flood and the restoration thereafter are seen as patterns of the final judgment and the new creation thereafter. It is also interesting how this retelling of the tale found in Gen 6:1–4 casts the angelic "sons of god" and their actions, which produced the giants, as the real causes of God's judgment upon the earth. This book clearly was written during a time of considerable speculation about angels and cosmic evil and their influence on the mundane realm. But it is not just that the fallen angels mated with human beings. They also taught them the black arts, magic, cosmology, as well as the secrets of metallurgy and mining so that they could, in the latter cases, make the tools of war and, in the former cases, learn the arts of seduction. This book "as a whole criticizes aspects of contemporary civilization, construing them as the result of heavenly rebellion that can be reversed and overcome only by divine judgment and reparation. The pervading sense of humanity's victimization by demonic forces and the necessity for direct divine intervention will continue to be a constitutive part of much of later apocalypticism."[16]

The author of the Book of the Watchers was not content to portray Enoch as a seer or sage; he was also to be portrayed as an Ezekiel-like prophet of judgment. Thus in chs. 12–16 we have the description of Enoch's ascension to the dazzling throne room of God, where he receives a sort of prophetic commissioning. From the throne room, Enoch will travel to the west (chs. 17–19) and to the east (chs. 20–36). At the western edge of the world, he sees the places of imprisonment of the rebel angels and some errant stars. But he will also come upon the mountain that contains the spirits of the dead awaiting their heavenly rewards or punishments (ch. 22), as well as the Eden-like mountain where God dwells and where the tree of life "is kept until it will be transplanted to the temple mount in the new Jerusalem, where it will nourish the righteous in the new age. [But] Enoch's vision of Jerusalem focuses on the cursed valley of Hinnom, where the wicked will be punished eternally in the presence of the righteous."[17] Nevertheless, the book closes on a positive note as Enoch tours the eastern spice orchards that lead to the new Eden, where the righteous dwell, and there at the center of this location is the tree of wisdom (32.3–6). The ending of this book shows that its aim is not speculation about the otherworld but reassurance about the afterlife here on earth in the promised land. In other words, the book uses otherworldly journeys to offer up eschatological hope.[18] Our author does not see the otherworld as a final

---

[16] Ibid., 2:510.

[17] Ibid.

[18] This hope has some odd features, such as the tree of wisdom, which is surely the tree of the knowledge of good and evil. This tree is now seen as a good thing for the righteous to partake of. This transformation reflects the sapiential perspective of the author, who sees knowledge, including moral knowledge, as a desirable and good thing.

destination for the righteous, and indeed the deceased even now are in the land of the dead under the earth.

The next major section of the book for consideration contains the two apocalyptic visions found in chs. 83–90. These visions, which are cast as prophecy from the days of Enoch, are really a review of the history of humanity and, in particular, God's people, beginning with Gen 6:1–4 and continuing on to the Hellenistic era and beyond to the final restoration of God's people. The historical review provides a structure for determining the plausibility of the prophecy about the end or messianic age, which is recounted at 90:20–42. This segment contains once again the Enochic conviction that the mating of the angels with human beings was the real beginning of the downfall of the human race or at least the cause of God's acts of universal judgment upon it, beginning with the flood. The visions here take on something of a bizarre allegorical character, with stars (read angels) mating with cows (read humans). The imagery, then, is not simply an adaptation of Persian or Babylonian mythology but draws on prophetic images of God's people as cows or as sheep. The name Animal Apocalypse is apt for the second of these two visions, which begins in ch. 85 and continues through ch. 90.

The first vision, however, which is recorded in ch. 83, is somewhat different and serves as a precursor to the longer second vision. It is clearly labeled as a dream vision (83:3), with Enoch seeing the destruction of the world. Enoch's grandfather interprets the dream for him to refer to "all the sins of the whole world as it was sinking into the abyss and being destroyed with great destruction. Now then rise my son and pray to the Lord of glory, for you are a man of faith so that a remnant shall remain upon the earth and that the whole earth shall not be blotted out. My son all of the things upon earth will take place from heaven; and there will occur a great destruction upon the earth" (83:8–9).

Once again the theme of God's orchestration of human history and destiny is stressed, and Enoch himself expresses the fear that God's judgment will wipe the entire slate clean, leaving not even a remnant of Jews. The visions offered here also express the conviction, found elsewhere in *1 Enoch*, that God places the fallen angels in a holding tank or prison of sorts, a dark abyss in the pit of the earth, where they await final judgment (ch. 88). Final judgment and restoration beyond it are seen as the final sorting out of the human dilemma, and therefore the events before them do not provide a final solution. If this material was written during or after the Maccabean period, it was not written by a Zealot, for it offers a very sobering assessment of Israel's political potential to control its own fate and be a righteous nation. It is possible that the reference to the leading white bull toward the end of the second vision is a reference to a messianic figure,[19] but, if so, he does not provide the final solution; rather, God alone does.

---

[19] See J. C. VanderKam, "Messianism and Apocalypticism," in *Encyclopedia* (ed. Collins), 193–228, here 199–200.

A further, short historical apocalypse is found in 93:1–10 and 91:11–17.[20] This material is sometimes labeled the Apocalypse of Weeks. It contains a variety of intriguing features beyond the usual ones of Enoch speaking to his child or children. Here the course of history and its conclusion are divided into ten segments, called weeks. By week 8 one has reached the time of judgment, in which the righteous finally receive a sword to punish sinners.[21] By week 9 the entire world has been alerted that judgment is transpiring, and finally in week 10 there is eternal judgment on the fallen angels who were responsible for setting the calamities in motion in the first place. All of this is followed by the creation of a new heaven.

Once again a historical review, cast as prophecy from the time of Enoch, provides the necessary background and authority structure to allow the author to say something definitive about the future and how it will all end. Notice, too, that when the new creation arises, there will be uncounted numbers of weeks in which the world lives sin-free. Much of this is familiar material reused from chs. 6–11, but there is also a great deal of quarrying of images, ideas, and events from the extant prophetic corpus. Thus the shepherd's failure to do his duty reflects knowledge of Zech 11, and the appearance of the messianic figure may owe something to Ezek 34. The seventy shepherds and their four periods of rule echo Jer 25:11–12 and 29:10 and provide us with a chronological marker for Daniel's final form, for it reflects the four kingdoms of Dan 7 as well.[22] This sort of quarrying and reuse of prophecy characterize most of apocalyptic literature, precisely because the author believed he lived in the time when a good deal of what had been predicted had already or was coming to pass.

It is time to turn to perhaps the most controverted part of the Enochic literature—the Similitudes found in chs. 37–71. The date of this material has been variously evaluated, with most scholars thinking it is, at the very least, from before AD 70, and perhaps most likely from the first century BC. This conclusion is, in part, based on the fact that no fragments of this part of *1 Enoch* have been found at Qumran. The silence there is assumed to be telling.[23] But it appears rather certain that the ideas found in these chapters were already circulating in early Judaism before the time of Jesus.[24] The work shares the common apocalyptic theme that God will vindicate God's elect and righteous ones and punish

---

[20] The Aramaic fragments from Qumran have this order, which is to be preferred over the later arrangement in the Ethiopic version.

[21] There is an interesting juxtaposition of a militant ideology and, at the same time, a realization that such an approach will not solve anything before the time of the final judgment!

[22] See Nickelsburg, "Enoch, First Book of," 511.

[23] The only specific reference that would help to date this document is the mention of the "Parthians and Medes" at 56:5, which might refer to the invasion in 40 BC, before the reign of Herod the Great, but even this is uncertain.

[24] See further the discussion in Witherington, *The Christology of Jesus*, 234–35.

their oppressors—the kings and the mighty. But there is also something new and different about the Son of man figure of Dan 7, as we shall soon see.

The Similitudes are divided into three major sections called "parables" (chs. 38–44, 45–57, 58–69). Reference to the use of this term at 1:2–3 and 93:1, 3 has already been made, and there, as here, it means metaphorical speech in the form of revelatory visions and/or discourses. Notice that the author of this material entitles the work a "vision of Wisdom" (37:1). As before, we are dealing with a hybrid kind of material that is one part prophecy, one part sapiential material (of the revelatory and counterorder sort), one part apocalyptic. Just how counterorder this Wisdom really is comes to light in ch. 42, where there is a sort of parody of Sir 24 and perhaps Bar 3:9–4:4. The latter sources claim that Wisdom came and dwelled with/in Israel in the form of Torah. To the contrary, Enoch suggests that Wisdom does not now dwell in Israel. Israel's sin and corruption drove Wisdom back to heaven, and she can only be had through revelation—"a pithy and telling summary of the apocalyptic world view (cf. 94:5)."[25]

Once more the reader is taken on a journey with Enoch; this vision seems to have the same literary form as that in chs. 17–32, composed of the following elements—journey, vision, seer's question, and interpretation by an accompanying angel.[26] Once again, Enoch will visit the heavenly throne room (39:2–41:2), the celestial phenomena (41:3–44; 59–60), and the places of punishment (52.1–56:4). There is also the by now familiar material on Noah and the flood (chs. 65–68), seen as a type or foreshadowing of the final judgment of God. Enoch is made aware of a heavenly conflict that stands behind and indeed influences what is happening on earth. As C. Rowland has well said, the author envisions an open heaven, in which heaven and earth and the affairs of each are intertwined and should not be seen as two separate realities hermetically sealed off from one another.[27]

It is interesting how each of the three "parables" begins with a poetic section, suggesting traditional prophecy, followed by narrative about visionary material. It is also telling how deeply indebted this author is to sapiential literature that was written during the Hellenistic period. We have already noted above the allusion to Sirach, but notice also how in 1 En. 62–63 the judgment scene is indebted to the judgment scene in Wis 4–5. In both these works the servant figure is the persecuted righteous man who is exalted. In the parables of Enoch, the person in mind who embodies godly wisdom is, of course, Enoch himself, who in due course will learn that he himself is the son of man. The indebtedness to Wisdom of Solomon is shown in the fact that the persecuted righteous man is taken up and finally judges his persecutors.[28]

---

[25] G. W. E. Nickelsburg, *Jewish Literature between the Bible and the Mishnah* (Philadelphia: Fortress, 1981), 216.

[26] See ibid., 214.

[27] See C. Rowland, *The Open Heaven: A Study of Apocalyptic in Judaism and Early Christianity* (New York: Crossroad, 1982).

[28] See Nickelsburg, *Jewish Literature,* 219–20.

Primary among God's agents in the coming judgment on the world is a being called the Elect One. This particular character in Enoch's narrative seems to combine into one the titles, attributes, and functions of the Davidic messiah, the Servant of Second Isaiah, and the one like the son of man of Dan 7.[29] In this particular work, the phrase "Son of Man" is almost always qualified by the word "that" ("that Son of Man"), presumably not only to distinguish this figure from human beings in general but also to indicate that the Son of Man in mind is one who would be already familiar to the audience. There is debate about this text, as about the Daniel parallel, as to whether a human being is in mind, but at least in the mind of the author of *1 En.* 71, the answer is clear—the reference is not to an angel but to a human being, indeed to Enoch himself. This means that the final editor of this material saw the Son of Man as a human being who had been carried up into—and indeed glorified or beatified in—heaven, so that he gains a face "like one of the angels" (46:1). This Son of Man figure is assigned the judging roles that earlier in the Enochic corpus were predicated of God. In order to understand the scope and depth of what is predicated of the Elect One, it is necessary to consider in more depth some of the second and third parables in this portion of *1 Enoch*.

First Enoch 45:1–6 is a piece of poetry about the judgment day; it includes the assertion "my Elect One will sit on the seat of glory and make a selection of their deeds, their resting places will be without number." Thus, this being is seen as doling out the heavenly rewards. But the final state does not include just a new heaven; it also includes a new earth, and so we are told in vv. 4–5, "I shall transform earth and make it a blessing, and cause my Elect One to dwell in her. Then those who have committed sin and crime shall not set foot in her." There is perhaps an echo of this in Rev 21:27. Further details about this key figure are given in prose in *1 En.* 46. Enoch asks the angelic tour guide about the Elect One, "the One who was born of human beings," "Who is this, and from whence is he who is going as the prototype of the One who precedes time?" Enoch is told,

> This is the Son of Man, to whom belongs righteousness. . . . And he will open all the hidden storerooms, for the Lord of Spirits [the usual designation for God in this work] has chosen him, and he is destined to be victorious. . . . This Son of Man . . . is the One who would remove the kings and the mighty ones from their comfortable seats and the strong ones from their thrones. He shall loosen the reins of the strong and crush the teeth of the sinners.

Chapter 48 further informs the reader that the Son of Man was given a name "even before the creation of the sun and the moon, before the creation of the stars he was given a name in the presence of the Lord of Spirits." This rather strongly suggests the preexistence of this Son of Man figure. Nickelsburg is likely right that "language about the preexistence of that son of man and his name (vv. 3, 6), read in the context of the many references to wisdom in chaps. 48–49,

---

[29] Ibid., 215.

may indicate that this figure is in some sense identified with or related to preexistent Wisdom."[30]

Chapter 48 goes on to say that

> [the Son of Man] will become a staff for the righteous ones in order that they may lean on him and not fall. He is the light of the gentiles and he will become the hope of those who are sick in their hearts. All those who dwell upon the earth shall fall and worship before him; they shall glorify, bless and sing the name of the Lord of the Spirits. For this purpose he became the Chosen One; he was concealed in the presence of (the Lord of the Spirits) prior to the creation of the world, and for eternity. And he has revealed the wisdom of the Lord of the Spirits to the righteous and the holy ones. . . .

The fate of the wicked and lost is said to be determined because "they have denied the Lord of the Spirits and his Messiah" (48:10). The Messiah = the Son of man = the Elect One. About this Elect One, it is stressed at 49:3 that "in him dwells the spirit of wisdom, the spirit which gives thoughtfulness, the spirit of knowledge and strength, and the spirit of those who have fallen asleep in righteousness. He shall judge the secret things." To this is added in 51:3, "from the conscience of his mouth shall come out the secrets of wisdom, for the Lord of the spirits has given them to him and glorified him." The portrait continues to be a conglomerate one throughout this first parable, drawing on the three traditions previously mentioned, but especially stressing the sapiential characteristics and resources of the Son of man, always making clear it is revealed wisdom.

Some of the major themes about judgment are reiterated in the subsequent parables, but so are some of the basic remarks about the Son of Man. For example, his preexistence is remarked on again as well as his role as the world judge when we are told about the consternation of the ruling class when they see the Son of Man on the throne and the beatification of the righteous ones:

> One half portion of them shall glance at the other half; they shall be terrified and dejected; and pain shall seize them when they see the Son of Man sitting on the throne of his glory. (These) kings, governors, and all the landlords shall (try to) bless, glorify, extol him who rules over everything, him who has been concealed. For the Son of Man was concealed from the beginning, and the Most High One preserved him in the presence of his power; then he revealed him to the holy and the elect ones. (62:5–7)

The apocalyptic age will be a time not merely when secrets are revealed but also when saviors, and the identity of the savior, will be revealed as well, and many will be surprised. As for the oppressed righteous ones, "they shall eat and rest and rise with that Son of Man forever" (62:14). This is clearly literature for an oppressed minority. Part of the joy of the righteous ones is that "the name of the Son of Man was revealed to them. He shall never pass away or perish before the face of the earth" (69:27–28). The actual revelation of the identity of the Son of Man comes in ch. 71 in the splendid throne room scene where Enoch is him-

---

[30] Ibid., 217.

self called Son of Man, but not "that Son of Man," by an angel at v. 14, but this is probably because he is being addressed directly. This indeed is the surprise conclusion of Enoch's heavenly tour, and a secret that could only be revealed, not one that could be guessed.

In these parables the central figure is called Son of Man sixteen times, as many as the number of times the term "Chosen One" is used of him. Less frequently the terms "Righteous One" or "Anointed One" (Messiah) appear. It is especially clear that this person is a human being, a conclusion reinforced by the end of the parables, where he is identified with and as Enoch. Yet it can also be said of him that he preexists and furthermore will rule on into the future forever. He also has, then, some divine attributes, attributes not normally predicated of Jewish messianic figures.[31] It is also interesting that it is the later prophetic and apocalyptic material (Second Isaiah, Ezekiel, Daniel) and the sapiential portraits of Prov 8–9 and of Wisdom of Solomon that most shape this portrait, and not the Davidic material from the historical books. These points must be kept steadily in view when this study turns to the Jesus material, which manifests some of these same emphases.

IV. NOAH'S DAUGHTER-IN-LAW—THE SONGS OF THE SIBYL

Though the original sibylline oracles were not Jewish or Christian in character, it seems clear that the third *Sibylline Oracle* is Jewish and can be dated before the turn of the era, perhaps even to the second century BC. It seems clearly to have been composed or collected in Egypt.[32] The *Sibylline Oracles* reveal that oracular prophecy, of the sort one might get either from the classical Hebrew prophets or from Greco-Roman prophets or prophetesses, was seen as still a valid means of revelation, even if these oracles are of a literary kind rather than reflecting actual prophetic ecstatic experience. These oracles include no visions, nor any interpretations or interpreting angels. It is also interesting that these oracles do not mention anything like judgment of the dead or resurrection. One might conjecture that they reflect the sort of piety that characterized hellenized Diaspora Jews rather than the Pharisees. The motive for intimating that these oracles come from the sibyl was that Jewish perspectives might more readily be accepted by a non-Jewish audience as well as serve as a warning to overly hellenized Jews not to engage in idolatry and immorality. Yet there is no getting away from the cross-cultural nature of this material. At one moment in an oracle of historical review, one is hearing about the tower of Babel in a fashion that comports with Genesis (3:97–109), and in the very next breath one learns about the myth of Chronos and the Titans (vv. 110–155).

---

[31] See VanderKam, "Messianism and Apocalypticism," 206–7.
[32] See ibid., 203; J. J. Collins, "From Prophecy to Apocalypticism," in *The Encyclopedia of Apocalypticism,* 129–61, here 149.

The character of the prophecies in this third book of *Sibylline Oracles* can, in general, be said to be like the form and substance of earlier Jewish oracular prophecy, not like apocalyptic. There are prophecies about kings and kingdoms and their rise and fall, not about otherworldly journeys. There are prophecies explaining the factors that cause kingdoms to experience God's judgment, namely, idolatry and immorality. This book appears to share with other sibylline books the schema of ten world kingdoms, the last of which will involve some sort of messianic king, and surprisingly an Egyptian king seems to be meant. In short, there is a considerable interest in eschatology, and the "real" prophecy is when the author steps beyond the historical review and dares to say something about the final earthly future. There is also a considerable stress on the temple in Jerusalem, which has suggested to some that this work came out of Jewish priestly circles in Egypt.

As for the form of the material, there is usually an introductory formula that apparently is meant to be characteristic of the sibyl's experience rather than that of a Hebrew prophetess ("then the utterance of the great God rose in my breast and bade me prophesy," v. 162; "when indeed my spirit ceased the inspired hymn, and I entreated the great Begetter that I might have respite from compulsion, the word of the great God again arose in my breast," vv. 295–298). Notice that the oracles not only are in poetic form but are called hymns (cf. vv. 489–490). There is also in this work a not so subtle polemic against forms of discerning the future that are viewed as false by the Jewish author. In the course of recounting the ancient origins of the Jews in Ur at vv. 218–264, the author characterizes Jews as "a race . . . always concerned with good counsel and noble works for they do not worry about the cyclical course of the sun or the moon . . . nor portents of sneezes, nor birds of augurers, nor seers, nor sorcerers, nor soothsayers, nor the deceits of foolish words of ventriloquists. Neither do they practice the astrological predictions of the Chaldeans nor astronomy. For all these things are erroneous, such as foolish men inquire into day by day."

Notice by contrast what is said about the sibyl's own utterances: "These things will not go unfulfilled. Nor is anything left unaccomplished that he so much as puts in mind for the spirit of God which knows no falsehood is throughout the world" (vv. 699–701). This last remark is especially telling, for it indicates the relatively broad perspective of the author about prophecy. God's spirit could even speak true prophecy through the sibyl, much as God had done with Balaam. Here again we find a clear indication that prophecy was viewed as a cross-cultural phenomenon even with an author who is a strict monotheist, who believes only Yahweh inspires true prophecy.

In character, these oracles have the sort of specificity that near-horizon prophecy did in the classical period. The author is not afraid to name names and speak clearly, but that is, in part, because he speaks with the benefit of hindsight. When he does speak about the future, the prophecy becomes more allusive, elliptical, and metaphorical, at least in some respects. For example, in the description of the eschatological woes in vv. 635–651, there is one specific reference—"foreign rule will ravage all of Greece and drain off the rich land of its wealth"

(vv. 639–640). But then about the redeemer figure it is said, "And then God will send a King from the sun who will stop the entire earth from evil war, killing some, imposing oaths of loyalty on others; and he will not do all these things by his private plans but in obedience to the noble teachings of the great God" (vv. 652–656). In light of the Egyptian Potter's Oracle, which also speaks of a "king from the sun," referring to one of the Ptolemies, it seems likely that this is meant here as well. This oracle, then, would be comparable to what we find in Second Isaiah when Cyrus is seen as the anointed one of God restoring God's people (cf. Isa 45:1; and see here vv. 193, 318, 608).[33] The key, in the author's mind, to proper relationship with God is the offering of proper sacrifices in the Jerusalem temple, including making atonement for sin, and then faithfully obeying God's law, especially the Ten Commandments. This becomes especially clear when the author speaks of what incurs God's final wrath: "because they knew neither the law nor the judgment of the great God, but with mindless spirit you all launched an attack and raised spears against the sanctuary" (v. 685).

How, then, does the author view the final state of affairs? "But the sons of the great God will all live peacefully around the Temple, rejoicing in these things which the Creator, just judge and sole ruler, will give." And what of the pagan nations? How will they react to the establishment of Israel and its temple one final time in the land? "They will bring forth from their mouths a delightful utterance in hymns, 'Come let us all fall on the ground and entreat the immortal king, the great eternal God. Let us send to the Temple since he alone is sovereign and let us ponder the Law of the most high God. But we have wandered from the path of the Immortal. With mindless spirit we revered things made by hand, idols and statues of dead men'" (vv. 715–723). "From every land they will bring incense and gifts to the house of the great God. There will be no other house among men, even for future generations to know" (vv. 772–774).

Here are the old Hebrew notions of Torah, temple, and territory as the heart of the faith. Notice, too, a Jewish mission to be a light to the Gentiles, beaming out from Zion and attracting them to come and honor the true God. This material is old-fashioned also in its placing of God at the center of things, as the real judge and restorer, while any messianic figure plays a decidedly secondary role in the whole process. Equally old-fashioned is the view of the role of the prophets in this eschatological process: "Prophets of the great God will take away the sword for they themselves are judges of men and righteous kings" (vv. 781–782; cf. 1 Macc 14:41; Philo, *Mos.* 2.1). The author operates with something of an *Urzeit-Endzeit* schema and perhaps envisions an important role for people like himself in the *eschaton*.

The third book of *Sibylline Oracles* comes to a rather shocking conclusion. In an apologetic move to suggest that all good things, ancient lore, good law, and true prophecy ultimately go back to the ancient Jewish tradition, we hear not only that the sibyl has long prophesied divine riddles about all cultures and ages but also that

---

[33] See J. J. Collins, "Sibylline Oracles," *OTP* 1:356–57.

Throughout Greece mortals will say that I am of another country, a shameless one, born of Erythrae. Some will say that I am Sibylla born of Circe.... But when everything comes to pass, then you will remember me and no longer will anyone say that I am crazy, I who am the prophetess of the great God.... God put all of the future in my mind so that I prophesy both future and former things and tell them to mortals. For when the world was deluged with waters, and a certain single approved man was left ... I was his daughter-in-law and I was of his blood. The first things happened to him and all the latter things have been revealed, so let all these things from my mouth be accounted true. (vv. 811–829)

The sibyl turns out to be righteous Noah's daughter-in-law! No wonder she offered such correct prophecies. But perhaps the veil of pseudonymity also slips down a bit here in this conclusion, for we learn that this sibyl also speaks of "former things," not just of the future. Yet the book, like the Enochic literature, does not really go back to the Garden. It really begins with the flood and goes forward. If one is meant to think of the sibyl speaking from the time of Noah, then in fact she does not speak of former things from that perspective. Yet there is something important to learn from this conclusion. A historical review that leads up to remarks about the author's future is indeed seen as prophecy. For the true, inspired interpretation of history is viewed as just as much a gift of God's spirit as is clear prediction. Whether such insight should be called prophecy is another question. Probably it should not be seen as the work of a prophet; rather, it is the provenance of sages and scribes who pay attention to the meaning of traditions and text and learn how to apply them and say, "This is that." This must be borne in mind as we now turn to the Qumran literature.

V. POSTCARDS FROM THE EDGE—QUMRAN AND PROPHECY

In the *Damascus Document* (CD 7:15–17), one finds one of the more interesting fortuitous correspondences between material in the NT and that from Qumran. There is an exegesis of Amos 9:11 about the fallen booth of David, which is surprisingly understood to be the Law. This booth, it is said, has been restored or set up again by the "Seeker of the Law," apparently the Teacher of Righteousness. This same text is cited in Acts 15:16–17, where the application seems to be to the community of Christian believers, seen as the restored tent of God into which Gentiles may now go. In both cases, the OT prophetic texts are read as if they were being fulfilled in the era of the writer of these documents. In other words, in both cases they are read with an eschatological mind-set that assumes that author and the audience are already living in the end times.

Very few would dispute the eschatological *Gestalt* of the Qumran literature, and thus likely of the community that generated it. More controversial, however, is the question whether we can call this eschatological orientation apocalyptic. Is there such a thing as specifically apocalyptic eschatology? Or is apocalyptic a formal category? This is not an idle question, not least because the eschatology that we find in apocalypses we also find in other early Jewish and Christian documents that are clearly not apocalypses.

Furthermore, we would be very hard pressed to say that, among the myriad of documents and fragments found, an apocalypse has surfaced at Qumran. Indeed, the two texts from Qumran that have been labeled apocalypses do not meet the critieria of the definition offered earlier in this chapter. For example, the so-called *Messianic Apocalypse* (4Q521) simply mentions that the Messiah will be listened to by the heavens and earth and all those who dwell therein will keep the holy precepts. Likewise the so-called *Aramaic Apocalypse* (4Q246) certainly is messianic and eschatological, speaking of a ruler, called the Son of God, who will be great over all the earth and of a people of God who will arise and put the sword to rest throughout the world. There are no apocalyptic images or visions mentioned in either text.[34]

Can we, then, speak of an apocalyptic mind-set that influenced the Qumran community and their views of themselves and of their texts? On the one hand, one can certainly demonstrate the enormous popularity of Daniel at Qumran.[35] There have been found no less than eight manuscripts of the book of Daniel and a further three or four feature portions or parts of the book and its ideas in other documents. Not even Jeremiah is as well represented. Interestingly, every chapter is represented except ch. 12. The mere number of manuscripts, plus the way Daniel is cited (cf., e.g., 4Q174, "written in the book of the prophet Daniel"), strongly suggests that this work was seen as Scripture and also seen as prophecy (and not ex eventu prophecy either). For this reason among others, Collins is prepared to speak of the apocalyptic eschatology at Qumran.[36] It can be argued that although the Qumran community may not have produced an apocalypse, they certainly meditated on the forebear of all such works, Daniel, and so developed an apocalyptic mind-set about their own community and times. It is time to reflect on this possibility by examining some texts.

First, what is striking is not only the lack of apocalypses in general in the Qumran literature but also the lack of reference to otherworldly journeys. Indeed, Collins admits that there is no evidence of otherworldly tours of heaven and hell in the Scrolls.[37] This means that if one is looking for apocalyptic thinking or ideas at Qumran, it must have been derived from the more historically oriented style of apocalypse. Two fragmentary texts may seem to contradict this conclusion: 4Q491 and 4Q427 have a figure speaking in the first person who says, "I have sat on the throne in the heavens" (4Q491) or, "My office is among the gods" (4Q427). Part of the difficulty in dealing with this material is that it is

---

[34] See VanderKam, "Messianism and Apocalypticism," 219.

[35] See P. W. Flint, "The Daniel Tradition at Qumran," in *Eschatology, Messianism, and the Dead Sea Scrolls* (ed. P. W. Flint and C. Evans; Grand Rapids: Eerdmans, 1997), 41–60.

[36] See J. J. Collins, "The Expectation of the End in the Dead Sea Scrolls," in Flint and Evans, *Eschatology, Messianism*, 74–90.

[37] See the panel discussion, Flint and Evans, *Eschatology, Messianism*, 148.

difficult to say who the "I" is in these fragments. It could be God or an angel, but it seems an odd and superfluous claim if this is a reference to God. M. Abegg has suggested tentatively that the reference is to the Teacher of Righteousness.[38] This may be correct, but if so, there is nothing about an ascent into heaven or about a tour. Instead, this is what may be called a revelatory experience, where the figure stays on earth but receives a vivid vision of what is above, perhaps not unlike what we find in 2 Cor 12:2–5.

It is perhaps also worthwhile stressing that the evidence for the Qumran community being a community of prophets or seers is weak. Not even their founder was called a prophet, and it is doubtful that the sort of high-tech pesher interpretation of prophetic texts, including Daniel, at Qumran tells us that they saw themselves this way. Rather, they believed they were on the cusp of the age of fulfillment or living in the first days of the eschatological age, the age when the prophecies would all come true. Thus, it was their task to search the Scriptures in scribal fashion and discern when and where and how the fulfillments were happening and what stood for or referred to what in the earlier prophecies.[39] In such an approach to Scripture, a very this-worldly orientation prevails. The Qumranites were not seeking heavenly compensation for earthly disappointment. They were expecting the end to come on earth.

Sometimes the frequent use of Daniel at Qumran has led to overhasty generalizations about what the Qumran community thought about the imminence of the *end* of the eschatological period, the time when the tribulation and eschatological war would be over and the final state of affairs with new temple and new land would occur. But again, although the Qumran literature does deal with the broad periodizing concepts of Daniel, Collins rightly admits, "I see no evidence that anyone at Qumran ever counted the days, in the manner of the book of Daniel, or that their expectation ever focused on a specific day or year. Consequently it does not appear that they ever encountered the trauma of disappointment."[40] An eschatological mind-set is one thing, but specific date setting is something more than this, and if the latter is what characterizes apocalyptic thinking, the Qumran community does not seem to reflect it. If we look carefully at the pesher on Hab 2:3 (1QpHab 7:6–13), the interpreter is dealing with the issue of delay. The interpreter says, "the last end time will be prolonged, and

---

[38] M. Abegg, "Who Ascended to Heaven? 4Q491, 4Q427, and the Teacher of Righteousness," in Flint and Evans, *Eschatology, Messianism*, 61–73.

[39] I must, then, disagree with Aune, *Prophecy in Early Christianity*, 133, who follows G. Jeremias in contending that the Teacher of Righteousness was a prophet and was seen as such. Rather, he was an inspired or charismatic sage, scribe, priest, or teacher who knew how to "rightly divide the Word" and apply it to the current situation. Notice how he is described in 1QpHab 2:8–9 as "the Priest whom God placed in [the House of Jud]ah to explain all the words of His servants the Prophets." This is the role of the exegete or teacher, not the prophet.

[40] Collins, "The Expectation of the End," in Flint and Evans, *Eschatology, Messianism*, 85.

it will be greater than anything of which the prophets spoke." After quoting, "if it tarries, wait for it," the author reassures, "for all of God's end times will come according to their fixed order." But about the timing the author says nothing. He seems to believe what is expressed in Acts 1: it is not for the audience to know the precise times and seasons of the reestablishment of Israel, Jerusalem, the temple, or the full coming of the dominion of God upon the earth.

Miqsat Maaseh Torah (4QMMT), a unique Qumran document in that it is addressed to outsiders, suggests that some curses and blessings are already happening but that these are precursors to the end of days. As Collins says, "The point is not that signs of eschaton have already begun to appear, as is sometimes implied in apocalyptic texts, but that the time of decision [in preparation for the end] is now. It is time to usher in the end of days by returning to the covenant."[41] But this is about as far as one gets with realized eschatology. The eschatological war and the coming of the two messiahs are clearly seen as happening in the future. And furthermore, there is precious little reflection on resurrection of the dead, such as we find in the ex eventu portion of Daniel (Dan 12; cf. above) and in the apocalypses of *1 Enoch*. One can point to 4Q521 and perhaps 4Q385, but "the evidence suggests that resurrection was only a minority belief at Qumran, and was not typical of the eschatology of the sect."[42]

What may we conclude from this sort of data? First, when we get beyond the form-critical matters that characterize the genre apocalypse, including revelatory visions that have bizarre images, and possibly tours of otherworldly realms, it is hard to say with conviction that anything is apocalyptic. Eschatology does not necessarily express itself in apocalyptic forms, and as has been seen, there is precious little evidence of apocalyptic forms in the Qumran material. Furthermore, periodization of history, reflections on the end of the world, and the like are not distinctive or at least genre-specific features of apocalyptic material. Plenty of this sort of thing is found in material from this era that is not apocalyptic literature. Also the eschatological material found in some of the Hebrew prophets does not express their thought in apocalyptic form (e.g., Second Isaiah). But this we *can* say: the sense that one lived in the age of fulfillment does characterize both the Qumran community and the author(s) of material such as we find in *1 Enoch*. This can be called an eschatological consciousness, since it occurs in varying genres of material. By and large, we should not view the Qumran community as a prophetic sect or movement, although it is certainly an eschatological movement. It is not a sect led by prophets or seers but by teachers, scribes, and, presumably, descendants of priests. One must look elsewhere to find prophets and fresh prophecies or apocalyptic material. There is one important prophetic figure, however, who may, at some point, have had connections with Qumran and to whom this study now turns—John the Baptist.

---

[41] Ibid., 80–81.
[42] Ibid., 88.

VI. JOHN THE BAPTIZER—LAST OF HIS KIND OR ESCHATOLOGICAL PROPHET?

In a discussion I was having with Richard Bauckham, an expert in early Judaism and its Christian offshoot, the conversation turned to prophecy. He kept stressing that, clearly, once one gets beyond Daniel, something is very different. There is no more oracular prophecy where Yahweh is quoted by a known historical prophet who gives his own name. This is indeed a remarkable fact, and it has led to the suggestion that prophecy ceased before the Second Temple era. But there were not just prophets in antiquity; there were also seers, visionaries, and it appears they kept one sort of prophecy alive throughout the period under evaluation here. There was a tradition, already long established in Hebrew prophecy, of speaking about things eschatological, or the ideal future. Such prophecies were offered at least as early as the Babylonian exile and perhaps even earlier. But in the tradition's early stages, these sorts of prophecies were offered by those who could not really be called "eschatological" prophets if by that one means someone who is the herald of an imminent eschatological action of God.

It is possible to interpret the Hebrew portions of Daniel to suggest that there was such a person behind some of this material, but on the whole, the creation of the first apocalypse appears to be a literary exercise rather than one grounded in fresh inspiration and oration, except that once we get beyond the historical review presented as prophetic preview, there are some statements made about what is still in the author's future. Should this material be seen as mere speculation? Why would a real prophet need to use someone else's name in order to speak with authority? Is a disciple of a prophet who carries on the tradition and expands upon it also to be considered a prophet? These are difficult questions to answer. All we can say for certain is that apocalyptic seems to have worked on the basis of different conventions than ancient oracular prophecy, and yet Josephus, the tradents at Qumran, and those involved in the Jesus movement saw apocalyptic material as real prophecy.

It was pointed out above that there are difficulties with the suggestion that the Qumran community was a prophetic community. Rather, they seem to have been an eschatological sect who saw themselves on the cusp of the age of fulfillment and diligently searched the Scriptures to understand their contemporary situation as well as what they expected to soon come to pass. It is nonetheless possible that there were one or more eschatological prophets at Qumran who spoke of the future as an extension of the pneumatic exegesis of the scribes or tradents of the community. One of them may well have been John the Baptizer.

What is new about John is that he is the first eschatological sign prophet in early Judaism who does not cloak himself in a veil of anonymity, much less pseudonymity. His location in the Judean desert, his eschatological message, his baptismal practice, his ascetical lifestyle, his belief in the deep corruption of God's people and especially of their leadership, his offering of an alternative to the current temple apparatus's means of forgiving sins may all be seen as pointers that at one time John was connected to the Qumran community.[43] There is also Luke 1:80 to reckon with, which says that John was in the desert places until his manifestation to Israel. When we combine all this with Josephus's statement that the Essenes adopted children and brought them up in their traditions (*War* 2.8.2) and with the fact that the Gospels use the very text about John—Isa 40:3—that the Qumran community used of itself to describe its own mission or task (1QS 8:13–15; 10:19–20), a very plausible case can be made for John coming out of the Qumran community.

Still, of course, there are differences between John and Qumran, not the least of which is that John's water rite seems to have been an unrepeatable one. John also reached out to Israel rather than expecting Israel to come to him, and yet it appears that he confined himself to the margins of the land along the Jordan. This was presumably because of the sign he felt called upon to enact and perhaps also because of his view of the eschatological situation—the land was impure and imperiled, one needed to start again at the boundary, as Israel had done when it first entered the land, only now with a new boundary ritual (not an Ebenezer but a ritual cleansing). It was the people rather than the land that needed cleaning out this time.

It is interesting how Josephus very carefully skirts the issue of whether John was a prophet. He does not call him such in the crucial passage in *Ant.* 18.116–119; indeed, as Meier says, he presents him as a sort of popular Stoic moral philosopher.[44] John is presented in both Josephus and the Gospels as a man of both sign and words, but in neither case are John's words presented as either (1) like the oracular utterances of ancient prophets using the divine first person or (2) like the words of apocalyptic seers. Rather, his message is eschatological in content, much like what one finds at Qumran, and spoken apparently on his own authority, without messenger formula or citation of human authorities. His words were about preparation for the coming divine redemptive judgment or reign of God in the people's midst. John's praxis and his words will be considered in a moment, but it is appropriate to point out that possibly John set a precedent or pattern as an eschatological prophet, for there were other figures in this era who also could have been called eschatological sign prophets. Consider the chart in table 7-1.

Some of these prophets also may well have seen themselves in a messianic light, but they all fit a particular mold: believing they live in the dawning eschatological age, they play a role as prophets of sign and word about the inbreaking activity of God. None of them seem to have proclaimed their message in the form of the ancient oracular prophets, using the messenger formula and the divine "I." They were part of a new breed of prophets, yet they shared with the ancient classical prophets the use of sign acts to convey or dramatize their message. None of them left behind apocalypses either.

---

[43] See Witherington, *Christology of Jesus,* 34ff.; and J. Meier, *A Marginal Jew: Rethinking the Historical Jesus* (New York: Doubleday, 1994), 2:19ff.

[44] Meier, *Marginal Jew,* 2:21.

Table 7-1: Eschatological Sign Prophets at the Turn of the Era				
Ruler	Prophetic Figure	Prophetic Activity	Location	Audience
Pilate	John	baptize	wilderness	crowds
Pilate	Jesus	feed 5,000	wilderness	5,000 men
Pilate	Samaritan	reveal temple vessels	Mt. Gerizim	great crowd
Fadus	Theudas	divide Jordan	Jordan	great crowd
Felix	The Egyptian	Jerusalem walls collapse	wilderness to Jerusalem	4,000 men[45]

What can we say for sure about John's sign and words from a historical point of view? In view of the fact that both the NT and Josephus tell us that John was executed by Herod Antipas, we must assume that this was a well-known fact. What this fact necessarily suggests is that John had said and/or done something that was threatening enough that Herod felt compelled to imprison and then execute him. The considerable significance of John is also suggested by the fact that he spawned a movement that continued well after his death (cf. Acts 18–19). We must reckon, then, with the likelihood that John was indeed a very significant prophetic figure in early Judaism. We can also say with viritual certainty that John was a baptizer; indeed, this practice so characterized his ministry that he came to be known as the Baptist and continued to have this title even as late as Josephus's day (*Ant.* 18.116—"surnamed the Baptist").

In regard to John's sign, it must be admitted from the start that it differed from what is found at Qumran in several respects. It is similar in that the Qumran community seems to have treated all Jews entering the community as if they were proselytes and there was a water rite they went through when entering "the covenant of conversion" (CD 19:16). But then there were multiple lustrations, or purification baths, thereafter. John's rite seems to be, once for all time, promising deliverance from the coming judgment if one repents and prepares for the coming day. Furthermore, John's sign is not just a sign; it is a participatory symbol. It is not like, for example, a prophet building a model of a city and lying on his side representing the seige of a city. It has no precedent in the prophetic corpus. Indeed, in their recent magisterial study of the historical Jesus, G. Theissen and A. Merz are prepared to call John's baptism an eschatological sacrament.[46] It prepares for what is to come. The baptism of water averts having to undergo the fiery baptism of judgment.

What must be said about Jesus' submission to John's baptism? At the very least, this must imply an endorsement of John's message and ministry. Indeed,

---

[45] This is an adaptation of a chart created by P. W. Barnett, "The Jewish Eschatological Prophets" (Ph.D. diss., University of London, 1977), 182–83.

[46] G. Theissen and A. Merz, *The Historical Jesus: A Comprehensive Guide* (Minneapolis: Fortress, 1998), 200.

as shall be seen in the next chapter, Jesus seems to have seen John as the greatest of prophets, as the final eschatological prophet, the Elijah figure. The implicit endorsement of John's message and practices by Jesus in his submission to baptism makes very dubious the suggestion that Jesus' own message was not eschatological in character.[47] Our earliest Gospel suggests that, at least at the outset, Jesus' preaching was a reiteration of John's message: repent, for God's divine judging and redeeming activity is about to break into Israel's midst. What is especially radical about John's baptism is that he calls *all* to submit to it—not merely the wicked but even the righteous, even the leaders of the community. Not merely pagans but Jews, and even "good" Jews, are called upon to undergo this rite. This can only mean that John, like the Qumranites, saw Israel as in a desperately corrupt state.

Yet it would also seem to imply enormous authority on John's part that he felt he could offer a means of receiving forgiveness of sins apart from sacrifices and the temple apparatus. One may be confident this motif is historically genuine, for it is hardly likely early Christians would suggest either that forgiveness came through means other than, or in advance, of Jesus' death on the cross, or that John dispensed it, or that Jesus submitted to such a baptism. This suggests that John was a more radical reformer than is usually recognized and that, unlike some prophetic figures, he was not merely going to talk about coming judgment or reform in lieu of it.

This radical alternative may well explain why, in the tradition, tax collectors and even Roman soldiers are said to come to John for baptism (Luke 3:12–14). He was going to do something about the situation by offering God's people an alternative to facing the wrath to come. Notice, too, that there is nothing in the apocalyptic corpus that perpares us for a prophet doing such a thing. John is a man of action seeking to help God's people. He is not just a prophet of doom. In this action and in his critique of Herod's marriage to his brother's wife, he seems to be much more like the northern prophets who involved themselves in political actions (e.g., Elijah, Elisha).

What, then, of his message? Meier rightly notes that various crucial elements in apocalyptic are missing from John's proclamation—mystical visions interpreted by angels, otherworldly journeys, astrological speculation, periodization of history, bizarre symbols.[48] Indeed, John's message sounds far more like Amos's on the Day of Yahweh than like Daniel's message. Even the images he uses, such as the ax laid to the tree or the "brood of vipers," sound more like those of the classical prophets than of the apocalyptic seers. Not without reason, some have made the mistake of simply seeing John as a glorious anachronism—a throwback to an earlier era of classical prophecy.

This will not do on several grounds. Nothing in the evidence available suggests that John ever offered quotations from Yahweh, even though one is told,

---

[47] Rightly Meier, *Marginal Jew,* 2:28–38.
[48] Ibid., 31.

"the word of God came to John" (Luke 3:2).[49] Furthermore, his eschatological focus is far more like the exilic and postexilic prophetic figures. Third, so far as one can say, John was never a writing prophet. If one must use the sociological categories, he is in every sense a peripheral prophet, not a central one like Isaiah or Jeremiah, and like such prophets in earlier ages, he is marginalized and finally eliminated by the powers that be. The title of eschatological sign prophet best characterizes him, and this seems to be a new sort of prophet, like neither ancient *neviim* nor seers, whether apocalyptic or otherwise. John does not proclaim merely imminent judgment of some sort; rather, he proclaims imminent final judgment. Yet his focus remains on the historical stage and the climax of the human drama.

Notice, as J. B. Green rightly stresses, that since John's baptism is a repentance baptism, his proclamation and his praxis are intricately interwoven.[50] The Q material found in Luke 3:7–18 and par. is hortatory in character and is some form of direct address to John's immediate audience. About this material Aune says,

> In form this speech bears little resemblance to prophetic speeches in the OT; . . . [but] The speech does, however, have some interesting parallels with prophetic speeches in Amos. The pejorative address with which the speech begins resembles similar addresses in Amos 4.1; 8.4. Further, the admonition of John begins with a positive exhortation followed by a prohibition, a pattern also found in Amos 5:4–5. The rhetorical question "Who warned you to flee from the wrath to come?" calls to mind the OT prophetic speech form which has been designated the "summons to flee" (Jer. 4:4–5; 6:1; 48:6–8 . . .).[51]

In short, the content is, in various ways, like material in Amos and the classical prophets, except for the clear eschatological focus coupled with a stress on imminence. The form differs from classical prophecy not least in its prosaic, rather than poetic, form.

The message suggests that the crowd must bear fruit worthy of repentance, for at present they are alienated from God. They can not call upon their Abrahamic heritage as some sort of security blanket that will protect them from the wrath to come. Indeed, they are the offspring of snakes, rather than Abraham, at this point.[52] Verse 9 is especially important: "Even now the ax is lying at the root of the trees; every tree therefore that does not bear good fruit is cut down and thrown into the fire." This, in all likelihood, is an exhortation to indi-

---

[49] We must be exceedingly cautious about the way we read the Lukan data, because of Luke's well-known tendency to portray his minor and major positive figures as prophets—Simeon, Anna, John, Jesus, Peter, Paul, and so on. On this cf. pp. 335–38 below.

[50] J. B. Green, *The Gospel of Luke* (NIC; Grand Rapids: Eerdmans, 1997), 173

[51] Aune, *Prophecy in Early Christianity,* 130.

[52] Green, *Gospel of Luke,* 175: to be born of something is to share its character or nature, in ancient thinking.

vidual Israelites, since multiple trees are referred to. Repentance and forgiveness are an individual matter, and presumably what John is hoping for is a righteous remnant before the wrath comes. Lest they have too exalted a view of themselves, John reminds them they can be replaced by God with stones!

The direct warning about judgment includes the prophetic image of ax and tree found in Isa 10:33–34 (cf. its later use in Wis 4:3–5 and Sir 6:3 and by Jesus at Luke 13:6–9). The crowd must respond now because the judgment is imminent. Fruitless trees are not only chopped down but thrown into the fire (cf. Mal 4:1—on the Day of the Lord the arrogant will be burned up, leaving neither root nor branch). Yet there is still time to avoid such an unpleasant fate, and thus a series of persons question John, "What then should we do?" His teaching, in short, led not merely to baptism but also to a reform of practice. The ordinary person who has clothing and food should share them. The tax collector is to practice extortion no longer, nor are the soldiers, who are also exhorted not to misuse their power or grumble about their wages.

Luke 3:16/Matt 3:11 introduces us to something else that John has to say about the future. There is one stronger than he is who is coming after him. Although it is possible that this is a reference to God, if so, it seems almost an innocuous comment. Would John really have compared himself to God? As Meier says, if the subject is the eschatological judgment, no one would ever have thought otherwise than that God is stronger than all mortals.[53] The comparison becomes even more nonsensical with the next clause, where John says he is not worthy even to untie the thong of this stronger one's sandal. The image is of a slave in relation to a master, but a master who still needed sandals as the slave did. Nothing in this metaphor suggests a being of another order, much less the Almighty.

Who then, if not God, might John have in mind who would come and offer a more efficacious baptism? If indeed John came out of the Qumran community, he could well have had a messianic figure of some description in mind—a priestly messiah, a royal messiah, perhaps even another eschatological prophet. The implication is, of course, that John himself is not strong enough to complete the eschatological agenda God has in mind.[54] There is considerable debate whether the further baptism that is to come is simply the baptism with or by the Spirit or whether "with fire" is a clause that goes back to the Baptist's teaching. Probably the original simply contrasted water and spirit, but it may be that John had the purgative work of the Spirit especially in view, hence the addition "and with fire."

In any case, notice the prophetic style of John.

There is no arguing with John, because he presents no arguments to establish his position. There is no explicit argument from Scripture, no invocation of a previous rabbinic teacher, not even prophetic legitimation, "The word of the Lord came to

---

[53] Meier, *Marginal Jew*, 2:34.
[54] Ibid., 35.

me saying . . ." John knows the end is near, he knows the conditions for escaping destruction, and that is the end of the matter. . . . [John has] a forceful and striking
personality [and] claims direct, intuitive knowledge of God's will and plans—
knowledge unmediated by the traditional channels of law, temple, priesthood, or
scribal scholarship—and is able to draw notable crowds of people to himself and his
message, the label "charismatic" may be added to "eschatological" as part of this
prophet's description.[55]

What John also knows is that the one who comes after him, whether final prophet
or messiah or angel or deity, will pour out on God's people what the prophet Joel
and others promised—the Spirit. But John seems also to believe that only those
repentant Israelites who submit to water and repentance now will be imbued with
Spirit later.

John the Baptist is a crucial figure to help us understand a new breed of eschatological prophets who nonetheless have various things in common with
some of the older classical prophets—both in their use of signs and in some of
the content of, and metaphors within, their utterances. Still, on the whole, these
figures are not merely classical prophets with the volume or sense of urgency
turned up. They will speak of the *eschaton* as something on the near horizon that
they, as named prophetic figures, will help usher in. This is *not* the stuff of the
idealized final future prophecy of a Second Isaiah, or of an apocalyptic seer, or of
a classical prophet who spoke only to his own age and the near horizon of his
situation. This is something new. It is this eschatologically intense environment
that produced both a Qumran and John—and I would add a Jesus, but the latter
is the subject for our next chapter.

VII. CONCLUSIONS

Without question, in the period leading up to the NT era, some old forms
of prophecy seem to have been left behind, and some new forms seem to have
arisen. To be specific, the old "thus says Yahweh" formula, followed by first-person discourse presented by a named prophet, is nowhere to be found; on the
other hand, with at least John the Baptist, if not before him, we see the rise of the
eschatological prophet. The evidence is convincing, from this Baptist material
and the Qumran material as well as other sources, that various early Jews were
convinced they lived in the age of the fulfillment of the old prophecies, which
may help explain why they were less concerned about the generation of new
prophecies. Nevertheless, the living voice of prophecy had not died out; it had
just changed its voice.

Another phenomenon that arose at least as early as the Maccabean era was
the literary or scribal exercise of creating ex eventu prophecy, often drawing on
older prophetic material. This development is primarily witnessed in the growing apocalyptic tradition, for example, in Dan 8–12, which expands on Dan 7, or

---

[55] Ibid., 40.

in the Enoch corpus. Yet it was to be the case, as the book of Revelation in the NT shows, that not all apocalyptic literature involved ex eventu prophecy, but this should not surprise the attentive student of this material, for there were already apocalyptic visions in Ezekiel and Zechariah that were not of the ex eventu variety. Even in a work that was largely ex eventu prophecy, the author often would summon up his courage and say a few things, at the end of the work or visionary cycle, about what still lay in his own future.

The cross-cultural nature and influence of prophecy is clearly evidenced in *Sibylline Oracles,* of which a sample was examined in this chapter. The assumption behind these compilations seems to be that true or valid prophecy comes from a variety of sources or, if one sees this as an apologetic venture, that Jewish prophecy (and later Christian prophecy) is just as valid as Greco-Roman prophecy. The attempt to claim the sibyl for the Jewish tradition must surely be seen as an apologetic device. Nevertheless, this material amply illustrates the cosmopolitan environment in which early Jews lived and in which prophecy arose near the turn of the era. This must be borne in mind as this study now turns to consider once more Jesus, this time as a Jewish seer indebted to the apocalyptic tradition.

CHAPTER 8

Jesus the Seer

*I*N A PREVIOUS STUDY I ARGUED that Jesus should be seen as a sage, albeit a prophetic sage.[1] It is the intent of this chapter to explore further the adjective in this last description, for no one title or label adequately explains a figure as complex as Jesus. Multiple complementary models are required to deal with the man who fits no one formula, as E. Schweizer once called him. The matter is complicated by the considerable cross-fertilization of things prophetic, sapiential, and apocalyptic by the time Jesus comes on the stage of early Judaism. The question then becomes, What sort of prophetic figure might he have been?

I. JESUS, JOHN, AND THE CLASSICAL PROPHETS

My previous work suggested strongly that Jesus could not simply be seen as standing in the line of the classical prophets. The form of most of his probably authentic utterances does not allow this conclusion, and notice that all of his utterances lack a messenger formula. Further, he was certainly not among the writing prophets. Yet in ch. 7, above, it was pointed out that Jesus' "mentor," John, was surely a prophet and, as an eschatological prophet, spoke on his own authority. Could Jesus have simply followed in the footsteps of John in this regard? This is possible, but then how do we explain all the counterorder wisdom material that goes back to Jesus? How do we explain the significantly different lifestyles of John and Jesus? Why does Jesus perform miracles and John does not? One can not

---

[1] Witherington, *Jesus the Sage,* 147–208.

conclude that Jesus *simply* followed in the footsteps of John. It is one thing to talk about John as Jesus' mentor, as Meier does; it is another to call Jesus a carbon copy of John.

Aune has made a detailed form-critical analysis of the Gospels, sifting the material for evidence that Jesus' utterances were prophetic in character. But this sort of critical sifting comes to a far from compelling conclusion: "The evidence *though slim* does suggest that Jesus regarded himself as a prophet in the OT tradition, and in the framework of current Jewish expectation he must have thought of himself as an eschatological prophet."[2] The question is, Which OT traditions, and what sort of eschatological prophet? Aune admits that Jesus nowhere directly calls himself a prophet and that there is no evidence in the Gospels of a prophetic call narrative for Jesus, for the baptismal scene can not be counted as such.

Aune then points to the popular assessments of Jesus found in texts such as Mark 6:14–15 and Mark 8:28. But in fact, in the narrative context of both passages, both assessments are presented as being incorrect or at least inadequate. On the basis of this evidence and the non-Markan material found in Matt 21:46, Luke 7:39, and John 6:14; 7:40, 52, we could conclude that this was a popular way in which Jesus was viewed during his day. He was doing or saying something that suggested this to some people. To this we could add Luke's systematic attempt to portray Jesus as a prophet, about which I will have occasion to say more in a later chapter.[3] None of this material helps very much to get a clearer fix on what sort of prophet Jesus may have thought himself to be. What people believe about themselves and how others assess them can certainly be two different things. It is important also to inquire into Jesus' narrative thought world. What role did Jesus see himself playing in the drama of God's people?

Two direct pieces of evidence require attention first—Mark 6:4 (Matt 13:57; Luke 4:24) and Luke 13:31–33. What we discover from this material is that Jesus, during his Galilean ministry, may have presented himself as like other northern prophets who performed miracles and were without honor in their own land and time—Elijah and Elisha. The first text is, in all likelihood, the citation of a proverbial expression, and Aune says its proverbial character means "not that Jesus regards himself as a prophet, but that he is one who is not accepted in his own homeland."[4] But it could be said that the Markan text at least indirectly suggests that Jesus was comparing his experience to that of earlier prophets.

Luke 13:31–33 is a pericope unique to Luke. In view of Luke's clear agenda to present Jesus as some sort of prophet, coupled with its lack of multiple attestation, scholars have been loath to consider this authentic Jesus material. It can, in any case, reveal no more than that Jesus saw himself as likely to face the same

---

[2] Aune, *Prophecy in Early Christianity*, 187.

[3] Pp. 330–43 below.

[4] Aune, *Prophecy in Early Christianity*, 156. Cf. C. K. Barrett, *The Holy Spirit and the Gospel Tradition* (London: SPCK, 1947), 94–95.

fate as earlier prophets, especially those who proclaimed judgment in the vicinity of Jerusalem. It does not tell us what sort of prophet he thought he was. Nonetheless, this text does indicate something quite important. It suggests that Jesus saw himself in the prophetic tradition that had some connection with Jerusalem, and that he expected a tragic end there.[5]

Possibly much more helpful is the Q material in Luke 7:24–28/Matt 11:7–11, a text that, as Meier says, has the earmarks of an authentic word of Jesus, especially in view of the total focus on, and praise for, John without any obvious christological counterpoint or any attempt to cast John as the Messiah's forerunner.[6] This text has recently been illuminated by G. Theissen's interesting discussion about Herod Antipas's coins that have a reed on them. Theissen explains, "If a personal attribute can replace a portrait, then conversely everything that appears in place of the usual portrait can be regarded as a personal attribute, even if it is intended otherwise by the coining monarch. People could have bestowed minute scrutiny and comment on the first coins of Antipas to appear in the country. Would not some wit have made the joke: look at Antipas, the wavering reed?"[7] This is certainly possible, and so Jesus' saying means that the crowd did not go out to the river to see a king or someone wearing a royal robe. To the contrary, they went out to see a prophet the likes of whom had not been seen in that region in a while. This attests not only to John's considerable popularity (and his lack of need to seek out disciples or audiences for his teaching and rite, unlike Jesus) but also to a contrast between Jesus' estimation of Herod and his estimation of John. There is, however, something else going on here. It suggests that John should not be seen as a ruler figure or even as a messianic figure. One would expect to find them elsewhere.

John, to use the earlier categories of this study, is not a central or court diviner or court prophet. He is a peripheral prophet—the sort that made rulers most nervous. Since he had a following, John can certainly also be called a leadership prophet.[8] John and Jesus seem to have had a relationship with Herod Antipas rather like Elijah had with Ahab, except that neither Jesus nor John seems to have confronted Herod in his own capital city or court. They both seem to have condemned Herod's incestuous marriage. This led to the arrest of

---

[5] It is not sufficient to say that this is merely Luke's agenda here, since there is evidence, presented below, that Jesus himself saw his ministry in some sort of Jewish prophetic light.

[6] Meier, *Marginal Jew,* 2:139.

[7] G. Theissen, *The Gospels in Context* (Edinburgh: T&T Clark, 1992), 34.

[8] Not much is gained from the paradigm that suggests John could be seen as a clerical prophet. It might be better to say he was prophet who was from a clerical line and who, like the Teacher of Righteousness, became an anticlerical leader, reacting to the existing temple setup. But see R. L. Webb, *John the Baptizer and Prophet: A Socio-historical Study* (Sheffield: Sheffield Academic Press, 1991); and more recently his "John the Baptist and His Relationship to Jesus," in *Studying the Historical Jesus* (ed. B. Chilton and C. A. Evans; Leiden: E. J. Brill, 1994), 179–230.

John, and if Luke 13:30–33 has any echo of the truth, Jesus himself may have felt pursued or under the ominous surveillance of Herod, whom Jesus apparently called "that fox" (13:32). This leads to a discussion of a crucial verse a bit more closely—Luke 7:26/Matt 11:9.

It is, frankly, surprising how many scholars have paid attention only to the second half of this logion—"and more than a prophet." This phrase is important, but the whole enigmatic saying needs to be taken together: "A prophet? Yes, I tell you, and more than a prophet." Jesus' high estimation of John is clear here and elsewhere (cf. the logion in Luke 7:28; Matt 11:1). He affirms that John is indeed a prophet, but lest the crowds simply rank John as another in the long line of Hebrew prophets, Jesus adds, "and more than a prophet." Thus we are left with a riddle: what sort of prophet is more than a prophet? One possible answer would be a messianic prophet, or another might be an, or *the,* eschatological prophet. Is there other evidence that may help sort this matter out?

Mark 1:14–15 provides a sort of summary of Jesus' early preaching. It has often been remarked that this summary suggests that Jesus was following in the footsteps of John, at least in his early preaching. But while acknowledging that there may be some truth to this, Crossan and others have suggested that Jesus abandoned this sort of preaching for a very different style of utterance.[9] The problem with this suggestion is that we find this very same sort of eschatological message on Jesus' lips later in parabolic form, and one could list a variety of other similar traditions that manifest the eschatological thematic motifs that characterized Jesus' message (cf. below). Consider, for example, not only that there is the phrase "kingdom of God" throughout the Jesus tradition but also that the theme of repentance comes up in a wide variety of material, some of which has a Galilean and some of which likely has a Judean provenance (cf. Luke 10:13–15 and par.; Luke 11:32; 13:3–5; 15:7–10; Mark 6:12). The lament for Jerusalem and the utterance about the temple's destruction surely both come from late in the ministry. In other words, there is eschatological continuity between Jesus' and John's message in various regards, both from the material that likely came from the beginnings of Jesus' ministry and from the later material as well. But greater clarity about Jesus' view of John, and so of himself, is still needed.

The discussion by Meier at this point is helpful. There was a tradition in Mal 4:5 that Elijah would return before the great and terrible Day of the Lord. There was not, however, so far as we can tell, a tradition in early Judaism before or during the time of Jesus about Elijah being the forerunner of the Messiah.[10] An implicit contrast between Herod Antipas and John could have conjured up "echoes of Elijah, the prophet who had struggled with and been persecuted by the evil monarchs of the northern kingdom of Israel."[11] Did Jesus identify John as the Elijah redivivus figure? This may well be the case. It is even possible that

[9] J. D. Crossan, *The Historical Jesus* (San Francisco: Harper, 1991), 238.

[10] See J. Fitzmyer, *The Gospel according to Luke I–IX* (Garden City: Doubleday, 1981), 672.

[11] Meier, *Marginal Jew,* 2:140.

John, near the close of his life, returned the favor when he asked, "Are you the one who is to come or should we look for another?"[12]

What is interesting about this is that J. J. Collins has suggested, in the light of the *Messianic Apocalypse,* that there was a messianic expectation in which "the messiah is more likely to be an eschatological prophet in the manner of Elijah. The royal messiah is never said to raise the dead. Elijah was credited with raising the dead during his historical career (1 Kgs 17)."[13] As Collins goes on to say, both the *Messianic Apocalypse* and Luke 4:17–19 use Isa 61:1–2 to describe the tasks of the Messiah. This text is also clearly alluded to in Jesus' response to the query from prison, found in the Q material in Matt 11:2–6/Luke 7:22–23. I have argued elsewhere for the authenticity of the latter text, not least because it shows that John had doubts about who Jesus was.[14]

The nature of John's quandary seems to have been that he expected the coming one to bring or usher in judgment, whereas Jesus had set out on a healing ministry. Jesus, in his quotation from Isaiah, carefully omits the parts of the text that refer to judgment. Thus, Jesus would apparently be suggesting he was indeed an Elijah-like figure who healed and raised the dead, fulfilling an Isaianic prophet's vision of what would come when God's dominion dawned. What is important about all this is that Jesus sees his ministry as in continuity with, if not a continuation of, John's Elijah-like ministry. In Jesus' view John was, in some sense, the Elijah figure. But there was more to Elijah than thundering doom on wicked leaders and Israelites. Jesus was filling out the portrait more fully.

Another pointer in this direction is the shocking Q saying in regard to filial piety, found at Matt 8:21–22/Luke 9:59–60. As M. Hengel long ago saw, Jesus is here advocating behavior that Jews and non-Jews would have seen as scandalous (cf. m. *Ber.* 3.1).[15] Here is not the place to argue again for the authenticity of this utterance.[16] It is sufficient to say that this remark clearly meets the criterion of embarrassment, whether one is thinking of early Jews or early Christians. As N. T. Wright puts it, "The only explanation for Jesus' astonishing command is that he envisaged loyalty to himself and his kingdom-movement as creating an alternative family."[17] This is true enough, and one would have to ask what kind of person had that sense of authority, that he could redefine the most basic so-

---

[12]See N. T. Wright, *Jesus and the Victory of God* (Minneapolis: Fortress, 1996), 166–67.

[13]J. J. Collins, "Jesus and the Messiahs of Israel," in *Geschichte—Tradition—Reflexion: Festschrift für Martin Hengel zum 70. Geburtstag* (Tübingen: Mohr, 1996), 287–302, here 296–97.

[14]See Witherington, *Christology of Jesus,* 42–43.

[15]M. Hengel, *The Charismatic Leader and His Followers* (New York: Crossroad, 1981), 9ff.

[16]See Witherington, *Christology of Jesus,* 137–40; and the arguments by Hengel, *Charismatic Leader,* 9ff.

[17]Wright, *Jesus and the Victory,* 401.

cial unit of his society, and redefine it around himself. More importantly, one should hear in this saying a definite echo of the Elijah tradition and Elijah's call of Elisha (see 1 Kgs 19:19–21). Jesus, in fact, as the eschatological Elijah, made even more stringent demands than did the original northern prophet. Nonetheless, this saying suggests that Jesus, while in the north, acted out the part of a northern prophet.[18]

The upshot of this for Jesus' self understanding is that he was also presenting himself in Galilee as some sort of eschatological and messianic prophet in the Elijah mold. It is believable that a Galilean, such as Jesus, would take precisely such a tack, considering his *Sitz im Leben.* Elijah and Elisha were northern prophets. Indeed, they were the great northern prophets. As northern prophets, they had no associations with Jerusalem and basically little or no contact with Judah or Judeans. It appears that both John and Jesus broke this mold, John by being in the Judean wilderness, Jesus not only by spending some time in the wilderness with John (John 3) but by making one or more trips to Jerusalem. Nevertheless, it is difficult to doubt that the majority of Jesus' ministry transpired in Galilee.

Furthermore, it is likely that Jesus understood enough about his social setting to present himself differently as a prophetic figure in Jerusalem than he did in Galilee. There was not a strong heritage of oracular prophets in the north. Elijah and Elisha were famous not for their oracles but for their actions, both real and symbolic. Notice that it took a southern prophet, Amos, to come and address a northern king with oracles.[19] This meant that Jesus could feel free in Galilee to pursue whatever form of discourse he saw most suitable—in this case, parables, aphorisms, riddles. By contrast, there was a very strong tradition of oracular prophets in the south. If Jesus wanted to present himself as any sort of prophet when he visited Judea and Jerusalem, he would need to use some conventional prophetic forms—such as woe oracles and the like. This is precisely what the synoptic tradition suggests Jesus did.[20]

When we return to Aune's critical analysis of the probably authentic Jesus material that manifests a prophetic form, we discover the kind of distinctions suggested above.[21] For example, the *Sitz im Leben* for any of the Markan apocalypse in Mark 13 that goes back to Jesus is surely Jerusalem, and in proximity to the temple. It was something that Jesus said about the temple that

---

[18] Luke, perhaps because of his schematized travel narrative, has this episode in Samaria, although I would not automatically rule out this locale as the original setting for this saying. Matthew rather clearly has it in Galilee, since Capernaum has just been mentioned (see Matt 8:5).

[19] See pp. 106–16 above.

[20] The Johannine tradition, to the extent it offers authentic words of Jesus, represents Jesus' utterances mainly made in Judea. The social setting helps to explain the lack of parables in John. See B. Witherington, *John's Wisdom* (Louisville: Westminster John Knox, 1995).

[21] Aune, *Prophecy in Early Christianity,* 171–87.

helped precipitate his being taken prisoner (cf. the witnesses in Mark 14:58). In this same material, for example, Mark 13:28–31 offers the sort of prediction, using metaphors, that was typical of southern prophets, who were often critical of the temple and Jerusalem.

Second, there is the judgment oracle about Jerusalem, found in the Q material at Luke 13:34–35/Matt 23:37–39, where, using *qinah* rhythm, a lament is offered for the Holy City, which kills its own prophets. One may compare this to the lament for the city, followed by a threat, found in Luke 19:41–44. There is, furthermore, the oracle for the daughters of Jerusalem about the coming demise of Jerusalem (Luke 23:28–31). There is the response of Jesus to the Pharisees about the future in Luke 17, which has as its most natural setting the primary domain of the Pharisees—Judea. One may also note that the material, drawing on Dan 7, on the future coming of the Son of man occurs in Judea and Jerusalem (Mark 13–14). This is not to say that there were not occasions when Jesus used prophetic forms, such as woe oracles, in Galilee (cf., e.g., the Q pericope Luke 10:13–15/Matt 11:21–22) or told parables in or especially pertinent to Judea or even Samaria (Luke 10:25–37— the Good Samaritan). The point is the dominant form of discourse chosen in each setting.

If Jesus had a prophetic ministry in both Galilee and Judea and perhaps also briefly in Samaria, did Jesus go back and forth between the regions regularly, or was there a turning point in Jesus' Galilean ministry when he felt he left Galilee behind and went up to Jerusalem, perhaps through Samaria and then on to Judea? There are several possible pointers that there was indeed a turning point or a series of turning points in the Galilean ministry.

The incarceration and death of John the Baptist could have been one precipitating factor. Second, there is the Galilean woe oracle already mentioned (Luke 10:13–15/Matt 11:21–22). The likely authenticity of this saying is widely recognized, not least because it is hardly likely that Christians were later making up oracles of woe for lowly Chorazin. This oracle anathematizes not only Chorazin but also Bethsaida and Capernaum—the fishing villages, on the northern shores of the sea of Galilee, that Jesus frequented and obviously had little success in winning over. D. C. Allison intimates that such texts as this may suggest one reason for Jesus' going up to Jerusalem—to find a better audience.[22] "Certainly the woes upon the cities of Galilee show us that certain high hopes or expectations of Jesus fell to the ground."[23] There is, third, the reaction of Jesus to the response to his miracles in Galilee, which seems to have been rather different from the response to his preaching in some other places. For example, Mark paints a picture of a Jesus who can hardly get away from the crowds (cf. Mark 3:7–12; 6:30–31 [immediately after the death of the Baptist], 53–56; 8:8–10).

---

[22] D. C. Allison, *Jesus of Nazareth: Millenarian Prophet* (Minneapolis: Fortress, 1998), 144 n. 177.

[23] Ibid., 150.

An even closer look shows that Jesus seems to have had to go in and out of the Galilean region to escape the crowds. Notice the alternation: after various miracles and teachings, he takes a trip across the sea to Gerasa (Mark 5:1ff.) and then returns across the sea (5:21); after miracles and a controversy with the Pharisees (Mark 6:53–7:23), he goes away into the region of Tyre and Sidon; after feeding the four thousand (Mark 8:1–10), he goes away into the district of Dalmanutha. The impression left is that once Jesus' reputation spread, especially as a healer, he had to present a moving target to get anything accomplished. Mark's presentation suggests that he did not want to be known primarily as a healer but as a proclaimer. He went out to teach; when people came to him and asked for physical help, he also healed. The reactions to the healings may be another reason he eventually left Galilee.

Finally, there is also Luke's suggestion that, at some definitive point, Jesus set his face like a flint to go up to Jerusalem, although the Lukan presentation suggests that he took a long time getting there and indeed went through Samaria to do so (Luke 9:51–52). There are also the various traditions about Jesus' rejection in his hometown (Mark 6:1–6 and par.; the rather different Luke 4:16–30).

Putting these disparate traditions together, and perhaps throwing in John 6:15 for good measure,[24] we are left with the conclusion that there likely was some sort of turning point in Jesus' ministry after which he largely left Galilee behind for a variety of reasons. It is possible that one of these is that he had fulfilled his prophetic responsibility there to that part of God's people and now must discharge his office elsewhere. Certainly, the traditions about how Jesus taught his followers to react to rejection, namely, to shake the dust off their feet and move on (Mark 6:6–13 and par.), is probably advice that Jesus himself would not only have given but have followed.

Where has this brought the discussion thus far? Jesus seems to have been some sort of prophet with an eschatological message who presented himself somewhat differently in different social settings. The Qumran material may suggest that such an eschatological prophet was also a messianic figure.[25] Jesus' message was in considerable continuity with that of John the Baptist, it would seem, both early and late.

There seems to have been a turning point in Jesus' ministry. Seen and welcomed largely as a healing prophet in Galilee but discovering his kingdom message of repentance and redemption was often unwelcome, he decided not to change his message but to change his audience, leaving Galilee behind. Thereafter he primarily concentrated on oracles of various sorts and prophetic sign acts (although there were some miracles performed), a presentation that would comport with that of southern prophets. But can we be even more specific? It is time to consider the powerful proposal of D. C. Allison.

---

[24] Which seems to confirm Jesus' withdrawing from Galilean crowds, especially when they sought to make him out to be something other than what he believed himself to be.

[25] See pp. 234–37 above.

II. JESUS THE MILLENARIAN APOCALYPTIC PROPHET?

The most recent notable attempt to pin down what sort of prophetic figure Jesus was has come from D. C. Allison, who suggests that Jesus was much as
A. Schweitzer depicted him at the beginning of this century—an apocalyptic or
millenarian prophet believing the end of the world would come at any moment.
It will be helpful to have an extended dialogue with his arguments at this juncture to help us get a clearer picture of what sort of prophet Jesus might have
been. Building on his earlier work, *The End of the Ages Has Come*, Allison has
now produced a more comprehensive proposal that challenges the noneschatological Jesus of Crossan, Borg, Patterson, and Wright while reviving the older
proposal of Schweitzer and J. Weiss. In *Jesus of Nazareth: Millenarian Prophet*,
Allison seeks to read the Jesus tradition with the help of sociological studies of
millenarian sects of various ages and locales.[26]

In one sense, *Jesus of Nazareth* is a prequel to Allison's earlier work, as it
deals with matters methodological and contextual, while also discussing some
particular Gospel texts. Allison opens this recent study by saying that, on the one
hand, if Jesus was indeed an eschatological prophet "who lived in the imaginative world of the apocalypses, we should not expect much consistency from him,
for the essential irrationality of apocalyptic is manifest from the history of messianic and millenarian movements."[27] While I grant that those who write apocalypses manifest considerable struggle in dealing with the apparent contradictions
between life and their faith in God, Jesus' form of public discourse was apparently not the apocalypse or the apocalyptic vision. Thus, the genre of his speech
itself need not lead us to expect the expression of irreconcilable opposites, although one can argue for a considerable degree of paradox in his counterorder
wisdom (first shall be last, least shall be greatest). It is, however, precisely the apparent absence of apocalyptic visions, date setting, apocalyptic mythological
symbols, and the like in the probably authentic Jesus tradition that makes it difficult to prove Jesus was a millenarian prophet of the sort Schweitzer envisioned.

Allison professes misgivings about using the criteria of dissimilarity (do
we really know enough about early Judaism or early Christianity to use it?), coherence (what counts as the core to which the rest coheres?), and embarrassment as ultimate litmus tests of authenticity, but he does affirm that a
judicious use of such criteria is the best hope one has of getting at the authentic
logia of Jesus.[28] The reason for some of his doubts about the criteria seems to
be that he has accepted the argument that there were various early Christian

---

[26] D. C. Allison, *The End of the Ages Has Come* (Philadelphia: Fortress, 1985), did
not receive the full attention it deserved, but now, in the wake of the Third Quest and with
major figures in that quest, such as E. P. Sanders and Meier, already suggesting that Jesus
should be seen as some sort of eschatological prophet, while other major figures are denying that this paradigm works, Allison's new work should become a focus of discussion.

[27] Allison, *Jesus of Nazareth*, 4.

[28] See ibid., 5–8.

prophets speaking words of the risen Jesus that eventually, because of the earliness of such oracles, intermingled with the Jesus tradition at the oral stage and ended up in the Gospels.[29]

Later in this study, there will be an occasion to deal with a rather widespread scholarly assumption about the role of Christian prophets, but for now the following must be stressed: (1) Prophets, to judge from the NT itself, were not a dime a dozen, as some have thought, in the earliest stages of the post-Easter Jesus movement. Indeed, to judge from the books that ended up in the canon itself (none of which are prophetic books or collections of oracles as we find in the OT, with the exception of Revelation), prophets played a secondary role to apostles, teachers, evangelists, elders, and other leader figures in this movement. (2) Even if there were some genuine prophets speaking words of the risen Lord (cf., e.g., John of Patmos in Rev 1–2), sufficient historical evidence is lacking that there was any felt need for, or actual practice of, retrojecting such words into the mouth of the historical Jesus in either Q collections or Gospels.[30] Indeed, words of the risen Lord appear in Paul and in Acts and in Revelation as words of the risen Lord. (3) Even authentic words of prophets in the NT era were not viewed as having the same authority as the words of Jesus or of apostles. In 1 Cor 14 Paul suggests that prophetic words need to be sifted or weighed, and in Rom 12 prophets are exhorted to prophesy according to the measure of their faith. On the one hand, this suggests that such utterances are to stand or fall on their own merit, and on the other hand, it suggests that oration might exceed inspiration, in which case such sayings could never have the same authority as the oracles offered by Jesus or the OT prophets. A plausible social process by which oracles of such prophets might end up as sayings of the historical Jesus has yet to be revealed or even really argued for.[31]

The critique by Allison of Crossan's methodology is telling and deserves an extended treatment, for it helps to demonstrate why the approach Crossan uses to come up with a noneschatological Jesus is deeply flawed.[32] First of all, there is the problem of dividing the Gospel material into four or five strata as if literary archaeology could have the same sort of sure results as archaeology. Allison

---

[29] Ibid., 8–9.

[30] If one points to the prologue of the *Gospel of Thomas* and P.Oxy. 654 ("these are the words which . . . the living Jesus spoke"), one first has to demonstrate that this material is not from the second century, and more important, one must demonstrate that it does not represent an esoteric and eccentric gnostic approach to the Jesus tradition. Probably most NT scholars think there are various features of the *Thomas* tradition that suggest it is not representative of how such material was normally handled or passed on in early Christian circles.

[31] The main concern here is not whether NT prophets' words had authority in early Christianity, for they did, but whether they were equated with the words of Jesus and had the same authority as the latter. In any event the issue concerns placing the words of the exalted Lord on the lips of the pre-Easter Jesus, and the evidence for this is weak at best (see below).

[32] Allison, *Jesus of Nazareth*, 11–39.

rightly asks, What is the justification for sorting our sources into four periods, and why are the time blocks set as they are (why not a line at AD 70 or 100)? As Wright observes, "Crossan's cut-off points for dating are of course arbitrary. The first two strata consist of twenty years each, the third forty, thus enabling him to imply, say, that a document written in 81 belongs with one written in 119 rather than with one written in 79."[33] There is also the problem of critical judgment, as Allison shows.

Crossan stands in a distinct minority of scholars who think that the so-called Cross Gospel (embedded in the *Gospel of Peter*) could provide earlier, more authentic material about Jesus than the canonical Mark. In fact, Crossan would include in his earliest strata of material *Thomas*, the Egerton Gospel, P.Oxy. 1224, the *Gospel of the Hebrews*, the Cross Gospel, the *Gospel of the Egyptians*, and the *Secret Gospel of Mark*. To this suggestion Allison rightly remarks, "It is surely better to be circumspect in this matter and err on the side of caution. If a document can be plausibly dated later rather than earlier, is it not safer, on methodological grounds, to prefer the later date? For this reason many of us would exclude all of Crossan's noncanonical proposals from the first stratum."[34] But even if the material could be included in the first stratum, the real question is not the date of the material but its quality. Indeed, as Allison shows, Crossan himself would seem to agree with this dictum, for while Crossan finds 22 percent of the sayings attested only in L (a third-stratum source) as going back to Jesus, he finds 28 percent of sayings attested only in Q (a first-stratum source) as from Jesus. This is not much of a difference.[35] Thus, while there may be a general plausibility in arguing that the earlier the material, the more likely it may be authentic, even those who most stress this rule do not always follow it.

What, then, of the criteria of multiple independent attestation? It is assumed that something attested only once is less likely to be original. But why should this be? Multiple independent attestation might only demonstrate the wider usefulness of a tradition. But even if one allows that this may be a useful criterion, Crossan himself uses it very inconsistently when it comes to Son of Man material. On the one hand, Crossan finds that there are ten earthly Son of Man complexes, of which only one is multiply attested (Luke 9:58 and par.), yet Crossan thinks five of these complexes are likely authentic. But in the same breath, Crossan finds eighteen apocalyptic Son of Man complexes, of which six are plurally attested and half are from Crossan's earliest-stratum category. Yet he sees none of these as going back to Jesus, at least if the phrase "Son of Man" is involved.[36] Something has gone awry here. As Allison says, this criterion ends up in a tug of war with the criterion of double dissimilarity (at least in regard to continuity between Jesus and his post-Easter followers).[37] He is also able to show

---

[33] Wright, *Jesus and the Victory*, 49 n. 102.

[34] Allison, *Jesus of Nazareth*, 17.

[35] Ibid., 19.

[36] Crossan, *Historical Jesus*, 238–55. Cf. Allison, *Jesus of Nazareth*, 116–19.

[37] Allison, *Jesus of Nazareth*, 20.

that, in Crossan's analysis, "nothing seems to be gained when something is witnessed to three times instead of two, or four times instead of three, or five times instead of four."[38] But if this is the case, then the only thing that multiple attestation seems to mean is that single attestation is a weakness by comparison.

There is a further crucial problem with Crossan's whole approach to multiple attestation, and here is where it most affects the Jesus-as-eschatological-prophet proposal. Crossan limits the use of the concept of multiple attestation to sayings or complexes but does not include key phrases or ideas, such as Son of Man. No particular apocalyptic Son of Man saying has multiple independent attestation, and so Crossan regards them all as secondary. But equally clearly, the phrase "Son of Man" certainly is multiply attested.[39] And one can understand well why individual sayings might not be multiply attested. The concept of the Son of Man was not seen to be useful for early Christian confession. This is demonstrated by the fact that it nowhere appears in Paul, or indeed outside the Gospels, except once in Acts, and even there it is not part of a confession.[40] The phrase, with a Danielic background, was too obscure to be understandable in the larger Greco-Roman world once the Gospel was taken beyond Israel and beyond the synagogue.

It is a revealing exercise to see how Luke, who may be the only Gospel writer writing purely to a Gentile (or Gentiles), handles eschatological matters, and especially eschatological Son of Man sayings. In general, he plays down the future eschatology he found in his sources, and when it comes to sayings about the Son of Man in the future, we discover the following: (1) At the crucial interrogation before the high priest, instead of Mark's climactic "and you will see the Son of Man seated at the right hand . . . and coming with the clouds of heaven" (Mark 14:62), Luke leaves the last clause about the coming Son of Man out altogether and concludes the interrogation with a question about whether Jesus is the Son of God (Luke 22:69–70). (2) Unlike Mark's threefold prediction of the suffering, death, and resurrection of the Son of Man (Mark 8:31; 9:31; 10:33–34), the second occurrence in Luke omits any reference to the future resurrection (although the first occurrence is repeated at Luke 9:22): "The Son of Man is going to be betrayed into human hands" (Luke 9:44). In the final occurrence of the prediction, Luke feels compelled to inform his audience, in a way that Mark does not, that "everything that is written about the Son of Man *by the prophets* will be accomplished" (Luke 18:31; my italics). He assumes that his audience will not know where this phrase comes from unless he tells them.

---

[38] Ibid., 21.

[39] See B. Witherington, *The Jesus Quest* (Downers Grove, Ill.: InterVarsity, 1995), 66–67.

[40] The use of the phrase in Revelation twice is simply in a quote of Dan 7, and the use once in Hebrews is similar. These authors knew well whom the phrase referred to in the synoptic tradition, but they felt compelled to put it back in its original setting if they were to use it at all. This shows the handicap the phrase had in the Greco-Roman world if it was used without its scriptural context.

(3) After the transfiguration story (Mark 9:1–8/Luke 9:28–36) in Mark, we have the order not to tell about the transfiguration until after the rising of the Son of Man, and then there is the discussion between Jesus and the disciples about Elijah and about the Son of Man suffering and being treated with contempt (Mark 9:9–13). Luke omits this discussion altogether. Instead he presents a highly condensed version of Mark's subsequent exorcism story, followed by the second passion prediction. (4) The important passion saying at Mark 10:45 is a Son of Man saying, but in Luke 22:26–27 we have an "I" saying. (5) Again, Mark 14:21b is a Son of Man saying, but Luke drops the phrase in Luke 22:22b.[41] (6) In view of the above, it is likely that when we find the Son of Man phrase in Luke 12:8–9 but not in the Q parallel (Matt 10:32–33), this is because Luke found the phrase in his Q source, not because he introduced it here, transforming an original "I" word.[42]

The upshot of this is twofold: (1) We should be wary of judging the original form of any eschatological saying of Jesus, including the Son of Man sayings in Mark or Q, on the basis of their Lukan presentation. (2) As interested as Luke is in presenting Jesus as a prophet, he seeks to do so in a form that does not emphasize the Son of Man or future eschatology material. In this regard he is rather like Josephus, who avoids referring to the Dan 7 material so that his Gentile audience will not think him a proponent of the notion of a coming Jewish messianic world ruler figure.

One must, in any case, stress with Allison that even if one or another eschatological and/or Son of Man saying does not go back to Jesus, there are far too many eschatological remarks in the synoptic tradition attributed to Jesus—about punishment and reward, resurrection and messianic woes, the latter days and the coming Son of Man, the messianic banquet and coming eschatological catastrophe—to dismiss all of this material.[43] And since nearly all scholars agree that both Jesus' mentor, John the Baptist, and various of Jesus' followers offered eschatological pronouncements, to "reconstruct a Jesus who did not have a strong eschatological orientation entails unexpected discontinuity not only between him and people who took themselves to be furthering his cause but also between him and the Baptist, that is, discontinuity with the movement out of which he came as well as the movement that came out of him."[44] The earliest

---

[41] The one notable place where Luke inserts the phrase "Son of Man" into his Markan source is at Mark 14:45//Luke 22:48. But notice that this is a present Son of man saying—Judas is betraying him now as the Son of man. Luke is happy to talk about Jesus as Son of man during his ministry in the same way he avoids having Jesus called Lord during his ministry in the narrative dialogue. Luke is attempting a historically careful and nuanced presentation of his material. Luke emphasizes the true humanity of Jesus (see the genealogy in Luke 3). He is son of Adam and so Son of Man. The title emphasizes his humanity in Luke's view—it is about his living, his suffering, his dying primarily.

[42] See Allison, *Jesus of Nazareth*, 118.

[43] Ibid., 34.

[44] Ibid., 40.

followers of Jesus were Jews thoroughly grounded in the eschatological hope of early Judaism, which included the notions of judgment and resurrection. It is not surprising they understood the end of Jesus' life and its sequel in light of these categories. It would be surprising if they did not get at least some of this orientation from Jesus himself.

There is a further problem with the noneschatological, non-prophetic Jesus model. As H. Koester has demonstrated, the Roman world itself was increasingly influenced by imperial eschatology. This was a prophetic eschatology that included pronouncement of good news about various emperors.[45] There was also a concern among Romans that a Jewish prophecy about coming Jewish world rulers might come true (cf. Tacitus, *Hist.* 5.13; Suetonius, *Vesp.* 4). To judge from Jewish literary output, many early Jews were caught up in this environment and felt they needed to respond in some way. One such response is seen in the book of Revelation, but we could as readily turn to some of the Jewish *Sibylline Oracles, 4 Ezra, 2 Baruch,* or the *Apocalypse of Abraham* and even some of the Dead Sea Scrolls to show what such folk were thinking during the first century AD.

Josephus tells us how very popular the book of Daniel was in his era, and he feels compelled to use quite a lot of it in his chronicles, damping down current eschatological hopes of a Jewish messianic sort (*Ant.* 10.268). In short, both the larger milieu in which Jesus lived and the more particular milieu associated with the Baptist and Jesus' followers were eschatologically charged. To strip the sayings of Jesus from this literary and historical context is a precarious procedure if one really wants to understand the historical Jesus. "If Jesus was . . . either a violent revolutionary or a secular sage, then the tradition about him is so misleading that we cannot use it for investigation of the pre-Easter period—and so we cannot know that Jesus was either a violent revolutionary or a secular sage."[46]

Allison lists the following items, which frequently recur in the synoptic tradition. These motifs strongly suggest that Jesus was some kind of eschatological prophet who made strong demands and had a strong following: (1) the dominion of God, (2) future reward, (3) future judgment, (4) suffering/persecution of the saints, (5) victory over evil powers, (6) a sense that something new is here or near, (7) the importance of John the Baptist, (8) reference to the Son of Man, (9) God as Father, (10) loving/serving/forgiving others, (11) special regard for the poor and unfortunate, (12) intention as what matters most, (13) hostility to wealth, (14) extraordinary requests/difficult demands, (15) conflict with religious authorities, (16) disciples as students and helpers, (17) Jesus as miracle worker. All of these items are multiply attested.[47] Also multiply attested are certain characteristic speech forms—parables, antithetical parallelism, rhetorical questions, initial amen, use of the divine passive, hyperbole, aphoristic formulation,

---

[45] H. Koester, "Jesus the Victim," *JBL* 111 (1992): 10–11.

[46] Allison, *Jesus of Nazareth,* 45.

[47] Ibid., 46–49.

use of paradox.[48] These last items, however, do not simply point to Jesus as an eschatological prophet; indeed, most of them suggest he was a sage of some sort. This varied and mixed material shows why multiple overlapping complementary paradigms are necessary to explain the historical Jesus. "Prophetic sage" or "apocalyptic prophetic sage" more nearly suggests the hybrid nature of the evidence than just "prophet" or even "eschatological prophet."[49]

Allison's strong case for Jesus being an eschatological prophet does, however, have some difficulties. He maintains that the best way to explain Jesus' use of the Son of Man phrase is to opt either for the old Bultmannian option (Jesus referred to a future redeemer figure other than himself) or for the view that Jesus did not use the phrase exclusively of himself but, rather, inclusively of the saints of the latter days.[50] But the earliest Christian interpreters of this phrase, namely, the Gospel writers, feel free to use this phrase interchangeably with "I" to refer exclusively to Jesus. Furthermore, when the earliest canonical interpreter of the tradition, Paul in 1 Thess 4–5, uses language taken from future Son of Man sayings, he assumes that the reference is clearly to Jesus, as must have those Aramaic-speaking early Christians who prayed *marana tha.*

Allison further argues that in Dan 7 "son of man" refers to the saints of the Most High. This interpretation of Dan 7 is severely problematic in light of the fact that the son of man's counterparts in the previously mentioned beastly empires are the rulers of these empires.[51] It may be added that this is clearly not how the author of *1 Enoch* understood the son of man reference in Daniel, for in that work Enoch is the Son of Man and the faithful as a group are not. An individual is also in view in the Son of Man material in *4 Ezra.* Jesus is seen in the synoptic tradition as the Son of Man who is the representative of God's people, not merely one among their number.

It is also a mixed blessing when Allison tries to compare the Jesus movement to millenarian movements across many centuries and cultures. There are too many variables and differences to make most of these sorts of parallels very helpful or convincing.[52] It is not clear, in the first place, that Jesus was a millenarian prophet, if a prerequisite for that is a belief that the end of the world is necessarily just around the corner. Various of the probably authentic words of

---

[48] Ibid., 49–50.

[49] At one point Allison (ibid., 114) seems to see the force of this thesis, for he notes that subversive wisdom utterances and prophecies about the possibility of imminent judgment could well go together on the lips of Jesus as means of denying the validity of the status quo. On p. 129 he adds, "So why play down one side of the tradition at the expense of the other, or play the sage against the prophet? Should we not rather decide that Jesus was an eschatological prophet who sometimes expressed himself as an aphoristic sage?" Just so, but then why settle for a phrase such as "apocalyptic" or "millenarian prophet" as adequate in itself to describe the historical Jesus?

[50] Ibid., 65–66.

[51] See pp. 199–207 above.

[52] See Allison, *Jesus of Nazareth,* 80–95.

Jesus, including sayings such as Mark 13:32, suggest that Jesus did not go the route of date setting, periodization of history, or offering of a purely interim or utopian ethic. A further weakness of using this model is the assumption that Jesus must be seen as an ascetic, like the Baptist.[53] Some of these criticisms will be unpacked in what follows, but it is important to recognize that this does not constitute a critique of the eschatological prophet paradigm per se—only of the millenarian apocalyptic prophet subset of this larger category.

That Jesus was a sort of eschatological prophet can be confirmed from the fact that Jesus not only chose twelve disciples as his inner circle but predicted that they would play a crucial role at the *eschaton* in relationship to Israel. The case for Jesus choosing the Twelve has been made compelling by Meier.[54] It is difficult to get around the fact that both Paul in 1 Cor 15 and the Gospels know that there was such a group during and even after Jesus' ministry.[55] The Q saying in Luke 22:28–30 and par. indicates that he expects his inner circle to play important roles when the kingdom comes in Israel.[56] This tradition has some confirmation of its authenticity from the independent tradition found in Mark 10:37 and par. Jesus not only spoke of the restoration and judging or ruling of Israel; this tradition implies that Jesus also assumed or taught something positive about the resurrection of the righteous and/or their return to Israel. Here we see how eschatologically focused and prophetic Jesus' teaching was.

Allison also offers a telling critique of the work of S. Patterson, who leans too heavily on the *Gospel of Thomas* in order to build his case for the noneschatological Jesus. Patterson's view overlooks what Koester had already pointed out, namely, that "the *Gospel of Thomas* presupposes, and criticizes, a tradition of the eschatological sayings of Jesus."[57] Allison adds the point that when Mark, Q, M, L, and Paul agree on an apocalyptic tradition or eschatological motif and the only dissenting voices are *Thomas* and possibly the hypothetically reconstructed first stratum of Q, the latter can not outweigh these other sources.[58]

Interestingly, Allison offers a valid critique of his own proposal that Jesus should be viewed with Schweitzerian spectacles when he says, "Although Jesus lived out of an eschatological hope, he was not, all would agree, a cartographer of future states. According to the extant evidence, eschatology was for him not a subject for recondite curiosity but part of his native religious language."[59] But aren't cartography, date setting, specific details about the future, and recondite curiosity about the future precisely what one would expect of an apocalyptic or

---

[53] See ibid., 172–216.

[54] J. Meier, "The Circle of the Twelve: Did It Exist during Jesus' Public Ministry?" *JBL* 116 (1997): 635–72.

[55] This fact must also count against another component of the millenarian prophet paradigm as applied to Jesus—the tendency toward egalitarianism among the followers.

[56] See Witherington, *Christology of Jesus*, 126–30.

[57] Koester, "Jesus the Victim," 7 n. 16.

[58] Allison, *Jesus of Nazareth*, 124–25.

[59] Ibid., 130.

millenarian prophet? They are what one finds in the final form of the book of Daniel and in some of *1 Enoch* and in *4 Ezra* and *2 Baruch*. Would it not be better accordingly to call Jesus an eschatological prophet, since it is agreed that his words do not suggest these sorts of speculative interest? What, then, does Jesus say about such things as final judgment, resurrection, and the like? Consider the following.

The reversal motif is familiar from a variety of the Jesus material: the exalted will be humbled and the humble exalted, the first will be last and the last first, those who try to keep their lives will lose them and vice versa. This material is found in both Q and Mark, as well as elsewhere (Luke 14:11 and par.; Matt 23:12; Luke 18:14; Luke 17:33 and par.; Mark 8:35; 10:31; *Gos. Thom.* 4). Bultmann once said of this sort of material, "Here if anywhere we can find what is characteristic of the preaching of Jesus."[60] The vast majority of scholars agree, but what does this material portend? Notice that the second member of each of these sayings involves a comment about the future—what will be the case at some time later.

As Allison stresses in his discussion of this material, "The sentiments of Q and Mark are implausible as generalizations about experience. Like Lk. 6.20 and 24, which bless the poor and censure the rich, they say that those on top will not be on top forever, and that those on the bottom will not always be on the bottom. . . . What is envisaged is the final judgment, a staple of Jewish eschatology in the Hellenistic period and ever since" (cf. *T. Jud.* 25:4; *b. Pesaḥ* 50a).[61] Allison is also right to add that this material would serve as comfort to the oppressed but as warning, rebuke, or exhortation to the oppressor.[62] Consider, for example, the warning to Chorazin and Bethsaida about their standing on judgment day in comparison with Tyre and Sidon (Luke 10:13–14 and par.) or the warning about blaspheming the Holy Spirit (Mark 3:29; Luke 12:10 and par.).

But for there to be a final judgment of the dead as well as the living, there must be a resurrection, and Jesus refers to such in a saying about the queen of the South rising in judgment to testify against this wicked generation (Luke 11:31–32 and par.).[63] This may be compared not only to the saying about Tyre and Sidon in Luke 10:13–14 and par., but also to the likely authentic material in Mark 12:18–27, where the reality of the resurrection is defended. One may go on to point out a saying such as Luke 14:12–14, which refers to recompense at the resurrection of the righteous (cf. Acts 24:15, and compare the broader concept of resurrection of both the condemned and the righteous in John 5:29).

Equally telling for the case that Jesus had a robust view of the afterlife—an afterlife that included resurrection and then one's eternal destiny—is a saying such as Luke 12:5 and par., which speaks of the destruction of the body in hell.

---

[60] R. Bultmann, *History of the Synoptic Tradition* (New York: Harper, 1963), 105.

[61] Allison, *Jesus of Nazareth*, 133

[62] Ibid., 135.

[63] See B. Witherington, *Women in the Ministry of Jesus* (Cambridge: Cambridge University Press, 1984), 44–45.

As Allison rightly stresses, one must first be raised and have a body before one can be dispatched to hell in a body.[64] This interpretation is confirmed independently by Mark 9:43–48, which speaks of being thrown into hell with a whole body.[65] The roles envisaged for the Twelve at the *eschaton* in Luke 22:28–30 and par., to which we have already referred, also imply, of course, the resurrection of both these twelve and of Israel's tribes. As Allison stresses, this same sort of thing is said about Judah and his brothers in *T. Jud.* 25:1–2 and *T. Benj.* 10:7. Whether a saying such as Luke 13:28–29 has to do with the gathering of dispersed Israel to the messianic banqueting table or of righteous Gentiles who will join the patriarchs there, in either case the scenario is eschatological, and Israel is seen as the center of all this final activity.[66] Allison goes on to demonstrate at length that Jesus also affirmed the coming tribulation or messianic woes that the faithful must prepare to endure.[67] In short, the belief in a coming crisis followed by resurrection and judgment was common in early Judaism, and Jesus shared these beliefs, as did his disciples, some of whom asked for favored spots in the kingdom. The difference between Jesus and others is that, as an eschatological prophet, he believed that the end times were already breaking in during his lifetime.

Allison points to the Q saying in Luke 16:16 and par. to suggest that Jesus believed the messianic woes were already upon God's people. "Eschatological violence is not confined to the future but belongs to the here and now. . . . Jesus did not proclaim that eschatological peace had arrived but rather that the eschatological sword had been drawn."[68] There is, however, a problem with this assessment. Jesus apparently is talking about violence that is happening to the kingdom or to its bearers—John and Jesus himself, and perhaps also to those who are trying to force their way into the kingdom. Wright offers a different plausible reading of this verse: Jesus is referring obliquely to the fact that the Zealots, violent men, are trying to hijack the kingdom of God for their own nationalistic ends.[69] Either of these readings suggests that a very different matter is at issue than the tribulation that will fall on God's people near the end. There is also the further problem that the Markan apocalypse suggests that such messianic woes are still in the future.

Allison then goes on to make the case for Jesus believing not only that eschatological tribulation had already come into the picture but that, in fact, the end, including final judgment, would come in his own time. Sometimes this argument suffers from the usual failure to distinguish between the beginning of the end and the end of the end, between the beginnings of the eschatological age

---

[64] Allison, *Jesus of Nazareth,* 139.

[65] Notice the converse of this, that in the resurrection life, the parts of one's body that have been destroyed during earthly life will be restored (2 Macc 7:10–11).

[66] See Allison, *Jesus of Nazareth,* 143–44.

[67] Ibid., 144–47.

[68] Ibid., 146.

[69] Wright, *Jesus and the Victory,* 468.

and its climax. The language of imminence about the dominion of God does not necessarily tell us anything about the timing of the final judgment and the like, which is to come after the dominion has been established on earth.

It is interesting that Allison fails entirely to see the irony of the imagery Jesus uses in his parables about sowing and the harvest (cf. Mark 4:2–9; *Gos. Thom.* 9; Mark 4:26–29; Matt 13:24–30; *Gos. Thom.* 37). He is quite right that images of threshing, winnowing, and harvesting regularly occur in Jewish prophecies about coming judgment and eschatological consummation. We see this not only in apocalyptic contexts such as *4 Ezra* 4:30–39 but also on the lips of the Baptist (Luke 3:17 and par.). But Jesus uses these images to talk about redemption or the rescuing of God's people. He uses them to talk about a harvest of wheat, not a harvest of chaff fit to be burned. Using these images, Jesus proclaimed the dawn of the good news about this radical rescue. In short, he turns the images on their heads.[70]

This confusion is compounded when Allison takes Mark 9:1 to refer to the end of the world.[71] What this text says is that some of Jesus' immediate audience will live to see the kingdom come with power. Mark himself seems to see this as a reference to the transfiguration, which he recounts next and which is presented as a resurrection or Parousia preview. It may have originally been a reference to the coming vindication beyond death that Jesus expected in Jerusalem. In any event, it is not about the final judgment or the end of the world.

Nor, for that matter, should Mark 13:30 be read in this fashion. Here Jesus is referring to the traumatic events that will lead up to the destruction of the temple. The temple destruction is presented as the end of *a* world, the world of early Judaism, but not the end of the world. If indeed Mark 13:30 goes back to Jesus, then this is a remarkable prophetic utterance that was fulfilled not during Jesus' lifetime but in the events that led up to AD 70. The amalgamation of these predictions with the Mark 13 references to what will happen at some unspecified time (see Mark 13:32) *after those days* when the Son of Man comes is a mistake. Like many prophetic figures, Jesus, or at least Mark, juxtaposes events from the nearer and further horizons, not least because he believes the eschatological age, the coming of the kingdom, has already begun. Nor will it do to suggest that Mark 13:30 is just a variant of Mark 9:1 and Matt 10:23. The focus of each of these is different unless one strips them of their context, in which case one can make them mean most anything.

Matthew 13:30 says that there are plenty of places for the disciples to flee to, as cities of refuge, just in Israel, indeed enough to last "until the Son of Man comes." This could be a reference to Jesus coming to help them during the ministry, for there is no reference here to coming with angels or coming on clouds

---

[70] See Allison, *Jesus of Nazareth*, 148. He is, however, clearly right to stress that the imminence or presence of the kingdom is talked about in terms of its advent or arrival, not in terms of its having always been there. In other words, the kingdom language can not be "de-eschatologized," despite the best efforts of Crossan, Borg, and Funk.

[71] Ibid., 149.

and, furthermore, there are plenty of "coming" sayings that refer to Jesus' earthly ministry (cf. Matt 11:19; Luke 7:34). Another good possibility is raised by S. McKnight in an extensive source- and redaction-critical investigation of Matt 13:30. He concludes that Matt 13:30's original setting is with the sort of material we find in Mark 13, which means that it is referring to what will be the case during the final intense persecution before the Parousia.[72] Even if this is not correct, no timetable is set up here for when the Son will come. The focus is not on eschatological speculation but on survival strategies and on suggesting that the disciples will always have a place to go when they are persecuted.

It is odd that Allison should be so adamant about a Schweitzerian interpretation of Matt 13:30, for two reasons. First, Schweitzer thought that Jesus said this but realized his error and so went to Jerusalem to set the end in motion, presumably by sacrificing himself. It is difficult to imagine Matthew's community in the last third of the first century thinking that Jesus had said the Parousia would come within the first generation. The presence of this saying in a Gospel written AD 80 or later suggests that the saying was not understood by the earliest Christians in the way Schweitzer thought. Second, in his earlier work Allison stressed that "the seeming contradiction between the presence of the kingdom of God and its futurity is dissolved when one realizes that Jewish thinking could envision the final events—the judgment of evil and the arrival of the kingdom of God—as extending over time, and as a process or series of events that could involve the present" (cf. *Jub.* 23; *1 En.* 91:12–17; 93).[73] This is true, but it means that the language of imminence about the kingdom does need to refer to the imminence of the whole eschatological scenario.

In large part because Allison thinks Jesus did see all the eschatological events as clustered together on the near horizon, he takes up the Schweitzerian argument that Jesus thus offered an interim ethic, and as it turns out, Allison thinks it is an ascetical one like the Baptist's. Allison shows at some length that millenarian sects often do have a tendency toward asceticism, but "often" does not mean "always" (e.g., the Jehovah's Witnesses are not ascetical), and thus one would have to demonstrate this was the case with Jesus and his movement.

Allison begins his argument by trying to discredit the usual conclusions drawn from the Q saying in Luke 7:31–35 and par. This saying suggests that Jesus ate and drank with various people, including sinners and tax collectors. He makes the valid point that the charge that Jesus was a glutton and a drunkard (v. 34b) probably reflects the polemical exaggerations of his opponents.[74] This is fair enough, but what can not be denied is that Jesus ate and drank with a variety of people, including the ritually and morally unclean—sinners and tax collectors. This notion is found independently in Mark 2:15–17 and par. and in the L material in Luke 19:1–10. In addition, one must take into account the material

---

[72] S. McKnight, "Jesus and the Endtime: Matthew 10.23," *SBL Seminar Papers, 1986* (Atlanta: Scholars Press, 1986), 501–20.

[73] Allison, *The End,* 105.

[74] Allison, *Jesus of Nazareth,* 173.

in Mark 7 and elsewhere that suggests that Jesus, at a minimum, was not observant of various rules about ritual purity and, at a maximum, thought such purity rules had been abrogated with the coming of the dominion of God. Thus, while "life of the party" may be an exaggerated way to describe Jesus' lifestyle, so would "ascetic," to judge from this material.

It is true that a text such as Mark 2:18–20 is not a blanket prohibition of all fasting under any circumstances. The issue is whether Jesus' life was regularly *characterized* by fasting rather than feasting. There is no positive evidence to suggest such a thing, although we may suspect that the temptation story is grounded in history enough to suggest that once in a while Jesus himself did fast. It is interesting that the two places where there is a suggestion that Jesus fasted both have to do with times of crisis at the beginning and at the end of Jesus' ministry (compare Luke 4 and par. with Mark 14:25). This is something different from even the suggestion that Jesus regularly observed the weekly Jewish fasts, which no Gospel text indicates.

Most importantly, Jesus distinguishes his ministry from that of the Baptist in regard to the issue of lifestyle—the Baptist's ascetical style was like the behavior of those who are in mourning, while Jesus' style was like those who are celebrating, complete with music for dancing (Luke 7:32 and par.). This chosen course of life has independent confirmation not only in the Zacchaeus story (Luke 19), or the Simon the Pharisee story (Luke 7), or the Mary and Martha story (Luke 10), but also independently in the Johannine tradition in John 2. The evidence is too widespread to ignore or dismiss.

Consider next the notion that Jesus and his disciples, while on the road, committed themselves to poverty and asceticism.[75] There are several serious problems with this conclusion. First, the disciples could have gotten to almost anywhere in lower Galilee and back again to Capernaum in a day or two. There is no reason to envision them spending weeks on the road without provisions. Furthermore, we are told that when they traveled, they were supported—by women (Luke 8:1–3)! Whether this means that they were financially supported by them or that material provisions such as food were given, in either case this must count strongly against seeing the first disciples as wandering mendicants or medieval Franciscan friars. Third, the mission charge of Jesus to his disciples calls upon them not to go hungry but, to the contrary, to rely on the system of standing ancient Near Eastern hospitality in whatever town they visit (Mark 6:10–13 and par.). Indeed, his instructions are to stay in the first home they are guests in until they leave. This is likely because Jesus does not envision them staying long periods in a town and, more important, does not want them to shame their host by moving on to someone else's house.

What about sexual asceticism? Allison bases much on his reading of Matt 19:10–12.[76] These verses do likely teach that sexual activity is not necessary for all, although it is unlikely that Jesus is simply referring to literal eunuchs. But

---

[75] Ibid., 174ff.
[76] Ibid., 175–76.

what Allison fails to say is that Jesus also, and in this same context, manifests a robust theology of the goodness of marriage and the one-flesh union. Indeed, the text suggests that the eunuch option is offered by Jesus to those who find it impossible to confine themselves to one wife for life. In short, Jesus is providing an early version of the dictum of complete fidelity in marriage and of celibacy in singleness. This is hardly asceticism; rather, it is a carefully refined and defined sexual ethic. His teaching on lust simply reinforces this ethic (Matt 5:27–28). Jesus rejects the early Jewish notion that the mandate to marry and procreate is incumbent on all persons,[77] but he in no way rejects either the goodness of marriage or of sexual sharing within marriage. What is radical about Jesus' teaching is his argument for the viability of singleness as a legitimate life calling.

Allison tries, then, to use the argument about levirate marriage in Mark 12:18–27 to maintain that Jesus believed there would be no sex or marriage in the kingdom of God but, rather, people would be like the angels.[78] In the first place, the discussion is about levirate marriage, not all marriages, and in a deathless state there would be no more point to levirate marriage. Levirate marriage is unlike regular marriage because it only exists because of death: the obligation to raise up an heir for a deceased brother was felt to require such an institution. Furthermore, Jesus does not say there will be no more state of marriage in the kingdom; he says there will be no more new acts of marrying—no marrying (the male's role in a patriarchal situation) or being given in marriage (the bride's role). To this one may add that early Jews did not generally think that angels were sexless creatures (cf. *2 Bar.* 56:14).[79] There is thus nothing in Mark 12 to support the notion that Jesus saw marriage as ceasing in the resurrection. What Jesus taught was that there would be no more change of status in the resurrection. Thus, while one may agree with Allison's urging that the texts just discussed do likely go back to Jesus in some form, they do not indicate what Allison has argued they do.[80]

Finally, Allison also maintains that Jesus' radical teaching about, and hostility to, money reflects an ascetical mentality. To this one must say the following: (1) The story of the rich young ruler can not be globalized as if it reflected Jesus' entire view of money. The Zaccheus story and the stories about Jesus, Mary, and Martha (Luke 10; John 11) show Jesus did not require such total renunciation of money, houses, and land in every case or even perhaps in the majority of cases. (2) Jesus commends a widow for self-sacrificial giving of all her coins (Mark 12:41–44). But to whom is he commending this example? To the disciples surely, in which case Jesus must assume that they also have something to sacrifice so that they could follow this example, even if they are relatively or even extremely poor as the woman was. This, in turn, means that even the inner circle of the Twelve

---

[77] See Witherington, *Women in the Ministry of Jesus,* 32–35.

[78] Allison, *Jesus of Nazareth,* 177–78; contrast Witherington, *Women in the Ministry of Jesus,* 32–34.

[79] See pp. ix–xii above.

[80] See Allison, *Jesus of Nazareth,* 182ff.

likely had not permanently sacrificed everything. (3) Jesus allows the paying of taxes to Caesar (Mark 12:13–17). Again, one must ask, for whom is this teaching? In this case, the teaching is apparently not for the disciples originally, but the fact that it is included in Mark's Gospel means Mark thinks it is appropriate to be applied to them. But again, one must have assets to pay taxes. (4) The attempt to suggest that the earliest Jewish Christian community reflected an ethic of total poverty and renunciation of possessions, based in their memory of Jesus' ethic, is simply false. The earliest Christians seem to have affirmed a theology of both stewardship and no exclusive right to property so that there would be no one among them in need, and all must be prepared to share to meet needs. The contrasting stories of Ananias and Sapphira, on the one hand, and Barnabas, on the other, in Acts 4:32–5:11 show that the former were not condemned for not giving all but for lying about what they gave, and the latter was commended for selling a piece of land and giving the proceeds. Nothing is said about Barnabas liquidating all his assets.[81] It is true that Jesus rightly contrasts the serving of God and money, with the emphasis on serving rather than having or using. It is also true that Jesus makes abundantly clear how hard it is for a rich person to enter the kingdom of God, although he does not suggest it is impossible.

In this material, as in his sexual ethic, Jesus indicates that self-sacrificial service of others is what it is all about. Such an ethic can be called a service-driven ethic, but it does not appear to be a utopian interim ethic, much less an ascetical one of total renunciation of the world. Nonetheless, texts such as Mark 9:42–48 do show where Jesus' priorities lie. It is far better to lose even major body parts than to fail to enter God's kingdom because of the indulging of various lusts.[82] Renunciation as a last resort so that one does not miss the kingdom is hardly a call to asceticism as a first resort, or a viewing of asceticism as the highest and best for all Jesus' followers. It is precisely the fact that Jesus does *not* universalize the eunuch teaching or the renunciation-of-money teaching or the teaching on the renunciation of homes and businesses and families that makes clear he is not instituting some utopian interim ethic, imposed on all regardless of their makeup or circumstances. Had Jesus really believed that the end of the world was necessarily right around the corner, perhaps he might have urged such a complete renunciation of human social institutions by all his followers for the sake of a time of fasting, repentance, and prayer. But we find no such universal pronouncements, and this in itself calls into question not only the notion that Jesus was an ascetic seeking only ascetical followers but also the eschatological premise behind such a notion—the belief that Jesus proclaimed the end of the world in his age.[83]

---

[81] See B. Witherington, *The Acts of the Apostles* (Grand Rapids: Eerdmans, 1997), 213–20.

[82] On the literalness of this text, see Witherington, *Women in the Ministry of Jesus*, 19–20.

[83] It is interesting to reflect on what is found a Qumran. Notice that even though there were surely those who believed that the end was near, they did not call for the renunciation of all things by all their adherents.

One final telltale sign that Jesus was *not* cultivating in the wilderness near the Jordan a small group of itinerant male celibates who had renounced all things is the presence of women among his traveling companions (Luke 8:1–3) and indeed among his disciples in general (Luke 10).[84] The presence of women at all as disciples, never mind as his traveling disciples, would have sent just the opposite signal to Jesus' culture—that, far from being ascetical, Jesus' sexual ethic was likely too liberal! This, coupled with Jesus' willingness to have contact with prostitutes and other unclean women and even to allow them to touch him (see Luke 7:36–50; Mark 5:24–34), would have made it impossible for Jesus to assert an ascetical ethic and be believed by friends or foes, much less gain adherents. The case for Jesus as an ascetical millenarian prophet, then, must be said to fail to pass muster. One must look elsewhere to get greater precision on the sort of prophet Jesus was. Nonetheless, Allison has advanced the discussion because he has shown that the noneschatological interpretation of Jesus and his ministry also will not do.

III. JESUS THE PROPHET OF REALIZED ESCHATOLOGY?

In his underappreciated study on Jesus' aims, B. F. Meyer draws the following conclusions about the nature of prophecy:

> To judge . . . from the whole biblical tradition, it belongs essentially to the phenomenon of prophecy that the message be expressed in symbols. . . . In prophecy what the symbol intends is identical with what God, for whom the prophet speaks, intends. This may enter the prophet's own horizon only partially and imperfectly. If the question "Was Jesus mistaken about the future?" is accordingly recast, it may be put this way: "Did Jesus have determinate knowledge of what God intended by the symbolic scheme of things which Jesus himself was commissioned to announce?" The answer, again, would seem to be no. Prophetic knowledge thus appears as limited knowledge. . . . It is a mistake to conceive of prophetic knowledge . . . as if prophetic knowledge were a kind of empirical-knowledge-by-anticipation but with symbolic frills and trimmings. We should not imagine that any prophet ever had before his inner eye the kind of scenario that history, on cue and according to schedule, might literally follow.[85]

In short, Meyer conceives of a prophet as being rather like the blind man who was healed by Jesus in two stages in Mark 8:22–26. Only the prophet would have achieved a vision about the future equivalent to what that man gained in the first stage of healing (Mark 8:24). He saw reality, but not with complete clarity of detail. There is likely some truth to this claim, but generally speaking, prophets were more specific about events on the near horizon, and when they spoke of more distant things, the descriptions tended, not surprisingly, to be more generalized. Meyer, however, is claiming that prophecy, though by nature

---

[84] See Allison, *Jesus of Nazareth*, 203, for this suggestion.
[85] B. F. Meyer, *The Aims of Jesus* (London: SCM, 1979), 246.

symbolic in character, does not merely contain symbols, apocalyptic or otherwise. It has a built-in indeterminacy or inexactness. If this is true, then many
today, ranging from fundamentalists to Schweitzerian scholars, have badly misunderstood the character of prophecy, including Jesus' prophecy, and apocalyptic even more, especially its periodization and the function of the numbers and
dates within it.[86]

Thus, while there is some justice to Meyer's claim, especially when it
comes to apocalyptic's dealing with the endgame, the question then becomes, Is
indeterminancy also really true about prophecy in a more classic form about the
near or far horizon that does not have an apocalyptic or visionary form? Should
we, for example, not take rather literally Jesus' talk about the coming destruction
of the temple, or the resurrection of the dead, or the persecution of the saints, or
the return of the Son of Man on the clouds, or the like? Responding with a re-
sounding no seems to be the heart of the case that Wright wants to make, having
been influenced by Dodd and G. B. Caird and others about the metaphorical
character of much eschatological language.[87]

It is a mistake to equate all prophecy with apocalyptic visions or to conclude that just because prophecy takes a poetic form, it must not ever be taken
to have a significant quotient of literal content. I agree with Allison that the ideas
of the final judgment, the resurrection of the dead, the suffering or tribulation of
God's people, the restoration of Israel, and various other eschatological ideas are
found both within and outside apocalyptic literature and should not be labeled
apocalyptic symbols simply because they sometimes show up in apocalypses.
Nor should the notion of the kingdom of God be seen as a description of heavenly existence rather than of God's saving activity in space and time. In fact, one
should not even assume that apocalyptic language had no historical referents.

Some time ago W. D. Davies warned, "Much modern discussion of the
meaning of apocalyptic language which overmuch spiritualizes it must be regarded as misguided. For example, to understand the term 'kingdom of God' as
used in early Christianity, as nonpolitical and nonterrestial, is unjustifiable, if it
be taken to have been so universally. . . . There was a literal dimension to apoca-

---

[86] One could envision an argument that maintained that the dates in apocalyptic,
for example, simply serve the purpose of indicating that God was in control and had set a
definite limit to the time evil would prevail or justice would be delayed. It wasn't about calculation but about consolation. See pp. 192–205 above.

[87] G. B. Caird, *The Language and Imagery of the Bible* (Philadelphia: Westminster,
1980), 243–71. Caird's argument is a bit more nuanced. He maintained that although the
biblical writers believed the world would literally come to an end someday, they nonetheless often used end-of-the-world language to refer to a crisis even they knew was not the
end of the world. He then says that the Gospel passages that have been assumed to speak of
the end's imminence have a metaphorical sense. Perhaps these passages do refer to imminence, but there is an indeterminacy not about all the events but about the chronological
links between the nearer and further events. The prophets reckoned with the possible imminence of it all but offered chronological and descriptive precision only about things on
the more immediate horizon.

lyptic language which must not be evaded."[88] Nevertheless, apocalyptic visions contain far more symbolic language and images than do ordinary eschatological prophecies, and it is largely the latter we find on the lips of Jesus. It is time to look at Wright's arguments at some length.

First of all, Wright does not argue, as do M. Borg or R. Funk, for a noneschatological Jesus. Most of his most recent detailed Jesus study focuses on Jesus as an eschatological prophet.[89] He says that Jesus "was announcing a prophetic message after the manner of the 'oracular' prophets, and that he was inaugurating a renewal movement after the manner of 'leadership' prophets."[90] He adds,

> Jesus adopts the style of, and consciously seems to imitate, Elijah. . . . It is clear from all three synoptics that they . . . regarded John the Baptist as in some sense Elijah *redivivus*. [But they] nevertheless portray Jesus as acting in Elijah-like ways, and show that the disciples were thinking of Elijah-typology as giving them a blueprint for his, and their own, activity. Jesus himself, explaining the nature of his work, is portrayed using both Elijah and Elisha as models.[91]

Wright insists that Jesus was "a prophet of the eschaton . . . [who] summoned Israel to a once-for-all national repentance, such as would be necessary for the exile to end at last. This was not simply the 'repentance' that any human being, any Jew, might use if, aware of sin, they decided to say sorry and make amends. It is the single great repentance which would characterize the true people of YHWH at the moment when their god became king."[92]

Wright goes on to say that, as an eschatological prophet announcing the in-breaking of God's kingdom (God becoming king), Jesus saw various of the major symbols of Israel as being not shoddy or wicked but obsolete.[93] This does not mean for Wright that Jesus spoke only in a realized eschatological mode, as if everything were already happening during Jesus ministry. No, Wright allows that Jesus predicted what would transpire during the coming generation (forty years or so) but did not speak beyond that horizon. Jesus speaks of the end of the world of early Judaism. This end was caused by the disaster in AD 70 when the Romans destroyed the temple and, in due course, banned Jews from entering, much less reconstructing, the city and its temple. Jesus does not speak of the END of the world writ large, much less the end of the space-time continuum. Once more let Wright speak for himself:

> As a prophet, Jesus staked his reputation on his prediction of the Temple's fall within a generation; if and when it fell, he would thereby be vindicated. As the kingdom-bearer, he had constantly been acting . . . in a way which invited the

---

[88] W. D. Davies, *Jewish and Pauline Studies* (Philadelphia: Fortress, 1984), 267.
[89] Wright, *Jesus and the Victory*, 147–474.
[90] Ibid., 163.
[91] Ibid., 167.
[92] Ibid., 251.
[93] Ibid., 400.

conclusion that he thought he had a right to do and be what the Temple was and did, thereby implicitly making the Temple redundant. The story he had been telling, and by which he ordered his life, demanded a particular ending. If, then, the Temple remained for ever, and his movement fizzled out . . . he would be shown to have been a charlatan, a false prophet, maybe even a blasphemer. But if the Temple was to be destroyed and the sacrifices stopped; if the pagan hordes were to tear it down stone by stone; and if his followers did escape from the conflagration unharmed, in a re-enactment of Israel's escape from their exile in doomed Babylon—why, then he would be vindicated, not only as a prophet, but as Israel's representative, as (in some sense) the "son of man."[94]

What this means for Wright is that the discussions in Mark 13 and elsewhere about the coming of the Son of Man on the clouds and the other events that have normally been taken to be events that would follow the destruction of the temple have been collapsed into being fulfilled in AD 70 in some sense. The destruction of the temple is the vindication of Jesus, which is spoken of metaphorically as his coming on the clouds as the Son of Man for judgment. This is an interesting argument, not least because of what it wants to maintain. Wright argues not merely that there is a largely metaphorical or even indeterminate content to Jesus' future prophecies (see Meyer above, this chapter) but that while one must take Jesus' prediction of the destruction of the temple more literally, the description of the events said to transpire after that in Mark 13 must be taken purely figuratively. Or to put it another way, one can take them as alternate metaphorical descriptions of the meaning of the destruction of the temple for an early Jew. It would be a catastrophic and earth-shattering event, and the end of an early Jewish world, without being the end of the world. Before focusing on Wright's understanding of eschatology and metaphorical language, some of the broader contours of his case need to be brought into the picture.

Wright makes some astute observations about the relationship of parable and allegory. He argues correctly that a hard and fast distinction can not be made between the two, but he also asserts that the world of apocalyptic provides the closest parallel to the parables.[95] He claims that "the most immediate literary background to the parables is that of apocalyptic. . . . Like the apocalyptic genre to which they belong, [they are] subversive stories, told to articulate and bring to birth a new way of being the people of God."[96] If he means no more than that they both are forms of figurative language, this is not very informative. But in fact, parables existed before there ever were any apocalyptic visions or literature. The parable of the ewe lamb by Nathan[97] reflects no apocalyptic traits nor any eschatological language. Narrative parables are a sapiential form of literature. We should not be misled by the fact that the term *meshalim* is used in *1 Enoch* to refer to the apocalyptic material there, for all

---

[94] Ibid., 362.
[95] Ibid., 177.
[96] Ibid., 181.
[97] See pp. 75–79 above.

that is meant is that it is metaphorical or figurative language. This does not mean that we find narrative parables in *1 Enoch* that could be compared to the parables of Jesus.

In the second place, Jesus' parables are not visionary in character, nor do they generally involve descriptions, much less tours, of the otherworld (the parable of the Rich Man and Lazarus is an exception). They are not a regular part of prophetic experience as apocalyptic visions are. The most that one could say is that parables, which are a sapiential form of discourse, were occasionally used by prophets before the time of Jesus, and even used by prophets, such as Ezekiel, who also had apocalyptic visions. To judge from Jesus' own era, they were more characteristic of sages or hasidim than of prophets.[98]

The message of Jesus in the parables is about God's divine saving and judging activity in Israel during and after the ministry of Jesus. That it has an eschatological content, as apocalyptic often does, is neither here nor there because both narrative parables and apocalyptic material exist without eschatological content.[99] That both parables and apocalyptic can be cryptic and can be used to undermine the dominant culture's paradigms is true, but they are cryptic for different reasons. About narrative parables, one asks primarily what the story means, what is its major thrust. About apocalyptic visions, one asks primarily what the symbols represent. There is, however, this in common between parables and apocalyptic visions: they both, on occasion, tell us something about events looming on the horizon or even at the end of history. Yet it would be a category mistake to see them both as part of one genre of material. Wisdom literature is a product of reflection on, and insight into, reality. Apocalyptic is a revelatory genre.

Yet it is worth pondering whether Jesus consciously chose to couch his teaching in the form of parables and aphorisms so as to appear somewhat less cryptic than an apocalyptic seer. Wright suggests that Jesus' parables rework, reappropriate, and redirect Israel's prophetic and apocalyptic traditions.[100] One can make a case for the reuse of prophetic ideas (Israel as a vineyard, etc.), but apocalyptic images and symbols seem to be generally lacking in Jesus' parables. Nor do his parables appear to be interpretations of visions or dreams; they are, rather, interpretations of prophetic and eschatological ideas about God's saving and judging activities.[101]

The most important observations that distinguish Wright's approach to Jesus as an eschatological prophet from that of others begin to occur about

---

[98] See Witherington, *Jesus the Sage,* 117ff.

[99] No one is talking about ex eventu parables either.

[100] Wright, *Jesus and the Victory,* 180.

[101] It is surely a mistake to follow John Drury, *The Parables in the Gospels* (London: SPCK, 1985), at this point, who wants to lump together parables and apocalyptic visions of the sort we find in Dan 7 and Zechariah. Apocalyptic visions are not allegories with odd imagery, but clearly some parables are allegorical in character, as is true in Ezek 17.

halfway through his treatment of the subject.[102] Wright stresses that Jesus' Jewish contemporaries who were looking for a great event to happen in the near future to and for Israel were not looking for a "cosmic meltdown" or the end of the space-time continuum.[103] This observation, while largely correct in itself, is then parlayed into a theory of eschatological language that suggests that it is simply figurative language always meant to talk about a significant crisis within human history, although it was fully expected that history would go on. If some of Jesus' disciples then took him too literally about the coming of the Son of Man on the clouds, or the future resurrection of the dead, or the Twelve sitting on thrones judging Israel, this was a result of their muddled thinking.[104]

To be absolutely fair, Wright insists that he, following Caird, is not saying that this language Jesus was using was merely metaphorical or nonreferential but that it refers to events within history, not events that end history. Wright categorizes his own view of eschatology as language about "the climax of Israel's history, involving events for which end-of-the-world language is the only set of metaphors adequate to express the significance of what will happen, but resulting in a new and quite different phase *within . . .* history."[105]

Yet it is odd that just when one thinks one has understood Wright's view, he proceeds to say that the present kingdom is the firstfruits of the future kingdom (having just discussed 1 Cor 15) and then he proceeds to say that the future kingdom involves "the abolition, not of space, time, or the cosmos itself, but rather of that which threatened space, time, and creation, namely, sin and death"[106] Yet surely Wright does not think that this outcome transpired when the temple was destroyed in AD 70, or does he? At another juncture in the argument, he refers to Jesus' welcoming of the poor and the outcast as a sign of the real return from exile, the new age: "The 'resurrection', was coming into being; and if the new age was dawning, those who wanted to belong to it would . . . have to repent."[107] The crucial question to be asked, which is not adequately answered, is, What does Wright think the earliest Christians thought would happen after the destruction of the temple? Indeed, what did the early Gospel writers, writing after AD 70, think still lay in their future when they included discussion about the resurrection of the dead, judgment day, the coming of the Son of Man, and the like? Did they think they were living in a posteschatological era, a post-Parousia era?

Wright goes on to stress that the early Christians reappropriated and reused early Jewish apocalyptic and eschatological language to interpret the death and resurrection of Jesus and the sending of the Spirit. In doing so, "they expressed their belief that the decisive 'end' for which Israel had longed *had al-*

---

[102] Wright, *Jesus and the Victory*, 207ff.

[103] Ibid., 207.

[104] See ibid., 207–29.

[105] Ibid., 208.

[106] Ibid., 218.

[107] Ibid., 255.

ready happened, and that the consummation for which they still waited was simply the final outworking of that now-past event."[108] This is true enough, but the question is, In what does this consummation consist? In view of the fact that language about the future coming Son of Man draws on the *Yom Yahweh* language about last judgment, when God will come and judge in person, it is difficult to doubt that something more final than the destruction of the Jerusalem temple was in mind when this language was used by Jesus. As C. S. Lewis said, when the author steps on the stage, then the play is truly over. It does not continue thereafter in the fashion it was going before.

Wright quite properly makes much of Jesus' kingdom teaching and preaching as eschatological in character and therefore having the implicit claim that Jesus himself was bringing Israel's history to a climax. Further, like the Baptist, he was offering eschatological forgiveness outside the structure of the temple apparatus.[109] "Jesus was replacing adherence or allegiance to Temple and Torah with allegiance to himself. Restoration and purity were to be had, not through the usual channels, but through Jesus."[110] It is here that the term "eschatological prophet" does not fully capture the significance of what Jesus was doing. "Leadership prophet" or "messianic prophet" comes closer at this juncture.

The messianic-prophet suggestion is given further plausibility when we reflect on Jesus' radical use of family language. In texts such as Mark 3:31–35 and par., we find Jesus redefining the family as those who are his disciples, those who do the will of God. "In a peasant society, where familial relations provided one's basis identity, [such talk] was shocking in the extreme. In first-century Jewish culture, for which the sense of familial and racial loyalty was a basic symbol of the prevailing worldview, it cannot but have been devastating."[111] Wright does not water down the radical nature of some of Jesus' claims just because he does not think he spoke of the end of the world. In other words, he does not think a radical ethic need be an interim ethic, meant for the short time remaining, and on this point I must agree.

It becomes clearer how Wright reads Jesus' eschatological language when he begins to deal with the Markan apocalypse (Mark 13). Here he quotes Caird approvingly that Dan 7 is not referring to a primitive form of space travel but, rather, is presenting a symbol of the great reversal of Israel's fortunes within history. The prediction about the Son of Man answers the question, When will the temple fall?[112] Then Jesus will come to Jerusalem as vindicated prophet and king: "The temple's destruction would constitute his

---

[108] Ibid., 322.

[109] Ibid., 272.

[110] Ibid., 274. It is Wright's view that Jesus did indeed perform a symbolic act in the temple and that it was a sign of coming judgment on that establishment. In this Jesus was claiming prophetic and messianic authority to pronounce judgment on the temple, which eventually led to his demise.

[111] Ibid., 278.

[112] Ibid., 341.

own vindication."[113] If this is indeed what Jesus meant by the coming of the Son of Man, one wonders how Paul so misunderstood it, as 1 Thess 4–5 must suggest that he did. One also wonders why, outside the Gospels, the NT is so eerily silent about the fall of the temple if it was such an important event for understanding matters christological.

But Wright's interpretation, whatever its merits in general, must be said not to be Mark's own interpretation. For, on the one hand, Mark insists that the coming of the Son of Man will happen only after the tribulation and after the abomination of desolation (see Mark 13:24—"after that suffering"); and further-more, Mark says that the temple will fall within a generation, but of the second coming he says all must be alert, since no one knows the timing, not even the Son of man (cf. vv. 32–34). The problem with seeing Jesus as simply inaugurat-ing the age of fulfillment is that Jesus seems to have thought it was also the age when further prediction was required, prediction even unto the ends of the ages.[114]

Wright, in order to make his case about Mark 13, is prepared to cite R. Horsley, whom he otherwise strongly criticizes for de-theologizing the mean-ing of Jesus' pronouncements and especially his kingdom language. He quotes Horsley approvingly as follows:

> The language of the end refers not to the end of history or of creation but to the reso-lution of the historical crisis. . . . What earlier biblical scholarship labeled as expecta-tions of "cosmic catastrophe" typical of Jewish apocalypticism would be called, in ordinary contemporary language, eager hopes for anti-imperial revolution to be ef-fected by God. . . . Jesus' proclamation . . . far from being an expectation of an im-minent cosmic catastrophe . . . was the conviction that God was now driving the satan from control over personal and historical life, making possible the renewal of the people of Israel. The presence of the kingdom of God meant the termination of the old order.[115]

This just proves that reductionistic eschatologies create strange bedfellows.

At the end of the day, the problem with Wright's proposal is not so much that he wants to read some of Jesus' eschatological remarks in a nuanced rather than a crassly literal fashion. It is true that poetical and parabolic speech does often occur in prophetic discourses. The problem lies primarily in what he wants

---

[113] Ibid., 342.

[114] In perhaps the clearest summary of Wright's view of Mark 13 (ibid., 361), he argues that it is crass literalism to take the references to falling stars and a descending Son of Man to mean future cosmic events. He adds that the Son of Man does not appear as a superhuman figure in Daniel or in Mark 13. He is wrong about Daniel—in that text, no human figure can rule as long as the Son of Man is said to rule. And God would turn over to no merely human figure the job of final judgment and the discerning of all hearts. And finally, Dan 7 is about a descent of the Son of Man, not an ascent. Cf. pp. 197–210 above.

[115] R. Horsley, *Jesus and the Spiral of Violence* (New York: Crossroad, 1987), 157–60; cited by Wright, *Jesus and the Victory*, 449.

these symbols or metaphors or images or phrases to refer to, for he is not arguing for a nonreferential use of the language. He is arguing for an interpretation that neither Paul nor other early Christians seem to have accepted of the coming of the Son of Man and other eschatological events.[116] There is also a problem with the confusion of apocalyptic, prophetic, and the parabolic, from a form-critical point of view.

Nevertheless, there is a wealth of valuable material in Wright's study, and he has gone some considerable way in delineating what Jesus as an eschatological prophet might look like, so long as he is dealing with the realized eschatological side of the equation. Ironically, he is also right that the end of the space-time continuum is never contemplated in the NT. But a drastic transformation of creatures and creation at the return of Christ is contemplated, not merely a major historical crisis surrounding the fall of the temple. The question is whether there is a way to construe Jesus as an eschatological prophet without making the errors of either Schweitzer, reducing Jesus to an end-time fanatic who was convinced he knew exactly when the end would come, or of Caird, reducing Jesus to never having spoken of the end at all. I think that there is a way, and it entails taking very seriously both Jesus' apocalyptic experience and self-concept and also his prophetic expression in both word and deed.

IV. JESUS THE SEER

The general argument for Jesus as a prophet has both promise and problems and that some specific proposals have their own difficulties as well;[117] now it is time for the fine-tuning of this study's proposal. Perhaps the most helpful question is, Where do we find the combination of revelatory and counterorder wisdom coupled with deep indebtedness to the prophetic tradition and a strong interest in things eschatological and otherworldly as well? The answer, surprisingly enough, is in the historical form of the apocalyptic tradition, in the material we find in Daniel and in some of the material in Zechariah and *1 Enoch*. There the hybrid form is already evident, and it has been noted earlier in this study how prophets, even those who had apocalyptic visions, could on occasion tell parables (e.g., Ezekiel).[118] It is time to press the

---

[116] On this, see rightly Allison, *Jesus of Nazareth*, 160. It will also not do to first argue, on the basis of the data we find in the Gospels, that Jesus did not predict the end of the world, and then turn around and argue that some of the same data, plus Paul, shows that some of Jesus' earliest followers were muddled on what Jesus meant (Wright, *Jesus and the Victory*, 318). We have access to the former only through the latter.

[117] See Meyer, *Aims of Jesus*, 245, whose conclusion, in my judgment, is correct: "On the level of historical-critical interpretation it is hardly possible to excise 'imminence' from Jesus' proclamation. At the opposite extreme, Schweitzer's reconstruction of Jesus' eschatology is exegetically and historically indefensible."

[118] See pp. 175–78 above.

case for seeing Jesus as a seer.[119] In my view, it explains a great deal, though not all, of the probably authentic Jesus tradition.

It turns out that Jesus' mixed genre of teaching material and, to some extent, his deeds and also his self-presentation followed an apocalyptic script. This should not entirely surprise anyone about the man whose most characteristic phrases were "Son of Man" and "Dominion of God," both found together in only one place in the OT—Dan 7. It should not surprise anyone because in *1 Enoch* a *mashal* amounted to a prophetic unveiling, though in metaphorical language, of the secrets of the future and the otherworld, as is also the case with Jesus' parables.[120] Could it be that Jesus, like the Enoch figure in *1 Enoch*, believed that it had been revealed to him that he indeed was "that Son of Man" to whom the secrets about the coming Dominion of God had been shown?[121] The case for a positive response to this question must now be laid out.

First, it will be remembered that it was argued above that Jesus generally offered two different sorts of prophetic performances, one in Galilee and another in Judea. If we ask what ties the two prophetic performances of Jesus together (Elijah-like performance in Galilee, oracular prophet in Judea), it is the use of Son of Man and Kingdom of God concepts in both the more sapiential material, such as the parables and aphorisms, and the more prophetic material, such as the predictions and laments and judgment sayings. Thus some phrases from an apocalyptic vision are used as the main themes of Jesus' discourse, but the form of that discourse is generally *not* apocalyptic, if by that one means the recounting of apocalyptic visions.

Theissen and Mertz put it this way: "In substance Jesus presents a variant of apocalyptic expectation, but formally it appears as prophecy—not in the form of an esoteric secret writing from dim prehistory but as a proclamation (in oral form) tied to his person. His preaching is a revitalization of apocalyptic in prophetic form."[122] This is correct if one simply means that Jesus has taken apocalyptic leitmotivs and applied them to himself and his ministry. It is not correct if one means that Jesus' message was one that included a focus on the world above (rather than on human history), the calculation of time until the final judgment, historical determinism, or pseudonymous esoteric material. To the contrary, Jesus believed the Dominion of God was breaking into human history then and there through his ministry. The woes and judgments Jesus pronounces (at least before the last week of his life) are, as in the classical prophets, conditional, in

---

[119] One can agree with Wright, *Jesus and the Victory,* 313, that Daniel's apocalyptic visions are not examples of wisdom. "It is the other way around. Daniel's wisdom is the thing which enables him to grasp the secrets of what Israel's God is doing with Israel and the world."

[120] I am referring here to some of the content, rather than formal similarities. The point is that *meshalim* is a term used to refer to widely divergent literary forms. It is an umbrella term referring to figurative or metaphorical language.

[121] See Witherington, *Jesus the Sage,* 201–2.

[122] Theissen and Mertz, *The Historical Jesus,* 249.

the sense that if Israel repents and responds to the stern warnings, they will not inevitably happen. And it is true that Jesus made pronouncements about the present and future in his own name.

What we can say is that Jesus had apocalyptic visions, he was indeed a seer, but that he translated that phenomenon into another form of discourse, retaining the "Son of Man" and "Dominion of God" phrases, which serve as telltale signs of the origins of Jesus' thinking and self-concept. His prophetic visionary experience did not translate directly into apocalyptic expression. Since I have elsewhere argued that Jesus was indeed a man of the Spirit, a seer who at least occasionally had visions (cf., e.g., the baptismal scene in Mark 1 or Luke 10:18),[123] it will be more helpful at this juncture to ask what kind of seer, what kind of apocalyptic or eschatological prophet Jesus was.

It will be profitable to consider one further narrative that suggests Jesus was an apocalyptic seer. Allison observes that fasting and acts of self-negation are regularly the regimen for visionary experiences (cf. Dan 9:3; 10:2–3; 4 *Ezra* 5:13, 20; 2 *Bar.* 9:2). This suggests that one should take the story of the temptation in the wilderness in Luke 4/Matt 4, which refers to extended fasting, as an account of an apocalyptic vision that Jesus had.[124] Strong support for this suggestion comes from the Antiochean church fathers and from Origen (*First Principles* 4.3.1), who saw the temptation narrative as a report of a vision.[125] The following elements in the story suggest that Jesus had a Danielic experience on this occasion: (1) Two sources report this event, Q (Luke 4/Matt 4) and Mark. While Mark does not recount the event in detail, nonetheless he speaks of Jesus' being driven into the wilderness by the Spirit, being tempted by the devil, being waited on by angels, and being accompanied by wild animals. The Markan description is reminiscent of Daniel's vision about what would happen to King Nebuchadnezzar, who is consigned to fraternize with the wild animals and is subject to the decree of the angelic watchers (Dan 4:15–17, cf. v. 33). This suggests that Mark knew of a tradition about an apocalyptic vision Jesus had while in the wilderness (cf. Ps 91:9–14). (2) Notice that the Matthean account, which seems more primitive and less schematized than the Lukan account, says that Jesus fasted for forty days and *then* the devil came to him and tempted him (Matt 4:2–3). This accords with what was said above about fasting as preparation for a vision. (3) The story includes the sort of transport in the Spirit, or visionary transport, characteristic of apocalyptic seers and visions. Jesus is transported not only to the pinnacle of the temple (Matt 4:5) but also to a high mountain (v. 8). (4) The devil plays the role of the interpreting angel. In this case, since he is a fallen angel, he does not explain but, rather, reveals and exhorts to get Jesus to act. He reveals to Jesus that he has supernatural powers even over stones and gravity. He reveals the kingdoms of

---

[123] See Witherington, *Christology of Jesus*, 145–55.

[124] Allison, *Jesus of Nazareth*, 193.

[125] See V. Kesich, "The Antiocheans and the Temptation Story," in F. L. Cross (ed.), *Studia Patristica* 7 (TU 92; Berlin: Akademie Verlag, 1966), 496–502.

the world to Jesus' mind's eye. Although Matthew mentions a mountain, there was no mountain anywhere in the then known world from which one could see all the surrounding kingdoms. Rather, this is the very stuff of visions and is reminiscent of the heavenly tours, but in this case it is an earthly tour. (5) Notice that the last temptation contains an offer of *all* the kingdoms of the world. This is what was promised, in essence, to the Son of Man in Dan 7.[126] This would have been a severe temptation if indeed Jesus believed it was his role to play the part of the Danielic Son of Man. The devil then would be offering a shortcut to how the prophecy of Dan 7 could be fulfilled for him. (6) The story, in its Lukan form, ends with the words that the devil departed from Jesus until an opportune time. This comports with the information we find in Luke 10:18, that Jesus again saw the devil, apparently in a vision, but this time he saw the devil as falling like lightning. (7) In this testing, Jesus responds in all three cases by quoting Scripture and thus passing the test, much as Enoch passed the test and so it was revealed to Enoch that he was the Son of Man. (8) As Wright notes, it would seem required that Jesus had some such visionary experience, as is recounted here, prior to his exorcisms, for in the Beelzebul controversy Jesus says that he has already bound the strong man.[127] What this experience likely meant to Jesus is that he had successfully resisted adopting any messianic Son of God styles of acting that would have accorded with the popular expectation of a Davidic ruler who would come and conquer the pagan occupiers. He would, in addition, perform no miracles simply to demonstrate who he was or for the purpose of self-gratification. Jesus believed that the real battle needed to be waged with the powers and principalities, not the Pilates and Antipases of this world. (9) Inasmuch as the domain of devils and angels is the cosmic realm, the mention of both in this account points us in the direction of this being an account of a visionary experience. About this story, M. Barker, who sees a strong connection between the Gospel Son of Man material and the Enochic material about the Son of Man, says this:

> A visionary experience of all the kingdoms of the world . . . was certainly not out of place in the world of Enoch. (Enoch had a similar experience, 1 Enoch 87.3. From a high place he saw history unfold before him.) Nor are the expelled demons and the vision of Satan falling from heaven out of character (Luke 10.18). What happens to our picture of Jesus . . . if we bring back the insights and ideas of 1 Enoch? . . . We should have a Messiah figure, a son of man, who was the intermediary between heaven and earth, a figure who functioned in both worlds. He was a priest who interceded in the heavenly temple. On earth he was the messenger who announced the great judgement, and in heaven he was the agent of that judgement. He was the centre of the great cosmic covenant which kept the creation in its appointed order. He was the bastion against the forces of evil which threatened the people of God, and the order of creation. His was the name which could bind the unruly forces of evil, and expel the demons which infested

---

[126] See pp. 197–210 above.
[127] Wright, *Jesus and the Victory*, 457–58.

the earth. . . . The reign of this son of man was a time when nature was restored to fertility, and humankind to peace.[128]

Certainly, one does not find all of these themes in the Synoptics, but the above is suggestive of how Jesus might have viewed himself if he saw himself as the Danielic Son of Man and was also influenced by the Enochic material. In particular, the idea of his having one foot in each world would illuminate some of the exorcism tales and the criticisms of Jesus' exorcisms. The exorcism data must be considered at this juncture. To anticipate: when Jesus practiced exorcisms, he was at the same time liberating the captives and enacting judgment on the powers of darkness. In short, he was beginning to exercise the role of the Son of Man in judging the spiritual realm before pronouncing judgment on the human domain.

A detailed study of the synoptic exorcism texts has been undertaken by G. Twelftree.[129] He demonstrates at some length that the exorcism stories generally are very primitive in character and are not found in the later forms of the Gospel tradition (see, e.g., John's Gospel). He also demonstrates that Jesus was well and widely known to be an exorcist and was still being criticized for this in later Jewish literature and that his name was used in exorcistic rites long after he died (cf. *b. Sanh.* 43a and *PGM* IV. 3019ff.; see IV. 127). But the most important of Twelftree's conclusions is that, unlike other early exorcists in early Judaism, Jesus connected his exorcisms explicitly with his eschatological message about the coming of the Dominion of God. "It was he who associated the notion of the cosmic, supernatural battle against the kingdom of Satan in the eschaton with the very act of an ordinary exorcism."[130] In other words, as Wright says, these were not just private cures; they were victories in the war against the kingdom of Satan.[131] Once the authenticity of at least some of these exorcism tales is granted, it becomes difficult indeed to conjure up a noneschatological Jesus. But unlike Wright, Twelftree recognizes that Jesus' exorcisms clearly imply that a further stage of eschatology will be required beyond the current efforts. This stage will entail not merely the liberation of the captives but the eventual destruction of Satan.[132]

Few scholars deny that Jesus was an exorcist. The notion is attested in nearly all levels of the Gospel tradition and is also alluded to in sayings, narratives, and summaries (cf. Acts 10:38; Mark 1:21–28 and par; Mark 3:22b and par.; Luke 11:20 and par.). Furthermore, the church had little reason to make such claims about Jesus if they were not true, for there is little evidence that it was characteristic of the ministry of early Christians. Paul never mentions the

---

[128] M. Barker, *The Lost Prophet: The Book of Enoch and Its Influence on Christianity* (Nashville: Abingdon, 1988), 111.

[129] G. Twelftree, *Jesus the Exorcist* (Tübingen: Mohr-Siebeck, 1993).

[130] Ibid., 227.

[131] Wright, *Jesus and the Victory*, 195.

[132] Twelftree, *Jesus the Exorcist*, 218.

practice, and it is notably absent from the other Epistles and from the Fourth Gospel and gets only brief mention in Acts 8:7 and 16:16–18.[133]

In another study I have argued for the authenticity of Luke 11:20[134] and here reiterate what this text suggests: (1) The reference to the finger of God suggests that Jesus sees that an epoch-making deliverance by God is in progress, as in the Exodus reference (Exod 8:15; cf. Deut 9:10; Exod 31:18). (2) It also shows that Jesus is concerned to indicate that the source of this action is God, not some magical incantation or ritual but also not his own innate human power or strength or skill. (3) Because Jesus is performing exorcisms, something is now true about the eschatological reign and saving activity of God—it is breaking into human history here and now. (4) This text indicates that Jesus is an action prophet, not merely a sign or oracular prophet. He not merely announces the coming of God's dominion; he brings it in. (5) So far as can be determined, the interconnection between exorcism and eschatology is distinctive of Jesus' interpretation of such events, and it suggests that Jesus saw himself bringing in the final reign of God. (6) This last point dovetails nicely with the early Jewish expectation that Satan would be vanquished at the end of the age (Isa 24:21–22; *1 En.* 10:4ff.; *Jub.* 23:39; 1QS 4:18–19; *T. Mos.* 10:1; *T. Levi* 18:12; *T. Jud.* 25:3; Rev 20:2–3). The significance of this should not be underplayed. A noneschatological interpretation of Jesus makes no sense of the exorcism texts, and furthermore, one has also missed a significant clue that Jesus viewed himself as an eschatological power broker. The exorcism texts also reveal how Jesus may be distinguished from the eschatological prophet John the Baptist. G. Theissen stresses,

> Jesus is unique in religious history. He combines two conceptual worlds which had never been combined in this way before, the apocalyptic expectation of universal salvation in the future and the episodic realization of salvation in the present through miracles. . . . Before Jesus there was no comparable combination of apocalyptic and the charism of miracle-working. . . . The eschatological view of miracles is generally and rightly held to be a peculiarity of Jesus' preaching. . . . Because the negative web of evil has already been broken it is possible for salvation to come in individual instances. Because individual instances of salvation occur, the presence of the end can be proclaimed here and now.[135]

The Beelzebul controversy must be considered at this point. A careful comparison of Matt 12:25–30, Mark 3:23–37, and Luke 11:17–23 suggests there is a complicated tradition history here, and it may be doubted that the finger saying already examined was originally a part of this complex, for Mark knows nothing of it. What are shared by these texts are the brief parables about the house divided and about the binding of the strong man. In part, the parables are

---

[133] One could also point to Acts 19:11–20 and Justin, *Dial.* 2.8. But only a distinct minority of early Christian texts suggests Christians were exorcists. The motive for gratuitously predicating an exorcist claim about Jesus is lacking.

[134] See Witherington, *Christology of Jesus*, 201–2.

[135] G. Theissen, *The Miracle Stories of the Early Christian Tradition* (Philadelphia: Fortress, 1983), 278–80.

meant to fend off the criticism that Jesus is performing his exorcisms while in league with Satan. The house divided parable is meant to indicate that Jesus is no part of that household, that indeed he is attacking that household or kingdom in the service of a very different kingdom. This coheres nicely with the implication of the independent logion in Luke 11:20 and par.[136] The implication of the house divided parable, as Meier suggests, is that "the exorcism of demons means that the kingdom or royal house of the prince of demons is being destroyed—certainly not by the prince himself, which would be absurd—but by the opposite royal power seizing control of human beings through a striking miracle."[137]

The parable in Mark 3:27 and Luke 11:21–22 adds a bit more to the picture. Meier is likely right that Mark presents the more primitive form of this saying. The parable indicates that Jesus is the stronger one who binds the strong one (Satan) and frees his captives, as is demonstrated by Jesus' exorcisms. The binding language is typical of stories about demons or fallen angels, as we have already seen in Isa 24:21–22.[138] Indeed, this is an allusion to the story about the fallen angels that was popular throughout a wide variety of Jewish and early Jewish Christian literature (cf. Jude 6–7; 1 Pet 3; 2 Pet 3:4–5).[139] The parable offers yet further evidence that no hard-and-fast division between parable and allegory can be made in early Jewish literature.[140] The question then becomes, What sort of person thinks that he is stronger than Satan and can deliver his captives? The answer is surely some sort of ruler figure who can take on and rule over other rulers and realms. This notion coheres with the idea that Jesus acted out the apocalyptic script he found in Daniel, with himself playing the role of Son of Man. Mention has already been made of the evidence from 4Q521, that the messianic one was likely to be an Elijah-like prophet who performed miracles.[141] It must not be forgotten that the Son of Man is likewise a ruler figure of some sort.

Thus, converging lines of evidence from both the eschatological, Elijah-like prophet side of the equation and the Son of Man–ruler–exorcist side of the equation, coupled with the evidence that Jesus had apocalyptic visions, suggest the interesting conclusion that Jesus saw himself as both an apocalyptic seer and a central player in an apocalyptic drama: he was a messianic prophetic figure, the Son of Man, who, in performing miracles and exorcisms and offering parables, oracles, and signs, was inaugurating the eschatological saving reign of God. This reign entailed redemption and judgment, not just one or the other: the liberation of the captives meant the binding of the powers of darkness, the extending of the reign of the Son of Man over God's people.

---

[136] See rightly Meier, *Marginal Jew*, 2:416–17.

[137] Ibid., 417.

[138] See pp. 123–25 above.

[139] See pp. ix–xii above on the development of this trajectory.

[140] See Witherington, *Christology of Jesus*, 210–15.

[141] See pp. 235–37 above.

There are very good reasons Jesus might have avoided publicly recounting apocalyptic visions. By the time one gets to the turn of the era, apocalyptic, as was seen in the previous chapter, had come to be especially associated with various themes that Jesus is studiously avoiding: (1) periodization of history; (2) date setting for the end of the world; (3) determinism and fatalism; (4) abandoning of hope for history, in particular the history of God's people; (5) ex eventu pseudonymous prophecy. Even Allison (who wants to argue for Jesus being an apocalyptist going for the eschatological jackpot of prophesying the imminent and necessary end of the world), when he deals with Jesus' future prophecies, says that they should not be taken as "obviously symbolic prophecies in a visionary context" but as general eschatological prophecy that is more literal in form and content.[142] Part of the confusion on all these issues is due to a failure to distinguish prophetic experience and prophetic expression. In the realm of prophetic experience, Jesus is an apocalyptic seer, but in the realm of prophetic expression and action, he appears as a messianic eschatological prophet, an Elijah-like figure. In this he has both continuity and discontinuity with what was the case with John the Baptist.

At this juncture it is necessary to stress the fact that when Jesus went up to Jerusalem as a prophet, he deliberately undertook a series of symbolic sign acts, unlike anything he undertook in Galilee, and he also deliberately assumed a more classical form of prophetic discourse—largely leaving parables and aphorisms and, for that matter, exorcisms and most cures behind. Attention will be given first to the signs—the triumphal entry on the donkey and the cleansing of the temple.

The seldom disputed fact that Jesus was crucified as a Jewish messianic figure nonetheless requires some significant explanation. There has to have been some connection between things Jesus said or did and this conclusion to his life. The evidence does not encourage us to think that it was what Jesus said or did while in Galilee that led to his demise. According to Luke 23:6–12, Herod passed on the opportunity to execute final judgment on Jesus, which, if historically true, must intimate that at least Antipas did not think Jesus' Galilean ministry suggested the need to turn him over to the Roman authorities for the "extreme" penalty. Even if this is only Luke's view, it means that he does not evaluate Jesus' Galilean ministry as connected to his untimely demise in Jerusalem. We must turn to the words and deeds of Jesus offered in Judea during that last week or so of his life.

In another study, I dealt with the triumphal-entry story in Mark 11:1–11 and par. and its critical problems.[143] There is no good reason Jesus and his disciples could not have followed the common practice of *angaria,* the borrowing of means of transportation for a specific limited time and use, for J. D. M. Derrett has shown that such practices were known among Jewish teachers and their followers in this era.[144] Notice that while no doubt Zech 9:9 is alluded to in the way the story is told in Mark, the allusion is not elaborated on in the earliest account

---

[142] Allison, *Jesus of Nazareth,* 157.

[143] Witherington, *Christology of Jesus,* 104–5.

[144] J. D. M. Derrett, "Law in the New Testament: The Palm Sunday Colt," *NovT* 13 (1971): 241–58.

in the way it is in Matthew and John. Jesus is also not acclaimed Lord in the Markan account; indeed, it can be argued that Jesus is simply accompanying those pilgrims into the city who are singing the ascent psalms, in this case Ps 118:26ff. There is also no evidence from Jesus' day or before that early Jews associated Zech 9:9 with the Messiah. For the purposes of this study, all that needs to be historically substantive about this event is that Jesus rode into town on an ass. M. Hooker puts it this way: "The united testimony of the four evangelists that Jesus—after trudging so many miles on foot!—rode this final stage of the journey is remarkable, and indicates that we are here on firm historical ground, since pilgrims normally all entered Jerusalem on foot. Far from being the act of humility which Christian tradition has made it, this was an extraordinarily bold and ostentatious gesture."[145] If indeed Jesus did this, he was playing out a script that he knew from the apocalyptic sources that most influenced him—in this case Zech 9:9.

What is the significance of this sign act? Bearing in mind Hooker's definition that such sign acts are the dramatic equivalent of the spoken oracle, not a mere visual aid to the teaching,[146] this must be seen as a prophetic act, albeit an apocalyptic prophetic one. It is, in fact, a prophetic drama in which Jesus acts out his self-understanding. It is also one that has echoes of the story of Solomon being mounted on David's own mule by Nathan and Zadok under the orders of the king to escort him to Gihon, where he was to be anointed and then brought back into the city to the acclaim of the residents (1 Kgs 1:32–40). Is this the juncture where Jesus finally reveals indirectly he is not just a prophet but, at the least, a messianic prophetic figure?

But what a strange gesture riding into town on a donkey is, for it seems anti-revolutionary in character. Jesus will not ride into town on a warhorse but as a man of peace. It may be that Jesus was the first to base messianic self-expression on Zech 9:9. In any case, this story simply confirms at the end of Jesus' ministry, as at the beginning, that Jesus did not intend to conform to popular messianic expectations, and further it confirms the notion that his self-understanding was grounded in the late apocalyptic prophets. If there is an allusion to the Solomon story as well, then Jesus as prophetic messianic sage might also come into the picture once more.

Since writing *The Christology of Jesus,* I have become more persuaded that Jesus' action in the temple was a prophetic sign of judgment.[147] This comports well with Jesus' lament over Jerusalem and also the ominous parable of the vineyard. Wright has ably shown that there is some consensus among major commentators from a wide variety of perspectives, including Crossan, Borg, Sanders, Neusner, and Wright himself, that Jesus was dramatizing the coming destruction of the temple itself.[148] In other words, this was no mere symbolic housecleaning.

---

[145] Hooker, *Signs of a Prophet,* 43.

[146] Ibid., 38.

[147] See Witherington, *Christology of Jesus,* 114–15.

[148] Wright, *Jesus and the Victory,* 413.

It could, as Hooker has suggested, be taken as a prophetic warning,[149] but more likely at this late juncture, it should be seen as a sort of figurative last rites, indicating the temple's fate was sealed. This comports with the fig tree sign, the saying in John 2 about the destruction and rebuilding of the temple, the synoptic testimony of the false witnesses, and the words predicated of Jesus himself in Mark 13:2. The temple action also has clear echoes of earlier prophetic oracles on this subject (cf. Isa 56:6–8; Jer 7:3–15). Perhaps most important, the whole scenario here seems to be redolent of Zechariah, in this case Zech 6:12 and the scene of destruction conjured up in Zech 14:1–5.[150] On the one hand, destruction is going to come on Jerusalem and its temple. On the other hand, a Branch is coming to town who will build a new temple of some sort.

Notice what Jesus actually did—he briefly stopped some of the activities in the temple. The cutting off of some of the temple's activities symbolizes the severing of the positive link with God. Notice the horror reflected in Dan 8:11f., 11:31, and 12:11 (cf. 1 Macc 1:45–46) about the cessation of the regular sacrifices. The only time sacrifices ceased would be when a temple was either abandoned or destroyed. Meyer puts the import of this succinctly: "To evoke, even conditionally, the destruction of 'this temple' was to touch not just stone and gold and not only the general well-being but history and hope, national identity, self-understanding, and pride."[151] What Jesus said and did in regard to the temple is what seems to have precipitated his demise: he would suffer a prophet's fate because of a prophetic sign and some oracular words he had spoken about the fate of the temple. What is the significance of that prediction in the so-called Markan apocalypse?

Almost all scholars agree that Mark 13 should likely be seen as a composite discourse. It consists of a discussion of both preliminary events (called signs) and apparently final events. The discourse, in its present form, has something of a chiastic structure. After the preliminary remarks about the destruction of the temple, the disciples ask about the timing and the signs of what is to come. The response discusses first the signs, then the issue of time or timing. In other words, the response is given in the reverse order of the questions. Almost all scholars concur, first, that there are some things that will occur within a generation, or about forty years, and, second, that Jesus professes agnosticism about the timing of the coming of the Son of Man.

Whatever the origins of all this material, it is a misnomer to call it an apocalyptic discourse, for the following very good reasons: (1) it is not visionary in form; (2) it does not contain apocalyptic symbols such as those found in Daniel (unless one counts as such some of the material in Mark's parenthetical insertion or in vv. 24–27, but in fact it is perfectly possible that this material is meant quite literally); (3) what it does contain are woe oracles (v. 17) and warnings

---

[149] Hooker, *Signs of a Prophet*, 45–46.
[150] Wright, *Jesus and the Victory*, 422–23.
[151] Meyer, *Aims of Jesus*, 183.

about coming suffering and persecution, which are some of the stock items found in classical OT prophetic sources.

One further preliminary remark is in order. Whatever the original provenance of this material, it has been put together in an A, B, A, B pattern. The A section is far longer than the B section and has to do with a rather long litany of preliminary events. The B section has to do with the final events. Thus one finds this schema: (1) A: vv. 5–23; (2) B: vv. 24–27; (3) A′: vv. 28–31;[152] (4) B′: vv. 32–37. If this observation is correct, then nothing specific at all is said about when the final events will take place—v. 24 simply says, "but in those days, after that suffering," with no specificity at all as to how long *after* is meant. Likewise, in regard to the timing of the second coming, v. 32 predicates ignorance on the part of all (even including the Son) save God the Father. This is definitely not the stuff of Dan 8–12 or *1 Enoch* or other date-setting apocalypses.

Indeed, when the preliminary events are examined more closely, they include remarks such as, "the Gospel must first be preached to all nations," which suggests a considerable period of time even for the preliminary events, extending well beyond the time of Jesus' ministry. The overall impact of vv. 5–23 is to suggest that there will be wars, false messianic claims, earthquakes, persecutions, and family betrayals, but these are but the earliest preliminary events (the beginning of the birth pangs). None of the above, however, is meant to deny that this passage is in some ways indebted to Dan 7–12. Of course it is, especially in its use of the Son of Man language and the abomination of desolation discussion (Dan 11:31–35). But there is nothing about beastly empires or calculations here, and no attempt to recount this data in visionary form.

The one preliminary event that signals an especially difficult time of suffering from which no one can escape is referred to in v. 14 (as in v. 2), and it augurs the end of the temple and of life as they knew it in Jerusalem. Yet even this is not a final event but a part of the preliminary birth pangs. The reference to "all these things" occurring within a generation refers to the events leading up to the desolating sacrilege, which is seen as the sign of the end of Zion. The preliminary events accomplish the end of a world of Torah, temple, and territory, but the author goes on to say things about the end of the world writ large as well. There is nothing said about the timing of the final events of human history that compares to what is said about the timing of the preliminary events.

---

[152] It is one of the regular mistakes of commentators to take vv. 28–31 as being about the same subject as vv. 32–37. The key point to be mentioned at this juncture is that v. 29 should not be translated, "you know that he is near." Rather, it should be rendered, "you know it is near." As Wright, *Jesus and the Victory*, 364, points out, Luke clearly understands the meaning here is that "the kingdom of God is near" (Luke 21:31). Furthermore, the oft repeated phrase "these things" or "all these things" refers, in each and every case in this discourse, to preliminary events, not to the final events. Compare v. 4: "all these things" that are to be accomplished are the preliminary events, which, when completed, will be followed by the final events "in those days" after the messianic suffering (v. 24). See also v. 23, which brings to a close the first telling of all the preliminary things.

It is also worth noting that literal eclipses of sun and moon were regularly taken as signs foreshadowing the death of kings or the destruction of cities (cf. Eusebius, *Praep. ev.* 395d; Plutarch, *Caes.* 69; Dio Cassius 56.29.3; Josephus, *Ant.* 17.167). It is also true that the ancients viewed meteorites as stars, and so when they spoke of falling stars, most often they quite literally meant what they said.[153] Furthermore, many early Jews (though not apparently the Sadducees) believed in literal angels and demons and their involvement in human history, and evidence has already been presented that Jesus himself believed in such supernatural beings. There is no compelling reason, then, to think that any of the material in vv. 24–27 is not meant literally.

As for the material in vv. 32–37, there is some parabolic speech in vv. 34–36, signaled by the normal parabolic introduction, "it is like," but again this is not the same as apocalyptic visionary material. It is basically an extended analogy. This material bears little resemblance to "obviously symbolic prophecies in a visionary context" (e.g., *4 Ezra* 11–12).[154] The point, however, to be made is that the parable in the Markan text is referential language and the reference has to do with an event that was seen as historical—the coming of the Son of Man (see v. 26). There is in this Markan discourse a mixture of prophetic and sapiential speech, which is precisely what characterized Jesus' public utterances, as already pointed out.

With this general introduction, we must consider what is said about the final events in vv. 24–27 and vv. 32–37. Whatever else we may say, this material is not a creation of Mark, for, as G. R. Beasley-Murray showed in some detail a long time ago, Paul knows these very portions of this discourse in some form. Consider the following: (1) 1 Thess 4:15ff. = Mark 13:26–27; (2) 1 Thess 5:1–5 = Mark 13:32–33; (3) 1 Thess 5:6ff. = Mark 13:35–36; (4) 2 Thess 2:1–2 = Mark 13:26–27; (5) 2 Thess 2:13 = Mark 13:27.[155] The two most solid parallels are the coming of the Son/Lord from heaven and the surprising nighttime intruder motif. Nor should we assume that Mark 13 is history poorly remembered in the guise of ex eventu prophecy. The lack of precision about what finally happened to Jerusalem does not reflect poor memory on the part of the evangelist but, rather, reflects the very nature of predictions in the classical mode, especially predictions as deeply indebted to previous prophetic material as this collection of materials is. As Wright puts it, Mark 13 is "a first-class example of Jesus picking up a storyline from the prophetic tradition and retelling it so as to focus on his own work"[156] In particular, this passage is indebted to the earlier descriptions of the fall and sacking of great cities and the turmoil that surrounded such events, including the fall of Jerusalem and the fall of Babylon, both of which are mentioned in the OT (cf., e.g., Mic 7:2–10).

---

[153] On this see the discussion by Allison, *Jesus of Nazareth*, 161–62.

[154] Ibid., 157.

[155] G. R. Beasley-Murray, *Jesus and the Future* (London: Macmillan, 1954), 226–30.

[156] Wright, *Jesus and the Victory*, 348.

First, we must note that the ignorance expressed here is not merely about the exact time of the coming but about the general time.[157] The phrase "day or hour" must be compared to the reference to the *kairos* in the next verse.[158] Jesus is professing general ignorance of the timing of this climactic eschatological event. This is all the more shocking because the verse seems to present an ascending order of knowledge about the mind and plan of God for human history: human beings have some knowledge, angels have more, the Son even more, but only the Father knows all, including the timing of this event. It is difficult to imagine anyone in the early church inventing this saying and placing it on Jesus' lips.[159]

Whatever else we may gather from this, it is appropriate to conclude the following: (1) However near Jesus may have thought some preliminary eschatological events may have been, and however much he may have believed God's Dominion was already breaking into human history during his ministry, he did not offer up a timetable for the conclusion of the eschatological events, nor did he make specific predictions about the timing of some of the individual things he believed would happen at the end of human history. (2) This means, in turn, that Allison's case for Jesus being not merely apocalyptic but also millenarian and Schweitzerian about the imminence of the end is simply incorrect. It does not follow from this, however, that Dodd was right that Jesus was an advocate of mere realized eschatology or that Caird or Wright are correct that it is necessary to interpret all this eschatological language largely figuratively, referring to the end of a world of early Judaism due to the temple's demise.

Focusing for a moment on Mark 13:26, it is germane to point out that this does not appear to be simply an alternate form of the saying found in 14:62. There is no doubt, however, that there is a close match in the theme of these two verses. In one saying, the Son of Man will come with power; in the other, he is seated at the right hand of the Great Power; and in both, he will come on the clouds. The reference is clearly to Dan 7:13, which, as previously discussed, even in its original context was about a coming to earth for the *Yom Yahweh*.[160]

---

[157] There is nothing, in principle, against the idea that at least a goodly portion of this material goes back to the historical Jesus, especially vv. 26–27 and vv. 32, 35–36. Focusing first on v. 32, the most crucial verse, I have argued for its authenticity elsewhere. See Witherington, *Christology of Jesus*, 228–33.

[158] Meier's detailed study of the verse has led him to also conclude that this is a word of Jesus, not least because it meets the criterion of embarrassment. Notice that Luke omits this verse altogether, John has no hint of anything like this, and a significant number of manuscripts of the parallel Matthean text (Matt 24:36) omit the phrase "nor the Son." All of this reflects the embarrassment of the later tradents about this verse, which clearly predicated ignorance of Jesus about something, indeed about an important eschatological matter involving his own future. See J. Meier, *A Marginal Jew: Rethinking the Historical Jesus*, vol. 1: *The Roots of the Problem and the Person* (New York: Doubleday, 1991–1994), 169–70.

[159] See Meier, *Marginal Jew*, 2:347.

[160] See pp. 208–9 above.

Consider for a moment the old Bultmannian question of whether Jesus could have been thinking of someone other than himself as this particular future Son of Man. This is possible, but the evidence that Jesus called himself Son of Man in a variety of genres of material and a variety of settings is too strong to dismiss. Jesus nowhere suggests there will be two Sons of Man. If it is indeed possible that Jesus believed that he was the Danielic Son of Man, a belief confirmed through visionary experiences among other things, then he would have anticipated playing a role in the final judgment and the ruling of the world. If he saw the eschatological ruling already beginning during his lifetime in part through such things as the exorcisms, it would be natural for him to be confident that God would allow him to complete the tasks of the Danielic Son of Man at some point.

But as Meier argues, Jesus, as a prophetic figure, anticipated a violent end to his life in Jerusalem, coupled with some form of vindication by God thereafter.[161] If Jesus could believe that his own disciples would one day play a role at the *eschaton*, sitting on thrones judging the twelve tribes, it is not much different from this for Jesus to have envisaged himself playing a role in that final judging process. But in order to do that, he would have to come back to earth from the place of vindication. How would he have viewed this?

Suppose for a minute that Jesus did see himself as the eschatological prophet cut in the mold of Elijah. The story of the end of Elijah's life was, of course, famous—he was taken up into heaven to dwell with God. If Jesus saw himself playing the eschatological role as the latter-day Elijah or even as the Enochic Son of Man, he could well have believed that he would one day be sitting on the right hand of the Great Power after he experienced the death of a prophet in Jerusalem. The final stage in his long, strange journey would find him back on earth in the kingdom of God, playing an important role on the Day of the Lord and partaking of the messianic banquet (cf. Mark 14:25). The script laid out for Jesus was found in texts from Zechariah, Daniel, *1 Enoch*, but also in the Elijah-Elisha cycle, especially with its early Jewish interpretation that suggested an eschatological role for Elijah. Jesus' prophetic experience located him within this script, and his prophetic expression revealed the eschatological roles he chose to assume. The failure to see Jesus within this matrix of ideas has led to the failure to recognize Jesus as the seer and eschatological prophet he was.

V. CONCLUSIONS

The measure of the value of a hypothesis is how much of the available evidence it explains. It is the contention of this study that the thesis of Jesus the seer/eschatological prophet explains the majority of the authentic synoptic tradition. It explains how Jesus viewed himself, why he acted as he did in regard to

---

[161] See Meier, *Marginal Jew*, 2:337ff.

the signs, exorcisms, and miracles, why he took the steps he did during the last week of his life, and why he suffered a violent end as a result.

Jesus lived at a time when the rivers of the prophetic, apocalyptic, and sapiential traditions had already flowed together; indeed, apocalyptic was itself a hybrid of wisdom and prophetic materials. It is not surprising that Jesus himself reflected this situation in his words and deeds and in his self-understanding as a messianic prophet, a northern prophet, an apocalyptic eschatological sage, a Son of Man.

If we take multiple lines of evidence, the lines eventually converge at the same conclusion. The Elijah-like eschatological and messianic prophet was also the apocalyptic Son of Man. The latter best described Jesus' prophetic experience and visions. The former reflected his prophetic expression, first as a northern prophet in the mold of Elijah and then as a more classical eschatological sign prophet during his tenure in Judea and Jerusalem.

The conclusions of this chapter are based not just on a close analysis of places where the term "prophet" crops up in the Gospel material. They are based, in part, on a reading of the Jesus materials in light of the history of the prophetic corpus—in other words, in light of the discussions in the earlier chapters in this study. If one fails to exegete Jesus in light of the northern prophetic traditions and the late apocalyptic traditions, one has missed an enormous clue to how Jesus presented himself.

The conclusions of this chapter are also based on a vigorous interaction with other similar proposals about Jesus as an eschatological prophet, especially the recent works of Allison, Theissen and Mertz, and Wright. All of these scholars have made helpful contributions to the discussion, but all suffer, to one degree or another, from a failure to really understand the enigmatic character of Hebrew prophecy and/or of eschatological language, or they simply overread the data.

On the one hand, the Jesus of Schweitzer can not simply be dusted off and represented today as the historical Jesus. There are still too many problems with that theory. On the other hand, the failure to take it seriously and, in some cases, to take it literally that Jesus spoke about the end time and not just the end of a world of early Judaism through the destruction of the temple also leads to inadequate and, in some cases, inaccurate conclusions about the historical Jesus. For example, Jesus did affirm the future resurrection of the dead and the final judgment as events in space and time. He did affirm that the Son of man would return to earth and have a role in those events. He did *not* simply see this sort of discourse as an alternate, metaphorical way of describing the events surrounding the destruction of the temple within a generation. Jesus taught that there would indeed be life and eschatological events after the temple's demise. But unlike those who engaged in the forms of apocalyptic that entailed ex eventu prophecy, Jesus set no dates, offered no periodized timelines, but instead warned that one must always be ready, for the end could come at any time, whether sooner or later.

Jesus' language was indeed referential, but like the prophetic discourse that influenced him, it had an indeterminacy and lack of specificity about it. I suggest that his predictions had this quality at least in part because prophecy was given in a relational context (what would happen if Israel should indeed repent?) and, as such, it had a conditional or contingent character insofar as the timing was concerned. These important conclusions must be borne in mind as this study now turns to examine the role of prophecy in the movement that Jesus inaugurated.

CHAPTER 9

Prophets, Seers, and Dreamers at the Dawn of the Christian Era

ERE THE FIRST POST-EASTER FOLLOWERS of Jesus prophets? Did they follow in the footsteps of Jesus, offering various predictions and warnings about the future? Was prophecy so ubiquitous that one could call the Jesus movement, in essence, a prophetic movement, perhaps something like Elijah and his followers? On first blush, the evidence for such a conclusion seems lacking. It is true that there are various references to prophets in early Christian literature (e.g., 1 Cor 14; Acts 11:27–30), but apart from the book of Revelation, there are no books in the canon of the NT that could be called prophetic books on the order of the OT prophetic books or that could be called apocalypses.

Furthermore, even within the canonical NT books, only a distinct minority of the material found there could be called oracular or visionary in form. Thus, if there were creative Christian prophets in the early church offering up new words of Jesus that ended up in the Gospels, either they chose to express themselves in non-prophetic forms (in which case it will be virtually impossible to prove the material came from a prophet) or they did not make an enormous impact on the Jesus tradition. Even if one were to argue that *all* the prophetic material in the Gospels comes from a situation in the life of the church and not from Jesus, the quantity of relevant data is not enormous.

Outside the canon as well, there is some data about Christian prophets, particularly traveling ones (e.g., in the *Didache*), but if prophets were so omnipresent in early Christianity, why is it that the sources speak so little of local prophets as opposed to itinerant ones (again Acts 11:27–30; *Didache*)? Were the earliest leaders of the Jesus movement (such as Peter, James, John, and Paul) prophets? It so, why are apostles and prophets distinguished in the earliest lists of church functionaries (e.g., 1 Cor 12)? It is these kinds of questions that will be addressed in this chapter. Before doing so, however, it will be well to take a look at both Jewish and Greco-Roman prophecy in the first century AD as a context for better evaluating Christian prophecy.

I. FROM JERUSALEM TO ATHENS

It would be difficult to overestimate how highly prophecy was valued throughout the Roman Empire during the first century AD. As was pointed out earlier in this study, there was a variety of early Jewish sign prophets, and there were also eschatological prophets such as John the Baptist.[1] This phenomenon continued even in Jerusalem right up to the time of the fall of the temple. There was, for example, the prophet Jesus ben Ananiah, who began in AD 62 to offer oracles of woe against Jerusalem until the fall of the city in AD 70, despite persecution and torture. Basically, his oracles are a refrain of Jeremiah's woe oracle, for they take the form "a voice from the east, a voice from the west, a voice from the four winds, a voice against the bridegroom and bride, a voice against all the people" (cf. Josephus, *War* 6.300–309).

Josephus himself claims to have been a seer, a receiver of night visions or dreams, and a diviner of the meaning of obscure utterances. He not only prophesied that Vespasian would be emperor (as apparently did Johanan ben Zacchai as well) but believed that it had been revealed to him that he was to willingly surrender to the Romans and agree to go on living so that he could be God's minister and witness (*War* 3.351–354, 399–408).[2] Josephus's value judgment that figures such as Theudas and the various sign prophets he mentions were *pseudoprophētai* (*Ant.* 20.97–98, 168–169) does not erase the fact that these figures existed and that they evaluated their own activities differently than Josephus did.

A case can also be made that Philo saw himself as a prophet, for he speaks of having been seized from time to time by the divine, leaving him unconscious (*Migr.* 35). He goes on to liken himself to a person possessed with divine frenzy "even as prophets are inspired" (*Her.* 69f.). Almost the entire vocabulary that Philo uses to describe these experiences is derived from nonbiblical Greek and from ideas that come from prophecy in the Greco-Roman world. This reflects how hellenized a Jew he was.[3] Philo appears to regard the Therapeutae, who,

---

[1] See pp. 238–46 above.

[2] It is intriguing that Josephus reserves the term *prophētēs* for the OT prophets, perhaps because he believed that he lived in an age in which biblical prophecy in the classical style had largely ceased—dreams and visions being what remained as God's vehicle of revelation.

[3] See rightly D. Hill, *New Testament Prophecy* (London: Marshall, Morgan & Scott, 1979), 33; E. Boring, *The Continuing Voice of Jesus* (Louisville: Westminster, 1991), 53.

among other things, are noted for their singing, as prophetesses (*Contempl.* 83–87). This is the only reference from non-NT Jewish sources to women with the prophetic gift in the first century AD.

Overall, the evidence is sufficient to make clear that the prophetic gift had not died out in early Judaism during the first century AD, but the evidence does not at all suggest that these prophetic figures dominated the landscape or controlled the passing on of sacred traditions and texts. Furthermore, with the exception of Philo and the Therapeutae, the evidence is connected specifically with Jerusalem or activities in Israel (even in the case of Josephus, he is reminiscing about his time in the Holy Land).

If we bring the Qumranites, John the Baptist, the sign prophets, and even Jesus into the picture, we are still dealing with prophecy in, or on the borders of, Israel. Thus, although Jewish prophecy was highly regarded throughout the empire,[4] its provenance seems to be highly localized. This may, in turn, suggest that we should expect much of the Jewish apocalyptic literature to come out of this same geographical region in the eastern empire.

What we do not find is any hard evidence of Jewish prophets in the major pagan cities of the empire, such as Ephesus or Athens or Rome.[5] The provenance of some of the Jewish *Sibylline Oracles* may be debated, but even if one considers this material real prophecy and not just literary artifice, it does not substantially alter the above picture. This evidence does not need to be belabored, because the character of such material is very much like what has already been discussed at length in the preceding chapters. More attention at this juncture needs to be paid to pagan prophecy and divining.

If we turn to Hellenistic or Greco-Roman prophecy, the evidence becomes more abundant, especially if we include diviners as well as oracular prophets in the discussion. Throughout Greek literature, it seems to be regularly assumed that the person who had close contact with a god was not necessarily able to speak clearly about or at least properly interpret what had been heard, and so needed a second person to interpret the messages received.[6] This need not mean that the oracle had spoken in strange or foreign languages or had simply uttered nonsensical syllables; it simply meant that the prophecy, though in plain speech,

---

[4] See the judgments of Tacitus and Suetonius, p. 259 above.

[5] Acts 19:11–20 does provide a brief glimpse of some Jewish exorcists, but notice that even they are said to be itinerant. We cannot rule out Jewish prophets appearing elsewhere in the empire than in Israel and its borders (down into Egypt as far as Alexandria, and north perhaps as far as Antioch, and west into the regions just beyond the Jordan), but the evidence for Jewish prophets being widespread throughout the empire is lacking. The case of Simon Magus comes to mind, since he is supposed to have gone to Rome and spoken there, but he was never a person who was a part of mainstream early Judaism, and at least the NT portrays him as a magician or thaumaturge rather than a prophet (Acts 8). See Witherington, *The Acts of the Apostles*, 283–84.

[6] See rightly D. Potter, *Prophets and Emperors* (Cambridge: Harvard University Press, 1994), 11.

required further explanation to make sense. It had a vague or multivalent quality to it that could be interpreted several ways. For this reason, it is not surprising that it is frequently the interpreter of the oracles who is called the *prophētēs* in Greek literature.[7] "The failure to develop a precise terminology to distinguish between receivers and interpreters of divine communication is a result of a range of techniques available and underlines the basic point that definitions that insist upon direct divine contact as a feature of prophecy . . . will not do for the Greek and Roman world."[8]

Herein lies a significant difference between prophecy in the Jewish and Christian traditions and that in the Greco-Roman traditions. This may be one reason that Jewish or Christian prophecy was so widely appreciated—the prophet or prophetess did not require a second consultant to make plain what was meant. At the same time, one must stress that apocalyptic literature manifests some of the same qualities as Greco-Roman prophecy in this respect: further interpretation of the meaning of the revelation was often required, indeed required by the seer himself, to make sense of it. The angelic interpreter in apocalypses plays a role somewhat similar to the Greco-Roman interpreter of prophecies.

If we examine the map of the Greco-Roman world, we discover that there were only so many famous oracular sites, most of which, not surprisingly, were clustered in Greece or in hellenized Asia. The nearest Greek oracular sites, of any importance, to the Holy Land would be the shrines at Apamea and Mallos north and west of Antioch on the Orontes.[9] There were a couple of such shrines near Rome, but of course they did not have the antiquity or reputation of the shrines at Delphi in Greece or Claros or Myra in Asia. Because the famous oracular shrines were removed, in some cases far removed, from civilization, it became difficult for ordinary people who did not live near a shrine to consult oracles. Hence the need arose for traveling prophets.

Plutarch provides clear evidence about traveling prophets and would have been in a position to evaluate them, since he had served, at one point in his career, at the shrine at Delphi. In *Def. orac.* 421B he refers to a prophet he met near the Red Sea who held meetings with humans only one day of the year. He was seen as a sacred person because he had separated himself from human society and engaged in an ascetical lifestyle (cf., e.g., John the Baptist). Plutarch informs us this man was versed in many languages but spoke to him in Doric Greek that had a musical quality to it. Besides having great learning, he also was inspired to prophesy and did so one day a year when he went to the sea and predicted the future.

If one could not find a wandering prophet, one could resort to a divining device. One such device was the lot oracle, which Cicero speaks of with contempt (*Div.* 2.41.86–87). Yet clearly it was very popular, as is shown by the lot oracle (found in P.Mich. 1258) from Egypt in which Isis is petitioned for health. We may also refer to the use of dice by all sorts of people to make decisions or

---

[7] See below on the Pythia, pp. 318–20.

[8] Potter, *Prophets and Emperors*, 12.

[9] See the map, ibid., 14.

gain knowledge (cf. Suetonius, *Tib.* 14.3; Pausanias, *Desc.* 7.25.10). Nevertheless, in the Jewish tradition Urim and Thummim were respected, and it is noteworthy that there is a depiction of the earliest Christians using a lot oracle to determine membership among the Twelve (Acts 1:15–26). It is difficult to know whether Luke is himself apologetically viewing this as an inferior form of prophecy that Christians would only engage in before the Holy Spirit fell on them, or whether he saw this as viable for Christians.[10]

There was a tendency to trust the old shrines most, and since it was known that Jewish prophecy had a very long heritage, it was revered for its antiquity, just as Greco-Roman prophecy was. Even the skeptical Tacitus was willing to allow that the oracle of Apollo at Claros had accurately predicted the death of Germanicus, the nephew of Tiberius, a year in advance (in AD 19; *Ann.* 2.54.2–3). Greco-Roman prophecy was often about understanding the present, but it also definitely had a predictive element.

The interpretation of dreams was a major part of Greco-Roman prophecy, and there were even handbooks, such as Artemidorus Daldianus's *Onirocritica (The Interpretation of Dreams),* that served as guides. It is interesting that Artemidorus divides dreams into predictive and nonpredictive dreams (*Onir.* 1.1) and says they can be direct or allegorical and that they are seen by him as an accurate means of revelation, either as a clear vision from a god or as an oracle (1.2–4). Here again there is a similar attitude to what one finds in postexilic Jewish material that stands at the beginning of the apocalyptic genre (e.g., Daniel and Zechariah). One might hypothesize that the closer we get to the turn of the era and the more hellenized Judaism became, the more Jewish prophecy manifested some of the aspects of broader prophetic traditions, but we must be cautious about this judgment because dream interpretation and divining had a long history in the ancient Near East.[11]

Without question, the character of Greco-Roman prophecy was, more often than not, extremely mundane. A person wanted to know about his or her future or the way to go in regard to some major decision that needed to be made. The person then would go to an oracle and ask the sort of questions we find in P.Oxy. 1477: "Shall I get my pay? Am I to be sold as a slave? Shall I go on an embassy? Am I to become a town councilor? Shall I be separated from my wife? Am I under a spell?" The oracle or prophet played the role of advisor or consultant.

But suppose one could not go to an oracle. One could still consult a book such as that from which the above questions were taken—the *Sortes Astrampsychi.* This book was enormously popular, and it contained ninety-two standard questions, like those listed above, and, in the second part of the book, a series of answers arranged in groups of ten. The seeker would first pick a numbered question, then pick a number from 1 to 10, then add the number of the question to the number picked, and so one had one's answer. Since the second

---

[10] Notice there is no criticism of the lot casting or any later report that the selection of the Twelve's new member was done over because of the inadequacy of the lot casting.

[11] See pp. 13–19 above.

number was picked at random, it was thought that the god had placed that number in one's mind.[12] It is of importance that the questions and answers spanned the social spectrum. Some were those likely asked by slaves, others by the free working class, others by elite members of society. Thus, while consultative prophecy of the sort found at Delphi or Claros or Didyma was an expensive proposition involving travel, time, and money and thus was a practice that reinforced the stratified nature of society, some of these other means of getting answers were more readily and cheaply available, even to slaves.

Something more, however, needs to be said about the prophetic shrines and consultations at places such as Delphi. On the day when the Pythia would give oracles, the seeker sacrificed outside the shrine and choruses sang hymns to the gods. It was the role of the *prophētēs* to go in to the Pythia's shrine and ask her the questions that the one who came for consultation had asked. Once the Pythia responded, the *prophētēs* would then go forth and interpret the oracle to the client. Notice that if one had come to the shrine on behalf of another, the prophecy was written down and sealed, to be opened only by the original inquisitor. The agent would be warned of dire consequences if he opened the written-out prophecy in advance of its being seen by the originator of the request (Iamblichus, *Myst.* 3.10–12). It is also worth stressing that the oracle was written down in verse by the *prophētēs*.

These facts not only help explain why some of Paul's Corinthian Christians might well have thought it appropriate, and indeed a prophetic task, to ask questions during a worship service that included prophecy (cf. below on 1 Cor 14). They might also have seen interpretation as a prophetic task. The sealing up of the prophecy echoes what is found in Jewish and Christian apocalyptic material. There are a wide variety of social similarities between prophecy and its accouterments in all these cultures, especially in the eastern end of the empire, and thus the phenomena need to be compared and contrasted.

Potter has noted that inspired oracles "appear to have been a feature of religious life that was peculiar to the Eastern Mediterranean: their like appears on tablets from Mari and Assyria and from records of the earliest periods of recorded Greek history."[13] This is an important observation for this particular study because it means that, in the area in which early Jewish and Christian prophecy arose, there was an expectation of oracular performance from a prophet. One needed to speak like or as a prophet if one was to be recognized as such, and this meant, among other things, making pronouncements about the future in poetic form. Virgil was so successful in imitating the poetic form of prophetic oracles that his fourth *Eclogue* was often mistaken for a real prophecy.

But we must bear clearly in mind the differences from biblical prophecy as well. Plutarch puts the matter quite plainly when he says that the voice of the prophet is *not* the voice of the god, nor is the utterance or diction or meter from the god. Plutarch says the god puts visions in the mind of the Pythia and a light

---

[12] See Potter, *Prophets and Emperors*, 24–25.
[13] Ibid., 38.

in her soul in regard to the future, but the voice, the utterance, the meter, the diction all come from the Pythia herself. This poetic utterance then must be interpreted by a *prophētēs* (*Mor.* 397B-C). Plutarch is very insistent that gods do not enter human bodies and act like ventriloquists, using human mouths as instruments (*Mor.* 414E).

In general, there seems to have been a higher opinion of oracles than of diviners. Cicero admits, even though he is a supporter of diviners, that those who practice divination by "art" (as opposed to inspiration) were likely to make mistakes (*Div.* 1.55.24). There was an especially high appreciation of the accounts of fulfilled oracles. Indeed, one of the major reasons for writing down already fulfilled prophecies was the authentication of the art, but another reason was to reassure some that nothing further was to be feared from such fulfilled old prophecies (see *FGH* 257, frg. 36). One wonders if perhaps at least some of the material in the Markan apocalypse and its parallels may have been recorded for this reason, to reassure the audience that these various things were predicted and had already transpired and needed not to be feared any longer.

The case of the sibylline oracles deserves special mention. The earliest extant evidence of a prophetess named Sibylla comes from the fifth century BC.[14] Her words were collected and added to, over the course of time, by professional oracle collectors, known as "chresmologues."[15] One notable feature of her oracles seems to have been their conditional nature, in the form of conditional and final clauses. The gist of such oracles was that "when certain conditions arise, something will happen." There is perhaps only one fragment of the original oracles that has survived intact the burning of the Temple of Jupiter in 83 BC. It is preserved by Phlegon Trallianus and details the relationship of the sibyl with Apollo (her inspiring deity). The passage deserves to be quoted at some length.

> But why indeed all-sorrowful do I sing divine oracles about other peoples' suffering, holding to my fated madness? Why do I taste its painful sting, retaining my grievous old age into the tenth century, raging in my heart and speaking things that are not believed, having foreseen in a vision all the unendurable griefs of humankind? The one envious of my prophetic gift, the son of famous Leto, filling his destructive heart with passion, will loose my spirit, chained in its miserable body, when he will have shot through my frame with a flesh-piercing arrow. Then immediately, my spirit, having flown through the air, sends to the ears of mortals audible omens mingled with the breeze, wrapped in complex riddles. My body will lie shamefully unburied upon mother earth. No mortal will cover it with earth or hide it in a tomb. My black blood will trickle down through the broad pathways of the earth, dried by

---

[14] See ibid., 72.

[15] This practice raises the question whether there would have been Jewish or Christian oracle collectors as well. In regard to the latter, all one can say is that there is no evidence of them in the NT because there are no prophetic books except the Apocalypse, which represents not a collection from varied sources but material from one source. In any case, as Potter, ibid., 95, clearly reminds us, the oracle collector was *not* seen as a prophetic figure himself and did not claim authority as a prophet. He was, rather, a sage who conveyed ancient wisdom to others in the form of oracles.

time. From there thick grass will shoot up, which when the herds have grazed on it, will sink into their livers and show the purposes of the immortal gods by prophecies; and the birds in their feathered robes if they taste my flesh, will give true prophecy to mortals. (*FGH* 257, frg. 37V)

This passage is noteworthy not only for the light it sheds on ancient thinking about the connection of the entrails of animals or the flight of birds to prophecy but also because it stresses that the sibyl sang her oracles. The musical phenomenon or dimension is so widespread in connection with prophecy not only in the Greek and Roman world but also in the ancient Near East and in Jewish contexts that it sets up an a priori likelihood that Christians who inherited various eastern traditions and knew various western ones would likely have couched their prophecies in verse and have sung them as well.[16]

Notice, for example, in the eighth *Sibylline Oracle,* a Christian product, there is in the first 216 verses a prediction of the end of the world in the mid–second century AD, followed by a poem on Christ, another eschatological description, a hymn to God, and a discussion of Christ's incarnation. Lines 217–250 also include the famous acrostic on the words "Jesus Christ, son of God savior, cross." Hymnic material is considered prophetic by Christians and so is included in this collection. One must note as well that there were hymns, composed in honor of the emperor, that were sung in the emperor cult and in processions through the streets in the Greek east.[17]

Christians would and did quite naturally see the emperor cult as a rival claimant to their own worship of Christ, not least because both were touting "gods who walked upon the earth." In this environment and especially in the eastern end of the empire, where emperor worship had originated and flourished, it is understandable that Christians might compose prophetic hymns in honor of Christ.[18] This would place Christians in a precarious position because although Romans allowed a distinction between private religion and official cults, when a "private" religion made exclusive claims that conflicted with the emperor's claims, then that religion and its prophecies and songs would be seen as subversive of the political order. It was not for no reason that Augustus had, according to Suetonius, two thousand "false" (from his perspective) prophetic books burned in the Forum in Rome. He also moved other prophetic books to the Temple of Apollo on the Palatine from their previous Capitoline location (*Aug.* 31). Any sect offering up new prophecies about a Lord or world ruler would fall under suspicion during the empire.[19]

Both Jews and Christians, under the influence of Hellenistic culture, came in due course to adapt and add to the sibylline collections. It was only after the

---

[16] See pp. 17–19 and 37–39 above.

[17] See Potter, *Prophets and Emperors,* 129.

[18] See pp. 306–10 below.

[19] Notice the conclusion of Potter, *Prophets and Emperors,* 214: "The single most important development in the three centuries after Augustus was the growth of Christianity, a religion that was itself founded upon prophecies."

time of Augustus that the sibyl emerged as the preeminent prophetess, whose words had survived the centuries.[20] Once this happened, there would be considerable impetus and temptation for Jews and Christians to co-opt this tradition to validate their own traditions. This study has already seen evidence that this transpired,[21] and to this evidence we could add the testimony of Pausanias, who mentions a Jewess who was a sibyl named Sabbe and who grew up around Palestine among the Hebrews (*Desc.* 10.12.9). In fact, by the time we get to the turn of the era, there were already a variety of sibyls in a variety of places, all of whom were thought to contribute to the sibylline tradition. We must bear in mind that the sibylline oracles were seen as so important that in 76 BC an embassy was sent by the Senate to the east to collect and bring back a new set of her oracles to replace the ones lost in the Jupiter temple fire of 83 BC.

Collections of such prophecies were considered politically dangerous as well, as is shown by the action of the ever suspicious and paranoid Tiberius, who ordered an investigation of all books containing prophecies (Dio Cassius, 57.18.5). The re-collection of sibylline oracles in itself provided a window of opportunity for various traditions to be added to this material. This tradition continued to have considerable influence and authority even up to the time of the emperor Constantine, who commended the sibyllines as authentic, as was proved because they were morally uplifting (*Or. sanct.* 19.1). And the author of the Shepherd of Hermas had already (mis)identified the Spirit of the church as the sibyl of Cumae, perhaps the most famous of all the sibyls (Herm. *Vis.* 2.4.1).

Thus, the NT discussions of prophecy must be assessed in the light of not only the Jewish prophetic background but also the Greco-Roman prophetic foreground. While it is true that the NT authors, being Jews with the possible exception of Luke, reflect more indebtedness to the Jewish prophetic tradition than to the Greco-Roman one, nonetheless the influence of the latter can be seen, for instance, in the way the Corinthians approached prophecy and, in some respects, even in that Scripture-saturated book—Revelation. Bearing all this in mind, it is time to consider some of the Christian prophetic material, beginning with the earliest source of information—the Pauline corpus.

II. PAUL THE SEER AND PROPHET

Was Paul a prophet? This question is of crucial importance, not least because the earliest documents about early Christianity are Paul's letters. What follows is a review of the evidence that Paul was a seer and/or a prophet.[22] The first text of importance is Gal 1:15–16. This is not Paul's personal testimony in

---

[20] See ibid., 78.

[21] See pp. 231–34 above.

[22] This discussion is a somewhat different version of my discussion in B. Witherington, *The Paul Quest: The Search for the Jew from Tarsus* (Downers Grove, Ill.: InterVarsity, 1998).

anything like a full form. It is a highly selective and carefully couched presentation on a subject that the Galatians have already heard something about (1:13). Furthermore, the function of the autobiographical remarks is to substantiate a particular claim not so much about Paul and his Christian origins as about the nature and origins of his gospel and, secondarily, about his apostolic authority to preach it.

Galatians 1:12 offers two specific denials. Paul did not receive his gospel from human beings, nor was he taught it. On the contrary, it came through a revelation of Jesus Christ. Notice that the issue here is the source and nature of his gospel and the means and timing of its reception (namely, at the beginning of his Christian life). There is debate as to whether the last clause ("revelation of Jesus Christ") should be taken to refer to a revelation of which Christ is the content or a revelation that comes from or through Christ. In view of the rest of ch. 1, Paul is not likely denying that he ever received any information about Jesus from human beings. Verse 16 intimates that Paul is speaking of a revelation that came from or through his encounter with Christ on the Damascus road. The most reasonable suggestion is that this revelation entailed an indication not just of who Jesus was but also of what the message was that God wanted Paul to convey—the law-free gospel, proclaimed to the Gentiles, about redemption through faith in the crucified Christ. Paul admits that this sort of message is not the kind of thing human beings could come up with on their own. It had been revealed to Paul through a "revelation." The term *apokalypsis* refers to a revelation of a hidden secret about God's plan for human redemption.

Paul here describes his experience in prophetic terms. In particular, we should hear an echo of Jer 1:5—"Before I formed you in the womb I knew you, and before you were born I consecrated you; I appointed you a prophet *to the nations.*" Isaiah 49:1–6 may also be alluded to here. Paul then refers to his being called by grace. The point of the remark is that God has had his hand on Paul since even before the time of his birth and all along had in mind for him to be God's spokesman to the Gentile nations. Paul's current occupation and vocation as apostle to the Gentiles were not a result of careful career planning on his part. Indeed, it was against the flow of, and quite apart from, his pre-Christian behavior, especially his persecuting activities. The focus here is not on the personal salvific consequences of Paul's encounter with Christ but, rather, on the basis of his ministry and message. The description is task-centered, not focused on the effects on Paul as a person apart from such activities.

But it will not do to simply see this event as a matter of a prophetic call. Galatians 1:16 speaks of a revelation of the Son either to or in Paul, probably the latter in light of 2:20 and 4:6. The coupling of the word "revelation" with the phrase "in me" suggests that Paul had an apocalyptic vision of the risen and glorified Christ, which changed the character and course of his life and indeed his very identity. Paul is not talking about his "having made a decision for Christ" or his having voluntarily changed the course of his life. To the contrary, Paul is talking about God having made a decision about Paul being his witness to the Gentiles from before the time he was born!

One must compare what Paul says here with 1 Cor 9:1, where Paul speaks of having seen the risen Lord. Paul in all likelihood would have rejected modern distinctions between objective and subjective if asked about the nature of this revelation. It was objective in the sense that it was from God and was not a result of his fantasizing or dreaming or some sort of wish projection. It was subjective in that the revelation came to, and indeed even in, Paul. It was deeply personal and transforming. The purpose of the revelation was that Paul might preach Christ among the nations. Thus, there was a call that came with the conversion, not later. The verb "preach" is in the present tense, but the verbs "set apart" and "called" are aorist, or past, tenses.

If we were to do a careful sociological analysis of what happened to Saul on the Damascus road, we would have to conclude he underwent a thorough resocialization. His symbolic universe was not just altered; it was turned upside down. Those formerly thought to be insiders were out, and those thought to be out were found to be in the people of God! It reveals something crucial about Paul's new worldview that he can see the Jewish rite of passage, namely, circumcision, as not fundamental for marking out Christians or those who were truly in the assembly of God. Notice, too, that Paul focuses clearly on the spiritual experience that changed human lives (see Gal 3:2–8) and he was willing to de-emphasize or downplay the Christian initiation rite (1 Cor 1:13–17). Conversion, not initiation, was the truly crucial thing in his mind.

It has become common in some quarters, especially in the wake of the work of K. Stendahl,[23] to suggest strongly that all that happened to Paul on the Damascus road was a prophetic call, not a conversion from Judaism to something else. The evidence suggests that Stendahl is right in what he affirms but wrong in what he tries to deny. Even with all the diversity in early Judaism, neither Qumranites nor Samaritans nor Sadducees nor Pharisees were prepared to say what Paul in fact says—that the Mosaic covenant, though glorious, has been now eclipsed, indeed is now a glorious anachronism (2 Cor 3; see Gal 4). Nor were any of these groups prepared to say that full converts to their party would not have to be circumcised and keep the law. It is impossible to believe that Paul, the former zealous Pharisee, could have ever said, "neither circumcision nor uncircumcision matters" (Gal 6:15), had there not been a radical change in his worldview and symbolic universe. This change is quite properly called a conversion. But the concern here is to focus on the prophetic and pneumatic aspects of this experience that Paul had.

Apart from the seminal work of G. D. Fee, surprisingly few detailed works have been produced in the last two decades in English that meaningfully discuss Paul's own life in the Spirit.[24] This is, in part, because Paul himself seems reticent to talk about such things, not least because he is not like many a modern Western individual bent on revealing his innermost thoughts. Ancients went out of their way not to discuss their own "unique" experiences that

---

[23] See K. Stendahl, *Paul among Jews and Gentiles* (Philadelphia: Fortress, 1977).

[24] See G. D. Fee, *God's Empowering Presence* (Peabody, Mass.: Hendrickson, 1994).

distinguished them from the crowd. Such discussions would be seen as antiso-
cial to the ancient mind-set.

It is, then, not surprising that when Paul does boast about his own "personal" experiences (spiritual and otherwise), the boasting is clearly ironic or
tongue in cheek—for example, in 2 Cor 12:1–10. This text is set in a context in
which Paul has just "boasted" about his weaknesses and his trials and tribulations (2 Cor 11), mocking the opposite sort of all too common boasting about
one's great deeds. Paul here speaks of visions and revelations (12:1). While Paul
is really claiming to have had this sort of experience once in a while, which
makes him, in various respects, like John of Patmos, he is writing to a highly
"charismatic" audience who would be eager to hear about such experiences. Paul
knows the emotional impact of such claims on them, and so here he raises their
expectations but, in the end, just teases and shames them.[25]

In vv. 2–4 Paul says that he had a vision that was a source of revelation to
him (in other words, he not only saw but heard and learned), but coyly he says
he is not permitted to convey the contents of this revelation! It is possible that
his opponents, who were bewitching the Corinthians, were claiming such experiences as well and he was mainly trying to deflate their boasting. The reason Paul
puts the description of this experience in the third person is that he is following
the rules of inoffensive self-praise.[26]

This experience is said to have happened fourteen years prior to the writing of this letter—in other words, during the period AD 40–44, which probably
places it during Paul's "hidden" years in Syria and Cilicia.[27] It is possible that,
precisely because Paul was not a modern individualist, the Corinthians would
have been shocked to hear Paul recount this story, just as they may have been
shocked to hear what Paul says about tongues and prophecy in 1 Cor 14 (see
below). Some commentators have suggested that since Paul is able to mention
only an experience of fourteen years prior, such experiences must have been especially rare for him. On the other hand, Paul may mention this one because to
him it was especially notable and outstanding. In favor of the last suggestion is
the observation of A. T. Lincoln that the plural in 2 Cor 12:1 suggests that initially Paul thought about relating more than one such vision or revelation.[28]

In the course of his discussion of this event, Paul says twice that he does
not know whether he was in or out of the body when he was "caught up." The
language suggests an overpowering ecstatic experience that overtook Paul, much
like those said to overcome some prophets in the OT era.[29] It was not something
Paul deliberately worked his way into through some spiritual exercises or ascetical practices. Paul says also that he got as far as the third heaven, which he calls

---

[25] See Witherington, *Conflict and Community in Corinth*, 459–65.

[26] See pp. 305–7 below.

[27] On the so-called hidden years, see M. Hengel and A. M. Schwemer, *Paul between
Damascus and Antioch: The Unknown Years* (Louisville: Westminster, 1997).

[28] See A. T. Lincoln, "Paul the Visionary," *NTS* 25 (1979): 204–20.

[29] See pp. 50–57 above.

paradise, a term from the Genesis story about Eden (cf. Luke 23:43; Rev. 2:7). Paul is probably not suggesting that there are any levels above the third heaven, for if he shared such a notion with his audience, this would not be an unsurpassable mock boast. Paul's point is that he got all the way to the third heaven and that this was no planned trip. Perhaps, unlike the Corinthians, he was not seeking such adventures in the Spirit.

Paul says in v. 4 that he heard unutterable words, but he clarifies this by explaining that he was simply not permitted (by God? by the Spirit?) to repeat what he heard. The Corinthians might well understand this in terms of their knowledge of mystery religions, where secrets were only revealed to special initiates. The point of even mentioning this without disclosing the message is to make clear that God thought Paul was a special person. In short, the Corinthians had badly underestimated him, for he was a seer. Yet Paul also does not want them to overestimate him just because he has had an "excess" of revelations (v. 6).[30] The impression that Paul was a visionary is clearly confirmed in Acts (see, e.g., not only the account of his conversion in Acts 9 but also Acts 16:6–10; 23:11); in addition, one may point to the various texts where Paul himself indicates that he both knows and teaches mysteries and has special revelatory knowledge (cf. 1 Cor 2:1, 10, 16; 4:1, 15:51).

As a deflation device, God gave Paul a "stake" (a sharp wooden object) in the flesh lest he, too, give way to the wrong sort of boasting. This "stake" or "thorn" had the effect of bringing Paul down to earth. Despite repeated prayer, God chose not to remove this "stake" from Paul's flesh, likely a reference to a physical condition.[31] It appears Paul was a visionary with a vision problem (see Gal 4:11–15)! Clearly from 2 Cor 10:10, Paul's condition included something visible and obvious to an outsider that led to an evaluation that he was weak or sickly. Furthermore, as 12:12 will go on to say, when Paul was with the Corinthians, miracles happened. Paul may also have been a healer who himself was not entirely well! Yet it is clear from this same context (11:21–24) that Paul did not let this condition or other misfortunes slow him down. The point, in any case, would be that Paul's weaknesses would show that the power and the revelation came from God and not from the apostle. Indeed, God's power comes to full expression or completion precisely through and in the midst of human weakness. It is interesting that Paul says in 12:9 that this divine power made its home in him. This likely draws on the image of the Shekinah glory descending on the temple and its holy of holies.

The next point to make about Paul's life in the Spirit is that he did perform miracles, although once again he does not boast of such things but mentions them only in passing. For example, one can stress the reference to signs and wonders and mighty works in 12:12 and also point to Rom 15:18–19. The last text is important because it closely associates the performances of powerful

---

[30] "Excess" is another term that supports the idea that Paul was not suggesting in this text that such experiences were rare for him.

[31] On Paul's infirmities, see pp. 301–4 above.

works with the power of the Spirit working through Paul. This impression of Paul as a miracle worker, or thaumaturge, is confirmed by various texts in Acts (see, e.g., Acts 13:11; 14:10; 16:18; 19:11; 28:3–6).

It is in light of the above evidence that we come to the discussion in 1 Cor 14 that Paul both prophesied and spoke in tongues. The former is simply implied in this chapter (see, e.g., vv. 37–39, where prophets should recognize his prophetic utterances as God's word; and cf. 13:1–2, where Paul's remarks should be probably taken as autobiographical),[32] but the latter is specifically stated. Indeed, in an attempt to deflate the overly charismatic and chaotic Corinthians, Paul says, "I thank God I speak in tongues more than all of you" (14:18), not, mind you, more than *any* of the Corinthians but more than *all* of them! Nevertheless, it is quite clear that Paul affirms the gifts of prophecy and of tongues (cf. ch. 11 on the former, and on both, 14:39), both in his own life and in the lives of other Christians.[33]

Close scrutiny of a text such as 14:2 or 14:14 strongly suggests that Paul saw glossolalia as a prayer language, something prompted by the Spirit in the believer and uttered to God. The human spirit is involved in this kind of praying but not the human mind. This leads us to a text such as Rom 8:15, with which Rom 8:26 must compared. In the former verse, we have the coordinate efforts of the human spirit and the Holy Spirit within the believer, prompting the prayer "Abba, Father." Notice how this differs from Gal 4:6, where it is said that it is the Spirit who cries, "Abba, Father." This is, of course, an intelligible utterance or prayer, but in Rom 8:26 it appears that Paul is referring to glossolalia, where the Spirit helps the believer at a loss for words and intercedes through the believer with "inarticulate groanings or speech."[34]

This kind of utterance does have meaning, although it is not immediately intelligible to the human speaker. God, however, knows the mind of the Spirit and what the Spirit is saying through the believer. The Spirit intercedes for the saints according to God's will (v. 27). That is, while the human person may not know exactly how to conform a prayer to God's will, the Spirit indeed does and will do so for the believer so that a person may pray effectively.[35] What is important about this material is that Paul is speaking from experience, including his own here. The first person plurals ("when *we* cry . . . with *our* spirit . . . the Spirit helps *us* . . . for *we* do not know how to pray") must be taken quite seriously here.

Paul was not only a spirited man, as any reading of his more polemical letters will attest, but also a man of the Spirit. It is important that we not downplay

---

[32] See C. A. Holladay, "1 Corinthians 13: Paul as Apostolic Paradigm," in *Greeks, Romans, and Christians: Essays in Honor of Abraham J. Malherbe* (ed. D. L. Balch, E. Ferguson, and W. A. Meeks; Minneapolis: Fortress, 1990), 80–98.

[33] See Witherington, *Conflict and Community in Corinth*, 276–80.

[34] See Fee, *God's Empowering Presence*, 583.

[35] See the discussion, ibid., 586; and J. D. G. Dunn, *Romans 1–8* (Waco: Word, 1988), 479–80.

this factor, and it is equally important not to contrast it with the notion of Paul being a profound and rational thinker. Paul was a person who manifested both life in the Spirit and the life of the mind, and in fact one sees a marriage of the two in passages such as Rom 8. No doubt, Paul might have said that the only persons really in their right minds are those who are filled with, and inspired by, the Spirit to think God's thoughts after God has revealed them.

When we assess this data as a whole, it becomes clear that, despite Paul's reticence to talk directly about such matters,[36] he was much more like his Corinthian converts than many modern commentators would like to think. Paul was not being facetious in 1 Cor 1:4–7 when he thanked God for the Corinthians' spiritual gifts. Paul was indeed a man of the Spirit, a "charismatic" individual not just in the secular sense of that term. His Christian life was punctuated and enriched with notable spiritual and ecstatic experiences.

Perhaps even more revealing is what Paul says about himself in 1 Cor 13:2: "And if I have prophetic powers, and understand all mysteries and all knowledge, and if I have all faith so as to move mountains, but do not have love, I am nothing." Here the "if" with the present-tense verb does not connote a purely hypothetical possibility but rather, in all likelihood, a real condition.[37] Paul has prophetic powers and understands mysteries and matters of spiritual knowledge, but he had already told his converts about spiritual knowledge earlier, in ch. 3. Again one must take seriously what Paul says about himself in 14:6: "How will I benefit you unless I speak to you in some revelation or knowledge or prophecy or teaching?" These are not terms picked at random; they reflect the way Paul views the nature or form of some of what he had communicated to the Corinthians in the past.

To judge from recent scholarly work, there is, of late, among scholars a revival of interest in Paul as a prophetic figure. Earlier in this century, one heard many debates about Paul as an apostle, but precious little was said about Paul as a prophet. When there was some discussion about Paul as a prophet, he was mainly compared to prophets connected with various forms of Hellenistic religion, especially mystery religions,[38] despite the fact that Christian prophecy was directed to, and intended for, the edification of whole congregations and was not merely a response to an inquiry by a private individual.[39] There is now a full-length monograph by K. O. Sandnes on the subject of Paul as a prophet,[40] which simply confirms what most have been saying, namely, that Paul's understanding of prophecy and prophets owes far more to the Jewish tradition than to the

---

[36] See rightly Hengel and Schwemer, *Paul between Damascus and Antioch*, 1–10.

[37] See rightly Holladay, "1 Corinthians 13," 80–85.

[38] See, e.g., H. Leisgang, *Die vorchristlichen Anschauungen und Lehren vom Pneuma unter der mystisch-intuitiven Erkenntnis* (Leipzig: Hinrichs, 1919); and R. Reitzenstein, *Die hellenistichen Mysterienreligionen: Ihr Grundgedanken und Wirkungen* (Leipzig: Teubner, 1927).

[39] See rightly E. Boring, "Prophecy, Early Christian," *ABD* 5:495–502, here 498.

[40] K. O. Sandnes, *Paul: One of the Prophets?* (Tübingen: Mohr, 1991).

Greco-Roman tradition, and there have been other significant treatments of the subject as part of larger studies of prophecy in the NT era.[41]

E. E. Ellis and others who have followed him have urged that Paul's way of handling the OT manifests Paul to be a prophetic figure.[42] In an influential study on prophecy in the Corinthian church, W. Grudem argues that there was overlap in terminology and that "the New Testament can sometimes view apostles as 'prophets.'"[43] What is troubling about some of these studies is that the term "prophet" becomes a sort of catchall label to explain diverse activities and aspects of Paul's ministry.

Scholars have long noted that Paul speaks of his conversion and call in Gal 1 in prophetic terms. Hengel sums up the opinions of many when he says,

> For Paul the eschatological "apostolic" sending by God or Christ is orientated on the sending of the prophets of the Old Covenant, indeed it surpasses these. Now the sending relates to the eschatological final salvation and therefore to decision. . . . In other words, with the Christ event and Paul's present apostolic ministry, the prophetic promise is being fulfilled. For Paul, who like Jeremiah remained unmarried, entering into this service for the sake of this salvation is from the beginning like a compulsion which he cannot avoid without putting his existence at risk.[44]

The scholarly discussion raises a whole series of questions about Paul. On the one hand, since Paul so rarely identified himself as a prophet (but see 1 Cor 14), it could be argued that Paul simply used the prophetic language of the OT to characterize his call to be an apostle, which is a rather different role from that of a prophet. Grudem, for instance, has rightly pointed out that while Paul suggests that the words of the Corinthian prophets are expected to be weighed (1 Cor 14:29) and Paul says things such as that prophets should prophesy in proportion to their faith (Rom 12:6), by contrast Paul expects his own words to be seen as having the same authority as the words of Jesus or of the Hebrew Scriptures![45]

It is thus not enough to note that both prophets and apostles are Spirit-inspired authority figures who speak for the Lord. The same could be said of Jewish sages or teachers, as a careful reading of Sirach would show. Furthermore, when Paul does use a formula such as "the Lord says," he is not offering fresh revelations but quoting or interpreting the Jesus tradition (see 1 Cor 7:10–12; 11:23; and probably 1 Thess 4:15). What one does *not* find in Paul's letters is Paul speaking simply as the mouthpiece of God or the risen Christ, speaking in the first-person

---

[41] See especially Aune, *Prophecy in Early Christianity,* 195–262; and see the survey of literature by C. A. Evans, "Prophet, Paul as," *DPL* 763–65.

[42] E. E. Ellis, *Prophecy and Hermeneutic in Early Christianity* (Grand Rapids: Eerdmans, 1978).

[43] W. Grudem, *The Gift of Prophecy in 1 Corinthians* (Lanham, Md.: University Press of America, 1982), 53.

[44] Hengel and Schwemer, *Paul between Damascus and Antioch,* 95.

[45] Grudem, *The Gift of Prophecy,* 48–49.

singular for the divine figure.[46] It is also not enough to point out that Paul frequently alludes to the prophetic Scriptures in describing the condition of his converts or of himself.[47] This is also the case of the sage who wrote Wisdom of Solomon, but it does not make the author a prophet. Unlike an oracular prophet, Paul is quite prepared to speak on his own authority as an authorized agent of Jesus Christ and expects that to carry its own weight (see 1 Cor 7:12).[48]

Grudem has argued that Paul has authority like that of the OT prophets, whose word was not to be questioned.[49] This is true, but it seems to be a matter of analogy. How do we know that apostles in the early church were not viewed as having authority equivalent to, or even greater than, the OT prophets? In other words, Paul's authority does not necessarily provide evidence for Paul as a prophetic figure. Unlike most of the Israelite prophets, Paul saw it as his primary task not to confront Israel with her sin but to convert the pagans. Jonah is hardly much of a forerunner of Paul, but a case could be made that Paul was significantly affected by the prophecies found in Isa 40–55, in understanding his own call. Indeed, it could be urged that he saw himself as the Servant referred to in those texts or at least a servant modeled on Christ, whom he saw reflected in those texts (see, e.g., Phil 1:1; cf. Phil 2:1–11).

There is also the further problem, in identifying OT and NT prophets and prophecy, that prophecy in early Christianity seems to have had a liturgical setting—it happened in Christian worship services as a part of what was expected to be communicated there (see 1 Cor 14; cf. Acts 11:27–30). The political setting and political nature of much of OT prophecy are missing in Paul's letters.

Against the attempt to suggest that the early church simply identified or amalgamated the roles and functions of apostles and prophets, one must emphasize that they are *both* listed in Paul's lists of Spirit-led leaders, which suggests that he assumes his audience would understand the distinction between the two roles (see 1 Cor 12:10, 29; Rom 12:6; Eph 4:11). These same lists suggest a distinction between a prophet and a teacher or a prophet and an evangelist.[50] Nevertheless, it was possible for a person such as Paul to fulfill the role of both prophet and apostle. The upshot of all this is that there is far too much methodological confusion among scholars on how to evaluate the prophetic material in Paul and Paul as a prophetic figure.

Aune has pointed out the right path toward a more rigorous analysis of these issues, and he has shown that more methodological precision is necessary in evaluating early Christian prophets and prophetic speech. What is of importance

---

[46] A quotation of an OT prophetic "I" word, identified as such, probably should not count as a prophetic "I" word from Paul. See, for example, Rom 14:9, which is prefaced by "as it is written" to make clear it is a quotation of an older sacred tradition, not the spontaneous creation of a new one.

[47] But see Evans, "Prophet," 763.

[48] See the second half of this chapter.

[49] See Grudem, *The Gift of Prophecy*, 48–49.

[50] See Aune, *Prophecy in Early Christianity*, 203–11.

for the search for Paul the prophet is the following: (1) Christian prophets, to judge from texts such as 1 Cor 14 or Acts 11:27–30 or Acts 21:10–11, were figures who spoke intelligible, fresh messages that were spontaneously granted to them by God by means of the Holy Spirit. (2) On occasion, God might reveal truths or ideas to these prophetic figures in visions or dreams, and Paul claims to have occasionally had such visions and dreams (see 2 Cor 12:1–10), but again, this is not simply identical with evangelizing Gentiles or speaking in synagogues. (3) Prophets in the OT, while they can be said to be like prosecutors of the covenant lawsuit that Yahweh had against his people, are not, by and large, exegetes or scribes.[51] They are those who deliver a late, pertinent word from God to God's people. (4) In view of the third point, it is not clear that "charismatic" contemporizing or interpreting of OT texts at Qumran or by various NT figures should be seen as a prophetic activity. There were other persons filled with the Spirit—teachers, scribes, or sages—who are more likely candidates to have carried out such activities.[52]

In short, prophets were apparently distinguishable in function from apostles, scribes, teachers, and evangelists even if there was some occasional overlap between their roles and functions. The goal of the study of the prophetic material in Paul's letters should be to discern what is *distinctively prophetic* about Paul's activities.[53] One thing that can be said with some assurance is that prophetic figures in the NT era continued to offer oracles about the future, as had OT and intertestamental prophetic figures.

I have argued at length elsewhere that there is no clear evidence to support the conclusion that Paul was a mistaken prophet whose teaching on eschatological matters may be considered generally suspect, since he got the timing question all wrong.[54] The possible and the necessary imminence of the end are two

---

[51] Note that Jeremiah is not portrayed as being a scribe but as having one—Baruch.

[52] Aune's remarks are telling in *Prophecy in Early Christianity*, 205:

> Paul names a great many individuals in his letters, *but none of them are designated prophets.* Prophecy for Paul is a divinely bestowed gift, and the prophets who exercise that gift appear to do so only within the framework of services of worship [italics added].

Aune also notes earlier (p. 204):

> The prophet was unique among early Christian leaders in that, unlike other functionaries, he claimed no personal part in the communication which he conveyed. Prophets acted as leaders in many early Christian communities because they were regarded by themselves and others as inspired spokesmen for the ultimate authority God. . . . There is no evidence that prophets occupied a prophetic "office," nor is there evidence that they possessed personal or professional qualification or talents other than the ability to prophesy.

[53] There are hints in both 1 Thess 5:20 and 1 Cor 14 that Paul took a somewhat different view of Christian prophecy than did his converts. There were some converts who were in danger of ignoring or despising Christian prophecy, and there were others whose enthusiasm for it knew no bounds. Part of the danger in Corinth seems to have been that the partially socialized converts there continued to view prophecy according to the pagan models they were familiar with from their past.

[54] See B. Witherington, *Jesus, Paul, and the End of the World* (Downers Grove, Ill.: InterVarsity, 1992).

different things, and Paul only spoke of the former. Yet what does Paul's lack of calculations about the timing of the end tell us about Paul's character as a prophet and about the heart of his theology? Consider the words of J. C. Beker:

> Paul's Christian hope is a matter of prophecy, not a matter of prediction. The incalculability of this hope is for Paul one of its essential marks. . . . Whereas the apocalyptic composition often concentrates on a timetable of events or on a program for the sake of calculating apocalyptic events, Paul stresses to the contrary the incalculability of the end . . . the unexpected, the suddenness, and surprising character of the final theophany (1 Thess. 5:2–10). Moreover, the incalculable character of the end motivates Paul to restrain severely his use of apocalyptic language and imagery. . . .
>
> Thus the delay of the parousia is not a theological concern for Paul. It is not an embarassment for him; it does not compel him to shift the center of his attention from apocalyptic imminence to a form of "realized eschatology," that is, to a conviction of the full presence of the kingdom of God in our present history.[55]

There is much wisdom in these words, but we would also do well to remember that apocalyptic thinking and literature by no means always include calculations about the end; indeed, often they do not.[56] Thus, it is not necessary to conclude that Paul was *not* an apocalyptic prophet (like a John of Patmos) just because he doesn't offer calculations. Paul, in his letters, also does not provide us with a cornucopia of apocalyptic images, which might discourage us from seeing Paul as, on the whole, more like Daniel than, say, Amos. But perhaps one could say he was like Jesus in that he had apocalyptic experiences yet, by and large, he expressed his prophetic words in a more traditional or classical form.

Still, the apocalyptic dimension of Paul's thought and picture language should not be dismissed. Paul's admission to having visions and revelations seems to be the one really telling piece of evidence that he sometimes functioned as an apocalyptic seer (2 Cor 12), but what makes this whole matter devilishly difficult is that Paul lived at a time after the confluence of three great Jewish traditions—prophecy, apocalyptic, and wisdom. Sages could use prophetic ideas in their aphorisms. Prophets could use apocalyptic images. Seers could speak like sages. And apparently apostles could speak like all of the above. In short, Paul's occasional use of apocalyptic language may, in the end, tell us little or nothing about Paul as a prophet, but Paul's admission to having revelations and visions does indicate that he acted as a prophet from time to time (see 1 Cor 14:6).

It would be possible at this juncture to spend considerable time looking at the positive things Paul says, apparently as a prophet, about various future events, including the character of the return of Christ and the judgment and redemption it will entail, the future resurrection triggered by Christ's return, and the final coming of God's dominion on earth. There is little or no dispute

---

[55] J. C. Beker, *Paul's Apocalyptic Gospel: The Coming Triumph of God* (Philadelphia: Fortress, 1982), 48–49.

[56] See J. J. Collins, *The Apocalyptic Imagination* (New York: Crossroad, 1984).

among scholars that Paul believed in such future realities and discussed them, especially in his earlier letters. I have addressed these issues at length elsewhere.[57] What we learn from all this discussion is that Paul the prophet has very specific ideas and hopes about the future. His is not, or at least not primarily, a vision of "pie in the sky by and by." He looks forward to a new earth and new earthlings, not merely a new heaven. He is quite clear that the Pharisaic vision of the resurrection of the righteous is essentially a right one. Resurrection is something that happens to persons on earth, not in heaven. This condition will be triggered by the return of Christ. It will be followed by the judgment of believers, and then finally, as early Christians had long prayed, the kingdom of God will come on earth as in heaven.

Yet although the content of this material is precisely what we might expect an early Christian prophet to focus on, little or none of this Pauline material about the future comes to us in the *form* of a prophetic oracle, nor does it appear to be a mere recitation of a revelation. We must look more closely to find material in Paul's letters that takes the form of prophetic or apocalyptic material.

First, we may point to the use of the term *mystērion* in an introductory clause as a signal that what follows is a quoted oracle. For example, 1 Cor 15:51 says, "Behold! I tell you a mystery: 'We will not all die, but we will all be changed, in a moment, in the twinkling of an eye, at the last trumpet. For the trumpet will sound, and the dead will be raised imperishable, and we will be changed.'" There follows an explanation of this oracle, backed up by a supporting quotation from the OT. Unlike the material in 1 Cor 15:3–7, this information would come as news to Paul's converts. It is a "late word from God," a revelation of a mystery that would otherwise not be known. Another example of this phenomenon is found in Rom 11:25. Again there are the introductory remarks about a mystery, followed by the quotation of an oracle—"I want you to understand this mystery: 'a hardening has come upon a part of Israel, until the full number of the Gentiles has come in, and in like manner all Israel will be saved.'"[58] Once again this is backed up with two quotations from the Hebrew Scriptures (in this case Isa 40:13 and Job 35:7).[59]

It says something about Paul's view of prophecy and how he expects it to be received by his audience that he feels it necessary to back such revelations up with explanations and quotations from the Scriptures. It comports with what we hear in a text such as 1 Thess 5:19–21, where Paul feels compelled to urge his converts not to quench the Spirit or despise prophecy but instead to test it and hold fast to the part of it that is true and good.

As has been often noted in this study, the form-critical study of prophecy, whether Jewish, Christian, or pagan, shows that oracles were typically given in

---

[57] See Witherington, *Jesus, Paul, and the End of the World;* and also the relevant passages from 1 Corinthians in Witherington, *Conflict and Community in Corinth.*

[58] It is interesting that the term "mystery" is also used to introduce pagan oracles from time to time. See Aune, *Prophecy in Early Christianity,* 251.

[59] See ibid., 333.

poetic form.[60] It is one of the features we should look for in isolating prophetic oracles in the Pauline corpus. Yet another feature is direct speech by God such that the prophet simply serves as an instrument through which God speaks. We do find one example of the latter phenomenon in 2 Cor 12:9, where, as mentioned, Paul speaks coyly about a revelatory experience he once had without actually revealing its content except to say at the end, "But he said to me: 'My grace is sufficient for you, for my power is made perfect in weakness.'"[61] Furthermore, one can also cite 2 Cor 13:3, where Paul stresses that Christ is speaking in or through him. At the least Paul is implying that he occasionally delivers oracles from Christ not unlike the mysteries already mentioned.

A further probable example of material that meets the formal requirements of an oracle is 1 Thess 4:15–17, where we find an introductory formula, "For this we declare to you by the word of the Lord," and then the rest of the verses quote the content of the oracle about how the living and the dead in Christ will go forth to meet the returning Christ in the air. It is not incidental that there was a long-standing tradition among the Romans, dating to at least 88 BC, that the beginning of an era or golden age would be announced by trumpet blast (Tacitus, *Ann.* 14.10.3).

Sometimes Paul refers to times when he prophesied or predicted something while he was with his converts, and once he offers a fresh prediction in a letter. For the former, see 1 Thess 3:4, "For when we were with you we predicted 'We are about to suffer persecution,'" and 1 Thess 4:2–6, " 'No one should transgress and wrong his brother in this matter, because the Lord is an avenger in all these things,' as we predicted and testified to you." For the latter case, one may refer to Gal 5:21b, "I predict for you now, just as I predicted formerly that 'Those who do such things shall not inherit the Dominion of God.'"[62] Sometimes we also find direct commands from God in Christ, conveyed by Paul (see, e.g., 2 Thess 3:6, 10, 12).

There is one further form of material that is found in Paul's letters and that may have originated when Paul or another Christian prophet was speaking oracularly—the christological hymn fragments, particularly Phil 2:6–11 and Col 1:15–20. Certainly this material has distinctive formal and poetic features, and there is precedent both within and outside the OT for prophets singing their messages. Indeed, there may even be a hint of such on the part of Paul's own namesake—King Saul (compare 1 Sam 10:9–12 with 16:16; 2 Chron 25:1; 1QH 11:3–4). In addition, it would be surprising, in view of the references in the Pauline corpus to psalms, hymns, and spiritual songs (Col 3:16; Eph 5:19–20), if we found no traces of such forms in the letters.

---

[60] Here one may compare ibid., 335–42, to most any of the form-critical surveys of OT prophetic material, e.g., Westermann, *Prophetic Oracles of Salvation;* and the study of pagan prophecy in Potter, *Prophets and Emperors.*

[61] As discussed, this is part of a put-down by Paul of the Corinthians' overeagerness for things revelatory. See Witherington, *Conflict and Community in Corinth,* 442–64.

[62] See Aune, *Prophecy in Early Christianity,* 258–59.

What is not usually recognized in the discussions of christological hymns in the NT is that the likely candidates to have originated such forms are the Christian prophets. This is so on two accounts: (1) the poetic form of the utterances points us in this direction; (2) the profound christological message of the hymns, like some of the mysteries Paul refers to (see, e.g., Eph 5:32), appears to be a likely subject for a revelation, as such high Christology might not have naturally occured to some of the earliest Jewish followers of Jesus. If this conjecture has merit, then there is a further category of material within Paul's letters that provides formal evidence that Paul was himself a prophet, or at least given to repeating Christian prophetic utterances. The Pauline character of only a minority of the material in these hymns suggests that Paul is quoting prophetic hymns of others and adding to them.

There is solid confirmation from the author of the book of Acts that Paul was a prophet. It is in Acts that very little is said about Paul being an apostle (but see Acts 14:4, 14), but Paul is rather clearly identified as a prophet (13:1) and then portrayed as one in 13:9–11. We may further point to Paul's receiving revelations in 16:6–10, 23:11, and 27:23–25. This material provides some independent confirmation of Paul's prophetic status, since it appears that the author does not know Paul's letters, or at least the capital Paulines,[63] and, of course, is famous for saying nothing about Paul being a letter writer.

It is time to sum up the discussion of Paul the prophet. Paul was by no means shy about speaking with assurance about the future, and he even offered formal predictions, which are, from time to time, quoted in his letters. This is not unexpected, since, in the Greco-Roman world, one went to an oracle, whether at Delphi or elsewhere, or to a prophet to get answers to questions about one's future.[64] Paul would have been recognized as a prophet precisely because he answered the sort of questions we find him answering in texts such as 1 Thess 4–5 or 1 Cor 15. It was not absolutely necessary for him to say, "Thus saith the Lord," and then speak as the voice of God to be recognized as a prophet in a largely Gentile context, yet it appears that Paul did regularly preface his oracles with some sort of introductory formula about a mystery or a word from the Lord.

One further learns from this material that Paul was an eschatological prophet both in the character and in the content of his prophecy. Paul believed that the eschatological age had already dawned through the death and especially the resurrection of Jesus and that, as a result of this, the form of the old world was passing away and the new creation was already partly in evidence. Paul believed that the future was indeed as bright as God's promises, and what was promised was the sure return of the Lord Jesus, the resurrection of believers, the final judgment, and the coming of the kingdom of God on earth. Paul's words about the future, while they did include metaphors such as the "thief in the night" motif, were not meant to be taken as nothing more than vague hints

---

[63] See Witherington, *The Acts of the Apostles,* 51–64.

[64] See the discussion on prophecy in the Greco-Roman world in Witherington, *Conflict and Community in Corinth,* 276–82.

about what was to come. For Paul, who had been a Pharisee, the resurrection, and in particular the resurrection body, was no mere metaphor, nor a mere description of a spiritual state. Paul expected something just as dramatic to happen to believers and their bodies as had already happened to their Lord on Easter. The linking of Christ's resurrection with that of believers makes clear that Paul has something quite concrete in mind.

Paul was an apocalyptic prophet in the sense that, on occasion, he could use apocalyptic images to describe the future (2 Thess 2). He was an apocalyptic prophet also in that he believed he was conveying mysteries hidden from the human eye. We should not divorce what we learn about Paul as a man of the Spirit,[65] who on occasion was taken up by a vision into heaven and received revelations, from what we learn about him as a prophet. Paul was also an apocalyptic prophet in that he believed that it would take nothing less than direct divine intervention to finally and forever change the world and humankind into what they ought to be. No visit from an emperor could convey the state of blessedness humans needed in order to be in continual bliss. Yet Paul was not like a prophet who is all future promises and no present delivery. Believers would be exhorted to become what they already were beginning to be. Not just talk but power was already available through the Holy Spirit.

It is the combination of prophecy and the work of the Spirit that, among other things, made Paul a powerful figure to reckon with. Paul could deliver more than just spiritual words; he was a conduit for spiritual works as well. He was, in some respects, like the charismatic performance prophets of old, such as Elijah or Daniel. The reaction to Paul as depicted in Acts 14:8–18, as the true Hermes, the true messenger of God, was surely not all that untypical. If indeed Paul came with powerful words and powerful or even miraculous deeds to a Greco-Roman world starved for, and in need of, both, it is not surprising he was often welcomed with open arms. It is also not surprising that other authority figures and power brokers—in the synagogue, in the secular assembly, and even, sadly, within the church—saw him as a definite threat and danger. Charismatic leaders always rattle the cage of institutional leaders, especially when they claim to answer solely or almost solely to God directly.

Our discussion of the forms of prophetic speech in Paul's letters has suggested several important conclusions: (1) The majority of the content of Paul's letters is not oracular, but there is enough evidence of oracles to suggest that Paul did regularly offer such oracles. (2) It is possible that some of the hymn fragments in Paul's letters reflect prophetic activity. (3) There was a repeated emphasis on prediction in the passages that contained citation of mysteries or oracles. It appears that prophecy can not be simply equated with preaching the good news, which, as texts such as 1 Cor 15:3–8 suggest, was based largely on received tradition, not instantaneous oracles. (4) Paul, in his letters, often teaches on the basis of both received traditions and revelations about the future, but most of this material is now no longer in the form of prophecy but, rather, has been made serviceable for

---

[65] See pp. 303–8 above.

teaching and persuading Gentiles. It has the form of discourse, not poetry. A distinction can and should be made between a revelation, the conveying of a revelation in a prophecy, and teaching on the basis of a revelation. (5) Very little encouragement was found for the suggestion that "charismatic" interpretation of the Hebrew Scriptures should be seen as a prophetic activity, unless those texts where Paul cites creatively an OT text to back up a revelation count. (6) The description of the effect of prophecy in 1 Cor 14: 3 as something that builds up, encourages, and consoles and later, in 14:24, as something that reproves and calls to account suggests a strong ethical content to some prophecy, which is not surprising, since the major audience for Christian prophecy was the body of Christ and the occasional outsider who came and shared with them in worship.

On the issue of the office of prophet, Paul has little to say. He seems strangely reluctant to use the term *prophētēs* as a way of characterizing who he is and what his role is in his churches. This contrasts dramatically with his use of the term "apostle." This reluctance is understandable when we recognize that NT prophets did not have the same status, standing, or unquestioned authority as some of the OT prophets. Rather, there is evidence from Paul suggesting that the utterances of Christian prophets needed to be weighed, since it was possible for their prophecy, in the enthusiasm of the moment of revelation, to exceed the proportion of their faith and understanding. Thus, on the one hand, Paul has to encourage even the "charismatic" Corinthians to seek to prophesy, and on the other hand, he has to urge the Thessalonians not to despise prophecy or quench the Spirit. The prophet, it seems, did not have the highest honor rating in Paul's communities. Yet Paul clearly rated prophets as very important to the early church, placing them behind only the apostles in his lists of church roles and functionaries.

Finally, there is no reason to simply blend together the roles of prophet and apostle. Indeed, there are good reasons to distinguish the two, as Paul regularly does. In Paul's view, an apostle has more authority than a prophet and a wider scope of responsibilities and ministry. Nevertheless, when Paul seeks to characterize his conversion and call to ministry, not surprisingly he draws on the characterizations of the calls of some of the great OT prophets, such as Jeremiah, and he uses the language of the Servant Songs to speak of himself. It is difficult to tell whether this is just the use of biblical language to characterize his call to be an apostle or whether he sees himself as called to be a prophet at the same time he was called to be an apostle.

III. THE CORINTHIAN PROPHETS

Some of the sources that present us with a picture of Paul as a prophet also provide us with evidence about some of Paul's converts being prophets. It is time to consider what 1 Cor 14 reveals about prophecy as the Corinthians saw it.[66]

---

[66] What follows is found in a somewhat different form in Witherington, *Conflict and Community in Corinth.*

There are two important issues to be addressed: (1) how did the Corinthians view prophecy and tongues, and (2) how did Paul view them? It is easier to get at the latter than the former, but both are crucial to understanding this passage because Paul is definitely correcting abuses of these gifts, and this involves Paul in trying to persuade the Corinthians to view these gifts in a different manner than they had been doing. First Corinthians 14 is not just about the use of the gifts but also about the reasons they should be evaluated and used in certain ways, which requires a clear understanding of the nature of the phenomena in question.

One of the problems in various works by NT scholars on prophecy is that certain assumptions are made about the relationship between ecstasy and prophecy in the Greco-Roman world and at Delphi in particular and this understanding is then predicated of at least the Corinthians, if not Paul as well. For example, A. C. Wire assumes that the Corinthians experienced prophecy and tongues as an integrated phenomenon and suggests, "This movement into tongues could occur as the climax of prophecy when it reveals 'unspeakable speech' (2 Cor. 12:4) or as a final sign confirming to believers that the prophecy is divine."[67] Apparently, this is based on the assumption that ecstasy was the basis, if not the very essence, of pagan prophecy, particularly at Delphi. Or again, Boring suggests, on the basis of a certain reading of 14:13–19, that the interpretation of tongues is equivalent to prophecy, but in fact all that Paul says is that tongues can be edifying like prophecy and therefore can be expressed in worship if the tongue speaker interprets what he has just said.[68] The social effect of interpreted tongues and prophecy can be the same, but otherwise they are different phenomena.

---

[67] A. C. Wire, *The Corinthian Women Prophets: A Reconstruction through Paul's Rhetoric* (Minneapolis: Fortress, 1990), 140. Cf. B. A. Pearson, *The Pneumatikos-Psychikos Terminology in 1 Corinthians* (Missoula: Society of Biblical Literature, 1973), 44. Wire also seems to assume that all or nearly all of the Corinthian women were ecstatic prophetesses, and by an unfortunate bit of mirror reading argues, "It is possible that some of Paul's negative images for speaking in tongues are direct reversals of positive images used in Corinth: tongues seen as cultivated speech, as signs of maturity, as fruitful for the community, as special intelligence, as a music particularly appropriate to the revealing of God in Christ" (p. 143). This is part of her larger argument in support of a Corinthian theology supported by the prophetesses, which she finds more palatable than Paul's alternative. Against this sort of approach, Paul is not simply trying to correct women in this passage. Furthermore, he is not trying to stifle either prophecy or tongues in Corinth but to order their expression so *everyone* benefits from these gifts, not just the individual speaker. At the close of his argument, he makes certain no one misunderstands him to have been guilty of forbidding such expressions (14:39). It is a matter of prioritizing them according to what best edifies and witnesses to those present.

[68] E. Boring, *The Continuing Voice of Jesus* (Louisville: Westminster, 1991), 152–53; this provides grist for his mill that the prophets were also those who interpreted traditions and texts. But this is a real stretch on the basis of 1 Cor 14. One must argue this case on other grounds.

J. Fontenrose has stressed that assumptions about ecstasy and the oracle at Delphi need to be checked against what is actually known about the practices at Delphi as well as other similar Greek oracles.[69] Fontenrose argues that a "close study of all reliable evidence for Delphic mantic procedures reveals no chasm or vapors, *no frenzy of the Pythia, no incoherent cries interpreted by priests. The Pythia spoke clearly, coherently, and directly to the consultant in response to his question.*"[70] The oracles at Delphi took three basic forms: (1) commands, sanctions, or instructions to do something; (2) predictions; and (3) statements of past or present fact. The most common of these modes is the first.

One particular form of sanction is especially interesting for the study of 1 Corinthians. The sanction begins, "it is better and more good" *(lōon kai ameinon)* to do X (than Y). A good example of this form is found in L137, where the oracle tells the Heraklids, "it is better *[ameinon einai sphisin]* to bury Alkemene in Megara."[71] This should be compared to the "slogan" in 1 Cor 7:1: "It is good for a man not to 'touch' a woman." At least some of these so-called slogans may have begun life as prophetic words or sanctions, cast in one of the traditional forms used at Delphi. Delphi was Apollo's shrine, he was the god of prophecy, and the ancient temple in Corinth was likely his shrine. It is hardly surprising that the Corinthians might view prophecy in a Delphic light.

Category 2 includes the repeating of commonplaces or proverbs, but Fontenrose thinks the evidence is weak that the Pythia ever historically used such proverbs as a part of a response.[72] It is true that Delphi during the period of the empire was past its glory days, and there were certain tendencies manifested in this late period, such as responses in poetic form, that did not characterize the oracle's words in classical or Hellenistic times. It is not clear, however, that the *priests* or *prophētai* transformed the oracles of the Pythia into poetic form (hexameter).[73]

The procedure at Delphi entailed a person asking *questions* of the Pythia. This may provide a clue to the meaning of 1 Cor 14:35, for *eperōtatōsan* normally means to ask a question. The evidence suggests that the oracle responded in intelligible speech directly to the questioner, or if an ambassador had been sent to ask on someone else's behalf, a response would be given and perhaps written down by one of the priests.[74] Plutarch, as mentioned, had been one of

---

[69] For a sample oracular answer, promising guidance and prosperity to the inquirer, cf. *NewDocs* 2:37–44.

[70] J. Fontenrose, *The Delphic Oracle* (Berkeley: University of California Press, 1978), 10; emphasis added.

[71] Cited in Fontenrose. Fontenrose rightly takes a critical approach to the oracles at Delphi, dividing them up into clearly historical responses and legendary ones. The modes of command or sanction have a strong historical basis, whereas "obscure" or barely intelligible commands and instruction seem to have none. Cf. ibid., 14–15.

[72] Ibid., 87.

[73] Strabo, 9.3.5, speaks of poets who put the oracles into verse and worked for the sanctuary at Delphi. On oracles in verse with meter, cf. Plutarch, *Mor.* 623A.

[74] Cf. Fontenrose, *The Delphic Oracle*, 217.

the priests at Delphi (cf. *Mor.* 792–793; 700e; *SIG* 829A), and he witnessed consultations and heard responses. As Fontenrose says, Plutarch "says nothing about vapors, toxic or otherwise, nothing about a frenzy or trance of the Pythia, nothing about wild or incoherent speech from the Pythia's mouth except in one passage—a report of an *exceptional* consultation."[75] Plutarch does, however, speak about *pneumata* that affected the oracle (*Mor.* 402B; cf. 437c).

It is a mistake to draw conclusions on the basis of late Latin writers who had never visited Delphi, because the Greek word *mania* means "transport, rapture, ecstasy, inspiration," *not* "frenzy, delirium, hysteria, insanity." It was translated into Latin as *insania* or *vecordia,* with the result that Lucan and others described a mad or raving Pythia, which is not historically accurate.[76] There is no historically credible evidence of the Pythia taking leave of her senses when prophesying. "The Pythia's inspiration is not Dionysiac, but thoroughly Apolline in nature, i.e., mantic."[77]

While inspiration or ecstasy led to speech at the oracle at Delphi, the historical evidence for "ecstatic speech" that was then interpreted by a priest is lacking.[78] The Pythia gave her answer clearly and directly to the consultant. If the Corinthians were taking their cues from their larger culture in regard to ecstatic *speech,* which today is called glossolalia, they would likely have thought of it in light of what they knew about the Dionysiac rites and would have distinguished it from prophecy, which they would have associated with Apollo and Delphi. There is no hard evidence that the Corinthian Christians confused or fused prophecy and tongues. Paul's responses suggest that they had simply been practicing both in worship without regulation and order and that the tongues spoken in Corinth had gone uninterpreted.

Another important point is that at Delphi not only was the Pythia often called a *prophētis* (cf. Euripides, *Ion,* lines 42, 321) but so is the priest, although "in most instances a *prophetes* is not himself a mantis; he is a god's representative, a man who oversees and adminsters an oracular session. The priest-prophet who attended the Pythia presided over the mantic session at Delphi, answering all questions except the question put to the Pythia as the god's mouthpiece."[79] This likely means that, in addition to the female Pythia, the male priests were also viewed as holding the prophetic office and could answer some questions. What the priest did not do was answer *for* the Pythia when the oracle was being consulted directly.

---

[75] Ibid., 197. The one exceptional incident is recorded in Plutarch, *Mor.* 438b, and Plutarch stresses that the Pythia was not at all herself on this occasion. She even entered the *manteion* unwillingly, and the text says she became hysterical, gave a shout, and rushed for the door. It says nothing about ecstatic speech.

[76] On her intelligibility of response, cf. Plutarch, *Mor.* 407 BC.

[77] Cf. Fontenrose, *The Delphic Oracle,* 207. It is a mistake to associate too closely the Dionysiac rites and what went on at Delphi.

[78] Boring, *The Continuing Voice,* 49, falls into the trap many have fallen into: taking one account in Plutarch to represent the normal experience of the Pythia.

[79] Fontenrose, *The Delphic Oracle,* 218–19.

Finally, the questions most frequently asked of the Pythia fall into three categories: (1) religious matters, such as whether a sacrifice should be offered, a temple built, or a certain rite followed; (2) public matters, such as whether a city or colony should be founded, a war undertaken, and statements about rulers and ruling; (3) domestic matters, such as one's birth or origins, career or profession, whether one should buy some land, and death and burial. One of the most frequent sorts of question in the legendary sources, however, was about marriage and childbearing, and the papyri from Egypt show that questions and answers about marriage, separation, and the death of a spouse were not uncommon at other locations.[80] It is this third category—domestic questions—that most likely would have been asked of prophets in the Corinthian congregation. It is possible, too, that some of the other pronouncements in 1 Corinthians, such as, "there is no resurrection of the dead" or, "everything is permitted," were prophetic in character and thus, because of their supposed sacred origins, Paul had to counter them at length. This raises the question whether Paul would have seen his own teaching, for example, in 1 Cor 7 or 14, as inspired in character as he responded to the Corinthians' queries. First Corinthians 14:37 suggests yes is the proper answer to this question.[81] This, however, need not mean that Paul's inspired teaching should be seen as prophecy. Rather, it is pneumatic teaching. But this entire discussion raises major questions about how prophecy has been viewed in NT scholarship, especially by those who want to maintain that the continuing voice of Jesus speaking through Christian prophets was not usually distinguished from the utterances of the historical Jesus. This discussion must turn to these issues next.

IV. ECSTASY AND ENERGY—PROPHETS AND TRADENTS IN EARLY CHRISTIANITY

In what follows, the very important proposal of Boring will be the focus of attention. Boring, expanding on older ideas of Bultmann, argues that there were indeed many early Christian prophets, that they spoke the words of the risen Lord, and that in due course this material was blended with collections of the words of the historical Jesus (in part because prophets were those who transmit-

---

[80] Cf. *NewDocs* 2:42–43. The similarity of the questions here to those asked of the Pythia at Delphi in the legendary sources suggests that marriage and family questions *were* asked of her, since such questions seem to have been commonly asked of oracles in the Greco-Roman world, although we lack hard evidence for Delphi.

[81] On Paul as a prophet and on the prophetic claims he makes in 1 Cor 14, cf. H. Merklein, "Der Theologe als Prophet," *NTS* 38 (1992): 402–29, here 427. G. Dautzenberg, "Botschaft und Bedeutung der urchristlichen Prophetie nach dem ersten Korintherbrief (2.6–16;12–14)," in *Prophetic Vocation in the New Testament and Today* (ed. J. Panagopoulos; Leiden: E. J. Brill, 1977), 131–61, is hardly convincing when he argues that Christian prophecy barely outlived the time of Paul in the Pauline communities. This conclusion comes from too narrow a definition of what prophecy was.

ted the sayings of Jesus), so that one finds some of this data in the Gospels and elsewhere in the NT.[82] This proposal has been a major presupposition in a good deal of the scholarly study of Q and has strongly affected, among others, the Jesus Seminar. Thus, this thesis deserves to be examined very carefully.

There is much to be commended in Boring's work, not the least of which is his systematic approach to dealing with these complex issues. Boring is right that the discussion of early Christian prophecy has been plagued by problems of definition. What is this prophecy? Is it preaching? Is it a form of teaching? Is it apocalyptic revelations? Does it involve the exegesis and contemporizing of older prophetic texts? Boring offers the following definition: "The early Christian prophet was an immediately inspired spokesperson for the risen Jesus, who received intelligible messages that he or she felt impelled to deliver to the Christian community or, as the representative of the community, to the general public."[83] One of the most helpful aspects of this definition is that it makes evident that one is *not* talking about someone who has prepared a sermon in advance. Although preaching and prophesying both involve proclamations, their origins and their form and character differ from one another. Preaching from prophetic texts or on prophetic themes, such as justice for the poor, was still preaching; it was not prophecy.[84]

There are, however, two red flags raised by Boring's definition. In the first place, he says nothing about the form of prophetic communications. It appears that this is one of the reasons he is able to conclude that in the Gospels a great deal of material that one would otherwise not judge on form-critical grounds to be prophetic oracles or apocalyptic visions or dreams comes from Christian prophets. Second, Boring limits the Christian prophet to being a spokesperson for the risen Jesus—someone who speaks in the first person as the voice of the risen Lord. It is especially this conclusion that allows him to argue that the words of the historical Jesus and the risen Lord often got mixed together, were fused or confused at the stage of oral tradition, so that in due course both ended up in our Gospels. Part of the problem here lies in the fact that Boring assumes that in the early Church "the Lord was the Spirit," on the basis of a very dubious exegesis of 2 Cor 3:17.[85] In other words, in his view, there was no real distinction between the risen Lord and the Holy Spirit in the mind of the earliest Christians, and prophets spoke for the former under the influence of the latter, assuming that whatever the Spirit prompted them to say was actually the words of the risen Jesus.

The proof texts that prophets spoke for the risen Lord are chiefly texts from Revelation—for example, the material we find in Rev 1:17–3:22. The problem with the conclusion that this represents how prophets spoke whenever they

---

[82] This discussion will be interacting with the major presentation of Boring's case in *The Continuing Voice.*

[83] Ibid., 38.

[84] See ibid., 44.

[85] See Witherington, *Conflict and Community in Corinth,* 382.

addressed Christian audiences is fourfold: (1) Here the narrative context makes clear that it is the Son of Man who is speaking to John through this visionary experience. (2) This is a record of John's visionary experience; it is not simply prophetic expression. It is one of the regular confusions in Boring's work that he does not distinguish between prophetic experience and prophetic expression. It may be doubted that John would have expressed himself this way if he were simply delivering a prophetic oracle in the first person *without* a narrative context. (3) The assumption that visions and oracles worked in the same way is also not helpful. When one recounts a vision, one always has a narrative context that makes clear that it is someone other than the prophet who is ultimately speaking in the vision. This was not always the case with ordinary oracles, especially from the time of John the Baptist on, when the messenger formula was not always used. (4) It seems clear that Christian prophets and, indeed, others often spoke under the prompting of the Holy Spirit without reference to the voice of the risen Jesus. For instance, in a text Boring regularly cites, Acts 15:28, nothing is said about this judgment coming from the risen Jesus. What it says is that the Holy Spirit as well as the human authorities in Jerusalem produced this ruling. Agabus, who is mentioned in Acts 11:28, is said to predict by the Holy Spirit that a famine was coming. Nothing whatsoever is said about this being the continuing voice of Jesus. Or again, Boring makes a point of citing Acts 13:2 to prove that the prophet spoke through the Holy Spirit for the risen Jesus. This is not what the text says. It says, "While they were worshiping the Lord and fasting *the Holy Spirit said:* 'Set apart for me Barnabas and Paul.'" The Holy Spirit is the one said to be speaking in all these Acts texts that Boring cites, *not* the risen Jesus.

The risen Jesus speaks in visionary material, such as Paul's conversion or the vision Paul has during his journey to Rome. It is striking that the *only* time the risen Jesus clearly speaks either in Revelation or in Acts is in a vision or a dream, where the speech is a private communication to someone such as Paul or Peter, not in a public utterance (cf., e.g., Acts 22:6–10; 23:11). There is no clear or indisputable evidence in the NT of public oracles being delivered by Christian prophets to congregations or individuals as the voice or words of the risen Jesus.[86] Indeed, the only clear evidence for such a conclusion is found in *Odes Sol.* 42:6, where the risen Jesus is said to have remarked, "For I live and am resurrected, am with them and speak through their mouths." The *Odes of Solomon*, however, dates to either the late first century or early second century AD, and it is illegitimate to simply assume that such a statement was characteristic of the state of affairs during the time in which the collections of Jesus' sayings were being made and edited, an event that, even on Boring's own showing, took place fifty to sixty years earlier.

---

[86] Acts 1:7–8 is no exception. Here there are indeed words of the risen Jesus, but they are delivered before the ascension, by Jesus himself before he left earth, not through Christian prophets from a Jesus who is in heaven.

We must also ask about the psychological probability that utterances of genuine Christian prophets might end up on the lips of the Jesus who speaks in the Gospels. I have argued elsewhere,

> If the utterances of Christian prophets were valued as highly as the sayings of the earthly Jesus, then the rationale for retrojecting them back into the ministry of Jesus is lacking. Further, how has it happened, if the early church retrojected prophetic material into a ministry setting, that we have little or no Gospel material dealing with some of the major crises of the early church over circumcision, baptisms, the relationship of Jews to Gentiles . . . ? Can we legitimately assume that all these matters were settled when the Gospels were written or that none of them was an issue for the evangelists?[87]

A further problem with Boring's case is that he fails to distinguish between apocalyptic and prophecy sufficiently and indeed even takes the book of Revelation as the paradigm of what early Christian prophecy must have, in general, been like. This is a mistake. While apocalyptic is indeed a hybrid development of sapiential and prophetic concepts and forms, if we follow the definitions of the Society of Biblical Literature Seminar on apocalyptic,[88] this should lead us not to confuse or fuse eschatological prophecy, such as we find on the lips of John the Baptist or Jesus, and the recounting of apocalyptic visions or dreams.

The last preliminary problem with Boring's entire approach is that he mistakes the pneumatic interpretation of texts including prophecies with prophecy itself. For instance, he argues that the Teacher of Righteousness at Qumran must be seen as a prophet because of his inspired contemporizing of OT texts.[89] As has been pointed out earlier in this study's discussion of the Qumran material, this is an error. The Qumran community, like the early followers of Jesus, believed they lived in the age of the fulfillment of prophecy— the eschatological age. They thus also believed that God's Spirit helped them to understand the relevance of the Scriptures to their own situation through pesher exegesis and application. They read the Scriptures in light of their experience and vice versa. To judge from Qumran, but also from a book produced by a scribe or sage such as Matthew (cf. Matt 13:52, widely seen as a tip-off about the author of this Gospel), this sort of pneumatic activity was the work of teachers or sages, not prophets.

It is true that early Christians affirmed that all believers had the Spirit and that the Spirit could, on various occasions, inspire dreams, visions, or prophecies (Acts 2). It is not true that they believed that this was all the Spirit inspired people to do or that it was acceptable to amalgamate all Spirit-inspired activity under the heading of prophecy. There was pneumatic teaching, pneumatic praying, pneumatic preaching or evangelizing, pneumatic speaking in tongues, pneumatic prophesying. But Paul is quite clear that not all are

---

[87] Witherington, *Christology of Jesus*, 4.

[88] See pp. 217–23 above.

[89] See Boring, *The Continuing Voice*, 54–55.

prophets (1 Cor 12:29), even though he wished for the Corinthians to seek for the gift of prophecy (14:1).[90] There is, furthermore, nothing at all said in 1 Cor 14 to suggest that the prophecies are in the form of the continuing voice of the risen Jesus.[91] What Paul does insist on is that prophecy is, by nature, a public utterance in intelligible speech (v. 3). One must also reckon with the fact that, in the lists of early church functionaries, apostles, prophets, and teachers are listed separately even though there seems to have been some overlap. That is, some apostles seem also to have been prophets and teachers. This overlap may mean that there were fewer prophets rather than more, since apostles could function in several roles.

Having dealt with the broader or more general difficulties with Boring's approach, it is time to assess both the pluses and the minuses of some of his more detailed comments and arguments. One of the more basic assumptions of Boring, as of many post-Bultmannian form critics, is that the sayings of Jesus did not originally have a narrative context but that Mark and others gave these sayings such a context. This conclusion is drawn even in regard to narratives that climax in a memorable saying of Jesus—the so-called pronouncement stories.[92] It is assumed that Jesus' words existed in the period of about AD 40–70 without such narrative contexts and that during this period of time various utterances of Christian prophets intermingled or were identified with the historical utterances of Jesus.

First, it must be said that there is no hard empirical evidence about the state of the Jesus tradition prior to the formation of the Gospels. No one has found any Q documents from the pre-Gospel period. Thus, while there are no a priori problems with the notion that there was at least one collection, if not more, of Jesus sayings in the early church, it is interesting that Mark seems to know nothing about such a collection. It is plausible to argue that the material in the Sermon on the Mount in Matt 5–7, which is found in various places in Luke, originally was transmitted with little, if any, narrative framework. One may also argue the same about a collection of parables such as one finds in Luke 15. But it is far more difficult to accept this conclusion in regard to sayings that are embedded in, and crucial to, various of the Gospel narratives. In regard to the Markan material itself, it is far easier to believe that Mark did indeed have contact with one or more eyewitnesses of the historical Jesus and obtained at least the bulk of his pronouncement stories and controversy dialogues, which in-

---

[90] This in itself suggests that although there seem to have been a good number of prophets and prophetesses in Corinth, it was by no means the role all or perhaps even the majority of Corinthian Christians played.

[91] Notice that the only time the "Lord" comes into the conversation in 1 Cor 14 is when Paul cites Isaiah in v. 21, and there it can be debated whether we are meant to take "Lord" to mean the Father or the Son. The "command of the Lord" in v. 37 may refer to Jesus, but the instructions Paul has just given the Corinthians are just that—inspired instructions, not oracles.

[92] See Boring, *The Continuing Voice*, 24, 28.

cluded some teachings of Jesus, from such a source.[93] Even if his source was not an eyewitness source, if the Jesus tradition was passed down like traditions about other early Jewish hasidim or prophets, we would have expected special care and attention being paid to preserve stories about what he said and did—in other words, sayings in a narrative context. Mark would likely have been surprised to be credited with the creation of the narrative framework of the Gospel.[94] In short, the assumption of the artificiality of all the narrative frameworks of Jesus' sayings material is just that—an unproven assumption. Other explanations are equally plausible.

In the earliest source for data about Christian prophecy, written by someone himself a prophet, Paul in 1 Cor 7 distinguishes between his own teaching and the sayings of Jesus, whom, not surprisingly, Paul calls the Lord. That he thinks his teaching has the same authority for the Corinthian situation as Jesus' teaching is remarkable, but it does not suggest that he thinks his teaching *is* the teaching of the risen Jesus. Indeed, he says, "I say, not the Lord," to make the distinction clear. It is, furthermore, not quite correct to say, as Boring does, that there is no consensus on whether Paul understands himself to be quoting a traditional saying of Jesus.[95] The vast majority of Pauline scholars who have commented on this text think it is clear that Paul is drawing on traditional material here. The use of the term "Lord" certainly need not suggest that Paul thinks this is a teaching given by the exalted Lord. This is just Paul's most common way of referring to Jesus, whom he never knew personally until his encounter with the risen Lord. Indeed, D. Wenham and other scholars have provided us with extensive evidence that Paul does quote or paraphrase the Jesus tradition with some regularity, both sayings and narrative material (cf. 1 Cor 11).[96]

Boring seeks to draw an analogy between the way the Isaiah tradition developed and the way the Jesus tradition developed with later anonymous prophets adding to it.[97] Boring is forced to admit that Christian prophetic oracles were not, however, anonymous, unlike the material in second Isaiah, but are always identified with known persons in the NT. Furthermore, the Jesus tradition was not passed on as a prophetic book or a collection of prophecies. Indeed, the majority of the Jesus tradition was sapiential material and is more likely to have

---

[93] It is interesting that Q scholars often just dismiss or ignore such a possibility despite the fact that many Markan specialists take such ideas very seriously (V. Taylor, C. E. B. Cranfield, R. Pesch, and others).

[94] If, with most scholars, one grants the independence of the Fourth Gospel from the Synoptics, then one would have to ask where John got his own narrative framework for Jesus' ministry, especially since it is, at many points, very similar to Mark's (e.g., John the Baptist at the beginning; a similar account of the feeding of the five thousand in the same location).

[95] Boring, *The Continuing Voice*, 29.

[96] See, e.g., D. Wenham, "Paul and the Synoptic Apocalypse," in *Gospel Perspectives: Studies of History and Tradition in the Four Gospels* (ed. R. T. France; 4 vols.; Sheffield: JSOT Press, 1981), 2:345–75.

[97] Boring, *The Continuing Voice*, 30–31.

been handed on, like other early Jewish wisdom material, from sages. There is this further difference between the Isaiah tradition and the Jesus tradition. The historical Isaiah's prophecy was a word of Yahweh, and so is the lyrical prophecy found in Second Isaiah. For there to be a clear analogy, the material in First Isaiah would have to be his own utterances and that in Second Isaiah the post mortem utterances of the historical Isaiah![98] In the end, Boring is forced to admit that this analogy with Isaiah breaks down.[99]

Boring's treatment of Rom 12:3–8 is interesting. He apparently takes v. 6 to refer to some sort of *analogia fidei*, some received tradition about Jesus such that prophecy is seen as interpreting this tradition.[100] But in all likelihood, the Reformers were wrong in their translation and interpretation of this text. It refers to prophesying in proportion to the degree of one's faith.[101] This conjures up the scenario of prophets speaking in a fashion that exceeds their inspiration. Such a possibility might well explain why Paul says what he does in 1 Cor 14 about the need for the Corinthians to weigh or sift the prophecy offered by other Corinthians.

If this is a correct reading of Paul's meaning, then Grudem is likely right that Paul sees the prophecy of the Gentile churches as not having the same degree of inspiration or authority as either OT prophecy or his own teaching or, for that matter, Jesus' prophecy and teaching, none of which is said to need weighing or sifting (cf. 1 Cor 12:10; 14:29).[102] This sort of prophecy is also distinguished from both teaching and exhorting in Rom 12:6–7.

Several more things need to be said about Paul's view of these matters: (1) The prophecy Paul is referring to is unlike Greco-Roman prophecy in that it is communal in nature and is a part of Christian worship. (2) Prophecy is highly valued not least because of its potential moral effect, not merely on Christians but on non-Christian visitors, who are reproved and the secrets of their hearts revealed (1 Cor 14:24–25). These verses suggest that the content of such prophecy was not sayings of Jesus but words of insight about human vice and corruption, coupled with a call to repent of one's wickedness and idolatry (see 1 Thess 1:9). (3) Paul has to encourage both the Romans and the Thessalonians to prophesy; the latter he has to urge not to quench the Spirit or despise the words of prophets (1 Thess 5:19–20). If 1 Corinthians did not exist, it is hardly likely anyone would suggest that prophecy was a dominant phenomenon in Christian

---

[98] Aune, *Prophecy in Early Christianity*, 235–36, refers to the tradition that some Greek philosophers, on occasion, appeared to their disciples in dreams offering further teaching, which came to be considered authentic teaching of the philosopher.

[99] Boring, *The Continuing Voice*, 40.

[100] See ibid., 106, 150.

[101] See, e.g., J. D. G. Dunn, *Romans 9–16* (Waco: Word, 1988), 727–28, who rightly sees the key phrase as a close synonym of *metron pisteōs* in v. 3; and C. E. B. Cranfield, *Romans 9–16* (Edinburgh: T&T Clark, 1979), 620, who points out that the terms *metron* and *analogia* are both translated by the same word in the Peshitta Syriac.

[102] See Grudem, *The Gift of Prophecy*, 150–76.

worship or in the traditions in the churches to which Paul wrote. (4) Paul clearly values prophecy highly. But even in 1 Corinthians a few oracles, such as one probably finds in 1 Cor 15:51–55, are set in a larger context that is dominated by teaching both of Paul's own making and from Jesus and early Christian pedagogical traditions. Nothing suggests that one should use a prophetic model to gauge how the Jesus traditions were created, were transmitted, or found their way into Gospels. Only a very distinct minority of the Pauline corpus is oracular or apocalyptic in form. This leads to the conclusion that Paul's placing of prophecy high in the list of speech gifts reflects the rhetorical and social situation he is addressing in Thessalonike, Corinth, and Rome. Paul wishes to commend this gift, especially in comparison to tongues, and we must assume there was some need for such encouragement.

The picture one finds in Acts—in which prophets, prophecy, and visions are certainly present and possibly even prominent in a few locations but prophecy and prophets hardly dominate the landscape of church roles or activities—is likely to be nearer the historical mark than Boring wishes to admit.[103] This is especially likely to be the case in view of Luke's strong tendency to portray his leading figures as prophets, including Jesus and Paul, to better commend them and the faith they promote to his Gentile audience.[104] Luke would have played up their role even more had he had evidence to support such a presentation.

In addition, this study has noted regularly that, in the Jewish prophetic tradition, prophets were not rulers; at most they were the consultants to rulers. They were not leaders in the sense of those who controlled the structures or sacred traditions of Israel. One should not have expected them to do so with the Jesus tradition either, which largely bears a non-prophetic shape. Indeed, to judge from a figure like Agabus, Christian prophets filled the role prophets had always fulfilled for God's people—they offered, from time to time, a late word from God. They did not lead unless they were also apostolic figures or elders, nor should we conflate them with the teachers or Christian sages or the historians, such as Luke, who were the likely bearers, with the apostles, of the Jesus tradition. Much more will be said about the presentation of Jesus and other prophets in Luke–Acts in the next chapter.

V. CONCLUSIONS

It is a difficult and delicate matter to avoid saying either too little or too much about prophecy and prophets in the Pauline corpus. There is no denying either that Paul presents himself as a prophet or that there were some prophets in at least some of his congregations. Yet this does not lead to the conclusion that prophets dominated the Pauline churches or that they provide the explanation for the transmission of the Jesus tradition in these churches.

---

[103] See Boring, *The Continuing Voice,* 72–73, 97ff.

[104] On this, much more will be said in the next chapter, pp. 330–43.

There is sufficient evidence that Paul had some revelatory or ecstatic experiences during his Christian life and that he offered some oracles to his congregations. Yet nothing suggests either of these were everyday occurrences, and in fact the majority of the Pauline material is not in the form of oracles. Paul seems happy enough to quote and amplify prophetic material from others, including perhaps some of the christological hymns, but these materials can be isolated from their contexts, which are largely constituted by teaching or narrative material. Although prophecy is clearly alive and well in the Pauline churches, Paul's letters do not read like the works of a classical prophet—a collection of oracles offered on various occasions. Indeed, the works found in the NT do not, in general, suggest that early Christianity was dominated by prophets. One must be careful to define what one means if one contends that early Christianity was a prophetic movement. True, it was a movement that believed there was a living voice of prophecy addressing the churches, but to claim much more than this in regard to the early church's leadership or means of transmitting, never mind creating, sacred traditions goes beyond and, in some cases, against the evidence.

The study of Greco-Roman prophecy aids particularly in the discussion of how the Gentiles in Corinth may have mainly viewed prophecy as a consultative matter where questions would be asked and answered. Paul, by contrast, seems to have operated with a much more Jewish model of prophecy. Texts in both 1 Cor 14 and Rom 12 suggest that Paul thought that it was possible to prophesy beyond the extent of one's inspiration and faith, and so such prophecy had to be sifted or weighed. Paul encourages the Corinthians to pray and prophesy in the worship context, and urges them to distinguish how they should use the gift of tongues as opposed to the gift of prophecy. Nothing from the Delphic material or from Paul suggests that there was a reason to equate ecstasy and prophecy. Rather, the former has to do with prophetic experience, as this study has several times pointed out, and the latter has to do with prophetic expression.

The influential study of Boring was critiqued at some length. The chief thesis of his work, that sayings of the risen Lord were, in due course, placed on the lips of the historical Jesus and so fused or confused, not least because no distinction was made in the minds of early Christians between Jesus, the risen Lord, and the Holy Spirit, was shown to be significantly flawed in various regards. Boring is, however, right that the risen Lord did continue to speak to the churches, as a work such as Revelation shows. Such words were seen to have authority equal to those of the historical Jesus, without the two simply being identified. A late word of guidance or warning from the Lord was always welcome. When Gentiles reached a critical mass in the communities of early Christianity, it seems clear that this question came to be asked: how may the Christian faith be presented in a manner that pagans will find winning? One answer, to be explored in the next chapter, was to present Jesus and his movement both as prophetic in character and as the fulfillment of prophecy.

CHAPTER 10

Profile of a Prophet and His Movement:

Jesus and His Followers in the Greco-Roman World

THE LAST COUPLE OF CHAPTERS HAVE chronicled the wide-ranging fascination with matters prophetic in the Roman Empire during the first century AD. This fascination was felt by Gentile no less than Jew, although the two did not share exactly the same views on what prophecy was and how it worked. Some recently published papyri now make available some indications of the very practical nature of prophecy in the Greco-Roman world. It will be well to review some of this material briefly before considering the somewhat hellenized portraits of prophets and prophecy found in Luke–Acts.

It is not uncommon to find in the papyri the sort of questions that were asked of pagan oracles in the Greco-Roman world. But it is much rarer to find a record of their answers. One such record from the first century AD is found in P.Vindob.Sal.1.[1] The oracle responds to the practical and situation-specific questions as follows:

> Concerning the things about which you asked—
> You are well.
> What you desire night and day will be yours.
> As for what you want the gods will guide you
> and your livelihood will be for the better
> and your life will be distinguished.

---

[1] In what follows I am drawing on the material as it is reproduced and dealt with by *NewDocs* 2:37–44.

The oracle is cast in poetic form, with the speaker ringing the changes on the *eis* ending to various Greek words, and the answers being given in the personal form ("you" being repeated several times and ways). Notice the general character of the response. There is nothing specific about times or dates, or the form of the guidance from the gods, or how the inquirer's livelihood would improve, or how his life would be distinguished. The answer reflects the usual concerns of everyday life about health and wealth and decision making. It seems likely that it is recorded at all because this answer was given to some agent in written form to transmit to the original inquirer, as was not uncommon when ambassadors or the well-to-do sent someone else to consult the oracle.

This oracle hints at why there are not great quantities of Christian oracular material in the NT. It is because of the personal and specific nature of the oracles in the Greco-Roman world, which dealt with ordinary individual problems and puzzles but paradoxically often did so in very generic terms. Notice that, in the two clearest oracles in Acts, by Agabus, the matters that are dealt with are (1) a particular crisis for Christians, caused by a famine and the resulting food shortage, and (2) an even more individual crisis that Paul alone would face when he went up to Jerusalem. Such prophecies, in order to be words on target, had to be either very generic in form, as the one above is, or so situation-specific that they could not readily be reapplied to other situations. In either case, they hardly had an enduring or endearing ring to them.

As will be seen near the end of this chapter, the author of the *Didache* anticipates precisely these kinds of mundane matters to be dealt with in Christian prophecy—including asking for food or money while "in the Spirit." The personal, individual, mundane, and generic character of such utterances likely consigned most such remarks to oblivion when it came to the collecting of material of enduring worth to be included in various of the books of the NT—including, of course, Acts. Far from being scintillating, memorable words of the risen Jesus, the exalted Lord, most such prophecies would be ordinary words of comfort, counsel, or conviction, inspired by the Spirit to help Christians in their daily struggles and perhaps convict, convince, and even convert outsiders who might visit Christian worship and had some of the same anxieties. The prophecies that would usually be worth recording were those that had a more general or messianic or eschatological character, telling people about the future that would affect the community, not just individuals. Bearing this in mind, we will turn to a brief survey of the portrait of prophets and prophecy in Luke–Acts, including the notable portrait of Jesus as an eschatological prophet in Luke's Gospel.

I. JESUS—THE YOUNG AND FEARLESS PROPHET

Of all the NT writers, Luke seems most likely to have been a Gentile. He brings to his material the perspectives and methods of a Hellenistic historian, but also one who knows the LXX well and thus the history of God's people.[2] He is

---

[2] See Witherington, *The Acts of the Apostles*, 24–68.

concerned to portray Jesus and his followers as part of the larger sweep of salvation history; indeed, he wishes to show that in Jesus this history, and the divine prophecies and promises related to this history, come to fulfillment and fruition. But what sort of portrait of Jesus and his followers would play well with his Gentile audience?

To anticipate the conclusions, Luke chooses to present Jesus and his movement not only as the fulfillment of prophecies but also as prophetic in character. More specifically, he portrays Jesus, Peter, Paul, Agabus and others as prophets and seers much like various OT figures. In doing so, he was tapping into the profound interest of the Gentile world in Jewish prophets and their oracles and thereby helping to confirm to Theophilus the legitimacy of this ongoing movement. It appears that he was in the process also of removing some of the suspicion about early Christianity being a subversive phenomenon. Instead of being subversive of the divinely determined world order, it was a movement prompted and led by God's Spirit and the revelations God gave. To be disobedient to the leading and guidance that came from the heavenly realms would have been folly. R. H. Stein puts it this way:

> Just as later in the history of the Christian church the proof from prophecy argument was used both apologetically and even evangelistically to convince people of the truthfulness of the Christian faith, so in a similar although less developed way Luke sought to help his readers come to a greater assurance of the truthfulness of what they had been taught. He did this by showing that the events experienced by Jesus and the early church fit God's plan and were foretold by the prophets.[3]

Luke also did this by portraying Jesus and his best-known followers as prophets. This was a perspective that a Gentile, whether a Festus or a Theophilus, could easily understand and with which such a person could well agree.

Before discussing the presentation of prophets and prophecy in Luke–Acts, something should be said about where the emphasis lies. The purpose of the proof-from-prophecy motif in Luke–Acts is to explain two major things: (1) why Jesus was crucified if indeed he was whom the Gospel claims him to be; (2) why Judaism, to a large extent, had not accepted Jesus as the Messiah either during his life or through the later Christian proclamation of him. These would be major concerns of any person interested in the Christian movement. If Jesus and his movement were indeed a fulfillment of Jewish prophecies given to and by Jewish people, why had things turned out as they did? Thus, Luke seeks to show not only how Jesus' death and resurrection correspond to the prophetic Scriptures (Luke 24:32; Acts 8:27–30) but also how the rejection of Jesus by Israel was foretold (Luke 9:22; 13:32–34; 17:25; 18:31; 24:7), as were Jesus' delivery over to, and death by, the hands of Gentiles rather than Jews (Luke 9:44; 18:32), the future coming of the Spirit of prophecy to Jesus' followers (Luke 24:49; Acts 1:4–8; 11:16), and finally the destruction of Jerusalem (Luke 11:49–51; 13:5, 35; 19:27, 43–44; 21:5–24; 23:28–31). Furthermore, these things were prophesied not just

---

[3] R. H. Stein, *Luke* (Nashville: Broadman, 1992), 38–39.

by human prophets but also by angels (Luke 1:14–17, 20, 31–33; 2:11–12; Acts 27:23–24) and indeed by God directly (Luke 2:26; Acts 9:15–16; 18:9–10).[4] Luke clearly knows he has obstacles to overcome in the crucifixion and in the largely non-Jewish character of Christianity in his day if he is to confirm a Gentile like Theophilus in his new Christian faith. He plays the prophetic card heavily to accomplish this aim.

Perhaps a piece of evidence pointing to the primitive character of the Christology in Luke–Acts is that, more than many NT writers, Luke places a strong emphasis on Jesus as a prophet, indeed perhaps as the great prophet like unto Moses whom God would raise up.[5] As such, he is seen as the last great eschatological and messianic prophet or, to put it the other way around, a prophetic Messiah.[6] Perhaps the easiest point of entry into this form of christological thinking is to examine Acts 2:22–24, where we read about "Jesus of Nazareth, a man attested to you by God with mighty works and wonders and signs which God did through him in your midst . . . this Jesus you crucified. But God raised him up." This must be compared to Deut 34:10–12: "There has not arisen a prophet since in Israel like Moses, whom the Lord knew face to face, none like him for all the signs and wonders which the Lord sent him to do." It must be remembered as well that this prophecy is given in the context of the statement about Joshua (in Greek, Jesus) that he was "full of the Spirit of wisdom, for Moses had laid his hands upon him."

In early Judaism it was not believed that Joshua completely fulfilled what Deut 34:10–12 predicted, and so an eschatological fulfillment in a latter-day Moses/Joshua figure was looked for (cf. 4QTestim 1–5; John 1:21; 4:19; 6:14). In the Acts passage cited above, the deeds of Jesus during his ministry, coupled with his being "raised up" (in a nonmetaphorical sense) by God, are seen as clear evidence that the prophecy in Deuteronomy has come to fulfillment in Jesus. Once we recognize that this is one of the ways Luke is portraying Jesus, it is then possible to go back to his Gospel and make sense of a variety of other pieces of data.[7]

---

[4] So rightly Stein, ibid., 38.

[5] J. D. Kingsbury thinks that "prophet" is not a christological title for Luke even though Luke casts Jesus' ministry in a prophetic light. Kingsbury prefers the term "prophetic Messiah." The reason for this seems to be that Kingsbury rightly recognizes that to call Jesus prophet, even the Prophet, was insufficient from Luke's perspective. See J. D. Kingsbury, "Jesus as the 'Prophetic Messiah' in Luke's Gospel," in *The Future of Christology: Essays in Honor of Leander E. Keck* (ed. A. J. Malherbe and W. A. Meeks; Philadelphia: Fortress, 1993), 29–42.

[6] This discussion may be found in a somewhat different form in B. Witherington, *The Many Faces of the Christ* (New York: Crossroad, 1998), 162–65.

[7] E. Richard, *Jesus: One and Many: The Christology Concept of New Testament Authors* (Wilmington, Del.: Michael Glazier, 1988), 179, rightly stresses that, on the whole, in his Gospel Luke follows Mark's use of titles with only minor modifications, although these modifications are not insignificant. For example, the title "Son of God" is extended into Jesus' childhood (1:32, 35).

For example, not only is Jesus, like Joshua, said to have received the Spirit bodily (Luke 3:22); it is also said that he was "full of the Spirit" when tempted (4:1) and that he began his preaching "in the power of the Spirit" (4:14). The paradigmatic sermon in Jesus' hometown (Luke 4), which sets the agenda for what follows in the Gospel, depicts Jesus as reading from Isaiah and claiming not only that he understands prophecy but that he fulfills it (4:21). Jesus is the one anointed by God with the Holy Spirit and power (Acts 10:38; cf. Acts 4:27) to prophesy great things, do mighty works, and even bring to fulfillment God's eschatological promises.[8] Luke–Acts is written with the understanding that something fundamental is being revealed about Jesus' prophetic character in Luke 4. Indeed, he calls himself prophet at v. 24. Near the end of the speech in ch. 4, Jesus compares himself to Elijah and Elisha in his deeds (vv. 25–27). But his deeds are also like Joshua, who took on the foes of the people of God and triumphed, leading God's people into the promised land. Jesus will do so as well, but now the foes are the devil and his minions, as well as the devil's tools—sin, disease, demonic possession, death. Triumph comes by means of salvation, which has both a spiritual and a social dimension here and now, creating a new or renewed people of God, and in due course it comes by means of resurrection.

Notice how in Luke 7 the comparison between Jesus and other great prophets is fully fleshed out. There Jesus heals a Gentile centurion because of Jews interceding for him (7:1–10), just as Elisha healed a foreigner in like fashion through the intercession of a Jewish girl (2 Kgs 5:1–14), and then, just as Elijah had raised a widow's son from the dead (1 Kgs 17:17–24), Jesus raises the widow of Nain's son (Luke 7:11–15), after which the response to these sorts of deeds is that a "great prophet whom God raised up" is in their midst and through him "God is visiting his people" (7:16).[9] It is precisely at this juncture that Jesus sends word to the Baptist that "the poor have good news preached to them," fulfilling the prophecy announced in Luke 4.[10]

Equally important to the discussion of this christological theme in Luke–Acts is what one finds in Luke 13:33–34. The lament over Jerusalem, which begins in v. 34, is Q material also found in Matt 23:37–39. But Luke has prefaced this with 13:33, which is found only in his Gospel and reads, "Yet today and tomorrow and the next day I must be on my way, because it is impossible for a prophet to be killed outside of Jerusalem." Here Jesus is not merely called a prophet; he calls himself a prophet as he nears the climax of his ministry, and he looks to suffer a prophet's fate. Thus, the two great OT prophetic figures are said only in Luke to discuss with Jesus his coming "exodus," or departure (9:31).

---

[8] See ibid., 185.

[9] Here I am following the helpful discussion of L. T. Johnson, "Luke–Acts, Book of," *ABD* 4:412–15.

[10] J. H. Neyrey, *Christ Is Community: The Christologies of the New Testament* (Wilmington, Del.: Michael Glazier, 1985), 137, points out that there is overlap between the Son of Man and prophet images of Jesus in Luke–Acts, particularly in the depiction of Jesus as judge.

This theme becomes even more explicit in Acts, where, in Stephen's speech in Acts 7, Stephen, himself a prophetic and visionary figure, speaks of a twofold sending of Moses to God's people, first in weakness, then in power, with two offers of salvation to God's people (vv. 23–43). Those who reject Moses after the second offer of salvation and the great signs and wonders he worked are themselves to be rejected by God. Stephen makes the connection with Jesus crystal clear in Acts vv. 35–37, especially when he says, "This is the Moses who said to the Israelites, 'God will raise up for you a prophet from your brothers as he raised me up.'"

Even in some of the apparently passing comments, Luke tailors his account to reveal the prophetic character of Jesus. For example, Luke 9:51, in contrast to the Markan account (cf. Mark 9:9), speaks of "the days of his being taken up," surely an echo of 2 Kgs 2:1: "When the Lord was about to take Elijah up to heaven" (cf. Sir 48:9; 1 Macc 2:58).[11] One begins to see that the ascension in Luke–Acts is crucial precisely because it will demonstrate that Jesus is indeed the Elijah-like latter-day prophet. But as J. B. Green points out, one must also remember that it was only at Elijah's ascension that Elijah's spirit was passed on to Elisha (2 Kgs 2:9–15), and this is likewise the case with Jesus' disciples. Jesus must go on high before they receive power from on high.[12] There is also the matter of Jesus setting his face like a flint to go up to Jerusalem (Luke 9:51). One may compare, for instance, the command to Ezekiel, the other Son of Man, who is told to "set his face against Jerusalem" in Ezek 21:7–8. Or one may compare the passage about the Servant in Isa 50:7: "The Lord God helps me; therefore I have not been disgraced; therefore I have set my face like flint, and know that I shall not be put to shame; he who vindicates me is near." This text, then, has echoes of the coming suffering that the prophet must steel himself to face. Thus, Luke 9:51 is not just a passing comment. It is a turning point in the narrative, where Jesus takes one more step forward toward fulfilling his prophetic role.[13]

But as it turns out, Jesus is not only a prophet; he is the one who, in the church age, sends the Spirit of inspiration and prophecy to Christians so that they may offer prophetic witness as well. L. T. Johnson says, "The power active in their prophetic witness is the Spirit of Jesus (Acts 2:33; 3:13; 4:10; 13:30–33),"[14] although it would be better to say it is the Spirit that Jesus sent.[15] This image, then,

---

[11] See L. T. Johnson, *The Gospel of Luke* (Collegeville, Minn.: Liturgical Press, 1991), 162.

[12] J. B. Green, *The Gospel of Luke* (Grand Rapids: Eerdmans, 1997), 403.

[13] Ibid., 402–3.

[14] Johnson, *Luke*, 18; cf. 19–20. Throughout this section on Jesus as prophet the discussion is indebted to Johnson's presentation.

[15] This comports with Luke's major emphasis throughout his two volumes, that it is the Spirit that brings salvation as well as its announcement. Jesus, like his disciples, must be full of the Spirit to perform their ministries. Jesus himself provides the paradigm of the Spirit-anointed, -appointed, and -empowered person. It is not, however, true to say, as R. Schnackenburg, *Jesus in the Gospels: A Biblical Christology,* (Louisville: Westminster John Knox, 1995), 138, does, that Jesus is the only Spirit-filled and -driven person during Jesus'

of Jesus as the eschatological or Mosaic prophet who is also therefore the prophetic Messiah is an important one for Luke, and it serves to bind his christological presentation in Luke–Acts together, to some degree. Luke stresses that Jesus is not only prophet but also Messiah throughout his earthly career and beyond (at birth, Luke 2:11; cf. 1:35; during the ministry, Luke 4:21, 41; 7:20–23; 9:20; at his death, Luke 24:26, 46; Acts 3:18; 17:3; 26:23; at the resurrection he becomes both Lord and Messiah, Acts 2:36). As such, he is the object of the proclamation (Acts 5:42; 8:5; 9:22; 18:5, 28), and he will come again as Messiah one day (Acts 3:20; cf. 1:11).[16] It is understandable why Luke might highlight this theme if he wrote to Gentiles, among whom there were a great respect for, and interest in, prophecy, especially Jewish prophecy.[17]

II. JESUS IN A PROPHETIC ENVIRONMENT

The presentation of the story of Jesus by Luke is part of his larger presentation of the story of salvation history, as it begins with the story of John the Baptist and continues on until Rome is reached by Paul. There is a suggestion that the story continues into the author's own time and, furthermore, that this story is grounded in hoary antiquity, indeed is the fulfillment of divine prophecies and promises and long-cherished hopes. We are told from the very first verse of Luke's Gospel that this account is going to be about the "things that have been fulfilled among us." The theme of fulfillment runs like a red thread throughout Luke–Acts, making clear that all the characters in the narrative are caught up in a drama that is the plan of God. Jesus is the most important character in the drama, but nonetheless the narrative is about salvific events. The account is a history, not a biography, even in the Lukan Gospel. Thus, one could say it is an account about the fulfillment in history of God's long-standing salvific plan.

The story begins with an angelic appearance to Zechariah the priest, forecasting the birth of a son who, even before he is born, will be full of the Holy Spirit. The reader is told quite specifically that this child is to be a prophet, and not just any sort of prophet but one who, according to 1:17, will go before God "with the spirit and power of Elijah." In light of the subsequent account, this can not mean that John will do miracles like Elijah but that he will engage in prophetic, Spirit-inspired speech. The allusion here is to the text of Malachi, and if we include v. 16 as well as v. 17, we have allusions to Mal 2:6–7; 3:1, 18; 4:5–6.[18]

---

life. This overlooks Mary, Anna, Simeon, John the Baptist, and others. Luke's view of the Spirit, like his view of prophets and prophecy, owes much to the OT presentation of these matters.

[16] See ibid., 150–51.

[17] Consider, for example, the famous story of Josephus saving his own life by prophesying that his captor, Vespasian, would become emperor, which in fact did happen.

[18] See Green, *Luke*, 77–78.

The point is that the eschatological age has dawned, the age when promises and prophecies would come true. This dual character—an age both of the offering of eschatological prophecies and of the fulfillment of eschatological prophecies—must be kept steadily in view. The angelic messenger tells Zechariah that his words will be fulfilled in their time (v. 20) and that time is obviously soon, very soon.

This scenario is repeated with Mary of Nazareth, but unlike Zechariah, she is obedient to and believes the words of promise of the angelic messenger. As with John, the Holy Spirit will come upon Mary so that she may bear the promised child (v. 35). In the age of fulfillment, the Spirit is precipitating the coming to pass of all the promises and prophecies. Both men and women prophesy and will prophesy. This is already evidenced with Elizabeth, who in v. 41 is said to be filled with the Holy Spirit and is given divine insight into the truth about Mary and the fruit of her womb. We see it again with Zechariah, who is filled with the Holy Spirit and speaks a prophecy that includes the revelations that the time that the prophets of old spoke of has come (v. 70) and that John will be the great prophet, mentioned in Malachi, who will go before the Lord and prepare his ways (v. 77). The perspective throughout presents a variety of figures who are much like the OT prophets, for whom to be filled with the Spirit means to be inspired, not to be saved or sanctified, and the outcome of such filling is that both men and women prophesy. It is as if the promise mentioned in Acts 2 as fulfilled at Pentecost had already been fulfilled thirty-five years earlier.

This observation is only further confirmed when we look at Luke 2 and find the two prophetic figures of Simeon and Anna. Of the former, it is said he is looking for Israel's consolation and the Holy Spirit rested on him (2:25). It is made clear in the next verse that he is indeed a prophet, for we are told that he had received a revelation that he would not die before seeing the Messiah. Guided by the Spirit (v. 27), he comes into the temple precincts and does see the Messiah. His concluding words are a prophecy offered to Mary: "This child is destined for the falling and rising of many in Israel, and to be a sign that will be opposed so that the inner thoughts of many will be revealed—and a sword will pierce your own soul too" (v. 35). Perhaps the most telling remark is that Jesus is a prophetic sign that will serve either as a stone of stumbling for those with untoward thoughts or a foundation stone for those who will be favorably inclined toward Jesus.

Simeon is, in turn, followed by another prophetic figure, Anna, who is explicitly called a prophet (unlike Simeon), and while the seeing of the Messiah causes Simeon to say that he is now prepared to die happy, the sight causes Anna to go forth and proclaim the good news to all looking for the redemption of Israel (2:38). One of Luke's important themes is that in the eschatological age both men and women will reveal God's will and word. In both Luke and Acts, both men and women are portrayed as prophetic figures.

Lest we think that this prophetic and prophet-saturated kind of narrative is peculiar to the birth narratives, the account of the ministry is not presented in any different manner. Indeed, immediately in 3:2 we are told that the word of

God came to John and he went forth prophesying in
in 3:4 to be an explicit fulfillment of Isa 40:3, whic'
tory formula "as it is written in the book of the wc
tice the emphasis on Isaiah being a prophet. Mei..
sermon earlier in this study.[19] Here it is sufficient to sa,
prophetic form, that the message of coming judgment is mu.
the classical prophets, and finally that John's ascetical lifestyle a..
ent him as not only a person who lives on the margins of society but ..
whom society has marginalized very much like the one in whose power he .
to operate—Elijah.

In this prophetic context, it is difficult not to hear the baptismal story about Jesus as the prophetic empowerment of Jesus—"and the Holy Spirit descended on him in bodily form" (3:22). Green's comment here is apposite:

> This is a pivotal experience for Jesus that (1) sets in motion the sequence of events to follow and, by implication, sets the course of his entire mission (cf. 4:1, 14, 18–19); (2) is expounded as the event that determines his understanding of his divine mission and empowers him to perform accordingly (4:18–19; Acts 10:37–38); and (3) anticipates the analogous empowering of Jesus' followers in Acts (e.g., Acts 1:8 . . .). . . . Luke's "in bodily form" emphasizes the materiality of this apocalyptic scene in a characteristic way (cf. 22:43–44; 23:44–45; 24:50–53; Acts 1:9–11; 2:1–4).[20]

Armed with this Spirit, indeed "full of the Spirit," Jesus is led by the Spirit into the wilderness to be tested by the powers of darkness while fasting. Yet he comes forth from this testing still filled with the power of the Spirit (4:14) and thus enabled to undertake his ministry. This brings the discussion once more to the text that is programmatic for the entire rest of Luke, and some would also say Acts—Luke 4:16–30. To be stressed here is that the prophetic foreground in the early part of Luke, which has just been rehearsed above in cursory fashion, leads to a particular reading of this key text.

When one examines Luke 4:16–30 closely, one discovers that D. Tiede is right when he says,

> Jesus' claim to embody the fulfillment of the eschatological promises of the Isaiah text could hardly be more direct: "Today this scripture has been fulfilled in your hearing." And that "today" clearly articulates Luke's eschatological conviction that the present is the arena of the deployment of the reign of God and his anointed one. Only a few chapters later, Jesus is already pointing back to what has been accomplished, using scriptural phrasing that is closely related to the first statement of the agenda: "Go and tell John what you have seen and heard: the blind receive their sight . . ." (7:22).[21]

---

[19] Pp. 238–44 and above.

[20] Green, *Luke*, 186–87.

[21] D. L. Tiede, *Prophecy and History in Luke–Acts* (Philadelphia: Fortress, 1980), 19–20.

rst four chapters of Luke's first volume set the tone for the rest of
Acts: the era of prophecy, fulfillment, Spirit, salvation has arisen. Which
od's people is not at least potentially a prophet or prophetess in such
ge?

The discussion of the Gospel material about prophecy will now conclude
with a brief consideration of Luke 24:13–32. Here it is reiterated at the end of the
Gospel that Jesus is a prophet (v. 19), and the followers of Jesus are chided for
not believing the prophets (v. 25), for not seeing that their oracles were being
fulfilled even as Jesus spoke. Both the pneumatic interpretation of Scripture and
further prophecy were to characterize the Christian era.[22] We must, in a moment, consider some aspects of the prophetic portrait of the material in Acts, but
before doing so, it will be instructive to contrast the material just discussed from
Luke's Gospel with what we find in Matthew.

In the first place, the beginning of Matthew's Gospel is consumed with
making clear that the prophecies are all coming true in the events surrounding
the coming of Jesus. It is the prophecies of old and their fulfillment, announced
by a formula citation ("then was fulfilled what had been spoken through the
prophet[s]"—Matt 1:22; 21:15, 17, 23; 4:14), that concerns the first evangelist.
While John the Baptist is certainly presented as a prophet in 3:1–12, he is seen as
the last of the great OT prophets, who offers words that are about to be fulfilled
in Jesus. Thus, at the baptism of Jesus, Jesus is presented not as a prophet but as
one who fulfills God's will, the Scriptures, for only Matthew has him speak of
fulfilling all righteousness.

As is well known, what leads up to the Sermon on the Mount is a stress
on Jesus teaching in the synagogues and proclaiming the kingdom and healing
(3:23–25), but nothing at all suggests a presentation of Jesus as a prophet.
In the Sermon of the Mount, Jesus is seen as a great sage who offers be-
atitudes and practical teaching and, when he does mention prophets or prophecies, simply affirms what Matthew has already said, that he comes to fulfill
the law and prophets (5:17). Jesus does intensify or reapply or add to the
teachings of Moses but not in oracular form. There is, near the end of the sermon, the warning about false prophets (7:15–19), and even those who may
have, in some sense, been true prophets prophesying in Jesus' name (which
likely means under his authorization or using his name as a word of power—
7:22) are not guaranteed a place in the kingdom of God. There is not much encouragement to be a prophet in ch. 7, to say the least. The commissioning of
the disciples in ch. 10 is to proclaim and to cure, but nothing is said about
prophesying. When John's disciples come asking about Jesus, he does not claim
to be a prophet but one through whose ministry the prophecies come true
(11:2–6).

Especially telling is the entire discussion of John the Baptist in 11:7–19.
The crucial verses are vv. 13–14, which, not accidentally, have no parallel in the
parallel passage in Luke 7. Here one learns that "all the prophets and the law

---

[22] See Boring, *The Continuing Voice*, 145.

prophesied until John, and if you are willing to accept it, he is Elijah."[23] It is odd that, in his entire study, Boring does not discuss these verses, perhaps because they must count against any case that Matthew supports the notion that prophets were passing on the Jesus tradition. What these verses suggest is that John is the last of the prophets of old, the Elijah figure who would come, according to Malachi, before the great and terrible day of the Lord (cf. Matt 17:12–13). When we couple this with the warnings against false prophets (which does not provide evidence that there were true ones in Matthew's audience), we find in Matthew a suspicion about prophets after the time of the Baptist, a suspicion similar to what we find in the *Didache* (cf. below).

It is true that Matthew goes on to portray Jesus as using prophetic diction (woe oracles in ch. 11, cf. also chs. 23–25), but this is the same Jesus who refuses to perform a sign, except the sign of Jonah (12:39–40; cf. 16:1–4), and furthermore the Jesus who speaks mainly as a sage, or as Wisdom come in the flesh, in this Gospel.[24] One can argue that the presentation is of a revelatory sage (see 11:25–27, with disciples who receive revelatory wisdom, as well as 16:17–20) who occasionally uses prophetic diction but never the citation formula for oracles. He speaks in his own voice, which is sometimes the same as the voice of Wisdom. Notice that, in the scene of the rejection at Nazareth, Jesus does not call himself a prophet, at least not directly, but refers to the fact that prophets, in general, are not without honor except in their own region and among their own kin (cf. Mark 6). This is a general maxim, the point of which seems to be that the rejection of Jesus is like the rejection of the prophets.

How very different is the Matthean presentation of the transfiguration from the Lukan one. There is in Matt 17:1–13 no reference to Jesus' exodus, no mention of his being taken up, like Elijah. Further, unlike what one finds in Luke 9:36, in Matt 17:9 Jesus commands the disciples *not* to report this "vision" until after the Son of Man has been raised from the dead. The disciples are not sent out during the ministry to recount visions or new prophecies.

One may also contrast the concluding postresurrection scene in Matthew with that in Luke. In Luke 24 the scene is full of discussion of Jesus as prophet and of prophecies being fulfilled. In Matt 28:16–20 the disciples are commissioned to make disciples of all nations, not by prophesying but by baptizing and teaching. Nothing is said about the sending of the Spirit of prophecy, nor is there any suggestion of the starting of a prophetic movement by such a sending. In regard to prophecy and prophets, the portrait could hardly be more different from what one finds in Luke. In Matthew Jesus is Emmanuel, Wisdom, the Davidic Messiah, God's Son, the Son of Man, but there is hardly a mention of Jesus as a prophet. "Prophet" does not seem to have been seen by this evangelist as either a christological or an eschatological term. Instead, John is seen as the

---

[23] Contrast Luke 16:16: "the law and the prophets were *in effect* until John." Luke does not suggest that prophesying stopped with John but, rather, that the old covenant did.

[24] See Witherington, *Jesus the Sage*, 335–80.

last hurrah of prophecy—the Elijah figure who comes before the one who embodies God's very presence on earth and brings God's salvation and judgment to
earth. The church age will indeed be a time of false prophets (compare 24:24
with 7:15–19), but nothing is said about disciples being true prophets. They are,
rather, teachers and scribes and healers and proclaimers. Finally, in Matthew one
sees a people of God living in the age where prophecy is fulfilled, but there is certainly no real hint that new prophecy is encouraged or seen as vital to the faith.
While Matthew's Gospel could be seen somewhat as a preparation for what one
finds in the *Didache* (cf. below), it is impossible to imagine Matthew's volume as
the prelude to Acts, in view of the presentation of Christian prophecy there; to
Acts this chapter must now turn.

In his helpful study on dreams and visions, M. T. Kelsey notes that "beginning with what happened at Pentecost, every major event in Acts is marked by a
dream, a vision, or the appearance of an angel, and it is usually upon this experience that the coming events are determined."[25] This correct assessment makes
evident that we can not focus just on those who are called prophets. Luke is intimating that we must also consider the visionaries and seers to understand the
prophetic character of the early Christian movement. For example, in Acts 2
Kelsey observes that when the disciples are filled with the Spirit, tongues of fire
were *seen* to rest on various people. This is the language of vision. Kelsey stresses
the visionary nature of any encounter with an angel; thus twice the church leaders escape from prison with the assistance of God's divine messengers, who are
seen by these Christians (Acts 5:19; 12:6–11). Indeed, in the account of Peter's
stay in prison, it is said that Peter did not realize that what was happening was
real, for "he thought he was seeing a vision *(horama)*." As Kelsey says, whatever
else we make of Acts 12:9, this surely indicates that the normal assumption was
that when one saw an angel, one was having a vision. Or again, in the story of
Stephen, the visionary aspect of the moments before his death are clear—the
heavens are opened, he sees the Son of Man standing, and he dies asking the one
he sees in the vision for forgiveness for his tormentors (7:55–8:1).

Paul is depicted as a visionary in several places in Acts, not only in his Damascus road experience (ch. 9). When he recounts the experience to Agrippa in
26:12–23, he makes very certain to emphasize that he was speaking of a heavenly
vision *(optasia)* that he had received (26:19). Peter likewise has a vision in a
dream in ch. 10, but in fact the story is about a double vision, for Cornelius has
one as well, and it is these two visions that bring about the recognition by Peter
of the acceptability of Gentiles to God. God engineers God's will through dreams
and visions. Again, at a significant turning point in his ministry, Paul has a vision *(horama)* in which he is bidden to come across the Hellespont and help
those in Macedonia (16:9). In 18:9–11 Paul is given courage to continue to speak
the Gospel in Corinth by means of a vision from or of the Lord, who reassures
him. Finally, near the end of his trek to Rome, Paul is encouraged by a vision or a
dream of the angel of the Lord, which enabled him to proceed on his journey

---

[25] M. T. Kelsey, *God, Dreams, and Revelation* (Minneapolis: Augsburg, 1991), 90.

to Rome and not fret about falling short of the goal (27:23–25).[26] The two major human figures in Acts, Peter and Paul, are, then, presented to us as visionaries, as those who have dreams, as those who receive guidance like the seers of old. But there is another aspect to the portrayal of things prophetic in Acts. There is one vivid portrait of a figure much like the traditional oracular Hebrew prophet— Agabus. Still, it must be stressed that he is not an isolated phenomenon.

Prophets in Acts are portrayed, in general, very much like OT prophets and prophets in Luke's Gospel. One would be hard pressed to call any of the dreams and visions or oracles or signs in Acts apocalyptic in character. Luke strives to present Jewish Christian prophecy in a light that shows its continuity with OT prophecy and with the larger prophetic context of the Greco-Roman world. Nor does Luke suggest that those specifically designated prophets in the Christian era are interpreters of Scripture, as even Boring recognizes.[27] Nonetheless, "the immediate authority with which prophets act in Acts is illustrated by Agabus, especially in the introductory formula 'thus says the Holy Spirit' (21.11)."[28] Perhaps this is why prophets in Acts "are portrayed by Luke as having no particular relation to church tradition"; indeed, they "certainly have nothing to do with the transmission of Jesus' words."[29]

This is not unimportant, since Luke presents us with the only "historical" presentation and analysis of what prophecy in the early church was like. He is suggesting it was much like it had always been since Jewish antiquity. While it was Jesus who appeared in visions to various prophetic figures to call or confirm them in their faith, whether one thinks of Stephen (ch. 7), or possibly Peter (10:9–16), and certainly Paul (9:22; 23:11, 26), it was not the voice of the risen Jesus who offered oracles but prophets being prompted by the Holy Spirit and speaking for the Spirit. Agabus uses quite intentionally the formula "thus says the Holy Spirit" instead of "thus says the Lord" or "thus says Jesus" (21:11).

On a closer inspection, Agabus provides an interesting model of prophecy. Agabus comes down from Jerusalem, apparently being familiar with Philip's house as a center of prophecy, and performs a prophetic sign act according to 21:10. It is a dramatization of what is to come for Paul (cf. Jer 19:1–13; Ezek 4:1–7). Paul will indeed be put in a bind by the Jews of Jerusalem, and he will be bound by the Gentile authorities, but he will not literally be bound hand and foot, nor will Jews hand him over to the Gentile authorities. What is presented here is much like the way OT prophecy and prophetic sign acts worked. The word had a general authority, not a specific one. This metaphorical sign act warns Paul, in a general way, of significant trouble and bondage awaiting him in Jerusalem.[30] There is a similar phenomenon in Acts 21:4, where, through the Spirit, some warn Paul not to go to Jerusalem, even though Paul himself feels led

---

[26] On all this, see ibid., 92–94.

[27] Boring, *The Continuing Voice*, 131.

[28] Ibid.

[29] Ibid., 115.

[30] See Witherington, *The Acts of the Apostles*, 634.

by God to do so. I suggest that, in these two texts, Luke is telling us much the same as what we find in 1 Cor 14. "NT prophecy would seem to have had an authority of general content and was not taken as a literal transcript of God's words, but rather was something that needed to be weighed or sifted (see 1 Cor. 14.29)."[31] What does have absolute authority, in Luke's view, is (1) the OT prophecies and (2) the words of Jesus, whether during his ministry or as conveyed in visions from the exalted Christ. In the age of prophecy fulfillment, there was indeed new prediction, but it had to be weighed carefully. One might prophesy beyond the measure of one's faith.

At Acts 11:27 Agabus predicts a coming famine "over all the world," and Luke says that this famine took place during the reign of Claudius, in the late 40s AD. This may provide us with yet another example of prophecy that is generally correct but must be allowed some poetic and prophetic license. This could, however, be a reference to a famine that affects the whole Roman Empire.[32] It is not an example of exaggeration but a statement that recognizes that if there is a drought in Egypt, the breadbasket of the empire, then there are famine and food shortage throughout the empire. The prophecy suggests that many Christians, perhaps especially in Jerusalem, were poor.

Notice that Luke says that Agabus came in the company of prophets from Jerusalem to Antioch. This suggests that Luke sees Jerusalem not only as the center from which God's word goes out but as "prophecy central." Philip, who has several prophesying daughters (21:9–10), also comes from Jerusalem (6:5; ch. 8). Peter begins his prophetic career in Jerusalem, where he received the Spirit (ch. 2), and Paul has his encounter with the heavenly Christ while going forth from Jerusalem to Damascus. The first significant city center, other than Jerusalem, with a Christian presence is Antioch, and it is there that one hears about prophets and teachers whom the Holy Spirit instructs to set aside Paul and Barnabas for a specific mission (13:1–3). The impression left is that they are sent out as prophets and teachers. But Barnabas and Paul also have links with Jerusalem and the Jerusalem community (11:30; 12:25). Aune's summary is apt at this point:

> The book of Acts depicts prophets, as well as apostles and teachers, as constantly on the move. Yet this movement at least so far as the prophets are concerned, is limited to the region of Syria-Palestine. Acts 11.27ff. reports that a group of prophets, including Agabus traveled from Jerusalem to Antioch. . . . Later Agabus went from Judea (presumably Jerusalem) to Caesarea for the specific purpose of delivering a prophetic warning to Paul (Acts 21.8–11). Judas and Silas, both designated prophets in Acts 15.32, were sent to Antioch from Jerusalem to interpret and expand on the letter which they had carried from the apostles and elders in Jerusalem to the Antiochean Christian community (Acts 15.22–35). These three instances of prophetic itinerancy are the only NT examples of trips taken by prophets for the specific purpose of exercising their prophetic gifts. The last two examples, and

---

[31] Ibid., 631.
[32] Ibid., 372–73.

probably the first as well, are not instances of aimless wandering, but each trip is apparently undertaken for a specific purpose.[33]

But what would happen to early Christian prophecy when it lost its home base in Jerusalem? Would it continue to be a phenomenon mainly localized in the eastern end of the empire, or would a real itinerancy develop? To judge from material ranging from the *Didache* to the Montanist movement, early Christian prophets did begin to wander in and from the Syrian and Palestinian region. At least as Christianity gained a stronger and stronger foothold in Asia and the west, even in Rome, a prophetic presence became part of the church in those places as well. But we must consider first itinerant prophets within the Syrian-Palestinian region.

III. MOVING PROPHETS RATHER THAN PROPHETIC MOVEMENT

It will be useful at this juncture to compare Luke's portrait of a prophetic movement based in, and moving out from, Jerusalem with the picture one gets in another important early Christian document that is probably roughly from the same period as Luke–Acts but did not find its way into the canon—the *Didache*. Probably written near the end of the first century AD or, at the latest, in the first few years of the second century, the *Didache* paints a portrait of itinerant prophets whose actions as well as words are to be scrutinized. The question of the provenance of this document has been debated, with the vast majority of scholars being convinced that this document comes from the Syrian-Palestinian part, or perhaps the Egyptian part, of the empire.[34] It certainly leaves the impression that it is dealing with an area with small towns and villages that may be visited by prophets and teachers. The reference to mountains in *Did.* 9:4 perhaps would favor the Syrian-Palestinian setting.

The ecclesial structure manifested in the book, with local bishops and deacons (*Did.* 15:1; cf. Phil 1:1), and resident ministers of other kinds (*Did.* 15:2) alongside itinerant apostles and prophets (11:1–7; 13:1), suggests that at least the advice offered in chs. 11–15 (coupled with the eschatology at the end of the book) dates from the first century, perhaps as early as the 70s or 80s, whenever the final form of this document was assembled.[35] More importantly, the portrait of prophets in this book, in comparison with Acts, suggests a time when they were less prevalent and likely to be more marginalized even within the Syrian-Palestinian region. In other words, one may doubt that Luke, rather than the *Didache*, is reflecting what was the case in the last third of the first century AD in the east. Instead Luke is reflecting on the historical period about which he purports

---

[33] Aune, *Prophecy in Early Christianity*, 212.

[34] See R. Kraft, "Didache," *ABD* 2:197–98.

[35] The very lack of reference to Jerusalem as a home base for traveling prophets and apostles suggests a time after the fall of Jerusalem in AD 70. See M. W. Holmes, "Didache, The," *DLNT* 300–302.

to be writing. The *Didache* reflects a somewhat later time, when the church seems to be less of a prophetic movement and more of a localized phenomenon, with local church officials controlling the day-to-day operations of things.

The advice given in *Did.* 11–13 basically has to do with how to handle prophets and teachers who might occasionally show up. The especial concern is with those who might want to locate in a particular congregation or area. This is a very different approach to the management of the prophets and prophecies from what one finds in 1 Cor 14, where prophecy and desiring to be a prophet are encouraged but organized. Boring is right that in the *Didache* "prophets are not only highly esteemed, they also present problems for the community, particularly when they are traveling prophets wanting to settle down in the community. This is the reason for the intense interest of the author(s) in prophecy, an interest that causes the instructions on prophets to be elaborated far beyond what is said about 'apostles' and 'teachers.'"[36] When prophets and prophecy are seen more as a problem than a sign of the promise of the new age, one is a long way from the atmosphere in Luke 1–2.

The first reference to prophets in the *Didache* comes at 10:7, where the discussion is about the fellowship meal and prayers for it. The author instructs the congregation to "permit the prophets to give thanks as much as they wish." This may suggest localized prophets rather than itinerant ones,[37] but notice that while, as in 1 Corinthians, the locale of the prophets' proclamation is the Christian worship service, someone is being told in the *Didache* to "allow" the prophets to act in this fashion, which suggests a person who has authority over the prophets.

Didache 11:1–3 reflects a situation where there is a standard of "dogma" (see v. 3) by which the teaching and the prophecies of itinerants should be measured (cf. vv. 1, 3). Notice the language that concludes ch. 10—"but permit the prophets to hold the eucharist as they will." Those who are in control of this situation are not the prophets themselves but those who grant them permission, to whom the author of the *Didache* is writing. The same applies to the advice given in 11:5: if an apostle comes and visits, he is to be welcomed, but if he stays more than one or two days, he is a false prophet *(pseudoprophētēs)*. If he asks for money, he is a false prophet (v. 6). Clearly, there is a considerable suspicion about the moral integrity of such itinerants, and it is the local officials who are expected to be discerning and make decisions about the matter.

At 11:7 we come to the imperative not to test or examine any prophet speaking *en pneumati*, which presumably means "in the Spirit." To this is appended the warrant "for every sin will be forgiven except this one," a variant of Matt 12:31–32. The point is that one dare not speak a word against the Holy Spirit and, for fear of that, one shall not examine the prophets *speaking* in the Spirit. This might mean—indeed, seems likely to mean—do not test their utterances while they are in a pneumatic state. This is so for two reasons. First, 11:8

---

[36] Boring, *The Continuing Voice,* 83.
[37] Ibid., 94.

goes on to say that not everyone who speaks in a spirit is a prophet, and the proof of the true prophet will be his behavior, which must model the behavior of the Lord. This again likely echoes the discussion in Matt 12:31–32, where the context is that Jesus has said that he acts by the Spirit of God and that while a person may be forgiven a word against the Son of Man, the person may not be forgiven a word against the Spirit of God. In short, the *Didache* reflects the kind of high respect for the Holy Spirit that the Lord's teaching demanded, but there is clearly a significant suspicion about the wandering prophet himself. Second, one has already been told that the local officials are indeed to act according to a preexisting "dogma" of the Gospel when a wandering prophet comes to town.

For fear of judging the Spirit, the instructor in this manual urges close scrutiny of the prophet's behavior—this is the ultimate litmus test, aiding the discernment of who is a true and who a false prophet. For example, if a prophet orders a meal "in the Spirit" and eats of it, he is a false prophet. Every prophet who teaches the truth but does not do what he teaches is a false prophet. This is not to say that his utterances are false but that he is a fake. The focus here is on moral discernment in regard to the prophets rather than on the prophecies. The authentic prophets who have passed these behavioral criteria are not to be judged even if they perform a "worldly mystery of the church," *so long as* they do not teach others to do so as well (11:11). It is not clear what a worldly mystery of the church is, but perhaps the best guess is that the Eucharist is meant (cf. 10:7). *Didache* 11:1 is also interesting because it compares Christian prophets to the prophets of old and says that both have God as their ultimate judge.

Didache 11:12 urges, "whoever shall say in the spirit, 'Give me money or something else,' you shall not listen to him; but if he urges you to give on behalf of others you shall not judge him." What this verse must mean is that indeed some words of prophets, even if spoken in the Spirit, are not truly from God and are not to be heeded or complied with. This, in turn, means that our author is not just saying, "Judge what he does, not what he says." There is to be a sifting even of what he says. The prophet's words are not to be taken as the Gospel if they do not comport with the "dogma" of the Gospel. The situation here does not seem to be significantly different from that found in 1 Cor 14, for in neither case is it simply assumed that what the prophet says in a pneumatic state is necessarily the very words of God. Again, we are dealing with a different situation from that found in the early church when it treated prophecy found in Scripture and apparently also the prophetic teaching and utterances of at least the original apostles.

It comes as something of a surprise, in light of the tone of suspicion found in *Did.* 11, that in 13:1 we hear, "every true prophet who wishes to settle among you is worthy of his food." The quotation is a version of Matt 10:10/Luke 10:7, and it begins to become clear that the Gospel "dogma" that is the measuring stick for prophets is indeed the teaching of Jesus about such matters. The suspicion only applies to someone who is an itinerant, not an itinerant who has proved himself a true prophet and wishes to become a local prophet, for one can not observe the words and deeds of an itinerant over a period of time to see if they comport with the Gospel.

Indeed, the proven itinerant prophet turned local prophet becomes something of a local celebrity. But notice that it is not this prophet who is the bearer or applier of the Gospel "dogma" or teaching of Jesus but, rather, the local church leaders. If this is even close to representing the situation in general in the early church, it bodes ill for Boring's thesis that the prophets transmitted and had much influence on the developing Gospel tradition. As Boring himself recognizes, the itinerant nature of various of these prophets must also count against their playing such a role.[38]

To this one may add that the sociological profile of the prophet in the *Didache* stands against his playing such a role. The prophet is a person depicted in this work as one who is in need of food, shelter, funds. The prophets are poor, but clearly they are not ascetics, as they are expected to ask for food and funds. It is not accidental that the author says to give to the poor if not to the prophet (cf. below). The prophet is ranked among the poor. In short, the prophet is marginalized, and the author must even exhort the community that if he is willing to localize, he should be fed. This does not suggest a situation where either the laity or the local officials would have seen the prophet as the sort of authority figure who would be entrusted with the "dogma" of the Gospel, and in fact it is not the prophet who applies this "dogma" in this work but the church officials.

Prophets were worship leaders (10:7, 13:3), "with nothing suggesting that prophets function outside the worship setting. This latter view is specifically opposed in Hermas who considers the context of worship by the holy community as the sine qua non (Mandate 11.1–9), while false prophets avoid congregations (Mandate 11.13)."[39] But if this is correct, then the social venue in which prophets operate is not the scriptorium or places where manuscripts were copied or the Jesus tradition was written down for the first time. The prophets were oracles, conveyors of the spoken word, including spontaneous prayers. They were not sages or scribes.

The advice given in 13:3, 6 is to treat the prophet like a priest and give him the firstfruits of the winepress and of the grain and of the animals. Indeed, they are called "your high priests," those who bring you into the presence of God. It is interesting that something similar seems to be the premise behind 1 Macc 14:41, where one hears that the Jews decided that Simon should be "their leader and high priest for ever, until a trustworthy prophet should appear." The assumption seems to be that prophets, like priests, are holy men, extremely close to God, and from them one can hear the word of God. It appears that the ecclesial process mentioned in Maccabees is going in the opposite direction from what one finds in the *Didache*, where it is intimated that the prophetic office can be assumed and succeeded by other officials.

---

[38] Ibid., 95.
[39] Ibid., 109.

Notice, however, that the imperative is given in the *Didache:* "But if you do not have a (local) prophet, give to the poor" (13:4). This suggests that it was not expected that every local village or congregation would have such a prophet. But it was expected of the local congregation that they would appoint overseers/bishops and deacons (15:1), and in fact, their presence makes unnecessary having a local prophet, because "they minister to you the ministry of the prophets and teachers." In other words, the important functions of itinerant teachers and prophets can be assumed by other local ecclesial authorities. The command "do not despise them for they are the ones to be honored among you, along with the prophets and teachers" (15:2) speaks volumes about the attitude of the author of this material, for whom local church leaders are the primary authorities in the church, but true teachers and prophets are certainly to be honored as well.

The impression given by both the material in Luke–Acts and the material in the *Didache* is that prophets had authority in the early church, but not absolute authority. They are seen as inspired but not infallible, and they are held responsible for what they say (*Did.* 11:8–12). They are not, in other words, seen as ecstatics who can not help what they say or do.[40] The words of the prophets spoken in the Spirit were to be respected and not tested while being uttered, but they seem, at most, only to have had an authority of general content rather than an absolute "thus saith the Lord" quality. Prophets were distinguishable from apostles, bishops, deacons, and even teachers, and in regard to comparison with these other functionaries, Hill's summary seems judicious: "The prophet disclos[es] the revealed will of God for and in a certain set of circumstances, and the teacher [is] more concerned with the exposition of Scripture and the transmission of the tradition concerning Jesus."[41] One such teacher is the author of our material in the *Didache*, who measures prophets by the sayings of Jesus, seeing the latter as a higher authority.

One may also agree with the assessment of Hill when he says that the *Didache* seems to reflect a time when the number of the prophets was dwindling, and it could not be assumed that there would be a prophet in every local congregation, so their roles were to be assumed by overseers and deacons. It is also true that the

> author of the *Didache* allows the supreme value and unique prestige of a true prophet; but experience has by this time proved that self-authenticated wandering prophets are a doubtful blessing. . . .
> The aim, therefore, of the author of the *Didache* is to create, wherever it did not yet exist, a *resident ministry of episkopoi and deacons.* Where it already exists, he tries to raise its status; congregations are bidden to regard these as their "honorable men along with the prophets and teachers."[42]

---

[40] Ibid., 128.

[41] Hill, *New Testament Prophecy,* 104.

[42] B. H. Streeter, *The Primitive Church* (London: Macmillan, 1929), 155–56.

The *Didache* reminds us of the ongoing presence of prophets in the church. It does not suggest that we should see Christianity as a prophetic movement or one led by prophets at the end of the first century or into the second century.

IV. THE MONARCHIAL PROPHET

Going a little further down the time line to Ignatius of Antioch, we can see where the sort of thinking found in the *Didache* can lead—in particular, the concept that non-prophets can take over the prophetic roles or functions. Ignatius of Antioch died a martyr's death sometime near the end of the reign of Trajan, or in about AD 115–117. Like Paul, he was taken into Roman custody and extradited to Rome, where he was executed. Along the way of his journey through Asia Minor, he wrote the letters to the churches in western Asia (as well as in Rome), some of which are the same churches addressed in Revelation. Ignatius placed strong emphasis on the near total authority of the local bishop, who is supported by a circle of elders and deacons, all of whom together are seen as carrying on the apostolic tradition and perhaps also, in the case of the bishop, the apostolic office. Ignatius hardly mentions prophets (only once—Ign. *Phld.* 5:2), and that one time he does mention them, he may well be referring to OT prophets. As Aune's careful study has shown, however, Ignatius himself speaks in oracular form at various points in these letters. The basic pattern is a narrative introduction followed by an oath or revelation formula and concluding with admonitions:

> *Narrative:* But some suspected that I said these things because I already knew of the division caused by some people.
>
> *Oath and revelation formula:* But he is my witness in whom I am bound that I had learned nothing from any human being, but the Spirit was proclaiming by speaking in this manner.
>
> *Admonitions:*
>
> "Apart from the bishop do nothing"
>
> "Guard your flesh as the temple of God"
>
> "Love unity"
>
> "Flee divisions"
>
> "Be imitators of Jesus Christ as he was of the Father."

Immediately preceding this is another oracle introduced with the formula "I cried out . . . I spoke with a great voice, with the voice of God" (Ign. *Phld.* 7:1–2). As Aune says, the loud voice indicates some sort of pneumatic state, and the form of this introduction in Greek is a poetic triplet, which is a trait of some prophetic speech.[43] This is consistent with claims Ignatius makes elsewhere in his letters,

---

[43] Aune, *Prophecy in Early Christianity*, 292.

where we hear, "though I am in chains and can understand heavenly things, and the places of angels and the gatherings of principalities, and 'things seen and unseen'" (Ign. *Trall.* 5:2, LCL). This is surely a claim to be a sort of seer, having knowledge and presumably visions of the heavenly world. The example cited in the chart above shows the highly practical and ethical content of such prophecy, addressing particular problems in a particular church. Indeed, as Aune stresses, prophecy here functions much as Paul states it should in 1 Cor 14:25, for the Philadelphians suspected that Ignatius had prior knowledge of their problems, since his admonitions were so clearly on target in addressing the difficulties in that church.[44]

What we should make of this is that Ignatius himself is manifesting the traits of prophet and seer and apparently does not refer to any other church functionary doing so. There is nothing in his letters about dealing with itinerant prophets or even localized prophets, but there is certainly some revealing material about the bishop assuming prophetic functions and roles. It is difficult to know whether we might read this as something of a power play or not, but we would expect that if there were prophets who could have rivaled Ignatius as "the voice of God" to these Christian groups, he would surely have had to mention them in one or more of these letters. His silence is eloquent that prophecy offered by noninstitutional figures seems to be missing in these churches, only a very short time after the seer John of Patmos had addressed the churches in an apocalyptic form and warned them against false prophets. It is to the latter subject we must turn in our next chapter as we examine apocalyptic at the end of the first century AD—from Revelation to Hermas. While, in the eastern end of the empire (as in *Didache*, Matthew, Antioch), oracular Christian prophecy by those who were designated prophets seems to have been on the wane at the end of the first century AD, prophecy's flamboyant child, apocalyptic, appears to have been gaining new life from Asia to Rome.

V. CONCLUSIONS

Prophecy manifested itself in various forms at the end of the first century AD and into the second century, but the impression left by the data is that while Christianity started out with prophets playing some important roles in various locales, by the end of the century, the presence and authority of such figures had waned. Luke, to be sure, presents early Christianity as a sort of prophetic movement led by a notable messianic prophet, Jesus, and his ablest prophetic successors, Peter and Paul, but Luke is speaking as a historian and apologist, not as an exegete of his own experience at the end of the first century. The *Didache* more accurately portrays that later period, as do the letters of Ignatius of Antioch. Prophecy and the role of prophet were not dead, but they were being marginalized in various ways as the second century got under way.

---

[44] Ibid.

In the literature discussed in this chapter, prophecy appeared as a phenomenon including prediction, but expressed in general or generic terms. It had an authority of general content but seldom offered clear specifics, and in any case, the prophet might say more than his inspiration warranted in the excitement of the moment. The author of the *Didache* respects prophets and their oracles and is fearful of judging their utterances, but suggests a lifestyle test to discern if a prophet is a true prophet. This differs from what we find in 1 Cor 14. In the latter text a congregation is encouraged as a whole to be prophets, utter oracles, and weigh them. In the *Didache* we get the distinct impression the congregation is not prophetic at all, and indeed it is called to be wary of itinerant prophets. In the case of Ignatius, we find the office of the prophet assumed by the monarchial bishop, a new sort of central prophet who makes possible the further marginalizing of those prophets at the periphery of Christian communities.

Prophecy throughout the material scrutinized in this chapter is seen as a community phenomenon that transpires in worship, including worship where the Lord's Supper is involved. In the *Didache* the prophet is said to be like a priest, performing a worldly mystery. Nothing in any of this material suggests that prophecy was, in the main, seen as words of the risen Lord spoken to the congregation. Rather, it was words of the Spirit. It is telling that in Acts the risen Lord speaks through visions and dreams but the Spirit speaks through traditional oracular prophets. This perhaps in part reflects Luke's theological cosmology: Christ is in heaven and therefore accessible through visions and dreams, while the Spirit is on earth inspiring prophets to speak and thus is directly accessible even in the conscious state. Luke, in his apologetic efforts to portray Christianity as a venerable movement grounded in, and characterized by, prophecy, paints a winsome picture of visions, dreams, and oracles guiding the early church, a picture geared to intrigue and attract the prophecy-hungry pagan world. But although we would not guess this from Acts, apocalyptic was also alive and well in early Christianity, even well into the second century. This study must now turn to the remarkable phenomenon of Christian apocalyptic.

CHAPTER 11

From the Seer to the Shepherd:

Apocalyptic at the End of the New Testament Era

*I*N VIEW OF THE DIFFICULTIES IN understanding the book of Revelation, it will come as no surprise that the discussion of Christian apocalyptic must begin with some disclaimers. In light of the discussion in the previous two chapters, it will not do to suggest either that Revelation provides the sole or necessarily even the primary model of what "prophecy" was like among Christians in this era. At the same time, it will not do to dismiss the prophetic character of Revelation either, as if the hybrid-form apocalyptic was not grounded in the prophetic tradition.[1] The older influential differentiation of P. D. Hanson between prophecy and apocalyptic,[2] which was grounded in a distinction between history and myth, has rightly been rejected of late by R. P. Carroll and L. Grabbe. As Grabbe asks, "Do the apocalypses depend a lot on visions? So do many prophecies. Do many apocalypses describe an ideal world to come? So do many prophetic passages. . . . [Furthermore,] many of the prophecies without visionary frameworks may

---

[1] It is one of the main errors of Boring, *The Continuing Voice*, 79ff., that he tries to take the book of Revelation, which does indeed have sayings of the exalted Lord (presented as just that, not as sayings of the historical Jesus) as *the* main paradigm for what early Christian prophecy was like. This means accordingly that he must devalue the evidence of Acts and, to some extent, that of Paul as not in accord with the earliest reality of the church. But in fact both oracular prophets and apocalyptic seers existed in the early church, and we must not underestimate or ignore either of these traditions if we wish to understand the prophetic phenomenon in this era.

[2] Hanson, *Dawn of Apocalyptic,* 126–32, 299–315.

nevertheless have been received via visions."[3] To this one may add that both prophecy and apocalyptic use mythical concepts and images.

It is, however, possible to make a literary distinction between a book or document that has the form of an apocalypse and one that has the form of classical prophecy. The latter may contain apocalyptic material, such as visions, within it without being an apocalypse as a whole. Apocalypses are developments of the prophetic tradition and, like that tradition, are concerned with predicting the future, but they also draw on other traditions as well, both sapiential and even epistolary traditions. Thus, the difficulty is to neither underplay the continuity nor overplay the discontinuity between prophecy and apocalyptic. On the whole, one may agree with Grabbe that apocalyptic can likely be seen as a specialized form of prophecy, but it is perhaps pushing things too far, in view of its hybrid nature, to call an *entire work* in the form of an apocalypse simply a subset of the larger category, prophecy. How does this aid in the understanding of Christian prophecy and apocalyptic?

On the one hand, the evidence does suggest that early Christians believed that the risen Lord spoke through dreams and visions, including apocalyptic ones, to both seers and Christian leaders who occasionally experienced such phenomena. The NT tradition, however, regularly distinguishes between such visionaries and oracular prophets such as Agabus, who spoke under the inspiration of the Spirit and not as the risen Jesus. The question then becomes, Is the book of Revelation, in the main, a work of Christian prophecy that is essentially like classical prophecy but uses apocalyptic forms to accomplish its aims, or is it primarily an apocalypse that draws on prophetic and other sorts of forms to achieve its goals? In my view, the answer must be the latter. Revelation is not the paradigm of early Christian prophecy writ large; rather, it is an excellent example of what the hybrid apocalyptic form was like and, as such, deserves to be seen as a particular and, in many ways, peculiar kind of development of the prophetic tradition and also other traditions.[4] Recently J. J. Collins has suggested that works such as Daniel and *1 Enoch* are experimental compositions where features of other genres are used to create a new whole. They are, then, works in prog-

---

[3] L. Grabbe, "Poets, Scribes, or Preachers? The Reality of Prophecy in the Second Temple Period," *1998 SBL Seminar Papers* (Atlanta: Scholars Press, 1998), 524–45, here 527. Carroll, *When Prophecy Failed,* 206–7. Carroll's thesis is that apocalyptic arose to resolve the cognitive dissonance caused by the failure of prophecy to be fulfilled in the postexilic period. This ignores that there were already apocalyptic visions before the postexilic period, and it also ignores the character of the book of Revelation, which involves apocalyptic prophecy. Apocalyptic can not be reduced to *ex eventu* prophecy plus pseudonymity, nor does it deserve, in every case, the label of representing the triumph of imagination over reality (see ibid., 213).

[4] Contrast Boring, *The Continuing Voice,* 80: "Though the apocalyptic form of sealed scroll and interpreting angel is retained, it is subordinated to the understanding of revelation in Christian prophecy, in which the risen Lord speaks through the prophet. . . . The apocalyptic materials can be incorporated in a Christian prophetic framework."

ress. One wonders if one could not say the same about Revelation with its use of epistolary conventions and its naming of an actual author.[5]

The roots of the Jewish apocalyptic mind-set have been discussed in an earlier chapter, and there can be no doubt that Revelation's author is mainly indebted to the Jewish tradition, in particular the Danielic, rather than the Enochic, tradition (so also *4 Ezra*).[6] It has been argued that apocalyptic is a development primarily of the Jewish prophetic tradition but with some considerable influence from both Jewish sapiential traditions and also non-Jewish materials and ideas that Jews first came into contact with in and after the Babylonian exile. Contact with nonbiblical and non-Jewish materials did not, however, cease when the NT era began; indeed, perhaps especially in the missionary religion known as Christianity, such contacts increased during the course of the NT era.

Before turning to discuss a document such as Revelation, it is necessary to be fully cognizant of the environment in which the audience of such a document would have lived. How would John's largely Gentile audience in the cities of western Asia have heard such a document as Revelation? What mental resources and traditions would they have drawn on to understand it? Were there pagan traditions about the succession of world empires and the "end of the world" that may have guided how they would read such a document? How did pagans view visions and dreams? These sorts of questions must be addressed first.

I. DREAMS, VISIONS, AND APOCALYPTIC NOTIONS IN PAGAN ANTIQUITY

For those who have delved into classical Greek and Roman literature, it will come as no surprise when it is asserted that, with rare exception, the ancients believed that dreams, as well as visions, were real means by which the gods and other semidivine beings could reveal their truths and instructions to human beings. In early Greek literature, including the Homeric corpus, such means of revelation have rather stereotyped forms, as is ably summed up by E. R. Dodds:

> [They take] the form of a visit paid to a sleeping man or woman by a single dream-figure (the very word *oneiros* in Homer nearly always means dream-figure, not dream-experience). This dream-figure can be a god, or a ghost, or a pre-existing dream-messenger, or an "image" *(eidolon)* created specially for the occasion; but whichever it is, it exists objectively in space and is independent of the dreamer. It effects an entry by the keyhole . . . it plants itself at the head of the bed to deliver its message; and when that is done, it withdraws by the same route. The dreamer, meanwhile, is almost completely passive.[7]

---

[5] J. J. Collins, "Genre, Ideology, and Social Movements in Jewish Apocalypticism," in *Mysteries and Revelations: Apocalyptic Studies since the Uppsala Colloquium* (ed. J. J. Collins and J. Charlesworth; Sheffield: JSOT Press, 1991), 11–32, here 20.

[6] See pp. 216–22 above.

[7] E. R. Dodds, *The Greeks and the Irrational* (Boston: Beacon, 1957), 104–5.

It is a stock item in Greek plays that the characters regularly receive revelations and warnings from above in the form of symbolic dreams, not unlike the sort Joseph or Nebuchadnezzar had in the biblical tradition. For example, in Aeschylus's *Choephori*, when Arestes learns that his mother has dreamed that she would give birth to an asp who would be breast-fed by her, he finally understands the tragic role he is to play in relationship to his mother (lines 523–552).

But it is hardly just in plays that we find these mirrors of Greek social existence. Herodotus tells us that Pheidippides, who made the famous 150-mile run before the battle of Marathon, was inspired and aided by a vision of the god Pan as he sought to reach Sparta and give aid (*Hist.* 5.105). The father of Greek history also tells the tale of the Nasmonians in western Africa, who would return to the graves of their ancestors for the purposes of divination. They would pray, and after lying down to sleep on the grave, it is said that dreams came to them that would guide their future conduct (*Hist.* 4.172). It was widely believed that dreams revealed the future. Thus Pindar wrote that when one is dreaming, "each one's body follows the call of overmastering death; yet still there is left alive an image of life, for this alone is from the gods. It sleeps while the limbs are active; but while the man sleeps it often shows in dreams a decision of joy or adversity to come" (frg. 131, 116B).

The legendary Socrates is said by Plato to have had a dramatic premonition of his coming death, in the form of a very vivid dream. Socrates tells Crito he has had a vision in a dream, and is asked what the nature of the dream was. To this Socrates replies, "There appeared to me the likeness of a woman, fair and comely, clothed in bright raiment, who called to me and said: 'O Socrates, the third day hence to fertile Pythia shall thou come.'" Socrates then adds, "There can be no doubt about the meaning, Crito, I think." Crito urges Socrates to try to escape his fate, but to no avail (Plato, *Crito* 44B).

But it was recognized by Plato that not all dreams told the truth. The classic example is the lying dream that Zeus sent to Agamemnon (*Resp.* 2.382). Nonetheless, it is important to stress that Plato does not deny for a minute that the gods could and did reveal things to people in dreams. There are, in addition, some very revealing comments about the Greek view of the nature of prophecy in Plato's *Symposium,* where Socrates relates what the prophetess Diotima told him:

> God mingles not with man; but through love all the intercourse and converse of gods, with men, whether they be awake or *asleep,* is carried on. The wisdom which understands this is spiritual; all other wisdom, such as that of arts and handicrafts, is mean and vulgar. . . . God has given the art of divination not to the wisdom, but to the foolishness of human beings. No one, when in his wits, attains prophetic truth and inspiration, but when he receives the inspired word, either his intelligence is enthralled in sleep, or he is demented by some distemper or possession. (203)

Plato is very clear that the diviners should not be called prophets: "they are only the expositors of dark sayings and visions . . . interpreters of prophecy"

(*Tim.* 71–72). It would be interesting to know what Plato thought of the Delphi tradition in which the priests who conveyed the message of the oracle were indeed called *prophētēs*.[8]

There was a minority tradition in Greek literature, represented chiefly by Aristotle and those he influenced, that maintained that people are in contact only with the empirical world even in their dreams, and not with the world of the supernatural. Dreams are seen as natural phenomena, not messages sent by the gods. This he maintained throughout his major discussions on this subject in *Sleep and Waking, Dreams,* and *Prophesying by Dreams.* He does allow a certain clairvoyance during sleep, as he believes the soul is more sensitive when the body is asleep and so more attuned to what is happening in the outside world. It is safe to say, in view of what we find in subsequent Greek and Roman literature, that few shared Aristotle's views about dreams not being divine or prophetic in character.

Hippocrates, whose work became the basis for both Greek and Roman medicine, has a good deal of positive remarks to make about dreams, especially in *On Regimen* 4. For example, he says there, "Such dreams as are divine, and foretell to cities or private persons things evil or things good, have interpreters in those who possess the art of dealing with such things. But all the physical symptoms foretold by the soul . . . these also the diviners interpret, sometimes with, sometimes without success." The scepticism here expressed is not about the dreams themselves and their divine origins but about some of their interpreters—the diviners.

It is interesting that none of the Greek historians except Thucydides seem to have agreed with Aristotle's views about dreams, for all the rest present dreams as a means of divine revelation to human beings. The Roman historians were largely in agreement with the dominant Greek historical tradition on these matters. Even sceptical Tacitus does not deny that sometimes gods may reveal themselves or messages through dreams. Suetonius tells us that Alexander the Great was guided by divine dreams and omens that served as premonitions of what was to come (*Aug.* 94.5). Plutarch in his *Parallel Lives* time and again recounts how in dreams famous people have premonitions of important events, especially of coming great victories or their coming deaths (cf., e.g., *Luc.* 11.1–2; *Ant.* 75.3–4).

But it is not just dreams and visions that are of relevance to the discussion of how Gentiles would hear Revelation; there is also the larger tradition, in the Greco-Roman world, of oracles about the succession and end of empires and emperors and even of the world. There was, for example, speculation that Rome would come to an end nine hundred years after the foundation of the city, which prompted debates about the exact date when the city was begun. In the eighth *Sibylline Oracle,* one has a prophecy concerning that end, which seems to be connected with the emperor Hadrian. It thus comes from within about twenty years of the date of Revelation itself and reads,

---

[8] See pp. 317–20 above.

When the sixth generation of Latin kings will complete its last life and leave its scepter, another king of this race will reign, who will rule over the entire earth, and hold power over the scepter; and he will rule well in accord with the command of the great god; the children and the generation of children of this man will be safe from violation according to the prophecy of the cyclic time of years.

When there will have been fifteen kings of Egypt, then, when the phoenix of the fifth span of years will have come . . . there will arise a race of destructive people, a race without laws, the race of the Hebrews. Then Ares will plunder Ares, and he will destroy the insolent boast of the Romans, for at that time the luxuriant rule of the Romans will be destroyed, ancient queen over conquered cities. The plain of fertile Rome will no longer be victorious when rising to power from Asia, together with Ares, he comes. He will arise arranging all these things in the city from top to bottom. You will fill out three times three hundreds and forty and eight cycling years when an evil, violent, fate will come upon you, filling out your name. (*Sib. Or.* 8.131–150, trans. Potter)

As Potter points out, "the sixth generation of Latin kings" is a rather clear reference to the Flavians, with Nero being the sixth Caesar, who in turn is part of the sixth generation (cf. the number 666 of the Neronian antichrist figure in Revelation). Potter conjectures that this part of the eighth *Oracle* may in fact date from the reign of Vespasian, since it mentions his children without saying they reigned (which Titus did).[9] One of the coordinating factors is the rising of the phoenix from the ashes, which was believed to happen every 540 years. But the number 900 or its multiples kept coming up—for example, in Juvenal's mention of nine ages of iron followed by a golden age (*Sat.* 13.28–30). There had long been the speculation, found as early as Hesiod, that there would be four kingdoms corresponding to ages of gold, silver, bronze, and iron (*Op.* 106–201). John of Patmos's near contemporary, Dionysius of Halicarnassus, in the preface to his *Roman Antiquities* kept this tradition alive by pointing out that Rome was superior to these aforementioned four "metal" kingdoms.

Dio Cassius mentions another oracle, reportedly of the sibyl, that said, "when thrice three hundred revolving years have run their course civil war and the folly of Sybaris will destroy the Romans" (57.18.3–5). Tiberius took pains to try to disprove this prophecy by calling it a fake, but apparently not many were convinced. After the fire of AD 64 in Rome, this same prophecy cropped up again, and in addition, there was a further sibylline verse that appeared at this time that said, "last of the sons of Aeneas, a mother-slayer will rule" (Dio Cassius, 62.18.3–4). About the latter, Dio remarked that even if it was not an ancient oracle, it proved true and so may have been divinely inspired by contemporary events.[10]

A good deal more could be said along these lines, but perhaps this will suffice to make clear that what we find in books such as Daniel and that latter-day work it heavily influenced, Revelation, was not so foreign, in its content and

---

[9] Potter, *Prophets and Emperors*, 104.
[10] See ibid., 100.

character, to the Gentile mind as we might have suspected. The apocalyptic imagery and features offered a new twist, but the story was still about political matters and the rise and fall of rulers and realms and times and seasons. In addition, the evidence also strongly suggests that John's work would not have been seen as a literary creation of a nonreferential variety. To the contrary, it would have been seen as some sort of symbolic but nonetheless real prophetic or visionary material involving the history of the period in which the audience lived and the future of that period. As Grabbe says, to the ancient writers, the heavenly council to which the seer may have access and the invasion of Israel by Assyria are equally real things that can be seen. Also one must not distinguish between prophecy and apocalyptic as if only the latter uses metaphorical or hyperbolic or disclosure language (cf. Isa 2:2–4, Mic 4:1–5).[11] It is the almost exclusive reliance on visionary material and apocalyptic images and ideas that distinguishes an apocalypse from prophecy, which simply includes the odd apocalyptic vision or image. Bearing this in mind, it is time to consider some aspects of the Christian apocalypse known as Revelation.

II. JOHN THE SEER'S VISIONS AND EXPRESSION

A. A Tour Guide's Map.   Though we can not be sure, it appears likely that John's apocalypse has the epistolary framework it does purely because the author is at some distance from his audience, for one normal way to communicate with an audience at a distance in antiquity was through a letter or letters. A normal way to communicate with several different but related audiences in several different locales was a circular letter. This may lead to the conclusion that the epistolary framework to this particular document is incidental rather than essential to the apocalyptic form. The seer has adapted things because of his social situation, but then, of course, apocalypses were rather plastic hybrid forms, in any case. The narrative portions that preceded most of the visions in Daniel provided a certain precedent for such an adaptation, but the author of Revelation is not slavishly following Daniel's pattern. There is nothing like the wisdom tales of Dan 1–6 in Revelation.

A further consequence of recognizing the epistolary form of some of Revelation's framework is that it reveals again the importance of distinguishing prophetic experience and prophetic expression. The seer experienced visions. Revelation is not merely a transcript of those visions, in all likelihood, but instead an incorporating of those visions and some oracular and epistolary and other material into a literary whole. John the seer did not likely experience an apocalypse. He had apocalyptic visions and then fashioned an apocalypse to express what he had seen, as he felt it had bearing on his audiences. This is an important distinction, for it means that we might well not have an apocalypse at all if John had not been at a distance from his audience. He might have simply

---

[11] Grabbe, "Poets," 526.

shared one or more of his visions orally with his churches as they came, without resorting to a literary creation.

The question, then, must be raised again about whether the inscribing of these visions in a book is itself a prophetic activity. Surely, it need not be, for a person might well use a scribe to accomplish this task and this would not, in itself, make the scribe a prophet.[12] Reasons to distinguish between inspired or pneumatic interpretation of prophecy and prophecy itself have been mentioned,[13] and now it must be stressed that it is perfectly possible to distinguish between having apocalyptic visions and the literary task of forming an apocalypse, which may or may not have been done by a seer or prophet. Doubtless some seers or prophets could write and did indeed do so, but doubtless others relied on their Baruchs or had their oracles recorded by others along the way. While it is likely a mistake to see John's Apocalypse as the result of a purely literary exercise (unlike most apocalypses which are pseudonymous in character), we must not underestimate the literary character of the text as it now stands.

The recent work of S. Niditch is helpful at this point, especially in the present postmodern environment, which wrongly stresses that all we have to connect the modern reader with antiquity is texts. Niditch stresses that we must ask the proper questions about how texts function in a largely oral culture where the vast majority of people could not read or write.[14] While the elite were likely to dominate and to be far more literate than others in a highly stratified society, nonetheless oral culture shaped even the literate in regard to what they did with, and how they used, texts. Texts were often just tools for further oral performances. "Very few people in the culture we are envisioning know written works because they have seen and read them; they have received the works' messages and content by word of mouth. Even if they have read the works themselves, they quote from memory."[15] This means that we must not imagine John on Patmos poring over a multitude of OT scrolls and then creating an imaginative literary pastiche. The visions that came to John came to a Scripture-saturated mind, but also to a mind well acquainted with popular and mythical images of the larger Greco-Roman world. The resulting attempt to explain or express these visions in writing drew on this deep reservoir of images and ideas. What John *heard* he might well transcribe almost verbatim, especially if he wrote it down soon after the experience. But what John *saw* he had to describe, and here he drew on the resources he already had.

One of the likely giveaways that we must see prophecy as an essentially oral phenomenon is it poetic form. It was intended to be spoken, not read.

---

[12] See Grabbe, *Priests, Prophets,* 180ff.

[13] See pp. 234–37 above.

[14] Niditch, *Oral World and Written Word.*

[15] Ibid., 5. Niditch is also right to emphasize that memory in an oral culture was often a sharper and more reliable tool than it is in a modern text-reliant culture. John may well have given us descriptions of his visions and oracles very close to the way he experienced them, perhaps especially in regard to what he heard.

Whether this is also true with apocalyptic visions or dreams may be debated. On the one hand, there is the experience of Ezekiel, who has a vision that renders him speechless for a period of time, and also we may think of the command in some apocalyptic literature to record but seal up the vision for a later time. On the other hand, the nature of apocalyptic is the disclosure of secrets. Apocalyptic visions are not usually just intended to inform a seer about his own fate or future. His revelations are meant to be shared and thus become common coin in an oral culture.[16] Revelation itself, in contrast to the command in Dan 12:9, is about the unsealing of the scrolls because the eschatological age has indeed dawned (Rev 6 and following).

While a prophet could hear and simply repeat an oral communication, it is not possible to simply "repeat" a vision verbatim. It must be described or drawn, and when what one sees is images and symbols, one must grope for analogies ("It was like . . .") and resort to aspective and metaphorical and multivalent language. There is an elusive and allusive character to the description of any vision, and one must use universal symbols or at least familiar types in order to communicate. This was good news in some respects because it made it easier for visions to communicate across time and helps explain why apocalypses were preserved. What was said in the Pentateuch of all prophets other than Moses was certainly true of seers: while Moses may well have received direct revelation, seers experienced the divine communication, to some degree, as enigma, as a dark and parabolic thing.[17] Apocalyptic material always required interpretation or explanation. It is indeed a kind of coded language, and those not familiar with the universe of discourse would not likely get the point.

It is plausible to imagine an extended process such as J. Crenshaw has suggested for the composition of works of prophecy: (1) putative revelatory moment, (2) reflection, (3) articulation, (4) refining of word by poetry, (5) adding of supporting arguments, (6) performance. But this process might well be telescoped considerably in the case of an apocalyptic work such as Revelation.

For one thing, the prophetic experience may have included hearing poetry, perhaps in the form of songs (cf. Rev 4:8–11; 5:9–14). For another thing, at least in the case of Revelation, the seer himself did not perform this work in part or in toto so far as one can tell, although it is likely his messenger or some other Christian did. In view of all that has been seen in this study of prophetic materials, it also appears likely that various prophets and seers *experienced* their revelations as poetry. Poetry was not necessarily the later refinement of an inchoate word. But one must also make no mistake that what we find in Revelation is not just a transcript of experience. Whatever the content of these pneumatic

---

[16] Perhaps one reason there seems to be no concern about grammatical infelicities and the like in Revelation is that it was meant to be read aloud and so heard, not merely read.

[17] So rightly J. Crenshaw, in his important "Transmitting Prophecy across Generations" (paper presented at the annual meeting of the Society of Biblical Literature, Orlando, Fla., November 23, 1998).

experiences ("I was in the Spirit on the Lord's day," Rev 1:10), the book, as it now exists, is a literary attempt to use such materials to persuade and exhort several groups of Christians who were apparently badly in need of some reassurance and encouragement and instruction. The rhetorical dimensions and function of the book must not be overlooked.

Bearing these things in mind, it is time to reflect on some of the general aspects of this book. First, while it is certainly true that there are various examples of otherworldly visions in Revelation, it is crucial to bear in mind that this work is not just about what is transpiring in heaven. The seer is not simply a mystic like other early Jewish or Christian mystics.[18] There is a historical and eschatological dimension to this book not only in the opening letters but also in the descriptions of destruction followed by a new earth as well as a new heaven. The seer is concerned not just about a heaven that is spatially near but about events that are thought to be at least possibly temporally near. His focus is not just "up there" but also "out there." It is perhaps a product of modern tendencies to separate the social and the spiritual, or the mundane and the supernatural, that we find the notions of traffic between heaven and earth, or of an open heaven and an influenced earth, or indeed of a merger between heaven and earth (Rev 21–22) somewhat off-putting. John has not substituted an otherworldly view of eternity for an earlier more temporal, historical, eschatological one. Rather, the two are intertwined here. A quick comparison with the Shepherd of Hermas or, even better, Dante's *Divine Comedy* will show just how eschatological John's Revelation actually is.[19]

On the other hand, it also will not do to assume that John himself believed he was simply using mythical images to describe all too mundane realities. John really believed not merely in God and the Christ and angels but in their regular interaction with humankind in the earthly sphere. The angels, for instance, are not symbols or figures of human beings. We should not be misled by the hyperbolic nature and rhetorical dimensions of various of the apocalyptic images into thinking that this material is not intended to be referential. Indeed it is, but the references are sometimes to human figures and sometimes to superhuman ones.

---

[18] Here is where C. Rowland's otherwise helpful work goes somewhat awry, but see Rowland, *The Open Heaven;* and "Apocalyptic, Mysticism, and the New Testament," in *Judentum,* vol. 1 of *Festschrift für M. Hengel: Geschichte—Tradition—Reflexion* (ed. P. Schafer; Tübingen: J. C. B. Mohr, 1996), 405–430.

[19] It is interesting to compare Revelation to Hebrews. The latter work has a very clear emphasis and focus on the otherworld and the heavenly realm *as destination,* to a stronger degree than Revelation, and accordingly the eschatological realities receive far less treatment in Hebrews than they do in Revelation. Hebrews is more of a harbinger than Revelation of the later less eschatological, more otherworldly, Christian literature of the second through fourth centuries. One may, in part, recognize in Hebrews the same sort of influence of Neo-Platonism and its speculations about the heavenly perfect realm as we find in Philo, but the same could not be said about Revelation.

That this material is multivalent and not literally descriptive should not lead us to assume that it is not referring to *some* reality John believed existed. John's focus, like that of most biblical writers, is on the redemption and judgments of God in space and time. He thus shares an essential kinship with other prophets and seers in the Jewish and Christian tradition who are concerned about the future of God's people not merely in heaven but on earth. This is one of the things that distinguishes John from those who simply have mystical visions of heaven or go on ecstatic otherworldly tours of heaven and its occupants and activities. Indeed, it could be debated whether John even had an otherworldly tour in the Spirit. It appears more likely that John's experience was simply a matter of receiving certain revelations seriatim. His account does not read like Enoch's tour of heaven. One must, then, allow John to have his say about the historical future and indeed the conclusion of human history at the return of Christ, however wrong some may think he was not only about the timing but also about the substance of his predictions.

E. Schüssler Fiorenza's conclusion is worth pondering at this point: "Early Christian prophecy is expressed in apocalyptic form and early Christian apocalyptic is carried on by early Christian prophets. Early Christian prophecy is an ecstatic experience 'in the Spirit' . . . and the revelation of divine mysteries."[20] What is not so apt about this statement is the assumption that all early Christian prophecy took this form or was an expression of apocalyptic or that apocalyptic is the mother genre and prophecy a subset under it. But this much is absolutely correct—apocalypses like that of John are not purely literary products of tradents. They are generated by prophets and grounded in prophetic experience of an apocalyptic sort. Schüssler Fiorenza is also quite right that Revelation shares with early Christian prophecy the following: it is an eschatological revelation of or about Jesus Christ that has as a main purpose exhortation and strengthening of communities and is meant to be read aloud or performed in Christian worship, for, unlike much of Greco-Roman prophecy, it is not individual but communal in nature. Christian prophecy and apocalyptic were not, in general, matters or products of private consultation.

It should be added that one of the functions of a work such as Revelation is to give early Christians perspective. It seeks to peel back the veil and reveal to the audience the underlying supernatural forces at work behind the scenes, affecting what is going on at the human level. In short, a certain limited dualism is evident in this literature. The message is often this: "Though it appears that evil is triumphing, God is still in his heaven, and all in due course will be right with the world." It is stressed that the goal of life is ultimately beyond death in the afterlife, the afterworld on earth, or both. There is also usually a strong sense of alienation and loss of power in these documents, and thus a major stress on God's sovereignty and divine intervention in human affairs. The stress is on transcendent solutions to human dilemmas, although human efforts have not been rendered either meaningless or pointless.

---

[20] E. Schüssler Fiorenza, *The Book of Revelation* (Philadelphia: Fortress, 1985), 149.

Here is a good place to say something about the use of multivalent symbols and gematria in Revelation. It is true that the wounded beast in Rev 13 and 17 probably alludes to Nero, but with the help of mythological imagery Nero is portrayed as but a representative example of a higher supernatural evil—the antichrist figure. The author knows that Nero does not exhaust the meaning of the beast, but he certainly exemplifies it well. There could be other such figures as well, for the author is dealing with types. These symbols are plastic, flexible, and on the order of character analysis rather than literal descriptions. Christ can be depicted in Revelation as the blood-drenched warrior, or a lamb who was slain, or a lion, or an old man with snow-white hair. All these descriptions are meant to reveal some aspect of his character and activity. In this respect, these symbols are very much like some modern political cartoons.

Apocalyptic literature is basically minority literature, and often even sectarian literature, the product of a subset of a subculture in the Greco-Roman world. While it is not always true that such literature is written in a time of crisis or for a people experiencing crisis or persecution at that specific point, it is certainly written for people who feel vulnerable in a world that largely does not concur with their own worldview.[21] In the case of Revelation, there is probably enough internal evidence to suggest that there had been some persecution and even martyrdom and more was expected.

It is not surprising, then, that apocalyptic prophecy often has a political dimension, dealing with the dominant human powers that appear to be shaping the destiny of God's people. Whether it is Revelation portraying Rome as a modern-day Babylon or Daniel portraying a succession of beastly empires, there is frequent discussion of these matters in such literature but always under the veil of apocalyptic symbols and images. One must be an insider to really sense the referents and the drift of the polemic and promises.

This aspect of apocalyptic literature grows directly out of the classical Jewish prophetic material, where nations and rulers, including Israel's, are critiqued, but here this is carried out by "outsiders" (those who do not have controlling access to the political process) using "insider" language. It is not just the loss of the monarchy that changed Jewish prophecy and prophets but its replacement by a not infrequently hostile and anti-Semitic foreign power. All Jewish or Christian prophets in such a situation are peripheral prophets and often must resort to coded language to express their message. From a psychological point of view, one might wish to consider the suggestion that when they were cut off from their spiritual center in Jerusalem (or, in John's case, in the Christian communities in western Asia Minor), revelation was expected to come to God's people in

---

[21] The attempt to dismiss almost entirely the context of actual persecution, suffering, and even martyrdom in which Revelation was written is not convincing, especially in light of Rev 11–12 (cf. below), but see A. Y. Collins, *Crisis and Catharsis: The Power of the Apocalypse* (Philadelphia: Westminster, 1984); W. J. Harrington, *Revelation* (Collegeville, Minn.: M. Glazier, 1993), 9ff. True, persecution was not likely systematic or continuous, but it was a real enough prospect to be taken very seriously.

less clear and more enigmatic ways, for they were farther from the perceived central locale of the divine presence.[22]

There is certainly a great fascination, in apocalyptic literature, with symbolic numbers, and so something must be said about gematria. There are, of course, some oft-repeated numbers—4, 7, 10, 12, and their multiples. Knowing that 7 means completion or perfection helps one to understand not only why there are the number of seals that one has in Revelation (a complete and comprehensive set of judgments) but also why the antichrist figure is numbered 666, which signifies chaos and incompletion. There is also a tendency in this literature to speak of time elusively or elliptically—such as Daniel's "a time, a time and a half, and a time" or his famous interpretation of Jeremiah's seventy weeks. Yet it is surprisingly rare to find in either Jewish or Christian apocalypses any sort of precise calculations about how many days or years are left before the end. Scholars have often puzzled over the two different numbers, apparently referring to the same time period, in Dan 12:11–12, but it need not be a case of recalculation or later editorial emendation. If the numbers are symbolic in nature (e.g., multiples of 7, or one-half of 7), they should probably not be taken as attempts, much less failed attempts, at precise calculation.[23] What such numbers do suggest when they describe periods of time is that matters are determined or fixed already by God and thus God is still in control, so that evil and suffering will, at some point in time, cease. The message of such numbers is "This too will pass" or "This too will come to pass." They were not meant to encourage ancient or modern chronological forecasting.

But what if justice is indeed deferred, or not seen to be done in a reasonably short period of time? Certainly, one of the major impetuses producing apocalyptic literature is this sense of justice deferred for the minority group, which has led to a robust emphasis on vindication both in the afterlife and, more important, in the end times. It is not an accident that apocalypses often manifest interest in justice and political issues, on the one hand, and the otherworld and the afterlife, on the other. There is a relationship between these two interests—if there is no life to come, then many of the wrongs done in this life will never be rectified, and God's justice will be called into question. Apocalyptic literature is often an attempt to deal with the issue of theodicy; for instance, Revelation reassures the saints not only about personal individual vindication in the afterlife but about justice for God's people in the end time. Indeed, it is at the point where cosmology and history meet, when heaven comes down to earth in the form of the Messiah and the new Jerusalem, that there are finally resolution and reward for the saints and a solution to the human dilemma caused by suffering and evil. Suffering and death are overcome by resurrection and everlasting life,

---

[22] See pp. 165–70 above.

[23] This is a common mistake made by some scholars. See, e.g., Carroll, *When Prophecy Failed,* although Carroll is right that there is and was such a thing as failed predictive prophecy. The point here is simply that one must be wary of evaluating apocalyptic prophecy, and especially its use of symbolic numbers, in a literal manner.

and evil is overcome by the Last Judgment. Obviously, the persuasiveness of this schema depends entirely on the audience's belief in not only a transcendent world but also a God who cares enough to intervene in human history and set things right once and for all.

But the very fact that this sort of information is only conveyed through visions and dreams and oracles makes clear that without revelation, without the unveiling of divine secrets and mysteries, humans would be in the dark about such matters. It is the message of apocalyptic literature that the meaning and purpose of human history can not finally be discovered simply by an empirical study or analysis of that history. This does not mean that the author has given up on history, as is sometimes asserted, but that he is placing his trust in what God can finally make of history rather than in what humans can accomplish in history.

B. A Brief Tour of Revelation's Character and a Part of Its Content.   At this juncture, it will be well to take some core samplings from Revelation and analyze them closely. In the first place, as Aune has demonstrated at some length, while Revelation certainly contains oracles, it can not be simply said to be oracles and so is not just like a classical collection of oracles, such as that found in Amos. For example, we find embedded within the narrative of John's commissioning experiences quotations of God's direct words to the seer in 1:8, "I am the Alpha and Omega," and in 1:17b–20, "Do not be afraid; I am the first and the last, and the living one. I was dead, and see, I am alive forever and ever; and I have the keys of Death and Hades. Now write what you have seen, what is, and what is to take place after this." It is no accident that, at the inception of this remarkable book, John says that when he was in a pneumatic state, he first heard something and then saw something (vv. 10–11). Although this is mostly a visionary work, it has its aural and oracular dimensions, and the visionary material is set within the context of the interpreting oracles.

In vv. 17b–20 the revealer is the exalted Christ, who identifies himself as one who was once dead but is now alive. In short, he speaks appropriately according to the time in which John lives. There is nothing here that suggests that sayings of the risen Lord that would be appropriate to place on the lips of the historical Jesus were conveyed in this way. Indeed, a saying such as vv. 17b–20 would not have been appropriate if found on Jesus' lips before he died. The same may be said about the oracle in 16:15, where we hear, "Behold, I am coming like a thief" (cf. 22:7, 12–14), an oracle that is appropriate on the lips of the exalted Christ but different from the ones found on the lips of the historical Jesus, who speaks in the third person when referring to a future coming of the Son of Man. One could also point to other examples of oracular speech in 13:9–10; 14:13; 18:21–24 (words of an angel); 19:9; 21:3–4, 5–8; and 22:18–20, and one should certainly note that there is a concentration of such oracles at the beginning and end of the book, making clear the prophetic character of the work.[24]

---

[24] See Aune, *Prophecy in Early Christianity*, 280–88.

To such oracles one could add the clearly demarcated prophetic character of the oracles to the seven churches in chs. 2–3, all of which have a shared prophetic pattern including (1) an introductory commissioning word, (2) a middle portion, and (3) a double conclusion containing a call for vigilance and a saying about conquering. In each oracle John is commanded to write to each of these churches, which, because of his exile, is "a functional equivalent to the sending of prophetic messengers in the OT."[25]

Notice that there is a citation formula here, "thus says" *(tade legei)*, after which the exalted Christ speaks in each case.[26] Of course, the content of each oracle, after the citation formula in the central or middle "I know" part of the oracle, varies according to the situation of each church. The exhortative nature of the central section of these prophecies is clear, and the often strongly negative tone reminds us that Christian prophets and seers, such as John, saw themselves having a similar role to OT prophets as "guardians and preservers of Christian behavior, beliefs, and customs."[27] They, too, could be prosecutors of the covenant lawsuit, but in this case it is the new covenant lawsuit. One may conjecture, as Aune does, that there must have been a dearth of leadership in these churches, which, in turn, necessitated prophetic intervention by John. Prophets and seers could be seen as crisis intervention specialists, especially when there was a power or leadership vacuum. This appears likely to have been the case in John's churches, for he does not really appeal to local leadership to solve problems, but rather, like Paul, exercises leadership from a distance.

It is time to consider a specific sample of visionary material from Revelation to get a sense of its character. Scrutiny will be given to two consecutive sections—ch. 11, which presents the tale of the two witnesses, and ch. 12, the story of the woman and the dragon. It is possible to see ch. 11 as a continuation of ch. 10, but this may be debated. In any case, there is no debate about the indebtedness of ch. 11 to Ezek 40–48. In the vision, John is given a staff and told to rise and measure the temple of God and its surroundings. There have been at least four basic suggestions as to what this measuring means: (1) It is the preliminary to rebuilding and restoring the temple. This is certainly true in the case of Ezek 40–48, and it is understandable that a Jewish Christian prophet who is in exile after AD 70 might see himself as being in the same position as Ezekiel. How, then, would this square with the fact that John seems to see the church as the new temple of God, such that any restoration of the old temple would be superfluous? (2) The temple is being sized up for destruction. This makes especially good sense if this book was written in the 60s rather than the 90s as is usually thought and if our author was familiar with the Jesus tradition on this subject

---

[25] Ibid., 275.

[26] On all of this, one should compare F. Hahn's helpful study "Die Sendschreiben der Johannesapokalypse: Ein Beitrag zur Bestimmung prophetischer Redeformen," in *Tradition und Glauben* (ed. G. Jeremias et al.; Göttingen: Vandenhoeck & Ruprecht, 1971), 357–94.

[27] Aune, *Prophecy in Early Christianity*, 277.

(see Mark 13). On the whole, the arguments for a date in the 60s do not convince. (3) The measurements are taken to indicate the parts to be protected from physical harm. This does not seem to fit with the theme, found earlier in Revelation, of partial judgments even on God's people. (4) Measuring refers to protection from spiritual rather than physical harm.

One clue to unraveling this mystery is found at 11:14, where we discover that what is recounted as happening to the temple and to its worshipers (the latter being a point against this being a retrospective remark about AD 70) is said to be the second woe, not the last woe. Notice that this event is clearly identified as happening in Jerusalem, for there is mention of the place where the Lord was crucified. We must now broach the subject of the two witnesses. Whoever they are supposed to represent, it is clear enough that they are presented here as being at least like Moses and Elijah, the two witnesses who stood with Jesus on the Mount of Transfiguration according to the synoptic tradition, found in Mark 9 and par. Notice that these witnesses bring the fire-breathing word of God to earth, including plagues and the like, but they are also taken back up into heaven. If this is a prophecy of Jerusalem's fall, why has it been placed in this locale in Revelation and called the second woe? If this is a prophecy about the final preservation of the Jewish people, why are the witnesses identified with the figure used in the letters to identify the church? A more probable explanation than that this is about Jerusalem or Jews is that this is about the universal church and its task of witnessing or, more specifically, about the churches at Smyrna and Philadelphia, which were undergoing persecution and perhaps enduring instances of martyrdom as John wrote. This would explain why the number 2 is used of the witnesses here, rather than the earlier 7 of all the churches John is addressing.

Some have seen here an allusion to Deut 19:15, where it is said that the verification of the truth of anything requires the validating testimony of two witnesses. But if John believed this was still true, would this not imply he would need a second witness to validate his own testimony, something this prophet doesn't appear to think he needs? His words appear to have independent authority for the seven churches, and he expects them to be unchallenged. It is surely easier to see here a reference to two of John's churches undergoing persecution. This fits with the reference in the text to the lamp stands (cf. Rev 2–3). If John could cast his own role in the light of the prophet Ezekiel, there is no reason why he could not cast the role of two of his churches in the light of the experiences of Elijah and Moses.[28] The implication is that not only John's life but that of his churches bears prophetic witness to God's revelation or truth. In this view, the idea of outward harm and even physical death is meant to suggest that even such extreme persecution can not harm such witnesses spiritually.

The witnesses are called olive trees, for they carry within them the fuel they need to light their candlesticks. The reference to Daniel's three and a half years suggests that the church will go through such persecution, not be

---

[28] See Aune, *Revelation 6–16* (Nashville: Nelson, 1998), 600.

raptured out of it. One must also see the reference to Sodom and Egypt as a statement about the spiritual status of Jerusalem—a city occupied and trampled underfoot by Gentiles in the last decade of the first century. In other words, it is a place of oppression, slavery, and immorality. That the bodies of the witnesses are not allowed to be buried was considered one of the utmost indignities or crimes that could be perpetrated against a people in the ancient Near East (cf. *Pss. Sol.* 2:30ff.).

Again Ezekiel is drawn upon in 11:11 to speak of the resurrection of the two witnesses, possibly alluding to the resurrection of the martyrs, which will be referred to in 20:2. According to v. 13, once the witnesses were vindicated by being taken to heaven, judgment fell upon a tenth part of the unholy city during a supernaturally induced upheaval, and seven thousand are said to be killed. Perhaps not coincidentally, this would have been about a tenth of the nonfestival season population of Jerusalem. The upshot of this is that John is suggesting that Jews, symbolized by Jerusalem, are the persecuting agents troubling the churches in this case. There is here a coded message of great relevance to the present and future situation of at least two of John's churches, offering them future hope of vindication despite present difficulties.

Of a similar sort and with a similar point is the much controverted revelation about the woman and the dragon in ch. 12. Here is a classic case where the author has drawn on various sources, including pagan myths, to make a Christian point. One gets the feeling in apocalyptic, especially when its audience is largely Gentile, that any and all sources are fair game for raw material so long as they can be christianized. A. Y. Collins has spent considerable time in a booklength treatment of this material demonstrating that the story line in this chapter is based, in part, on the ancient combat myth, probably in its Babylonian form.[29] The myth, in its basic form, concerns a dragon threatening the reigning gods or the supreme god. Sometimes in these myths the supreme god is even killed, which results in the dragon reigning in chaos for a time. Finally the dragon is defeated by the god who had ruled before or one of his allies.

Perhaps the closest form of the myth to the text of Revelation is the Greek version, which contains the birth of the god Apollo from the goddess Leto. One form of this tale speaks of the great dragon Python, who pursued Leto because he learned that she would bear a child who would kill him. Leto was carried off to Poseidon, the god of the sea, who placed her on a remote island and then sank the island beneath the sea for good measure. After a vain search, Python went away to Parnassus, and Leto's island was brought back up to the surface of the sea. When the infant was born, he immediately gained full strength, and thus within four days Apollo went and slew Python at Mt. Parnassus. An even more primitive version of this story, this time from Babylonia, speaks of war between Tiamat the seven-headed sea monster and the gods of heaven. Tiamat's flaunting of these gods was ended by Marduk, a young god of light, who hewed the sea

---

[29] See A. Y. Collins, *The Combat Myth in the Book of Revelation* (Missoula: Scholars Press, 1976).

monster in pieces. In the war with Tiamat, a third of the stars were thrown from the sky. Interestingly, Marduk's mother is portrayed in a fashion similar to the way the woman is portrayed in Rev 12. One may also point to the Egyptian story about Osiris, whose wife, Isis, gives birth to the sun god, Horus. Isis is portrayed with the sun on her head. The dragon Typhon is portrayed as red in color (but is sometimes represented as a crocodile or a serpent). In this Egyptian myth, the dragon slays Osiris and pursues Isis, who is about to give birth. In a miraculous manner, she does give birth and escapes to an island in a papyrus boat. The son, Horus, eventually overcomes the dragon, which is destroyed through fire (cf. Rev 20:1ff.).

Clearly enough, the parallels between these various myths and the visionary materials found in Rev 12 are too striking to be accidental and are, in most forms, too early for one to argue they were derived from Revelation. Rather, John has freely drawn on elements of these myths, adding certain elements to conform the tale to the Christian story about the Savior. It is probable that John's audience would have been familiar with at least one form of this myth, if not more, and would recognize what the seer was doing. The implication, in part, would be that in Christ all the primal myths and the truths they enshrine come true. He proves to be the archetype of which all these others are mere types or fictional copies.

Yet there is a further and more ominous undercurrent here, for various emperors saw these myths as referring to themselves (being the incarnation of divine Apollo, for example). It is probable that the woman in our chapter is portrayed as the queen of heaven. On Roman coins the emperor and his wife were portrayed as the sun and the moon. Roma, the patron goddess, was represented as the queen of the gods and mother of the savior, the emperor. Here, then, in Rev 12 we find a counterclaim. Jesus, the male child, is the real conqueror, not the emperor, and the woman from whom he comes, either the people of God or Mary, is the real queen of heaven, the real mother of the Savior instead of Roma. This is an antiestablishment story borrowing from classical myths but also grounded in the story of Jesus and in the Hebrew Scriptures (e.g., Dan 7).

One of the keys to understanding this and other texts in Revelation is the notion of the intertwined nature of things heavenly and earthly. Thus, one must disagree with G. B. Caird that John is simply describing earthly realities and struggles, using mythical or heavenly symbols.[30] Rather, John believed he was describing supernatural as well as earthly realities though freely using metaphorical and mythical language of these realities. It is not that John is describing a sort of heavenly parallel universe to earth so that war in heaven mirrors war on earth. Rather, in his view, there is but one struggle, both heavenly and earthly, both supernatural and natural, both divine and human, and these forces interact with each other.

---

[30] See G. B. Caird, *The Revelation of St. John the Divine* (BNTC; Peabody, Mass.: Hendrickson, 1966), 147ff.

Chapter 12 begins by saying that the seer saw a great portent or sign in the heavens, the normal place where such portents were expected to appear (cf., e.g., Matt 2). We hear of a woman clothed with the sun, with the moon under her feet, and a crown with twelve stars. Some have suggested that this crown might represent the constellations or, more to the point, the twelve signs of the zodiac. If so, the point seems to be that in this woman lies the whole destiny or fate of the race, drawing on the astrological notion that stars controlled one's future (but cf. below). Although it is possible that we have a reference to Mary here, it is more probable that we do not, for several reasons: (1) Notice in v. 17 that one hears about the rest of her offspring. This is unlikely to be a reference to Jesus' natural brothers and sisters. It is far more likely to refer to Christ's brothers and sisters in the faith, who are being addressed in this book, perhaps especially those facing or even enduring persecution. (2) The echoes of Isa 66:6–9 here are loud, which means echoes of the Zion tradition. Notice that Paul in Gal 4:26 refers to the new heavenly Jerusalem as "our mother." What is likely in view here, then, is the community of God's people, portrayed as a woman (cf. Rev 21:9–14).[31] There is an implied continuity between the OT and NT people of God, at least in the sense that Jesus came forth from the Jewish people of God and that his brothers and sisters did likewise.

The woman is depicted as being in anguish to give birth. The red or fiery (or bloody) dragon is said to be a second portent in the sky or heavens. That he has ten horns suggests one of awesome strength, and clearly the imagery of Dan 7–8 is drawn on here, although in Daniel the reference is to beastly empires and their rulers. That the dragon has seven crowns may suggest he has usurped all power, but notice that his crowns are called *diadēmata* while that of mother Zion is called a *stephanos* (the laurel wreath crown of those who are victors). The twelve stars in the woman's crown are likely to refer to the twelve tribes of Israel and thus are a symbol that one is dealing with a community—the whole people of God.

It is clear enough that this apocalyptic vision involves more than just predictive prophecy, for in fact it describes an event that had already transpired—the birth of the male child or Savior. Revelation 12:4b depicts the dragon as almost hovering in front of the woman who is about to give birth so that it can devour the child as soon as it is born. Drawing on Ps 2, the male child is depicted as destined to be a shepherd who would rule the nations with an iron hand or, as the text says, an iron rod. The image conveys his absolute power over the nations and perhaps also his power to judge.

The text goes on to say that, at the crucial moment, the child was seized by God and carried off to God and his throne. John has skipped from the Savior's birth to his death and ascension and exaltation. The point for Christians under pressure or persecution is that what the powers of darkness may have seen as the end of Jesus, and as intended for evil, God used for good, indeed used in order to give the male child more power over the forces of darkness. What might have

---

[31] See the exposition of Harrington, *Revelation*, 130–31.

been thought to diminish the power of the male child actually further empowered him. By his being taken away from earth by God, he was enthroned in heaven.

In v. 6 the woman flees into the desert, and since this woman represents the people of God, we are meant to hear echoes of the exodus here (note how exodus imagery crops up again in vv. 13ff.). There in the desert this woman is nurtured just as the Israelites were by God during their wilderness wandering period. It is not said here that the church is raptured into heaven. Rather, it is protected, while on earth, from the wrath of the dragon. The woman is put in a place prepared by God and made to stay there a definite period of time—Daniel's three and a half years (1,260 days). In view of 13:5 and 11:1–13, what is probably in view here is the great tribulation, when Satan is viewed as trying to crush the church out of existence.[32]

At v. 7 the scene shifts to war in heaven. While we might expect this war to be waged by Christ against the dragon, instead Michael the archangel leads the fighting for the saints. Here again this author is adopting and adapting traditional material. In *T. Dan.* 6:2, Michael is seen as a mediator between God and humankind. In the canonical Daniel, Michael is seen as the guardian angel of Israel, fighting against the angelic leaders of the Gentile nations (Dan 10:13ff.; 12:1). Here in Rev 12, his task is to take on the adversary of the people of God. In general, Michael prevails, and the Devil and his minions are cast down to earth. There is, in fact, a threefold fall of Satan in Revelation: (1) from heaven to earth (12:9), (2) from earth to the abyss (20:2), and (3) from the abyss to the lake of fire (20:10).

Satan is not just seen as a prosecuting attorney or the accuser of the people of God. Rather, he has lost his role in the heavenly court, and now in v. 9 he is seen as the deceiver of the whole *oikoumenē*, a term for the civilized or human world. At v. 10 a song is sung in heaven, and note that salvation and kingship and power come when Satan is cast down to earth. The "our brothers" in v. 10 may well be those who have already been martyred (cf. 6:9–11).[33] The accuser is no longer allowed to accuse because of the atoning death of the Lamb and because of the word of his testimony. The author seems to suggest that the casting down of Satan took place at the death of Christ or immediately thereafter, when the benefits of his death began to accrue for God's people. Verse 12 makes clear that Satan's days are numbered, and he knows it as a result of Christ's death. Some have seen John 12:13ff. as a useful commentary on this text, or the saying of Jesus about seeing Satan fall like lightning from the sky[34] as a possible source of some of this imagery.

---

[32] See rightly G. R. Beasley-Murray, *The Book of Revelation* (London: Marshall, Morgan & Scott, 1974), 191ff.

[33] Aune sees vv. 10–12 as redactional or later additions to this text but admits that they, along with 12:17, clearly refer to martyrdom. In view of 2:10, however, there is little reason to doubt that John believed some martyrdoms not only had happened but also were likely to continue to happen in Asia. The question is, At whose hands? See Aune, *Revelation 6–16*, 702–3; and cf. Beasley-Murray, *Revelation*, 202–3.

[34] See pp. 250–90 above.

Notice, however, that Satan is not prevented from pursuing the woman but that she is aided in her flight, being given the wings of eagles (cf. Exod 19:4). Verse 15 says that Satan produces a river to flush the woman out of the wilderness or desert, another possible allusion to the exodus/Sinai events. Since, in the primal myth, the sea monster is the evil one, it is not surprising that here water is his modus operandi to try to do in the woman. But unable to destroy the church collectively, Satan contents himself with attacking individual Christians—the ones keeping God's commandments and bearing the testimony of Christ. The section concludes with the sea monster or dragon standing next to his native element, the sea (often a symbol of chaos and the locus of evil things and creatures in the Hebrew tradition).

In these two chapters, there is a rich intertextual feast with echoes of both biblical and nonbiblical, both Jewish and Gentile, traditions. The author hears oracles and songs and sees visions, but he chooses to relate these visions in language his mostly Gentile audience can understand and apply to themselves. The language is definitely referential, although it is also symbolic and metaphorical and even mythic in character. It can not be taken literally, but it must be taken seriously, for the author believes he is depicting, in apocalyptic language, some truths and realities his audience needs to know about. This is not merely heavenly language with an earthly meaning but, rather, apocalyptic language about the interplay of heaven and earth, time and eternity, history and the supernatural. If our study pressed on further to investigate Rev 19–22, we would see that our author can indeed offer predictions about the future in apocalyptic form, as well as descriptions of the past and present in that same visionary form. The eschatological as well as the otherworldly, the horizontal as well as the vertical dimensions of this author's vision of the final solution are prominent throughout. It is time to turn to a somewhat later Christian work that is also an apocalypse and has some similarities and some differences with Revelation—the Shepherd of Hermas.

III. THE SHEPHERD'S TOWER, THE SHEPHERD'S OUTLOOK

This discussion of the Shepherd of Hermas must begin by mentioning some of the things the work has in common with Revelation. Helpful morphological studies of apocalyptic give us a basis for seeing some of the essential traits of Revelation as well as Hermas and contrasting these works with other early Christian apocalyptic works, such as the *Ascension of Isaiah* or the *Apocalypse of Peter*.[35] For example, neither Revelation nor Hermas is pseudonymous, and thus neither contains *ex eventu* prophecy. It is interesting that neither has any significant recollection of the past, whether of primordial events or of salvation-historical events that run up to the author's present day. Neither author is at all

---

[35] These studies appeared in *Semeia* 14 (1979). Here I am relying on the helpful charts found on pages 104–5.

concerned with issues of theogony or cosmogony. The contrasts with parts of the Enochic literature are clear.

Both Hermas and Revelation have paraenesis by a mediator and instructions to the recipient; both speak of persecution and judgment of the wicked (the latter being one of the most universal elements in Jewish and Christian apocalypses, for theodicy is a major concern). Both works give prominence to visions, epiphanies, otherworldly beings, and mediators and broach the subject of the afterlife. Both mention the process of writing and thus apparently the necessity to preserve the revelation. There is this salient difference, however, between Revelation and Hermas: the latter has no reference to resurrection or cosmic transformation. Hermas seems to reflect a somewhat later stage of Christian apocalyptic where eschatological fervor has waned somewhat.

If we take a moment to compare and contrast these works with the Christian compositions *Apocalypse of Peter* and *Ascension of Isaiah*, we discover that these two works are both pseudonymous and that at least *Ascen. Isa.* 6–11 also engages in presenting ex eventu prophecy. While the *Apocalypse of Peter* does mention resurrection, it omits cosmic transformation, and *Ascen. Isa.* 6–11 is silent on both these matters. Primordial events, cosmogony, and recollection of the past do not really figure in either of these works, and in fact, such subjects are rare in any Christian apocalypses of this period. Christians were concerned with redemption and judgment—in other words, with what was coming afterwards—not what had come before, whereas various Jewish apocalypses had a significant concern with the past and cosmogony.

This brings to light an important conclusion: early Christianity was a forward-looking movement insofar as it reflected on divine activity in human history, and it thus comes nearer to being appropriately called a prophetic movement than early Judaism writ large. Early Judaism had prophetic movements like that of John the Baptist, or one may wish to point to Qumran, but unlike early Christianity, it could not be called, as a whole, a prophetic movement, in contrast to what Luke's presentation of early Christianity suggests. There is, furthermore, this crucial difference between Christian and Jewish apocalypses—the figure of Jesus Christ and, more particularly, the idea that all such eschatological and apocalyptic events are grounded in, and were set in motion by, a set of historical events that culminated in the death of Jesus and changed the course of salvation history. Bearing these things in mind, it is time to consider some aspects of the Shepherd of Hermas.

In various regards, the social location of the author of the Shepherd of Hermas seems to be similar to that of the author of Revelation at least in this respect: both are suffering from social deprivation and have little sympathy for the rich and complacent. Both are alienated from their kin—whether fictive or real. It appears that Hermas was a freedman at the point when he wrote, but he had been a slave sold to the lady Rhoda (Herm. *Vis.* 1.1.1). Since he had been freed, he had toiled apparently in an agricultural pursuit (3.1.2). He had recently been suffering some "great trials of [his] own because of the transgressions of [his] family" (2.3.1). His wife had a sharp tongue (2.3.1), and his children were accused of rejecting God, blaspheming, betraying their parents, indulging in debauchery, and participating in orgies (2.2.2; Herm. *Sim.* 7.2). I agree with J. Christian Wilson against M. Dibelius that we must take this social data very seriously and not treat it as allegory.[36] There is also no reason to dispute the Roman locale of Hermas. Since both Clement of Alexandria and Origen quote this work, it must be dated prior to their time. An internal clue is probably found in the reference to Clement in *Vis.* 2.4.3, which strongly suggests that our author is a contemporary of Clement of Rome, who wrote *1 Clement* during the last decade of the first century AD. This is so not least because that text in Hermas refers to a Clement who has some sort of official church position, such that he sends documents to Christians in other cities.[37]

Thus, this work is not likely from a time earlier than the 90s AD, but it may well be from the early second century. Notice that it reflects the persecution of Christians. In *Vis.* 3.2.1, when Hermas asks what kind of sufferings Christians seated at the elderly lady's right hand had endured, she replies, "whips, prisons, great persecutions, crosses, wild beasts, for the sake of the name." Like Revelation, Hermas must deal with those who apostasize under pressure. Thus we hear in *Sim.* 9.21.3, "the double-minded, whenever they hear of persecution, worship idols because of their cowardice and are ashamed of the name of the Lord" (cf. *Sim.* 9.28.1–4). If we compare this with *1 Clem.* 5, which refers to calamities and reversals amongst the Roman Christian community, it is believable that there was some sort of crackdown during the time of Domitian in Rome, if not also elsewhere (cf. Dio Cassius, 67.14; Eusebius, *Hist. eccl.* 3.17).

Although one should not exaggerate either the extent or the duration of such a persecution, the recent attempt to exonerate Domitian of all such persecuting activities is simply not convincing.[38] Nevertheless, it is quite possible that Hermas was written at a somewhat later date, and his references to persecution may reflect the known persecutions of Trajan in AD 113–115. By the time Ignatius of Antioch wrote, he had a rather clear catalog of what he, like other Christian martyrs, could expect in Rome—fire and cross, wild beasts, the mangling of one's body, and finally death (Ign., *Rom.* 5). It is not convincing to argue that Hermas obtained his images of persecution from the now distant Neronian persecutions in the 60s. The references are too fresh and too pointed, and the whole social character of Hermas as literature for the pressured and persecuted speaks against this.

---

[36] See J. C. Wilson, *Five Problems in the Interpretation of the Shepherd of Hermas* (Lewiston, Me.: Mellen Biblical Press, 1995), 5.

[37] But see C. Osiek, *Rich and Poor in the Shepherd of Hermas* (Washington, D.C.: Catholic Biblical Association, 1983), 20–21.

[38] But see J. Jeffers, *Conflict at Rome: Social Order and Hierarchy in Early Christianity* (Minneapolis: Fortress, 1991).

What may one say about the genre of this work? As Wilson avers, it seems, like other apocalypses, to be a strange mixture of literary types.

> The overall literary genre of the document might be termed "apocalyptic," because Hermas receives a series of visions from two apocalyptic revelators, an elderly lady and the Shepherd. However, the apocalyptic theological content of the Shepherd of Hermas is minimal. The book is virtually devoid of apocalyptic eschatology. About the best Hermas can offer us is one 100-foot-long sea monster which has "a head like a jar" and which does nothing but lie on the ground and stick out its tongue (Vis. 4.1:6–9).[39]

It is uncertain that the description "apocalypse" is apt for the Shepherd as a whole. The lack of eschatology suggests that at least the final form of this document comes from the early second century, perhaps during the reign of Trajan.

The mixed nature of this work is clear, especially when we examine the *Mandates,* which are basically a series of ethical principles and imperatives that Christians are expected to live by and that bear some similarities to the material we find in the *Didache.* This is very different material from the *Visions* of the first section of the work, or the so-called *Similitudes* of the last section. This is why some scholars would prefer to call the Shepherd a mixed, perhaps even a composite, work that includes apocalyptic visions but is not, as a whole, an apocalypse.

In his helpful study, Wilson suggests that Hermas had read (or heard?) Revelation but had not accepted its eschatology. Hermas writes, says Wilson, during or at the "twilight of apocalyptic."[40] This seems correct, which is even more reason to see this as an early-second-century document when "the prophetic, charismatic, eschatological Christian Church of the first century is giving way to the institutional Church of the second century."[41]

The formal apocalyptic features of the Shepherd of Hermas can be listed as follows: (1) Hermas gets his knowledge through mediators who convey divine wisdom to him through visions and words; there are three mediators—the Shepherd (*Vis.* 5 through *Sim.* 10), the elderly Lady (*Vis.* 2–4), and even Rhoda (*Vis.* 1). Though Rhoda seems clearly to be a human being, all three of these revelators appear to Hermas while he is praying or is in the Spirit. (2) Hermas has visions of a book, a tower, and a beast (*Vis.* 2–4). (3) Like Zechariah in Zech 1–8, Hermas requires an angelic interpreter to make sense of his visions. (4) Hermas feels compelled to write down his revelations and their interpretations so that copies may be sent to churches (*Vis.* 2.4.2–3; *Sim.* 10.1.1).[42] A case can be made that at least one vision of Hermas has eschatological content, *Vis.* 4, and it must now be examined. Its similarities to, and yet differences from, earlier apocalyptic literature are both striking and revealing of the character of this work.

---

[39] Wilson, *Five Problems,* 41.
[40] Ibid., 80.
[41] Ibid., 82.
[42] See ibid., 83–84.

Hermas says at the outset of this vision that it concerns a type of the persecution that is to come (*Vis.* 4.1.1). What distinguishes this vision from what we find in Revelation is the suggestion that if one has faith and prays, one will not be harmed or have to suffer. There is also this interesting distinction: the revelations have come to Hermas "by his holy Church" (4.1.3).

As Hermas proceeds down the Via Campana in Italy, he encounters a huge dust cloud (4.1.5) and thinks at first there is a cattle drive going on, but he discovers that the cloud of dust is being stirred up by a beast like Leviathan who has fiery locusts coming out of his mouth (4.1.6). The beast is one hundred feet long with a head like a piece of pottery. This head also has four colors on it—black, red, gold, and white (4.1.10). When Hermas takes courage and faces down the beast, it lies down like a tame dog and merely sticks out its tongue, not moving until he has passed it (4.1.9).

Having passed the beast by about thirty feet, Hermas encounters a young woman "adorned as if coming forth from a bridal chamber" (4.2.1), who is all in white and even has white hair, a symbol of purity. The young woman queries Hermas as to whether he has encountered anything along the road, and he admits he has met a monster that could destroy nations but that the Lord's strength and mercy allowed him to escape it. The young woman explains that because Hermas trusted the Lord, the Lord sent an angel to shut the mouth of the beast.

The echoes of the story of Daniel in the lion's den are clear, but what is noteworthy by contrast with Revelation is the emphasis on escape rather than on faithful endurance through suffering. The young woman then commissions Hermas to go tell his fellow Christians that this beast is a type of the great persecution that is to come and that, with like faith and trust in the Lord and especially purity of heart, the outcome can be the same for them (4.2.5). "You will have the type of the great persecution which is to come but if you will it shall be nothing." (4.3.6). This is hardly the martyrological theology about witness one finds in Revelation.

The third portion of this vision also includes the satisfying of Hermas's curiosity about the four colors on the beast's head. Black represents the character of the world in which Hermas lives (4.3.2). Red is the color of fire and blood and signifies the way the world must be destroyed (4.3.3). Gold represents the saints themselves, who must have their dross burnt off, their metal tested (although nothing is said about being tested by physical suffering). They will put off all sorrow and tribulation (4.3.4), after which, being pure, they will be useful as building materials for the "tower," an image of the people of God to come. White is said to represent the color of the pure or crystal-clear world that is to come (4.3.5). After revealing this, the maiden disappears, and because there is still a cloud, Hermas turns back, fearing the beast is coming (4.3.7). Notice that there is nothing here about the second coming of Christ.

As Wilson says, the transformation of the old woman into the young bride after the facing down of the tribulation suggests that Hermas is well familiar with the sequence and content of the material of the closing chapters of the book of Revelation.[43] He is also right that although Hermas mentions the dissolution of the world (cf. 2 Pet 3:10–13), he makes nothing of it and sees the tribulation that precedes it as overrated if one has faith and a pure heart. This is not the stuff of the canonical apocalypse, even though it uses some of the same forms and materials.

G. F. Snyder is surely right that the monster here represents the ominous power of the state, which is perceived as having an adversarial relationship with Christians. He concludes, "The beast is a threatened persecution against the city (i.e., Zion, or the church: cf. Sim. I). We have taken this threat to be that of Trajan."[44] This conclusion is plausible though not necessarily compelling, for, as Wilson says, the persecution of Trajan's time may have been confined to Asia Minor. On the other hand, Trajan's policy in Asia Minor would also have likely been Trajan's policy in Rome and Italy as well when it came to Christians. The fact that Hermas was not, at the time, noting any persecution where he was situated may have led to the character of the conclusion of this vision. The saints will go through the tribulation time but will be protected from harm if they are pure of heart and trusting. Hermas does believe that the wicked or apostates will be judged at some point when the "summer" comes (*Sim.* 4.4–5), but there is no sense that he feels he is already in either the end times or the last tribulation or that "summer" is imminent. Nor does he see this *eschaton* as a threat to Christians.

The eternal reality that Hermas sets before his audience is not the new heaven and new earth but the church as tower or the church as eternally youthful bride. "Hermas has read Revelation, but Hermas has seen that life goes on. . . . Unlike the apocalypse, which would break in all at once from outside the present reality, the Church is already here, in the present reality, and in the process of growth and change. The Church is like the tower under construction in Vis. III and Sim. IX. . . . It is not too much to say that for Hermas the Church has replaced the apocalypse"[45] or, at the least, it has rendered it harmless and remote.

Were one to explore Hermas more widely, examining the considerable corpus of material in the *Mandates* and *Similitudes,* one would discover a work that has much more in common with the moralizing of the *Didache* or the *Epistle of Barnabas,* with their two-ways schema about good and evil, than with Revelation.[46] The author of Hermas is more concerned with dealing with the issue of postbaptismal sin than with the second coming, more concerned with purity of heart than the pure realm of the new Jerusalem coming to earth. The form may suggest apocalypse, but the content is largely of another ilk.

---

[43] Ibid., 91–92.

[44] G. F. Snyder, *The Shepherd of Hermas,* vol. 5 of *The Apostolic Fathers* (ed. R. M. Grant; Camden: Nelson, 1966), 57.

[45] Wilson, *Five Problems,* 94.

[46] See rightly M. W. Holmes, "Hermas, Shepherd of," *DLNT* 469–71.

As this discussion draws to a close, we must inquire in regard to what Hermas tells us about prophets and whether he sees himself as a prophet. This requires an examination of the problematic Herm. *Mand.* 11. This section of the book opens with a vision of a false prophet sitting in a chair (the seat of the instructor?) and acting as a consultant to those coming to him asking about their futures (11.1–2). The complaint is that double-minded Christians come to him as to a wizard (read "diviner"—*mantis* in the Greek). The false prophet is one who does not have the Holy Spirit and so speaks to his inquirers in a flattering way—according to their desires and requests (11.2), "for he is empty and makes empty answers to empty people" (11.3).

The problem is, however, that the false prophet also sometimes speaks true words, and amazingly this is said to happen when "the devil fills him with his spirit, to see if he can break the righteous" (11.3). It seems clear that Hermas sees divining as a purely pagan art that Christians should shun (11.4): "For he who acts a false prophet concerning any act is an idolator, and empty of the truth and foolish." Hermas states unequivocally his understanding of the difference between a true and a false prophet: "For every spirit which is given from God is not asked questions, but has the power of the Godhead and speaks all things of itself, because it is from above, from the power of the divine spirit. But the spirit which is questioned and speaks according to the lusts of man is earthly and light, and has no power, and does not speak at all unless questioned." (11.5–6). But this is not all. Hermas also says that one can tell a true prophet by his character: "he who has the spirit from above, is meek . . . gentle . . . lowly-minded . . . refrains from all wickedness . . . and makes himself poorer than all men, and gives no answers when he is consulted, nor does he speak by himself (for the Holy Spirit does not speak when a person wishes to speak), but he speaks at that time when God wishes him to speak" (11.7–8).

This is in contrast to the false prophet, who exalts himself, wishes to have first place, is impudent, shameless, talkative, lives in great luxury, and accepts payments for his prophecy, indeed requires them in advance (11.12). True inspiration is described as when "the angel of the prophetic spirit rests on him and fills the man" (11.9), but a false prophet shuns the assembly of the righteous because the earthly spirit in him flees and he is rendered mute and he will be found to be empty (11.14). A prophet is to be judged on the basis of his life, character, actions (11.16).

In various ways, this segment of the Shepherd is like the material already discussed from the *Didache*.[47] Prophets and their words are seen as possibly problematic, and so criteria have to be set up to discern true from false prophets. The baneful influence of a false prophet is feared, especially on the "double-souled" believers. There is nothing, however, in this material to suggest that such prophets, whether true or false, are itinerants, unlike what is found in the *Didache*. Hermas seems to recognize prophets as valid functionaries in the Church (*Sim.* 9.15.4), but he does not mention them as church officials (*Vis.*

---

[47] See pp. 343–48 above.

3.5.1). It is notable that *Sim.* 9.15.4 is the only mention of prophets in this entire long work except *Mand.* 11, but in view of the latter text, it is not necessary to conclude that the text in *Sim.* 9 refers to OT prophets, though it may.[48]

As Wilson suggests, while Hermas is opposed to the paid or professional prophets who are self seeking, *Mand.* 11 seems to suggest that he has no problems with the notion of prophecy itself or the idea that any Christian, in principle, might prophesy when the Spirit came upon him or her. It was not that the prophet himself had authority like a church official but that his words had authority.[49] Hermas does not call himself a prophet, and on the showing of *Mand.* 11, he may not have viewed himself that way. Rather he is a visionary, who has visions while alone, unlike the prophet, who is inspired to speak while in the congregational worship.

One reason Hermas may have avoided calling himself a prophet is pointed out by J. Reiling: some Christian prophets were acting more and more like pagan mantic prophets or diviners during Hermas's day, and so the prophetic office was falling into disrepute.[50] Hermas's description of true prophecy is reminiscent of the description of 1 Cor 14,[51] which suggests that while Hermas has not entirely given up on the early Christian prophetic or, for that matter, the apocalyptic tradition, nonetheless he finds himself in a situation where he must marginalize a significant portion of such Christian prophets and omit them from the list of foundational church officials. He also finds himself the recipient of visions that are largely noneschatological in character. This best fits the situation in second-century Christianity, where we may truly speak of the twilight of Christian apocalyptic and, to some degree, of Christian prophecy. But as shall be seen in the next chapter, the process of marginalizing Christian prophecy would go even further toward the end of the second century, when the Montanist movement arose and challenged the authority of the growing church.

IV. CONCLUSIONS

Christian apocalyptic literature was, without a doubt, an offspring of Jewish apocalyptic, and we can say that both grew out of, or were one form of, the prophetic tradition. There is a sense in which the Christian movement after AD 70 remained more prophetically, and so more apocalyptically, inclined than did the Judaism that reestablished its identity at Jamnia. The bar Kokhba revolt in the early second century and its defeat basically led to the end of an eschatologi-

---

[48] See M. Dibelius, *Der Hirt des Hermas,* vol. 4 of *Die Apostolischen Väter* (ed. K. Bihlmeyer; Tübingen: Mohr, 1923), 624–25.

[49] J. C. Wilson, *Toward a Reassessment of the Shepherd of Hermas: Its Date and Its Pneumatology* (Lewiston, Me.: Edwin Mellen Press, 1993), 92.

[50] J. Reiling, *Hermas and Christian Prophecy: A Study of the Eleventh Mandate* (Leiden: E. J. Brill, 1973), 121.

[51] Wilson, *Toward a Reassessment,* 96.

cally oriented Jewish community. Christian prophecy and apocalyptic and eschatological thinking continued on well into the second and even third and fourth centuries.

Nonetheless, in the production of apocalyptic works, Christianity and Judaism at the end of the first century shared many of the same concerns about the minority audience for which the material was written. The problems of justice and vindication, the problems of God's character in view of a difficult and dangerous world, were as real for Christians as for Jews. If one was going to be critical of the powers that be and the existing historical situation, one would need to look above and/or beyond it for solutions and perhaps use coded language to communicate one's message of triumph over evil and darkness. Apocalyptic provided a vehicle to meet some of the social needs of early Christians and offer them hope as the first century concluded and the second century began. In a largely pagan environment where dreams and visions were regarded highly, it is not surprising that visionary literature such as apocalyptic was popular among the largely Gentile congregations of early Christianity at the end of the first century.

In this chapter, two samples of Christian apocalyptic have been considered—the book of Revelation and the Shepherd of Hermas. These two works share a number of notable features. Neither Revelation nor Hermas is pseudonymous, and thus neither involves ex eventu prophecy. It is interesting that neither has any significant recollection of the past, whether of primordial events or of salvation-historical events that run up to the author's present day. Neither author is at all concerned with issues of theogony or cosmogony. The contrasts with parts of the Enochic literature are clear. Both Hermas and Revelation have paraenesis by a mediator and instructions to the recipient. Both speak of persecution and judgment of the wicked (the latter being one of the most universal elements in Jewish and Christian apocalypses, for theodicy is a major concern). Both give prominence to visions, epiphanies, otherworldly beings, and mediators and broach the subject of the afterlife. Both mention the process of writing and thus apparently the necessity to preserve the revelation. There is this salient difference, however, between Revelation and Hermas: the latter has no reference to resurrection or cosmic transformation. Hermas seems to reflect a somewhat later stage of Christian apocalyptic where eschatological fervor has waned somewhat. For Revelation's author, the final solution seems to lie in the future and in God's hands. For the author of the Shepherd, the final solution seems to lie in the church. The Shepherd is apocalyptic with very little future eschatology, and in this regard, it contrasts notably with Revelation.

The language used in both of the works examined in this chapter is indeed referential but nonetheless not literally descriptive. It is, rather, symbolic disclosure language, metaphorical in character, even though its referents are hardly just ideas. The dragon represents the beastly empire, which was all too real to these authors and their fellow Christians. In the case of Revelation, there seems little doubt that actual visionary experiences are the origin of the material found in the book, and this appears to be the case with the Shepherd as well, although one is less confident it is not simply a literary exercise. These two works differ significantly in their approach to the issue of potential suffering and martyrdom, and so also their portraits of Christ differ as well. The slaughtered Lamb who is a Lion in Revelation is very different from the angelomorphic speculations about Christ found in the Shepherd. But neither of these works can be said to be either pseudonymous or to involve *ex* eventu prophecy. In the next chapter, there will be an occasion to see what a Christian apocalyptic work that does have these two features looks like.

CHAPTER 12

From Mari to Montanus

*T*HIS STUDY OF THE DEVELOPMENT of prophecy in the ancient Near East and the eastern end of the Greco-Roman world, especially in Jewish and Christian contexts, has journeyed in many directions and through many texts. It would not be appropriate to conclude this study, however, with the end of the NT period lest this simply continue to perpetuate the myth that prophecy ceased at the end of the "canonical" period. Indeed, it did not, as the sort of material we will examine in this concluding chapter will show. One may certainly talk about the development or diminution of prophecy and its proliferation or marginalization across various periods of time, but one can not talk about its extinction, so far as I can tell, for any considerable time in the period 1600 BC to AD 300.

I. THE *ASCENSION OF ISAIAH*

This fascinating composite work may well date, at least in part, to a time before the end of the first century AD and before the Shepherd of Hermas.[1] The judgment of R. J. Bauckham seems sound that it is a Christian work that draws on earlier Jewish tradition about the martyrdom of Isaiah. Bauckham conjectures that possibly a genuine prophetic experience is described in *Ascen. Isa.* 6 and predicated of

---

[1] See, e.g., J. Pelikan, *The Emergence of the Catholic Tradition (100–600)*, vol. 1 of *The Christian Tradition: A History of the Development of Doctrine* (Chicago: University of Chicago Press, 1971), 99; R. J. Bauckham, "Apocryphal and Pseudepigraphal Writings," *DLNT* 69–70; C. D. G. Müller, "Ascension of Isaiah," in *Writings Relating to the Apostles, Apocalypses, and Related Subjects*, vol. 2 of *New Testament Apocrypha* (ed. W. Schneemelcher; trans. R. McL. Wilson; Louisville: Westminster John Knox, 1992), 603–5; J. L. Trafton, "Isaiah, Martyrdom and Ascension of," *ABD* 3:507–9.

Isaiah.[2] Generally the work has been divided into two major sections—chs. 1–5 and chs. 6–11, with the former being an account of the martyrdom and the latter an account of the ascension of Isaiah. But *Ascen. Isa.* 3:13–5:1 seems to interrupt the first half of the book, and some have seen 11:2–22 as an insertion in the second half of the book. The work was clearly very popular among Christians in various parts of the empire well into the Middle Ages, and it appears in Ethiopic, Greek, and Latin, although the entirety is only found in Ethiopic at this point. It may also be that the martyrdom section, if Jewish, was originally in Hebrew.

The final Christian form of the work has various interesting christological features: (1) Christ is called the "Beloved" throughout. (2) The V pattern of the christological hymns such as Phil 2 is replicated in the discussion about the descending then ascending Savior (see 3:13–4:1). (3) But extracanonical traditions are also drawn on, such as the notion that the angel of the Holy Spirit and Michael are those who open Christ's grave on the third day and on whose shoulders Christ will sit and come forth to send out the twelve disciples to the world. (4) The virginal conception is described by drawing on Matthean traditions (11:2–8), but the birth is not described; indeed, it is said that Joseph, without cohabiting with her, lived with Mary for two months after she became pregnant and "when Joseph was in his house, and his wife Mary, but both alone, it came to pass, while they were alone, that Mary straightway beheld with her eyes and saw a small child, and she was amazed. And when her amazement wore off, her womb was found as it was before she was with child" (11:7–9). (5) The presentation of what happened to Isaiah is that he had a vision of, or mystical rather than literal ascent to, heaven in a fashion similar to what we find in Revelation (6:10–15), and the scene of worship in heaven around the throne (7:10–20) is also reminiscent of what is found in Revelation. (6) The relationship of Isaiah and the tour guide angel also echoes Revelation, for Isaiah says he was not allowed to worship the angel and was told, "Worship neither the angel nor the throne" (7:21). (7) As in the perspective of the NT, Christ's coming to earth is seen as the beginning of the eschatological age (9:13). (8) The work contains ex eventu prophecy up to the point when the author speaks, with the mission to the world and the second coming and final events still yet to come. (9) The mission of Christ to earth is seen as a struggle against the principalities and powers, to such an extent that Christ himself is an apocalyptic secret—"so his descent . . . is hidden from the heavens so that it remains unperceived who he is" (9:15)—and indeed, his identity is not recognized, even at the point of his death, by those who crucified him. (10) Christ is said to remain in the world after his resurrection for 545 days (9:16). (11) There continues to be an emphasis that Jesus was incognito: Joseph's eyes had to be opened to see that the Lord had come to his portion (11:10), Jesus was breast-fed by Mary so that he might maintain the guise of being a normal infant and not be recognized for who he was (11:17), and during Jesus' ministry, it was kept from the devil who he was so that eventu-

---

[2] See the entire chapter on this work in R. J. Bauckham, *The Fate of the Dead* (Leiden: E. J. Brill, 1998), 363–90.

ally the devil and his human adjuncts would kill Jesus and so bring about salvation unknowingly. (12) The emphasis lies on the *ex eventu* prophetic narrative about Jesus' descent, ministry, and ascent, and these events are seen as the end of the world and the consummation of the last generation (11:37–38). (13) It is only in the earlier Christian material in ch. 4 that we really hear about the second coming with the angels and the heavenly saints (4:14), at which point Satan will be dragged off to Gehenna (compare Rev 20:2 with *Ascen. Isa.* 4:14). (14) It is also in ch. 4 that we hear that Satan, coming down to earth in the antichrist figure who demands to be worshiped as a divine being (4:2–12), causes apostasy or fleeing of the saints (4:13). (15) The upshot of the previous two observations is that there is a historical-apocalypse fragment in chs. 3–4 but an otherworldly vision-journey apocalypse in *Ascen. Isa.* 6–11.[3]

It is clear that the final Christian compiler or composer of this document had a robust eschatology, was well attuned to apocalyptic literature, and, unlike the author of the Shepherd of Hermas, had not given up on the primitive eschatological views of the early church and indeed had further elaborated them. Yet the author also believes that, in the last days, there will be a waning of prophecy and true prophets, for he describes the following scenario as transpiring after the church age has been going on for a while:

> And in those days there will not be many prophets nor such as speak reliable words, except here and there, on account of the spirit of error, of fornication, of boasting and of covetousness which shall be in those who yet will be called his servants and who receive him. Great discord will arise among them, between shepherds and elders. . . . And they will set aside the prophecies of the prophets which were before me and also pay no attention to these my visions, in order to speak [forth from the] torrent of their heart. (3:27–29, 31, trans. Müller)

We see what can be called an anxiety about the loss of the prophetic and eschatological character and vision of the early church, in very similar fashion to what we see in the Montanist literature, for it is difficult to resist the suggestion that this last quotation has to do, in part, with the author's own day, especially if this part of the book was composed in the second century AD.

One further aspect of the *Ascension of Isaiah* calls for comment, and it, too, manifests similar ideas to the later Montanist material. The description of the ecstatic state of Isaiah, found in 6:10–15, reads as follows:

> And while he was speaking by the Holy Spirit in the hearing of all, he [suddenly] became silent and his consciousness was taken from him and he saw no [more] the men who were standing before him: his eyes were open, but his mouth was silent and the consciousness in his body was taken from him; but his breath was [still] in him, for he saw a vision. . . . And the people who were standing around, with the exception of the circle of the prophets, did (not) think that the holy Isaiah had been taken up. And the vision which he saw was not of this world, but

---

[3] See pp. 381–82 above.

from the world which is hidden from. (all; *Ethiopic also:* his) flesh (*Ascen. Isa.* 6:10–12, 14, trans. Müller)[4]

The description of the ecstatic transport of Isaiah no doubt owes something to similar descriptions in the canon (cf., e.g., Ezekiel, John the Seer), but one must agree with Bauckham that the author is likely also drawing on contemporary experience within his own day and circle. Ecstatic transport entails a certain degree of loss of contact with the mundane realm, perhaps in order to focus on the otherworld. We hear more about this from Montanists, such as Tertullian, to whom this chapter must now turn.

II. THE MONTANIST MOVEMENT

It comes as something of a surprise to discover that, in the past one hundred years, there is a dearth of detailed critical studies of the Montanist movement.[5] It is surprising precisely because of the Montanist movement's geographical scope, chronological duration, and depth of impact on Christianity. Begun by a Phrygian Christian named Montanus, who started to prophesy in the village of Ardabav in Phrygian Mysia around AD 172, the movement not only grew to have influence throughout much of Asia Minor but also exported itself to Rome and later had a large impact in North Africa, even claiming the significant church father Tertullian among its adherents. Thus its presence and impact were still being felt a century after Montanus had begun to prophesy.

Tertullian tells us that even one of the bishops of Rome (possibly Zephyrinus, bishop AD 198–217; possibly Victor) was prepared to recognize the New Prophecy and so bring peace to the churches in Asia and Phrygia, until one

---

[4] Elsewhere in this section, the translation of Bauckham, with minor variations, is followed.

[5] Aside from F. C. Klawiter, "The New Prophecy in Early Christianity: The Origin, Nature, and Development of Montanism, A.D. 165–220" (Ph.D. diss., University of Chicago, 1975), and the presentation of the Montanist oracles (without detailed critical analysis) in R. E. Heine, *The Montanist Oracles and Testimonia* (Macon, Ga.: Mercer, 1989), we have to go back seventy years to W. Schepelern, *Der Montanismus und der phrygischen Kulte: Eine religionsgeschichtliche Untersuchung* (Tübingen: Mohr, 1929), and before that to the work of P. de Labriolle, *La crisis montaniste* (Paris: Gabalda, 1913), and *Les sources de l'histoire du montanisme* (Paris: Gabalda, 1913). There have been a few seminal articles along the way, but most focus on one specific aspect of the phenomenon; cf. K. Aland, "Bemerkungen zum Montanismus und zur frühchristlichen Eschatologie," in *Kirchengeschichtliche Entwürfe* (Gütersloh: G. Mohn, 1960), 105–48; R. E. Heine, "The Role of the Gospel of John in the Montanist Controversy," *SecCent* 6 (1987–1988): 1–19; D. Powel, "Tertullianists and Cataphrygians" *VC* 29 (1975): 33–55; and W. Tabbernee, "Early Montanism and Voluntary Martyrdom," *Colloq* 17 (1985): 33–45. To this we can finally add a full monograph—but only on the later stages of the Montanist movement in North Africa—C. M. Robeck, *Prophecy in Carthage* (Cleveland: Pilgrim, 1992); and R. E. Heine's survey article "Montanus, Montanism," *ABD* 4:898–902.

Praxeas came from Asia and argued that the bishop must not recognize the prophetic gifts of figures such as Montanus, Maximilla, and Priscilla (*Prax.* 1). Interestingly, the confessors of Lyons also sent a letter via Irenaeus to Rome, urging Pope Eleutherius and the church of Asia not to quench the Spirit by condemning the Montanists.

The New Prophecy was found difficult, not chiefly because of the views expressed but because of the challenge it posed to the authority structure of the church in Asia Minor. N. G. Bonwetsch puts the matter well when he defines Montanism as "an effort to shape the entire life of the church in keeping with the expectation of the return of Christ, immediately at hand; to define the essence of true Christianity from this point of view; and to oppose everything by which conditions in the church were to acquire a permanent form for the purpose of entering upon a longer historical development."[6] In a sense, then, Montanism was the last gasp of the more pneumatic and less institutional approach to the Christian movement; or put another way, it was the last manifestation of Christianity *as a charismatic movement* in reaction to the idea of it as an established, ongoing institution with a preset authority structure, which inherently assumes that Christ is not likely coming back soon.

While the church fathers tended to call the movement the Cataphrygians, Montanus and his followers seemed to prefer to call what they did "the New Prophecy" and their movement Montanism, after their founder. The movement was notable for the fact that it had as prophetic leaders both men and women (notable among the women would be Maximilla and Priscilla in the first stage of the movement, and one may perhaps name Perpetua in the latter stages in North Africa). It is difficult to evaluate the nature of the movement and its prophecy precisely, because none of its oracles have been preserved in neutral or positive sources, with the exception of some material in Tertullian's work, and even his work must be evaluated critically, for he modified various elements of the Montanist beliefs and ideas that he received. We are almost wholly dependent on Eusebius (AD 263–340) and Epiphanius (AD 315–403) for the discussion of the early period of this movement, but both of these authors must be treated as, to some extent, hostile witnesses. Yet what we do learn even from these witnesses does not suggest that Montanists were guilty of any theological or christological heresy.

The Montanists did, like many other early Christians, predict the second coming of Christ as happening in their lifetime, and there is even an oracle locating Pepuza in Asia Minor as the spot where the new Jerusalem would come down (Epiphanius, *Pan.* 49.1). Note that Tertullian as well speaks of the new Jerusalem descending for one thousand years but does not mention Pepuza as the locale (*Marc.* 3.24). There is another oracle from Maximilla saying, "after me there will be no longer a prophet, but the consummation,"[7] indicating that they thought the *eschaton* was at hand. This same oracle reveals that they were

---

[6] N. G. Bonwetsch, *Geschichte des Montanismus* (Erlangen, 1881), 139.

[7] See Aune, *Prophecy in Early Christianity,* 315.

dependent on a certain reading of Revelation and also on the Farewell Discourses in the Gospel of John for their views of things. They seem to have believed that the Paraclete had revealed to them deeper truths about matters
eschatological than had been revealed to the apostles and so their New Prophecy
was needed to supplement earlier revelation.

The fact that they seem to have experienced ecstasy and what has been
called spirit trance does not distinguish them from some other early Christian
prophets, but the failure of some of their predictions to come true because they
involved date and place setting would distinguish them from some earlier
Christian prophets. We could say of them, as could be said of other early Christian prophets, that their zeal and enthusiasm for their subject exceeded their
inspiration and thus they were sometimes guilty of saying too much. On the
whole, one must agree with Aune that neither the form of their prophesying
nor its content gives any warrant for the suggestion that Montanist prophecy
was a form of pagan prophecy.[8] Certainly Tertullian did not view Montanist
prophecy that way.

The conclusion of W. Schepelern is apt: "Montanism arose from ground
soaked with blood—not the blood of the raging slashed adherents of the cult of
Cybele, but the blood of the Christian martyrs; and Montanism grew in an atmosphere saturated not with Phrygian mystery ideas, but with the apocalyptic
conceptions of Judaism and Christianity."[9] Equally apt is the conclusion of J.
Pelikan:

> The decline in the eschatological hope and the rise of the monarchical episcopate
> are closely inter-related phenomena . . . both indicate a process of settling already at
> work in the second-century church, and perhaps earlier, by which many Christians
> were beginning to adjust themselves to the possibility that the church might have to
> live in the world for a considerable time to come. Part of that process of settling was
> the gradual decline, both in intensity and in frequency, of the charismata that had
> been so prominent in the earlier stages of the Christian movement.[10]

This eschatological millenarian prophetic movement also had, as one of its
essential features, certain ascetic tendencies that Tertullian, among others, found
attractive. The movement did not permit a second marriage after the death of
one's spouse (Epiphanius, *Pan.* 48.9), it inaugurated various new fasts beyond
what the church had commended (Eusebius, *Hist. eccl.* 5.18.2), and it held martyrdom in extremely high esteem (5.16.20). It saw martyrdom as a validation of
the truth of its faith and witness.

Some of the oracles of Montanism and the beliefs that lay behind them
must now be examined. It is perhaps correct to say that the Montanist movement was a response not just to the waning of eschatology in the church but also
to the oppressive social environment outside the church, due to the way Marcus

---

[8] Ibid., 311, against J. Lindblom and E. Fascher.

[9] Schepelern, *Der Montanismus*, 162.

[10] J. Pelikan, *Emergence of the Catholic Tradition*, 98–99.

Aurelius chose to act as emperor in relationship to such religious phenomena. The blood of the martyrs was the seed of the Montanist movement.[11] The focus of most of Montanist teaching and prophecy had to do with ethical rigorism in the face of the coming end, not with doctrinal matters.

First, one must note that Montanus himself appears to have spoken like the oracles of old, not in his own voice or in the third person but as the mouthpiece of God. Thus one of his oracles says, "I am the Father, the Son, and the Paraclete." The explicitly trinitarian preface for the following utterances is noteworthy. In fact, Epiphanius was forced to admit that the Montanists did not hold any different doctrine of the Trinity than the "orthodox," but he argued they erred in regard to the spiritual gifts (*Pan.* 48.1.4). He especially argued that the OT and the NT teach that prophets were always in possession of their understanding when they uttered their prophecies (48.3.3). This polemical claim was not true at least about all the cases of prophetic experience recorded in the Bible, but it appears that he was leaning heavily on 1 Cor 14 in regard to prophetic expression; it provides some justification for this argument. In any case, as Aune says, oracles are rarely attributed to God in early Christianity, although we do find instances not only here in Montanism but also in Rev 1:8 and 21:5–8 and possibly in Ignatius (*Phld.* 7.1).[12]

Montanus is also credited with saying, "Behold, humankind is like a lyre, and I rush thereon like a plectrum. Humans sleep and I awake. Behold the Lord is he who arouses the hearts of human beings and gives a heart to a person."[13] This oracle is especially crucial, for it reveals several aspects of Montanist belief, some of which was found especially objectionable by other Christians. The first of these is that the prophet does not have control over the revelation. Nothing, however, is said here about not having control over prophetic expression of the truths received. The prophet receives his or her revelation either in a state of ecstasy or in an unconscious state (while asleep or in a trance). According to Epiphanius (*Pan.* 48.3.3; 48.7ff.), the Montanists had appealed to Gen 2:21, which they understood to say, "and God cast a state of ecstasy on Adam and he slept," which text they juxtaposed with Eph 5:31–32. They also appealed to Ps 115:2 and Acts 10:10–14 to justify ecstatic prophecy, and they saw themselves as the successors of such prophets as Philip's prophesying daughters and Christian prophets of the earlier second century such as Ammia and Quadratus.

Another significant oracle that speaks to the martyrological ethos of the Montanist movement is the one where the Spirit is said to speak, "Desire not to die in bed, nor in the delivery of children, nor by enervating fevers, but in martyrdom, that He may be glorified who has suffered for you." Notice here the reference to the suffering of Christ plus the same sort of desire for martyrdom that we find in orthodox writers such as Ignatius of Antioch.

---

[11] See Aune, *Prophecy in Early Christianity*, 313.

[12] See ibid., 315.

[13] Here and afterwards I am following Aune, ibid., 314–15, and Aland, "Bemerkungen zum Montanismus," 105–48, in their presentations of these oracles.

It is important not to underestimate the significance of the roles women played in this movement, and it is remarkable that even some of their oracles have been preserved. Unfortunately, the reaction against Montanism also likely meant a reaction against women exercising spiritual gifts not only in Montanism but in the larger church. Notice the ascetical cast of the following oracle: One must be pure to receive a holy vision. The holy prophetess Prisca proclaims, "A holy minister must understand how to minister holiness. For if the heart gives purification, they will also see visions, and if they lower their faces, then they will hear the saving voices, as clear as they are secret" (Tertullian, *On Exhortations* 10.5). There is a strong stress here on submission of the person to the process and to the revelation in order to receive the message clearly.

Priscilla (or possibly Quintilla) was also credited with this remarkable revelation about the descent of the Holy City: "In the form of a woman arrayed in shining garments, came Christ to me and set wisdom upon me and revealed to me this place [i.e., Pepuza] is holy and that Jerusalem will come down hither from heaven." In regard to the ethos of the Montanist movement so far as the involvement of women is concerned, it seems quite similar to what we find in the *Acts of Paul,* where Thecla is able to carry on a ministry insofar as she is ascetical and denies her sexual nature. In other words, it is well before the Middle Ages that holiness was associated with the absence of human sexual expression, especially in the case of women. This was not seen as a problem or a violation of the creation order mandate precisely because it was believed that the end was near and one must live accordingly in a state of spiritual rigor in preparation for the Parousia.

Tertullian makes evident that the central content of most of the prophecies and visions of the Montanists had to do with establishing a new moral rigor and a new devotion to spiritual disciplines in light of the coming end, not with establishing new doctrine (*Jejun.* 1.3). He says clearly that the function of the coming of the Paraclete to the Montanists was to establish not a new teaching but a new discipline. It was apparently believed that the Paraclete had manifested itself fully in and through the oracles of Montanus.[14] This does not mean that Montanus saw himself as the Paraclete, nor does Tertullian suggest this, but there is some evidence, from an inscription from Numidia, that later generations of Montanists drew such a conclusion. The inscription in question reads, "Flavius, grandsire of the household. In the name of the Father, and the Son [and] of the Lord Muntanus. What he promised he performed."[15]

It is possible to add an "and" after the Son, and so make the reference to Montanus correlate with the spot in the formula where the Spirit would be mentioned. On the other hand, it may just be a binitarian formula with a reference to the fact that Montanus acknowledged the Father and the Son and so was inspired by them. One notable overreaction to Montanism was that of Hippolytus, who, in order to refute the Montanists, insisted that inspiration and revelation

---

[14] See Pelikan, *Emergence of the Catholic Tradition,* 102–3.
[15] Ibid., 103.

from the Holy Spirit ceased with the book of Revelation (*Antichr.* 47–48). The price of this refutation was that Hippolytus both admitted Christianity to be no longer a prophetic movement (prophecy was now in the past) and, at the same time, was willing to push the second coming off into the indefinite future.[16] It is time to consider some of the material about the later stages of the Montanist movement, as manifested in Perpetua and Tertullian.

The backdrop to this later manifestation of the Montanist movement in North Africa is the edict of Septimus Severus, probably issued about AD 200, which is said to have forbidden all conversions to both Judaism and Christianity. Tertullian says that Severus had ordered straightforward condemnation for those who confessed their guilt in violating the edict, and torture of those who denied having done so (*Scap.* 4.2). Among those caught in the crossfire of this crackdown were one Vibia Perpetua, a well-educated young woman with a newborn child, and her slave Felicitas, along with two men, Saturninus and Revocatus. These Christians lost their lives in March of either 202 or 203 in Carthage. The document of most importance in discussing these matters is the *Passion of Perpetua and Felicitas,* the second part of which is in the first person and is plausibly argued to go back to Perpetua herself. There is some scholarly debate as to whether Perpetua should actually be seen as one of the Montanists, but it appears that not only the final redactor of the tract about her martyrdom thought so, and the character of her visions as well as the attitude about ecstasy suggest Montanist influence. It must be remembered, however, that Montanism did not arise in North Africa, any more than it did in Asia Minor or Rome, as a religious phenomenon competing with orthodoxy. Rather, it arose within the context of the existing Christian community in North Africa. There were both Montanists and other sorts of Christians in the church in North Africa.[17]

Consider first one of Perpetua's visions, which she had shortly before martyrdom while she was imprisoned and which, fortunately, she recorded in a diary. The account begins with the a discussion between Perpetua and her sister about her requesting a vision from God to let her know whether she would be freed or condemned. She makes the request and the result is as follows:

> I saw a ladder of tremendous height made of bronze, reaching all the way to the heavens, but it was so narrow that only one person could climb up at a time. To the sides of the ladder were attached all sorts of metal weapons: there were swords, spears, hooks, daggers, and spikes; so if anyone tried to climb up carelessly or without paying attention, he would be mangled and his flesh would adhere to the weapons. At the foot of the ladder lay a dragon of enormous size, and it would attack those who tried to climb up and try to terrify them from doing so. And Saturus [the leader of this group of Montanists] was the first to go up, he who was later to give himself up of his own accord. He had been the builder of our strength, although he was not present when we were arrested. And he arrived at the top of the staircase and he looked back and said to me: "Perpetua, I am waiting for you. But take care;

---

[16] See ibid., 106.

[17] See Robeck, *Prophecy in Carthage,* 14–15.

do not let the dragon bite you." "He will not harm me," I said, "in the name of Christ Jesus." Slowly, as though he were afraid of me, the dragon stuck his head out from underneath the ladder. Then, using it as my first step, I trod on his head and went up. Then I saw an immense garden, and in it a grey-haired man sat in shepherd's garb; he was tall and milking sheep. And standing around him were many thousands of people clad in white garments. He raised his head, looked at me, and said: "I am glad you have come my child." He called me over to him and gave me, as it were a mouthful of milk he was drawing; and I took it into my cupped hands and consumed it. And all those who stood around said: "Amen." At the sound of this word I came to, with the taste of something sweet still in my mouth. I at once told this to my brother, and we realized we would have to suffer and that from now on we would no longer have any hope in this life.[18]

If we analyze this vision carefully, it apparently reflects the fact that Perpetua is familiar with another apocalyptic work, the Shepherd of Hermas. The dragon and its ultimate harmlessness despite its size are very reminiscent of Hermas's account,[19] as is the reference to the shepherd. Although Perpetua was a relatively new convert and was baptized while in prison, she had gone through the catechetical process beforehand, in which she would have been instructed in early Christian teaching, both canonical and extracanonical. It is, however, interesting to note the contrast between this vision of Perpetua, which is vertically or otherworldly oriented, and the eschatological prophecies of Montanus and Priscilla, but this is, in part, explained by the difference between oracles and visionary material. The influence of Revelation on Perpetua should also be mentioned, not just because of the dragon, which is surely the symbol for the devil here (cf. Rev 20:2), but also because of the character of at least one of her other visions, the vision of the Egyptian, which has descriptions very reminiscent of some of those we find of Christ and angelic figures in Revelation.

There may also be some influence from the *Ascension of Isaiah*, another apocalyptic work, which also uses the ladder image when talking about a person ascending to God's presence. One must also refer to Luke 10:19–20, where Jesus gives the disciples authority to tred on snakes and scorpions. Robeck suggests as well that there may be an echo of *4 Ezra*, another apocalyptic work that includes the passage that Israel must tred a narrow path between fire and water to reach the Holy City and that "between the fire and the water . . . is this path, that it can contain only one person's footstep at once" (*4 Ezra* 7:6–8). The description of the shepherd seems to owe something to Dan 7's description of the Ancient of Days or, perhaps more likely, to the imagery of that text as it is applied to Christ in Rev 1:14.

Notice that the function of this vision is to prepare Perpetua for martyrdom. It is not, in the first instance, for the public or for Christian worship. Had she not recorded the vision, the church would not have known about it. This reminds us that oracles were always public revelations but this was not always the

---

[18] Following here Robeck's presentation (ibid., 206–7) with minor emendations.
[19] See pp. 371–78 above.

case with visions (cf. 2 Cor 12:1–10). The distinction between prophets and visionaries is an important one even though sometimes prophets have visions and sometimes visionaries offer oracles.

Turning now to Tertullian himself, it is appropriate to review what he says about prophecy, and necessary to consider if Tertullian himself was a prophet or visionary. On the latter score, there is no clear evidence that Tertullian himself had visions or offered oracles, but equally clearly he believed God was still giving them to various Christian believers in his era. For example, in *De exhortatione castitatis* 10.4, Tertullian quotes the oracle cited above about how purification or holiness makes one ready and receptive to receiving oracles or visions. But it is the context of this quotation that is significant. Tertullian cites this revelation from the living voice of prophecy immediately after quoting "the prophetic voice" of the OT in Lev 11:14 and then citing Ps 18:25–26 and Rom 8:6.

"From Tertullian's perspective, then, Prisca continued to function in the same tradition as the prophets and apostles, the primary difference being that she prophesied later."[20] This does not seem to be because Tertullian believed in an open canon, as if he were arguing for Prisca's words to be included in Scripture, but he did believe that these words are a fresh revelation from God and so have the same authority as earlier true prophetic utterances. Tertullian believed God had not finished speaking to the church. It could be argued that since the oracle of Priscilla was from several decades before Tertullian wrote the aforementioned tract, he was not in fact speaking about the living voice of prophecy in his own day. This conclusion, however, is easily dismissed, for we also have from about AD 212, in Tertullian's tract *De anima,* the record of a vision had by a woman whom Tertullian knew personally. So convinced was he of the authenticity of this and other such oracles in his day that he was willing to speak of "the true system of prophecy which has arisen in this present age" (*An.* 2.3).

In the course of an argument about the corporeal nature of the soul (that it has substance), Tertullian cites the account of a woman he knew and her vision. In this vision, the woman also received an oracle from God to the following effect: "A soul was exhibited to me in bodily form, and a spirit appeared but it was not of an empty and vacuous quality but rather of a quality that would suggest it could be grasped being soft and bright and of the color of air and resembling the human form in all respects" (*An.* 9.4). This revelation was given during a worship service in Carthage, but it was not disclosed by the prophetess during the Sunday service but afterwards to a group that stayed to hear it, including Tertullian.

Tertullian tells us all this, and it suggests several things: (1) The Montanists were still part of the larger orthodox congregation. (2) They did not, however, want to disrupt or disturb the regular worship service. (3) It appears also that the regulation about women not speaking during the church service, a point on which Tertullian himself insisted, was being followed here. What is interesting about this is that, on the one hand, Tertullian was very restrictive about

---

[20] Robeck, *Prophecy in Carthage,* 121.

his views of women's roles in the proper worship service but, on the other hand, he was quite prepared to recognize them as prophetesses who should express their gifts. (4) Notice that Tertullian has no problem with the notion that persons who were not ordained clergy, much less bishops, might have the Spirit in its fullness and speak with authority to the church. Tertullian did not support the tendency in the church to assume that the gifts of the Spirit were held only by the ordained or recognized male leaders of the church.

The attendant circumstances of this particular revelation to Tertullian's contemporary also merit discussion. Tertullian describes her as being "by ecstasy in the Spirit" when she received this revelation (9.4). This transpired during the worship, but it did not lead to any immediate outbursts or even controlled speech because "the spirit of prophets is subject to the prophets" (1 Cor 14:32). Tertullian says she received this revelation sometime between the reading of the Psalms and the conclusion of the sermon, but he was not quite sure of the precise moment. Tertullian also makes clear that the oracle was not simply accepted on face value but, rather, closely scrutinized, tested, probed (9.4). "Tertullian's convictions that the Spirit's most recent revelations must be consistent with all previous revelations and that the genuine prophet said only what God wanted to be said, not inserting his or her 'conceits,'" are crucial.[21]

This last observation leads to some more general points about how Tertullian approached the matter of prophecy. First, the importance, for this theologian, of the Farewell Discourses in John, and in particular John 16:12–14, needs to be recognized. Tertullian believed that this text makes evident that there would be revelation given later by the Paraclete to Jesus' disciples because, at the time the Paraclete spoke this, they were unable to bear it. The Paraclete was promised to come and guide the church into all truth. Tertullian believed such guidance, offered through the prophetic voice, was still ongoing in his day.

But equally clearly, the Spirit would not guide anyone to say anything that was contrary to what Scripture had already said. "The continuing gift of prophecy was secondary in its authority since it was secondary to Scripture."[22] The *regula fidei*, or rule of faith, was the assumed norm by which such prophecies could and should be judged. In substance, such new prophecies were cases of the Spirit illuminating or expanding upon earlier truth or applying that previously given truth to new situations.[23] In Tertullian's view, the charismata were necessary if the church was to go on to perfection in its walk with Christ. The New Prophecy was not new in the sense of introducing new theological notions, for the most part, but new in its enforcement and application of an ethical and even ascetical rigor necessary for the church to be Christ's holy bride on earth. The Paraclete, then, had a teaching role in regard to matters such as marriage or fasting (*Virg.* 1.5).

---

[21] Ibid., 131.
[22] Ibid., 143.
[23] See ibid., 145.

If we ask about Tertullian's view of the experience of ecstasy itself, he draws an analogy with the person who is asleep and dreaming. The ecstatic in the visionary moment loses a certain amount of contact or sensation of the outside world, like the sleeper (*Marc.* 4.22.5). Accordingly, ecstatics bear a certain resemblance to someone who is mad, even though this is not the case and even though they are not raving (*An.* 45.3). Dreams or visions are produced by external forces and, as such, the soul has no mastery over them; they are simply received (45.5). In Tertullian's view, one must enter an ecstatic state in order to receive a revelation from God, and in order to enter such a state, one must first be in the right moral condition (48.3).

One of the most interesting observations by Tertullian to justify his views on ecstasy is his exegesis of the transfiguration story found in Mark 9 and par. Peter is taken by Tertullian as an example of an ecstatic, not merely because of the account in Acts 10 but because of his encounter on the Mount of Transfiguration. Tertullian reasoned that since Peter saw Moses and Elijah, he must surely have been "in the Spirit" not only to be able to see them at all but to be able to recognize them for who they were, for there were no descriptions of these prophets in the Scriptures. Then, too, Peter's response to what he saw was much like the *amentia* the ecstatic experienced—he was dumbfounded and did not know what he said. The words came to him spontaneously as a revelation (*Marc.* 4.22.5). Since prophetic knowledge was revealed knowledge that comes from God in the ecstatic state, this explains how it is possible for the prophet to predict the future and expose the secrets of human hearts (things only God could know and share—5.8.12).

It is clear that Tertullian had carefully thought through the possible problems the New Prophecy might create for the church's authority structure and the possible objections that might be raised to the expression of such new revelation. Yet he was not prepared to give up on or quench the fresh work of the Holy Spirit. Rather, he would try to find a way to have such truths expressed without violating the regular order of worship or his views of what women's role could be in worship. In the end, however, his efforts must be seen as something of a rearguard action, a last great attempt to hold on to the prophetic heritage of the church, in the church, and for the church as a whole. His efforts did not succeed. Indeed, the dark cloud was on the horizon already in about AD 200 when various Asian synods condemned Montanism and its prophecies. Although this would not mean the end of prophecy in the church in the form of isolated prophets and visionaries, it seems, on the whole, to have meant the end both of the church as a prophetic movement continually open to new revelations from the Spirit and of a prophetic movement that could remain within the orthodox church and contribute to it.

If we ask, as this study draws to a close, what factors led to the decline of prophecy at the end of the period under scrutiny, several have been mentioned that are worthy of consideration. First, we may refer to the thesis of A. von Harnack that the decline was, in some fashion, related to the formation of the NT canon. He stresses that the canon's "creation very speedily resulted in the opinion that the time of divine revelation had gone past and was exhausted in the Apostles, that is, in the records left by them. . . . The New Testament, though not all at once, put an end to a situation where it was possible for any Christian under the inspiration of the Spirit to give authoritative disclosures and instructions."[24] There is some merit to this proposal, but it hardly explains everything.

Hill and Aune both suggest that the decline of prophecy was caused by an allergic reaction among the orthodox to Montanism.[25] Prophecy was the victim of this reaction, in a case of guilt by association. Aune also stresses that the rise of theologians and teachers displaced prophecy:

> Throughout the entire second century the phenomenon of prophecy was primarily tied to dissenting voices and movements within various phases of Christianity. This does not mean that prophets became an endangered species primarily because of their increasing association with heretical movements, but it does suggest that the earlier role of the prophets as articulators of the norms, values, and decisions of the invisible head of the church was taken over by the visible figures of the teacher, preacher, theologian, and church leader.[26]

What Aune fails to say but what certainly needs to be added is that the reaction to Montanism was also part and parcel with the reaction against imminentistic and chiliastic eschatology, which Montanism manifested, an eschatology largely in continuity with that of earlier Christianity. The death of eschatology in the second and third centuries contributed to the death or at least marginalization of eschatological prophecy. Here one must agree with the conclusions offered by Schepelern and Pelikan above.

Another thesis worthy of mention is that of J. Ash, who suggests that the role of the prophet was swallowed up or co-opted by the monarchial bishop, with the result that a separate prophetic role became superfluous. Anyone who has read the letters of Ignatius of Antioch can see why Ash might argue in this fashion. This is simply another form of the thesis that when the movement became an ecclesiastical institution with institutional authority figures, charismatic individuals had less of a role to play. H. von Campenhausen suggested a somewhat related thesis—that the transmission of the apostolic tradition by the church and the use of it as an arbiter of the truth against movements thought heretical, such as Montanism, led to the marginalization of prophecy.[27]

Most likely some combination of these factors must be credited with the decline of prophecy in the third century. In the fourth and fifth centuries, the ecumenical councils, which helped to define orthodoxy, and the rise to promi-

---

[24] A. von Harnack, *History of Dogma* (trans. N. Buchanan; 2 vols.; New York: Dover, 1961), 2:53.

[25] See Hill, *New Testament Prophecy*, 191; Aune, *Prophecy in Early Christianity*, 338.

[26] Aune, *Prophecy in Early Christianity*, 338.

[27] Cf. J. Ash, "The Decline of Ecstatic Prophecy in the Early Church," *TS* 37 (1976): 227–52; compare this to H. von Campenhausen, *Ecclesial Authority and Spiritual Power in the Church in the First Three Centuries* (trans. J. A. Baker; Stanford: Stanford University Press, 1969), 178ff.

nence of a history of early Christianity by Eusebius, who took a dim view of chiliasm and charismatic figures, were also contributing causes. Yet even so, prophecy never entirely disappeared, and there would always be the visionary, such as Hildegaard of Bingen, or other more oracular prophets throughout the ensuing ages of church history. What can be said is that we can no longer with any accuracy call Christianity, as a whole, a prophetic movement once we get beyond the second century AD.

It appears that this decline of prophecy was already foreseen or predicted at the end of the canonical period, for in the Christian apocalypse known as the *Ascension of Isaiah,* which may date to the last decade of the first century, we find these words: "And there will be a great contention about his advent and his coming. . . . And the Holy Spirit will withdraw from many. Nor will there be in those days many prophets or those who speak things confirmed, except a few in a few places. . . . And they will neglect the prophecy of the prophets who were before me [i.e., before Isaiah], neglecting my visions as well" (3:22–31). In what is likely the latest book in the NT, it is not a surprise to hear the reassurance that with the Lord one day is as a thousand years and vice versa, as a response to the complaint that is said to be typical of scoffers in the last days: "Where is the promise of his coming?" (2 Pet 3:3–8).

Montanism was perhaps the last major reaction to such skepticism inside and outside the church, and thus it is ironic that it was branded a heretical movement when it stood closer in spirit to the eschatological nature of early Christianity than did those who claimed the ecclesiastical and doctrinal high ground for themselves. The conclusion of K. N. Giles is worth quoting here:

> The fundamental issue raised by Montanism was whether or not the church should be led by prophets. The verdict was a resounding no. In the face of this threat to its institutional life, the church closed ranks. The Montanists and prophecy itself were pushed to one side. Thus Montanism represents the last flare-up of prophecy in the early church and its virtual demise. Eventually Montanism, and by implication prophecy itself, was condemned in about A.D. 200 by Asian synods.[28]

III. CONCLUSIONS

Prophecy was not a phenomenon that ceased to characterize early Christianity at the end of the first century AD. Indeed, the evidence suggests that both prophecy and its offspring, apocalyptic, continued to be viable means of Christian expression long after the NT era. In the *Ascension of Isaiah,* we find a robust example of Christian apocalyptic, while in the oracles from the Montanus movement, we see the continuation of oracular prophecy. Other early Christian documents could have been examined, but these are sufficient to reveal the continuing living presence of both oracular prophecy and its written residue during the period under discussion.

---

[28] K. N. Giles, "Prophecy, Prophets, False Prophets," *DLNT* 970–77, here 976

It is entirely possible that at least part of the *Ascension of Isaiah* was a first-century document, not least because its eschatology has closer affinities with early Christian eschatology, as manifested in, for example, Mark 13 or Revelation, than with what one finds in the Shepherd of Hermas. The conjecture of Bauckham that there is a literary record of a genuine prophetic call experience in the *Ascension* is probably correct and means that, even in documents that are largely ex eventu prophecy, there may also be some genuine prophetic material that speaks of the present or future. This, in turn, means that the judgment that apocalyptic was a response to the demise or failure of predictive prophecy is probably incorrect. Apocalyptic could be a genuine form of prophecy, or it could be of the literary ex eventu variety.

It is intriguing that when the Montanist movement arose in the second century, the major complaint about it was not its eschatological views but its claims to authority and its call for radical asceticism. Unfortunately, when this movement was branded heretical by the orthodox church, prophecy itself suffered a decline through guilt by association. It was never entirely eliminated but became a minority voice in a largely non-prophetic movement becoming an institution.

The Montanist movement also included visionaries who received apocalyptic revelations. So far as we can tell, this did not lead to the production of a Montanist apocalypse, which reminds the student of this material once again that the literary genre labeled apocalypse is neither the origin of apocalyptic visions nor the only locale in which we find them. Indeed, apocalyptic visions even existed before the postexilic period of Jewish history (e.g., Ezekiel).

Prophecy was not, during the period this study has examined, a gender-specific phenomenon, and this is especially evident in Christian contexts, whether we think of Philip's daughters, or Corinthian prophetesses, or someone like Perpetua or Maximilla. The attentuation of women and their roles in general in the church as we get further and further from the first century, except insofar as they practiced extreme asceticism, apparently helped to accelerate the marginalization of women prophets in the church.

Both the *Ascension of Isaiah* and the Montanist materials appear to be reactions, in part, to the demise of early Christian eschatological thinking and perhaps also to the growing skepticism about the roles of prophets witnessed in documents such as the *Didache*. Both the *Ascension of Isaiah* and the Montanist material bear witness to the continual reality of ecstasy as part of the prophetic experience. Both of these documents also bear witness to the fact that Christianity continued to be a minority phenomenon that faced ridicule and persecution from other segments of society.

Prophecy and apocalyptic appear to have declined in early Christianity for a variety of reasons. Association with a "heretical" movement, the challenge it brought to the growing institutional authority structure of the church, the prominence it gave to women and their roles in the church, the assumed challenge that the living voice of prophecy offered to accepted sacred traditions, and other complex reasons as well led to the gradual decline, though not to the death, of prophecy in early Christianity. The prophetic movement had gradually become a movement with the occasional prophetic voice and finally, by at least the time of Constantine if not before, changed into an established institutionalized religion. Yet the ongoing living voice of prophecy continued to remind the church that neither God nor God's word had ceased to be active well into the church's history, and it could neither be tamed, domesticated, nor entirely placed under human control.

CHAPTER 13

The Progress of Prophecy:
Conclusions

*I*T IS POSSIBLE TO GENERALIZE ABOUT prophecy over so long a period as two millennia in limited but important ways. The subtitle of this study rightly intimated from the start that we must reckon with growth and change in regard to the practice and the perception of prophecy over this extended period. Yet clearly there was enough continuity across these varied cultures in the understanding of prophets and prophecy that a prophet could be recognized across cultural boundaries and through time.

This study began by mentioning Grabbe's definition of a prophet. A prophet is a person who speaks in the name of a god (usually Yahweh) and claims to pass on a revelation from that god. Divine revelation—or at least the belief that one has received a revelation—is a sine qua non of prophecy. On this showing, divination is not prophecy, and neither is what has come to be called literary prophecy (ex eventu prophecy). This definition grounds the prophetic expression in prophetic experience. It is possible to sharpen these remarks by adding that there is a difference between a mediator or intermediary and a prophet.

On the one hand, there are times and places where a prophet is simply a mouthpiece for the deity and does not intercede with the deity on anyone's behalf. The communication flows in one direction and is not prompted by any attempts at consultation by a human party. On the other hand, there are obviously also times when a prophet does beseech the deity or inquire of the deity on behalf of some human person or group. What needs to be emphasized about the latter is that this may be a role that a prophet plays, but it is not specifically a prophetic role. Moses appears largely as an intermediary and leader in the relevant data, but one could say that Moses and Aaron together fulfill the whole role of a prophet—having both the experience of revelation and the expression. But precisely these data equally make clear that we must distinguish between prophetic experience and prophetic expression.

The definition mentioned above also makes clear that one must distinguish between prophets and scribes or exegetes, or what are today called preachers. A prophet was not offering conscious reflection on preexisting sacred texts. There is an element of spontaneity that must not be missed in the prophetic experience. The prophet offered a late or up-to-date or fresh word from the deity. Of course, if the prophet had a mind already saturated in some holy texts, it is not surprising that such materials became part of visions or oracles when they were articulated.

As a social phenomenon, prophets and their colleagues, diviners, seem to have played both central and peripheral roles in their societies. Court prophets and diviners were found both within and outside Israel, and diviners in particular seem to have been far more prevalent outside Israel and the early church than within it. Yet it is certainly not the case that there was no use of divination in Israel or in the early church. At the same time, it must be stressed that the seeking and interpreting of omens and the consultative process involved have some features that distinguish them from prophecy—not the least of which is the absence of the prophetic experience and the spontaneous prophetic expression. Divination was more of an art or a skill in interpretation; prophecy was more of an experience and spontaneous expression, and to judge from what evidence we have, divination was far more prevalent and valued outside the biblical tradition than within it. There are some texts, such as some of the ancient Near Eastern ones investigated in this study, that suggest that prophecy was only a backup or supplement to divination. This is clearly not what the biblical evidence suggests about the Jewish and Christian tradition.

In regard to the prophetic experience, there is more than ample evidence that ecstasy or trance was a regular aspect of what happened to one who became a prophet, whether one was a prophet in the ancient Near East, in Israel, in the church, or at Delphi. It is not the case, then, that only nonbiblical prophets experienced ecstasy or trance, and we can certainly not distinguish between true and false prophets on this basis, which provides more than sufficient warrant to justify a cross-cultural approach to studying this phenomenon.

Some of the terminology used of prophets, such as *hozeh*, suggests there was often, though apparently not always, a visual aspect to the prophet's experience, but equally clearly, there are texts where the auditory aspect of the prophet's experience is emphasized. A hard-and-fast distinction between prophets and seers can not really be made, and more importantly, visions and visionary aspects of prophecy are present as far back as one cares to study prophecy. Thus, we can not say that visions are something new with the rise of apocalyptic. Apocalyptic literature is, clearly enough, visionary literature, but it is visionary literature of a specific sort even while it stands in a long tradition of prophets experiencing such pictures or images.

But precisely at this point in the discussion of the prophetic experience, an important observation comes to light. When a prophet hears something, it is possible for the prophet or seer to simply report what has been heard, perhaps even verbatim. The first-person speech of the deity we see as early as Mari and as late as Montanus, and it is only sometimes accompanied by some sort of messenger formula. But when a prophet sees something, unless he also hears a description of what he sees, he must then try to describe what has been seen. This does not amount to a verbatim transcript, for one could always say more or less about what one saw, and often one must use analogies ("It was like . . ."), especially if it is bizarre or unexpected or out of the ordinary. It is one thing to hear Amos describe seeing a basket of summer fruit, quite another to listen to Ezekiel or John of Patmos say, "It was like . . . ," describing his apocalyptic visions.

This last observation brings to the surface a crucial point. Prophetic expression often had a significant human component. One could describe more or less adequately what one saw. One could interpret it more or less adequately. A true prophet who had had a genuine prophetic experience might well, in the enthusiasm of the moment, overshoot the mark in the way he expressed or interpreted his experience. Perhaps it was because of the increasingly visual components to prophecy, together with the popularity of apocalyptic, that we find remarks such as those in 1 Cor 14 or Rom 12, where prophets are urged to prophesy in proportion to their faith, and, their utterances are to be weighed or sifted. We do not find similar advice concerning oracles. The oracle was either true or false, as subsequent events would bear out. A distinction, then, must be and, on some occasions, was made between oracles and vision reports. It was the latter that most often required further interpretation or elaboration.

Another facet of the discussion of prophetic expression follows from these remarks. While it is certainly true that there were sometimes quite specific oracles about matters on the near horizon that affected one's immediate audience, it is also true that prophets often spoke about the more distant horizon, and when they did so, they spoke in more general or idealized or metaphorical terms. The form of prophetic expression of such matters was, in addition, often poetic and could not, in any event, simply be understood literally. Across a wide range of times and cultures, prophetic expression took poetic forms. It has been seen in this study that there seems often to have been some connection with music, whether as an inducement to prophetic experience or as a means of expressing one's prophetic oracles. Prophets might well be singers, or at least creators of songs. This raises significant questions about material ranging as wide as from the Song of Deborah to the christological hymns in the NT. In all cases, while the prophet did intend for his or her remarks to be referential, it was seldom the case that such poetry or song or idealized forms of speech were meant to be taken literally. This is one of the reasons it is more than a little unwise to speak too quickly about false prophecy or unfulfilled prophecy. No prophet offering a poetic or nonliteral prophecy would have been happy with attempts to prove or refute that a literal fulfillment had or had not transpired.

This, in turn, brings up another regular feature of prophetic expression. Prophecies were often conditional in nature. Especially when one is dealing with prophecy offered to a group or in the context of some sort of covenantal relationship, one must allow for the dynamism of the relationship to come into play, and one must regularly ask what has been said for rhetorical effect, what has been said unconditionally, what has been said conditionally. If a conditional prophecy is offered ("If my people who are called by my name will repent, then I will pardon their offenses") and the condition suggested is met, then one can perhaps speak of fulfillment, but if the condition is not met and something else transpires, one can not speak of false prophecy or failed prophecy. One can only speak of prophecy that had a possible positive or negative outcome that went unfulfilled because the conditions were not met. Prophecy was always a complex matter, and it is probably incorrect to suggest that a phenomenon as varied and as rich as apocalyptic chiefly arose because of the failure of prophecy to come true. False prophecy and unfulfilled prophecy there always were, but only history and time would potentially reveal what was the case about some predictive prophecy, and even then, if it was conditional, it might not be clear the conditions had been met.

Something must also be said about the prophetic tradition. This phrase could, on the one hand, refer to the passing on of written prophetic material, but it could also refer to the development of a social movement of prophets, such that one could speak of disciples of prophets or the sons of prophets. The historical evidence for a continuously ongoing prophetic movement in Israel, with things being passed down through many generations, is, frankly, lacking. There are some clues in the Elijah and Elisha material and a few other places suggesting that, for some periods of time, there was something that could be called a prophetic movement, but this material is only of limited usefulness to explain multi-source prophetic documents, or documents that kept being added to over the course of time. As Grabbe suggests, scribes and tradents could as well be responsible for the expansion of the prophetic corpus as the sons of prophets. A social movement does not always produce a literary residue or a written tradition of the pronouncements of the leaders of the movement, though sometimes this is the case.

But in the case of the Israelite tradition, in a way that was not as true of other traditions, including the Christian tradition, there was indeed a literary residue of the passing on of prophetic traditions. Such a large portion of the Hebrew canon is devoted to collections of oracles, visions, and narratives about prophets that it would be most unwise to ignore that this suggests they played a very important role in Israelite society before, during, and even after the monarchy. The demise of the monarchy did not lead to the demise of the prophetic office. It may, however, have accelerated the process of collecting prophetic oracles into something like the form of a book.

Certainly, some things changed during and after the exile. For one thing, the rise of apocalyptic as a new hybrid form of prophetic (and sapiential) expression tells us that some things had changed. Israel was no longer in charge of its own destiny. Indeed, Jews were an oppressed group in their own land as well as in exile. The voice of prophecy did not die as a result of this sea change, but it certainly changed pitch and key. As has been noted in this study, once one gets to the postexilic situation, the prophet who is known by name, uses the messenger formula, and speaks oracles is difficult, if not impossible, to find. Instead, there is not only apocalyptic but even literary prophecy as the faithful strain to explain what a sovereign and just and loving God is doing in an age where God's people feel they are receiving not manna from heaven but, rather, a stone.

During the postexilic age, not only were there apocalyptic visionaries; a new, hybrid form of literature, apocalyptic, was born. The composite document Daniel became a paradigm of sorts for a plethora of documents from *1 Enoch* to the *Ascension of Isaiah* and beyond. It would be difficult to overestimate the influence of Daniel on a variety of groups in early Judaism and Christianity. Whether we think of the Qumran community, or the Baptist movement, or the Jesus movement, or Josephus, or the early church, the indebtedness to Daniel is considerable. No wonder Josephus ranked it as one of the most popular prophetic books of his day.

The postexilic and the NT eras saw the rise not only of the literary-form apocalypse but also of a great concern for matters eschatological. To some extent, these two growth trends intertwined, although eschatology is found in many sources that are not apocalypses and, on the other hand, there are apocalypses of the heavenly-tour sort that do not focus on eschatological matters at all. It is doubtful, then, that one should really talk about apocalyptic eschatology, for there is no such distinctive thing, although eschatological ideas were regularly expressed using these sorts of forms in historical apocalypses.

It is after the confluence of sapiential, prophetic, and apocalyptic ideas in early Judaism that John the Baptist and Jesus come on the stage of history. In part because of this confluence, new sorts of prophets came to light—eschatological sign prophets or leadership prophets. There was Jesus, who in his experience was deeply indebted to the apocalyptic tradition but chose as his way of self-expression forms that were most often sapiential even if the content was often eschatological. It is true that he also occasionally spoke woe and weal oracles like the prophets of old. But he was no millenarian prophet, and the attempt to portray him as such fails. It was John, not Jesus, who was the ascetic, and it was John, not Jesus, whose ministry was characterized by a sign act that prepared for and symbolized the coming time of judgment. John, unlike Jesus, was not a proclaimer of the good news.

Members of the early church—like the Qumran community, like John, like Jesus—believed that they lived in the age of fulfillment of God's promises and of the prophet's oracles. They diligently sought correspondences between the Hebrew Scriptures and their own day. This was the primary thrust of these early Jewish and Christian groups. They were all concerned with matters eschatological. In such an environment, while there was, to be sure, new prophecy and new prophets, this is not where the emphasis lay with any of these groups, with the possible exception of the Baptist movement. Even a work such as Revelation is ultimately about the coming to fruition of all the old concepts and ideas found in the Hebrew Scriptures and now reconfigured in new ways. John sees this as having already begun to happen in his day and to be consummated in the future—an extension of the already extant eschatological age. It is a confirmation of the above thesis that we find in the NT no prophetic books other than Revelation. Early Christianity was a group of communities largely led by apostles but occasionally given a fresh word from God by prophets.

And what was the character of those prophetic utterances by Christian prophets? To judge from a text such as 1 Cor 14, it was words of encouragement, exhortation, revelation about human character that were generic enough to have wide but deeply personal application. There were also some prophets, such as Agabus, who offered fresh predictions apropos to that age and time. But these figures are distinguished from the apostles and their coworkers who preached the word based on sacred traditions both Jewish and Christian. Early Christianity was a movement largely of preachers and teachers as well as some prophets. Prophets, when performing their distinctive tasks, were not preachers or teachers or exegetes, although there were various figures, such as Paul, who could assume multiple roles in early Christianity.

Nothing in the evidence examined in this study encourages the assumption that Christian prophets were the parties responsible for generating historical Jesus traditions. A prophet or seer might well speak a word of the risen Lord to a congregation, but it was presented as just that—not as a word of the historical Jesus. Furthermore, no justification is seen for assuming that whenever a prophet was inspired, what he spoke was words of the Lord. Just as often, it appears, the Spirit may have inspired a person to tell the congregation what the Spirit was saying, and the Spirit was not simply equated with the Lord in early Christianity.

Documents such as the *Didache* remind the student of this period that prophets could be seen as a problem as the movement became more of a localized and institutionalized phenomenon; yet there were prophets who continued to itinerate, and room was left to accord them at least some respect in local congregations. The Shepherd of Hermas says precious little about prophets, and it shows, in contrast to the *Ascension of Isaiah*, that it was possible to write in a manner following the apocalyptic forms and without much eschatological content. The *Ascension of Isaiah*, by contrast, stands in strong continuity with Revelation in its eschatological focus, but one can not say it is any more apocalyptic in form than the Shepherd. Meaningful distinctions must be made between form and content when we deal with prophetic and apocalyptic materials. Both forms could have eschatological content; neither always did.

In the second century of the Christian era, it appears that some, if not most, of the roles of the prophet were taken over by figures such as the monarchial bishop. As eschatological fervor faded in the second and third centuries, this became increasingly easy to do, and one must surely see the Montanist movement as a sort of last strong prophetic and eschatological challenge to a church settling down for a long winter's nap.

But what we learn from a close scrutiny of this entire period from Mari to Montanus is that there were always prophetic figures cropping up in religious settings. Prophets might appear sporadically in some eras or more frequently in others, but we can never say that the prophetic phenomenon entirely died out over the course of nearly two millennia. In the biblical tradition, prophets were often crisis intervention specialists and so seem to have more often arisen when trouble was brewing. To some extent, the same must be said about apocalyptic seers. Their literary work is a clear sign of dysfunction and difficulties for the people of God, in one form or another.

There is a sense in which prophecy continued to be an important phenomenon for early Christianity from about AD 70 to AD 300 in a way that was not so much the case for early Judaism. Judaism became more Torah-centric in character, just as Christianity would gradually become more ecclesiocentric as the Middle Ages drew nigh. Christianity, by nature, continued to be strongly forward-looking for a longer period of time than early Judaism. It would be difficult to imagine the Qumran community arising after the disastrous failure of the bar Kokhba revolt.

Yet just when one might think that prophecy had ceased altogether, a Jesus ben Ananiah or a Montanus would arise and raise all the hopes of the ordinary folk and all the hackles of the religious powers that be. Prophets were always a threat to the status quo, a threat to attempts at human control of religious power. Prophets could not sustain a consensus and mostly could not have cared less. Throughout the period under discussion in this study, both women and men were involved in offering oracles and visions. It was clearly not a gender-specific activity, which is another reason it was often perceived as a threat by the patriarchal power structures.

Unless we are talking about court prophets in some monarchy from whom never was heard a discouraging word, prophets, in general, were always viewed with suspicion by the power brokers of the day. Yet whether peripheral prophet or court prophet, whether professional oracle for hire or part-time intervention specialist, prophets were remembered, often by name, and they left their legacies of oracles and visions. They stood as constant reminders that God was not finished with God's people just yet, nor had God left them without a living witness. To a significant degree, both Judaism and Christianity can be called communities of the word, and one form in which the word often came to these communities was through prophets and prophetesses. They reminded them not merely that "in the beginning was the word" but also that God would have the last word.

Whether threat or promise of new light, prophets played an important role in ancient societies. They remind one and all that religion and matters religious were at the very heart of what ancient societies were about. If we miss this factor in a social analysis of antiquity, we have missed something crucial to the understanding of these cultures. If this study has contributed in some small way to highlighting the importance of prophets and prophecy in all these ancient cultures, this author will be content.

Bibliography

PROPHECY

This bibliography is not intended to be exhaustive. It includes only a representative sampling of materials that deal directly with the issues of this book. Accordingly, the standard commentaries, which are referred to from time to time in the notes, are not included in this bibliography. My teaching assistant Andrew Spore must be thanked for helping me assemble some of the materials for this bibliography. For those interested in pursuing only the matter of prophecy and apocalyptic especially as it relates to Daniel and other canonical literature, I provide a separate smaller bibliography at the end of this larger one.

Abegg, M. "Who Ascended to Heaven? 4Q491, 4Q427, and the Teacher of Righteousness." Pages 61–73 in *Eschatology, Messianism, and the Dead Sea Scrolls*. Ed. P. W. Flint and C. Evans. Grand Rapids: Eerdmans, 1997.

Ahlstrom, G. W. *Royal Administration and National Religion in Ancient Palestine*. Leiden: E. J. Brill, 1982.

Aland, K. "Bemerkungen zum Montanismus und zur frühchristlichen Eschatologie." Pages 105–48 in *Kirchengeschichtliche Entwürfe*. Gütersloh: G. Mohn, 1960.

Albright, W. F. "The Oracles of Balaam." *JBL* 63 (1944): 207–33.

Allison, D. C. *Jesus of Nazareth: Millenarian Prophet*. Minneapolis: Fortress, 1998.

Arnold, B. T. "The Use of Aramaic in the Hebrew Bible: Another Look at Bilingualism in Ezra and Daniel." *JSNT* 22 (2, 1996): 1–16.

Ash, J. "The Decline of Ecstatic Prophecy in the Early Church." *TS* 37 (1976): 227–52

Aune, D. E. *Prophecy in Early Christianity and the Ancient Mediterranean World.* Grand Rapids: Eerdmans, 1983.

Barker, M. *The Lost Prophet: The Book of Enoch and Its Influence on Christianity.* Nashville: Abingdon, 1988.

Barnett, P. W. "The Jewish Eschatological Prophets." Ph.D. diss., University of London, 1977.

Barrett, C. K. *The Holy Spirit and the Gospel Tradition.* London: SPCK, 1947.

Battenfield, J. "Isaiah 63.10: Taking the 'if' out of the Sacrifice of the Servant." *VT* 32 (1982): 485.

Bauckham, R. J. *The Fate of the Dead.* Leiden: E. J. Brill, 1998.

———. "The Rise of Apocalyptic." *Them* 4 (2, 1979): 10–23

Beasley-Murray, G. R. "The Interpretation of Daniel 7." *CBQ* 45 (1983): 44–58.

———. *Jesus and the Future.* London: MacMillan, 1954.

Beker, J. C. *Paul's Apocalyptic Gospel: The Coming Triumph of God.* Philadelphia: Fortress, 1982.

Beyer. B. E. "Aspects of Religious Life at Mari." Ph.D. diss., Hebrew-Union College, 1985.

Birch, B. *The Rise of the Israelite Monarchy: The Growth and Development of 1 Samuel 7–15.* Missoula: Scholars Press, 1976.

Block, D. L. "Deborah among the Judges: The Perspective of a Hebrew Historian." Pages 229–53 in *Faith, Tradition, and History.* Ed. A. R. Millard et al. Winona Lake, Ind.: Eisenbrauns, 1994.

Bonwetsch, N. G. *Geschichte des Montanismus.* Erlangen, 1881.

Boring, E. *The Continuing Voice of Jesus.* Louisville: Westminster, 1991.

Broneer, L. *The Stories of Elijah and Elisha.* Leiden: E. J. Brill, 1968.

Brueggemann, W. "Unity and Dynamic in the Isaiah Tradition." *JSOT* 29 (1984): 89–107.

Buss, M. J. "The Social Psychology of Prophecy." Pages 1–11 in *Prophecy: Essays Presented to Georg Fohrer on His Sixty-fifth Birthday, 6 September 1980.* Ed. J. A. Emerton, Berlin: de Gruyter, 1980.

Caird, G. B. *The Language and Imagery of the Bible.* Philadelphia: Westminster, 1980.

Campenhausen, H. von. *Ecclesiastical Authority and Spiritual Power in the Church in the First Three Centuries.* Trans. J. A. Baker. 1969; Peabody, Mass.: Hendrickson Publishers, 1998.

Carlson, R. A. *David the Chosen King: A Traditio-historical Approach to the Second Book of Samuel.* Stockholm: Almqvist & Wiksell, 1964.

Carroll, R. P. "The Elijah-Elisha Sagas: Some Remarks on Prophetic Succession in Ancient Israel." *VT* 19 (1969): 400–415.

———. *When Prophecy Failed: Cognitive Dissonance in the Prophetic Traditions of the Old Testament.* New York: Seabury, 1979.

Casey, M. *Son of Man: The Interpretation and Influence of Daniel 7.* London: SPCK, 1979.

Cazelles, H., and A. Gelin. *Moïse: L'homme de l'alliance.* Paris: Desclée, 1955.

Chadwick, N. K. *Poetry and Prophecy.* Cambridge: Cambridge University Press, 1942.

Clements, R. E. *Old Testament Prophecy: From Oracle to Canon.* Louisville: Westminster, 1996.

Clifford, R. J. "The Roots of Apocalypticism in Near Eastern Myth." Pages 3–38 in vol. 1 of *The Encyclopedia of Apocalypticism.* Ed. J. J. Collins. New York: Continuum, 1998.

Clines, D. J. A., and D. M. Gunn. "Form: Occasion and Redaction in Jeremiah 20." *ZAW* 88 (1976): 390–409.

Collins, A. Y. *The Combat Myth in the Book of Revelation.* Missoula: Scholars Press, 1976.

———. *Crisis and Catharsis: The Power of the Apocalypse.* Philadelphia: Westminster, 1984.

Collins, J. J. *The Apocalyptic Imagination.* New York: Crossroad, 1984.

_____ . "The Expectation of the End in the Dead Sea Scrolls." Pages 74–90 in *Eschatology, Messianism, and the Dead Sea Scrolls.* Ed. P. W. Flint and C. Evans. Grand Rapids: Eerdmans, 1997.

_____ . "Genre, Ideology, and Social Movements in Jewish Apocalypticism." Pages 11–32 in *Mysteries and Revelations: Apocalyptic Studies since the Uppsala Colloquium.* Ed. J. J. Collins and J. Charlesworth. Sheffield: JSOT Press, 1991.

_____ . "Jesus and the Messiahs of Israel." Pages 287–302 in *Geschichte—Tradition— Reflexion: Festschrift für Martin Hengel zum 70. Geburtstag.* Tübingen: Mohr, 1996.

_____ . "Sibylline Oracles." Pages 356–57 in vol. 1 of *The Old Testament Pseudepigrapha.* 2 vols. Ed. J. Charlesworth. Garden City: Doubleday, 1983.

———, ed. *Apocalypse: The Morphology of a Genre. Semeia* 14 (1979).

Craigie, P. "The Conquest and Early Hebrew Poetry." *TynBul* 20 (1969): 76–94.

Cross, F. M. *Canaanite Myth and Hebrew Ethic.* Cambridge: Harvard University Press, 1973.

_____ . "The Stele Dedicated to Melcarth by Ben-Hadad of Damascus." *BASOR* 205 (1972): 36–42.

Crossan, J. D. *The Historical Jesus.* San Francisco: Harper, 1991.

Dahood, M. "Isaiah 53.8–12 and Masoretic Misconstructions." *Bib* 63 (1982): 566–70.

Daiches, D. *Moses: The Man and His Vision.* New York: Praeger, 1975.

Dautzenberg, G. "Botschaft und Bedeutung der urchristlichen Prophetie nach dem ersten Korintherbrief (2.6–16;12–14)." Pages 131–61 in *Prophetic Vocation in the New Testament and Today.* Ed. J. Panagopoulos. Leiden: E. J. Brill, 1977.

Derrett, J. D. M. "Law in the New Testament: The Palm Sunday Colt." *NovT* 13 (1971): 241–58.

Dibelius, M. *Der Hirt des Hermas.* Vol. 4 of *Die Apostolischen Väter.* Ed. K. Bihlmeyer. Tübingen: Mohr, 1923.

Dodds, E. R. *The Greeks and the Irrational.* Boston: Beacon, 1957.

Ellis, E. E. *Prophecy and Hermeneutic in Early Christianity.* Grand Rapids: Eerdmans, 1978.

Fee, G. D. *God's Empowering Presence.* Peabody, Mass.: Hendrickson, 1994.

Fleming, D. E. "The Etymological Origins of the Hebrew Nabi: The One Who Invokes God." *CBQ* 55 (1993): 217–24.

_____ . "Nabu and Munabbiatu: Two New Syrian Religious Personnel." *JAOS* 113 (1993): 175–83.

Flint, P. W. "The Daniel Tradition at Qumran." Pages 41–60 in *Eschatology, Messianism, and the Dead Sea Scrolls.* Ed. P. W. Flint and C. Evans. Grand Rapids: Eerdmans, 1997.

Fontenrose, J. *The Delphic Oracle.* Berkeley: University of California Press, 1978.

Freedman, D. N. "Pottery, Poetry, and Prophecy: An Essay on Biblical Poetry." *JBL* 96 (1, 1977): 5–26.

Gelston, A. "A Note on 2 Samuel 7.10." *ZAW* 84 (1973): 92–94.

Gerlmann, G. "Schuld und Sühne: Erwagungen zu 2 Sam. 12." Pages 132–39 in *Beiträge zur alttestamentlichen Theologie: Festschrift für Walther Zimmerli.* Ed. H. Donner et al. Göttingen: Vandenhoeck & Ruprecht, 1977.

Gese, H. "Bemerkungen zur Sinai-Tradition." *ZAW* 79 (1967): 137–54.

Gitay, Y. *Prophecy and Persuasion: A Study of Isaiah 40–48.* Bonn: Linguistica Biblica, 1981.

Gordon, R. P. "From Mari to Moses: Prophecy at Mari and in Ancient Israel." Pages 63–79 in *Of Prophets' Visions and the Wisdom of Sages.* Ed. H. A. McKay and D. J. A. Clines. Sheffield: JSOT Press, 1993.

_____. "Where Have All the Prophets Gone?" *BBR* 5 (1995): 67–86.

Grabbe, L. L. "Poets, Scribes, or Preachers? The Reality of Prophecy in the Second Temple Period." Pages 524–45 in *SBL Seminar Papers, 1998*. Atlanta: Scholars Press, 1998.

_____. *Priests, Prophets, Diviners, Sages: A Socio-historical Study of Religious Specialists in Ancient Israel*. Valley Forge, Pa.: Trinity, 1995.

Greene, J. T. *Balaam and His Interpreters: A Hermeneutical History of the Balaam Traditions*. Atlanta: Scholars Press, 1992.

Grudem, W. *The Gift of Prophecy in 1 Corinthians*. Lanham, Md.: University Press of America, 1982.

Haag, H. *Der Gottesknecht bei Deuterojesaja*. Darmstadt: Wissenschaftliche, 1985.

Habel, N. "The Form and Significance of the Call Narratives." *ZAW* 77 (1965): 297–323.

Hackett, J. A. *The Balaam Text from Deir 'Alla*. Chico, Calif.: Scholars Press, 1980.

Hahn, F. "Die Sendschreiben der Johannesapokalypse: Ein Beitrag zur Bestimmung prophetischer Redeformen." Pages 357–94 in *Tradition und Glauben*. Ed. G. Jeremias et al. Gottingen: Vandenhoeck & Ruprecht, 1971.

Haldar, A. *Associations of Cult Prophets amongst the Ancient Semites*. Uppsala: Almqvist & Wiksell, 1945.

Hanson, P. D. *The Dawn of Apocalyptic*. Philadelphia: Fortress, 1979.

Hasel, G. "The First and Third Years of Belshazzar (Dan. 7.1; 8.1)." *AUSS* 15 (1977): 173–92.

Heine, R. E. *The Montanist Oracles and Testimonia*. Macon, Ga.: Mercer, 1989.

_____. "The Role of the Gospel of John in the Montanist Controversy." *SecCent* 6 (1987–1988): 1–19.

Hengel, M. *The Charismatic Leader and His Followers*. New York: Crossroad, 1981.

Hengel, M., and A. M. Schwemer. *Paul between Damascus and Antioch: The Unknown Years*. Louisville: Westminster, 1997.

Hill, D. *New Testament Prophecy*. London: Marshall, Morgan & Scott, 1979.

Holladay, C. A. "1 Corinthians 13: Paul as Apostolic Paradigm." Pages 80–98 in *Greeks, Romans, and Jews: Currents of Culture and Belief in the New Testament World*. Ed. J. D. Newsome.

Hooker, M. D. *The Signs of a Prophet: The Prophetic Actions of Jesus*. Harrisburg, Pa.: Trinity, 1997.

Horsley, R. *Jesus and the Spiral of Violence*. New York: Crossroad, 1987.

Huffmon, H. B. "The Origins of Prophecy in Israel." Pages 172–86 in *Magnalia Dei: The Mighty Acts of God*. Ed. F. Cross et al. Garden City: Doubleday, 1976.

Hugenberger, G. P. "The Servant of the Lord in the 'Servant Songs' of Isaiah: A Second Moses Figure." Pages 105–40 in *The Lord's Anointed*. Ed. P. E. Satterthwaite et al. Carlisle: Pater Noster, 1995.

Hultgard, A. "Persian Apocalypticism." Pages 39–83 in vol. 1 of *The Encyclopedia of Apocalypticism*. 3 vols. Ed. J. J. Collins. New York: Continuum, 1998.

Jeffers, J. *Conflict at Rome: Social Order and Hierarchy in Early Christianity*. Minneapolis: Fortress, 1991.

Kelsey, M. T. *God, Dreams, and Revelation*. Minneapolis: Augsburg, 1991.

Kingsbury, J. D. "Jesus as the 'Prophetic Messiah' in Luke's Gospel." Pages 29–42 in *The Future of Christology: Essays in Honor of Leander E. Keck*. Ed. A. J. Malherbe and W. A. Meeks. Philadelphia: Fortress, 1993.

Klawiter, F. C. "The New Prophecy in Early Christianity: The Origin, Nature, and Development of Montanism, A.D. 165–220." Ph.D. diss., University of Chicago, 1975.

Koch, K. *The Prophets*. 2 vols. Philadelphia: Fortress, 1983.

Koester, H. "Jesus the Victim." *JBL* 111 (1992): 10–11.

Kraus, H.-J. *Die prophetische Verkündigung des Rechts in Israel.* Zollikon, Switzerland: EVZ, 1957.

_____. *Worship in Israel.* Richmond: John Knox, 1966.

Kruse, C. G. "The Servant Songs: Interpretive Trends since C. R. North." *SBT* 8 (1978): 1–27.

Labriolle, P. de. *La crisis montaniste.* Paris: Gabalda, 1913.

_____. *Les sources de l'histoire du montanisme.* Paris: Gabalda, 1913.

LeCocque, A. *Daniel in His Time.* Columbia: University of South Carolina Press, 1988.

Leisgang, H. *Die vorchristlichen Anschauungen und Lehren vom Pneuma unter der mystisch-intuitiven Erkenntnis.* Leipzig: Teubner, 1919.

Lewis, T. J. *Cults of the Dead in Ancient Israel and Ugarit.* Atlanta: Scholars Press, 1989.

Lincoln, A. T. "Paul the Visionary." *NTS* 25 (1979): 204–20

Lindars, B. "Deborah's Song: Women in the Old Testament." *BJRL* 65 (1982–1983): 158–75.

Lindblom, J. *Prophecy in Ancient Israel.* Philadelphia: Fortress, 1962.

Lipinski, E. "Recherches sur le livre de Zecharie." *VT* 29 (1970): 38.

Longman, T., and D. Reid, *God Is a Warrior.* Downers Grove, Ill.: InterVarsity, 1995.

Luckenbill, D. D. *Ancient Records of Assyria and Babylonia.* 2 vols. Chicago: University of Chicago Press, 1926–1927.

Malamat, A. *Mari and the Israelite Experience.* Oxford: Oxford University Press, 1989.

_____. "Mari Prophecy and Nathan's Dynastic Oracle." Pages 68–82 in *Prophecy: Essays Presented to Georg Fohrer on His Sixty-Fifth Birthday, 6 September 1980.* Ed. J. A. Emerton, Berlin: de Gruyter, 1980.

_____. "The Origins of Statecraft in the Israelite Monarchy." Pages 195–99 in *The Biblical Archaeologist Reader 3.* Ed. E. F. Campbell et al. Garden City: Doubleday, 1970.

McKnight, S. "Jesus and the Endtime: Matthew 10.23." Pages 501–20 in *SBL Seminar Papers, 1986.* K. H. Richards, ed. (Atlanta: Scholars Press, 1986).

Meier, J. "The Circle of the Twelve: Did It Exist during Jesus' Public Ministry?" *JBL* 116 (1997): 635–72.

_____. *Jesus: A Marginal Jew: Rethinking the Historical Jesus.* Vol . 1, *Roots of the Problem and the Person.* New York: Doubleday, 1991. Vol. 2, *Mentor, Message, and Miracles.* New York: Doubleday, 1994.

Merklein, H. "Der Theologe als Prophet." *NTS* 38 (1992): 402–29.

Messner, R. G. "Elisha and the Bears." *Grace Journal* 3 (1962): 12–24.

Meyer, B. F. *The Aims of Jesus.* London: SCM, 1979.

Moore, M. S. *The Balaam Traditions: Their Character and Development.* Atlanta: Scholars Press, 1990.

Mowinckel, S. *He That Cometh.* New York: Abingdon, 1956.

Muller, C. D. G. "Ascension of Isaiah." Pages 603–5 in *Writings Relating to the Apostles, Apocalypses, and Related Subjects.* Vol. 2 of *New Testament Apocrypha.* Rev. ed. Ed. W. Schneemelcher. Trans. R. McL. Wilson. Louisville: Westminster John Knox, 1992.

Müller, K. "Der Menschensohn im Danielzyklus." Pages 37–80 in *Jesus und der Menschensohn.* Ed. R. Pesch et al. Freiburg: Herder, 1975.

Nickelsburg, G. W. E. *Jewish Literature between the Bible and the Mishnah.* Philadelphia: Fortress, 1981.

_____. "Social Aspects of Palestinian Jewish Apocalypticism." Pages 641–54 in *Apocalypticism in the Mediterranean World and the Near East.* Ed. D. Hellholm Tübingen: Mohr, 1989.

Niditch, S. *Oral World and Written Word: Ancient Israelite Literature.* Louisville: Westminster John Knox, 1996.

Nissinen, M. *References to Prophecy in Neo-Assyrian Sources.* SAA 7. Helsinki: Helsinki University Press, 1998.

Noort, E. *Untersuchungen zum Gottesbeschied Mari: Die Mariprophetie in der alttestamentlichen Forschung.* Neukirchen-Vluyn: Neukirchener, 1977.

Noth, M. "David and Israel in II Samuel VII." Pages 250–59 in *The Laws in the Pentateuch and Other Studies.* Trans. D. R. Ap-Thomas. Edinburgh: Oliver & Boyd, 1966.

Osiek, C. *Rich and Poor in the Shepherd of Hermas.* Washington: Catholic Biblical Association, 1983

Overholt, T. *Channels of Prophecy: The Social Dynamics of Prophetic Activity.* Minneapolis: Fortress, 1989.

Parker, S. B. "Possession Trance and Prophecy in Pre-exilic Israel." *VT* 28 (1978): 271–85

———. "Prophecy at Mari and in Israel." *VT* 43 (1, 1993): 50–68.

Parpola, S. *Assyrian Prophecies.* SAA 9. Helsinki: Helsinki University Press, 1997.

Pearson, B. A. *The Pneumatikos-Psychikos Terminology in 1 Corinthians.* Missoula: Society of Biblical Literature, 1973.

Petersen, D. L. *Late-Israelite Prophecy: Studies in Deutero-prophetic Literature and in Chronicles.* Missoula: Scholars Press, 1977.

Phillips, A. "The Interpretation of 2 Sam. xii.5–6." *VT* 16 (1966): 242–44.

Potter, D. *Prophets and Emperors.* Cambridge: Harvard University Press, 1994.

Powel, D. "Tertullianists and Cataphrygians." *VC* 29 (1975): 33–55;

Raabe, P. "The Effect of Repetition in the Suffering Servant Song." *JBL* 103 (1984): 77–81.

Rad, G. von. *The Message of the Prophets.* San Francisco: HarperCollins, 1962.

Reid, S. B. *Enoch and Daniel: A Form Critical and Sociological Study of Historical Apocalypses.* Berkeley: Bibal, 1989.

Reiling, J. *Hermas and Christian Prophecy: A Study of the Eleventh Mandate.* Leiden: E. J. Brill, 1973.

Reiner, E. "Fortune-telling in Mesopotamia." *JNES* 19 (1960): 22–35.

Reitzenstein, R. *Die hellenistichen Mysterienreligionen: Nach ihren Grundgedanken und Wirkungen.* Leipzig: Teubner, 1927.

Rendtorff, R. "Reflections on the Early History of Prophecy in Israel." Pages 14–34 in *History and Hermeneutic.* Ed. R. W. Funk. New York: Harper & Row, 1967.

———. "Zur Komposition des Buches Jesaja." *VT* 34 (1984): 295–320.

Renteria, T. H. "The Elijah/Elisha Stories: A Socio-cultural Analysis of Prophets and People in Ninth-Century B.C.E. Israel." Pages 75–126 in *Elijah and Elisha in Socioliterary Perspective.* Ed. R. B. Coote. Atlanta: Scholars Press, 1992.

Richter, W. *Die sogenannten vorprophetische Berufsberichte.* Göttingen: Vandenhoeck & Ruprecht, 1970.

Robeck, C. M. *Prophecy in Carthage.* Cleveland: Pilgrim, 1992.

Rofe, A. "The Classification of the Prophetical Stories." *JBL* 89 (1970): 427–40.

Rowland, C. "Apocalyptic, Mysticism, and the New Testament." Pages 405–430 in *Judentum.* Vol. 1 of *Festschrift für M. Hengel: Geschichte—Tradition—Reflexion.* Ed. P. Schafer. Tübingen: Mohr, 1996.

———. *The Open Heaven: A Study of Apocalyptic in Judaism and Early Christianity.* New York: Crossroad, 1982.

Sakenfeld, K. D. *The Meaning of Hesed in the Hebrew Bible: An Inquiry.* Missoula: Scholars Press, 1978.

Sandnes, K. O. *Paul: One of the Prophets?* Tübingen: Mohr, 1991.

Schepelern, W. *Der Montanismus und der phrygischen Kulte: Eine religionsgeschichtliche Untersuchung.* Tübingen: Mohr, 1929.

Schibler, D. "Messianism and Messianic Prophecy in Isaiah 1–12 and 28–33." Pages 87–104 in *The Lord's Anointed.* Ed. P. E. Satterthwaite et al. Carlisle: Paternoster, 1995.

Schlisske, W. *Gottessöhne und Gottesohn im Alten Testament.* Stuttgart: Kohlhammer, 1973.

Schüssler Fiorenza, E. *The Book of Revelation.* Philadelphia: Fortress, 1985.

Seybold, K. *Das davidische Königtum im Zeugnis der Propheten.* Göttingen: Vandenhoeck & Ruprecht, 1972.

Simon, U. "The Poor Man's Ewe-Lamb: An Example of a Juridical Parable." *Bib* 48 (1967): 207–42.

Snyder, G. F. *The Shepherd of Hermas.* Vol. 5 of *The Apostolic Fathers.* Ed. R. M. Grant. Camden: Nelson, 1966.

Starr, I. *Queries to the Sungod: Divination and Politics in Sargonid Assyria.* SAA 4. Helsinki: Helsinki University Press, 1990.

Stendahl, K. *Paul among Jews and Gentiles.* Philadelphia: Fortress, 1977.

Stone, M. E., and J. Strugnell. *The Books of Elijah, Parts 1–2.* Missoula: Scholars Press, 1979.

Tabbernee, W. "Early Montanism and Voluntary Martyrdom." *Colloq* 17 (1985): 33–45.

Theissen, G. *The Gospels in Context.* Edinburgh: T. & T. Clark, 1992.

_____. *The Miracle Stories of the Early Christian Tradition.* Philadelphia: Fortress, 1983.

Theissen, G., and A. Merz. *The Historical Jesus: A Comprehensive Guide.* Minneapolis: Fortress, 1998.

Tiede, D. L. *Prophecy and History in Luke–Acts.* Philadelphia: Fortress, 1980.

Tigray, J. H. "'Heavy of Mouth' and 'Heavy of Tongue': On Moses' Speech Difficulty." *BASOR* 231 (1978): 57–65.

Tsevat, M. "The House of David in Nathan's Prophecy." *Bib* 46 (1965): 353–56.

_____. "Marriage and Monarchial Legitimacy in Ugarit and Israel." *JSS* 3 (1958): 237–43.

_____. "Studies in the Book of Samuel. III. The Steadfast House: What Was David Promised in II Samuel 7.13b–16?" *HUCA* 34 (1963): 71–82.

Tucker, G. M. "Prophecy and Prophetic Literature." Pages 325–68 in *The Hebrew Bible and Its Modern Interpreters.* Ed. G. M. Tucker and D. A. Knight. Philadelphia: Fortress, 1985.

Twelftree, G. *Jesus the Exorcist.* Tübingen: Mohr-Siebeck, 1993.

Uhlshofer, H. K. "Nathan's Opposition to David's Intention to Build a Temple in the Light of Selected Ancient Near Eastern Texts." Ph.D. diss., Boston University, 1977.

VanderKam, J. C. "Messianism and Apocalypticism." Pages 193–228 in volume one. *The Encyclopedia of Apocalypticism.* 3 vols. Ed. J. J. Collins. New York: Continuum, 1998.

Vaux, R. de. *The Bible and the Ancient Near East.* Garden City: Doubleday, 1971.

Vondergeest, C. "A Question of Loyalty: Prophets and Kings in Israel and Mesopotamia." Paper presented at John Wesley Fellows meeting. Duke University. December 12, 1998.

Webb, R. L. "John the Baptist and His Relationship to Jesus." Pages 179–230 in *Studying the Historical Jesus.* Ed. B. Chilton and C. A. Evans. Leiden: E. J. Brill, 1994.

_____. *John the Baptizer and Prophet: A Socio-historical Study.* Sheffield: Sheffield Academic Press, 1991.

Weinfeld, M. "The Covenant of Grant in the OT and in the ANE." *JAOS* 90 (1970): 184–203.

Westermann, C. *Prophetic Oracles of Salvation in the Old Testament.* Louisville: Westminster, 1991.

Williams, J. G. "The Prophetic 'Father': A Brief Explanation of the Term 'Sons of the Prophets.'" *JBL* 85 (1966): 344–48.

Wilson, J. C. *Five Problems in the Interpretation of the Shepherd of Hermas.* Lewiston, Me.: Mellen Biblical Press, 1995.

_____ . *Toward a Reassessment of the Shepherd of Hermas: Its Date and Its Pneumatology.* Lewiston, Me.: Edwin Mellen Press, 1993.

Wilson, R. R. *Prophecy and Society in Ancient Israel.* Philadelphia: Fortress, 1980.

Wire, A. C. *The Corinthian Women Prophets: A Reconstruction through Paul's Rhetoric.* Minneapolis: Fortress, 1990.

Witherington, B. *The Jesus Quest.* Downers Grove, Ill.: InterVarsity, 1995.

_____ . *Jesus, Paul, and the End of the World.* Downers Grove, Ill.: InterVarsity, 1992.

_____ . *The Many Faces of the Christ.* New York: Crossroad, 1998.

_____ . *The Paul Quest: The Search for the Jew from Tarsus.* Downers Grove, Ill.: InterVarsity, 1998.

_____ . *Women in the Ministry of Jesus.* Cambridge: Cambridge University Press, 1984.

Wright, N. T. *Jesus and the Victory of God.* Minneapolis: Fortress, 1996.

Zobel, K. *Prophetie und Deuteronomium.* Berlin: de Gruyter, 1992.

APOCALYPTIC AND PROPHECY

Monographs

Caragounis, C. C. *The Son of Man.* WUNT 38. Tübingen: Mohr-Siebeck, 1986.

Casey, P. M. *Son of Man: The Interpretation and Influence of Daniel 7.* London: SPCK, 1979.

Coppens, J. *La relève apocalyptique du messianisme royal. II. Le fils d'homme vetero et intertestamentaire. Le fils d'homme danielique. Le fils d'homme hénochique.* BETL 61. Leuven: Peeters, 1983.

Coppens, J. and L. Dequeker. *Le fils de l'homme et les saints du Très-haut en Daniel VII.* ALBO 3/23. Leuven: Publications Universitaires, 1961.

Ferch, A. J. *The Son of Man in Daniel 7.* Andrews University Seminary Doctoral Dissertation Series 6. Berrien Springs, Mich.: Andrews University Press, 1979.

Articles

Barr, J. "Jewish Apocalyptic in Recent Scholarly Study." *BJRL* 58 (1, 1975): 9–35.

Bauckham, R. J. "The Eschatological Earthquake and the Apocalypse of John." *NovT* 19 (3, 1977): 224–33.

_____ . "The Rise of Apocalyptic." *Them* 3 (2, 1978): 10–23.

Baumgartner, W. "Das Aramaische im Buch Daniel." *ZAW* 45 (1927): 81–133.

Beasley-Murray, G. R. "The Interpretation of Daniel 7." *CBQ* 45 (1983): 44–58.

Betz, H. D. "Zum Problem des religionsgeschichtlichen Verstandnisses der Apokalyptic." *ZTK* 63 (1966): 391–409.

Bruce, F. F. "A Reappraisal of Jewish Apocalyptic Literature." *RevExp* 72 (3, 1975): 305–15.

Caragounis, C. C. "The Interpretation of the Ten Horns of Daniel 7." *ETL* 63 (1987): 106–12.

Casey, P. M. "The Corporate Interpretation of 'One Like a Son of Man' (Daniel VII 13) at the Time of Jesus." *NovT* 18 (1976): 167–80.

Collins, J. J. "Cosmos and Salvation: Jewish Wisdom and Apocalyptic in the Hellenistic Age." *HR* 17 (2, 1977): 121–42.

_____ . "The Court-Tales in Daniel and the Development of Apocalyptic." *JBL* 94 (2, 1975): 218–34.

_____ . "The Jewish Apocalypses." *Semeia* 14 (1979): 21–59.

_____ . "Jewish Apocalyptic against Its Hellenistic Near Eastern Environment." *BASOR* 220 (1975): 27–36.

_____ . "The Mythology of Holy War in Daniel and the Qumran War Scroll: A Point of Transition in Jewish Apocalyptic." *VT* 25 (3, 1975): 596–612.

_____ . "Persian Apocalypses." *Semeia* 14 (1979): 207–17.

_____ . "The Son of Man and the Saints of the Most High in the Book of Daniel." *JBL* 93 (1, 1974): 50–66.

_____ . "The Symbolism of Transcendence in Jewish Apocalyptic." *BR* 19 (1974): 5–22.

Coppens, J. "Le fils d'homme danielique vizir céleste?" *ETL* 49 (1964): 72–80.

_____ . "Les origines du symbole du fils d'homme en Daniel VII." *ETL* 44 (1968): 497–502.

_____ . "Les saints du Très-haut sont-ils à identifier avec les milices célestes?" *ETL* 37 (1961): 94–100.

Davies, G. I. "Apocalyptic in Historiography." *JSOT* 5 (1978): 15–28.

Delcor, M. "Les sources du chapitre VII de Daniel." *VT* 18 (1968) 290–312.

Dequeker, L. "Daniel 7 et les saints du Très-haut." *ETL* 36 (1960): 353–92.

Di Lella, A. A. "The One in Human Likeness and the Holy Ones of the Most High in Daniel VII." *CBQ* 39 (1977): 1–19.

Dumbrell, W. J. "Daniel and the Function of Old Testament Apocalyptic." *RTR* 34 (1, 1975): 16–23.

Eerdmans, B. D. "Origin and Meaning of the Aramaic Part of Daniel." *Actes du XVIIIe Congrès international des orientalistes* (1932): 198–202.

Emerton, J. A. "The Origin of the Son of Man Imagery." *JTS* 9 (1958): 225–42.

Ferch, A. J. "Daniel 7 and Ugarit: A Reconsideration." *JBL* 99 (1980): 75–86.

_____ . "The Two Aeons and the Messiah in Pseudo-Philo, 4 Ezra, and 2 Baruch." *AUSS* 15 (2, 1977): 135–51.

Flusser, D. "The Four Empires in the Fourth Sibyl and in the Book of Daniel." *Israel Oriental Society* 2 (1972): 148–75.

Freedman, D. N. "The Flowering of Apocalyptic." *JTC* 6 (1969): 157–65.

Glasson, T. F. "Apocalyptic Ideas of Judaism Contemporary with Our Lord." *London Quarterly and Holborn Review* (1960): 166–70.

_____ . "The Son of Man Imagery: Enoch XIV and Daniel VII." *NTS* 23 (1976–1977): 82–90.

Goldingay, J. E. "Holy Ones on High in Daniel 7:18." *JBL* 107 (1988): 497–99.

Hanson, P. D. "Old Testament Apocalyptic Reexamined." *Int* 25 (4, 1971): 454–79.

_____ . "Rebellion in Heaven, Azazel, and Euhemeristic Heroes in 1 Enoch 6–11." *JBL* 96 (2, 1977): 195–233.

Hasel, G. F. "The Identity of 'the Saints of the Most High' in Daniel 7." *Biblica* 56 (1975): 173–92.

Hill, D. "Prophecy and Prophets in the Revelation of St. John." *NTS* 18 (4, 1972): 401–18.

Hook, S. H. "Life after Death: VI. The Extra-canonical Literature." *ExpT* 76 (1965): 273–76.

Howard, G. "Jewish Apocalyptic Literature." *ResQ* 6 (1962): 77–84.

Kallas, J. "The Apocalypse—an Apocalyptic Book?" *JBL* 86 (1, 1967): 69–80.

Kuanvig, H. S. "An Akkadian Vision as Background for Daniel 7." *StTh* 35 (1981): 85–89.

——. "Struktur und Geschichte in Dan 7, 1–4." *StTh* 32 (1978): 95–117.

Lebram, J. C. H. "Apokalyptek als keerpunt in het Joodse denken." *NedTT* 30 (4, 1976): 271–81.

Lenglet, A. "La structure littéraire de Daniel 2–7." *Biblica* 53 (1972): 169–90.

Lindars, B. "Re-enter the Apocalyptic Son of Man." *NTS* 22 (1, 1975): 52–72.

Loader, W. R. G. "The Apocalyptic Model of Sonship: Its Origin and Development in New Testament Tradition." *JBL* 97 (4, 1978): 525–54.

Luck, U. "Das Weltverständnis in der jüdischen Apokalyptik." *ZTK* 73 (3, 1976): 283–305.

Lust, J. "Daniel 7,13 and the Septuagint." *ETL* 54 (1978): 62–69.

Morenz, S. "Das Tier mit den Hörnern: Ein Beitrag zu Dan 7, 7f." *ZAW* 63 (1951): 151–54.

Morgenstern, J. "The Son of Man of Daniel 7:13f.: A New Interpretation." *JBL* 80 (1961): 65–77.

Muilenberg, J. "The Son of Man in Daniel and the Ethiopic Apocalypse of Enoch." *JBL* 79 (1960): 197–209.

Murdock, W. "History and Revelation in Jewish Apocalypticism." *Int* 21 (2, 1967): 167–87.

Nickelsburg, G. W. E. "Apocalyptic and Myth in 1 Enoch 6–11." *JBL* 96 (3, 1977): 383–405.

——. "The Apocalyptic Message of 1 Enoch 92–105." *CBQ* 39 (3, 1977): 309–28.

Perkins, P. "Apocalypse of Adam: The Genre and Function of a Gnostic Apocalypse." *CBQ* 39 (3, 1977): 382–95.

Reicke, B. "Official and Pietistic Elements of Jewish Apocalypticism." *JBL* 79 (1960): 137–50.

Rowland, C. "The Visions of God in Apocalyptic Literature." *JSJ* 10 (2, 1979): 137–54.

Smith, P. K. "The Apocalypse of St. John and the Early Church." *JBR* 25 (1957): 187–95.

Stagg, F. "Interpreting the Book of Revelation." *RevExp* 72 (3, 1975): 331–42.

Towner, W. S. "Retribution Theology in the Apocalyptic Setting." *USQR* 26 (3, 1971): 203–14.

Vawter, B. "Apocalyptic: Its Relation to Prophecy." *CBQ* 22 (1980): 33–46.

Wilder, A. N. "The Rhetoric of Ancient and Modern Apocalyptic." *Int* 25 (4, 1971): 436–53.

Willi-Plein, I. "Das Geheimnis der Apokalyptik." *VT* 27 (1, 1977): 62–81.

——. "Ursprung und Motivation der Apokalyptik im Danielbuch." *TZ* 35 (5, 1979): 265–74.

Wolff, H. W. "Prophecy from the Eighth through the Fifth Century." *Int* 32 (1, 1978): 17–30.

Yuzon, L. A. "The Kingdom of God in Daniel." *South East Asia Journal of Theology* 19 (1, 1978): 23–27.

Index of Modern Authors

Index of Ancient Sources